The Defaulting State and the South China Sea Arbitration

Alfredo C. Robles Jr.

The Defaulting State and the South China Sea Arbitration

DE LA SALLE UNIVERSITY
RELIGIO MORES CULTURA
MANILA

palgrave
macmillan

Alfredo C. Robles Jr.
De La Salle University
Manila, Philippines

ISBN 978-981-19-6396-4 ISBN 978-981-19-6394-0 (eBook)
https://doi.org/10.1007/978-981-19-6394-0

Jointly published with De La Salle University Publishing House
The print edition is not for sale in the Philippines. Customers from the Philippines please order the print book from: De La Salle University Publishing House.
ISBN of the Co-Publisher's edition: 978-971-555-711-5

This Palgrave Macmillan imprint is published by the registered company Springer Nature Singapore Pte Ltd.
The registered company address is: 152 Beach Road, #21-01/04 Gateway East, Singapore 189721, Singapore

Preface

From the very moment when China rejected in February 2013 the Philippine Notification and Statement of Claim that initiated the *South China Sea Arbitration* on 22 January 2013, I knew that a separate study devoted solely to the issues raised by China's default would be necessary, but it did not seem to me that the scope of such a study would differ greatly from that of commentaries published on cases of default before the International Court of Justice ("ICJ") in the 1970s and the 1980s.

I first had an inkling that the proceedings in the *Arbitration* would not unfold in the way that default proceedings did before the ICJ when I tried in vain to access the website of the Permanent Court of Arbitration ("PCA"), the Registry in the *Arbitration*, during the Hearing on Jurisdiction and Admissibility in July 2015. I e-mailed the PCA to inform it of the problem and inquired half in jest whether China had anything to do with it. The news that the website had been hacked by Chinese actors alarmed me and forced me to scan my hard disk as a precaution.

The next surprise came with the publication of the Award on Jurisdiction and Admissibility in October 2015, which revealed that on several occasions China had secretly lobbied the Tribunal for unknown purposes. Just when it seemed that China's behavior could no longer shock, China launched slanderous attacks against the appointing authority and the judges several months after the issuance of the Award on Jurisdiction. The attacks were amplified by Chinese journalists and scholars in the wake of the issuance of the Award of 12 July 2016. It turned out that the attacks were only the first salvos in a wide-ranging campaign of misinformation and disinformation that now ignored China's default and gave the impression that the Tribunal had rejected the arguments of a party that had appeared before it. The scale of the Chinese misinformation and disinformation campaign on China's default and its consequences for the proceedings convinced me that a full-length study would have to be devoted to them.

The effort to engage with Chinese authors has had the effect of expanding the scope of the book to cover the legal and procedural issues that they raise and the conduct of the defaulting State that they ignore. The few scholarly articles that have been published outside China focusing on China's default rarely make references to their work. Perhaps this attitude stems from a mistrust of Chinese authors, who can be expected to express (and do express) unconditional support for official Chinese positions. After reading the artfully woven web of half-truths and counter-truths that is presented to the reader by Chinese authors, one cannot help but feel that the mistrust is fully justifiable. Nevertheless, one must still engage with them, for at least two reasons. First, they must be held accountable for their views, regardless of their publication record or membership in learned societies. It matters little whether the points they make seem to be quibbles that do not deserve an extended response. If Chinese authors harped on these points, these were obviously thought to be important; hence they deserve to be exposed as canards, whether served Peking style or not. A second reason is captured in the Latin adage *verba volant, scripta manent*, lit. "words fly away, writings remain." The fanciful claims and malicious allegations spread by Chinese authors cannot be erased from the record, despite the warming of Sino-Philippine relations, and may always be unearthed by anyone should these relations take a different turn. In the absence of a rebuttal, the passage of time, rather than rendering them less plausible, may lend credibility to them, particularly in the minds of those who are exposed only to Chinese official media or of those who are unfamiliar with international law and the law of the sea. One of the strengths of this book is precisely that it takes seriously all, not just some, of the objections formulated by Chinese scholars to the Tribunal's handling of procedural issues. As far as I know, I am the only scholar outside China to do so.

Unlike other scholarly studies of China's default, this book also reviews the caselaw of the ICJ going back to 1948 and the associated scholarly commentary, together with hundreds of official documents of the

Arbitration, thus making it possible to avoid factual errors or misunderstanding of important points that have also appeared in some scholarly studies published outside China. Unlike other studies on the *South China Sea Arbitration*, the book does not discuss issues relating to the jurisdiction of the Tribunal, the merits of Philippine claims, the dispute settlement system under the United Nations Convention on the Law of the Sea, and the various territorial and maritime disputes in South China except to the extent that is necessary to facilitate comprehension of the legal issues arising from China's default and its practical consequences for the proceedings. Having acknowledged these limitations, I remain hopeful that anyone interested in the *Arbitration* or in China will be able to grasp the book's arguments.

I have explained in Chapter 1 my reasons for preferring the word "default" to "non-appearance." To these reasons, I will add my belief that "default" is more immediately comprehensible to the ordinary reader than "non-appearance" and my desire to avoid the awkwardness associated with a negative expression. The main exceptions to this usage are direct quotations from texts that use the expressions "non-appearance" or "non-participation."

This is my fourth book on the *South China Sea Arbitration*. Inevitably, it covers some of the substantive issues that were covered in the earlier books. Nevertheless, I have made an effort to avoid repetition. In particular, I have not repeated my refutation of two erroneous ideas relating to fact-finding. The first is that the Arbitral Tribunal, when deciding whether Chinese fishers resorted to dangerous or harmful fishing methods, refused to make a finding in the absence of expert testimony. The second is that the Arbitral Tribunal, when examining the Philippine submission that China's island-building had caused harm to the environment, advocated a new kind of fact-finding, "hard fact-finding." The reader interested in my refutations of these erroneous ideas should consult the book, *Endangered Species and Fragile Ecosystems in the South China Sea: The Philippines v. China Arbitration.*

Repetition has also been avoided as a result of the different perspective adopted in this book, yielding fresh insights that had not occurred to me when I was writing the first three books.

This book draws on sources in English, French, German, Italian, Portuguese, and Spanish.

I hope this book will convince the reader that China's conduct in the *South China Sea Arbitration* provides more trustworthy evidence of its true attitude to international law than its self-serving and implausible protestation, made at the UN General Assembly in 2014, that it is a staunch defender and builder of the rule of law in international relations.

Acknowledgments

It is my pleasure to acknowledge the assistance that I received in the writing of this book.

Dr. Thaemar Tana of the University of the Philippines facilitated access to a wide range of materials in various languages, without which this book, and indeed, my entire research on the *South China Sea Arbitration*, would have been impossible.

Kareff Rafisura's gift of the *Commentary* on the United Nations Convention on the Law of the Sea edited by Alexander Proelss is the gift for which I will never cease to be grateful.

In Japan, Darren Mangado located and scanned for me articles and books in English, French, and German that were published long before the digital age.

Dr. Tara Davenport of the National University of Singapore provided me with a copy of her book chapter entitled "Procedural Issues Arising from China's Non-Participation in the *South China Sea Arbitration.*"

Dr. Raymond Girard R. Tan, Member of the National Academy of Science and Technology (Engineering Sciences and Technology Division), University Fellow, and Vice President for Research and Innovation (VPRI) of De La Salle University, very kindly took the time to go through my sections on remote sensing and satellite-derived bathymetry and suggested corrections and improvements of the text.

Dr. Francis Rico Domingo of the Department of International Studies of De La Salle University discussed with me the hacking of the Permanent Court of Arbitration's website and China's cyberwarfare strategies.

Comments from an anonymous reviewer for Palgrave-Macmillan spurred me to clarify my main arguments and my methodology.

De La Salle University awarded me in 2020 a year-long research grant intended for University Fellows who are no longer teaching.

Dr. David Jonathan Bayot, Director of De La Salle University Publishing House (DLSUPH), once again proved to be the publisher that any academic would dream of having: he expressed interest in my manuscript, started the review process in the Philippines during the prolonged quarantine, and established contact with Palgrave-Macmillan for the publication of an international edition of the book.

Last but not least, the production teams of Palgrave-Macmillan and the DLSU Publishing House deserve thanks for their painstaking work in preparing the book for publication.

The usual caveats apply.

Contents

About the Author

Alfredo C. Robles Jr. is a University Fellow at De La Salle University. He holds doctorate degrees from the Université Paris 1 (Panthéon-Sorbonne) and Syracuse University. He is the author of *French Theories of Regulation and Conceptions of the International Division of Labour* (Macmillan, 1994), *The Political Economy of Interregional Relations: ASEAN and the EU* (Ashgate, 2004), *The Asia-Europe Meeting: The Theory and Practice of Interregionalism* (Routledge, 2008), *The South China Sea Arbitration: Understanding the Awards and Debating with China* (De La Salle University Publishing House and Sussex Academic Press, 2018), *Endangered Species and Fragile Ecosystems in the South China Sea: The Philippines v. China Arbitration* (Palgrave Macmillan, 2020) and *Vessel Collisions in the Law of the Sea: The South China Sea Arbitration* (Palgrave Macmillan, 2022).

ABBREVIATIONS, ACRONYMS, AND TERMS

ABLOS	Advisory Board on the Law of the Sea
AFDI	*Annuaire français de droit international* [French Yearbook of International Law]
AFRC	Armed Forces Revolutionary Council (Sierra Leone)
AJIL	*American Journal of International Law*
AMTI	Asian Maritime Transparency Institute
AOI	Area of Interest
APIIL	Asia-Pacific Institute of International Law
ASEAN	Association of Southeast Asian Nations
ASIPI	Inter-American Association of Intellectual Property
BRP	*Barko ng Republika ng Pilipinas* [Vessel of the Republic of the Philippines]
BYIL	*British Yearbook of International Law*
C(T)SIL	Chinese (Taiwan) Society of International Law
C(T)YILA	*Chinese (Taiwan) Yearbook of International Law and Affairs*
CBD	Convention on Biological Diversity, signed at Rio de Janeiro on 5 June 1992, entered into force on 29 December 1993
CCP	Chinese Communist Party
CE90	circular error at the 90th percentile
CJIL	*Chinese Journal of International Law*
CLCS	Commission on the Limits of the Continental Shelf
CMS	China Marine Surveillance
COLREGS	International Convention on the Regulations for Preventing Collisions at Sea, adopted at London on

	20 October 1972, entered into force 15 July 1977, amended in 1981, 1987, 1989, 1993, 2001 and 2007
Convention	United Nations Convention on the Law of the Sea, concluded at Montego Bay on 10 December 1982, entered into force on 16 November 1994
CPPCC	Chinese People's Political Consultative Conference
CSIL	Chinese Society of International Law
DEM	Digital Elevation Modeling
DOC	ASEAN-China Declaration on the Conduct of the Parties in the South China Sea, 4 November 2002
ECHR	European Convention on Human Rights
ECtHR	European Court of Human Rights
EEZ	Exclusive Economic Zone
EIA	Environmental Impact Assessment
ERTS	Earth Resources Technology Satellite
ETM+	Enhanced Thematic Mapper Plus
FAO	United Nations Food and Agriculture Organization
FCO	Foreign and Commonwealth Office (UK)
FCTC	Framework Convention on Tobacco Control, done at Geneva on 21 May 2003, entered into force on 27 February 2005
FLEC	Fisheries Law Enforcement Command (China)
FRG	Federal Republic of Germany
FTC	NAFTA Free Trade Commission
GCP	Ground Control Point
GCRMN	Global Coral Reef Monitoring Network
GESAMP	Joint Group of Experts on the Scientific Aspects of Marine Environmental Protection
GIS	Geographic Information System
GYIL	*German Yearbook of International Law*
IACtHR	Inter-American Court of Human Rights
ICC	International Criminal Court
ICJ	International Court of Justice
ICRI	International Coral Reef Initiative
ICSID	International Centre for the Settlement of Investment Disputes
ICTR	International Criminal Tribunal for Rwanda
ICTY	International Criminal Tribunal for the Former Yugoslavia
IDI	*Institut de droit international* [Institute of International Law]
IHO	International Hydrographic Organization
ILA	International Law Association

ILC	United Nations International Law Commission
IMCO	Intergovernmental Maritime Consultative Organization
IMO	International Maritime Organization
IOC	Intergovernmental Oceanographic Commission
ITLOS	International Tribunal for the Law of the Sea
IUCN	International Union for the Conservation of Nature
IUSCT	Iran-United States Claims Tribunal
JIDL	*Journal of International Dispute Settlement*
LE90	90th percentile linear error
LPICT	*Law and Practice of International Courts and Tribunals*
MCS	Monitoring, Control, and Surveillance (Philippines)
MP	*Memorial of the Philippines* (30 March 2014)
MSS	Multispectral Scanners
NAFTA	North American Free Trade Agreement
NASA	National Aeronautics and Space Administration (US)
NPC	National People's Congress (China)
NSA	Non-State Actors
OAS	Organization of American States
PAHO	Pan-American Health Organization
PAMH	*The Philippines' Annexes cited during Merits Hearing* (30 November 2015)
PCA	Permanent Court of Arbitration
PCIJ	Permanent Court of International Justice
PLA	People's Liberation Army (China)
PPLC	Party Political-Legal Committee (China)
RCADI	*Recueil des Cours de l'Académie de droit international de La Haye* [Collected Courses of the Hague Academy of International Law]
RGDIP	*Revue générale de droit international public* [General Journal of Public International Law]
RIAA	*Reports of International Arbitral Awards*
RMSE	Root mean square error
ROC	Republic of China
RTRC	*Responses of the Philippines to the Tribunal's 5 February 2016 Request for Comments* (11 March 2016)
RTRC French Archives	*Responses of the Philippines to the Tribunal's 26 May 2016 Request for Comments on Materials from the French Archives* (3 June 2016)
RTRC Itu Aba	*Responses of the Philippines to the Tribunal's 1 April 2016 Request for Comments on Additional Materials regarding the Status of Itu Aba* (25 April 2016)

RTRC UKHO	*Responses of the Philippines to the Tribunal's 1 April 2016 Request for Comments on Materials from the Archives of the United Kingdom Hydrographic Office* (28 April 2016)
RUF	Revolutionary United Front (Sierra Leone)
SCSL	Special Court of Sierra Leone
SDP	*Supplemental Documents of the Philippines* (19 November 2015)
SOA	State Oceanic Administration (China)
SOE	State-owned Enterprise (China)
SOLAS	International Convention for the Safety of Life at Sea, adopted at London on 1 November 1974, entered into force on 25 May 1980
SPC	Supreme People's Court (China)
SWSP	*Supplemental Written Submission of the Philippines* (16 March 2015)
TM	Thematic Mapper
UKHO	United Kingdom Hydrographic Office
UNCITRAL	United Nations Commission on International Trade Law
UNCLOS I	First United Nations Conference on the Law of the Sea, Geneva, 24 February–27 April 1958
UNCLOS II	Second United Nations Conference on the Law of the Sea, Geneva, 17 March–26 April 1960
UNCLOS III	Third United Nations Conference on the Law of the Sea, 1973–1982
UNCSW	United Nations Commission on the Status of Women
UNDP	United Nations Development Programme
WGS	World Geodetic Survey
WHO	World Health Organization
WTO	World Trade Organization
WWF	World Wide Fund for Nature

List of Tables

CHAPTER 1

Introduction

The proper administration of justice would seem to require the simultaneous appearance before the judge of the two parties, each of which would present its arguments and evidence as well as contest those of the other party. In pre-Roman times, the absence of one party prevented the court from reaching a decision.[1] The requirement that both parties appear had disappeared in ancient Rome when the law envisaged situations in which either the plaintiff or the defendant defaulted.[2] It was only in modern times that the principle, already present in Roman law, that judgement could not be rendered against the party that had not appeared

[1] Claude-Albert Colliard, "La non-comparution [Non-appearance]," in Société française pour le droit international [French Society for International Law] ("SFDI"), Colloque de Lyon [Lyons Colloquium], *La juridiction internationale permanente* [Permanent International Jurisdiction] (Paris: Éditions A. Pedone, 1987), 167; Adhémar Enstein, *Histoire de la procédure criminelle en France et spécialement de la procédure inquisitoriale, depuis le XIIIe siècle jusqu'à nos jours* [A History of Criminal Procedure in France, and Particularly of the Inquisitorial Procedure, from the 13th Century to the Present] (Paris: L. Larose et Forcel, 1882), 60, https://archive.org/details/histoiredelapro00esmegoog/page/n10/mode/2up, accessed 11 March 2020.

[2] Pierre Boncenne and Olivier Bourbeau, *Théorie de la procédure civile, précédée d'une introduction* [Theory of Civil Procedure, Preceded by an Introduction], vol. III (2nd ed.; Paris: Videcoq père et fils Libraires, 1844), 2–6, https://ia800209.us.archive.org/7/items/thoriedelaproc03bonc/thoriedelaproc03bonc.pdf, accessed 9 March 2020. According to the authors, defaulting individuals sometimes hid behind the columns and statues of the Roman Forum.

A. C. Robles Jr., *The Defaulting State and the South China Sea Arbitration*, https://doi.org/10.1007/978-981-19-6394-0_1

or defended itself without further examination of the case by the judge, became widely accepted.[3]

At the international level, as arbitration became more widely accepted as a means of dispute settlement from the mid-nineteenth century onwards, States anticipated situations in which one or the other of the parties would fail to defend its case. These agreements provided for default judgments. For example, a special agreement between Great Britain and Portugal, signed in 1861, stipulated that the Hamburg Senate, which had been empowered to settle the dispute, would give a decision by default if either or both parties failed to reply to the Memorandum of the other party.[4] In the twentieth century, Article XV of the

[3] Ibid., 6, 11; Géraldine Haas, "La procédure par défaut et l'opposition. Notions générales et contradictions [Default and Opposition Procedure. General Notions and Contradictions]," unpublished master's thesis, Faculty of Law and Criminology, Catholic University of Louvain, 2013, 6, https://dial.uclouvain.be/downloader/downloader.php?pid=thesis%3A1842&datastream=PDF_01, accessed 11 March 2020; Heinrich Mitteis, "Studien zur Geschichte des Versäumnisurteils, besonders im französischen Recht [Studies on the History of Default Judgments, Particularly in French Law]," *Zeitschrift der Savigny-Stiftung für Rechtsgeschichte. Germanistische Abteilung* [Journal of the Savigny Foundation for Legal History. German Department] 42 (1921): 141.

[4] "Memorandum para ser transmitido au Senado da Cidade Libre de Hamburgo, para se encarregar da arbitragem relativamente à reclamação dos Sres Yuille, Shortridge e Cia [Memorandum to Be Transmitted to the Senate of the Free City of Hamburg, to Take Charge of the Arbitration Relating to the Claim of Messrs. Yuille, Shortridge and Co.] [8 March 1861]," in Henri La Fontaine (ed.), *Pasicrisie internationale 1794–1900. Histoire documentaire des arbitrages internationaux* [Compendium of International Caselaw 1794–1900. A Documentary History of International Arbitrations] (Berne: Imprimerie Stampfli & Cie, 1902), 377, https://ia600205.us.archive.org/9/items/pasicrisieinter00fontgoog/pasicrisieinter00fontgoog.pdf, accessed 11 March 2020. The Portuguese text uses the expression "*ex parte*," "in part," "with only one party or side present before a tribunal." Aaron X. Fellmeth and Maurice Horwitz, *Guide to Latin in International Law* (New York: Oxford University Press, 2009), 97. Hans von Mangoldt, "Versäumnisverfahren in der internationalen (Schieds) Gerichtsbarkeit und souveräne Gleichheit [Default Procedures in International Arbitration and Adjudication and Sovereign Equality]," in Rudolf Bernhardt (ed.), *Völkerrecht als Rechtsordnung, internationale Gerichtsbarkeit, Menschenrechte. Festschrift für Hermann Mosler* [International Law as a Legal Order, International Adjudication, Human Rights. Festschrift for Hermann Mosler] (Berlin: Springer Verlag, 1983), 504, cites another special agreement between the same States, signed in 1855 ("1955" is erroneously substituted for "1855"), but the English and Portuguese versions of the agreement seem to differ. The French translation of the English text is identical to the text of the later agreement. Albert Geouffre de Lapradelle and Nicolas Politis (eds.), *Recueil des arbitrages internationaux* [Compilation of International Arbitrations], vol. II, *1856–1872* (Paris: A. Pedone Éditeur, 1923), 12, https://ia802607.us.archive.org/3/items/recueildesarbitr02lapruoft/recueildesarbitr02lapruoft.pdf, accessed 11 March 2020. The Portuguese text, on the other hand,

Convention for the Establishment of a Central American Court of Justice of 1907 provided that if the defendant State (mistranslated in the English text as "complainant") failed to respond to a complaint within 80 days, the Central American Court was authorized to render a decision "in view of the evidence presented and of such evidence as it may ex officio have seen fit to obtain."[5]

In the absence of *travaux préparatoires* we can only speculate about the rationale for Article XV, but whatever the rationale for it may have been, Article 53 of the Statute of the Permanent Court of International Justice ("PCIJ"), established in 1922, marked a departure from these earlier agreements, in that it imposed on the PCIJ an obligation to satisfy itself not only that it had jurisdiction over the dispute but also that the claim of the appearing party was "well founded in fact and law" if one of the parties did not appear before the Court or failed to defend its case. The same obligation was imposed on the International Court of Justice ("ICJ"), the PCIJ's successor, by Article 53 of its Statute. Although largely inspired by Article 53 of the PCIJ and ICJ Statutes, Article 28 of the Statute of the International Tribunal for the Law of the Sea ("ITLOS") and Article 9 of Annex VII of the United Nations Convention on the Law of the Sea ("the Convention"), which governs arbitration, differ from Article 53 of the PCIJ and ICJ Statutes in that they provided a title to the article concerned and explicitly used the term "default" and "default of appearance," respectively, to refer to the phenomenon that in the PCIJ and ICJ contexts is known as "failure to appear" or "non-appearance."[6] The use of the expression "default of

suggests that the Free Senate could decide *ex parte* only if the claimant, Croft, failed to transmit his response to the Portuguese Memorandum to the Senate. "Memorandum pour soumettre au Sénat de Hambourg en qualité d'arbitre la réclamation Croft [Memorandum submitting the Croft Claim to the Senate of Hamburg as Arbitrator][9 July 1861]," in La Fontaine, *Pasicrisie internationale*, 371–72. It is probably these two types of provision that justified Fitzmaurice's contention that the drafters of Article 53 of the PCIJ and ICJ Statutes could not have had in mind a total boycott by the respondent of proceedings. Gerald Fitzmaurice, "The Problem of the 'Non-appearing' Defendant Government," *British Yearbook of International Law* 51 (1980): 93 ("*BYIL*").

5 *Convention for the Establishment of a Central American Court of Justice*, *American Journal of International Law*, 2, No. 1/2, *Supplement: Official Documents* (1908): 237 ("*AJIL*").

6 *United Nations Convention on the Law of the Sea*, concluded at Montego Bay on 10 December 1982, entered into force on 16 November 1994 ("Convention"), http://www.un.org/Depts/los/convention_agreements/texts/unclos/closindx.htm, accessed 21

appearance" in the title of Article 9 of Annex VII thus justifies the designation of the State that conducts itself in the manner described in that Article as "the defaulting State."[7] As we shall see, the interpretation and application of Article 9 of Annex VII are central to the understanding of the proceedings in the *South China Sea Arbitration*.

The territorial and maritime disputes in the South China Sea, a semi-enclosed sea of 2.74 million square kilometers and with dozens of insular features, mainly the Paracel Islands, Scarborough Shoal, and the Spratly Islands, are among the most complex disputes of their kind at the present time.[8] Five states (Brunei Darussalam, China, Malaysia, the Philippines, and Vietnam) as well as Taiwan (Republic of China) have territorial and maritime claims of varying geographic scope and legal foundations. Three categories of disputes in the South China Sea have been identified by scholars, each involving different sets of States.[9] The sovereignty disputes encompass both islands and insular features in the South China Sea. As Jayakumar et al. rightly observe, the most complicated sovereignty disputes are over the Spratly Islands, as they involve the greatest number of claimants and maritime features.[10] Maritime entitlement disputes revolve around the legal capability of maritime features in the South China Sea to generate maritime zones—territorial sea, exclusive economic zone ("EEZ"), and/or continental shelf—under the Convention. The most prominent of these disputes arise over China's claim that the Spratly Islands "as a whole" are entitled to all maritime zones under the Convention. The third category of disputes, maritime delimitation

March 2019; United Nations Division for Ocean Affairs and the Law of the Sea, *Annex VI. Statute of the International Tribunal for the Law of the Sea*, http://www.un.org/depts/los/convention_agreements/texts/unclos/annex6.htm, accessed 11 March 2020.

[7] It should be noted that in French, the term "État défaillant" (defaulting State) is used to designate the State that does not appear before a court or fails to defend its case.

[8] *South China Sea Arbitration, Memorial of the Philippines* (30 March 2014), vol. I, 3, para. 9 ("*MP*"), https://files.pca-cpa.org/pcadocs/Memorial%20of%20the%20Philippines%20Volume%20I.pdf, accessed 27 March 2019.

[9] The following discussion relies mainly on S Jayakumar et al., "The *South China Sea Arbitration*: Laying the Groundwork," in S. Jayakumar et al. (eds.), *The South China Sea Arbitration: The Legal Dimension* (Cheltenham: Edward Elgar Publishing, 2018), 2–9, and Michael Sheng-Ti Gau, "The U-Shaped Line and a Categorization of the Ocean Disputes in the South China Sea," *Ocean Development and International Law* 43 (2012): 62–64.

[10] Jayakumar et al., "The *South China Sea Arbitration*," 3.

disputes, can only be resolved once the first two categories of disputes have been settled, and even then, maritime delimitation would hardly be a straightforward exercise.[11] In all categories of disputes, the issues, as China put it, are "compounded by a complex historical background and sensitive political factors."[12]

This tangled skein was shaken on 22 January 2013, when the Philippines initiated arbitration under Annex VII of the Convention by means of a Notification and Statement of Claim addressed to China.[13] On 19 February, China rejected and returned the Philippine Notification and Statement of Claim.[14] On the same day, the Philippines responded that China's rejection of the *Arbitration* would not interfere with the proceedings and that the Tribunal would be constituted, with or without China's participation.[15] The following day a Chinese spokesperson forcefully expressed China's disapproval of and opposition to the initiation of the *Arbitration*.[16] On 26 March, China reiterated its preferred scenario, in

[11] Ibid., 9.

[12] *South China Sea Arbitration, Supplemental Written Submission of the Philippines* (16 March 2015), Annex 467, People's Republic of China, Position Paper of the Government of the People's Republic of China on the Matter of Jurisdiction in the South China Sea Arbitration Initiated by the Republic of the Philippines (7 December 2014), vol. VIII, 32, para. 92 ("*SWSP*"), https://files.pca-cpa.org/pcadocs/The%20Philippines%27%20Supplemental%20Written%20Submission%20-%20Volume%20VIII%20%28Annexes%20466-499%29.pdf, accessed 10 March 2020.

[13] *MP*, Annex 1, Notification and Statement of Claim of the Republic of the Philippines (22 January 2013), vol. I, 11–32, https://files.pca-cpa.org/pcadocs/Memorial%20of%20the%20Philippines%20Volume%20I.pdf, accessed 27 March 2019. For the text of Annex VII, see United Nations Division for Ocean Affairs and the Law of the Sea, *Annex VII. Arbitration* ("*Annex VII*"), http://www.un.org/depts/los/convention_agreements/texts/unclos/annex7.htm, accessed 10 March 2020.

[14] *MP*, Annex 3, *Note Verbale* from the Embassy of the People's Republic of China in Manila to the Department of Foreign Affairs of the Republic of the Philippines, No. (13) PG-039 (19 February 2013), vol. I, 39, https://files.pca-cpa.org/pcadocs/Memorial%20of%20the%20Philippines%20Volume%20I.pdf, accessed 27 March 2019.

[15] *The Department of Foreign Affairs' Statement on China's Response to the Philippines' Arbitration Case* (19 February 2013), https://tokyo.philembassy.net/02events/the-department-of-foreign-affairs-statement-on-chinas-response-to-the-philippines-arbitration-case/, accessed 18 August 2020.

[16] Embassy of the People's Republic of China in the United States of America, *Foreign Ministry Spokesperson Hong Lei's Regular Press Conference on February 20, 2013* (21 February 2013), http://www.china-embassy.org/eng/fyrth/t1015425.htm, accessed 10 March 2020.

which the Philippines would "return to the right track" of bilateral negotiations.[17] In a statement devoted exclusively to the *Arbitration*, China declared the Philippine recourse to arbitration "absolutely unacceptable to China."[18] China's default would condition decisively the conduct of the arbitral proceedings in the following three and a half years.

The *South China Sea Arbitration* was the first instance of default in arbitration under Annex VII of the Convention and in proceedings under any of the Convention's compulsory dispute settlement mechanisms. It is also the first major instance of default before an international court since the US withdrawal in 1984 from the proceedings on the merits in the *Nicaragua Case* before the ICJ.[19] These circumstances would suffice to justify a full-length study of China's default in the *South China Sea Arbitration*. Other considerations militate in favor of such a study. The challenges posed by the default of the respondent State (the State against which proceedings are instituted), for the applicant State (the State instituting proceedings), and for an international court were magnified in the *South China Sea Arbitration* by several circumstances. The first is the sheer number and the breadth of the claims of the Philippines. The fifteen submissions ranged from China's claim of historic rights under the Convention (Submissions No. 1 and 2) to China's conduct endangering the safety of navigation (Submission No. 13), including the status of maritime features as low-tide elevations or rocks (Submissions No. 3, 4, 5, 6, and 7), interference by China in the exercise by the Philippines of its sovereign rights in its EEZ and continental shelf (Submissions No. 8, 9, and 12(a)), China's interference with traditional fishing in the territorial sea of Scarborough Shoal (Submission No. 10), China's violation of its

[17] Ibid., *Foreign Ministry Spokesperson Hong Lei's Regular Press Conference on March 26, 2013*, (27 March 2013), http://www.china-embassy.org/eng/fyrth/t1025838.htm, accessed 10 March 2020.

[18] Ministry of Foreign Affairs of the People's Republic of China, *Foreign Ministry Spokesperson Hua Chunying's Remarks on the Philippines' Efforts in Pushing for the Establishment of the Arbitral Tribunal in Relation to the Disputes between China and the Philippines in the South China Sea* (26 April 2013), https://www.fmprc.gov.cn/mfa_eng/xwfw_665399/s2510_665401/2535_665405/t1035577.shtml, accessed 10 March 2020.

[19] "Text of US Statement on Withdrawal from Case Before the World Court," *New York Times*, 19 January 1985 ("U.S. Statement on Withdrawal"), http://www.nytimes.com/1985/01/19/world/text-of-us-statement-on-withdrawal-from-case-before-the-world-court.html?pagewanted=all&pagewanted=print, accessed 13 March 2020.

obligation to protect and preserve the marine environment (Submissions No. 11 and 12(b)), the aggravation of the dispute by China (Submission No. 14), and an undertaking by China to respect Philippine rights and freedoms under the Convention (Submission No. 15).[20]

Second, the Philippines presented complex scientific and technical evidence in support of some of its claims. To take just one example, to support its claim that Second Thomas Shoal was a low-tide elevation (Submission No. 4), the Philippines submitted two images of the Shoal. The first was in Band 1 (blue–green), corresponding to shorter wavelength light (0.45–0.52 μm) in the electromagnetic spectrum, which penetrates water better than other bands. In that image, the underwater structure of Second Thomas Shoal was visible.[21] The second image was in Band 4 (near infrared), corresponding to longer wavelengths (0.76–0.90 μm) that are almost entirely absorbed by water. Only features above water are visible in Band 4, which allegedly makes clear that there are no features above water at Second Thomas Shoal.[22] On the basis of images of this type, the Philippines requested that the Tribunal declare that Second Thomas Shoal, Mischief Reef, and Subi Reef are low-tide elevations—naturally formed areas of land that are above water at low tide and that are submerged at high tide. The Philippines submitted evidence that was no less complex in support of its Submissions No. 11 and 12(b) on the marine environment and Submission No. 13 on the near collisions between Chinese and Philippine vessels in 2012.

Third, the litigation strategy of the defaulting State differed markedly in certain respects from that of defaulting States in previous cases before the ICJ. China exerted pressures on the Tribunal that recall the pressures to which the Chinese government and the Chinese Communist Party ("CCP") subject Chinese judges. When the pressures failed to intimidate the judges, China undertook a defamation campaign against the judges that assumed that international judges are as corrupt as Chinese judges.

[20] *South China Sea Arbitration*, Award of 12 July 2016, 41–42, para. 112, https://pcacases.com/web/sendAttach/2086, accessed 27 August 2020.

[21] The symbol "μm" refers to a micrometer, defined as one-millionth of a meter (10^{-6} m). It was formerly referred to as "micron." *Larousse Dictionary of Science and Technology* (Edinburgh: Larousse plc, 1995), 700.

[22] *MP*, vol. I, 132–36, paras. 5.59–5.73. The images of Second Thomas Shoal and of other features are in volume II, which is not available on the website of the Permanent Court of Arbitration ("PCA"), the Registry in the case.

Fourth, the Arbitral Tribunal, in fulfillment of its duty to satisfy itself not only that it had jurisdiction over the dispute but also that the Philippine submissions were well founded in fact and in law, adopted a number of procedural innovations, notably in fact-finding, that took account of the difficulties posed by default to the appearing State and to the Tribunal. At the same time, the Tribunal acted as the de facto counsel of the defaulting State.

Existing scholarly studies of China's default in the *South China Sea Arbitration* are far from satisfactory. With one exception,[23] Chinese scholars defend China's default and criticize the Tribunal's fact-finding and handling of procedural matters. Chinese scholar He Tiantian, describing the case as "exceptionally fact-intensive," believes that the magnitude of the task facing the Tribunal in evaluating an enormous amount of material was such that it could not have been carried out without China's cooperation.[24] Interestingly, the book-length critique of the Tribunal's decisions by the Chinese Society of International Law ("CSIL") raises issues of due process and evidence without acknowledging China's default.[25] Had one not known any better, one might get the impression that the Tribunal had ignored arguments and evidence

[23] Mincai Yu, "China's Responses to the Compulsory Arbitration on the South China Sea Dispute: Legal Effects and Policy Options," *Ocean Development and International Law* 45 (2014): 1–16; Mincai Yu, "China's Informal Participation in the Annex VII Philippines v. China Arbitral Tribunal's Proceedings," *International Journal of Marine and Coastal Law* 30 (2015): 54–92.

[24] He Tiantian, "Commentary on Award on Jurisdiction and Admissibility of the Philippines-instituted Arbitration under Annex VII to the UNCLOS: A Discussion on Fact-Finding and Evidence," *Chinese Journal of Global Governance* 2 (2016): 103–04. See also Yen-Chiang Chang, "China's Non-participation Approach Toward the South China Sea Arbitration," *Chinese (Taiwan) Yearbook of International Law and Affairs* 34 (2016): 56–72 ("*C(T)YILA*"); Shiping Liao, "Fact-Finding in Non-appearance Before International Courts and Tribunals," unpublished ms., Beijing Normal University, 2018, https://ssrn.com/abstract=3187971, accessed 22 March 2020; Xinjun Zhang, "Nonappearance and Procedural Delicacy: Some Observations on the Tribunal's Handling of Jurisdiction in the South China Sea Arbitration," unpublished ms., Tsinghua University, September 2018, https://papers.ssrn.com/sol3/papers.cfm?abstract_id=3205321, accessed 16 July 2020; and Xinjun Zhang, "Bifurcation in Inter-State Cases" *University of Pennsylvania Journal of International Law* 40 (2018–2019): 937–88, https://scholarship.law.upenn.edu/cgi/viewcontent.cgi?article=1991&context=jil, accessed 24 October 2019.

[25] Chinese Society of International Law ("CSIL"), "The South China Sea Arbitration Awards: A Critical Study," *Chinese Journal of International Law* 17 (2018): 620–39, paras. 886–947 ("*CJIL*").

that had been presented by a respondent that had appeared before it. Yet if one examines closely the CSIL's criticisms, one immediately realizes that they can often be refuted by referring to China's default. Chinese accounts of China's default are usually ignored in writings by non-Chinese scholars. Perhaps the one-sided character of nearly all Chinese accounts explains the absence of reference to them. The unfortunate result of this understandable neglect is that many misconceptions purveyed by Chinese scholars remain unanswered. Outside China, an effort is made to explain the motivations for China's default and to determine whether it portends fundamental changes in China's attitude toward international law.[26] Even among non-Chinese scholars, criticism of China's default is rare.[27] Only occasionally does scholarly commentary analyze China's default in the broader context of the phenomenon, with reference to ICJ cases.[28] Several authors examine the procedural issues arising from China's default

[26] Isaac B. Kardon, "China Can Say No: Analyzing China's Rejection of the South China Sea Arbitration. Toward a New Era of International Law with Chinese Characteristics," *University of Pennsylvania Asian Law Review* 13 (2018): 1–46, https://scholarship.law.upenn.edu/cgi/viewcontent.cgi?article=1037&context=alr, accessed 23 June 2019; Julian Ku, "The Significance of China's Rejection of the South China Sea Arbitration for Its Approach to International Dispute Settlement and International Law," *C(T)YILA* 34 (2016): 73–103; Bing Ling, *China's Attitude to the International Legal Order in the Xi Era: The Case of the South China Sea*, Japan Institute of International Affairs (JIIA) Indo-Pacific Focus Policy Brief No. 4 (27 June 2018), https://www2.jiia.or.jp/en/article_page.php?id=7, accessed 7 February 2019.

[27] The notable exceptions are Elena Pineros Polo, "Arbitraje del mar del sur de China. la estrategia procesal de la República Popular de China [The South China Sea Arbitration. The Procedural Strategy of the People's Republic of China]," *Revista Electrónica de Estudios Internacionales* [Electronic Journal of International Studies] 35 (2018): 1–23, http://www.reei.org/index.php/revista/num35/notas/arbitraje-mar-sur-china-estrategia-procesal-republica-popular-china, accessed 10 June 2020, and Otto Spijkers, "Non-participation in Arbitral Proceedings Under Annex VII United Nations Convention on the Law of the Sea: *"Arctic Sunrise"* and *South China Sea* Compared," in Angela Del Vecchio and Roberto Virzo (eds.), *Interpretations of the United Nations Convention on the Law of the Sea by International Courts and Tribunals* (Cham, Switzerland: Springer International Publishing, 2019), 171–90.

[28] Alexander Wentker, *Nichtteilnahme als Grenzphänomen zwischenstaatlicher Gerichts- und Schiedsverfahren – die Fälle South China Sea und "Arctic Sunrise"* [Non-participation in Inter-State Proceedings Before International Tribunals – the South China Sea and "Arctic Sunrise" Cases] (Heidelberg: Max Planck Institute for Comparative Public Law and International Law, 2018), https://papers.ssrn.com/sol3/papers.cfm?abstract_id=3248261, accessed 17 March 2020.

and the procedural innovations adopted by the Tribunal.[29] It is to be regretted, though, that noteworthy aspects of the Tribunal's approach to fact-finding are neglected (e.g., the treatment of submissions by self-proclaimed *amicus curiae*, "friends of the court"), misunderstood (e.g., the Tribunal's independent fact-finding), not fully explored (e.g., the expert evidence), or not further explained (e.g., the Tribunal's evaluation of expert evidence). China's efforts to pressure and defame the Tribunal are for the most part passed over in silence. Finally, the English-language literature makes very little reference to scholarly writings in languages other than English.

This book focuses on the legal issues raised by China's default in the *South China Sea Arbitration* and its practical consequences for the proceedings. Examining the record of default before the ICJ between 1948 and the 1980s, it accepts that in some respects China's litigation strategy resembled that of other defaulting States; but in other respects, it diverged significantly from that of these other States. Faced with the litigation strategy of the defaulting State, the Arbitral Tribunal could only respond using its procedural powers and could only address those issues that came within the scope of its procedural powers, in order to fulfill its duty under Article 9 of Annex VII of the Convention to satisfy itself not only that it had jurisdiction but also that the claims of the Philippines were well founded in fact and in law.

Like defaulting States before the ICJ, China sought to exempt itself from the proceedings by affirming the absence of a duty to appear, but unlike most other defaulting States, it went further and asserted the existence of a right not to appear. In effect, China denied the principle that a Tribunal has jurisdiction to determine its jurisdiction, a principle that has been established for over 150 years. One course of action that could not be incorporated in China's litigation strategy was withdrawal from the dispute settlement mechanism of the Convention. As that mechanism

[29] Tara Davenport, "Procedural Issues Arising from China's Non-participation in the *South China Sea Arbitration*," in S. Jayakumar et al. (eds.), *The South China Sea Arbitration: The Legal Dimension* (Cheltenham: Edward Elgar Publishing, 2018), 65–98; Jacqueline Joyce F. Espenilla, "Judicial Fact-Finding Initiatives in the *South China Sea Arbitration*," *Asian Journal of International Law* 9 (2019): 20–30; Judith Levine and Garth L. Schofield, "Navigating Uncharted Procedural Waters in a Rising Sea of Cases at the Permanent Court of Arbitration," in Stephen Minas and H. Jordan Diamond (eds.), *Stress Testing the Law of the Sea: Dispute Resolution, Disasters and Emerging Challenges* (Leiden: Brill Nijhoff, 2018), 95–149.

was an integral part of the Convention, withdrawal from it would have required withdrawal from the Convention. Faced with a defaulting State that denied its competence to decide on jurisdiction, the Tribunal could only respond by bifurcating the proceedings and devoting a separate phase thereof to the question of its jurisdiction.

Default raised for the Tribunal the twin problems of acquiring knowledge of the facts and maintaining the equality of the parties. Like other defaulting States before the ICJ, China was unable to adhere to its position not to participate in the proceedings, transmitting informal communications to the Tribunal and making public statements on the *Arbitration*. Unlike other defaulting States, China tacitly allowed entities that presented themselves as "*amici curiae*" ("friends of the court") to submit their views to the Tribunal. It cannot be excluded that China was responsible for the hacking of the website of the Permanent Court of Arbitration ("PCA"), the Registry in the case, during the Hearing on Jurisdiction and Admissibility in July 2015. The Tribunal, like the ICJ in cases of default, took account of China's informal communications and public statements. Unlike the ICJ, it tacitly admitted submissions by *amici curiae*. Unlike the ICJ, the Tribunal used the full range of its procedural powers to acquire knowledge of the facts: it permitted the appearing State to make a supplemental written submission; it put a large number of oral and written questions to the appearing State; it appointed independent experts; and it carried out independent fact-finding on behalf of the defaulting State and in pursuit of a line of inquiry that was different from that of the Philippines. In practice, as the Philippines admitted, the Tribunal acted as de facto counsel for the defaulting State, but it also introduced procedural innovations that alleviated the difficulties created by default for the appearing State.

Particular attention is paid to the exercise by the Tribunal of its power of appointing independent experts, for several reasons: the technical nature of several Philippine submissions; the introduction by the Tribunal of procedural innovations designed to ensure the independence and impartiality of the independent experts and to enable the parties to challenge their reports; the Tribunal's detailed examination of the evidence presented by the experts appointed by the Philippines and the independent experts; the CSIL'S post-litigation critique of the exercise of this power; and the scholarly debate on the independence and impartiality of international experts. Since China failed to have recourse to the procedures for ensuring the independence and impartiality of the experts appointed by the Tribunal, as well as those appointed by the Philippines, and the CSIL's critique was only put forward after the proceedings, it will be the task of this book to examine the issue of the independence and impartiality of the experts in the context of the practice of other international tribunals and the scholarly debate on the subject matter.

Unlike other defaulting States, China adopted a litigation strategy that involved questioning the composition of the Tribunal, undermining the independence of the judges, and challenging their impartiality. China sought to achieve the first goal by pointing out that the Tribunal had no Chinese or Asian member. The second goal was pursued through secret lobbying of the Tribunal and the organization of an international campaign that questioned the Award on Jurisdiction. The third goal alleged corruption of the judges, based on a deliberate misunderstanding of the nature of arbitral proceedings in which one party refuses to pay its share of the expenses. As in the case of the independent experts, China refused to have recourse to the procedures provided for in the Rules of Procedure of the *Arbitration* in order to ensure the independence and impartiality of the judges. This being the case, it will be the task of the book to examine these issues in the context of the practice of other international tribunals and of the scholarly debates on the subject matter.

This Chapter will present the legal framework of default under Annex VII of the Convention. It will then outline the practical consequences of default for the appearing State, the defaulting State, and the Tribunal. The third part will recapitulate the history of China's default in the arbitral proceedings. The fourth part will provide an overview of the book.

I. The Legal Framework of Default

Article 9 of Annex VII is the logical starting point of any study of China's default in the *South China Sea Arbitration*. Annex VII is an element of the unique dispute settlement mechanism of the Convention. The fact that the mechanism is incorporated in Part XV of the latter, rather than in an optional protocol, means that the procedures are binding on all States parties to the Convention as soon as they ratify the Convention. Part XV is also unique in that it provides for compulsory dispute settlement for most disputes that may arise in the interpretation and application of the Convention. The system is compulsory in that it permits initiation of procedures by a State party without further consent of another party, subject only to certain preconditions (laid out in Section 1 of Part XV) and to certain limitations and exceptions (laid out in Section 3 of Part XV). Section 2 of Part XV provides States parties to the Convention with a wide range of choices of the procedure for compulsory settlement of disputes, although arbitration under Annex VII is presumed to be the procedure chosen by the States parties if the States parties to the dispute have not chosen a procedure under Section 2 or they have not chosen the same procedure under Section 2. Decisions of judicial bodies under Section 2 are binding on the States parties to the dispute.

Article 9 of Annex VII reads as follows:

Article 9
Default of Appearance

> If one of the parties to the dispute does not appear before the arbitral tribunal or fails to defend its case, the other party may request the tribunal to continue the proceedings and to make its award. Absence of a party or failure of a party to defend its case shall not constitute a bar to the proceedings. Before making its award, the arbitral tribunal must satisfy itself not only that it has jurisdiction over the dispute but also that the claim is well founded in fact and law.

It follows from Article 9 that the proceedings may continue despite one State's default if the appearing State so requests. In this way, as the Tribunal explained, Article 9 protects the appearing State by ensuring that the proceedings will not be frustrated or paralyzed by the other party's decision to default.[30] Default of one party will not have the effect of depriving the appearing State of its right to obtain adjudication of its claim.[31] At the same time, Article 9 does not permit a default judgment. Rather it imposes on the tribunal the duty to satisfy itself not only that it has jurisdiction over the dispute but also that the claims of the applicant

[30] *South China Sea Arbitration*, Award on Jurisdiction and Admissibility (29 October 2015), 40, para. 115, https://pcacases.com/web/sendAttach/2579, accessed 10 March 2020.

[31] Gaetano Arangio-Ruiz, "Notes on Non-appearance Before the International Court of Justice," in *Le droit international à l'heure de sa codification. Études en l'honneur de Roberto Ago* [International Law at the Time of Its Codification. Studies in Honour of Roberto Ago], vol. II, *Les différends entre États et la responsabilité* [Inter-State Disputes and Responsibility] (Milano: Dott. A. Giuffrè Editore, 1987), 25.

are well founded in fact and in law. Article 9 protects the right of the defaulting State by ensuring that the tribunal will not simply accept the claim of the appearing State by default.[32] The price of the protection of the defaulting State is a heavy obligation imposed on the tribunal.

A. The Scope of Application of Article 9 of Annex VII

According to Article 9, default may occur in two situations. Article 9 leaves open its application to any phase of arbitral proceedings.

In the first situation identified by Article 9, a State does not appear before the Tribunal. Interpretations of Article 53 of the ICJ Statute, upon which Article 9 is based, may help us to understand what it means to say that a State "does not appear before the Tribunal." For Lamberti Zanardi, this means that a State has omitted an activity relating to the proceedings that constitute an obligation for it and that must be carried out within a certain time limit.[33] In Thirlway's view, a State that does not appear before the ICJ has not taken some action that is assumed to form part of the normal procedure: it has not informed the Court of its agent's name; it has not attended meetings with the Court's President to settle questions of procedure; it has not filed a *Counter-Memorial*; it has not addressed arguments to the Court at the oral hearings; and it has not replied to questions put to it.[34] Default in this situation may be partial or complete. It may occur in the written proceedings or in the oral proceedings.[35] Rosenne distinguishes between three situations: withdrawal of a

[32] Award on Jurisdiction, 40, para. 115.

[33] Pierluigi Lamberti Zanardi, "Forme nuove di contestazione della competenza della Corte internazionale di giustizia e potere della Corte di aprire d'ufficio un procedimento sulla competenza [New Forms of Challenge to the Jurisdiction of the International Court of Justice and the Court's Power to Open ex officio Jurisdictional Proceedings]," *Comunicazioni e studi* [Communications and Studies] 14 (1975): 458.

[34] H.W.A Thirlway, *Non-appearance Before the International Court of Justice* (Cambridge: Cambridge University Press, 1985), 2.

[35] Hermann Mosler, "Nichtteilnahme einer Partei am Verfahren vor dem Internationalen Gerichtshof [Non-participation of a Party in Proceedings before the International Court of Justice]," in Ingo von Münch (ed.), *Staatsrecht – Völkerrecht – Europarecht. Festschrift für Hans-Jürgen Schlochauer* [Constitutional Law – International Law - European Law. Festschrift for Hans-Jürgen Schlochauer] (Berlin: Walter de Gruyter, 1981), 446, it is difficult to imagine that a State that does not file a *Counter-Memorial* will then decide to participate in the oral proceedings.

party that has participated in an earlier phase of the proceedings; entry into the case after appearance in an earlier phase; and refusal to participate in any way.[36] The exact scope of the "failure to defend its case" is less clear. Lamberti Zanardi believes that in this situation a respondent has presented its *Counter-Memorial* or carried out some other act in the proceedings from which one may deduce the appearance of that State but has subsequently omitted an act in the proceedings that it is under an obligation to carry out within a certain timeframe. Even understood in this way, the difference between the two situations is not very clear. Ultimately, the distinction seems to matter little, as the two situations produce the same legal effects.[37] Rosenne lays stress on the motivations of a State that does not appear before an international court or fails to defend its case. A State may have objective reasons that prevent it from appearing or defending its case, or it may deliberately decide not to appear or defend its case. Regrettably, Rosenne does not provide any illustrations in State practice of this twofold distinction.[38]

The question of the phase in the proceedings in which provisions on default are applicable had triggered a lively debate among judges and scholars in the 1970s, when a State defaulted completely for the first time in proceedings before the ICJ. The debate would not seem to be of interest in the context of the *South China Sea Arbitration*, had it not been for a passing remark by Sienho Yee that "usually, the opening of the merits hearing would be finally the time to see for sure that a State would appear or not."[39] He was objecting to the fact that the Tribunal had scheduled the Hearing on the Merits only three weeks after the issuance of the Award on Jurisdiction and Admissibility. Alleging that three weeks would have been insufficient time for China to prepare its arguments and marshal evidence, he implies that China's repeated statements that it would not participate in the proceedings should not have been taken at face value. In his view, the Tribunal would have been able to determine that China had indeed defaulted only if it did not participate in the oral

[36] Shabtai Rosenne, with the assistance of Yaël Ronen, *The Law and Practice of the International Court, 1920–2005*, vol. III, *Jurisdiction* (Leiden: Martinus Nijhoff Publishers, 2006), 1360–61.

[37] Lamberti Zanardi, "Forme nuove," 459–60.

[38] Rosenne, *The Law and Practice*, 1360.

[39] Sienho Yee, "The South China Sea Arbitration Decisions on Jurisdiction and Rule of Law Concerns," *CJIL* 15 (2016): 224.

proceedings, which would have been the last opportunity for China to defend its case. In short, the Tribunal should not have taken a procedural decision that assumed that China would persist in its default. Sienho Yee's reasoning reminds us that certain ICJ members in the 1970s were of the view that the Statute provisions on default could not be applicable before the merits phase of the proceedings. They explained that a State cannot be compelled to give an account of itself before an international court until that court has decided that it has jurisdiction. They added that a respondent cannot decide whether it should default or not unless it has full knowledge of all the arguments and evidence submitted by the appearing State. Such full knowledge can only be attained after submission of the written pleadings on the merits.[40] The implication is that there can be no default in the phases devoted to a request for provisional measures and to jurisdiction and admissibility.[41] This reasoning forgets that at the jurisdictional phase, there is already jurisdiction—the jurisdiction of the court to determine its own jurisdiction.[42] This being the case, default may occur at any phase of the proceedings. This debate has been resolved in favor of

[40] *Fisheries Jurisdiction (United Kingdom v. Iceland), Order of 18 August 1972*, Joint Dissenting Opinion of Judges Bengzon and Jiménez de Aréchaga, *I.C.J. Reports 1972*, 184–86, https://www.icj-cij.org/en/case/55/orders, accessed 11 August 2019. This view was supported by Lamberti Zanardi, "Forme nuove," 458; Pierre-Michel Eisemann, "Les effets de la non-comparution devant la Cour internationale de Justice [The Effects of Non-appearance Before the International Court of Justice]," *Annuaire français de droit international* [French Yearbook of International Law] *AFDI* 19 (1973): 356–57 ("*AFDI*"), https://www.persee.fr/docAsPDF/afdi_0066-3085_1973_num_19_1_2217.pdf, accessed 23 March 2020; Louis Favoreu, "Les arrêts de la Cour Internationale de Justice relatifs à la compétence en matière de pêcheries (Royaume-Uni c/Islande et République fédérale d'Allemagne c. Islande – Arrêts du 25 juillet 1974) [The Judgments of the International Court of Justice on Fisheries Jurisdiction (United Kingdom v. Iceland and Federal Republic of Germany v. Iceland – Judgments of 25 July 1974]," *AFDI* 20 (1974): 258, http://www.persee.fr/doc/afdi_0066-3085_1974_num_20_1_2271, accessed 17 March 2020; and Louis Favoreu, "Les ordonnances des 17 et 18 août 1972 dans les affaires relatives à la compétence en matière de pêcheries - Contribution au droit procédural de la Cour en matière de mesures conservatoires, exceptions préliminaires et compétence en cas de défaut (Royaume-Uni c. Islande et République fédérale d'Allemagne c. Islande) [The Orders of 17 and 18 August 1972 in the Cases relating to Fisheries Jurisdiction – Contribution to the Procedural Law of the Court with respect to Provisional Measures, Preliminary Objections and Jurisdiction in case of Default]," *AFDI* 8 (1972): 320–21, http://www.persee.fr/doc/afdi_0066-3085_1972_num_18_1_3855, accessed 4 March 2018.

[41] Eisemann, "Les effets," 356.

[42] Thirlway, *Non-appearance*, 40.

the thesis that the provisions on default apply whenever an international court has to take a decision of any kind in which the respondent State is not cooperating.[43]

Returning to Sienho Yee's argument: China had already been given time to prepare a *Counter-Memorial* following the submission of the Philippine *Memorial*. Instead of filing a *Counter-Memorial*, China transmitted a Position Paper to the Tribunal. Subsequently, China was given the opportunity to respond to the supplemental written submissions of the Philippines; to submit observations on the Hearing on Jurisdiction as well as to the transcripts thereof; to comment on the schedule of the Hearing on the Merits; and to comment on the list of questions formulated by the Tribunal prior to the Hearing on the Merits. China had not responded to any of the requests for comments and had repeatedly declared that it would not change its position. Having all these circumstances in mind, the Tribunal, while indicating to China that it was open to it to participate in the proceedings at any time and that the Tribunal would adjust the schedule of the hearings if China changed its mind, must have concluded that China had already defaulted and that it would persist in its default. Following Sienho Yee's logic would have delayed the proceedings, the continuation of which is authorized by Article 9.

B. The Continuation of the Proceedings

The first consequence of default is that upon the request of the appearing party, the proceedings will continue, notwithstanding the default of the respondent State. As a result of the continuation of the proceedings, the defaulting State remains a party to the case. As such, it enjoys the same rights and is subject to the same obligations as the appearing State.

The first sentence of Article 9 replaces the phrase of Article 53 of the ICJ Statute, which authorizes the appearing State to request that the ICJ decide in favor of its claim. In this manner, Article 9 of Annex VII spells out the right of the appearing State in a more neutral way, avoiding the possible tension between the right of the appearing State to request that the Tribunal decide in favor if its claim and the Tribunal's duty to satisfy itself not only that it has jurisdiction but also that the claim is

[43] Ibid., 140.

well founded in fact and in law. For a judge of the ITLOS, this formulation represents an improvement over Article 53 of the ICJ Statute.[44] The second sentence of Article 9 has no equivalent in Article 53. It is understood in Article 9 that the proceedings will continue provided there is a title to jurisdiction. If, for instance, the defaulting State were not a party to the Convention, then there would obviously be no basis at all for an arbitral tribunal's jurisdiction, making it impossible for the proceedings to continue.[45] The Philippines expressly requested, for the avoidance of doubt, that the proceedings continue.[46] Consequently, the *South China Sea* Tribunal continued the proceedings.[47]

Yet the Tribunal did not give up hope that China might change its decision taken at the time of the constitution of the Tribunal and participate in the subsequent phases of the proceedings. During both Hearings, the Tribunal declared that it was open to China to participate in the proceedings at any stage; as we shall see, the Tribunal expressed its willingness to modify the schedule of the Hearing on the Merits in the event that China decided to take part in the Hearing.[48] The reminder was not a pure formality. It has happened in three cases before the ICJ that as the proceedings continued and the Court made a decision that was unfavorable to the defaulting State, the latter changed its mind and participated in the subsequent proceedings. In the *Nottebohm Case*, Liechtenstein

[44] *"Arctic Sunrise" (Kingdom of the Netherlands v. Russian Federation), Provisional Measures, Order of 22 November 2013*, Separate Opinion of Judge Paik, *ITLOS Reports 2013*, 273, para. 2, https://www.itlos.org/fileadmin/itlos/documents/cases/case_no.22/published/C22_Paik_221113.pdf, accessed 19 March 2020; Wentker, *Nichtteilnahme*, 27.

[45] C. Amerasinghe, Letter of 19 October 1990, in Gaetano Arangio-Ruiz, "Non-appearance Before the International Court of Justice. Final Report," *Annuaire de l'Institut de droit international* [Yearbook of the Institute of International Law], Session de Bâle [Basel Session], 64-I (1991), 344 ("Non-appearance Final Report"), http://www.gaetanoarangioruiz.it/publications/non-appearance-before-the-international-court-of-justice/, accessed 13 October 2019.

[46] *MP*, vol. I, 6, 230, paras. 1.21, 7.39.

[47] Award on Jurisdiction, 39, para. 113; Award of 12 July 2016, 45, para. 118.

[48] *South China Sea Arbitration*, Hearing on Jurisdiction and Admissibility, Transcript, Day 1 (7 July 2015), 2 ("Hearing on Jurisdiction"), https://pcacases.com/web/sendAttach/1399, accessed 19 March 2020; *South China Sea Arbitration*, Hearing on the Merits and Remaining Issues of Admissibility, Transcript, Day 1 (24 November 2015), 2 ("Hearing on the Merits"), https://pcacases.com/web/sendAttach/1547, accessed 19 March 2020; Award on Jurisdiction, 12, para. 18; Award of 12 July 2016, 47, para. 121(k).

had instituted proceedings against Guatemala in 1951 for the detention, internment, and expulsion of Friedrich Nottebohm and for the sequestration and confiscation of his property as an enemy alien during World War II.[49] Guatemala denied that the Court had jurisdiction to hear the case, citing the expiry of its declaration of acceptance of the ICJ compulsory jurisdiction by the time of the filing of the Application; at the same time, it denied that its attitude was one of voluntary absence.[50] Guatemala did not attend the Hearing on Jurisdiction. After the Court ruled that it had jurisdiction to hear the case, Guatemala decided to participate in the proceedings. Undoubtedly Guatemala took full advantage of the opportunity to present its case, as the ICJ ended up dismissing Liechtenstein's claim.[51]

In the *Anglo-Iranian Oil Co. Case*, the UK instituted proceedings against Iran for the nationalization of the Anglo-Iranian Oil Co. on 1 May 1951, which allegedly amounted to a unilateral annulment of a Convention signed in 1933 between the Company and Iran.[52] Iran did not attend the Hearing on the UK request for provisional measures, but it did send a telegram to the ICJ arguing that nationalization was a matter exclusively within its jurisdiction and that there existed no dispute between the UK and Iran.[53] Following the Court's issuance of an Order indicating provisional measures on 5 July 1951, Iran decided to participate in the proceedings on Iranian's objection that the Court lacked jurisdiction because the Convention between the Anglo-Iranian Oil Co. and Iran

[49] Liechtenstein, *Application Instituting Proceedings* (17 December 1951), *I.C.J. Pleadings, Nottebohm Case (Liechtenstein v. Guatemala)*, vol. I, 8, https://www.icj-cij.org/files/case-related/18/018-19511217-APP-1-00-BI.pdf, accessed 19 March 2020.

[50] Letter from the Minister of Foreign Affairs of Guatemala to the President of the International Court of Justice, 9 September 1952, *I.C.J. Pleadings, Nottebohm Case (Liechtenstein v. Guatemala)*. Vol. I, 162–69. https://www.icj-cij.org/files/case-related/18/10985.pdf, accessed 8 January 2020.

[51] *Nottebohm Case (second phase), Judgment of April 6th, 1955, I.C.J. Reports 1955*, 4, http://www.icj-cij.org/files/case-related/18/018-19550406-JUD-01-00-BI.pdf, accessed 19 March 2020.

[52] United Kingdom, *Application Instituting Proceedings* (26 May 1951), *I.C.J. Pleadings, Anglo-Iranian Oil Co. Case (United Kingdom v. Iran)*, 8, https://www.icj-cij.org/files/case-related/16/016-19510526-APP-1-00-BI.pdf, accessed 19 March 2020.

[53] Communication from the Minister of Foreign Affairs of Iran to the President of the International Court of Justice, dated 29 June 1951, with Three Annexes, *I.C.J. Pleadings, Anglo-Iranian Oil Co. Case (United Kingdom v. Iran)*, 679, https://www.icj-cij.org/files/case-related/16/8987.pdf, accessed 19 March 2020.

was not a treaty. Iran's decision to appear before the Court paid off, for the Court declared that it lacked jurisdiction.[54] In *Maritime Delimitation and Territorial Questions between Qatar and Bahrain*, relating to sovereignty over the Hawa Islands, sovereign rights over the Shoals of Dibal and Qit'al Jaradah, and the delimitation of maritime areas between the two States, Bahrain, which denied that there had been an agreement to submit their dispute to the ICJ, refused to appear before the Court in the second phase of the proceedings on jurisdiction.[55] Nearly a year after the Court issued its ruling on jurisdiction, based on Qatar's unilateral application, and two months before the time limit for the submission of Qatar's Memorial, Bahrain decided to participate in the hearings on the merits.[56]

China's default did not and could not mean that China was not a party to the case, as it insisted. The very text of Article 9 makes clear that the defaulting State remains a party, in that it refers to "[a]bsence of a *party* or failure of a *party* [italics supplied]." It acquires the status of a party as soon as the proceedings are initiated, for the simple reason that the defaulting State, by ratifying the Convention, gave its advance consent to the jurisdiction of a court to which a dispute is properly submitted by

[54] *Anglo-Iranian Oil Co. Case (Jurisdiction), Judgment of July 22, 1952: I.C.J. Reports 1952*, 93, https://www.icj-cij.org/files/case-related/16/016-19520722-JUD-01-00-BI.pdf, accessed 19 March 2020. At the Hearings on Jurisdiction, Iran was represented by no less than the Prime Minister, Dr. Mossadegh, who would a year later be the target of a CIA-sponsored coup to overthrow him. Minutes of the Public Sittings from June 9th to 23rd and July 22nd, 1952, *I.C.J. Pleadings, Anglo-Iranian Oil Co. Case*, 437–44, https://www.icj-cij.org/files/case-related/16/016-19520609-ORA-01-00-BI.pdf, accessed 8 January 2020.

[55] State of Bahrain, Ministry of State for Legal Affairs, Minister's Office, *Comments by the State of Bahrain on the Qatari "Act" of 30th November, 1994* (5 December 1994), 3, para. 8, https://www.icj-cij.org/files/case-related/87/13263.pdf, accessed 16 August 2020; *Maritime Delimitation and Territorial Questions between Qatar and Bahrain, Jurisdiction and Admissibility, Judgment, I.C.J. Reports 1995*, 9–10, paras. 12–14, https://www.icj-cij.org/files/case-related/87/087-19950215-JUD-01-00-BI.pdf, accessed 17 August 2020.

[56] Emmanuel Decaux, "Affaire de la délimitation maritime et des questions territoriales entre Qatar et Bahreïn, Fond (arrêt du 16 mars 2001 Qatar c. Bahreïn) [Case concerning Maritime Delimitation and Territorial Questions between Qatar and Bahrain, Merits (Judgment of 16 March 2001) Qatar v. Bahrain]," *AFDI* 47 (2001): 179, 181, https://www.persee.fr/doc/afdi_0066-3085_2001_num_47_1_3660, accessed 27 August 2020.

another State party to the Convention.[57] The defaulting State remains a party until the court or tribunal decides that it lacks jurisdiction or that the claims of the appearing party are inadmissible. Should the tribunal decide that it does have jurisdiction and/or the appearing party's claims are admissible, then the defaulting State remains a party in the merits phase of the proceedings. That the *South China Sea* Tribunal had to restate the obvious in both the Award on Jurisdiction and the Award of 12 July 2016 may be explained by China's insistence that it was not a party to the proceedings and that it could not be bound by any decisions of the Tribunal.[58]

In all instances of default before the ICJ, the defaulting State has asserted that it was not a party to the case. Occasionally individual judges have adopted the views in this respect of the defaulting State. In the *Nuclear Tests Cases*, Australia and New Zealand had sought in 1973 a declaration from the Court that further atmospheric testing of nuclear weapons in the South Pacific was incompatible with international law as well as an order that France cease carrying out such tests.[59] France denied that the Court had jurisdiction, invoking its reservation to the acceptance of the Court's compulsory jurisdiction that excluded matters relating to national defense. Eventually, the Court decided that a decision was moot following declarations of French leaders that the Court interpreted as unilateral commitments to cease atmospheric nuclear testing.[60] In his separate opinion on the Judgment, Judge Gros, a French national,

[57] *MP*, vol. I, 218, para. 7.5; Mincai Yu, "China's Responses," 5.

[58] Award on Jurisdiction, 39, para. 114; Award of 12 July 2016, 45, para. 118. One is surprised to read that the Tribunals in the *South China Sea Arbitration* and the *"Arctic Sunrise" Arbitration* "continued the proceedings *as if* [italics supplied] the respondents [China and Russia, respectively] were actually still part of them." Ciarán Burke, "Annex VII. Article 9," in Alexander Proelss et al. (eds.), *The United Nations Convention on the Law of the Sea: A Commentary* (Munich: E.H. Beck, 2017), 2843. The formulation implies some doubt as to the status of the respondents as parties. In fact, the two respondents continued to be parties to the arbitrations, despite their default.

[59] Australia, *Application Instituting Proceedings* (9 May 1973), *I.C.J. Pleadings*, *Nuclear Tests*, vol. I, 28, https://www.icj-cij.org/files/case-related/58/13187.pdf, accessed 19 March 2020; New Zealand, *Application Instituting Proceedings* (9 May 1973), *I.C.J. Pleadings*, *Nuclear Tests*, vol. II, 9, https://www.icj-cij.org/files/case-related/59/9447.pdf, accessed 19 March 2020.

[60] *Nuclear Tests (Australia v. France)*, *Judgment*, *I.C.J. Reports 1974*, 253, http://www.icj-cij.org/files/case-related/58/058-19741220-JUD-01-00-BI.pdf, accessed 17 March 2020; *Nuclear Tests (New Zealand v. France)*, *Judgment*, *I.C.J. Reports*

argued that the Court would have done well not to treat France as a party to the case:

> To speak of two parties in proceedings in which one has failed to appear, and has on every occasion re-affirmed that it will not have anything to do with the proceedings is to refuse to look facts in the face. The fact is that when voluntary absence is asserted and openly acknowledged there is no longer more than one party in the proceedings. There is no justification for the fiction that, so long as the Court has not recognized its lack of jurisdiction, a State which is absent is nevertheless a party in the proceedings.... In the present case, by its reasoned refusal to appear the Respondent has declared that, so far as it is concerned, there are no proceedings, and this it has repeated each time the Court has consulted it.[61]

This view has never been followed by the Court. As a German scholar who subsequently became an ICJ judge observed, it did not make sense to characterize the defaulting State as a non-party, a status that was undefined in the Statute and would only generate legal uncertainty in procedural law.[62]

As a party, the defaulting State enjoys the same rights as the appearing State. It must be afforded the same opportunities as the latter to express its views on procedural steps. It must be granted the same time limits for the submission of its written pleadings and the same amount of time for its oral presentations if it appears in the hearings. It must be provided copies of tribunal orders, submissions made by the appearing State, and transcripts of oral hearings.[63] The equal treatment of the appearing and defaulting States in the procedure is not a minor point. On the occasion

1974, 457, https://www.icj-cij.org/files/case-related/59/059-19741220-JUD-01-00-BI.pdf, accessed 19 March 2020.

[61] *Nuclear Tests (Australia v. France), Judgment, I.C.J. Reports 1974*, Separate Opinion of Judge Gros, 290, para. 25, http://www.icj-cij.org/files/case-related/58/058-19741220-JUD-01-04-BI.pdf, accessed 19 March 2020.

[62] Mosler, "Nichtteilnahme," 447.

[63] Stefan Talmon, *The South China Sea Arbitration: Is There a Case to Answer?* (Bonn: Universität Bonn, Institute for Public International Law, 2014), 12, https://papers.ssrn.com/sol3/papers.cfm?abstract_id=2393025, accessed 13 March 2020. This piece is reproduced in Stefan Talmon and Bing Bing Jia (eds.), *The South China Sea Arbitration: A Chinese Perspective* (Oxford: Hart Publishing, 2014), 15–79. On this point see also CSIL, "The South China Sea Arbitration Awards," 414, para. 888; Levine and Schofield, "Navigating," 107; and Jun Zhao and Jiang Li, "The *"Arctic Sunrise"* Case and Its Implications

of the first complete default (i.e., default in all phases of the procedure) before the ICJ, a French commentator was surprised that in spite of the respondent's default, the ICJ regularly transmitted to it the different documents relevant to the proceedings and continued to set time limits for its response to the arguments of the appearing States. The same commentator believed that granting the same time limit for the submission of its arguments to the defaulting State unnecessarily prolonged the proceedings.[64]

As a party to the proceedings, the defaulting State is also subject to the same obligations as the appearing State. The most important is certainly compliance with decisions of the Arbitral Tribunal: any decision will be binding on the defaulting State. China's denial of this obligation compelled the Arbitral Tribunal to reiterate that China is bound under international law by any awards rendered by the Tribunal.[65] It might be naïve to expect a defaulting State to comply with any decisions of an international court or tribunal, particularly if we accept the argument that one purpose of default is to signal the defaulting State's intention not to comply with the appearing State, the court, and the domestic and international audience.[66] To expect or demand compliance might seem like an effort to square the circle.

Yet it is precisely the hope that any decisions of the international court or tribunal will be acceptable to the defaulting State that justifies the

for China," in Shicun Wu and Keyuan Zou (eds.), *Arbitration Concerning the South China Sea. Philippines Versus China* (London: Routledge, 2016), 123.

[64] Favoreu, "Les arrêts," 258.

[65] Award on Jurisdiction, 39, para. 114; Award of 12 July 2016, 55, para. 143. The *Institut de droit international* (Institute of International Law, "IDI") stressed in its 1991 resolution on non-appearance before the ICJ that "notwithstanding the non-appearance of a State before the Court in proceedings to which it is a party, that State is, by virtue of the Statute, bound by any decision of the Court in that case, whether on jurisdiction, admissibility, or the merits." *Institut de droit international*, Session de Bâle [Basel Session], *Non-appearance Before the International Court of Justice* (1991), https://www.idi-iil.org/app/uploads/2017/06/1991_bal_01_en.pdf, accessed 16 March 2020.

[66] Bernard H. Oxman, "Nonparticipation and Perceptions of Legitimacy," *Ecology Law Quarterly* 46 (2019): 81–94, https://www.ecologylawquarterly.org/wp-content/uploads/2020/03/11_ELQ_Oxman_Final_Redacted.pdf, accessed 8 May 2022. Oxman was a member of the legal team of the Philippines in the *Arbitration*.

obligation imposed on the court to satisfy itself not only that it has jurisdiction but also that the appearing State's claims are well founded in fact and in law.

C. The Obligations of the Arbitral Tribunal under Article 9 of Annex VII

Default does not automatically result in a judgment in favor of the appearing State. The Arbitral Tribunal is under a duty to satisfy itself not only that it has jurisdiction but also that the claims of the appearing State are well founded in fact and in law.

It might seem at first glance that the first paragraph of Article 53 of the ICJ Statute, which provides that the appearing State "may call upon the Court to decide in favour of its claim,"[67] grants it the right to demand a default judgment. In reality, this provision has become a dead letter.[68] In the first cases of default, the appearing State had invoked it, but the Court had never acceded favorably to such a request, for the simple reason that the second paragraph of Article 53 requires the ICJ to satisfy itself that it has jurisdiction and that the appearing State's claims are well founded in fact and in law. In subsequent cases of default, appearing States understandably refrained from invoking it. Hence it is just as well that Article 9 of Annex VII contains no equivalent stipulation. The *South China Sea* Tribunal expressly recognized that China's default imposed a special responsibility on it. It recalled that there is no system of default judgment under the Convention, so that it did not simply adopt Philippine arguments or accept its assertions untested.[69]

The Tribunal actively sought to satisfy itself that it had jurisdiction over the disputes submitted by the Philippines in the first phase of the

[67] ICJ, *Statute*, Article 53(1), http://www.icj-cij.org/en/statute, accessed 10 March 2020; PCIJ, *Statute*. https://www.icj-cij.org/files/permanent-court-of-international-justice/serie_D/D_01_1e_edition.pdf, accessed 25 March 2020.

[68] Joe Verhoeven, "Le droit, le juge et la violence (les arrêts *Nicaragua c. États-Unis)* [The Law, the Judge and Violence (The *Nicaragua v. United States* Judgments)]," *Revue générale de droit international public* [General Journal of Public International Law] 91 (1987): 1196.

[69] Award on Jurisdiction, 11, para. 12; Award of 12 July 2016, 49, para. 129.

proceedings and that Philippine claims were well founded in fact and in law in the second phase of the proceedings.[70]

As Amerasinghe succinctly put it, facts are for the actor to prove; the law is the province of the tribunal.[71] It is a general principle that a State party to a dispute making a claim must prove the facts necessary to prevail on its claim. A dispute usually involves disputed facts, but it may happen that the disagreement between parties on the facts is the manifestation of a desire to see different legal rules applied to them. The reasons for this are the existence of contradictory rules or the existence of exceptions to the rule.[72] Proving facts requires the production of evidence, while combining facts to reach a conclusion entails argument.[73] It is then for international judges, who enjoy wide discretion in the assessment of evidence, to decide cases on the basis of evidence submitted to them by the States parties to the dispute.[74] Judges are presumed to know the law, as expressed in the maxim *jura novit curia*, defined more formally as the power of the judge to seek and apply the law independently of the parties.[75] For this reason, international courts are not limited in applying the law by the parties' contentions.[76]

As we shall see in the body of the book, it is the obligation imposed on the Tribunal to satisfy itself that the Philippine claims were well founded

[70] Award of 12 July 2016, 49–50, paras. 129–31.

[71] Chittaranjan F. Amerasinghe, *Evidence in International Litigation* (Leiden: Martinus Nijhoff Publishers, 2005), 57.

[72] Jean J.A. Salmon, "Le fait dans l'application de droit international [Facts in the Application of International Law]," *Recueil des cours de l'Académie de droit international de La Haye* [Collected Courses of the Hague Academy of International Law], vol. 175 (1982-II), 305 ("*RCADI*").

[73] Richard M. Mosk, "The Role of Facts in International Dispute Resolution," *RCADI*, vol. 304 (2003-IV), 29–40.

[74] Rüdiger Wolfrum, "Taking and Assessing Evidence in International Adjudication," in Tafsir Malick Ndiaye and Rüdiger Wolfrum (eds.), *Law of the Sea, Environmental Law and Settlement of Disputes. Liber Amicorum Judge Thomas A. Mensah* (Leiden: Martinus Nijhoff Publishers, 2007), 344. Wolfrum was a member of the *South China Sea* Arbitral Tribunal.

[75] Giancarlo Venturini, "Il principio 'jura novit curia' e il processo internazionale [The Principle of "Jura Novit Curia" and International Judicial Proceedings]," *Comunicazioni e studi* [Communications and Studies] 14 (1975): 971.

[76] Amerasinghe, *Evidence*, 51.

in fact that would be the object of most of the Tribunal's procedural decisions in the *South China Sea Arbitration*.

II. The Practical Consequences of China's Default in the *South China Sea Arbitration*

The practical consequences of default for the appearing State, the defaulting State, and an international court were concisely stated in a separate opinion appended to an ITLOS Order for provisional measures in the *"Arctic Sunrise" Arbitration*.[77] Non-appearance hampers the appearing party in pursuit of its rights and interests; it weakens the legal position of the defaulting party; and it hinders the work of the international court or tribunal hearing the dispute.[78] At least for the appearing State and the international court, the practical difficulties are the logical, if not inevitable, consequences of the obligations imposed on the court or tribunal. The following paragraphs give an overview of these practical consequences, which will be examined in the context of the *South China Sea Arbitration* in greater detail in the following Chapters.

A. The Practical Consequences for the Appearing State

At first glance, it might seem that the appearing State finds itself in a favorable position vis-à-vis the defaulting State—only its written pleadings are before the court and only its oral arguments are heard by the court. Such a favorable position is illusory, given the obligations imposed on the Tribunal by Article 9 of Annex VII. In the event of default, the appearing

[77] Under Article 290(5) of the Convention, pending the constitution of an Annex VII arbitral tribunal, any party to the dispute may request provisional measures from the ITLOS. The ITLOS ordered that the *Arctic Sunrise* and the persons detained by Russia be released and allowed to leave Russia. *"Arctic Sunrise" (Kingdom of the Netherlands v. Russian Federation), Provisional Measures, Order of 22 November 2013, ITLOS Reports 2013*, 252, para. 105(1) (*"Arctic Sunrise" Provisional Measures*), https://www.itlos.org/fileadmin/itlos/documents/cases/case_no.22/published/C22_Order_221113.pdf, accessed 20 November 2018.

[78] *"Arctic Sunrise" Provisional Measures*, Joint Separate Opinion of Judges Wolfrum and Kelly, *ITLOS Reports 2013*, 256 ("Joint Separate Opinion, Judges Wolfrum and Kelly"), https://www.itlos.org/fileadmin/itlos/documents/cases/case_no.22/published/C22_Wolfrum_Kelly_221113.pdf, accessed 16 March 2020. Wolfrum was a member of the Tribunal in the *South China Sea Arbitration*.

State is bound to encounter difficulties in proving that the court has jurisdiction and that its claims are well founded in fact and in law.[79] Such difficulties may be alleviated, but only to a certain extent, by informal communications or public statements issued by the defaulting State.

Default places a heavy burden on the appearing State. In the first place, some of the evidence required to support its submissions might well be in the possession or under the control of the defaulting State. The US found itself in this predicament in the *United States Diplomatic and Consular Staff in Tehran Case*. In 1979, the US had brought a case against Iran before the ICJ over the detention of US diplomatic and consular staff as hostages in the US Embassy in Iran.[80] The US explained to the Court that owing precisely to the situation of which it complained, it was unable to have access to its diplomatic and consular staff, premises, and archives in Iran. Consequently, it was unable to provide detailed factual evidence on such matters as the treatment and conditions of the hostages.[81] In the *South China Sea Arbitration*, the Philippines encountered similar difficulties in its efforts to provide evidence in support of certain of its submissions, particularly those on the harmful effects of China's island-building on the marine environment of the South China Sea. The Philippines reminded the Tribunal that it was China that had information on the nature and purpose of its activities in the Spratly Islands. The Philippines was not in a position to verify China's claim that their main purpose was to meet civilian demands and better perform China's international obligations in areas such as maritime search and rescue,

[79] It is somewhat surprising to read, from the pen of a former member of the ITLOS, that the non-appearance of Iceland in the *Fisheries Jurisdiction Cases* before the ICJ did nothing to make more difficult the positions of the appearing States, the UK and the Federal Republic of Germany. David Anderson, *Modern Law of the Sea: Selected Essays* (Leiden: Brill – Nijhoff, 2008), 200.

[80] United States, *Application Instituting Proceedings* (29 November 1979), *I.C.J. Pleadings, United States Diplomatic and Consular Staff in Tehran*, 3–8. https://www.icj-cij.org/files/case-related/64/9545.pdf, accessed 20 March 2020.

[81] *United States Diplomatic and Consular Staff in Tehran, Judgment, I.C.J. Reports 1980*, 10, para. 11, https://www.icj-cij.org/files/case-related/64/064-19800524-JUD-01-00-BI.pdf, accessed 11 October 2019.

disaster prevention and mitigation, marine scientific research, meteorological observation, environmental conservation, navigation safety, and fishery production services.[82]

Second, the appearing State is under an obligation to prove to the international court that the latter has jurisdiction and that its claim is well founded in law, without the benefit of hearing the defaulting State's arguments. The appearing State finds itself compelled to raise before the international court or tribunal arguments on matters that should have been brought to it by the defaulting State.[83] In the *United States Diplomatic and Consular Staff Case*, the US was faced with a situation in which Iran had apparently not put forward at any time an opposing claim, which could have made it impossible to circumscribe the dispute.[84] In the *South China Sea Arbitration*, the Philippines declared that it found itself in a similar situation: it would be "in the position of having to guess what China's arguments might be and formulate arguments for both States."[85] The appearing State's difficulties have been steadfastly ignored by the ICJ, according to an ICJ judge.[86] In contrast, the two Awards in the *South China Sea Arbitration* are remarkable for explicitly acknowledging the difficulties encountered by the appearing State in sections entitled "The Legal and Practical Consequences of China's Non-Participation."[87]

The difficulties encountered by the appearing State may be alleviated somewhat by the defaulting State's informal communications to the international court or tribunal and public statements if these set out the main theses of the defaulting State and contain some facts in support of these theses. In the *United States Diplomatic and Consular Staff Case*, Iran

[82] *South China Sea Arbitration*, Hearing on Jurisdiction and Admissibility, Transcript, Day 2 (8 July 2015), 76, https://pcacases.com/web/sendAttach/1400, accessed 16 March 2020.

[83] D.P. O'Connell, Fifth Public Sitting, 9 October 1978, *I.C.J. Pleadings*, *Aegean Sea Continental Shelf*, 318, https://www.icj-cij.org/files/case-related/62/062-19781009-ORA-01-00-BI.pdf, accessed 20 March 2020.

[84] Vincent Coussirat-Coustère, "L'arrêt de la Cour internationale de Justice sur le personnel diplomatique américain à Téhéran [The Judgment of the International Court of Justice on American Diplomatic Staff in Teheran]," *AFDI* 26 (1980): 210, https://www.persee.fr/doc/afdi_0066-3085_1980_num_26_1_2388, accessed 20 March 2020.

[85] *MP*, vol. I, 231, para. 7.42.

[86] Fitzmaurice, "The Problem," 91, 111–12.

[87] Award on Jurisdiction, 39–42, paras. 112–23; Award of 12 July 2016, 45–56, paras. 115–44.

sent telegrams to the Court on 9 December 1979 and on 16 March 1980, in which it argued that the question of hostages only represented "a marginal and secondary aspect of an overall problem...[one] which involves more than 25 years of continual interference by the United States in the internal affairs of Iran..."[88] During the oral hearings, the US noted "the total absence [in the two telegrams] of any legal or factual argumentation to the effect that the Iranian seizure of the hostages and the Embassy was lawful," concluding that Iran had "virtually conceded the total illegality" of its conduct.[89] In the *South China Sea Arbitration*, a number of China's informal communications and public statements went some way toward informing the Philippines of China's arguments and evidence.

As we shall see in the succeeding Chapters, the litigation strategy of the Philippines sought to alleviate the practical difficulties created for it by China's default in ascertaining China's position and formulating arguments against these putative arguments, primarily through the recourse to the special procedure under Article 25 of the Rules of Procedure, and to a lesser extent, to its agreement to the Tribunal's consideration of China's informal communications and public statements, the statements of Taiwan, and the statements of putative "*amici curiae*."

It is tempting to ask whether on the other side of the coin are advantages of default for the defaulting State.

B. The Practical Consequences for the Defaulting State

The ICJ has stated on one occasion that the first consequence of a decision to default is that "the case will continue without its [the defaulting State's] participation."[90] There is some disagreement on the point whether this consequence is advantageous or not for the defaulting State.

[88] *United States Diplomatic and Consular Staff in Tehran, Judgment*, 19, para. 35.

[89] Mr. Owen, Third Public Sitting, 18 March 1980, Oral Arguments, *I.C.J. Pleadings, United States Diplomatic and Consular Staff in Tehran*, 266, https://www.icj-cij.org/files/case-related/64/064-19800318-ORA-01-00-BI.pdf, accessed 11 October 2019.

[90] *Military and Paramilitary Activities in and Against Nicaragua (Nicaragua v. United States of America), Merits, Judgment, I.C.J. Reports 1986*, 24, para. 28, http://www.icj-cij.org/files/case-related/70/070-19860627-JUD-01-00-BI.pdf, accessed 17 March 2020.

Those who argue that default is disadvantageous for the defaulting State aver that the main practical disadvantage for the latter may lie in the fact-finding phase.[91] In discussions within the *Institut de droit international* (Institute of International Law, "IDI") on non-appearance before the ICJ, at least one member was of the view that default did not release the defaulting State from the obligation to clarify the factual situation objectively.[92] Whether or not such an obligation exists, defaulting States have in practice communicated facts that support their legal position to the ICJ. In addition, the ICJ has also sought out facts that are in the public domain, but this strategy, as the ICJ itself has admitted, might not fully compensate for the absence of the defaulting State's version of the facts.[93]

Another possible disadvantage is that the defaulting State loses the chance to present its own arguments and refute those of the appearing State. But if a judge or court is assumed to know the law, will a defaulting State suffer from the loss of opportunities to present its legal arguments and to refute those of the appearing State? One clear legal disadvantage for the defaulting State appears to lie in the inability to present a counterclaim, which would allow it the opportunity to turn against its adversary in the course of the same proceedings and pursue its own outstanding claims.[94] Under Article 80 of the ICJ Rules of Court, a counterclaim may be submitted only if it comes within the jurisdiction of the Court and is directly connected with the subject matter of the other party's claim.

[91] Observations of Mr. E. McWhinney (18 November 1985), in Gaetano Arangio-Ruiz, "Non-appearance Before the International Court of Justice. Preliminary Report," *Annuaire de l'Institut de droit international* [Yearbook of the Institute of International Law], Session de Bâle [Basel Session], 64-I (1991), 258 ("Non-appearance Preliminary Report"), http://www.gaetanoarangioruiz.it/publications/non-appearance-before-the-international-court-of-justice/, accessed 13 October 2019. The Institute is a learned society independent of governmental influence; it was founded in 1873 to promote the progress of international law. It received the Nobel Peace Prize for its work in 1904. Institut de droit international, *About the Institute* (2019), https://www.idi-iil.org/en/a-propos/, accessed 16 March 2020.

[92] Observations of Mr. K. Doehring (15 November 1985) in Arangio-Ruiz, "Non-appearance Preliminary Report," 275.

[93] *Nicaragua*, *Merits*, 25, para. 30.

[94] Constantine Antonopoulos, *Counterclaims Before the International Court of Justice* (The Hague: T.M.C. Asser Press, 2011), 1.

The counterclaim must be made in the *Counter-Memorial*.[95] It has to be said that this disadvantage is purely theoretical if the defaulting State has no intention in the first place of complying with the Court's final judgment.[96]

On the other hand, there is considerable scholarly support for the view that the defaulting State enjoys a great part of the benefits of appearance while insisting that it is not bound by the Court's decision.[97] The defaulting State often presents its version of the facts and its arguments through informal communications to the Court and public statements. It has sometimes been suggested that default frees the defaulting State from the obligation to justify doubtful legal theses,[98] but Talmon reminds us that default cannot be taken as an admission of facts or the appearing State's legal views or as an indication that the defaulting State has no convincing legal arguments.[99] More importantly, an international court or tribunal is bound to protect the defaulting State as part of its obligation to satisfy itself not only that it has jurisdiction but also that the appearing State's claims are well founded in fact and in law. The lengths to which the ICJ could go in order to protect a defaulting State prompted a former judge to declare, half in jest, that he would advise a State with a shaky legal case to default, because the Court would in practice substitute itself for the defaulting State against the appearing State.[100]

[95] ICJ, *Rules of Court*, Article 80(1) and (2), https://www.icj-cij.org/en/rules, accessed 22 March 2020.

[96] D. W. Bowett, "Contemporary Developments in Legal Techniques in the Settlement of Disputes," *RCADI*, vol. 180 (1983-II), 208–09.

[97] Fitzmaurice, "The Problem," 106; Mr. E. McWhinney, Letter of 18 November 1985, 258.

[98] Favoreu, "L'arrêt," 277.

[99] Talmon, *The South China Sea Arbitration*, 3. Interestingly, another author who defends China's positions asked "[i]f China is so convinced that its substantive legal arguments and claims against the Philippines are sound, why should it be so unwillingly [sic] to allow international legal authority to adjudicate in its favor?" Anthony Carty, "The South China Sea Disputes Are Not Yet Justiciable," in Shicun Wu and Keyuan Zou (eds.), *Arbitration Concerning the South China Sea. Philippines versus China* (London: Routledge, 2016), 24. One might add that the Tribunal's two Awards demonstrate that most of China's arguments were not convincing.

[100] Mohammed Bedjaoui, "Introduction from the Bench," in Edgardo Sobenes Obregón and Benjamin Samson (eds.), *Nicaragua Before the International Court of Justice. Impacts on International Law* (Cham, Switzerland: Springer International Publishing AG, 2018), 9.

Unfavorable outcomes for defaulting States are often put forward as evidence of the disadvantages of default.[101] The US "disappearance" in the *Nicaragua Case* was said to have made an unfavorable judgment against the US "almost inevitable."[102] In the *South China Sea Arbitration*, a Chinese scholar has not hesitated to affirm that China's decision not to appear in the proceedings was an unmitigated disaster, given that the Tribunal overwhelmingly decided against China on almost all the Philippine claims.[103] Such arguments would not account for ICJ decisions that may be deemed to be favorable to the defaulting State and are tantamount to charging the court or tribunal concerned with failing to comply with its obligations.

As we shall see in the following Chapters, China's litigation strategy combined a refusal to appear in the formal proceedings with informal participation. The latter consisted of the publication of a position paper on the jurisdiction, public statements by Chinese officials, secret lobbying of the Tribunal, the organization of an international campaign against the Award on Jurisdiction and Admissibility, the orchestration of an international campaign of defamation against the appointing authority and the judges, and, possibly, the hacking of the PCA website.

One can only determine whether default has placed the defaulting State at a disadvantage by examining each case and the way in which the international court in question dealt with the practical consequences of default[104]—hence the importance of analyzing the court's conduct of the proceedings.

[101] Shiping Liao, "Fact-Finding," 2; Spijkers, "Non-participation," 187.

[102] Keith Highet, "Nonappearance and Disappearance Before the International Court of Justice," *AJIL* 81 (1987): 250. The US was said to have "disappeared" because it participated in the proceedings on jurisdiction and admissibility but withdrew from the proceedings after the ICJ had issued its judgment on jurisdiction and admissibility.

[103] Bing Ling, *China's Attitude*, 4. The author is based in Australia, which might explain why he did not hesitate to make such a statement. Chinese-language versions of the author's argument are cited in Anthea Roberts, *Is International Law International?* (Oxford: Oxford University Press, 2017), 249, note 159.

[104] Observations of Mr. E. McWhinney (18 November 1985), 257.

C. The Practical Consequences for the Arbitral Tribunal

An arbitral tribunal applying Article 9 of Annex VII faces two practical challenges. First, it must determine the standard for "satisfying itself" that it has jurisdiction and that the applicant State's claims are well founded in fact and in law. Second, it must respect the principle of equality of the parties in its efforts to acquire knowledge of the facts of the case.

Determining the standard for "satisfying itself" represents a challenge because Article 9 of Annex VII, like Article 53 of the PCIJ and the ICJ Statutes as well as Article 28 of the ITLOS Statute, does not establish what is to be regarded as satisfactory when determining that a claim is well founded in fact and in law.[105] Consequently, the standard of "satisfying itself" might appear to be subjective rather than objective. In the *Nicaragua Case*, the Court explained that the phrase "to satisfy itself" in Article 53 of the ICJ Statute means that the Court must attain the same degree of certainty as in any other case (i.e., in cases in which both parties appear) that facts on which a claim is based are supported by convincing evidence, "so far as the nature of the case permits," and that the claim is sound in law.[106] A court's conviction that a claim is sound in law rests on the assumption that it knows the law, but the standard to be applied to determine whether a claim is well founded in law has not been made explicit.[107] Second, Article 9 of Annex VII, like Article 53 of the Statute, does not lay down any procedural rules for situations of default.[108] To this it may be retorted that default does not entail any special form of proceedings,[109] but how can one apply Article 9 in the event of default if Article 9 contains no provision on the sources that the arbitral tribunal should consult in case of default?[110]

The second practical challenge is a consequence of the ICJ's explanation that in case of default, the general principles underlying the conduct of international judicial proceedings continue to be applicable. Notwithstanding a party's default,

105 Thirlway, *Non-appearance*, 120.

106 *Nicaragua, Judgment, Merits*, 24, 25, paras. 28–30.

107 von Mangoldt and Zimmerman, "Article 53," 1490.

108 Eisemann, "Les effets," 354.

109 Hugh Thirlway, "The Law and Procedure of the International Court of Justice 1960–1989. Part Twelve," *BYIL* 71 (2000): 157.

110 Mosler, "Nichtteilnahme," 450.

> equality of the parties must remain the basic principle for the Court. In a case of non-appearance neither party should be placed at a disadvantage; therefore the party which declines to appear cannot be permitted to profit from its absence, since this would amount to placing the party appearing at a disadvantage.[111]

The Rules of Procedure of the *South China Sea Arbitration* reaffirm the principle that the parties must be "treated with equality" and that at each stage of the proceedings each party must be "given a full opportunity to be heard and to present its case."[112] Yet in the event of default, one party does not present its case, with the result that the equality of the parties is compromised by that party's default. For the IDI, the two main difficulties that non-appearance generates for the ICJ, and by implication, other international courts and tribunals, lie in the full implementation by the ICJ of the equality of the parties and its acquisition of knowledge of the facts of the case.[113]

Equality of the parties is a basic requirement of a fair trial; there can be no fair trial and *a fortiori*, no fair outcome, if the parties are not treated equally.[114] In the international order, which is based on the principle of sovereign equality, equality of the parties is the fundamental principle of international justice. In the event of default, an international court must reestablish and maintain the equality of the parties. The court must take into account the defaulting State's arguments and proceed in the defaulting State's place with the critical analysis of the arguments and evidence submitted by the appearing State that the defaulting State would

[111] *Nicaragua*, *Judgment*, *Merits*, 26, para. 31.

[112] *South China Sea Arbitration*, Rules of Procedure (27 August 2013), Article 10(1), 5, https://pcacases.com/web/sendAttach/233, accessed 11 May 2020.

[113] IDI, *Non-appearance*, 2.

[114] This principle has been well-established in the caselaw of the European Court of Human Rights ("ECtHR") for nearly fifty years now. Jean-Pierre Dintilhac, "L'égalité des armes dans les enceintes judiciaires [Equality of Arms in Judicial Bodies]," in Cour de Cassation [Supreme Court], *Rapport de la Cour de Cassation 2003* [Report of the Supreme Court 2003] (Paris: La Documentation française, 2004), 129, https://www.courdecassation.fr/publications_26/rapport_annuel_36/rapport_2003_37/deuxieme_partie_tudes_documents_40/tudes_theme_egalite_42/enceinte_judiciaires_6255.html, accessed 16 March 2020; Robert Kolb, *The Elgar Companion to the International Court of Justice* (Cheltenham: Edward Elgar, 2014), 217. Dintilhac also argues that equality of the parties is a principle of natural law (129).

have undertaken if it had appeared.[115] For some scholars and judges, the practical consequence is that the court must act as the counsel of the defaulting State: the court must assume that the defaulting party is right, not wrong, until the appearing State has proven it to be wrong.[116] This conception of the court's role is not shared by other judges and was understandably rejected by the appearing State in the *Nicaragua Case*.[117] At the other extreme is the view that the international court must reestablish equality in favor of the appearing State, for instance, by declaring that it has jurisdiction and proceeding forthwith to the merits.[118] This approach is tantamount to imposing sanctions on the defaulting State, which would infringe the principle of equality and might only provide

[115] Mohammed Bedjaoui, "L'égalité des États dans le procès international, un mythe [Equality of States in International Judicial Proceedings, a Myth?]?" in *Le procès international. Liber Amicorum Jean-Pierre Cot* [International Judicial Proceedings. Liber Amicorum Jean-Pierre Cot] (Bruxelles: Établissements Émile Bruylant, 2009), 22; Vincent Coussirat-Coustère and Pierre-Michel Eisemann, "La procédure devant les juridictions internationales permanentes [Procedure before Permanent International Jurisdictions]," in SFDI, Colloque de Lyon [Lyons Colloquium], *La juridiction internationale permanente* [Permanent International Jurisdiction] (Paris: Éditions A. Pedone, 1987), 141.

[116] James Brown Scott, *The Project of a Permanent Court of International Justice and Resolutions of the Advisory Committee of Jurists. Report and Commentary* (Washington, D.C.: Carnegie Endowment for International Peace, Division of International Law, 1920), 125, https://ia800205.us.archive.org/12/items/cu31924016941142/cu31924016941142.pdf, accessed 24 September 2019; *Military and Paramilitary Activities in and Against Nicaragua (Nicaragua v. United States of America), Merits, Judgment*, Dissenting Opinion of Judge Schwebel, *I.C.J. Reports 1986*, 319, para. 25, http://www.icj-cij.org/files/case-related/70/070-19860627-JUD-01-09-BI.pdf, accessed 31 March 2020.

[117] Bedjaoui, "L'égalité des États," 22; Mr. Argüello Gómez (Nicaragua), *I.C.J. Pleadings, Military and Paramilitary Activities in and Against Nicaragua (Nicaragua v. United States of America)*, Vol. V, Oral Arguments on the Merits, Public Sitting of 20 September 1985, 238, https://www.icj-cij.org/files/case-related/70/070-19850912-ORA-01-00-BI.pdf, accessed 17 March 2020.

[118] Fitzmaurice, "The Problem," 93, 120, 121; James D. Fry, "Non-participation in the International Court of Justice Revisited: Change or Plus Ça Change?" *Columbia Journal of Transnational Law* 49 (2010): 73.

further justification to the defaulting State for its default.[119] The international court must strike a balance between the procedural rights of the appearing State and those of the defaulting State.[120]

An international court faces a severe test in its efforts to reestablish and maintain the equality of the parties, in particular when it undertakes to acquire knowledge of the facts. The equality of the parties, by virtue of which each party is given the opportunity to be heard and to present its case, is in part justified because this is the way in which the court can obtain the factual information necessary to decide the case.[121] It is the responsibility of each party to provide the court with factual information in support of its case. Each party should bear the burden of proving its case. If one party defaults, the court is by force of circumstances obliged to take a more active role in the collection of factual information. As the ICJ observed, it "is not bound to confine its consideration to the material formally submitted to it by the parties."[122] In theory, international courts have considerable powers to investigate the facts of a dispute. They may ask the parties to produce documents or provide further explanations at any time, put oral questions to the parties and to witnesses, appoint experts, arrange site visits, and make other arrangements necessary to obtain evidence. The extensive use of such powers should not go so far as to amount to the court's assuming the burden of proof for the defaulting State or placing the appearing State in a situation in which it would have to imagine the defaulting State's arguments and respond to them.[123] Here, too, the international court should strike a balance—this time between the obligation to investigate the facts and the equality of the parties.[124]

[119] Arangio-Ruiz, "Notes," 87; Lambert Grasern, "Verfahrensboykott vor dem Internationalen Gerichtshof, Sachverhaltsermittlung und Beweiswürdigung [Boycott of Proceedings Before the International Court of Justice, Fact-Finding and Evaluation of Evidence]," *Archiv des Völkerrechts* [Archive of International Law] 25 (1987): 466.

[120] Bedjaoui, "L'égalité des États," 20.

[121] Coussirat-Coustère and Eisemann, "La procédure," 132; Dintilhac, "L'égalité des armes," 130.

[122] *Nicaragua*, *Judgment*, *Merits*, 30, para. 25.

[123] Bedjaoui, "L'égalité des États," 11.

[124] Matthias Goldmann, "International Courts and Tribunals, Non-appearance," *Max Planck Encyclopedia of Public International Law* (2006), 6.

The IDI stressed the difficulties encountered by the ICJ in obtaining the factual information necessary to enable it to reach a decision. It did not allude to the international court's efforts to determine that the appearing State's claims are well founded in law, on the assumption that the court knows the law. Nevertheless, the importance of reasoned presentation of the defaulting State's views as to the applicable law to the court cannot be underestimated.[125] In the absence of such presentations, the court might still encounter difficulties in applying the law to the dispute, placing the defaulting State at a disadvantage.

It is a matter of scholarly controversy whether the ICJ has successfully managed to maintain the equality of the parties in the eight cases of default of the 1970s and the 1980s.[126] Commentaries of individual cases do not fail to point out shortcomings of the ICJ on both counts, which more often than not tended to the advantage of the defaulting State. Only a sample of these criticisms can be provided here.[127] With respect to fact-finding, it is not too difficult to find instances in which the Court's approach in practice disadvantaged the appearing State(s). In the two *Nuclear Tests Cases*, the Court based its judgment that there was no longer any dispute for it to judge on unilateral declarations that had been made by French officials after the conclusion of the oral proceedings and had not been transmitted to the appearing states, Australia and New Zealand, for their comments. In the *Nicaragua Case*, the Court explicitly took into account in its judgment a substantial US document distributed on the first day of the oral proceedings, without informing

[125] *Nicaragua*, *Judgment*, *Merits*, 25, para. 29.

[126] The eight cases are the following: *Fisheries Jurisdiction (Federal Republic of Germany v. Iceland)* (1972–1974), https://www.icj-cij.org/en/case/56; *Fisheries Jurisdiction (United Kingdom v. Iceland)* (1972–1974), https://www.icj-cij.org/en/case/55; *Nuclear Tests (Australia v. France)* (1973–1974), https://www.icj-cij.org/en/case/58 *Nuclear Tests (New Zealand v. France)* (1973–1974), https://www.icj-cij.org/en/case/59; *Trial of Pakistani Prisoners of War (Pakistan v. India)* (1973), https://www.icj-cij.org/en/case/60; *Aegean Sea Continental Shelf (Greece v. Turkey)* (1976–1978), https://www.icj-cij.org/en/case/62; *United States Diplomatic and Consular Staff in Tehran (United States of America v. Iran)* (1979–1980), https://www.icj-cij.org/en/case/64; and *Military and Paramilitary Activities in and Against Nicaragua (Nicaragua v. United States of America)* (1984–1991), https://www.icj-cij.org/en/case/70.

[127] Other examples will be cited in Chapter 3.

Nicaragua that it would do so.[128] The Court's application of the law has at times appeared to redound to the benefit of the defaulting State. In the *United States Diplomatic and Consular Staff Case*, the Court, when considering its jurisdiction, examined *ex officio* whether its jurisdiction could be affected by a Commission of Inquiry set up by the UN.[129] In so doing, the Court in effect substituted itself for Iran.[130] In the *Nicaragua Case*, as a member of the Court admitted two decades after the judgment, the Court sought to make its judgment more palatable to the defaulting State. For this purpose, it gave a "strict, narrow, and rigorous" meaning to the concept of effective control of "paramilitary" operations to be able to determine whether the acts of the Contras directed against Nicaragua could be attributed to the US. The effect of this "strict, narrow, and rigorous" meaning was to limit the scope of US responsibility for the actions of paramilitary groups against Nicaragua.[131]

It is not necessary for the purposes of this book to assess the ICJ's success (or lack of it) in maintaining the equality of the parties and acquiring knowledge of the facts in cases of default. What is significant is that in the *South China Sea Arbitration*, counsel for the Philippines readily admitted that the Tribunal had acted as China's de facto counsel.[132] As we shall see, the Tribunal carried out a critical analysis of the Philippine arguments that China would have made had it appeared; put a large number of written and oral questions to the Philippines prior to and during the hearings on jurisdiction and on the merits; put a large number of written and oral questions to the experts presented by the Philippines for cross-examination; and appointed independent experts to assist it in the critical analysis of the technical arguments raised by

[128] Mr. I. Brownlie, Letter of 18 October 1990, in Arangio-Ruiz, "Non-appearance Final Report," 344. Brownlie considered this practice "obviously wrong in principle."

[129] *United States Diplomatic and Consular Staff in Tehran, Judgment*, 20–21, para. 39.

[130] Coussirat-Coustère, "L'arrêt," 203.

[131] This admission was first made in Bedjaoui, "L'égalité des États," 9. The motivation was explicitly stated in Bedjaoui, "Introduction," 9.

[132] Julie Makinen, "U.S. Lawyer Who Led Philippines' Case Says Beijing's Boycott Made His Job Harder in South China Sea Arguments," *Los Angeles Times*, 12 July 2016, https://www.latimes.com/world/asia/la-fg-south-china-sea-lawyer-20160712-snap-story.html, accessed 21 April 2020. As we have seen above, in the *Nicaragua Case*, Nicaragua protested against the views of Judge Schwebel, a US national, that the judge should in practice act as counsel for the defaulting State.

the Philippines on the status of maritime features, the protection and preservation of the marine environment, and navigational safety.

Having in mind the legal framework of default and its practical consequences, we may now recapitulate the history of China's default in the *South China Sea Arbitration*.

III. The History of China's Default in the *South China Sea Arbitration*

The history of China's default may be divided into three periods: the initiation of the *Arbitration*, the period following the constitution of the Tribunal to the issuance of the Award on Jurisdiction and Admissibility (June 2013–October 2015), and the period from the issuance of the latter to the issuance of the Award on the merits of the case (November 2015–July 2016).

A. The Initiation of the Arbitration

Despite the well-known opposition of China to binding dispute settlement, it seems that during this phase there was some scholarly debate in China about the appropriate litigation strategy to follow.

When it initiated the *Arbitration*, the Philippines was aware of the risk of China's default. As far back as 1998, China had stated in a bilateral meeting that "the important fundamental principle guiding our efforts" to address their dispute in the South China Sea was bilateral negotiations.[133] In January 2012, almost exactly a year before the Philippines initiated the *Arbitration*, China reiterated during high-level bilateral consultations that

> it is quite difficult to resolve this dispute through any legal procedure.... [T]he proposals that the Philippines made previously are not realistic or feasible whether it is about to refer the matter to any international mechanism or to hold any multilateral negotiations among claimant states....[I]t

[133] *MP*, Annex 184, Department of Foreign Affairs of the Republic of the Philippines, Record of Proceedings: 10th Philippines-China Foreign Ministry Consultations (30 July 1998), vol. VI, 248–49, https://files.pca-cpa.org/pcadocs/The%20Philippines%27%20Memorial%20-%20Volume%20VI%20%28Annexes%20158-221%29.pdf, accessed 10 March 2020.

> is our longstanding position that the dispute in the South China Sea should be properly resolved among parties directly involved through peaceful negotiations.[134]

On the same occasion, the Philippines declared that

> a rules-based approach is the only legitimate way in addressing the disputes in the West Philippine Sea [i.e., the South China Sea]….The dispute settlement mechanism established in the United Nations Convention on the Law of the Sea is the fundamental principle of the rules-based approach being espoused by the Philippines.[135]

A few months later, following incidents involving the naval vessels of the two States in the waters of Scarborough Shoal, the Philippines proposed to bring the matter of Philippine sovereign rights and jurisdiction over Scarborough Shoal and its EEZ "before an appropriate third-party adjudication body under international law, specifically the International Tribunal on the Law of the Sea (ITLOS)…."[136] China replied that the Philippine proposal to bring the issue to third-party arbitration had "none ground [sic]."[137]

China's apprehension of an unfavorable outcome in the *Arbitration* may have been responsible for the refusal to submit its disputes with the

[134] *MP*, Annex 204, Record of Discussion: 17th Philippines-China Foreign Ministry Consultations (14 January 2012), vol. VI, 367, para. 148, https://files.pca-cpa.org/pcadocs/The%20Philippines%27%20Memorial%20-%20Volume%20VI%20%28Annexes%20158-221%29.pdf, accessed 10 March 2020; quoted in Award on Jurisdiction, 118, para. 338.

[135] *MP*, Annex 204, 365, paras. 135–36; quoted in Award on Jurisdiction, 117, para. 337.

[136] *MP*, Annex 207, *Note Verbale* from the Department of Foreign Affairs of the Philippines to the Embassy of the People's Republic of China in Manila, No. 12–1137 (26 April 2012), vol. VI, 387, https://files.pca-cpa.org/pcadocs/The%20Philippines%27%20Memorial%20-%20Volume%20VI%20%28Annexes%20158-221%29.pdf, accessed 10 March 2020; quoted in Award on Jurisdiction, 119, para. 340. For details of the incidents, see Award of 12 July 2016, 417–21, paras. 1046–58, https://pcacases.com/web/sendAttach/2086, accessed 10 March 2020.

[137] *MP*, Annex 208, *Note Verbale* from the Embassy of the People's Republic of China in Manila to the Department of Foreign Affairs of the Philippines, No. (12) PG-206 (29 April 2012), vol. VI, 391, https://files.pca-cpa.org/pcadocs/The%20Philippines%27%20Memorial%20-%20Volume%20VI%20%28Annexes%20158-221%29.pdf, accessed 10 March 2020.

Philippines to third-party adjudication. In a confidential memorandum addressed to the Secretary of Foreign Affairs in July 2012, the Philippine Ambassador to China suggested that China may have already realized that the validity of its claims was doubtful:

> It is not absurd to suppose that, after having done the math and studied various independent analyses/commentaries of experts, academicians [sic] and think-tanks, China fears the uncertain outcome of international arbitration on the matter of sovereignty, and this drives China's strong negative response to any suggestion of international adjudication.[138]

The uncertainty to which the Philippine Ambassador alluded may explain what according to anecdotal evidence was disagreement within the Chinese Ministry of Foreign Affairs[139] and among academics[140] concerning the response to the Philippine Notification and Statement of Claim. Among the reasons that may have weighed in the minds of the opponents of appearance were the difficulty of proving China's claims,[141] for which some evidence would be in the possession of Taiwan,[142] China's lack of experience in international adjudication,[143] lingering fears of anti-Chinese bias,[144] and the short or limited period of time in which the decision to default or not had to be made.[145]

[138] *MP*, Annex 84, Memorandum from the Embassy of the Republic of the Philippines in Beijing to the Secretary of Foreign Affairs of the Republic of the Philippines, No. ZPE-110-2012-S (26 July 2012), vol. IV, 220, http://www.pcacases.com/pcadocs/The%20Philippines%27%20Memorial%20-%20Volume%20IV%20%28Annexes%2061-102%29.pdf, accessed 13 March 2020.

[139] Wim Muller, "China's Missed Opportunity in South China Sea Arbitration," *chathamhouse.org* (19 March 2015), https://www.chathamhouse.org/expert/comment/china-s-missed-opportunity-south-china-sea-arbitration, accessed 13 March 2020.

[140] Yu Mincai, "China's Responses," 8, 11–12, was in favor of China's participation, or "reparticipation" following its initial refusal.

[141] Sonya Sceats, "China's Fury Over South China Sea Belies Its Legal Insecurities," *chathamhouse.org* (4 July 2016), https://www.chathamhouse.org/expert/comment/chinas-fury-over-south-china-sea-belies-its-legal-insecurities%20, accessed 16 March 2020; Muller, "China's Missed Opportunity."

[142] Muller, "China's Missed Opportunity."

[143] *Ibid.*; Sceats, "China's Fury"; Bing Ling, *China's Attitude*, 6.

[144] Muller, "China's Missed Opportunity."

[145] Ling, *China's Attitude*, 5; Xinjun Zhang, "Bifurcation," 985.

The 30-day period and the timing of the Notification have been invoked by Chinese scholar Xinjun Zhang in order to lay some of the blame on the Philippines for China's decision to default. The Philippine Notification, which left China only 30 days in which to decide whether to appear, to appoint an arbitrator, and to discuss procedures with the Philippines, was described as "stunning" in its suddenness" and "procedurally hostile," comparable to a "legal ambush." Xinjun Zhang believes that the Philippine Notification was deliberately transmitted to China on 22 January 2013, only two weeks before the Lunar New Year, China's biggest festival and longest national holiday, thus making clear that the Philippines was not prepared for consultations on the constitution of the arbitral tribunal and the procedures of the *Arbitration*. The timing would allegedly explain why China did not approach the Philippines during the 30-day period and illustrate the Philippines' "firmly uncompromising" and "non-compromising" posture.[146] Needless to say, the author is unable to provide any evidence to support this creative interpretation of Philippine intentions, the reason for this being the non-existence of any such evidence.[147]

Some Chinese scholars envisaged an ingenious, if not cynical, solution to China's dilemma, involving imitation of US conduct in the *Nicaragua Case*. In 1984, Nicaragua had instituted proceedings against the US at the ICJ, for using military force against Nicaragua and intervening in Nicaragua's internal affairs.[148] The US appeared before the Court in the first phase of the proceedings, to contest the Court's jurisdiction and the admissibility of Nicaragua's claims. After the Court's judgment on jurisdiction and admissibility in October 1984 declaring that it had jurisdiction over some of Nicaragua's claims and that the claims were admissible, the US withdrew from the proceedings in January 1985.[149] The merits

[146] Xinjun Zhang, "Bifurcation," 985–86.

[147] The paranoia that gripped Chinese academics and ordinary citizens alike manifested itself in allegations that the Japanese were behind the case, that the US State Department wrote the Philippine *Memorial* and that the whole *Arbitration* was a vast conspiracy of Western States to use international law to discredit Chinese sovereignty in the South China Sea, is equally groundless. Kardon, "China Can Say No," 29.

[148] *Military and Paramilitary Activities in and Against Nicaragua (Nicaragua v. United States of America), Application Instituting Proceedings* (9 April 1984), https://www.icj-cij.org/files/case-related/70/9615.pdf, accessed 13 March 2020.

[149] "US Statement on Withdrawal."

phase was conducted in the absence of the US, whose "disappearance" in the proceedings was the object of widespread critical comment.[150] Some Chinese scholars advocated that China participate in the proceedings to challenge the Tribunal's jurisdiction, with the proviso, as Xinjun Zhang euphemistically put it, that such appearance would not prejudice default in the subsequent proceedings on the merits, following the US example in *Nicaragua*.[151] In other words, China could always withdraw from the proceedings and default in the merits phase if the Arbitral Tribunal decided that it had jurisdiction over the Philippine submissions.

Regardless of China's motivations for its default, the diplomatic exchanges between the two States convinced the Arbitral Tribunal that China was aware of the issues over which they disagreed and that for this reason it could not have been taken by surprise when the Philippines decided to proceed with arbitration.[152]

China described its position as non-acceptance of and non-participation in the proceedings, but subsequent events would prove that China, like other defaulting States in cases before the ICJ, was unable to refrain from participating in them in ways that were not in conformity with the Rules of Procedure of the *Arbitration*.

B. From the Constitution of the Tribunal to the Award on Jurisdiction (June 2013–October 2015)

As mentioned earlier, China's litigation strategy combined default with informal participation in the proceedings. During this phase, China refused to cooperate in the constitution of an arbitral tribunal and to respond to the Tribunal's requests for its observations on procedural matters, but it made known its views on jurisdiction through informal communications to the Tribunal, the publication of a Position Paper, and public statements. It also secretly lobbied the Tribunal for unknown purposes, and it may have instigated the hacking of the PCA website during the Hearing on Jurisdiction and Admissibility.

150 Keith Highet, "Litigation Implications of the U.S. Withdrawal from the Nicaragua Case," *AJIL* 79 (1985): 992–1005. Highet later remarked that the US "disappearance" conveyed the impression of a "sore loser." "Nonappearance and Disappearance," 249.

151 Xinjun Zhang, "Bifurcation," 940.

152 Award on Jurisdiction, 120, para. 343.

In its Notification and Statement of Claim, the Philippines appointed Judge Rüdiger Wolfrum, a German national and an ITLOS member, as its arbitrator. Since China refused to appoint its arbitrator, the Philippines requested the appointing authority designated in Annex VII of the Convention, the ITLOS President, to appoint a second arbitrator (22 February 2013). Judge Stanislaw Pawłak, a Polish national and another ITLOS member, was appointed in this manner on 23 March 2013. Two days later, in view of China's default, the Philippines requested the appointing authority to appoint the three remaining arbitrators. On 24 April, the ITLOS President announced the appointment of Jean-Pierre Cot, a French national and another ITLOS member; Alfred H.A. Soons, a national of the Netherlands; and M.C.W. Pinto, a national of Sri Lanka. The latter was also appointed President of the Tribunal. On 21 May 2013, Pinto resigned because his wife was Filipina. On 27 May, the Philippines requested that the ITLOS President fill the vacancy; the ITLOS President then appointed Judge Thomas A. Mensah, a Ghanaian national and a former ITLOS president, as a member and president of the Tribunal. China did not respond when the arbitrators' declarations of independence and impartiality were transmitted to the two parties.

Between July 2013 and October 2015, the Arbitral Tribunal made a number of important procedural decisions. It designated the PCA as Registry (12 July 2013); adopted its Rules of Procedure (27 August 2013); set 30 March 2014 as the deadline for the submission of the Philippine *Memorial* (27 August 2013); granted leave to the Philippines to amend its Statement of Claim (11 March 2014); granted Vietnam's request for copies of the pleadings and the annexes (12 April and 5 December 2014); set 15 December 2014 as the time limit for the submission of China's *Counter-Memorial* (2 June 2014); requested that the Philippines provide further written argument by 16 March 2015, following the receipt of China's Position Paper on 8 December 2014 (11 December 2014); took steps to engage technical experts (21 April 2015); decided to bifurcate the proceedings (21 April 2015); set the date for the Hearing on Jurisdiction and Admissibility (2 June 2015); provided the Philippines with a list of issues that it might wish to address during the Hearing on Jurisdiction (23 June 2015); approved requests for attendance at the Hearing on Jurisdiction by observers; conducted the Hearing on Jurisdiction (7–13 July 2015); requested payment of deposits for the costs of the *Arbitration*; and issued the Award on Jurisdiction (29 October 2015). Before all but the request for payment of deposits were adopted, the Tribunal sought comments from China, which refused to respond.[153]

Against this background of default, it becomes obvious that the CSIL's complaints that the Tribunal's adoption of the Rules of Procedure without China's consent and its handling of other procedural questions violated China's procedural rights are irrelevant as well as procedurally irregular.[154] The Tribunal had given China the opportunity to make its views known on the Rules of Procedure; China refused to respond. The Tribunal was well within its rights to adopt the decisions after having given the parties the opportunity to comment on the proposed decisions. After having refused to take advantage of the opportunity to object, China had in effect waived its right to object to the decisions taken by the Tribunal. That would certainly be the conclusion to be drawn from the silence of a party in proceedings in which both parties appeared. Obviously, China's preference would have been for the Tribunal not to make any decision at all on the matters for which its comments had been sought and ultimately for the proceedings to be paralyzed as a result of its default. It is equally obvious that under the terms of Article 9 of Annex VII of the Convention, the paralysis of the proceedings would have violated the procedural rights of the Philippines, which had specifically requested that the proceedings continue.

China's informal participation during this period took the form of letters to the Tribunal reiterating its non-participation in the *Arbitration* following the constitution of the Tribunal (29 July 2013),[155] in response to a letter from the Tribunal requesting its comments on procedural matters (6 February 2015),[156] and prior to the holding of the Hearing on Jurisdiction (1 July 2015).[157] The most important of China's informal communications to the Tribunal was its Position Paper, which was published by the Foreign Ministry on 7 December 2014 and transmitted to the individual members of the Tribunal by the PCA on 8

[153] Award on Jurisdiction, 15–19, 22, 26, 27, 28, 31, paras. 33, 34, 38, 42, 46, 47, 54, 60, 75, 79, 80, 90, 94.

[154] CSIL, "The South China Sea Arbitration Awards," 621, para. 892.

[155] Award on Jurisdiction, 17, para. 37.

[156] *SWSP*, Annex 472, *Letter* from H.E. Ambassador Chen Xu, Embassy of the People's Republic of China in The Hague, to H.E. Judge Thomas A. Mensah (6 February 2015), vol. VIII, 73–80; cited in Award on Jurisdiction, 22, para. 64.

[157] Award on Jurisdiction, 27, para. 83.

December 2014, one week before the expiry of the time limit set by the Tribunal for the filing of China's *Counter-Memorial.*[158]

It is interesting to note that in the 1920s, China also had recourse to informal communications in order to transmit its views on the proceedings initiated by Belgium against it before the PCIJ for China's unilateral termination of the Sino-Belgian Treaty of Amity, Commerce and Navigation of 1865. This Treaty belonged to the category of "unequal treaties," imposed on China by Western powers in the nineteenth century and restricting China's exercise of sovereignty in areas such as customs tariffs and jurisdiction over foreign nationals. In 1926, as part of China's campaign to achieve equality with Western States, China announced its intention to terminate the Treaty. Belgium, arguing that the Treaty gave only Belgium the power to terminate it, agreed to negotiate a new treaty and a provisional arrangement (modus vivendi) that would be in force during the negotiations. The negotiations failed because China set a six-month time limit for the conclusion of the negotiations, after which the modus vivendi would end; Belgium demanded that the modus vivendi be automatically renewed for six-month periods while the negotiations were ongoing. Belgium then proposed to submit the dispute over the Treaty's interpretation to the PCIJ. China refused, arguing that its position was founded on its aspiration for equality in relations with foreign powers, and that "national aspirations are scarcely suitable subjects for adjudication."[159] China refused to appoint an agent and to accomplish other

[158] Ibid., 20, para. 55; Award of 12 July 2016, 6, para. 13. Some confusion exists as to the timing of the Position Paper and the circumstances in which it was transmitted to the Tribunal. Ku claims that the time limit for the expiry of the filing of the Counter Memorial was 31 December 2014. Ku, "The Significance," 81. Now Procedural Order No. 2 of 2 June 2014, 3, para. 1.1, unambiguously set 15 December 2014 as the date by which China had to submit its *Counter-Memorial* (https://pcacases.com/web/sendAttach/1805, accessed 15 March 2020). Kuok asserts that the Position Paper was published on the MOFA website and not "filed" with the Tribunal, to avoid the impression that China had accepted the *Arbitration.* Lynn Kuok, *Tides of Change: Taiwan's Evolving Position in the South China Sea and Why Other Actors Should Take Notice* (Washington, D.C.: Center for East Asia Policy Studies, Brookings Institution, 2015), 19, https://www.brookings.edu/wp-content/uploads/2016/06/taiwan-south-china-sea-kuok-paper.pdf, accessed 15 March 2020. It is not clear what the author believes "filing" with the Tribunal would entail, but it does not seem that the Tribunal learned of the Position Paper by consulting it on the MOFA website. For the text of the Position Paper, see *SWSP*, Annex 467, Position Paper.

[159] "Statement of the Chinese Government Explaining the Termination of the Sino-Belgian Treaty of November 2nd 1865," in *Denunciation of the*

procedural acts, but it is not true that it refused to communicate with the PCIJ through its Registry.[160] In fact, it sent the same brochure twice to the PCIJ Registry, the first time from the Legation in The Hague[161] and the second time, from the Legation in Brussels.[162] In reply to an inquiry from the PCIJ Registrar, China's Minister declared that "all transmissions, communications or interviews take place, from my part, on a purely private basis, without any relationship to the issue of the dispute."[163]

If China had restricted itself to such communications, in both cases, there would have been little to deplore. Unfortunately, in 2013, as in 1926, China did not leave well enough alone. In 2013, China sought to lobby the Tribunal, an attempt that it thought it could keep secret from the Philippines. As recounted by the Award on Jurisdiction, on

Treaty of November 2nd, 1865, Between China and Belgium, Permanent Court of International Justice, Series C: Acts and Documents Relating to Judgments and Advisory Opinions Given by the Court. Pleadings, Oral Arguments and Documents (Leiden: A.W. Sijthoff's Publishing Company, 1930), 270–76 ("*Denunciation*"), https://www.icj-cij.org/files/permanent-court-of-international-justice/serie_C/C_16_01/C_16_01_04_Traite_sino-belge_autres_documents.pdf, accessed 13 March 2020. For overviews of the case see Manley O. Hudson, *The Permanent Court of International Justice. A Treatise* (New York: The Macmillan Company, 1934), 405–08, and Christoph von Katte, "Denunciation of Treaty of 1865 Between Belgium and China," in Rudolf Bernhardt (ed.), *Encyclopedia of Public International Law*, vol. II, *Decisions of International Courts and Tribunals and International Arbitrations* (Amsterdam: North-Holland Publishing Co., 1981), 75–76. On the "unequal treaties," see Wang Tieya, "International Law in China: Historical and Contemporary Perspectives," *RCADI*, vol. 221 (1990-II), 237–62; Xue Hanqin, "Chinese Contemporary Perspectives on International Law: History, Culture and International Law," *RCADI*, vol. 355 (2011-III), 60–61; and Phil C.W. Chan, *China, State Sovereignty and International Legal Order* (Leiden: Brill-Nijhoff, 2015), 63–107.

160 Talmon states that China never took any action in the proceedings or even communicated with the PCIJ. *The South China Sea Arbitration*, 5.

161 "Statement of the Chinese Government Explaining the Termination of the Sino-Belgian Treaty of November 2nd 1865," in *Denunciation*, 270–76; The Registrar to the Chinese Minister at The Hague, 3 December 1926, in *Denunciation*, 296, https://www.icj-cij.org/files/permanent-court-of-international-justice/serie_C/C_16_01/C_16_01_05_Traite_sino-belge_correspondance.pdf, accessed 13 March 2020.

162 Le Greffier au Ministre de Chine à La Haye [The Registrar to the Chinese Minister at The Hague], 13 December 1926, in *Denunciation*, 299.

163 The Registrar to the Chinese Minister at The Hague, 3 December 1926, and Le Ministre de Chine à La Haye au Greffier [The Chinese Minister at The Hague to the Registrar], 9 December 1926, in *Denunciation*, 296–97.

14 November 2013, the Chinese Ambassador to the United Kingdom requested a meeting with the President of the Tribunal.[164] It turns out that prior to November 2013, China had already attempted to contact the PCA, on at least two occasions, to discuss informal questions of a procedural nature with a Chinese representative.[165] In an admirably restrained response, the Tribunal merely reminded China that

> [i]f a Party wishes to express its position on matters in dispute, it should be aware that such statements will be made available to all members of the Tribunal, the Registry and the other Party, in accordance with the Rules of Procedure and the need to ensure that the Parties are treated with equality.[166]

These acts by China can only put China in the worst possible light. What was the purpose of the meeting that its Ambassador to the Netherlands requested with the President of the Tribunal? If China merely wished to obtain responses to procedural questions, why did China not adopt the easiest way to do so—to appear in the proceedings? And why did it seek to conceal its acts from the Philippines, as the Tribunal's reminder implied?

China's conduct recalls its conduct in January 1927, when a Chinese diplomat personally visited the PCIJ Registrar to inform him that Belgium, which had agreed to resume negotiations with it, no longer wished the proceedings to continue and that China would not respond to any communications from the Court.[167] The Registrar's response indicated that he did not understand that the visit's aim was to inform him that China would no longer respond to PCIJ communications. After all, if that had been the aim, China could have communicated it in writing or simply refused to respond. The Registrar understood that the diplomat's aim was to suspend the proceedings based on a Chinese approach to the Tribunal. Hence, the Registrar had to explain that proceedings

[164] Award on Jurisdiction, 18, para. 40.

[165] Ibid.

[166] Ibid.

[167] Le Greffier au Ministre de Chine à La Haye [The Registrar to the Chinese Minister at The Hague], 15 December 1927, in *Denunciation*, 317.

instituted could not be suspended, unless Belgium withdrew its application.[168] Less than a week later, the Chinese representative at The Hague wrote to the Registrar to inform him that Belgium and China had reached an agreement to suspend the proceedings during their negotiations.[169] The Registrar replied that he was not obliged to take any action on the basis of a letter that did not have an official character.[170]

One final form of China's participation in the proceedings may have been the hacking of the PCA website during the Hearing on Jurisdiction. On 6 July, the eve of the Hearing's opening, a vulnerability was spotted in Adobe Flash Player software by hackers. On 9 July, between the Hearing's first and second rounds, ThreatConnect, a cyber security firm based in Arlington, Virginia that scans websites for vulnerability, observed that an Adobe Flash Player zero-day exploit had been embedded within the PCA Website. An exploit is any attack that takes advantage of vulnerabilities in applications, networks, or hardware; an exploit usually takes the form of software or code that aims to gain control of computers or steal network data.[171] The vulnerability allowed for remote access to most computers that used the hacked website and were loaded with the Windows Operating system and Adobe Flash Player. The term "zero-day" refers to the fact that the vendor or developer has only just learned of the flaw—which means they have "zero days" to fix it.[172] The strategy behind the attack is known as "watering hole" because the hackers' goal is to access "creatures" who are drawn to "sip" at the watering hole. Foley Hoag, the law firm of one of the legal counsel of the Philippines, Paul Reichler, would have been one such "creature."[173] To protect visitors to the PCA

[168] Ibid.

[169] Le Ministre de Chine à La Haye au Greffier [The Chinese Minister at The Hague to the Registrar], 21 January 1927, in *Denunciation*, 322.

[170] Le Greffier au Ministre de Chine à La Haye [The Registrar to the Chinese Minister at The Hague], 25 January 1927, in *Denunciation*, 323.

[171] Avast, *Exploits: What You Need to Know* (2019), https://www.avast.com/c-exploits, accessed 23 March 2020.

[172] AO Kaspersky Lab, "Zero-day Meaning and Definition," https://www.kaspersky.com/resource-center/definitions/zero-day-exploit, accessed 8 May 2022.

[173] Michael D. Goldhaber, "China Denies Role in Hack Attack on Hague Peace Palace," *The American Lawyer*, 22 July 2015, https://www.law.com/americanlawyer/almID/1202732867280/china-denies-role-in-hack-attack-on-hague-peace-palace/?slr eturn=20200223044958, accessed 23 March 2020.

website from unwittingly downloading the malicious software on their own computers, the PCA website was shut down until 23 July.[174]

ThreatConnect believed that the exploit was not a random compromise of the PCA website, as the exploit was embedded within the very pages that described the *South China Sea Arbitration*. The exploit CVE-2015-5119 had been placed in a malicious URL that had been registered on 9 July 2015 by a Chinese domain reseller using falsified name and address in Xiamen, China. ThreatConnect attributed the attack to Chinese APT (Advanced Persistent Threat) groups.[175] The malware employed in The Hague was the hallmark of a specific APT group that focused on the South China Sea.[176] The attack would have enabled Chinese groups to obtain the names of diplomats, lawyers, journalists, and ordinary citizens in the Philippines and elsewhere who were following the case and to anticipate their reaction to any award by the Tribunal.[177] FireEye, a cybersecurity firm that became well known for publishing a report on Chinese cyberwarfare, agreed with ThreatConnect that China was in all likelihood responsible for the attack.[178]

[174] Luke Eric Peterson, "Permanent Court of Arbitration Website Goes Offline, with Cyber-security Firm Contending That Security Flaw Was Exploited in Concert with China-Philippines Arbitration," *Investment Arbitration Reporter* (23 July 2015), https://www.iareporter.com/articles/permanent-court-of-arbitration-goes-offline-with-cyber-security-firm-contending-that-security-flaw-was-exploited-in-lead-up-to-china-philippines-arbitration/, accessed 23 March 2020.

[175] ThreatConnect Research Team, "China Hacks the Peace Palace: All Your EEZ's Are Belong [sic] to Us," *ThreatConnect.com*, 20 July 2015, https://www.threatconnect.com/blog/china-hacks-the-peace-palace-all-your-eezs-are-belong-to-us/, accessed 23 March 2020.

[176] Goldhaber, "China Denies Role."

[177] Jason Healey and Anni Piiparinen, "Did China Just Hack the International Court Adjudicating Its South China Sea Territorial Claims?" *The Diplomat*, 27 October 2015, https://thediplomat.com/2015/10/did-china-just-hack-the-international-court-adjudicating-its-south-china-sea-territorial-claims/, accessed 23 March 2020.

[178] *APT1: Exposing One of China's Cyber Espionage Units* (2013), https://www.fireeye.com/content/dam/fireeye-www/services/pdfs/mandiant-apt1-report.pdf, accessed 23 March 2020; *Appendix C: The Malware Arsenal* (2013), https://www.slideshare.net/YuryChemerkin/appendix-c-digital-the-malware-arsenal, accessed 23 March 2020; Intel Team, *Mandiant APT1 Report Appendix F Update: SSL Certificate Hashes* (19 March 2013), https://www.fireeye.com/blog/threat-research/2013/03/md5-sha1.html, accessed 23 March 2020; *Appendix G (Digital) IOCs* (2013), https://www.slideshare.net/YuryChemerkin/appendix-g-iocs-readme, accessed 23 March 2020.

As was to be expected, China denied any responsibility for the hacking. The Chinese Embassy in the US declared that

> [t]he Chinese government and the personnel in its institutions never engage in any form of cyber attack and firmly oppose and combat all the forms of cyber attacks. Jumping to conclusion and making hypothetical accusation [sic] is meaningless and counterproductive.[179]

The voluminous scholarly literature on China's cyberwarfare and China's failure to investigate the incident, let alone prosecute the perpetrators, make it very difficult to take this denial seriously,[180] but as there is no way to prove conclusively China's responsibility in the hacking of the PCA website, the matter will be left here.

Following the issuance of the Award on Jurisdiction on 29 October 2015, China continued to pursue its litigation strategy combining default and informal participation in the proceedings.

C. From the Award on Jurisdiction to the Award of 12 July 2016 (October 2015–July 2016)

China persisted in its refusal to give its views on procedural matters. During this phase, its litigation strategy added new forms of informal participation. It organized an international campaign against the Award on Jurisdiction and Admissibility, tacitly allowed Taiwan to make submissions to the Tribunal, and organized a campaign of defamation against the appointing authority, the judges, and the Tribunal.

[179] Goldhaber, "China Denies Role."

[180] See, for example, Emilio Iasiello, "China's Three Warfares Strategy Mitigates Fallout From Cyber Espionage Activities," *Journal of Strategic Security* 9 (2016): 45–69, http://scholarcommons.usf.edu/jss/vol9/iss2/4, accessed 23 March 2020; G. Todd Puntney, *Chinese Cyber Economic Espionage: Motivations and Responses*, School of Advanced Military Studies United States Army Command and General Staff College Fort Leavenworth, Kansas, 2016, https://apps.dtic.mil/dtic/tr/fulltext/u2/1022202.pdf, accessed 28 July 2019; A. Segal, "The Code Not Taken: China, the United States, and the Future of Cyber Espionage," *Bulletin of the Atomic Scientists* 69 (2013): 38–45; Timothy Thomas, "China's Cyber Incursions: A Theoretical Look at What They See and Why They Do It Based on a Different Strategic Method of Thought," Foreign Military Studies Office (FMSO), United States Army Combined Arms Center, Fort Leavensworth, Kansas, 2013, http://indianstrategicknowledgeonline.com/web/Chinas-Cyber-Incursions.pdf, accessed 28 July 2019.

During this period, the Tribunal made further important procedural decisions. It appointed an expert hydrographer (August 2015); set the schedule for the Hearing on the Merits, with the possibility of a modification if China decided to appear in the proceedings (September 2015); approved the requests of several States to attend the Hearing on the Merits as observers; approved Philippine requests to present two experts and additional documentary evidence (6 and 14 November 2015); provided the Philippines with an "Annex of Issues the Philippines May Wish to Present" as guidance for the Hearing (10 November 2015); approved Philippine requests to present two experts and additional documentary and testimonial evidence and legal authorities (18 November 2015); conducted the Hearing from 24 to 30 November 2015; approved amendments to the Philippine Final Submissions; appointed coral reef experts (15 March and 12 April 2016) and a navigational safety expert (15 March 2016); provided the Philippines and China with documents that it had obtained from the archives of the UK Hydrographic Office ("UKHO") (1 April 2016) and French archives (26 May 2016); transmitted to the parties the navigational safety expert's report (18 April 2016) and the coral reef experts' report (29 April 2016); transmitted a communication from Malaysia to the two parties (23 June 2016); and issued the Award on the merits (12 July 2016).[181] On all but the last point, the Tribunal sought comments from China, which were not forthcoming. During this period, as in the earlier period, China refused to pay its share of the costs of the proceedings.[182] Once again, in view of China's refusal to comment on these matters, the objections by the CSIL to the appointment of independent experts and the Tribunal's search for documents on its own initiative ring hollow.[183]

The scheduling of the Hearing on the Merits three weeks after the Tribunal's decision on jurisdiction was the basis for two unfounded allegations by Chinese scholar Sienho Yee. First, it allegedly proved that the Tribunal was not sincere in reminding China that it was open to it to participate in the proceedings at any stage. Second, it allegedly indicated that the Philippines must have been told in advance of the decision on

181 Award on Jurisdiction, 21–22, paras. 64–65, 67–68; Award of 12 July 2016, 18–37, paras. 54–105.

182 Award on Jurisdiction, 32, para. 98; Award of 12 July 2016, 38, para. 110.

183 CSIL, "The South China Sea Arbitration Awards," 632, 637, paras. 924, 941.

jurisdiction and admissibility, given that the three-week period was insufficient for the Philippines to prepare its arguments on the merits.[184] Sienho Yee conveniently neglects several facts. The Tribunal had asked China and the Philippines as early as May 2015 whether the Hearing on the Merits should be scheduled within six to 12 months of its inquiry. When the Philippines expressed its preference for an early date, the Tribunal proposed the third week of November. China, of course, did not reply to any of the Tribunal's requests for its views on the schedule. When announcing the date of the Hearing on the Merits on the last day of the Hearing on Jurisdiction, the Tribunal explicitly stated that it was willing to adjust the schedule if China decided to participate in the proceedings.[185] Flexibility of this kind had also been demonstrated by the ICJ in the *United States Diplomatic and Consular Staff in Tehran Case*, when it informed Iran that it was willing to reconsider the time limit for the submission of the *Counter-Memorial* if Iran decided to appear in the proceedings.[186] In both cases, the Hearings on the Merits went ahead as scheduled because the defaulting States did not change their minds. The Philippines, which had not anticipated the bifurcation of the proceedings and had already submitted a *Memorial* as well as a *Supplemental Written Submission* dealing with both jurisdiction and the merits prior to the Hearing on Jurisdiction, did not need much more time to prepare its final arguments on the merits.

China's informal participation in the proceedings was manifested in further letters to the Tribunal following the issuance of Foreign Ministry statements (20 May 2016 and 3 June 2016), repeating its objections to jurisdiction, and transmitting a paper from the CSIL declaring that the Award on Jurisdiction was null and void. China also issued press statements reiterating its position upon the publication of the transcript of the Hearing on Jurisdiction (24 August 2015), the issuance of the Award on Jurisdiction and Admissibility (30 October 2015), and the publication of the transcript of the Hearing on the Merits (21 December 2015). Five

184 Sienho Yee, "The South China Sea Arbitration Decisions," 224.

185 Award of 12 July 2016, 18, 20, paras. 56, 57, 61.

186 *United States Diplomatic and Consular Staff in Tehran*, *Order of 24 December 1979*, *I.C.J. Reports 1979*, 23, http://www.icj-cij.org/files/case-related/64/064-19791224-ORD-01-00-BI.pdf, accessed 10 July 2020. H.W.A. Thirlway, *Non-appearance Before the International Court of Justice* (Cambridge: Cambridge University Press, 1985), 19 called this a "novel" procedure.

months after the closure of the oral proceedings, the Director-General of the Foreign Ministry's Department of Treaty and Law still thought it useful to provide a "Briefing on the South China Sea Arbitration Initiated by the Philippines." On 9 April, 27 May, and 18 June 2015 and 6 May 2016, Chinese statements presented brief responses to the Philippine submission that China's construction activities in the Spratly Islands had harmed the fragile ecosystem there and resulted in significant damage to the habitats of vulnerable species.[187]

During this period, China gave tacit approval to the presentation of views coinciding with its own by self-proclaimed *amici curiae*—Taiwan, the Chinese (Taiwan) Society of International Law ("C(T)SIL"), and the Asia–Pacific Institute of International Law ("APIIL"), contradicting its "firm opposition" expressed in 2015 to *amicus curiae* submissions to the Tribunal.[188] China's tacit approval of the participation of surrogates recalls its conduct in the 1920s, when an allegedly nongovernmental entity, the United Chambers of Commerce of China, sent a communication to the PCIJ.[189] The organization, which seemed to be a private entity, used stationery with the same letterhead as that of the Chinese Legation at The Hague.[190] China's Minister replied that it was a private legal person, having no relationship with the government, although it pointed out the importance of the entity as an association representing

[187] *South China Sea Arbitration, The Philippines' Annexes cited during Merits Hearing* (30 November 2015), Annex 820, Embassy of the People's Republic of China in Canada, An Interview on China's Construction Activities on the Nansha Islands and Reefs (27 May 2015), 5–9 ("*PAMH*"), https://files.pca-cpa.org/pcadocs/The%20Philippines%27%20Annexes%20cited%20during%20Merits%20Hearing%20%28Annexes%20820-859%29.pdf, accessed 15 March 2020; *PAMH*, Annex 821, China State Oceanic Administration, "Construction Work at Nansha Reefs Will Not Harm Oceanic Ecosystems" (18 June 2015), 11–16; *South China Sea Arbitration, Supplemental Documents of the Philippines* (19 November 2015), Annex 624, Ministry of Foreign Affairs of the People's Republic of China, Foreign Ministry Spokesperson Hua Chunying's Regular Press Conference on April 9, 2015 (9 April 2015), vol. I, 165–69 ("*SDP*"), https://files.pca-cpa.org/pcadocs/The%20Philippines%27%20Supplemental%20Documents%20-%20Volume%20I%20%28Annexes%20607-667%29.pdf, accessed 15 March 2020; cited in Award of 12 July 2016, 365–66, paras. 917–20.

[188] Award on Jurisdiction, 23, para. 64.

[189] Letter from the United Chambers of Commerce of China to the Permanent Court of International Justice, 20 November 1926, in *Denunciation*, 283.

[190] Le Greffier au Ministre de Chine à La Haye [The Registrar to the Chinese Minister at The Hague], 13 December 1926, in *Denunciation*, 298.

all traders in China.[191] Non-Chinese publications, however, stressed that the organization had very close connections with the government and that its political and legal functions, which were more important than its economic functions, transformed it into a quasi-governmental institution.[192]

In the twenty-first century, China extended its participation in arbitral proceedings in two ways that had never before been undertaken by any defaulting State in cases before the ICJ. Following the issuance of the Award on Jurisdiction in October 2015, China not only published a statement declaring that the Award was null and void. It also organized a vast international campaign in support of its position that the South China Sea dispute with the Philippines should be resolved exclusively by negotiations among the parties directly concerned and should not have been submitted to arbitration.[193] Two Chinese authors identified 70 States (39 in Africa, 23 in Asia, 4 in Europe, 3 in South America and the Caribbean, and 2 in Oceania) that supported China's position.[194] The geographic scope of China's international campaign, which invariably yielded unconditional support for China's position, far exceeded the usual efforts of a party to an inter-State dispute seeking international support for its position in the dispute. It is even more surprising in that it was launched and carried out at a time when the Tribunal had already issued its Award on Jurisdiction and it could no longer have had any impact on the Tribunal's decision-making.

[191] Le Ministre de Chine à La Haye au Greffier [The Chinese Minister at The Hague to the Registrar], 20 December 1926, in *Denunciation*, 308.

[192] "Extract from article on 'Changsha General Chamber of Commerce', published in Commerce Reports, Washington, March 30th. 1917," "Extracts from article on the 'Hankow Chinese General Chamber of Commerce', published in Commerce Reports, Washington, June 22nd, 1917," "Extracts from article on 'Chinese Guilds and Chambers of Commerce, published in the Commercial Handbook of China, Washington, 1920. (Vol. 2.)," in *Denunciation*, 284–286.

[193] Embassy of the People's Republic of China in the Republic of Iceland, *Foreign Ministry Spokesperson Hua Chunying's Regular Press Conference on May 25, 2016*, http://is.china-embassy.org/eng/fyrth/t1366744.htm, accessed 15 March 2020.

[194] Wang Wen and Chen Xiaochen, "Who Supports China in the South China Sea and Why," *The Diplomat*, 27 July 2016, https://thediplomat.com/2016/07/who-supports-china-in-the-south-china-sea-and-why/, accessed 16 March 2020.

The other manifestation of China's informal participation in the arbitral proceedings was an unprecedented campaign of defamation, beginning in April–May 2016, against the appointing authority, individual members of the Tribunal, and the Tribunal as a whole. The appointing authority, the ITLOS President, happened to be a Japanese national. He was accused of manipulating the composition of the Tribunal, which did not have a Chinese or Asian member.[195] Subsequently, two members of the Tribunal, Judges Cot and Soons, were singled out for allegedly contradicting their views expressed in academic writings that the determination of the status of maritime features was an integral part of maritime delimitation.[196] China, the Chinese media, and even Chinese scholars harped on these themes as part of the campaign launched against the Award of 12 July 2016, which was amplified to include the charge that the Tribunal had provided paid services to the Philippines.[197] The implication that the judges were bribed was so grave that several writers deemed it tantamount to "defamation,"[198] "slander,"[199] and "character assassination."[200] It should be noted in passing that this type of defamation was nothing new to the Philippines, whose leaders, including the President and the Secretary of Foreign Affairs, were habitually insulted in the

[195] Jesse Johnson, "Beijing Turns on Japanese Judge as Hague Tribunal Ruling Over South China Sea Nears," *The Japan Times*, 8 July 2016, https://www.japantimes.co.jp/news/2016/07/08/national/politics-diplomacy/beijing-turns-japanese-judge-hague-tribunal-ruling-south-china-sea-nears/#.XmEPWkpS-1s, accessed 5 March 2020.

[196] Xinhua, "Arbitral Tribunal on South China Sea Illegal, Ridiculous," *Global Times*, 8 July 2016, http://www.globaltimes.cn/content/993110.shtml, accessed 16 March 2020.

[197] Ministry of Foreign Affairs of the People's Republic of China, *Veil of the Arbitral Tribunal Must Be Tore [sic] Down [sic]---Vice Foreign Minister Liu Zhenmin Answers Journalists' Questions on the So-called Binding Force of the Award Rendered by the Arbitral Tribunal of the South China Sea Arbitration Case, 2016/07/13*, http://www.fmprc.gov.cn/mfa_eng/wjbxw/t1381879.shtml, accessed 16 March 2020. This article is no longer available online. The complete text is appended to Chapter 5 as Annex 5.1.

[198] Jerome A. Cohen, "South China Sea Ruling and Defamation," *jeromecohen.net*, 20 July 2016, http://www.jeromecohen.net/jerrys-blog/2016/7/20/south-china-sea-ruling-and-defamation, accessed 16 March 2020.

[199] Julian Ku, "China's Vice-Minister for Foreign Affairs Casually Slanders the South China Sea Arbitral Tribunal," *opiniojuris.org*, 26 July 2016, http://opiniojuris.org/2016/07/26/chinas-vice-minister-for-foreign-affairs-casually-slanders-the-south-china-sea-arbitral-tribunal/, accessed 16 March 2020.

[200] Ibid.

Chinese media. The level of abuse reached such a point that the Philippines had complained of it at a meeting with Chinese officials in July 2012. Philippine diplomats pointed out that Chinese leaders were not personally attacked in the Philippine media.[201]

Even assuming for the sake of argument that China could make a credible case against the independence and impartiality of the appointing authority and of the five members of the Arbitral Tribunal, its doubts should have been articulated at the commencement of the proceedings and not after the proceedings had been terminated. As in the case of China's other allegations of violations of its procedural rights, China can be deemed to have waived its objections to the independence and impartiality of the judges once it had failed to have recourse to the procedure that was offered to it for this purpose by the Rules of Procedure of the *South China Sea Arbitration*.

By this time, though, the defense of China's default had receded into the background. As mentioned earlier, there is no reference to it in the book-length critique of the two Awards published by the CSIL two years after the issuance of the Award on 12 July 2016.[202] The CSIL study may be properly considered as an authoritative work, representative of China's official position. As Bing Ling pointed out, it was carried out "under the supervision and leadership of the Foreign Ministry."[203] The silence over China's default may have been motivated by the desire to create the impression that the Tribunal had unjustifiably dismissed the arguments of a party that had actually appeared in the proceedings. It may

201 *MP*, Annex 84, Memorandum from the Embassy of the Republic of the Philippines in Beijing to the Secretary of Foreign Affairs of the Republic of the Philippines, No. ZPE-110-2012-S (26 July 2012), vol. III, 226, para. 20, https://files.pca-cpa.org/pcadocs/The%20Philippines%27%20Memorial%20-%20Volume%20III%20%28Annexes%201-60%29.pdf, accessed 15 March 2020.

202 This was first pointed out by Douglas Guilfoyle, "A New Twist in the South China Sea Arbitration: The Chinese Society of International Law's Critical Study," *ejil.talk*, 25 May 2018, ejiltalk.org/a-new-twist-in-the-south-china-sea-arbitration-the-chinese-society-of-international-laws-critical-study/, accessed 7 February 2018.

203 Quoted in Douglas Guilfoyle, "Taking the Party Line on the South China Sea Arbitration," *ejil.talk*, 28 May 2019, ejiltalk.org/taking-the-party-line-on-the-south-china-sea-arbitration/, accessed 16 July 2020. Roberts points out that the CSIL Secretariat is located in the China University of Foreign Affairs, which is governed by the Ministry of Foreign Affairs, and that its president in 2017 was a high official of the National People's Congress and was formerly a high-ranking legal official of the State Council. Roberts, *Is International Law International?* 241.

also flow from an awareness that many of China's objections, particularly those relating to procedural decisions, could be very easily refuted by pointing out that the Tribunal had given China the opportunity to express its views and it had refused to do so.

IV. Overview of the Book

Chapter 2 analyzes China's attempts to exempt itself from the jurisdiction of the Arbitral Tribunal. China's default draws the observer's attention to the scholarly consensus that there is no duty on the part of a State against whom a proceeding is initiated to appear before an international court if that State has given its prior consent to that court's compulsory jurisdiction. China's argument went much further than that of defaulting States in cases before the ICJ, for China affirmed the existence of a right not to appear before the Arbitral Tribunal, deliberately ignoring the fact that it had given its consent to the jurisdiction of international courts established under the Convention by ratifying the Convention. China's positions, like those of other defaulting States in cases before the ICJ, amounted to a denial of the well-established principle of an international court's power to determine its jurisdiction (*compétence de la compétence*). The Tribunal's response, following the precedent of the ICJ in default cases, was to treat China's arguments as a plea on jurisdiction and to bifurcate the proceedings, notwithstanding the opposition of the appearing State to bifurcation. At the ICJ, some defaulting States as well as some States that have appeared in proceedings and were dissatisfied with ICJ decisions have effectively deprived the Court of jurisdiction over subsequent disputes by withdrawing their acceptance of the Court's compulsory jurisdiction. Such an option was not available to China, which could have withdrawn from the dispute settlement mechanisms of the Convention only by withdrawing from the latter. The reason is that the Convention's dispute settlement mechanisms are an integral part of the Convention. In the end, China remained a party to the Convention. This was understandable, in view of the symbolic and material value of the Convention for China.

Chapter 3 discusses the efforts undertaken by the Tribunal to acquire knowledge of the facts in the *South China Sea Arbitration* while maintaining the equality of the parties. In several respects, the Tribunal's efforts were facilitated by the conduct of China. Like other defaulting States in cases before the ICJ, China made known its views through informal communications and public statements. Like the ICJ, the Arbitral Tribunal used the defaulting State's informal communications and public statements to assist it in ascertaining the latter's legal positions. Unlike the ICJ, the Tribunal explicitly acknowledged the practical difficulties caused by default to the appearing State and established a procedure to alleviate these difficulties, through permission granted to the Philippines to make a supplemental submission on issues that in the Tribunal's view had not been sufficiently canvassed or had not been canvassed at all by the Philippines in its *Memorial*. China's litigation strategy differed from that of defaulting States in cases before the ICJ in that it tacitly approved submissions by self-proclaimed *amici curiae*. There was no precedent in the ICJ caselaw for the handling of submissions of self-proclaimed *amici curiae*, and the Tribunal did not make explicit decisions granting them the status of *amici curiae*. The Chapter nevertheless makes an effort to assess the contribution of the putative *amici curiae* to the Tribunal's fact-finding on the basis of criteria derived from investor-State arbitration under the rules and practice of the North American Free Trade Agreement ("NAFTA") and the International Centre for the Settlement of Investment Disputes ("ICSID"). The final section of Chapter 3 discusses the Tribunal's exercise of its other fact-finding powers: the power to put questions to the parties during the oral proceedings, the power to appoint independent experts, and the general power to take all measures necessary to establish the facts. Chapter 3 pays particular attention to the Tribunal's independent fact-finding, which has been misunderstood by Chinese and non-Chinese scholars alike.

Chapters 4 and 5 examine aspects of the litigation strategy of the defaulting State in the *South China Sea Arbitration* that diverged sharply from that of defaulting States in cases before the ICJ and that occasionally went beyond the limits of international legal practice. By definition, such conduct could hardly be addressed, if at all, by recourse to the Arbitral Tribunal's procedural powers. Yet, it is precisely for these reasons that such conduct deserves scrutiny. The point of departure of Chapter 4 is the CSIL's critique of one of the fact-finding measures taken by the Tribunal—the appointment of independent experts. The CSIL questioned the independence and impartiality of the independent experts on coral reefs and asserted that the Tribunal had adopted their report without proper evaluation. In proceedings in which both parties appeared, China would have been construed as waiving its right to object to the qualifications, independence, and impartiality of the experts after having failed to communicate its views when given the opportunity to do so. The attention that the Chapter pays to this matter is justified by the judicial and scholarly debate of the last decade or so on the proper role of experts, whether they are appointed by a party or by a court, in international adjudication. Chapter 4 argues that the intervention of experts, particularly scientific experts, is an integral part of the Convention's legal framework and of the practice of Annex VII arbitral tribunals. It evaluates the independence and impartiality of the experts presented by the Philippines and those appointed by Tribunal on the basis of criteria that have been identified in the scholarly literature. The remaining three parts of the Chapter will summarize the complex scientific and technical evidence submitted by the Philippines, the independent experts' opinions, and the Tribunal's evaluation of the evidence presented by the two sets of experts in three areas: the determination of the status of features, the harm caused by China's island-building to the marine environment, and navigational safety.

The rationale for Chapter 5, like that for Chapter 4, is the conduct of China that has no parallel in the litigation strategy of defaulting States in cases before the ICJ. Strictly speaking, China's defamation campaign against the appointing authority, individual judges, and the Tribunal as a whole need not be addressed, given that China had failed to raise its objections to the independence and impartiality of the judges when given the opportunity to do so during the proceedings. The examination of China's charges in Chapter 5 is justified by the increased judicial and scholarly interest in the last two decades on the issues raised by the independence and impartiality of international judges. Chapter 5 first discusses China's criticism of the non-representative character of the Tribunal's composition. This critique is dismissed as irrelevant, as the representation of major civilizations, major legal systems, and nationals of the parties is not a requirement of arbitration in general or arbitration under Annex VII of the Convention, in particular. Chapter 5 then analyzes the scope of the concept of independence as it emerges from the scholarly literature. On this basis, it concludes that the appointing authority and individual judges were undoubtedly independent. Indeed, China did not criticize them for their independence; instead, it sought to undermine their independence through pressures similar to those exerted on Chinese judges by the Chinese government and the CCP as well as through "judicial populism." Chapter 5 then examines the scope of the concept of impartiality, identifying three approaches to determining the impartiality of international judges. Applying these three approaches to the appointing authority and the members of the Tribunal, Chapter 5 concludes that the appointing authority and the individual judges were impartial. The last part of the Chapter pays particular attention to China's attack on the impartiality of the Tribunal as a whole, based on the accusation that the Tribunal rendered decisions favorable to the Philippines in exchange for financial consideration. It argues that China's accusations of corruption manifest a deliberate and willful misunderstanding of arbitration and are nothing but manifestations of the reality of judicial corruption in China.

Chapter 6 summarizes the book's findings and concludes that China reaped the advantages of default anticipated in the scholarly literature; that China's contribution to international arbitral practice should be judged negatively; and that unlike dependent and corrupt Chinese judges, the Tribunal, confronted with the legal challenges and practical difficulties caused by China's default as well as the pressures exerted by the defaulting State, was able to perform successfully the judicial function.

This book does not address the legal issues, if any, that may have been raised by Vietnam's communications to the Arbitral Tribunal, which have sometimes been interpreted as attempts at intervention. If such had been indeed Vietnam's goal, the Tribunal would have had to deal with the issue of the legality of intervention in arbitral proceedings, whether or not China had defaulted. In any event, the question became moot when Vietnam did not follow up its communications with any application for intervention.

In the writing of this book the inductive method was adopted, rather than the deductive method. The research proceeded from the particular to the general, rather than from the general to the particular. Concretely, this meant that the starting points for discussion were particular acts—of China, Taiwan, the Philippines, the putative "*amici curiae*," and the Tribunal—that served as the bases for general conclusions about the litigation strategies of the first four actors and the exercise of its procedural powers by the last. The book relies primarily on the official documents of the *South China Sea Arbitration*, China's Position Paper and other public statements, Taiwan's position papers, and the position papers of the putative *amicus curiae* in order to analyze the positions of these actors. The official documents of the *Arbitration*, which constituted by far the bulk of the documents consulted in the writing of this book, encompass the *Memorial of the Philippines*; the *Supplemental Written Submission of the Philippines*; the hundreds of documentary annexes submitted by the

Philippines prior to, during, and after the Hearings on Jurisdiction and on the Merits; the Rules of Procedure; the Procedural Orders; the transcripts of the Hearings on Jurisdiction and on the Merits; the reports of experts engaged by the Philippines; the reports of the independent experts appointed by the Tribunal; the Philippine responses to the submissions of Taiwan, the reports of the independent experts, and the British and French archival materials transmitted to the parties by the Tribunal; the Award on Jurisdiction and Admissibility; and the Award of 12 July 2016. The book does not draw on general discussions of the South China Sea disputes, of the foreign policies of China and Taiwan, and the attitudes to international law of China and Taiwan for the purpose of analyzing China's default in the *South China Sea Arbitration*. On the contrary, the book's analysis of the acts of the differing actors will arguably shed new light on the South China Sea disputes, the foreign policies of China and Taiwan, and the attitudes to international law of China and Taiwan.

References

Aegean Sea Continental Shelf. I.C.J. Pleadings, https://www.icj-cij.org/files/case-related/62/062-19781009-ORA-01-00-BI.pdf, accessed 20 March 2020.

Amerasinghe, Chittaranjan F. *Evidence in International Litigation*. Leiden: Martinus Nijhoff Publishers, 2005.

Anderson, David. *Modern Law of the Sea: Selected Essays*. Leiden: Brill—Nijhoff, 2008.

Anglo-Iranian Oil Co. Case (Jurisdiction). United Kingdom. *Application Instituting Proceedings* (26 May 1951). *I.C.J. Pleadings, Anglo-Iranian Oil Co. Case*, 8–44, https://www.icj-cij.org/files/case-related/16/016-19510526-APP-1-00-BI.pdf, accessed 19 March 2020.

———. Communication from the Minister of Foreign Affairs of Iran to the President of the International Court of Justice, dated 29 June 1951, with Three Annexes. *I.C.J. Pleadings, Anglo-Iranian Oil Co. Case*, 672–98, https://www.icj-cij.org/files/case-related/16/8987.pdf, accessed 19 March 2020.

——— (Jurisdiction). *Judgment of July 22, 1952: I.C.J. Reports 1952*, 93–115, https://www.icj-cij.org/files/case-related/16/016-19520722-JUD-01-00-BI.pdf, accessed 19 March 2020.

———. Minutes of the Public Sittings from June 9th to 23rd and July 22nd, 1952. *I.C.J. Pleadings, Anglo-Iranian Oil Co. Case*, 426–669, https://www.icj-cij.org/files/case-related/16/016-19520609-ORA-01-00-BI.pdf, accessed 8 January 2020.

Antonopoulos, Constantine. *Counterclaims Before the International Court of Justice*. The Hague: T.M.C. Asser Press, 2011.

AO Kaspersky Lab. "Zero-day Meaning and Definition." https://www.kaspersky.com/resource-center/definitions/zero-day-exploit, accessed 8 May 2022.

APT1: Exposing One of China's Cyber Espionage Units (2013), https://www.fireeye.com/content/dam/fireeye-www/services/pdfs/mandiant-apt1-report.pdf, accessed 23 March 2020.

———. *Appendix C: The Malware Arsenal* (2013), https://www.slideshare.net/YuryChemerkin/appendix-c-digital-the-malware-arsenal, accessed 23 March 2020.

Arangio-Ruiz, Gaetano. "Non-appearance Before the International Court of Justice. Final Report." *Annuaire de l'Institut de droit international* [Yearbook of the Institute of International Law]. Session de Bâle [Basel Session], 64-I (1991), 280–339, http://www.gaetanoarangioruiz.it/publications/non-appearance-before-the-international-court-of-justice/, accessed 13 October 2019.

———. "Non-appearance Before the International Court of Justice. Preliminary Report." *Annuaire de l'Institut de droit international* [Yearbook of the Institute of International Law]. Session de Bâle [Basel Session], 64-I (1991), 193–279, http://www.gaetanoarangioruiz.it/publications/non-appearance-before-the-international-court-of-justice/, accessed 13 October 2019.

———. "Notes on Non-appearance Before the International Court of Justice." *Le droit international à l'heure de sa codification. Études en l'honneur de Roberto Ago* [International Law at the Time of Its Codification. Studies in Honour of Roberto Ago]. Vol. II. *Les différends entre États et la responsabilité* [Inter-State Disputes and Responsibility], 3–48. Milano: Dott. A. Giuffrè Editore, 1987.

"Arctic Sunrise" (Kingdom of the Netherlands v. Russian Federation). Provisional Measures. Order of 22 November 2013. ITLOS Reports 2013, 224–25, https://www.itlos.org/fileadmin/itlos/documents/cases/case_no.22/published/C22_Order_221113.pdf, accessed 20 November 2018.

———. Joint Separate Opinion of Judges Wolfrum and Kelly. *ITLOS Reports 2013*, 256–61, https://www.itlos.org/fileadmin/itlos/documents/cases/case_no.22/published/C22_Wolfrum_Kelly_221113.pdf, accessed 16 March 2020.

———. Separate Opinion of Judge Paik. *ITLOS Reports 2013*, 271–77, https://www.itlos.org/fileadmin/itlos/documents/cases/case_no.22/published/C22_Paik_221113.pdf, accessed 19 March 2020.

Avast. *Exploits: What You Need to Know* (2019), https://www.avast.com/c-exploits, accessed 23 March 2020.

Bahrain, State of. Ministry of State for Legal Affairs. Minister's Office. *Comments by the State of Bahrain on the Qatari "Act" of 30th November, 1994* (5

December 1994), https://www.icj-cij.org/files/case-related/87/13263.pdf, accessed 16 August 2020.

———. "Introduction from the Bench." *Nicaragua Before the International Court of Justice. Impacts on International Law*, 3–14. Eds. Edgardo Sobenes Obregón and Benjamin Samson. Cham, Switzerland: Springer International Publishing AG, 2018.

Bedjaoui, Mohammed. "L'égalité des États dans le procès international, un mythe [Equality of States in International Judicial Proceedings, a Myth?]?" *Le procès international. Liber Amicorum Jean-Pierre Cot* [International Judicial Proceedings. Liber Amicorum Jean-Pierre Cot], 1–27. Bruxelles: Établissements Émile Bruylant, 2009.

Boncenne, Pierre, and Olivier Bourbeau. *Théorie de la procédure civile, précédée d'une introduction* [Theory of Civil Procedure, preceded by an Introduction]. Vol. III, 2nd ed. Paris: Videcoq père et fils Libraires, 1844, https://ia800209.us.archive.org/7/items/thoriedelaproc03bonc/thoriedelaproc03bonc.pdf, accessed 9 March 2020.

Bowett, D. W. "Contemporary Developments in Legal Techniques in the Settlement of Disputes." *Recueil des cours de l'Académie de droit international de La Haye* [Collected Courses of the Hague Academy of International Law]. Vol. 180 (1983-II), 169–235.

Burke, Ciarán. "Annex VII. Article 9." *The United Nations Convention on the Law of the Sea: A Commentary*, 2482–83. Eds. Alexander Proelss et al. Munich: E.H. Beck, 2017.

Carty, Anthony. "The South China Sea Disputes Are Not Yet Justiciable." *Arbitration Concerning the South China Sea. Philippines Versus China*, 23–51. Eds. Shicun Wu and Keyuan Zou. London: Routledge, 2016.

Chan, Phil C.W. *China, State Sovereignty and International Legal Order*. Leiden: Brill-Nijhoff, 2015.

Chang, Yen-Chiang. "China's Non-participation Approach Toward the South China Sea Arbitration." *Chinese (Taiwan) Yearbook of International Law and Affairs* 34 (2016): 56–72.

China, People's Republic of. Embassy in the Republic of Iceland. *Foreign Ministry Spokesperson Hua Chunying's Regular Press Conference on May 25, 2016*, http://is.china-embassy.org/eng/fyrth/t1366744.htm, accessed15 March 2020.

———. Embassy in the United States of America. *Foreign Ministry Spokesperson Hong Lei's Regular Press Conference on February 20, 2013* (21 February 2013), http://www.china-embassy.org/eng/fyrth/t1015425.htm, accessed 10 March 2020.

———. Ministry of Foreign Affairs. *Foreign Ministry Spokesperson Hong Lei's Regular Press Conference on March 26, 2013* (27 March 2013), http://www.china-embassy.org/eng/fyrth/t1025838.htm, accessed 10 March 2020.

———. *Foreign Ministry Spokesperson Hua Chunying's Remarks on the Philippines' Efforts in Pushing for the Establishment of the Arbitral Tribunal in Relation to the Disputes between China and the Philippines in the South China Sea* (26 April 2013), https://www.fmprc.gov.cn/mfa_eng/xwfw_665399/s2510_665401/2535_665405/t1035577.shtml, accessed 10 March 2020.

———. *Veil of the Arbitral Tribunal Must Be Tore [sic] Down [sic]—Vice Foreign Minister Liu Zhenmin Answers Journalists' Questions on the So-Called Binding Force of the Award Rendered by the Arbitral Tribunal of the South China Sea Arbitration Case, 2016/07/13*, http://www.fmprc.gov.cn/mfa_eng/wjbxw/t1381879.shtml, accessed 16 March 2020.

Chinese Society of International Law. "The South China Sea Arbitration Awards: A Critical Study." *Chinese Journal of International Law* 17 (2018): 207–748.

Cohen, Jerome A. "South China Sea Ruling and Defamation." *jeromecohen.net*, 20 July 2016, http://www.jeromecohen.net/jerrys-blog/2016/7/20/south-china-sea-ruling-and-defamation, accessed 16 March 2020.

Colliard, Claude-Albert. "La Non-comparution [Non-appearance]." *La juridiction internationale permanente* [Permanent International Jurisdiction], 167–90. Société française pour le droit international [French Society for International Law]. Colloque de Lyon [Lyons Colloquium]. Paris: Éditions A. Pedone, 1987.

Convention for the Establishment of a Central American Court of Justice. *American Journal of International Law* 2, No. 1/2, *Supplement: Official Documents* (1908): 231–43.

Coussirat-Coustère, Vincent. "L'arrêt de la Cour internationale de Justice sur le personnel diplomatique américain à Téhéran [The Judgment of the International Court of Justice on American Diplomatic Staff in Teheran]." *Annuaire français de droit international* [French Yearbook of International Law] 26 (1980): 201–24, https://www.persee.fr/doc/afdi_0066-3085_1980_num_26_1_2388, accessed 20 March 2020.

———, and Pierre-Michel Eisemann. "La procédure devant les juridictions internationales permanentes [Procedure before Permanent International Jurisdictions]." *La juridiction internationale permanente* [Permanent International Jurisdiction], 103–66. Société française pour le droit international [French Society for International Law]. Colloque de Lyon [Lyons Colloquium]. Paris: Éditions A. Pedone, 1987.

Davenport, Tara. "Procedural Issues Arising from China's Non-participation in the *South China Sea Arbitration*." *The South China Sea Arbitration: The Legal Dimension*, 65–98. Eds. S. Jayakumar et al. Cheltenham: Edward Elgar Publishing, 2018.

Decaux, Emmanuel. "Affaire de la délimitation maritime et des questions territoriales entre Qatar et Bahreïn, Fond (arrêt du 16 mars 2001 Qatar c. Bahreïn) [Case concerning Maritime Delimitation and Territorial Questions between

Qatar and Bahrain, Merits (Judgment of 16 March 2001) Qatar v. Bahrain]. *Annuaire français de droit international* [French Yearbook of International Law] 47 (2001): 177–240, https://www.persee.fr/doc/afdi_0066-3085_2001_num_47_1_3660, accessed 27 August 2020.

Denunciation of the Treaty of November 2nd, 1865, Between China and Belgium. Permanent Court of International Justice, Series C: Acts and Documents Relating to Judgments and Advisory Opinions Given by the Court. Pleadings, Oral Arguments and Documents. Leiden: A.W. Sijthoff's Publishing Company, 1930, https://www.icj-cij.org/files/permanent-court-of-international-justice/serie_C/C_16_01/C_16_01_04_Traite_sino-belge_autres_documents.pdf, accessed 13 March 2020.

Dintilhac, Jean-Pierre. "L'égalité des armes dans les enceintes judiciaires [Equality of Arms in Judicial Bodies]." *Rapport de la Cour de Cassation 2003* [Report of the Supreme Court 2003], 129–40. Cour de Cassation [Supreme Court]. Paris: La Documentation française, 2004, https://www.courdecassation.fr/publications_26/rapport_annuel_36/rapport_2003_37/deuxieme_partie_tudes_documents_40/tudes_theme_egalite_42/enceinte_judiciaires_6255.html, accessed 16 March 2020.

Eisemann, Pierre-Michel. "Les effets de la non-comparution devant la Cour internationale de Justice [The Effects of Non-appearance before the International Court of Justice]." *Annuaire français de droit international* [French Yearbook of International Law] 19 (1973): 351–75, https://www.persee.fr/docAsPDF/afdi_0066-3085_1973_num_19_1_2217.pdf, accessed 23 March 2020.

Enstein, Adhémar. *Histoire de la procédure criminelle en France et spécialement de la procédure inquisitoriale, depuis le XIIIe siècle jusqu'à nos jours* [A History of Criminal Procedure in France, and Particularly of the Inquisitorial Procedure, from the 13th Century to the Present]. Paris: L. Larose et Forcel, 1882, https://archive.org/details/histoiredelapro00esmegoog/page/n10/mode/2up, accessed 11 March 2020.

Espenilla, Jacqueline Joyce F. "Judicial Fact-Finding Initiatives in the *South China Sea Arbitration*." *Asian Journal of International Law* 9 (2019): 20–30.

Favoreu, Louis. "L'arrêt de la Cour internationale de Justice dans l'affaire de la compétence en matière de pêcheries (Royaume-Uni c./Islande et Allemagne fédérale c./Islande)[The Judgment of the International Court of Justice in the Fisheries Jurisdiction Case (United Kingdom v. Iceland and Federal Republic of Germany v. Iceland]." *Annuaire français de droit international* [French Yearbook of International Law] 19 (1973): 272–89, http://www.persee.fr/doc/afdi_0066-3085_1973_num_19_1_2214, accessed 22 March 2020.

———. "Les arrêts de la Cour Internationale de Justice relatifs à la compétence en matière de pêcheries (Royaume-Uni c/ Islande et République fédérale d'Allemagne c. Islande — Arrêts du 25 juillet 1974) [The Judgments of the International Court of Justice on Fisheries Jurisdiction (United Kingdom v. Iceland and Federal Republic of Germany v. Iceland—Judgments of 25 July 1974]." *Annuaire français de droit international* [French Yearbook of International Law] 20 (1974): 253–85, http://www.persee.fr/doc/afdi_0066-3085_1974_num_20_1_2271, accessed 17 March 2020.

———. "Les ordonnances des 17 et 18 août 1972 dans les affaires relatives à la compétence en matière de pêcheries - Contribution au droit procédural de la Cour en matière de mesures conservatoires, exceptions préliminaires et compétence en cas de défaut (Royaume-Uni c. Islande et République fédérale d'Allemagne c. Islande) [The Orders of 17 and 18 August 1972 in the Cases relating to Fisheries Jurisdiction—Contribution to the Procedural Law of the Court with respect to Provisional Measures, Preliminary Objections and Jurisdiction in case of Default]. " *Annuaire français de droit international* [French Yearbook of International Law] 18 (1972): 291–322, http://www.persee.fr/doc/afdi_0066-3085_1972_num_18_1_3855, accessed 4 March 2018.

Fellmeth, Aaron X., and Maurice Horwitz. *Guide to Latin in International Law*. New York: Oxford University Press, 2009.

Fitzmaurice, Gerald. "The Problem of the 'Non-appearing' Defendant Government." *British Yearbook of International Law* 51 (1980): 89–122.

Fry, James D. "Non-participation in the International Court of Justice Revisited: Change or Plus Ça Change." *Columbia Journal of Transnational Law* 49 (2010): 35–74.

Gau, Michael Sheng-Ti. "The U-Shaped Line and a Categorization of the Ocean Disputes in the South China Sea." *Ocean Development and International Law* 43 (2012): 57–69.

Goldhaber, Michael D. "China Denies Role in Hack Attack on Hague Peace Palace." *The American Lawyer*, 22 July 2015, https://www.law.com/americanlawyer/almID/1202732867280/china-denies-role-in-hack-attack-on-hague-peace-palace/?slreturn=20200223044958, accessed 23 March 2020.

Goldmann, Matthias. "International Courts and Tribunals, Non-appearance." *Max Planck Encyclopedia of Public International Law* (2006).

Grasern, Lambert. "Verfahrensboykott vor dem Internationalen Gerichtshof, Sachverhaltsermittlung und Beweiswürdigung [Boycott of Proceedings before the International Court of Justice, Fact-Finding and Evaluation of Evidence]." *Archiv des Völkerrechts* [Archive of International Law] 25 (1987): 460–83.

Guilfoyle, Douglas. "A New Twist in the South China Sea Arbitration: The Chinese Society of International Law's Critical Study." *ejil.talk*, 25 May 2018, ejiltalk.org/a-new-twist-in-the-south-china-sea-arbitration-the-chinese-society-of-international-laws-critical-study/, accessed 7 February 2018.

———. "Taking the Party Line on the South China Sea Arbitration." *ejil.talk*, 28 May 2019, ejiltalk.org/taking-the-party-line-on-the-south-china-sea-arbitration/, accessed 16 July 2020.

Haas, Géraldine. "La procédure par défaut et l'opposition. Notions générales et contradictions [Default and Opposition Procedure. General Notions and Contradictions]." Unpublished master's thesis, Faculty of Law and Criminology, Catholic University of Louvain, 2013, https://dial.uclouvain.be/downloader/downloader.php?pid=thesis%3A1842&datastream=PDF_01, accessed 11 March 2020.

He Tiantian. "Commentary on Award on Jurisdiction and Admissibility of the Philippines-Instituted Arbitration Under Annex VII to the UNCLOS: A Discussion on Fact-Finding and Evidence." *Chinese Journal of Global Governance* 2 (2016): 96–128.

Healey, Jason, and Anni Piiparinen. "Did China Just Hack the International Court Adjudicating Its South China Sea Territorial Claims?" *The Diplomat*, 27 October 2015, https://thediplomat.com/2015/10/did-china-just-hack-the-international-court-adjudicating-its-south-china-sea-territorial-claims/, accessed 23 March 2020.

Highet, Keith. "Litigation Implications of the U.S. Withdrawal from the Nicaragua Case." *American Journal of International Law* 79 (1985): 992–1005.

———. "Nonappearance and Disappearance Before the International Court of Justice." *American Journal of International Law* 81 (1987): 237–54.

Hudson, Manley O. *The Permanent Court of International Justice. A Treatise.* New York: The Macmillan Company, 1934.

Iasiello, Emilio. "China's Three Warfares Strategy Mitigates Fallout from Cyber Espionage Activities." *Journal of Strategic Security* 9 (2016): 45–69, http://scholarcommons.usf.edu/jss/vol9/iss2/4, accessed 23 March 2020.

Institut de droit international [Institute of International Law]. *About the Institute* (2019), https://www.idi-iil.org/en/a-propos/, accessed 16 March 2020.

———. Session de Bâle [Basel Session]. *Non-appearance Before the International Court of Justice* (1991), https://www.idi-iil.org/app/uploads/2017/06/1991_bal_01_en.pdf, accessed 16 March 2020.

Intel Team. *Mandiant APT1 Report Appendix F Update: SSL Certificate Hashes* (19 March 2013), https://www.fireeye.com/blog/threat-research/2013/03/md5-sha1.html, accessed 23 March 2020.

———. *Appendix G (Digital) IOCs* (2013), https://www.slideshare.net/YuryChemerkin/appendix-g-iocs-readme, accessed 23 March 2020.

International Court of Justice. *Statute*, http://www.icj-cij.org/en/statute, accessed 10 March 2020.

Jayakumar, S. et al. "The *South China Sea Arbitration*: Laying the Groundwork." *The South China Sea Arbitration: The Legal Dimension*, 1–17. Eds. S. Jayakumar et al. Cheltenham: Edward Elgar Publishing, 2018.

Johnson, Jesse. "Beijing Turns on Japanese Judge as Hague Tribunal Ruling Over South China Sea Nears." *The Japan Times*, 8 July 2016, https://www.japantimes.co.jp/news/2016/07/08/national/politics-iplomacy/beijing-turns-japanese-judge-hague-tribunal-ruling-south-china-sea-nears/#.XmEPWkpS-1s, accessed 5 March 2020.

Kardon, Isaac B. "China Can Say No: Analyzing China's Rejection of the South China Sea Arbitration. Toward a New Era of International Law with Chinese Characteristics." *University of Pennsylvania Asian Law Review* 13 (2019): 1–46, https://scholarship.law.upenn.edu/cgi/viewcontent.cgi?article=1037&context=alr, accessed 23 March 2020.

Katte, Christoph von. "Denunciation of Treaty of 1865 Between Belgium and China." *Encyclopedia of Public International Law*. Vol. II. *Decisions of International Courts and Tribunals and International Arbitrations*, 75–76. Ed. Rudolf Bernhardt. Amsterdam: North-Holland Publishing Co., 1981.

Kolb, Robert. *The Elgar Companion to the International Court of Justice*. Cheltenham: Edward Elgar, 2014.

Ku, Julian. "China's Vice-Minister for Foreign Affairs Casually Slanders the South China Sea Arbitral Tribunal." *opiniojuris.org*, 26 July 2016, http://opiniojuris.org/2016/07/26/chinas-vice-minister-for-foreign-affairs-casually-slanders-the-south-china-sea-arbitral-tribunal/, accessed 16 March 2020.

———. "The Significance of China's Rejection of the South China Sea Arbitration for Its Approach to International Dispute Settlement and International Law." *Chinese (Taiwan) Yearbook of International Law and Affairs* 34 (2016): 73–103.

Kuok, Lynn. *Tides of Change: Taiwan's Evolving Position in the South China Sea and Why Other Actors Should Take Notice*. Washington, D.C.: Center for East Asia Policy Studies, Brookings Institution, 2015, https://www.brookings.edu/wp-content/uploads/2016/06/taiwan-south-china-sea-kuok-paper.pdf, accessed 15 March 2020.

Lamberti Zanardi, Pierluigi. "Forme nuove di contestazione della competenza della Corte internazionale di giustizia e potere della Corte di aprire d'ufficio un procedimento sulla competenza [New Forms of Challenge to the Jurisdiction of the International Court of Justice and the Court's Power to Open ex officio Jurisdictional Proceedings]." *Comunicazioni e studi* [Communications and Studies] 14 (1975): 439–76.

Larousse Dictionary of Science and Technology. Edinburgh: Larousse plc, 1995.

Levine, Judith, and Garth L. Schofield. "Navigating Uncharted Procedural Waters in a Rising Sea of Cases at the Permanent Court of Arbitration." *Stress Testing the Law of the Sea: Dispute Resolution, Disasters and Emerging Challenges*, 95–149. Eds. Stephen Minas and H. Jordan Diamond. Leiden: Brill Nijhoff, 2018.

Liao, Shiping. "Fact-Finding in Non-appearance Before International Courts and Tribunals." Unpublished ms., Beijing Normal University, 2018, https://ssrn.com/abstract=3187971, accessed 22 March 2020.

Ling, Bing. *China's Attitude to the International Legal Order in the Xi Era: The Case of the South China Sea*. Japan Institute of International Affairs (JIIA) Indo-Pacific Focus Policy Brief No. 4 (27 June 2018), https://www2.jiia.or.jp/en/article_page.php?id=7, accessed 7 February 2019.

Makinen, Julie. "U.S. Lawyer Who Led Philippines' Case Says Beijing's Boycott Made His Job Harder in South China Sea Arguments." *Los Angeles Times*, 12 July 2016, https://www.latimes.com/world/asia/la-fg-south-china-sea-lawyer-20160712-snap-story.html, accessed 21 April 2020.

Mangoldt, Hans von. "Versäumnisverfahren in der internationalen (Schieds)Gerichtsbarkeit und souveräne Gleichheit [Default Procedures in International Arbitration and Adjudication and Sovereign Equality]." *Völkerrecht als Rechtsordnung, internationale Gerichtsbarkeit, Menschenrechte. Festschrift für Hermann Mosler* [International Law as a Legal Order, International Adjudication, Human Rights. Festschrift for Hermann Mosler], 503–29. Ed. Rudolf Bernhardt. Berlin: Springer Verlag, 1983.

———, and Andreas Zimmerman. "Article 53." *The Statute of the International Court of Justice: A Commentary*, 3rd ed., 1467–98. Eds. Andreas Zimmermann et al. Oxford: Oxford University Press, 2019.

Maritime Delimitation and Territorial Questions Between Qatar and Bahrain. Jurisdiction and Admissibility. Judgment. I. C. J. Reports 1995, 6–26 https://www.icj-cij.org/files/case-related/87/087-19950215-JUD-01-00-BI.pdf, accessed 17 August 2020.

"Memorandum para ser transmitido au Senado da Cidade Libre de Hamburgo, para se encarregar da arbitragem relativamente à reclamação dos Sres Yuille, Shortridge e Cia [Memorandum to Be Transmitted to the Senate of the Free City of Hamburg, to Take Charge of the Arbitration Relating to the Claim of Messrs. Yuille, Shortridge and Co.] [8 March 1861]." *Pasicrisie internationale 1794–1900. Histoire documentaire des arbitrages internationaux* [Compendium of International Caselaw 1794–1900. A Documentary History of International Arbitrations], 377–78. Ed. Henri La Fontaine. Berne: Imprimerie Stampfli & Cie, 1902, https://ia600205.us.archive.org/9/items/pasicrisieinter00fontgoog/pasicrisieinter00fontgoog.pdf, accessed 11 March 2020.

"Memorandum pour soumettre au Sénat de Hambourg en qualité d'arbitre la réclamation Croft [Memorandum submitting the Croft Claim to the Senate of Hamburg as Arbitrator] [9 July 1861]." *Pasicrisie internationale 1794–1900. Histoire documentaire des arbitrages internationaux* [Compendium of International Caselaw 1794–1900. A Documentary History of International Arbitrations], 371–72. Ed. Henri La Fontaine. Berne: Imprimerie

Stampfli & Cie, 1902, https://ia600205.us.archive.org/9/items/pasicrisiein ter00fontgoog/pasicrisieinter00fontgoog.pdf, accessed 11 March 2020.

Military and Paramilitary Activities in and Against Nicaragua (Nicaragua v. United States of America). Nicaragua. *Application Instituting Proceedings* (9 April 1984), https://www.icj-cij.org/files/case-related/70/9615.pdf, accessed 13 March 2020.

———. *Merits. Judgment. I.C.J. Reports 1986*, 14–150, http://www.icj-cij.org/files/case-related/70/070-19860627-JUD-01-00-BI.pdf, accessed 17 March 2020.

———. Dissenting Opinion of Judge Schwebel. *I.C.J. Reports 1986*, 259–527, http://www.icj-cij.org/files/case-related/70/070-19860627-JUD-01-09-BI.pdf, accessed 31 March 2020.

Mitteis, Heinrich. "Studien zur Geschichte des Versäumnisurteils, Besonders im französischen Recht [Studies on the History of Default Judgments, Particularly in French Law]." *Zeitschrift der Savigny-Stiftung für Rechtsgeschichte. Germanistische Abteilung* [Journal of the Savigny Foundation for Legal History. German Department] 42 (1921): 137–239.

Mosk, Richard, M. "The Role of Facts in International Dispute Resolution." *Recueil des cours de l'Académie de droit international de La Haye* [Collected Courses of the Hague Academy of International Law]. Vol. 304 (2003-IV), 9–179.

Mosler, Hermann. "Nichtteilnahme einer Partei am Verfahren vor dem Internationalen Gerichtshof [Non-participation of a Party in Proceedings Before the International Court of Justice]." *Staatsrecht—Völkerrecht—Europarecht. Festschrift für Hans-Jürgen Schlochauer* [Constitutional Law—International Law - European Law. Festschrift for Hans-Jürgen Schlochauer], 439–56. Ed. Ingo von Münch. Berlin: Walter de Gruyter, 1981.

Muller, Wim. "China's Missed Opportunity in South China Sea Arbitration." *chathamhouse.org* (19 March 2015), https://www.chathamhouse.org/expert/comment/china-s-missed-opportunity-south-china-sea-arbitration, accessed 13 March 2020.

Nottebohm Case (Liechtenstein v. Guatemala). Liechtenstein. *Application Instituting Proceedings* (17 December 1951). *I.C.J. Pleadings, Nottebohm Case.* Vol. I, 9–20, https://www.icj-cij.org/files/case-related/18/018-19511217-APP-1-00-BI.pdf, accessed 19 March 2020.

———. Letter from the Minister of Foreign Affairs of Guatemala to the President of the International Court of Justice, 9 September 1952. *I.C.J. Pleadings, Nottebohm Case.* Vol. I, 62–69, https://www.icj-cij.org/files/case-related/18/10985.pdf, accessed 8 January 2020.

——— *(second phase). Judgment of April 6th, 1955. I.C.J. Reports 1955*, 4–27, http://www.icj-cij.org/files/case-related/18/018-19550406-JUD-01-00-BI.pdf, accessed 19 March 2020.

Nuclear Tests (Australia v. France). Australia. *Application Instituting Proceedings* (9 May 1973). *I.C.J. Pleadings, Nuclear Tests*. Vol. I, 2–79, https://www.icj-cij.org/files/case-related/58/13187.pdf, accessed 19 March 2020.

———. *Judgment*. *I.C.J. Reports 1974*, 253–74, http://www.icj-cij.org/files/case-related/58/058-19741220-JUD-01-00-BI.pdf, accessed 17 March 2020.

———. Separate Opinion of Judge Gros. *I.C.J. Reports 1974*, 276–97, http://www.icj-cij.org/files/case-related/58/058-19741220-JUD-01-04-BI.pdf, accessed 19 March 2020.

Nuclear Tests (New Zealand v. France). New Zealand. *Application Instituting Proceedings* (9 May 1973). *I.C.J. Pleadings, Nuclear Tests*. Vol. II, 3–45, https://www.icj-cij.org/files/case-related/59/9447.pdf, accessed 19 March 2020.

———. *Judgment*. *I.C.J. Reports 1974*, 457–78, https://www.icj-cij.org/files/case-related/59/059-19741220-JUD-01-00-BI.pdf, accessed 19 March 2020.

Oxman, Bernard H. "Nonparticipation and Perceptions of Legitimacy." *Ecology Law Quarterly* 46 (2019): 81–94. https://www.ecologylawquarterly.org/wp-content/uploads/2020/03/11_ELQ_Oxman_Final_Redacted.pdf, accessed 8 May 2022.

Permanent Court of International Justice. *Statute and Rules of Court*, 1st ed. Series D. N°.1 (1926). https://www.icj-cij.org/files/permanent-court-of-international-justice/serie_D/D_01_1e_edition.pdf, accessed 25 March 2020.

Peterson, Luke Eric. "Permanent Court of Arbitration Website Goes Offline, with Cyber-security Firm Contending That Security Flaw Was Exploited in Concert with China-Philippines Arbitration." *Investment Arbitration Reporter* (23 July 2015), https://www.iareporter.com/articles/permanent-court-of-arbitration-goes-offline-with-cyber-security-firm-contending-that-security-flaw-was-exploited-in-lead-up-to-china-philippines-arbitration/, accessed 23 March 2020.

Pineros Polo, Elena. "Arbitraje del mar del sur de China. la estrategia procesal de la República Popular de China [The South China Sea Arbitration. The Procedural Strategy of the People's Republic of China]." *Revista Electrónica de Estudios Internacionales* [Electronic Journal of International Studies] 35 (2018): 1–23, http://www.reei.org/index.php/revista/num35/notas/arbitraje-mar-sur-china-estrategia-procesal-republica-popular-china, accessed 10 June 2020.

Puntney, G. Todd. *Chinese Cyber Economic Espionage: Motivations and Responses*. School of Advanced Military Studies. United States Army Command and General Staff College, Fort Leavenworth, Kansas, 2016, https://apps.dtic.mil/dtic/tr/fulltext/u2/1022202.pdf, accessed 28 July 2019.

Roberts, Anthea. *Is international Law International?* Oxford: Oxford University Press, 2017.
Shabtai Rosenne, with the assistance of Yaël Ronen. *The Law and Practice of the International Court, 1920–2005*. Vol. III. *Jurisdiction*. Leiden: Martinus Nijhoff Publishers, 2006.
Salmon, Jean A. "Le fait dans l'application de droit international [The Fact in the Application of International Law]." *Recueil des cours de l'Académie de droit international de La Haye* [Collected Courses of the Hague Academy of International Law]. Vol. 175 (1982-II), 257–414.
Sceats, Sonya. "China's Fury Over South China Sea Belies Its Legal Insecurities." *chathamhouse.org* (4 July 2016), https://www.chathamhouse.org/expert/comment/chinas-fury-over-south-china-sea-belies-its-legal-insecurities%20, accessed 16 March 2020.
Scott, James Brown. *The Project of a Permanent Court of International Justice and Resolutions of the Advisory Committee of Jurists. Report and Commentary*. Washington, D.C.: Carnegie Endowment for International Peace, Division of International Law, 1920, https://ia800205.us.archive.org/12/items/cu31924016941142/cu31924016941142.pdf, accessed 24 September 2019.
Segal, A. "The Code Not Taken: China, the United States, and the Future of Cyber Espionage." *Bulletin of the Atomic Scientists* 69 (2013): 38–45.
South China Sea Arbitration. Award of 12 July 2016, https://pcacases.com/web/sendAttach/2086, accessed 27 August 2020.
———. Award on Jurisdiction and Admissibility (29 October 2015), https://pcacases.com/web/sendAttach/2579, accessed 10 March 2020.
———. Hearing on Jurisdiction and Admissibility. Transcript, Day 1 (7 July 2015), https://pcacases.com/web/sendAttach/1399, accessed 19 March 2020.
———. Transcript, Day 2 (8 July 2015), https://pcacases.com/web/sendAttach/1400, accessed 16 March 2020.
———. Hearing on the Merits and Remaining Issues of Admissibility. Transcript, Day 1 (24 November 2015), https://pcacases.com/web/sendAttach/1547, accessed 19 March 2020.
———. *Memorial of the Philippines*. Vol. I (30 March 2014), https://files.pca-cpa.org/pcadocs/Memorial%20of%20the%20Philippines%20Volume%20I.pdf, accessed 27 March 2019.
———. Vol. III (30 March 2014). Annexes, https://files.pca-cpa.org/pcadocs/Memorial%20of%20the%20Philippines%20Volume%20I.pdf, accessed 27 March 2019.
———. Annex 1. Notification and Statement of Claim of the Republic of the Philippines (22 January 2013), 11–32.

———. Annex 3. *Note Verbale* from the Embassy of the People's Republic of China in Manila to the Department of Foreign Affairs of the Republic of the Philippines, No. (13) PG-039 (19 February 2013), 37–42.
———. Vol. IV (30 March 2014). Annexes, http://www.pcacases.com/pcadocs/The%20Philippines%27%20Memorial%20-%20Volume%20IV%20%28Annexes%2061-102%29.pdf, accessed 13 March 2020.
———. Annex 84. Memorandum from the Embassy of the Republic of the Philippines in Beijing to the Secretary of Foreign Affairs of the Republic of the Philippines, No. ZPE-110-2012-S (26 July 2012), 217–28.
———. Vol. VI (30 March 2014). Annexes, https://files.pca-cpa.org/pcadocs/The%20Philippines%27%20Memorial%20-%20Volume%20VI%20%28Annexes%20158-221%29.pdf, accessed 10 March 2020.
———. Annex 184. Department of Foreign Affairs of the Republic of the Philippines. Record of Proceedings: 10th Philippines-China Foreign Ministry Consultations (30 July 1998), 248–49.
———. Annex 204. Record of Discussion: 17th Philippines-China Foreign Ministry Consultations (14 January 2012), 343–76.
———. Annex 207. *Note Verbale* from the Department of Foreign Affairs of the Philippines to the Embassy of the People's Republic of China in Manila, No. 12-1137 (26 April 2012), 385–88.
———. Annex 208. *Note Verbale* from the Embassy of the People's Republic of China in Manila to the Department of Foreign Affairs of the Philippines, No. (12) PG-206 (29 April 2012), 389–92.
——— *The Philippines' Annexes Cited During Merits Hearing* (30 November 2015), https://files.pca-cpa.org/pcadocs/The%20Philippines%27%20Annexes%20cited%20during%20Merits%20Hearing%20%28Annexes%20820-859%29.pdf, accessed 15 March 2020.
———. Annex 820. Embassy of the People's Republic of China in Canada. An Interview on China's Construction Activities on the Nansha Islands and Reefs (27 May 2015), 5–9.
———. Annex 821. China State Oceanic Administration, "Construction Work at Nansha Reefs Will Not Harm Oceanic Ecosystems" (18 June 2015), 11–16.
———. Procedural Order No. 2 (2 June 2014), https://pcacases.com/web/sendAttach/1805, accessed 15 March 2020.
———. Rules of Procedure (27 August 2013), https://pcacases.com/web/sendAttach/233, accessed 11 May 2020.
———. *Supplemental Documents of the Philippines*. Vol. I (19 November 2015), https://files.pca-cpa.org/pcadocs/The%20Philippines%27%20Supplemental%20Documents%20-%20Volume%20I%20%28Annexes%20607-667%29.pdf, accessed 15 March 2020.

———. Annex 624. Ministry of Foreign Affairs of the People's Republic of China. Foreign Ministry Spokesperson Hua Chunying's Regular Press Conference on April 9, 2015 (9 April 2015), 165–69.

———. *Supplemental Written Submission of the Philippines*. Vol. VIII (16 March 2015). Annexes, https://files.pca-cpa.org/pcadocs/The%20Philippines%27%20Supplemental%20Written%20Submission%20-%20Volume%20VIII%20%28Annexes%20466-499%29.pdf, accessed 10 March 2020.

———. Annex 467. People's Republic of China, Position Paper of the Government of the People's Republic of China on the Matter of Jurisdiction in the South China Sea Arbitration Initiated by the Republic of the Philippines (7 December 2014), 19–34.

———. Annex 472. *Letter* from H.E. Ambassador Chen Xu, Embassy of the People's Republic of China in The Hague, to H.E. Judge Thomas A. Mensah (6 February 2015), 73–80.

Spijkers, Otto. "Non-participation in Arbitral Proceedings Under Annex VII United Nations Convention on the Law of the Sea: *"Arctic Sunrise"* and *South China Sea* Compared." *Interpretations of the United Nations Convention on the Law of the Sea by International Courts and Tribunals*, 171–90. Eds. Angela Del Vecchio and Roberto Virzo. Cham, Switzerland: Springer International Publishing, 2019.

Talmon, Stefan. *The South China Sea Arbitration: Is There a Case to Answer?* Bonn: Universität Bonn, Institute for Public International Law, 2014, https://papers.ssrn.com/sol3/papers.cfm?abstract_id=2393025, accessed 13 March 2020.

———. "The South China Sea Arbitration: Is There a Case to Answer?" *The South China Sea Arbitration: A Chinese Perspective*, 15–79. Eds. Stefan Talmon and Bing Bing Jia. Oxford: Hart Publishing, 2014.

"Text of US Statement on Withdrawal from Case Before the World Court." *New York Times*, 19 January 1985, http://www.nytimes.com/1985/01/19/world/text-of-us-statement-on-withdrawal-from-case-before-the-world-court.html?pagewanted=all&pagewanted=print, accessed 13 March 2020.

Thirlway, Hugh. "The Law and Procedure of the International Court of Justice 1960–1989. Part Twelve." *British Yearbook of International Law* 71 (2000): 1–63.

Thirlway, H.W.A. *Non-appearance Before the International Court of Justice*. Cambridge: Cambridge University Press, 1985.

Thomas, Timothy. "China's Cyber Incursions: A Theoretical Look at What They See and Why They Do It Based on a Different Strategic Method of Thought." Foreign Military Studies Office (FMSO), United States Army Combined Arms Center, Fort Leavensworth, Kansas, 2013, http://indianstrategicknowledgeonline.com/web/Chinas-Cyber-Incursions.pdf, accessed 28 July 2019.

ThreatConnect Research Team "China Hacks the Peace Palace: All Your EEZ's Are Belong [sic] to Us." *ThreatConnect.com*, 20 July 2015, https://www.threatconnect.com/blog/china-hacks-the-peace-palace-all-your-eezs-are-belong-to-us/, accessed 23 March 2020.

United Nations Convention on the Law of the Sea. Concluded at Montego Bay on 10 December 1982. Entered into force on 16 November 1994, http://www.un.org/Depts/los/convention_agreements/texts/unclos/closindx.htm, accessed 21 March 2020.

United Nations. Division for Ocean Affairs and the Law of the Sea. *Annex VI. Statute of the International Tribunal for the Law of the Sea*, http://www.un.org/depts/los/convention_agreements/texts/unclos/annex6.htm, accessed 11 March 2020.

———. *Annex VII. Arbitration*, http://www.un.org/depts/los/convention_agreements/texts/unclos/annex7.htm, accessed 10 March 2020.

United States Diplomatic and Consular Staff in Tehran. United States. *Application Instituting Proceedings* (29 November 1979). *I.C.J. Pleadings, United States Diplomatic and Consular Staff in Tehran*, 3–8, https://www.icj-cij.org/files/case-related/64/9545.pdf, accessed 20 March 2020.

———. *Judgment. I. C. J. Reports 1980*, 3–48, https://www.icj-cij.org/files/case-related/64/064-19800524-JUD-01-00-BI.pdf, accessed 11 October 2019.

———. Oral Arguments. *I.C.J. Pleadings, United States Diplomatic and Consular Staff in Tehran*, 251–323, https://www.icj-cij.org/files/case-related/64/064-19800318-ORA-01-00-BI.pdf, accessed 11 October 2019.

Venturini, Giancarlo. "Il principio 'jura novit curia' e il processo internazionale [The Principle of "Jura Novit Curia" and International Judicial Proceedings]." *Comunicazioni e studi* [Communications and Studies] 14 (1975): 969–79.

Verhoeven, Joe. "Le droit, le juge et la violence (les arrêts *Nicaragua c. États-Unis)* [The Law, the Judge and Violence (The *Nicaragua v. United States* Judgments)]." *Revue générale de droit international public* [General Journal of Public International Law] 91 (19): 1159–1239.

Wang Tieya. "International Law in China: Historical and Contemporary Perspectives." *Recueil des cours de l'Académie de droit international de La Haye* [Collected Courses of the Hague Academy of International Law]. Vol. 221 (1990-II), 237–62.

Wang Wen, and Xiaochen Chen. "Who Supports China in the South China Sea and Why." *The Diplomat*, 27 July 2016, https://thediplomat.com/2016/07/who-supports-china-in-the-south-china-sea-and-why/, accessed 16 March 2020.

Wentker, Alexander. *Nichtteilnahme als Grenzphänomen zwischenstaatlicher Gerichts- und Schiedsverfahren—die Fälle South China Sea und "Arctic Sunrise"* [Non-participation in Inter-State Proceedings Before International

Tribunals—the South China Sea and "Arctic Sunrise" Cases]. Heidelberg: Max Planck Institute for Comparative Public Law and International Law, 2018, https://papers.ssrn.com/sol3/papers.cfm?abstract_id=3248261, accessed 17 March 2020.

Wolfrum, Rüdiger. "Taking and Assessing Evidence in International Adjudication." *Law of the Sea, Environmental Law and Settlement of Disputes. Liber Amicorum Judge Thomas A. Mensah*, 341–57. Eds. Tafsir Malick Ndiaye and Rüdiger Wolfrum. Leiden: Martinus Nijhoff Publishers, 2007.

Xue, Hanqin. "Chinese Contemporary Perspectives on International Law: History, Culture and International Law." *Recueil des cours de l'Académie de droit international de La Haye* [Collected Courses of the Hague Academy of International Law]. Vol. 355 (2011-III), 41–234.

Xinhua. "Arbitral Tribunal on South China Sea Illegal, Ridiculous." *Global Times*, 8 July 2016, http://www.globaltimes.cn/content/993110.shtml, accessed 16 March 2020.

Yee, Sienho. "The South China Sea Arbitration Decisions on Jurisdiction and Rule of Law Concerns." *Chinese Journal of International Law* 15 (2016): 219–37.

Yu Mincai. "China's Informal Participation in the Annex VII Philippines v. China Arbitral Tribunal's Proceedings." *International Journal of Marine and Coastal Law* 30 (2015): 54–92.

———. "China's Responses to the Compulsory Arbitration on the South China Sea Dispute: Legal Effects and Policy Options." *Ocean Development and International Law* 45 (2014): 1–16.

Zhang Xinjun. "Bifurcation in Inter-State Cases." *University of Pennsylvania Journal of International Law* 40 (2018–2019): 937–88, https://scholarship.law.upenn.edu/cgi/viewcontent.cgi?article=1991&context=jil, accessed 24 October 2019.

———. "Nonappearance and Procedural Delicacy: Some Observations on the Tribunal's Handling of Jurisdiction in the South China Sea Arbitration." Unpublished ms., Tsinghua University, September 2018, https://papers.ssrn.com/sol3/papers.cfm?abstract_id=3205321, accessed16 July 2020.

Zhao Jun, and Jiang Li. "The *"Arctic Sunrise"* Case and Its Implications for China." *Arbitration Concerning the South China Sea. Philippines Versus China*, 105–25. Eds. Shicun Wu and Keyuan Zou. London: Routledge, 2016.

CHAPTER 2

The Defaulting State and the Jurisdiction of Annex VII Arbitral Tribunals

Throughout the *South China Sea Arbitration*, China consistently declared as part of its litigation strategy that its rejection of and non-participation in the proceedings had a "solid basis" in international law, because the Tribunal lacked jurisdiction to hear the case.[1] The alleged reasons for the lack of jurisdiction were that the essence of the *Arbitration*'s subject matter was sovereignty; that China and the Philippines had agreed through bilateral and multilateral instruments to settle their disputes through negotiation; and that China had excluded maritime delimitation from the scope of the dispute settlement mechanisms of the United Nations Convention on the Law of the Sea ("the Convention").[2] China

[1] Ministry of Foreign Affairs of the People's Republic of China ("Foreign Ministry"), *Foreign Ministry Spokesperson Hua Chunying's Remarks on the Philippines' Efforts in Pushing for the Establishment of the Arbitral Tribunal in Relation to the Disputes Between China and the Philippines in the South China Sea* (26 April 2013), https://www.fmprc.gov.cn/mfa_eng/xwfw_665399/s2510_665401/2535_665405/t1035577.shtml, accessed 10 March 2020.

[2] *United Nations Convention on the Law of the Sea*, concluded at Montego Bay on 10 December 1982, entered into force on 16 November 1994, http://www.un.org/Depts/los/convention_agreements/texts/unclos/closindx.htm, accessed 21 March 2020; *South China Sea Arbitration, Supplemental Written Submission of the Philippines* (16 March 2015), Annex 467, People's Republic of China, Position Paper of the Government of the People's Republic of China on the Matter of Jurisdiction in the South China Sea Arbitration Initiated by the Republic of the Philippines (7 December 2014) ("Position

A. C. Robles Jr., *The Defaulting State and the South China Sea Arbitration*, https://doi.org/10.1007/978-981-19-6394-0_2

was in effect arguing that because in its view, the Arbitral Tribunal had no jurisdiction, China did not have any duty to appear before the Tribunal. Chinese scholars dutifully reaffirmed that "China's non-acceptance of and non-participation in the Arbitration and its non-recognition of any award made or to be made by the Tribunal have solid legal basis."[3]

But China went even further in defending its default. In May 2016, the Director-General of the Department of Treaty and Law of the Ministry of Foreign Affairs contended that

> not accepting or participating in arbitral proceedings is a right enjoyed by a sovereign State. That is fully in conformity with international law… by not accepting or participating in the arbitral proceedings, we aim to safeguard the solemnity [sic] and integrity of international law, including the UNCLOS, to oppose the abuse of the compulsory arbitration procedures.[4]

As was to be expected, Chinese scholars reiterated China's "legitimate right" under the Convention "not to accept any imposed solution or any unilateral resorting to a third- party settlement."[5] They have not hesitated to proclaim that "[n]on-appearance is an act within a State's sovereign competence and one of its legitimate rights."[6]

China's default has provided scholars the opportunity to revisit the debate on the existence of a duty to appear before an international court on the part of a State that has given its prior consent to that court's

Paper"), vol. VIII, 32, para. 86 ("*SWSP*"), https://files.pca-cpa.org/pcadocs/The%20Philippines%27%20Supplemental%20Written%20Submission%20-%20Volume%20VIII%20%28Annexes%20466-499%29.pdf, accessed 10 March 2020.

[3] Chinese Society of International Law ("CSIL"), "The Tribunal's Award in the 'South China Sea Arbitration' Initiated by the Philippines Is Null and Void," *Chinese Journal of International Law* 15 (2016): 487, para. 87 ("*CJIL*").

[4] Foreign Ministry, *Briefing by Xu Hong, Director-General of the Department of Treaty and Law on the South China Sea Arbitration Initiated by the Philippines 2016/05/12*, https://www.fmprc.gov.cn/nanhai/eng/wjbxw_1/t1364804.htm, accessed 16 January 2020.

[5] Chinese Ambassador's Second Letter, 1 July 2015, quoted in *South China Sea Arbitration,* Award on Jurisdiction and Admissibility (29 October 2015), 27, para. 83 ("Award on Jurisdiction"), https://pcacases.com/web/sendAttach/2579, accessed 10 March 2020.

[6] CSIL, "The South China Sea Arbitration Awards: A Critical Study," *CJIL* 17 (2018): 414, para. 888.

compulsory jurisdiction.[7] The International Court of Justice ("ICJ") has never made any pronouncement on the existence of a duty to appear or the existence of a right not to appear. A scholarly consensus, notably within the *Institut de droit international* (Institute of International Law, "IDI") exists as to the absence of a duty to appear before an international court on the part of a State that has given its prior consent to that court's jurisdiction, but the consensus does not extend to the affirmation of a "right" not to appear.

Whether a defaulting State merely denies the existence of a duty to appear or goes further by affirming the exercise of a "right" not to appear, it is clear that it is arrogating to itself the right to decide the issue of jurisdiction, with the aim of preventing proceedings from continuing. The defaulting State is in effect denying the jurisdiction of the international court to determine its own jurisdiction (*compétence de la compétence*), which is an inherent power of any international court. It is this inherent power that was challenged in the *South China Sea Arbitration* by a State that had no compunction about declaring that its position had a "solid basis" in international law.

The Arbitral Tribunal, like other international courts and tribunals, had no procedural powers that would have enabled it to compel a State that refused to recognize its jurisdiction to appear before it. Since default does not deprive an international tribunal of the *compétence de la compétence*, the Arbitral Tribunal had the power to organize a procedure to determine whether it had jurisdiction. In the exercise of this power, the Arbitral Tribunal, following the precedent set by the ICJ in default cases, decided to bifurcate the proceedings and to hold a separate hearing on jurisdiction and admissibility.

In anticipation of decisions rejecting its theses and presumably in order to free itself from the jurisdiction of any arbitral tribunals that might be established upon request of another party to the Convention, China was reported to have considered withdrawing from the Convention. In the end, despite its critique of the two Awards and the campaign of

[7] Alexander Wentker, *Nichtteilnahme als Grenzphänomen zwischenstaatlicher Gerichts- und Schiedsverfahren – die Fälle South China Sea und "Arctic Sunrise"* [Non-Participation in Inter-State Proceedings Before International Tribunals – the South China Sea and "Arctic Sunrise" Cases] (Heidelberg: Max Planck Institute for Comparative Public Law and International Law, 2018), 19–22, https://papers.ssrn.com/sol3/papers.cfm?abstract_id=3248261, accessed 17 March 2020.

defamation against the Arbitral Tribunal, China remained a party to the Convention. The reasons for remaining a party may lie in the symbolic and material value of the Convention for China.

I. Absence of a Duty to Appear, Absence of a Right Not to Appear

The existence or absence of a duty to appear before an international court on the part of a State that has given its prior consent to that court's jurisdiction was discussed by the drafters of the Statute of the Permanent Court of International Justice ("PCIJ"). As Article 53 of the PCIJ Statute has been reproduced in Article 53 of the ICJ Statute and has influenced the formulation of Article 9 of Annex VII of the Convention,[8] it is essential to reexamine the debates within the Advisory Committee of Jurists that drafted the PCIJ Statute from 16 June to 24 July 1920.

The absence of a duty to appear seems to be confirmed in subsequent State practice and in the practice of international courts and tribunals. States that have defaulted in cases before the ICJ have for the most part refrained from claiming that they are exercising a "right" not to appear. It was left to the IDI to take up the issue. For conceptual and practical reasons, the IDI declined to proclaim the existence of a "right" not to appear before an international court on the part of a State that has given its prior consent to that court's jurisdiction.

A. The Absence of a Duty to Appear

The regime of default has been an integral part of the structure of permanent international courts with general jurisdiction since their creation. The absence of a duty to appear seems to be confirmed in subsequent State practice and in the practice of international courts and tribunals.

[8] United Nations Division for Ocean Affairs and the Law of the Sea, *Annex VII. Arbitration* ("*Annex VII*"), http://www.un.org/depts/los/convention_agreements/texts/unclos/annex7.htm, accessed 10 March 2020 United Nations Division for Ocean Affairs and the Law of the Sea, *Annex VI. Statute of the International Tribunal for the Law of the Sea*, http://www.un.org/depts/los/convention_agreements/texts/unclos/annex6.htm, accessed 11 March 2020; *Statute of the International Court of Justice*, http://www.icj-cij.org/en/statute, accessed 10 March 2020; *Statute of the PCIJ*, https://www.icj-cij.org/files/permanent-court-of-international-justice/serie_D/D_01_1e_edition.pdf, accessed 25 March 2020.

1. The Origins of the Regime of Default

Within the Advisory Committee of Jurists, a regime for default was thought necessary in order to ensure that the appearing State could have its claim adjudicated, that the dignity of the defaulting State would be respected and that compliance with the court's decision would be promoted. The absence of a duty to appear may also be explained as a consequence of the progress embodied in the establishment of a permanent international court.

It seems that within the Advisory Committee of Jurists only one member indirectly argued for a duty to appear, by emphasizing that the League Covenant intended to limit the PCIJ's jurisdiction to cases submitted to it by both parties to the dispute.[9] This being the case, the PCIJ could only exercise its jurisdiction if both parties were present. The other Committee members did not wish to hinder the administration of international justice by making it dependent on the decision of a State unwilling to have its claims "tested by the rules of law."[10] The subsequent discussion on the future Article 53 centered not on the existence of a duty to appear but on the approach of the Court to a case of non-appearance. Mr. Hagerup pointed out the difference between the continental and the English approaches to non-appearance in a scenario in which a plaintiff claims to have delivered goods to a non-appearing defendant. In the continental legal system, a court would not be obliged to demand proof of the fact that the goods had been delivered; it would only have to consider whether in law and justice the fact was a sufficient basis for the plaintiff's conclusion. In the English legal system, the plaintiff would be called upon to prove that the goods had been delivered, obliging the plaintiff to prove even undisputed or well-known facts.[11]

[9] Mr. Adatoi (Japan), in PCIJ, Advisory Committee of Jurists, *Procès-verbaux of the Proceedings of the Committee, June 16th-July 24th, 1920, with Annexes* (The Hague: Van Langenhuysen Frères, 1920), 541 ("*Procès-verbaux*"), https://ia600900.us.archive.org/6/items/procsverbauxof00leaguoft/procsverbauxof00leaguoft.pdf, accessed 26 March 2020.

[10] James Brown Scott, *The Project of a Permanent Court of International Justice and Resolutions of the Advisory Committee of Jurists. Report and Commentary* (Washington, D.C.: Carnegie Endowment for International Peace, Division of International Law, 1920), 124, https://ia800205.us.archive.org/12/items/cu31924016941142/cu31924016941142.pdf, accessed 26 March 2020.

[11] 28th Meeting (20 July 1920), Annex No. 2, in Advisory Committee of Jurists, *Procès-verbaux*, 331.

Other Committee members reminded him that the parties to disputes to be heard by the PCIJ would be sovereign States, and that it would be a particularly serious matter to pronounce a judgment against them when they denied the Court's jurisdiction.[12] Hagerup himself admitted that it would not be in conformity with the dignity of sovereign States that an applicant State could be in a position to demand that the PCIJ, as in the continental system, admit its claims without proof.[13] It was recalled that in the US a case could be brought against a federal State without its consent before the Supreme Court but that the plaintiff was under a duty to show that its demands were well founded in fact and in law, "with the same care as if his opponent were in Court." Uppermost in the Committee members' minds was the need to make a judgment rendered in a situation of non-appearance acceptable to States, making compliance with the PCIJ's judgments more likely:

> To make the Court's judgment, even in the event of a refusal to appear, acceptable to the sensitiveness of sovereign States, the sentence pronounced on the State at fault must rest upon all desirable guarantees to give it moral force, and consequently to ensure that it is respected and more easily put into execution.[14]

The final text adopted by the Committee stipulated that before deciding in favor of the claim of the applicant State, the Court had to satisfy itself that it had jurisdiction and that the claim was well founded in fact and in law.[15]

In the regime of default, no sanctions are imposed on a State for failure to appear. The absence of sanctions for default underlines the absence of a duty to appear.[16] There do exist consequences of default, as already noted

[12] 34th Meeting (24 July 1920), Annex No. 1, in Advisory Committee of Jurists, *Procès-verbaux*, 740.

[13] 28th Meeting (20 July 1920), Annex No. 2, in Advisory Committee of Jurists, *Procès-verbaux*, 331.

[14] 34th Meeting (24 July 1920), Annex No. 1, in Advisory Committee of Jurists, *Procès-verbaux*, 740.

[15] 28th Meeting (20 July 1920), Annex No. 2, in Advisory Committee of Jurists, *Procès-verbaux*, 569, 590–91.

[16] Wentker, *Nichtteilnahme*, 20, 25. On this point see also Gaetano Arangio-Ruiz, "Notes on Non-Appearance Before the International Court of Justice," in *Le droit international à l'heure de sa codification. Études en l'honneur de Roberto Ago* [International

in the previous Chapter: the proceedings will continue without the participation of the defaulting State, which remains a party to the case and is bound by any decisions of the international court in question. There may be negative political consequences resulting from default, such as the loss of reputation, but the defaulting State is legally protected against unjustified claims through the obligation imposed on the ICJ and an Annex VII arbitral tribunal to satisfy themselves that they have jurisdiction and that the submissions of the appearing State are well founded in fact and in law.[17] As Thirlway put it succinctly, if non-appearance produces no distinct legal consequences, it is meaningless to talk of a duty to appear.[18]

Elkind challenges the above interpretation of the drafting history of Article 53. He points out that Article 53 was part of an original scheme that made compulsory the PCIJ's jurisdiction in disputes between League members. If indeed States were under a duty to submit their disputes to the PCIJ, then they would not have the opportunity to challenge the PCIJ's jurisdiction nor would they have a reason to default. Given this original scheme, it did not seem credible to him that the Committee intended to confer on the parties a right or privilege not to appear. He asserts that some Committee members wanted to punish a State for failure to appear, although this intention was abandoned because the Committee members felt that sanctions would not be feasible in international relations.[19] Unfortunately, Elkind does not explain how a duty to appear could have survived the elimination of the idea of the PCIJ's compulsory jurisdiction in disputes between League members. Moreover, if sanctions did not appear practical in the context of a draft that provided for the

Law at the Time of Its Codification. Studies in Honour of Roberto Ago], vol. II, *Les différends entre États et la responsabilité* [Inter-State Disputes and Responsibility] (Milano: Dott. A. Giuffrè Editore, 1987), 11–12; D.W. Bowett, "Contemporary Developments in Legal Techniques in the Settlement of Disputes," *Recueil des cours de l'Académie de droit international de La Haye* [Collected Courses of the Hague Academy of International Law], vol. 180 (1983-II), 205 ("*RCADI*"); and Hugh Thirlway, "The Law and Procedure of the International Court of Justice 1960–1989. Part Twelve," *British Yearbook of International Law* 71 (2000): 157 ("*BYIL*").

[17] H.W.A. Thirlway, *Non-Appearance Before the International Court of Justice* (Cambridge: Cambridge University Press, 1985), 67, 72 ("*Non-Appearance*").

[18] Thirlway, "The Law and Procedure," 916.

[19] Jerome B. Elkind, "Normative Surrender," *Michigan Journal of International Law* 9 (1988): 285–86, https://repository.law.umich.edu/cgi/viewcontent.cgi?article=1758&context=mjil, accessed 26 March 2020.

PCIJ's compulsory jurisdiction, it is difficult to see how they would have been any more feasible in a draft that excluded any idea of the PCIJ's compulsory jurisdiction. As Scott pointed out, it would not have been possible to compel the presence of a State that refused to appear—and one might add, that it would still not be possible at present.[20]

The IDI's Rapporteur on the question of non-appearance before the ICJ, the Italian scholar Gaetano Arangio-Ruiz, explains that the absence of a duty to appear was a concomitant of the progress embodied in the establishment of a permanent international jurisdiction. At first glance, this argument might seem paradoxical. After all, as C. Amerasinghe, a member of the IDI Commission on Non-appearance before the ICJ, observed in a communication to the Rapporteur, a party to proceedings would in any legal system have an obligation to appear. He described this obligation as the normal consequence of being a party to proceedings where the subject is part of the legal system.[21] Two other Commission members shared the view that appearance is the normal conduct expected under the ICJ Statute.[22]

To understand Arangio-Ruiz's argument, it is necessary to explain the difference between adjudication by a permanent international court, on the one hand, and arbitration, on the other. In the nineteenth century, the latter was based on the consent of both parties, as expressed in a

[20] Scott, *The Project*, 125.

[21] Observations of Mr. C. Amerasinghe (19 October 1990), in Gaetano Arangio-Ruiz, "Non-Appearance Before the International Court of Justice. Final Report," *Annuaire de l'Institut de droit international*, [Yearbook of the Institute of International Law], Session de Bâle [Basel Session], 64-I (1991), 345, ("Non-Appearance Final Report"), http://www.gaetanoarangioruiz.it/publications/non-appearance-before-the-international-court-of-justice/, accessed 13 October 2019.

[22] Santiago Torres Bernárdez, "Non-Appearance Before the International Court of Justice," *Annuaire de l'Institut de droit international* [Yearbook of the Institute of International Law], Session de Bâle [Basel Session], 64-I (1991), 352, http://www.gaetanoarangioruiz.it/publications/non-appearance-before-the-international-court-of-justice/, accessed 13 October 2019; Observations of Mr. W. Briggs (3 December 1985), in Gaetano Arangio-Ruiz, "Non-Appearance Before the International Court of Justice. Preliminary Report," Annuaire de l'Institut de droit international, [Yearbook of the Institute of International Law], Session de Bâle [Basel Session], 64-I (1991), 277 ("Non-Appearance Preliminary Report"), http://www.gaetanoarangioruiz.it/publications/non-appearance-before-the-international-court-of-justice/, accessed 13 October 2019.

special agreement (*compromis*). Since this agreement was a prerequisite to the establishment of an arbitral tribunal, it was in practice impossible for default to occur. If there was no agreement, the risk was not default, but the failure to establish an arbitral tribunal in the first place. A handful of agreements empowered the arbitrator to render a judgment if either of the parties failed to submit its reply to the submission of the other party.[23] They assumed that the agreement manifested in the *compromis* also entailed an agreement to achieve the aim of the arbitration—a judgment—so that if one party failed to appear or to defend its case, the arbitrator had the power to decide the case.[24] Notwithstanding such provisions, the compilations of international arbitrations published in the early twentieth century do not record any instances of default.[25] The only instance of default in arbitral proceedings occurred in the first half of the twentieth century and involved the USSR and a foreign company, rather than another State.[26]

[23] See, for example, "Memorandum para ser transmitido au Senado da Cidade Libre de Hamburgo, para se encarregar da arbitragem relativamente à reclamação dos Sres Yuille, Shortridge e Cia [Memorandum to Be Transmitted to the Senate of the Free City of Hamburg, to Take Charge of the Arbitration Relating to the Claim of Messrs. Yuille, Shortridge and Co.] [8 March 1861]," in Henri La Fontaine (ed.). *Pasicrisie internationale 1794–1900. Histoire documentaire des arbitrages internationaux* [Compendium of International Caselaw 1794–1900. A Documentary History of International Arbitrations] (Berne: Imprimerie Stampfli & Cie, 1902), 378, https://ia600205.us.archive.org/9/items/pasicrisieinter00fontgoog/pasicrisieinter00fontgoog.pdf, accessed 11 March 2020.

[24] Albert Geouffre de Lapradelle and Nicolas Politis (eds.). *Recueil des arbitrages internationaux* [Collection of International Arbitrations], vol. II, *1856–1872* (Paris: A. Pedone Éditeur, 1923), xxiii, https://ia802607.us.archive.org/3/items/recueildesarbitr02lapruoft/recueildesarbitr02lapruoft.pdf, accessed 26 March 2020.

[25] La Fontaine, *Pasicrisie internationale 1794–1900*; Albert Geouffre de Lapradelle and Nicolas Politis (eds.). *Recueil des arbitrages internationaux* [Collection of International Arbitrations], vol. I, *1798–1855* (Paris: A. Pedone Éditeur, 1905), https://ia600309.us.archive.org/19/items/recueildesarbit01lapr/recueildesarbit01lapr.pdf, accessed 26 March 2020; Lapradelle and Politis (eds.). *Recueil*, vol. II.

[26] This was the *Lena Goldfields Ltd v. USSR Arbitration* in the 1930s. The company, which had received an exploration, mining, and transportation concession in Siberia in 1925, sought damages from the USSR for the "total impossibility of either performing its obligations under the Concession Agreement, or enjoying its benefits." The USSR had agreed to set a date for the arbitral tribunal's first meeting, but it failed to put in a defense. The company ceased to finance the undertaking and the arbitration was cancelled. United Nations, *Commentary on the Draft Convention on Arbitral Procedure Adopted by the International Law Commission at its Fifth Session, prepared by the Secretariat* (New York: United

The possibility that a respondent State would fail to appear was anticipated in the Convention that established the first permanent international court, the Central American Court of Justice, in 1907.[27] Article XV of that Convention provided that if the defendant State failed to respond to a complaint within 60 days, the Central American Court could require the defendant to do so within a further 20 days. After 80 days, and in the absence of a reply from the defendant, the Central American Court, "in view of the evidence presented and of such evidence as it may ex officio have seen fit to obtain," would render a decision. No provision for enforcement of this provision was made. During the Central American Court's brief life, this provision was tested once.[28] In March 1916 Costa Rica filed a case alleging that Nicaragua's conclusion of a treaty with the US for the construction of an interoceanic canal violated Costa Rica's rights under several international instruments. Nicaragua requested that the Central American Court refuse to consider the complaint, but the latter declared that it had jurisdiction over the case. In May 1916, the Central American Court called upon Nicaragua to answer the case within 60 days, as required by the Convention of 1908. In August 1916, Nicaragua again denied the Central American Court's jurisdiction and declared that it would not abide by any adverse decision. The Central American Court, as required by the Convention of 1908, gave Nicaragua another 20 days within which to respond. When Nicaragua failed to do so, the Central American Court proceeded to hear the case and issued

Nations, 1955), 79, https://legal.un.org/ilc/documentation/english/a_cn4_92.pdf, accessed 26 March 2020. On the *Arbitration*, see Arthur Nussbaum, "The Arbitration Between the Lena Goldfields, Ltd. and the Soviet Government," *Cornell Law Quarterly* 36 (1950/1951): 31–53, https://scholarship.law.cornell.edu/cgi/viewcontent.cgi?article=1582&context=clr accessed 2 January 2020.

[27] *Convention for the Establishment of a Central American Court of Justice*, *American Journal of International Law*, 2, No. 1/2, *Supplement: Official Documents* (1908): 237, Article XVI ("*AJIL*"); Hans von Mangoldt, "Versäumnisverfahren in der internationalen (Schieds)Gerichtsbarkeit und souveräne Gleichheit [Default Procedures in International Arbitration and Adjudication and Sovereign Equality]," in Rudolf Bernhardt (ed.), *Völkerrecht als Rechtsordnung, internationale Gerichtsbarkeit, Menschenrechte. Festschrift für Hermann Mosler* [International Law as a Legal Order, International Adjudication, Human Rights. Festschrift for Hermann Mosler] (Berlin: Springer Verlag, 1983), 506–07.

[28] The Court ceased to exist in 1918, following Nicaragua's failure to renew the Convention in response to the Court's adverse judgment in the case filed against it by Costa Rica. James Brown Scott, "The Closing of the Central American Court of Justice," *AJIL* 12 (1918): 380–82.

a judgment in September 1916, declaring that Nicaragua had violated Costa Rica's rights under several international instruments.[29] Although the Convention of 1908 did not compel the Central American Court to consider Nicaragua's arguments, it did in practice take them into account and respond to them in the judgment.[30]

The Central American Court's experience, which does not seem to have had any influence on the work of the Advisory Committee of Jurists, suggests that even the threat of a decision based solely on submissions made by one party will not necessarily discourage default. More importantly, it illustrates *avant la lettre* the point made by Arangio-Ruiz that the permanent character of the PCIJ (and by extension, its successor, the ICJ) and the possibility that a State may unilaterally initiate proceedings against another State before the PCIJ excluded the need for the appearance of both parties.[31] The key consideration that unlocks the apparent paradox is that the right of unilateral initiative would already have been recognized by both parties when they agreed to accept the permanent international court's compulsory jurisdiction before any concrete dispute had emerged between them. Consequently, the appearance of the State against which a case is filed and which fails to appear is not required, as that State is already deemed to have given its consent to have proceedings instituted against it and to have the court hear the case. The proceedings will continue, both States—the appearing and the defaulting—will remain parties to the case, and the judgment will be binding on both. As Thirlway puts it, the appearance of both parties would be indispensable only if it were required for a court to make a decision. Since default neither prevents the court from taking a decision nor affects the decision's binding character for the defaulting State, the duty to appear is in no way necessary.[32] To make the appearance of both parties a requirement for the case to be heard would mean that the proceedings could not continue if

[29] Manley O. Hudson, "The Central American Court of Justice," *AJIL* 26 (1932): 774–76.

[30] von Mangoldt, "Versäumnisverfahren," 507–08.

[31] Arangio-Ruiz, "Notes," 11–12; Arangio-Ruiz, "Non-Appearance Preliminary Report," 290–91.

[32] Hugh Thirlway, "Normative Surrender' and the 'Duty' to Appear Before the International Court of Justice: A Reply," *Michigan Journal of International Law* 11 (1990): 913, 921, https://repository.law.umich.edu/cgi/viewcontent.cgi?article=1670&context=mjil, accessed 27 March 2020.

one party failed to appear and would deprive the appearing party, which had after all also given its consent in advance to the jurisdiction of the court concerned, of the right to have its claims adjudicated.

State practice and the practice of international courts and tribunals confirm the absence of a duty to appear.

2. State Practice and the Practice of International Courts and Tribunals

It may be assumed that a defaulting State, through its conduct, denies that it has a duty to appear before the international court concerned. More interesting is the attitude of the appearing States. They have generally refrained from asserting the existence of a duty to appear, as have international courts and tribunals.

With two exceptions, applicant States have refrained from making any pronouncements on the existence of a duty to appear or the violation of such a duty. At times, they have refrained from making any pronouncement at all on the respondent State's default. In the *Corfu Channel Case*, which had been initiated by the UK against Albania in 1947 for allegedly laying or causing to be laid mines in Albanian territorial waters in the Corfu Channel, Albania had appeared before the ICJ in the jurisdictional and merits phases of the proceedings.[33] When the Court then proceeded to evaluate the compensation due to the UK for the damage to British destroyers, Albania ceased its participation. During the oral hearings, the UK simply invoked Article 53 of the Statute, without any commentary on Albania's default.[34]

In other cases, the applicant States' responses suggest, as Arangio-Ruiz put it, that they were aware of the possibility of default when they became parties to the ICJ Statute and that default was a "*risqué du métier* [risk of the trade]."[35] Disappointment is one common response. In the *Nottebohm Case*, the applicant State, Liechtenstein, described the default of

[33] United Kingdom, *Application Instituting Proceedings* (13 May 1947), *I.C.J. Pleadings, Corfu Channel Case*, vol. I, 9, https://www.icj-cij.org/files/case-related/1/1499.pdf, accessed 27 March 2020.

[34] Sir Frank Soskice, Twelfth Public Sitting, 17 November 1949, Oral Proceedings (Second Part), *I.C.J. Pleadings, Corfu Channel Case*, vol. IV, 707, https://www.icj-cij.org/files/case-related/1/001-19491117-ORA-01-00-BI.pdf, accessed 8 January 2020.

[35] Arangio-Ruiz, "Non-Appearance Final Report," 318.

Guatemala as "much regretted" but did not go on at length about it.[36] On a number of occasions, the appearing State remained hopeful that the defaulting State could still be persuaded to change its mind. In the *Fisheries Jurisdiction Case*, the Federal Republic of Germany expressed the hope at the provisional measures stage that Iceland would appear at a later stage.[37] Similarly, in the hearing on its request for provisional measures in the *Nuclear Tests Case*, New Zealand expressed the "hope, expectation and belief that France will attend and participate in the later phases of the proceedings."[38] At the next stage, despite France's firmly declared intention not to participate in the proceedings, it was New Zealand's belief that the French decision remained and would continue to remain revocable "at the French Government's will."[39] On other occasions, the applicant State declared its readiness to provide assistance to the Court in reaching its judgment. In the *Fisheries Jurisdiction Case* between the UK and Iceland, the UK felt that it was its duty, in the light of Article 53 of the ICJ Statute, "to see that all necessary materials, whether they tell for or against the United Kingdom case, are put before the Court."[40] In the *Nuclear Tests Case*, New Zealand undertook "to present facts and

[36] Statement by E.H. Loewenfeld, Public Sitting of 10 November 1953, Oral Arguments concerning the Preliminary Objection, *I.C.J. Pleadings, Nottebohm Case (Liechtenstein v. Guatemala)*, 13, https://www.icj-cij.org/files/case-related/18/018-19531110-ORA-01-00-BI.pdf, accessed 8 January 2020.

[37] Argument of Mr Jaenicke, First Public Sitting (8 August 1972), Oral Proceedings on the Request for the Indication of Interim Measures of Protection, *I.C.J. Pleadings, Fisheries Jurisdiction (Federal Republic of Germany v. Iceland)*, vol. II, 42, https://www.icj-cij.org/files/case-related/56/056-19720802-ORA-01-00-BI.pdf, accessed 29 March 2020; Argument of Mr. Jaenicke, Third Public Sitting (8 January 1973), Oral Proceedings on the Jurisdiction of the Court, *I.C.J. Pleadings, Fisheries Jurisdiction*, vol. II, 120.

[38] Dr. Finlay, First Public Sitting (24 May 1973), Oral Proceedings on the Request for the Indication of Interim Measures of Protection, *I.C.J. Pleadings, Nuclear Tests (New Zealand v. France)*, vol. II, 100, https://www.icj-cij.org/files/case-related/59/059-19730524-ORA-01-00-BI.pdf, accessed 30 March 2020.

[39] Dr. Finlay, Fourth Public Sitting, 10 July 1974, Oral Proceedings on Jurisdiction and Admissibility, *I.C.J. Pleadings, Nuclear Tests*, vol. II, 252.

[40] Right Hon. Samuel Silkin, Fifth Public Sitting (25 March 1974), Oral Proceedings on the Merits, *I.C.J. Pleadings, Fisheries Jurisdiction (United Kingdom v. Iceland)*, vol. I, 440–41, http://www.icj-cij.org/files/case-related/55/055-19740325-ORA-01-00-BI.pdf, accessed 22 April 2020; see also Argument of Sir Peter Rawlinson, First Public Sitting (1 August 1972), Oral Proceedings on Interim Measures of Protection, *I.C.J. Pleadings, Fisheries Jurisdiction*, vol. I, 92, https://www.icj-cij.org/files/case-related/55/055-19720801-ORA-01-00-BI.pdf, accessed 29 March 2020; Argument of Sir Peter Rawlinson,

arguments fairly and to conceal nothing which may help the Court to arrive at an accurate assessment of the matters in issue."[41] On occasion, the applicant State explicitly mentioned the difficulties that default had caused for it. In the *Anglo-Iranian Oil Co. Case*, the UK admitted during the oral hearings on its request for provisional measures that it had not had the time to prepare a reply to a telegram sent by Iran to the Court the previous evening and begged leave from the Court "to say no more about this telegram at this stage."[42]

It seems that the duty of a respondent State to appear before the ICJ was first explicitly asserted by an applicant State in May 1973. Pakistan had instituted proceedings against India for proposing to hand over to Bangladesh 195 Pakistani Prisoners of War, who had been captured by India during the Bangladeshi war of independence against Pakistan (formerly West Pakistan), to be tried in Bangladesh for alleged acts of genocide.[43] India denied that there was any basis for the ICJ's jurisdiction and refused to attend the hearings on the provisional measures that Pakistan had requested. During the hearings, Pakistan expressed its astonishment that India had challenged the Court's jurisdiction by not appearing. Pakistan stressed that India, as a party to the ICJ Statute, was obliged to follow the procedure laid down by the ICJ Statute and Rules of Court for challenging the Court's jurisdiction. For Pakistan, it was not merely a matter of courtesy to the Court, but an "inescapable duty" imposed by law upon the parties to the State.[44] The proceedings were discontinued in December 1973 following negotiations between the two States, obviating the need for the Court to make a pronouncement

Third Public Sitting (5 August 1973), Oral Proceedings on the Jurisdiction of the Court, *I.C.J. Pleadings, Fisheries Jurisdiction*, vol. I, 242.

[41] Dr. Finlay, Fourth Public Sitting (10 July 1974), Oral Hearings on Jurisdiction and Admissibility, *I.C.J. Pleadings*, *Nuclear Tests*, vol. II, 252.

[42] *Anglo-Iranian Oil Co. (United Kingdom v. Iran)*, Oral Proceedings, Verbatim record (30 June 1951), *I.C.J. Pleadings*, *Anglo-Iranian Oil Co. Case (United Kingdom v. Iran)*, 424, https://www.icj-cij.org/files/case-related/16/016-19510630-ORA-01-00-BI.pdf, accessed 8 January 2020.

[43] Pakistan, *Application Instituting Proceedings* (1 May 1973), *I.C.J. Pleadings*, *Trial of Pakistani Prisoners of War*, 4–6, https://www.icj-cij.org/files/case-related/60/9461.pdf, accessed 27 March 2020.

[44] First Public Sitting (4 June 1973), *I.C.J. Pleadings*, *Trial of Pakistani Prisoners of War*, 26, http://www.icj-cij.org/files/case-related/60/060-19730504-ORA-01-00-BI.pdf, accessed 4 March 2018.

on Pakistan's assertions. A dozen years later, when the US withdrew from the proceedings in the *Nicaragua Case* after the Court's judgment on jurisdiction, Nicaragua asserted that "[o]nce jurisdiction has been found, there is no shadow of a doubt as to the obligatory nature of a country's appearance."[45] It is suggested here that following the reasoning of Arangio-Ruiz, the respondent State still had no duty to appear even after jurisdiction had been affirmed; its ultimate duty was to comply with the Court's judgment, whether or not it appeared before the Court.

As for the ICJ, the Court merely took note of the default of the respondent State in the first three cases, without further comment. In its judgment on compensation in the *Corfu Channel Case*, the Court observed that "the Albanian Government was absent and made no submissions."[46] In the *Nottebohm* judgment, the reference was even briefer: "The Government of Guatemala was not represented."[47] Beginning in the 1970s, in all cases of default, the Court expressed its regret, in practically identical terms:

> It is to be regretted that the Iranian Government has not appeared before the Court in order to put forward its arguments on the questions of law and of fact which arise in the present case; and that, in consequence, the Court has not had the assistance it might have derived from such arguments or from any evidence adduced in support of them.[48]

These formulations are the basis for divergent assessments of the Court's position on the (non) existence of a duty to appear. In the first view, the Court has never decided the theoretical question of whether

[45] Statement by Mr. Arguëllo Gómez, Seventeenth Public Sitting (7 September 1985), Oral Hearings on the Merits, *I.C.J. Pleadings, Military and Paramilitary Activities in and Against Nicaragua (Nicaragua v. United States of America)*, vol. V, 7, https://www.icj-cij.org/files/case-related/70/070-19850912-ORA-01-00-BI.pdf, accessed 17 March 2020.

[46] *Corfu Channel Case, Judgment of December 15th 1949: I.C.J. Reports 1949*, 247, http://www.icj-cij.org/files/case-related/1/001-19491215-JUD-01-00-BI.pdf, accessed 30 March 2020.

[47] *Nottebohm Case (Preliminary Objection), Judgment of November 18th, 1953: I.C.J. Reports 1953*, 117, https://www.icj-cij.org/files/case-related/18/018-19531118-JUD-01-00-BI.pdf, accessed 30 March 2020.

[48] *United States Diplomatic and Consular Staff in Tehran, Judgment, I. C. J. Reports 1980*, 48, para. 33, https://www.icj-cij.org/files/case-related/64/064-19800524-JUD-01-00-BI.pdf, accessed 30 March 2020.

there exists a duty to appear.[49] In the second view, the Court has not condemned non-appearance.[50] In the third view, it is an implicit negative judgment on non-appearance and is misplaced, given the existence of a right not to appear.[51] The most appropriate interpretation takes as its starting point the text itself: the Court regrets default because it deprives it of the assistance that the parties provide to the judge. In other words, the Court does not regret non-appearance because it is deplorable.[52]

The Tribunal in the *"Arctic Sunrise" Arbitration*, when explaining its decision regarding the duty of the defaulting party to contribute to the expenses of the *Arbitration*, affirmed that "the Convention may not oblige a party to appear before a Tribunal having jurisdiction under the Convention." Nevertheless, default did not mean that the defaulting State had no duty under the Convention's dispute settlement regime; in particular, it was bound by the Tribunal's Award and was under a duty to comply with it.[53] Prior to the constitution of this Tribunal, the International Tribunal for the Law of the Sea ("ITLOS"), upon the request of the Netherlands, had issued an order for provisional measures. Two judges appended a separate opinion to the order that diverges sharply from the positions adopted by the ICJ and the ITLOS. In the view of Judges Wolfrum and Kelly, where a State has given its consent to a dispute settlement system in general, such as that embodied in Part XV of the Convention, non-appearance is contrary to the object and purpose of

[49] Matthias Goldmann, "International Courts and Tribunals, Non-Appearance," *Max Planck Encyclopedia of Public International Law* (2006), 6.

[50] Gerald Fitzmaurice, "The Problem of the 'Non-Appearing' Defendant Government," *BYIL* 51 (1980): 106.

[51] Observations of Mr. S. Rosenne (25 November 1985), in Arangio-Ruiz, "Non-Appearance Preliminary Report," 267.

[52] Claude-Albert Colliard, "La non-comparution, [Non-appearance]" in Société française pour le droit international [French Society for International Law] ("SFDI"), Colloque de Lyon [Lyons Colloquium], *La juridiction internationale permanente* [Permanent International Jurisdiction] (Paris: Éditions A. Pedone, 1987), 189.

[53] *The "Arctic Sunrise" Arbitration (Netherlands v. Russia)*, Award on the Merits (14 August 2015), 91, para. 367, https://pcacases.com/web/sendAttach/1438, accessed 17 March 2020.

that dispute settlement system.[54] This view is reminiscent of the opinion expressed in the 1980s by German scholar Hermann Mosler, for whom non-appearance before the ICJ was contrary to the spirit of the UN Charter and the ICJ Statute, but was not a breach of the latter.[55] Mosler did not derive any practical consequences from his assessment of non-appearance.[56] It seems that the main consequences for Judges Wolfrum and Kelly of their position are twofold. First, the non-appearing State remains a party to the case; second, Article 28 of the ITLOS Statute on default should not be understood to confer a right not to appear. The first conclusion is entirely compatible with the view that there exists no duty to appear. The second conclusion is of fundamental importance, in view of China's declaration that it was exercising a "right" not to appear.

B. The Non-existence of a Right Not to Appear

It seems that prior to the *South China Sea Arbitration*, there was only one instance of a defaulting State explicitly asserting that it possessed a right not to appear. Bahrain invoked this "right" in 1995 to justify its decision not to participate in the second phase of the proceedings on the jurisdiction in the case concerning its dispute with Qatar over maritime delimitation and territorial questions.[57]

[54] *"Arctic Sunrise" (Kingdom of the Netherlands v. Russian Federation), Provisional Measures, Order of 22 November 2013*, Joint Separate Opinion of Judge Wolfrum and Judge Kelly, *ITLOS Reports 2013*, 258, para. 6, https://www.itlos.org/fileadmin/itlos/documents/cases/case_no.22/published/C22_Wolfrum_Kelly_221113.pdf, accessed 16 March 2020. Judge Wolfrum was a member of the *South China Sea* Tribunal.

[55] Hermann Mosler, "Nichtteilnahme einer Partei am Verfahren vor dem Internationalen Gerichtshof [Non-Participation of a Party in Proceedings before the International Court of Justice]," in Ingo von Münch (ed.), *Staatsrecht – Völkerrecht – Europarecht. Festschrift für Hans-Jürgen Schlochauer* [Constitutional Law – International Law - European Law. Festschrift for Hans-Jürgen Schlochauer] (Berlin: Walter de Gruyter, 1981), 443.

[56] Thirlway, *Non-Appearance*, 177.

[57] State of Bahrain, Ministry of State for Legal Affairs, Minister's Office, *Comments by the State of Bahrain on the Qatari "Act" of 30th November, 1994* (5 December 1994), 3, para. 8, https://www.icj-cij.org/files/case-related/87/13263.pdf, accessed 16 August 2020; *Maritime Delimitation and Territorial Questions Between Qatar and Bahrain, Jurisdiction and Admissibility*, Judgment, *I. C. J. Reports 1995*, 9–10, paras. 12–14, https://www.icj-cij.org/files/case-related/87/087-19950215-JUD-01-00-BI.pdf,

Very little attention has been paid to the *South China Sea* Tribunal's statement that

> China has been free to represent itself in these proceedings in the manner it considered most appropriate, including by refraining from any formal appearance, as it has in fact done. The decision of how best to represent China's position is a matter for China, not the Tribunal.[58]

It is possible that this statement has been ignored or overlooked by Chinese and other commentators because it was made in the context of the Tribunal's examination of the Philippine Submission that China, by its conduct, had aggravated the dispute and the Tribunal's conclusion that China had indeed aggravated the dispute.

The implications of the proclamation of a right not to appear had already been discussed by the IDI between 1985 and 1990. Ultimately, the IDI decided not to endorse the idea that a "right not to appear" was a corollary of the absence of a duty to appear. The debates revealed that affirming such a "right" was fraught with conceptual problems. It was also feared that recognition of a "right" not to appear might encourage more States to default, with the consequent undesirable consequences for the administration of international justice.

1. The Conceptual Problems Raised by a "Right" Not to Appear

Much of the debate within the IDI centered on the question of whether the existence of Article 53 of the ICJ Statute was tantamount to recognition of the "right" not to appear. Indeed, for a number of authors, the fact that an article is devoted to non-appearance implies recognition of non-appearance as a right or liberty or faculty.[59] However, the inability to specify the nature and content of such a right was put forward as grounds for rejecting the idea of a right not to appear.

In the 1970s, as the number of States that defaulted completely in proceedings before the ICJ increased, Shabtai Rosenne wrote that Article

accessed 17 August 2020. It should be noted, though, that Bahrain subsequently participated in the merits phase of the proceedings.

[58] *South China Sea Arbitration*, Award of 12 July 2016, 464, para. 1181, https://pcacases.com/web/sendAttach/2086, accessed 10 March 2020.

[59] Colliard, "La non-comparution," 190; Simone Dreyfus in SFDI, *La juridiction internationale permanente*, 266.

53 of the Court's Statute "confers a right on a party not to appear."[60] In his authoritative work on the PCIJ and the ICJ, he affirmed that a State is "entitled" to adopt whatever litigation strategy it finds appropriate to its circumstances, including a decision not to appear or to defend its case.[61] The IDI's Rapporteur, Arangio-Ruiz, drew from the idea that Article 53 excluded any condemnation of non-appearance the conclusion that non-appearance was legal. He asserted that non-appearance (or inactivity) before the ICJ was as discretionary and lawful as non-appearance before a national jurisdiction.[62] He dismissed attempts to draw a contrary conclusion on the basis of the United Nations Charter, in particular Article 2(3), on the obligation to settle disputes by peaceful means, and Chapter VI, on the pacific settlement of disputes. According to Arangio-Ruiz, only a very general obligation of respect for and recourse to the ICJ could be derived from such provisions and the obligation could be deemed to be fully complied with by any State that has accepted the Court's compulsory jurisdiction. Such acceptance included acceptance of the possibility of a judgment rendered in absentia and "obviously" implied the freedom to choose between appearing or not appearing. Lastly, the lawful character of non-appearance followed from the absence of sanctions against it.[63] In the same vein, Edward McWhinney contended that States retained the right "at all times" to choose as a tactical legal decision not to appear.[64] Invoking common law jurisprudence and legal history, he asserted that

[60] Shabtai Rosenne, "The Reconceptualization of Objections in the International Court of Justice," *Comunicazioni e studi* [Communications and Studies] 14 (1975): 749; Elkind, "Normative Surrender," 284.

[61] Shabtai Rosenne, with the assistance of Yaël Ronen, *The Law and Practice of the International Court 1990–2005*, vol. III, *Procedure* (4th ed.; Leiden: Martinus Nijhoff Publishers, 2006), 1360. Talmon reprises this theme: non-appearance is a procedural strategy available to a State to defend its rights and vital interests. Stefan Talmon, *The South China Sea Arbitration: Is There a Case to Answer?* (Bonn: Universität Bonn, Institute for Public International Law, 2014), 3, https://papers.ssrn.com/sol3/papers.cfm?abstract_id=2393025, accessed 13 March 2020.

[62] Arangio-Ruiz, "Notes," 11–12; "Non-Appearance Final Report," 291.

[63] Arangio-Ruiz, "Notes," 12–13; "Non-Appearance Final Report," 291–92.

[64] Observations of Mr. E. McWhinney (7 August 1985), in Arangio-Ruiz, "Non-Appearance Preliminary Report," 255.

any party to a case has the right, "within its own full discretion and political judgment," to opt not to appear or to terminate appearance after having already appeared in one phase of proceedings before the Court.[65]

Most IDI members were willing to concede that there was no duty to appear, but several were unable to agree with the Rapporteur on the legality of non-appearance. Herbert Briggs averred that Article 53 dealt with the possibility that contrary to normal expectations a State may not appear. In his view, Article 53 merely recognized the factual possibility, but this did not provide a basis for the conclusion that Article 53 conferred a legal right; the absence of sanctions could not be regarded as conferring a right.[66] C. Amerasinghe believed it would be "inaccurate" and "unnecessary" to declare that a State party to proceedings can "lawfully" not appear or had "liberty" not to appear. A respondent State is entitled not to appear only where the Court "manifestly" has no title to jurisdiction.[67]

Santiago Torres Bernárdez, a former ICJ Registrar, rejected Arangio-Ruiz's argument that any duty to appear that could be possibly derived from the UN Charter would be incompatible with Article 53, on the grounds that the Statute, as an annex to the UN Charter, should be interpreted in the light of the latter, and not vice-versa. He also argued that the mere existence of a non-appearance regime did not imply the lawfulness of non-appearance. The phrase in Article 53 that read "whenever one of the parties does not appear before the Court or fails to defend its case" did not constitute recognition of the "lawfulness" of non-appearance. Its intention was to determine a fact, the fact of non-appearance, as a material condition for a regime that would operate if the condition occurred. He stressed that until that time, no non-appearing State had ever asserted that non-appearance was the subjective exercise of its legal liberty to choose not to appear. In his experience, non-appearing States always invoked the manifest lack of jurisdiction by reference to a particular case.[68] Confirmation of this observation may be unexpectedly found in the dissenting

[65] Ibid. (18 November 1985), in Arangio-Ruiz, "Non-Appearance Preliminary Report," 255.

[66] Observations of Mr. W. Briggs (3 December 1985), in Arangio-Ruiz, "Non-Appearance Preliminary Report," 277.

[67] Observations of Mr. C. Amerasinghe (18 October 1990), in Arangio-Ruiz, "Non-Appearance Final Report," 345–46.

[68] Torres Bernárdez, "Non-Appearance," 354, para. 20.

opinion of Judge Schwebel, a US national, in the *Nicaragua Case*. It may be recalled that the US, after participating in the proceedings on jurisdiction and admissibility, refused to participate in the proceedings on the merits after the ICJ had issued its decision on jurisdiction and admissibility. Judge Schwebel simply said that the US did what Article 53 contemplated a party might do: it had not appeared, and it had failed to defend this case.[69] He did not defend US conduct on the grounds that the US had a "right" not to appear, confining himself to the observation that the US did what Article 53 contemplated a party might do.

The difficulty of specifying the nature and scope of a putative right not to appear was also emphasized in the IDI discussions. Eduardo Jiménez de Aréchaga, a former ICJ President, cautioned against reasoning in terms of a dichotomy, in which the choice of appearance is either a legal obligation or a discretionary right. He suggested that in international law, as in domestic law, appearance might be neither a duty nor a right but an "*onus probandi*," a condition to succeed in litigation.[70] Torres Bernárdez raised further unsettling questions. Were non-appearance to be declared "lawful," the scope of "lawfulness" would have to be determined against some reference. Was that reference to the Statute, the UN Charter, the treaty providing for the Court's jurisdiction, the substantive law to be applied by the Court, or the phase of the proceedings in which the non-appearance occurred?[71] He stressed that the Statute had to be interpreted in the light of the UN Charter, which could be construed to mean that States had a duty to appear before the ICJ. Torres Bernárdez did not elaborate on the conceptual difficulties that reference to a treaty, to the substantive law, or to a phase of the proceedings would have raised. It seems that only the problems surrounding the assertion of a putative right not to appear with reference to a treaty and to a phase of proceedings have been explored in the scholarly literature. It has been argued by at least one judge that a duty to appear may be derived from an agreement with a compromissory clause providing for the submission of the dispute to the

[69] *Military and Paramilitary Activities in and Against Nicaragua (Nicaragua v. United States of America), Merits, Judgment*, Dissenting Opinion of Judge Schwebel, *I.C.J. Reports 1986*, 316, para. 119, http://www.icj-cij.org/files/case-related/70/070-19860627-JUD-01-09-BI.pdf, accessed 31 March 2020. 7.

[70] Observations of Mr. E. Jiménez de Aréchaga, in Arangio-Ruiz, "Non-Appearance Preliminary Report," 273.

[71] Torres Bernárdez, "Non-Appearance," 353, para. 19.

ICJ.[72] This reasoning has not been followed by the ICJ. The conclusion might have been different if the treaty had expressly imposed a duty to appear in any proceedings instituted by virtue of that clause.[73] As for a putative right not to appear in a particular phase of the proceedings, we should recall Nicaragua's affirmation in the *Nicaragua Case* that once the ICJ has declared that it has jurisdiction, the respondent State has a duty to appear before the Court.

Torres Bernárdez identified one final conceptual difficulty, which arises from the fact that proceedings might be initiated at the ICJ by a State that has accepted the ICJ's compulsory jurisdiction against another State that has accepted the same obligation or by means of a special agreement between the two parties to the dispute. According to Torres Bernárdez, a declaration that default was lawful in the first situation would require that the IDI, to be consistent, also endorse the lawfulness of default in the second situation. Failure to do so would in effect "leave legality at the mercy of the way in which proceedings are instituted," something that was "unthinkable."[74] One may add that the declaration of the lawfulness of default might encourage default on the part of a State that is a party to proceedings initiated by special agreement and is having second thoughts about the wisdom of continuing the proceedings. No response was forthcoming from the Rapporteur or other IDI members to these penetrating questions.

In the end the IDI resolution adopted in 1991 refrained from proclaiming the lawfulness of non-appearance or the existence of a right not to appear. As Jiménez de Aréchaga suggested, its formulation was neutral: Article 53 implies that "a State may not appear before the Court." Yet the IDI resolution urged a State that has the intention of not appearing to have "regard to its duty to co-operate in the fulfilment of the Court's judicial functions."[75] The IDI was probably dissuaded from proclaiming a right not to appear not only by the conceptual problems

[72] *Fisheries Jurisdiction (United Kingdom v. Iceland), Merits, Judgment, I.C.J. Reports 1974*, Separate Opinion of Judge Sir Humphrey Waldock, 117–18, paras. 28–29, https://www.icj-cij.org/files/case-related/55/055-19740725-JUD-01-07-BI.pdf, accessed 24 March 2020,.3.

[73] Thirlway, "The Law and Procedure," 164.

[74] Torres Bernárdez, "Non-Appearance," 355, para. 22.

[75] IDI, *Non-Appearance Before the International Court of Justice*, 4th preambular paragraph and Article 2.

outlined above but also by the apprehension that proclamation of such a right would in effect encourage default, with the attendant undesirable consequences for the administration of international justice.

2. The Undesirable Consequences of Default for International Justice
There was a consensus among IDI members that the main unfavorable consequence of default was the risk that the ICJ might adopt a more lenient attitude toward the defaulting State. In this context one may cite the Court's judgments in the *Fisheries Jurisdiction Cases* and in the *Nuclear Tests Cases*.

Jiménez de Aréchaga was forthright in his opinion: if the proclamation of lawfulness of non-appearance came from the IDI, it would "encourage further boycott" of the Court by States, who would find in such a right a justification for denying the Court's power to determine its own jurisdiction. For this reason, he urged the IDI to avoid a pronouncement on the lawfulness of non-appearance.[76] Torres Bernárdez believed it would be dangerous for judicial settlement to recognize non-appearance as lawful, which would be tantamount to condoning it.[77] The Rapporteur, for his part, admitted the possible impact of non-appearance on even "the most able and conscientious of judges." Non-appearance and the attendant threat of non-compliance might induce them [i.e., international judges] to consciously or unconsciously "adopt a more lenient course or to use a softer hand towards the respondent than otherwise [they] might be inclined to do."[78] A court might be "seriously tempted to mitigate...the adversity of its judgment," in the name of the peaceful settlement of disputes, the promotion of international adjudication, and the rule of law. To put it bluntly, a court might bend over backward in order to appease the defaulting State. There were grounds for thinking that the ICJ had indeed bent over backward in the *Fisheries Jurisdiction Cases* and the *Nuclear Tests Cases*.[79] No further details were given over the way in which the Court mitigated "the adversity of its judgment," possibly because Arangio-Ruiz assumed that the cases were already familiar to

[76] Observations of Mr. E. Jiménez de Aréchaga, in Arangio-Ruiz, "Non-Appearance Preliminary Report," 273.

[77] Torres Bernárdez, "Non-Appearance," 348.

[78] Arangio-Ruiz, "Notes," 8; Arangio-Ruiz, "Non-Appearance Final Report," 286–87.

[79] Arangio-Ruiz, "Notes," 24; Arangio-Ruiz, "Non-Appearance Final Report," 331.

the IDI members. This presupposition is confirmed by the observations of Edward McWhinney, who noted that non-appearing States, far from being disadvantaged, may have benefited from the Court's indulgence. In his view, the high watermark of "manifest judicial favouring" of the non-appearing State was the *Nuclear Tests Cases*.[80] In this respect, at least, these members of the IDI agreed with those who deplored non-appearance and wished to impose sanctions on the non-appearing State.[81] The *compétence de la compétence* will be discussed in the following section. In the following paragraphs, an attempt will be made to examine the way(s) in which the ICJ may have mitigated its judgment to appease the defaulting States in the two sets of cases cited by Arangio-Ruiz.

Many commentators share the view that Iceland, which refused to appear throughout the entire proceedings in the *Fisheries Jurisdiction Cases*, enjoyed all of the benefits of the appearing State without the disadvantages of participation.[82] Evaluations of this type point, among others, to the way in which the Court handled informal communications from Iceland, examined the question of its jurisdiction, and exercised its power of putting questions to the appearing State(s). These issues will be discussed in the following section and the next Chapter. Attention here will focus on the Court's decision on the merits.

The UK and the Federal Republic of Germany (FRG) had filed separate cases against Iceland in 1972, requesting that the Court declare that Iceland's unilateral extension of its exclusive fisheries jurisdiction to 50 nautical miles had no basis in international law and could not be opposed to them. The FRG also sought a declaration that Icelandic interference with the operation of its fishing vessels was unlawful under international law and that Iceland was under an obligation to make compensation to it for these acts of interference. The two States founded the jurisdiction of the Court on separate Exchanges of Notes with Iceland (UK-Iceland Exchange of Notes of 13 July 1961 and FRG-Iceland Exchange of Notes

[80] Observations of Mr. E. McWhinney (21 August 1990), in Arangio-Ruiz, "Non-Appearance Final Report," 341.

[81] Fitzmaurice, "The Problem," 107, argued that the ICJ had "'bent over backwards' to ensure that no untoward consequences would ensue for the non-appearing State."

[82] Pierre-Marie Martin, "L'affaire de la compétence en matière de pêcheries (les arrêts de la C.I.J. du 2 février 1973) [The Fisheries Jurisdiction Cases (The I.C.J. Judgments of 2 February 1973)]," *Revue générale de droit international public* [General Journal of Public International Law] 78 (1974): 446 ("*RGDIP*").

of 19 July 1961). Under the two bilateral agreements, the UK and the FRG had undertaken not to object to Iceland's proclamation of a 12-nautical mile fishery zone in 1958. Iceland in return had undertaken to give the two States six months' notice of any further extension of its exclusive fisheries zone. In the event of a dispute relating to such an extension, the matter could be unilaterally submitted to the ICJ. In 1971 Iceland terminated the agreements with the UK and the FRG and extended its fisheries jurisdiction to 50 nautical miles. Following the failure of negotiations, the UK and the FRG instituted separate proceedings with the ICJ.[83]

In two judgments, the Court ruled that Iceland's extension of its exclusive fisheries zone to 50 miles was not opposable to the UK and to the FRG and held that the UK and Iceland, on the one hand, and the FRG and Iceland, on the other, were under mutual obligations to negotiate in good faith for the equitable solution of their differences concerning their respective fishery rights in the waters around Iceland. The Court identified the principles that these States should take into account in their negotiations, including the preferential rights of Iceland to fisheries resources based on its special dependence on fisheries for livelihood and economic development and the established rights of the UK and the FRG in the fishery resources of the waters around Iceland. The Court dismissed the FRG's request for a declaration of Icelandic responsibility under international law for interfering with the operations of FRG fishing vessels.[84]

The opinion of the Court's majority was criticized by Judge Gros for not deciding the precise legal question envisaged in the Exchanges of Notes of 1961 (and one might add, embodied in the submissions of the UK and the FRG)—the conformity with international law of

[83] *Fisheries Jurisdiction (United Kingdom v. Iceland), Merits, Judgment, I.C.J. Reports 1974*, 10–17, paras. 19–34, https://www.icj-cij.org/files/case-related/55/055-19740725-JUD-01-00-BI.pdf, accessed 17 March 2020; *Fisheries Jurisdiction (Federal Republic of Germany v. Iceland), Merits, Judgment, I.C.J. Reports 1974*, 182–89, paras. 20–33, http://www.icj-cij.org/files/case-related/56/056-19740725-JUD-01-00-BI.pdf, accessed 17 March 2020.

[84] *Fisheries Jurisdiction (United Kingdom v. Iceland), Merits*, 34–35, para. 79; *Fisheries Jurisdiction (Federal Republic of Germany v. Iceland), Merits*, 305–06, para. 77.

Iceland's extension of its exclusive fisheries zone to 50 nautical miles.[85] Judge Onyeama objected that the Court had redefined the dispute as one relating to the exercise of preferential rights that did not give due regard to established rights, when in fact it was a dispute involving an extension of the fisheries zone that was in conflict with international law.[86]

Scholarly commentary sought to explain the Court's transformation of an objective dispute (the conformity of the extension of the exclusive fisheries zone with international law) into a subjective dispute (the opposability of the extension of the exclusive fisheries zone to the UK and to the FRG).[87] The Court's aim in the judgments seems to have been a compromise that would satisfy the UK and the FRG without a thoroughgoing condemnation of Iceland's unilateral action.[88] The ICJ may have hoped that in this manner, it could gain the trust of Iceland. In fact, the Court avoided anything that could possibly offend Iceland, such as a declaration of Icelandic responsibility for a breach of international law or a declaration of an Icelandic obligation to pay compensation to the FRG for its interference with the operations of FRG fishing vessels.[89]

French default in the *Nuclear Test Cases* intensified the "severe test" that the case represented for the Court.[90] Australia had requested that

[85] *Fisheries Jurisdiction (United Kingdom v. Iceland), Merits*, Dissenting Opinion of Judge Gros, 128–29, https://www.icj-cij.org/files/case-related/55/055-19740725-JUD-01-08-BI.pdf, accessed 11 August 2019.

[86] Ibid., Dissenting Opinion of Judge Onyeama, 171, para. 16, https://www.icj-cij.org/files/case-related/55/055-19740725-JUD-01-10-BI.pdf, accessed 1 April 2020.

[87] Louis Favoreu, "Les arrêts de la Cour Internationale de Justice relatifs à la compétence en matière de pêcheries (Royaume-Uni c/ Islande et République fédérale d'Allemagne c. Islande — Arrêts du 25 juillet 1974) [The Judgments of the International Court of Justice on Fisheries Jurisdiction (United Kingdom v. Iceland and Federal Republic of Germany v. Iceland – Judgments of 25 July 1974]," *Annuaire français de droit international* [French Yearbook of International Law] 20 (1974): 263 ("*AFDI*"), http://www.persee.fr/doc/afdi_0066-3085_1974_num_20_1_2271, accessed 17 March 2020.

[88] Emmanuel Langavant and Olivier Pirotte, "L'affaire des pêcheries islandaises. L'arrêt de la Cour internationale de justice du 25 juillet 1974 [The Icelandic Fisheries Case. The Judgment of the International Court of Justice of 25 July 1974]," *RGDIP* 80 (1976): 81.

[89] Raymond Goy, "Le règlement de l'affaire des pêcheries islandaises [The Settlement of the Icelandic Fisheries Case]," *RGDIP* 82 (1978): 487.

[90] Jean-Pierre Cot, "Affaire des Essais nucléaires (Australie c. France et Nouvelle-Zélande c. France). Demandes en indication de mesures conservatoires. Ordonnances du

the Court declare that continued nuclear testing by France in the South Pacific violated international law and order that France cease testing.[91] New Zealand had requested a declaration that French nuclear tests in the South Pacific violated its rights under international law.[92] On 16 May 1973, a week after the initiation of the proceedings, France, invoking its reservation relating to questions of national defense attached to its declaration of acceptance of the Court's compulsory jurisdiction, declared that the Court manifestly did not have jurisdiction; France refused to appear before the Court throughout the entire proceedings. On 2 January 1974, France withdrew its declaration of acceptance of the Court's compulsory jurisdiction; this was the first instance of a State withdrawing its declaration during the actual proceedings.[93] The Court's response to the French demand that the case be immediately removed from the list of cases of the Court, the treatment of French informal communications to the Court, and the propriety of the Court's non-application of Article 53 at the stage of provisional measures, among others, attracted considerable controversy within the Court itself. These will be further discussed in the following section and in the next Chapter. The following paragraphs will concentrate on the controversy surrounding the Court's decision of 20 December 1974.

22 juin 1973 [The Nuclear Tests Cases (Australia v. France and New-Zealand v. France). Requests for the Indication of Provisional Measures. Orders of 22 June 1973]," *AFDI* 19 (1973): 255, https://www.persee.fr/docAsPDF/afdi_0066-3085_1973_num_19_1_2213.pdf, http://www.persee.fr/doc/afdi_0066-3085_1973_num_19_1_2213, accessed 1 April 2020.

[91] *Nuclear Tests (Australia v. France), Judgment, I.C.J. Reports 1974*, 256, para. 11, https://www.icj-cij.org/files/case-related/58/058-19741220-JUD-01-00-BI.pdf, accessed 1 April 2020.

[92] *Nuclear Tests (New Zealand v. France), Judgment, I.C.J. Reports 1974*, 460, para. 11, https://www.icj-cij.org/files/case-related/59/059-19741220-JUD-01-00-BI.pdf, accessed 1 April 2020.

[93] Barbara Kwiatkowska, "The International Court of Justice and the Law of the Sea. Some Reflections," in Jerzy Makarczyk (ed.), *Theory of International Law at the Threshold of the 21st Century. Essays in Honor of Krzysztof Skubiszewski* (The Hague: Kluwer Law International, 1996), 463. For the French perspective, see Guy de Lacharrière, "Commentaires sur la position juridique de la France à l'égard de la licéité de ses expériences nucléaires [Commentaries on the Legal Position of France with Respect to the Legality of Its Nuclear Tests]," *AFDI* 19 (1973): 235–51, http://www.persee.fr/doc/afdi_0066-3085_1973_num_19_1_2212, accessed 2 April 2020.

After issuing an order that France cease nuclear testing for a year, the Court had decided to devote the next phase of the proceedings to jurisdiction and admissibility. Accordingly, the two applicants submitted written and oral arguments on both matters. Yet in its judgments, the Court decided that French unilateral declarations made after the closure of the oral proceedings, which the Court interpreted as commitments to cease atmospheric nuclear testing, caused the dispute to disappear and deprived the Applications of any object.[94] The Court's judgments were harshly criticized, not without reason, by the dissenting judges and by commentators. The judge ad hoc designated by Australia and New Zealand objected to the fact that the Court had taken cognizance of events that had occurred after the closure of the oral proceedings; had not informed Australia and New Zealand of the French declarations that it had introduced into the proceedings; had decided on its own and without informing the two Applicants to consider the question whether the Applications had ceased to have an object; had not given them the opportunity to make submissions on this separate, different, and new question; and had avoided deciding questions of jurisdiction and admissibility that the two States had been directed to address.[95] These criticisms were sympathetically received in the scholarly literature.[96]

There is little doubt among scholarly commentators that French default and withdrawal of the French acceptance of the Court's compulsory jurisdiction, described as "body blows" to the Court from a State that had traditionally supported international adjudication in general and the Court in particular, decisively influenced the Court's approach to its

[94] *Nuclear Tests (Australia v. France), Judgment*, 270–71, paras. 52–56; *Nuclear Tests (New Zealand v. France), Judgment*, 474–75, paras. 53–59.

[95] *Nuclear Tests (Australia v. France), Judgment*, Dissenting Opinion of Judge Sir Garfield Barwick, *I.C.J. Reports 1974*, 391–92, http://www.icj-cij.org/files/case-related/58/058-19741220-JUD-01-09-BI.pdf, accessed 1 April 2020.

[96] See, e.g., Bowett, "Contemporary Developments," 201; Taslim O. Elias, *The International Court of Justice and Some Contemporary Problems. Essays on International Law* (Dordrecht: Springer Science + Business Media, 1983), 105, 117; R. St. J. Macdonald and Barbara Hough, "The *Nuclear Tests* Case Revisited," *German Yearbook of International Law* 20 (1977): 337–57 ("*GYIL*"); José Juste Ruiz, "Mootness in International Adjudication: The Nuclear Tests Cases," *GYIL* 20 (1977): 358–74; Ian Sinclair, "Some Procedural Aspects of Recent International Litigation," *International and Comparative Law Quarterly* 30 (1981): 348, 356 ("*ICLQ*"); and Thirlway, *Non-Appearance*, 152.

decision-making.[97] French scholar Serge Sur believes that the two French reactions convinced the Court that there was no point in allowing the proceedings to continue.[98] In the most plausible interpretation of the Court's approach to its decision-making, another French scholar, Hubert Thierry, argues that the Court had adopted a solution that did not give offense to French legal positions. The decision implied that the French reservation to the Court's compulsory jurisdiction had not been ignored or abrogated and that French theses, whether on jurisdiction or the merits, had not been rejected. Following the decision, France would not have been prevented from arguing that the Court would not have had jurisdiction to decide on the nuclear tests if they had been continued and that the nuclear tests were legal. In Thierry's view, underlying the decision was the Court's desire to calm things down in its relations with France. The resulting solution, though grounded in the law, was more diplomatic in nature.[99]

The suspicion that default may cause an international court to "bend over backward" to accommodate the defaulting State is not likely to serve the cause of international adjudication, as Arangio-Ruiz admitted.[100] This was probably the reason that weighed the most against the idea of proclaiming that States have a "right" not to appear before the ICJ. Another equally decisive reason is that the so-called "right" is invoked as a pretext to deny the power of international courts to determine their own jurisdiction.

[97] Edward McWhinney, "International Law-Making and the Judicial Process: The World Court and the French Nuclear Tests Case," *Syracuse Journal of International Law and Commerce* 3 (1975): 44, https://surface.syr.edu/cgi/viewcontent.cgi?article=1033&context=jilc, accessed 1 April 2020.

[98] Serge Sur, "Les affaires des essais nucléaires (Australie c. France, Nouvelle Zélande c. France), C.I.J. – arrêts du 20 décembre 1974 [The Nuclear Tests Cases (Australia v. France, New Zealand v. France), I.C.J. – Judgments of 20 December 1974]," *RGDIP* 79 (1975): 1022.

[99] Hubert Thierry, "Les arrêts du 20 décembre 1974 et les relations de la France avec la Cour internationale de justice [The Judgments of 20 December 1974 and French Relations with the International Court of Justice]," *AFDI* 20 (1974): 291–92, 298, http://www.persee.fr/doc/afdi_0066-3085_1974_num_20_1_2272, accessed 1 April 2020.

[100] Arangio-Ruiz, "Notes," 46; Arangio-Ruiz, "Non-Appearance Final Report," 331–32. At this point it is idle to speculate whether China was hoping or expecting that the Arbitral Tribunal would bend over backward to accommodate its legal positions. As we shall see in Chapters 3 and 5, China did not passively wait for the Tribunal to adopt its legal positions.

II. The *Compétence de la Compétence* and the Bifurcation of the Proceedings in the *South China Sea Arbitration*

A State that claims a right not to appear before an international court is in fact asserting that its subjective views on legal issues should prevail over the international court's decision. Such an attitude is incompatible with the principle of *compétence de la compétence*.[101] Under this principle, every international court has "the right to decide as to its own jurisdiction and has the power to interpret for this purpose the instruments which govern that jurisdiction."[102] This power does not contradict the consensual basis of international jurisdiction. In any given case, an international court or tribunal has to determine whether the parties to the dispute have given their consent to the dispute being heard by that court, but the consent in question is "the will of the parties as found and determined by the Court."[103] The principle is incorporated in the PCIJ Statute, the ICJ Statute, and in the Convention. Article 288(4) of the latter provides that "[i]n the event of a dispute as to whether a court or tribunal has jurisdiction, the matter shall be settled by decision of that court or tribunal." Accor[104]ding to an authoritative commentary of the Convention, Article 288(4) embodies the customary rule of international law that any international court has jurisdiction to determine the scope of its jurisdiction. The *compétence de la compétence* is now considered a fundamental principle of international law.[105]

An international court or tribunal exercises "jurisdiction over the jurisdiction" whenever a State against which proceedings have been instituted challenges the court's jurisdiction through a preliminary objection. In a

[101] Observations of Mr. E. Jiménez de Aréchaga, in Arangio-Ruiz, "Non-Appearance Preliminary Report," 273.

[102] *Nottebohm Case (Preliminary Objection), Judgment*, 119.

[103] Ibrahim F.I. Shihata, *The Power of the International Court to Determine Its Own Jurisdiction: Compétence de la Compétence* (Dordrecht: Springer Science+Business Media, 1965), 4.

[104] Myron H. Nordquist et al. (eds.), *United Nations Convention on the Law of the Sea 1982*, vol. V, *Settlement of Disputes, General and Final Provisions and Related Annexes and Resolutions* (Leiden: Brill, 1989), 48.

[105] Rosenne, *The Law and Practice*, vol. III, 812; Shabtai Rosenne, with the assistance of Yaël Ronen, *The Law and Practice of the International Court 1990–2005*, vol. I, *The Court and the United Nations* (4th ed.; Leiden: Martinus Nijhoff Publishers, 2006), 812.

situation of default, there is by definition no respondent State to file a preliminary objection. This circumstance cannot operate to deprive the court of its power to determine its own jurisdiction, as the Philippines pointed out.[106] In case of default, the ICJ practice has been to treat informal communications from the defaulting State that deny its jurisdiction as preliminary objections and to bifurcate the proceedings. It is this precedent that the *South China Sea* Tribunal followed.

A. The Compétence de la Compétence, *a Fundamental Principle of International Law*

The affirmation of the principle of *compétence de la compétence* is the product of a long process of evolution going back to the late eighteenth century and culminating in the nineteenth century. It is necessary to survey this historical development because the State that claimed that its default in the *South China Sea Arbitration* had a "solid basis" in international law seemed to be unaware that it was challenging this fundamental principle of international law.

1. The Evolution of the Principle of Compétence de la Compétence

The principle of *compétence de la compétence* emerged in arbitral practice in the eighteenth and nineteenth centuries and was progressively adopted in State practice until it was finally adopted in the Conventions for the Pacific Settlement of International Disputes of 1899 and 1907 ("the Hague Conventions").

The rationale for the principle of *compétence de la compétence* was first elaborated in the opinions filed by US commissioners in the context of arbitration with Great Britain under the Treaty of Amity, Commerce, and Navigation, widely known as Jay's Treaty or the Jay Treaty, after the US negotiator, Supreme Court Chief Justice, John Jay, concluded on 19 November 1794.[107] The Treaty's objective was to settle issues that had been left unresolved since the American War of Independence (1776–1783). Articles V, VI, and VII of the Treaty established three mixed

[106] *South China Sea Arbitration, Memorial of the Philippines* (30 March 2014), vol. I, 230, paras. 7.35, 7.39 ("*MP*"), https://files.pca-cpa.org/pcadocs/Memorial%20of%20the%20Philippines%20Volume%20I.pdf, accessed 23 April 2020.

[107] US Department of State, Office of the Historian, *John Jay's Treaty 1794–95*, https://history.state.gov/milestones/1784-1800/jay-treaty, accessed 2 April 2020.

commissions, composed of US and British representatives.[108] The mixed commission under Article V was to determine which river was intended to be the River St. Croix, which had been specified in the 1783 Treaty ending the War of Independence as part of the US northeastern boundary with Canada under British rule. The mixed commission organized under Article VI was to determine compensation to be paid by the US to British subjects who had failed to recover debts owed to them as a result of actions by States that later became part of the US. The mixed commission organized under Article VII was to determine compensation to be paid by Great Britain to American merchants and citizens whose vessels had been irregularly or illegally captured or condemned by the British in the course of the French Revolutionary Wars. In the commission established under Article VI, US commissioners denied the commission the right to determine its own jurisdiction and withdrew from it to destroy the quorum and to paralyze it. The question was never settled in this context. In the commission established under Article VII, the situation was reversed. Great Britain ultimately declined to support its commissioners and left it to the commission to determine its jurisdiction in relation to cases before it.[109]

The American members of the last Commission elaborated the rationale for "jurisdiction of the jurisdiction" that was gradually accepted in the nineteenth century. In their opinion, several considerations logically require that a tribunal have the power to decide its own jurisdiction. The broadest argument was that for a tribunal, determining whether it has jurisdiction is the first act that presents itself to the mind. It is a prerequisite to every other act and to the due exercise of every other authority.[110] Commissioner More reasoned in 1794 that the power to decide jurisdiction is necessary to enable a commission to reach its merits.[111] A commission that examined only the claims of the party that accepted its jurisdiction and did not examine the claim of the party that resisted its

[108] The following information is taken from John Bassett Moore, *The United States and International Arbitration* (Boston: The American Peace Society, 1896), 3–6.

[109] John Bassett Moore, *History and Digest of the International Arbitrations to Which the United States Has Been a Party*, vol. III (Washington, D.C.: Government Printing Office, 1898), 2133, https://ia800204.us.archive.org/18/items/historyanddiges01moorgoog/historyanddiges01moorgoog.pdf, accessed 2 April 2020.

[110] Ibid., 2282.

[111] Ibid., 2298.

jurisdiction would not be impartial and just. "The opinion of one ought to weigh as much and no more than the opinion of the other." Otherwise, the submissions to the commission would be under the control of only one of the parties, the party that accepted its jurisdiction.[112] Commissioner Gore articulated in June 1798 the now widely accepted view that the power to decide its jurisdiction is inherent in the very constitution of a commission and that it was "indispensably necessary" to discharge any duties.[113] For him, it was self-evident that the Jay Treaty gave a commission power to determine its jurisdiction. Even without a specific provision in the Treaty to that effect, arbitrators are always the judge on the scope of submissions to them. Otherwise, the submissions would be "idle and ineffectual."[114] More specifically, it would be a contradiction if a commission should have the power to decide on compensation and not the power to decide whether a complaint is within its jurisdiction.[115] It would be "absurd and inconceivable" if a commission had the power to examine and decide a claim yet had no power to decide whether there was a claim.[116]

Practical reasons also point to the conclusion that a court should have the power to determine its own jurisdiction. Earlier authors had contended that an arbitrator was a mandatory of the parties and would violate his mandate if he arrogated to himself the right to interpret the mandate.[117] Commissioner Gore pointed out that the US and Great Britain had not made provision for the Commissioners to refer to them to determine what cases should be submitted to a commission; it seemed to him to be hardly conceivable that if this had been the two parties' intention, they should have omitted it in the Treaty.[118] Commissioner Pinkney also observed in June 1798 that if a commission refused to decide on its jurisdiction, it would have to turn at every stage of the proceedings to the parties for instructions, which the parties were not obliged to give, or even worse, it would have to wait for further negotiations between the

[112] Ibid., 2281.

[113] Ibid.

[114] Ibid., 2296.

[115] Ibid., 2278.

[116] Ibid., 2284.

[117] Shihata, *The Power*, 24.

[118] Moore, *History and Digest*, vol. III, 2279.

parties, for which no provision had been made in the Treaty.[119] In any event, to grant one or both parties the right at all times to interfere in the proceedings would prevent a court from reaching a decision.[120] Of course, a tribunal faced with the question of its own jurisdiction could simply assume that the matter was within its jurisdiction, but such a way of proceeding would not be efficient or careful, and the result could be "great injustice." Unlike a domestic tribunal, a tribunal that was unable to address the question of its own jurisdiction could not turn to any other tribunal to settle the question, for there was no authority under the Jay Treaty for such a course of action; at any rate, there was no other tribunal authorized to make the decision for it.[121] Conceding that there was a risk that the arbitrators might exceed their powers, Commissioner Gore replied that the decision would be null and void but that the risk of such a decision could not be a reason for a commission to refuse to decide on its own jurisdiction.[122]

These opinions, which were opinions of individual commissioners designated by only one party and not of the commission as a whole, by no means settled the question.[123] As late as 1866, in an arbitration between the US and Colombia under the Convention of 10 February 1864 relating to the payment of Colombian bonds, the umpire (i.e., the neutral arbitrator) affirmed that in case of doubt as to the Commission's jurisdiction, the Commission was bound to decline to entertain a claim and to interpret its powers in a limited sense. A tribunal that adopted the contrary principle of interpretation would allegedly be assuming powers that States "jealously reserved" to themselves.[124] Despite this contrary example, the principle of *compétence de la compétence* was adopted in the nineteenth century by an increasing number of arbitral commissions, notably the US-Mexican Claims Commission of 11 April 1839, the US-Great Britain Commission of 8 February 1853, the US-Paraguay

[119] Ibid., 2311.

[120] Ibid., 2291.

[121] Ibid., 2282.

[122] Ibid., 2296.

[123] Shihata, *The Power*, 14.

[124] Moore, *History and Digest*, vol. IV, 3614, https://ia801404.us.archive.org/15/items/historyanddiges02moorgoog/historyanddiges02moorgoog.pdf, accessed 3 April 2020.

Commission of 4 February 1859, and the US-Costa Rica Commission of 2 July 1860.[125]

The next major milestone in the consolidation of the principle is conventionally held to be the *Alabama Arbitration* of 1871–1872 between the US and Great Britain. The *Alabama* was the most successful of several British warships that had been contracted during the US Civil War (1861–1865) by the secessionist South, the Confederacy, and that captured or sank over 150 Northern merchant ships. To evaluate US claims that Great Britain had violated neutrality laws by allowing the South to build a navy, the two States established an arbitral commission under the Treaty of Washington of 1871.[126] In addition to claims for direct damage, the US also claimed compensation for indirect damage—the prolongation of the Civil War. The Tribunal issued a confidential notification to the parties that it was not within its competence to adjudicate indirect claims, whereupon the US withdrew its claims and Great Britain withdrew its request for adjournment of the Tribunal. The value of the *Alabama Case* as a precedent is somewhat limited by several circumstances: Great Britain had not formally raised a preliminary objection alleging the incompetence of the Tribunal to adjudicate indirect claims, the notification of the Tribunal to the parties had in reality been drafted by the two parties, and the notification was still subject to their consent.[127]

Given these circumstances, the *Alabama Arbitration* may be more rightly considered a milestone because it stimulated scholarly reflection. The rationales provided by scholars for the principle of *compétence de la*

[125] Shihata, *The Power*, 15.

[126] United States Department of State, Office of the Historian, Foreign Service Institute, *The Alabama Claims, 1862–1872* (2017), https://history.state.gov/milestones/1861-1865/alabama, accessed 2 April 2020.

[127] Shihata, *The Power*, 18–19; Alexandre Mérignhac, *Traité théorique et pratique de l'arbitrage international: le rôle du droit dans le fonctionnement actuel de l'institution et dans ses destinées futures* [A Theoretical and Practical Treatise on International Arbitration: The Role of Law in the Present Operation of the Institution and in Its Future Destiny] (Paris: Librairie du Recueil général des Lois et des arrêts et du Journal du Palais, 1895), 81, 86, 254, https://ia601407.us.archive.org/14/items/traitthoriqueet00mrgoog/traitthoriqueet00mrgoog.pdf, accessed 3 April 2020; Thomas Balch, *The Alabama Arbitration* (Philadelphia: Allen, Lane & Scott, 1900), 125–26, https://archive.org/details/alabamaarbitrat00balcgoog, accessed 3 April 2020.

compétence reiterated the opinions first formulated by the US commissioners at the end of the eighteenth century. For instance, Merignhac explained that the arbitrator appointed to judge on the merits should also be considered as being invested with the power to determine his jurisdiction; he added that unlike in domestic systems, the question of jurisdiction of an international tribunal could not be referred to another tribunal.[128] Martens observed that the principle would obviate the need for the parties to negotiate a new agreement to settle questions of jurisdiction not provided for in the original agreement.[129] The IDI draft on the question prepared between 1873 and 1875 served as the basis for the work of further arbitral commissions, so that by the Hague Peace Conference of 1899 the *compétence de la compétence* was declared as a pre-existing rule.[130] At the Conference, it was explained that the principle was the very essence of the arbitral function and an inherent requirement for the exercise of the function.

> Not to accept this view would be to place the tribunal in the condition of a court incapable of acting and obliged to divest itself of the controversy, every time it might please one of the parties to maintain, even against the evidence, that the tribunal should not take cognizance of such a question.[131]

Under Article 48 of the Hague Convention of 1899 and Article 73 of the Hague Convention of 1907, an arbitral tribunal "is authorized to declare its competence in interpreting the 'Compromis' [special agreement] as well as the other Treaties which may be invoked in the case, and

[128] Mérignhac, *Traité théorique et pratique*, 215, 255.

[129] Fedor Fedorovich Martens, *Traité de droit international* [A Treatise on International Law], vol. III (translated from Russian by Alfred Léo; Paris: Chevalier-Marescq et Cie, Successeurs, 1887), 153, https://ia800902.us.archive.org/32/items/traitdedroitint00martgoog/traitdedroitint00martgoog.pdf, accessed 13 January 2020.

[130] Shihata, *The Power*, 19–21.

[131] Seventh Meeting, July 25, 1899, Annexes, in James Brown Scott (ed.). *The Proceedings of the Hague Peace Conferences. Translation of the Official Texts. The Conference of 1899* (New York: Oxford University Press, 1920), 147–48, https://ia802604.us.archive.org/18/items/proceedingshagu02scotgoog/proceedingshagu02scotgoog.pdf, accessed 3 April 2020.

in applying the principles of international law."[132] As mentioned above, the *compétence de la compétence*, stipulated in the Statutes of the PCIJ and the ICJ and in the Convention, is now considered a fundamental principle of international law.

It is this fundamental principle that the defaulting State refused to recognize in the *South China Sea Arbitration*.

2. China's Challenge to the Compétence de la Compétence

Seemingly unaware of the possible paradox, China claimed that its aim in refusing to participate in the proceedings was "to safeguard the solemnity [sic] and integrity of international law, including the UNCLOS...and to oppose the abuse of the compulsory arbitration procedures."[133] In its Position Paper, China had no qualms about declaring that it

> highly values the positive role played by the compulsory dispute settlement procedures of the Convention in upholding the international legal order for the oceans. As a State Party to the Convention, China has accepted the provisions of section 2 of Part XV on compulsory dispute settlement procedures.[134]

It then went on to say that it "respects that competence of judicial or arbitral bodies under the Convention."[135] Talmon concurred that non-appearance does not imply disrespect for the Arbitral Tribunal.[136] Needless to say, China's reasoning and litigation strategy contradict the profession of respect for the competence of courts or arbitral tribunals under the Convention. Notwithstanding the fact that Article 288(4) of the Convention confers on courts and tribunals established under the

[132] *1899 Convention for the Pacific Settlement of International Disputes*, 13, https://pca-cpa.org/wp-content/uploads/sites/6/2016/01/1899-Convention-for-the-Pacific-Settlement-of-International-Disputes.pdf, accessed 3 April 2020; *1907 Convention for the Pacific Settlement of International Disputes*, 18, https://pca-cpa.org/wp-content/uploads/sites/6/2016/01/1907-Convention-for-the-Pacific-Settlement-of-International-Disputes.pdf, accessed 3 April 2020.

[133] Foreign Ministry, *Briefing by Xu Hong*.

[134] Position Paper, 31, para. 79.

[135] Ibid., para. 82.

[136] Talmon, *The South China Sea Arbitration*, 3.

Convention the power to determine their jurisdiction,[137] China seemed to believe, as did other defaulting States at the ICJ, that its assertion that the Arbitral Tribunal "manifestly" lacked jurisdiction was sufficient to prevent the Tribunal from determining whether it had jurisdiction and to prevent China from being treated as a "non-appearing party." A State that truly sought to "uphold the international legal order for the oceans" and respected "the competence of the judicial or arbitral bodies under the Convention" would have had recourse to one or both of two procedures offered to it for challenging the Tribunal's jurisdiction—the filing of preliminary objections or the formulation of a request that the Tribunal examine its claim that the Philippines abused the Convention's dispute settlement procedures by initiating the *Arbitration*.[138]

China's Position Paper, which specified in advance that it should not be regarded "as China's acceptance of or participation" in the arbitral proceedings,[139] rationalized China's default as the consequence of the rightness of its arguments. As will be seen in the next section, the Tribunal responded to China's Position Paper by bifurcating the proceedings. What is of interest here is the CSIL's criticism that the Tribunal "mistreated China's non-acceptance and non-participation position and regarded China as a non-appearing party."[140] The unmistakable implication is that China should not have been treated a party at all and that the proceedings should have been halted.

The claim that China should not have been treated as a (non-appearing) party is reminiscent of the arguments of two defaulting States in three cases before the ICJ—France in the two *Nuclear Tests Cases* and Turkey in the *Aegean Sea Continental Shelf Case*. In these cases, the alleged manifest lack of jurisdiction of the Court was the ground for the defaulting State's request that the respective cases should be removed from the ICJ's General List.[141] In the General List, cases are numbered

[137] "In the event of a dispute as to whether a court or tribunal has jurisdiction, the matter shall be settled by decision of that court or tribunal."

[138] One also wonders how China would have behaved if it had *not* respected the competence of the Arbitral Tribunal.

[139] Position Paper, 21, para. 2.

[140] CSIL, "The South China Sea Arbitration Awards," 414, para. 888.

[141] *Nuclear Tests (Australia v. France), Interim Protection, Order of 22 June 1973, I.C.J. Reports 1973*, 100, para. 6, http://www.icj-cij.org/files/case-related/58/058-19730622-ORD-01-00-BI.pdf, accessed 3 April 2020; *Nuclear Tests (New*

successively according to the date of the document instituting proceedings. The purpose of the List is to prevent one case from being given preference over another that had been entered higher on the List, which determines the order in which cases that are ready for hearing will be heard by the Court.[142] Cases can only be removed from the General List by a Court decision. They are removed automatically following a final decision in a case or advisory opinion or through an order in the event proceedings are discontinued.[143] The removal from the General List would have been tantamount to a summary dismissal of the cases, without any examination by the Court of the question of its jurisdiction. In the three cases, the Court refused to remove the case from the General List, in this manner affirming that the defaulting States continued to be parties to the case and that the Court retained the power to determine its jurisdiction.[144]

The denial by China and Chinese scholars that China was a party to the case by reason of its refusal to recognize the jurisdiction of the Tribunal falls flat when one realizes that the ICJ only refuses to recognize the status of party to States who have not previously accepted the ICJ's jurisdiction and have refused an invitation by another State to accept the ICJ's jurisdiction. As explained in Judge Tarazi's separate opinion appended to the Order in the *Aegean Sea Continental Shelf Case*, the ICJ would have dismissed the application without examination of the question of jurisdiction only if the applicant State had merely invited the respondent State to accept the Court's jurisdiction, without invoking any legal instrument conferring jurisdiction on the Court, and the respondent State had

Zealand v. France), Interim Protection, Order of 22 June 1973, I.C.J. Reports 1973, 136, para. 7, https://www.icj-cij.org/files/case-related/59/059-19730622-ORD-01-00-BI.pdf, accessed 3 April 2020; *Aegean Sea Continental Shelf, Interim Protection, Order of 11 September 1976, I.C.J. Reports 1976*, 5, para. 8, http://www.icj-cij.org/files/case-related/62/062-19760911-ORD-01-00-BI.pdf, accessed 3 April 2020.

[142] Shabtai Rosenne, "The General List of the International Court of Justice," in Jerzy Makarczyk (ed.), *Theory of International Law at the Threshold of the 21st Century. Essays in Honor of Krzysztof Skubiszewski* (The Hague: Kluwer Law International, 1996), 806.

[143] Rosenne, *The Law and Practice*, vol. III, 1184.

[144] *Nuclear Tests (Australia v. France), Interim Protection, Order*, 105, para. 32; *Nuclear Tests (New Zealand v. France), Interim Protection, Order*, 141–42, para. 33; *Aegean Sea Continental Shelf, Interim Protection, Order*, 13, para. 46.

refused.[145] As long as the applicant State is able to invoke a basis for jurisdiction and the ICJ has not determined that the absence of jurisdiction is indeed manifest, the ICJ will not remove a case from the List. It will continue to treat the respondent State, defaulting or not, as a party to the case, and exercise its power to determine its jurisdiction.[146]

The CSIL's critique assumes that China was in the same legal position in relation to the Arbitral Tribunal as States that had been invited to accept the ICJ's jurisdiction and had refused the invitation. A brief overview of the five cases cited by Judge Tarazi will demonstrate that the analogy is a false one. In March 1954, the US instituted proceedings against Hungary and the USSR for having intercepted an American aircraft flying over Hungary and detaining its crew in Hungary. The US, which was aware that neither State had accepted the Court's compulsory jurisdiction, invited both States to accept the Court's jurisdiction.[147] When the two States refused, the Court had no choice but to remove the cases from the List.[148] Two years later, the US instituted proceedings against Czechoslovakia, whose aircraft had flown over the US zone of occupation in Germany in 1953, and invited Czechoslovakia, which had not accepted the Court's compulsory jurisdiction, to do so.[149] Following

[145] *Aegean Sea Continental Shelf*, *Interim Protection*, *Order*, Separate Opinion of Judge Tarazi, *I.C.J. Reports 1976*, 32, https://www.icj-cij.org/files/case-related/62/062-19760911-ORD-01-08-BI.pdf, accessed 3 April 2020.

[146] Rosenne, *The Law and Practice*, vol. III, 1189.

[147] United States, *Application Instituting Proceedings* (*United States of America v. Union of Soviet Socialist Republics)* (3 March 1954), *I.C.J. Pleadings*, *Treatment in Hungary of Aircraft of United States of America*, 59–60, https://www.icj-cij.org/files/case-related/23/023-19540303-APP-1-00-BI.pdf, accessed 5 April 2020; United States. *Application Instituting Proceedings* (*United States of America v. Hungarian People's Republic)* (3 March 1954), *I.C.J. Pleadings*, *Treatment in Hungary of Aircraft of United States of America*, 38–39, https://www.icj-cij.org/files/case-related/22/022-19540303-APP-1-00-BI.pdf, accessed 5 April 2020.

[148] *Case of the Treatment in Hungary of Aircraft of United States of America*, *Order of July 12, 1954: I.C.J. Reports 1954*, 99, https://www.icj-cij.org/files/case-related/22/022-19540712-ORD-01-00-BI.pdf, accessed 5 April 2020; *Case of the Treatment in Hungary of Aircraft of United States of America*, *Order of July 12, 1954: I.C.J. Reports 1954*, 103, https://www.icj-cij.org/files/case-related/23/023-19540712-ORD-01-00-BI.pdf, accessed 5 April 2020.

[149] United States, *Application Instituting Proceedings* (22 March 1955), *I.C.J. Pleadings*, *Aerial Incident of March 10th, 1953 (United States of America v. Czechoslovakia)*, 25–26, https://www.icj-cij.org/files/case-related/25/025-19550322-APP-1-00-BI.pdf, accessed 5 April 2020.

Czechoslovakia's refusal, the case was dismissed.[150] It was not just Cold War adversaries that disagreed over the submission of disputes to the ICJ. In 1956, the UK instituted proceedings against Argentina and Chile, arising from their competing claims to sovereignty over Antarctic and sub-Antarctic territories, and invited both to accept the Court's jurisdiction.[151] When Argentina and Chile refused to accept the UK invitation, the Court removed the two cases from the List.[152]

There is no doubt that these were not instances of default and that the States that refused the invitation to accept the Court's jurisdiction could not have been treated as parties to a case.[153] China is most certainly not in the same legal position in relation to the Arbitral Tribunal as Hungary, the USSR, Czechoslovakia, Argentina, and Chile before the ICJ in the above-mentioned instances, for the simple reason that China, by ratifying the Convention, had accepted the *compétence de la compétence* of courts and tribunals established under the Convention. When a State ratifies the Convention, it empowers a court or tribunal established under the Convention to open proceedings on the basis of a unilateral application by another State party to the Convention, before the existence of valid consent to the court or tribunal's jurisdiction has been admitted by the first State or ascertained by the court or tribunal.[154] This interpretation was confirmed by the Tribunal in the *"Arctic Sunrise" Arbitration*, which

[150] *Aerial Incident of March 10th, 1953 (United States of America v. Czechoslovakia). Order of March14, 1956: I.C.J. Reports 1956*, 6, https://www.icj-cij.org/files/case-related/25/025-19560314-ORD-01-00-BI.pdf, accessed 5 April 2020.

[151] United Kingdom, *Application Instituting Proceedings (United Kingdom v. Argentina)* (4 May 1955), *I.C.J., Pleadings, Antarctica Cases*, 36, para. 42, https://www.icj-cij.org/files/case-related/26/026-in19550504-APP-1-00-BI.pdf, accessed 5 April 2020; United Kingdom, *Application Instituting Proceedings (United Kingdom v. Chile)* (4 May 1955), *I.C.J., Pleadings, Antarctica Cases*, 73, para. 40, https://www.icj-cij.org/files/case-related/27/027-19550504-APP-1-00-BI.pdf, accessed 5 April 2020.

[152] *Antarctica Case (United Kingdom v. Argentina), Order of March 16th, 1956: I.C.J. Reports 1956*, 12, https://www.icj-cij.org/files/case-related/26/026-19560316-ORD-01-00-BI.pdf, accessed 5 April 2020; *Antarctica Case (United Kingdom v. Chile), Order of March 16th, 1956: I.C. J. Reports 1956*, 15, https://www.icj-cij.org/files/case-related/27/027-19560316-ORD-01-00-BI.pdf, accessed 5 April 2020.

[153] Observations of Mr. C. Amerasinghe, in Arangio-Ruiz, "Non-Appearance Final Report," 345.

[154] Arangio-Ruiz, "Notes," 16.

declared that the fact that a party may contest the Tribunal's jurisdiction is "not a basis on which it can frustrate the effective discharge of its functions by the Tribunal."[155]

It is precisely in a situation in which a respondent State contests an international court's jurisdiction that the *compétence de la compétence* is indispensable. The Philippines initiated arbitration because arbitration is deemed to be the mode of dispute settlement for States, such as the Philippines and China, that have not opted for one or more of the four modes of compulsory dispute settlement provided for under the Convention.[156] China affirmed that the Tribunal lacked jurisdiction; the Philippines on the contrary claimed that the Tribunal had jurisdiction. In this situation, as Commissioner Gore wrote in 1798, "[t]he opinion of one ought to weigh as much and no more than the opinion of the other." Why should greater weight be attached to one State's view that an international court lacks jurisdiction than the other State's view that the court does have jurisdiction? To concede the position of one over that of the other would be contrary to the sovereign equality of States. In proceedings before an international court, equal weight should be accorded to the views of both States.[157]

Of course, a State against whom proceedings are instituted has the right to challenge the jurisdiction of the international court concerned. At the ICJ, the classic method for challenging the Court's jurisdiction and/or the admissibility of a claim is through the raising of preliminary objections. If these are filed before a party has submitted its written pleadings, they suspend the proceedings on the merits until the challenge to jurisdiction and admissibility is dealt with.[158] Annex VII of the Convention contains no specific provisions establishing procedures to be

[155] *"Arctic Sunrise" Arbitration*, Award on the Merits, 368, para. 91.

[156] Ibid., Article 287(3).

[157] von Mangoldt, "Versäumnisverfahren," 514. Similarly, in the IDI commission on non-appearance before the ICJ, Torres Bernárdez stated that the unilateral arguments of one State on jurisdiction and admissibility do not have greater weight than the contrary unilateral arguments of another State. In this situation an international court has no alternative but to decide the dispute. Torres Bernárdez, "Non-Appearance," 362.

[158] Rosenne, *The Law and Practice*, vol. I, 805–06. Between 1946 and 2018, preliminary objections were raised in 47 out of 134 cases decided by the ICJ and were successful in approximately two-thirds of those cases. ICJ, *The International Court of Justice Handbook* (The Hague: International Court of Justice, 2019), 62, https://www.icj-cij.org/files/publications/handbook-of-the-court-en.pdf, accessed 7 September 2020.

adopted by arbitral tribunals on preliminary objections, but procedures for this purpose were established in the arbitral proceedings prior to the *South China Sea Arbitration* that were not transferred to the ITLOS or settled or terminated.[159] Similarly, a procedure for the filing of preliminary objections was laid down in the Rules of Procedure of the *South China Sea Arbitration*. The plea that the Tribunal lacked jurisdiction had to be raised at the latest by the time limit for the submission of China's *Counter-Memorial*. China's nomination of an arbitrator or its participation in the appointment of the other arbitrators would not have posed an obstacle to the filing of a preliminary objection.[160]

A State that professed to have respect for the Tribunal's jurisdiction, as China did in its Position Paper, would have filed a preliminary objection. In four arbitrations under Annex VII that were unilaterally initiated prior to 2013 and were not transferred to the ITLOS, settled, or terminated, preliminary objections were filed by the respondent State.[161] Instead of following the precedent set by these States, China, acting as a judge in its

[159] Not all of the Rules of Procedure of arbitrations under Annex VII have been published. All of those that have been published prior to the *South China Sea Arbitration* contain provisions on preliminary objections. *MOX Plant Case (Ireland v. United Kingdom)*, Rules of Procedure (25 October 2001), Article 11, 5, https://pcacases.com/web/sendAttach/848; *Guyana v. Suriname*, Rules of Procedure (24 February 2004), Article 10, 4–5, http://www.pcacases.com/web/sendAttach/882; *Barbados v. Trinidad and Tobago*, Rules of Procedure (23 August 2004), Article 10, 4, https://pcacases.com/web/sendAttach/1062; *Bay of Bengal Maritime Boundary Arbitration between Bangladesh and India*, Rules of Procedure (08 October 2009), Article 10, 7, http://www.pcacases.com/web/sendAttach/375; *Chagos Marine Protected Area Arbitration (Mauritius v. United Kingdom)*, Rules of Procedure (29 March 2012), Article 11, 6, https://pcacases.com/web/sendAttach/1567; and *The ARA Libertad Arbitration (Argentina v. Ghana)*, Rules of Procedure (31 July 2013), Article 13, 6–7, https://pcacases.com/web/sendAttach/427, all accessed 3 September 2020. Preliminary objections were filed in the *Southern Bluefin Tuna Case*, *Barbados v. Trinidad and Tobago*, *Guyana v. Suriname*, and the *Chagos Marine Protected Area Arbitration*. The preliminary objections were successful in the first case, were dismissed in the second and third cases, and were partially successful in the fourth case.

[160] *South China Sea Arbitration*, Rules of Procedure (27 August 2013), Article 20(2), https://pcacases.com/web/sendAttach/233, accessed 5 April 2020.

[161] These were the *Southern Bluefin Tuna Case between Australia and Japan and between New Zealand and Japan* (1998–2000), *Barbados v. Trinidad and Tobago Arbitration* (2004–2006), https://pca-cpa.org/en/cases/104/, *Guyana v. Suriname Arbitration* (2004–2007), https://pca-cpa.org/en/cases/9/, and the *Chagos Marine Protected Area Arbitration (Mauritius v. United Kingdom)* (2010–2015), https://pca-cpa.org/en/cases/11/, all accessed 3 September 2020.

own case, decided that the Arbitral Tribunal lacked jurisdiction to hear the Philippine claims. China's conduct reminds one of Pakistan's description of the legal position of India in the *Trial of Pakistani Prisoners of War* case. As Pakistan put it, a State that denies that an international court or tribunal lacks jurisdiction on the basis of its unilateral arguments is in effect arrogating to itself the functions of that court and purporting to determine jurisdictional issues that it is for the court or tribunal to determine. Such an attitude is "highly contemptuous" of the court or tribunal.[162] Regrettably, it seems that Yu Mincai was the only Chinese scholar willing to admit that it was the Arbitral Tribunal, and not China, that had the power to decide on the validity of China's claim that the Tribunal lacks jurisdiction.[163]

Another Chinese scholar attempted to explain China's default, including presumably its failure to file preliminary objections in the conditions laid down by the Rules of Procedure, by referring to the fear that notwithstanding China's position that the Tribunal lacked jurisdiction, the Tribunal might interpret its participation in the proceedings as acceptance of the Tribunal's jurisdiction under the principle of *forum prorogatum*.[164] A rapid overview of the issues raised by *forum prorogatum*, which cannot be discussed here at any length, should convince the reader that the explanation makes little sense. As already mentioned above, China had already conceded the Tribunal's power to determine its own jurisdiction as soon as it ratified the Convention. The Tribunal possessed that power, whether China defaulted or not.

Forum prorogatum is a summons to appear before an international court. It operates in a scenario in which a State initiates proceedings against another State at a time when the latter has not accepted the court's jurisdiction. The application is a mere invitation to the respondent State to accept the court's jurisdiction. If the invitation is accepted,

[162] First Public Sitting, 4 June 1973, *I.C.J. Pleadings*, *Trial of Pakistani Prisoners of War*, 26.

[163] Yu Mincai, "China's Responses to the Compulsory Arbitration on the South China Sea Dispute: Legal Effects and Policy Options," *Ocean Development and International Law* 45 (2014): 5.

[164] Yen-Chiang Chang, "China's Non-Participation Approach Toward the South China Sea Arbitration," *Chinese (Taiwan) Yearbook of International Law and Affairs* 34 (2016): 66. As we shall see in the following sub-section, it is possible for a defaulting State to file a preliminary objection.

then the court's jurisdiction is established. *Forum prorogatum* has been described as a form of jurisdiction based on an agreement between the parties after proceedings have been initiated.[165] The expression of consent is not subject to any particular form. It may be given explicitly, by means of an informal document, or it may be deduced from the conduct of the State invited to accept the court's jurisdiction.[166] A State that responds to the merits of a claim without making a reservation on the issue of jurisdiction is deemed to have consented to the jurisdiction of the international court.[167]

Cursory as this survey may be, it makes clear that there is no comparison possible between the legal position of a State that has been invited to accept the jurisdiction of an international court, on the one hand, and China in the *South China Sea Arbitration*, on the other. In the first scenario, the State has not accepted the jurisdiction of the court or tribunal at the time proceedings are initiated; in the second scenario, China, by virtue of being a State party to the Convention, has already accepted the power of courts or tribunals established under the Convention to determine their own jurisdiction. China's repeated protestations that its informal communications to the Tribunal do not constitute acceptance of or participation in the *Arbitration* do not change the legal situation or China's status as a party in any way. The real risk faced by China was not that appearance in the jurisdictional phase of the proceedings would be interpreted as acceptance of the Tribunal's jurisdiction. Rather it was that it would have been confronted with a dilemma had the Tribunal decided that it had jurisdiction to hear the case: should it continue to participate in the proceedings and risk an unfavorable decision on the merits? Or should it withdraw from the proceedings and risk additional opprobrium? As mentioned in Chapter 1, some Chinese scholars did advocate China's appearance in the jurisdictional phase, while reserving for itself the option to default in the event the Tribunal decided

[165] Rosenne, *The Law and Practice*, vol. II, 672–73.

[166] Ibid., 687; Mohammed Bedjaoui and Fatsah Ouguergouz, "Le forum prorogatum devant la Cour Internationale de Justice: Les ressources d'une institution ou la face cachée du consensualisme [Forum Prorogatum Before the International Court of Justice: The Resources of an Institution or the Hidden Face of Consensualism]," *African Yearbook of International Law* 5 (1997): 105.

[167] Sienho Yee, "Forum Prorogatum in the International Court," *GYIL* 42 (1999): 157.

that it had jurisdiction to hear the case.[168] China would have had to decide whether to follow the example of the US in the *Nicaragua Case*, when the US responded to the ICJ judgment on jurisdiction and admissibility by withdrawing from the proceedings.[169] China might have been subject to the same rebuke administered by the ICJ to the US following the latter's "disappearance" from the proceedings:

> Having taken part in the proceedings to argue that the Court lacked jurisdiction, the United States thereby acknowledged that the Court had the power to make a finding on its own jurisdiction to rule upon the merits. It is not possible to argue that the Court had jurisdiction only to declare that it lacked jurisdiction. In the normal course of events, for a party to appear before a court entails acceptance of the possibility of the court's finding against that party.[170]

The Philippines could also have insisted, as Nicaragua did at the ICJ, that appearance before the Tribunal was a duty once jurisdiction had been affirmed.

Consistently with its denial of the *compétence de la compétence*, China did not have recourse to the Tribunal to adjudicate its claim that the Philippine initiation of the proceedings was an abuse of the Convention's compulsory dispute settlement procedures. The Rules of Procedure had provided that a party may raise a plea that the Arbitral Tribunal was exceeding the scope of its authority, on condition that the plea is raised "as soon as the matter alleged to be beyond the scope" of the Tribunal's authority was raised during the proceedings.[171] One might ask whether the Tribunal would have been empowered under this provision to rule on

[168] Wim Muller, "China's Missed Opportunity in South China Sea Arbitration," *chathamhouse.org* (19 March 2015), https://www.chathamhouse.org/expert/comment/china-s-missed-opportunity-south-china-sea-arbitration, accessed 13 March 2020.

[169] "Text of US Statement on Withdrawal from Case before the World Court," *New York Times*, 19 January 1985, http://www.nytimes.com/1985/01/19/world/text-of-us-statement-on-withdrawal-from-case-before-the-world-court.html?pagewanted=all&pagewanted=print, accessed 13 March 2020.

[170] *Military and Paramilitary Activities in and Against Nicaragua (Nicaragua v. United States of America), Merits, Judgment, I.C.J. Reports 1986*, 23, para. 27, http://www.icj-cij.org/files/case-related/70/070-19860627-JUD-01-00-BI.pdf, accessed 17 March 2020.

[171] *South China Sea Arbitration*, Rules of Procedure, Article 20(2), 9.

China's allegation of abuse. We might surmise that this procedure was not entirely appropriate from China's perspective, considering that in China's view, the very initiation of the proceedings, and not a matter arising in the proceedings, constituted an abuse of rights.

The Tribunal itself interpreted China's claim of abuse with reference to Articles 294(1) (on preliminary proceedings) and 300 (relating to good faith and abuse of rights) of the Convention. Had China been serious about its profession of respect for the competence of courts and tribunals established under the Convention, it would have followed the procedure provided for in Article 294 of the Convention by requesting that the Tribunal examine its allegation. The Tribunal would then have given the parties a reasonable time within which to request that it determine whether the claim did indeed constitute an abuse of rights. In the event of a Chinese request, the Tribunal would have been obliged to rule on the plea. But China did not make any such request under Article 294 of the Convention; neither did China link its allegations of abuse to Article 300 of the Convention. China's failure to file a plea would not have prevented the Tribunal from determining, on its own initiative, whether or not the Philippine initiation of the *Arbitration* constituted an abuse of rights, but it declined to do so. The reason for this lay in the very serious consequences of such a ruling—the Tribunal would have been required to take no further action on the claim and the proceedings would have been discontinued.[172]

As China's default could not and did not deprive the Tribunal of the power to determine its own jurisdiction, the Tribunal decided to bifurcate the proceedings in order to examine the question of its jurisdiction.

B. Compétence de la Compétence *in Case of Default*

Article 20(3) and (4) of the Rules of Procedure of the *South China Sea Arbitration* provided that the Tribunal would rule on any objection relating to jurisdiction or admissibility as a preliminary matter, and for that purpose, would hold a hearing on jurisdiction or admissibility if the Tribunal determined that a hearing was necessary or useful, after seeking the parties' views. Article 25 of the Rules of Procedure did not prescribe the holding of a hearing on jurisdiction and admissibility in

[172] Award on Jurisdiction, 42–43, paras. 125–27.

the event of default. The Tribunal, invoking the practice of international courts and tribunals, decided to treat China's Position Paper and other informal communications as constituting a plea on the jurisdiction, i.e., as a preliminary objection, and to bifurcate the proceedings, suspending the proceedings on the merits of the Philippine claims. Taking into account the practical difficulties created by default for the parties to the case, the Tribunal exercised its procedural powers and organized the hearing with a view to addressing these difficulties.

1. Bifurcation of Proceedings in Case of Default

The term "bifurcation" is a neologism in the vocabulary of the law of the sea and indeed, of international law in general. It does not appear in the ICJ Statute, in the body of the Convention, or in any of its annexes; there is no mention of it in a dictionary of international law published in 2009.[173] Its use appears to be associated with the practice of some arbitral tribunals constituted under Annex VII of the Convention of "bifurcating," in the sense of splitting proceedings into a preliminary phase concerning jurisdiction and admissibility and the phase on the merits. It might seem anachronistic to use it retrospectively to refer to the practice of the ICJ, in whose case law the term does not appear. Yet it is a convenient term to designate the procedural response of international courts and tribunals to default. Given that this practice seems to be well-established, it remains to explain the opposition of the Philippines to bifurcation.

Until the 1970s the ICJ had no consistent procedural response to default. This may in part be explained by the circumstances of each case. In the *Corfu Channel Case*, the respondent, Albania, appeared in the first two phases of the proceedings and refused to appear only in the third phase. In the *Anglo-Iranian Oil Co. Case*, the ICJ, while acknowledging the first Iranian telegram challenging its jurisdiction, continued the written proceedings on the merits of the UK claims.[174] It was the

[173] One searches for it in vain in John P. Grant and J. Craig Barker, *Parry & Grant Encyclopaedic Dictionary of International Law* (3rd ed.; Oxford: Oxford University Press, 2009).

[174] Communication from the Minister of Foreign Affairs of Iran to the President of the International Court of Justice, dated 29 June 1951, with Three Annexes, *I.C.J. Pleadings, Anglo-Iranian Oil Co. Case (United Kingdom v. Iran)*, 679, https://www.icj-cij.org/files/case-related/16/8987.pdf, accessed 19 March 2020; *Anglo-Iranian Oil Co.*

Iranian explanation in "Preliminary Observations" of Iran's refusal to recognize the Court's jurisdiction that prompted the Court to suspend the proceedings on the merits, to request a UK response to what was in effect a preliminary objection from Iran, and to organize a hearing on jurisdiction.[175] In the *Nottebohm Case*, the applicant State, Liechtenstein, considered as a preliminary objection a letter from Guatemala, dated 9 September 1952, in which the latter argued, among others, that the Court no longer had jurisdiction to hear the case because its acceptance of the Court's compulsory jurisdiction had already expired. Thereupon the Court suspended the proceedings on the merits and decided to hold a hearing on jurisdiction. On the eve of the hearing, Guatemala requested that it be postponed or, if a postponement were not possible, that its letter be considered a preliminary objection.[176]

The practice of holding a separate hearing on jurisdiction in the event of default can be traced to the two *Fisheries Jurisdiction Cases* of 1972–1974, between Iceland, on the one hand, and the UK and the FRG, on the other. The Court, on the basis of a letter from Iceland, decided to suspend on its initiative the proceedings on the merits, to examine first of all questions of jurisdiction and admissibility, and to ask the UK and the Federal Republic to confine their first submissions to these questions as if a preliminary objection had been filed by Iceland. Under the Rules of Court in force at the time, only Iceland could have initiated a phase devoted to preliminary objections and the objection could only have been filed following the submission of the UK and FRG Memorials.[177] Despite the procedural irregularity, the Court's Orders were

Case, Order of July 5th, 1951: I.C.J. Reports 1951, 100–01, https://www.icj-cij.org/files/case-related/16/016-19510705-ORD-01-00-BI.pdf, accessed 6 April 2020.

175 "Observations préliminaires: Refus du Gouvernement impérial de reconnaître la compétence de la Cour [Preliminary Observations: Refusal by the Imperial Government to Accept the Jurisdiction of the Court]," (4 February 1952), *I.C.J. Pleadings, Anglo-Iranian Oil Co. Case*, 281–319, https://www.icj-cij.org/files/case-related/16/10980.pdf, accessed 6 April 2020; *Anglo-Iranian Oil Co. Case (Jurisdiction), Judgment of July 22, 1952: I.C.J. Reports 1952*, 93, https://www.icj-cij.org/files/case-related/16/016-19520722-JUD-01-00-BI.pdf, accessed 19 March 2020. In the end the Court declared that it lacked jurisdiction to hear the case.

176 *Nottebohm Case (Preliminary Objection), Judgment*, 114–17.

177 *Fisheries Jurisdiction (Federal Republic of Germany v. Iceland), Order of 18 August 1972, I.C.J. Reports 1972*, 188, https://www.icj-cij.org/files/case-related/56/056-19720818-ORD-01-00-BI.pdf, accessed 7 April 2020; *Fisheries Jurisdiction (United Kingdom*

justified by one commentator as being in conformity with the spirit of the reform of the ICJ Rules, the purposes of which were to avoid as much as possible repetition of the same arguments on the merits in the jurisdictional and merits phases and to oblige the Court to rule on its jurisdiction as a preliminary matter. The Orders began to define a procedure that the Rules of Court had not established.[178] The Court adopted the same approach in three subsequent cases of default—the two *Nuclear Tests Cases* (1973–1974) and the *Aegean Sea Continental Shelf Case* (1976–1978). A notable exception was the *United States Diplomatic and Consular Staff Case* (1979–1980), in which the Court did not institute a separate preliminary phase and considered preliminary objections and the merits in a single phase.[179] The Court's approach may have been prompted by the urgency of the case. Following the *Nicaragua Case*, the Court adopted the practice of bifurcation in cases where both parties appeared before it. Since the 2000 reform of the Rules of Court, the Court is authorized by Article 79(2), after receipt of the application instituting proceedings and in consultation with the parties, to decide separately questions of jurisdiction and admissibility.[180]

The practice of international courts and tribunals was invoked by the *South China Sea* Tribunal when it decided to hold a separate hearing

v. Iceland), Order of 18 August 1972, I.C.J. Reports 1972, 181, https://www.icj-cij.org/files/case-related/55/055-19720818-ORD-01-00-BI.pdf, accessed 7 April 2020.

[178] Louis Favoreu, "Les ordonnances des 17 et 18 août 1972 dans les affaires relatives à la compétence en matière de pêcheries - Contribution au droit procédural de la Cour en matière de mesures conservatoires, exceptions préliminaires et compétence en cas de défaut (Royaume-Uni c. Islande et République fédérale d'Allemagne c. Islande) [The Orders of 17 and 18 August 1972 in the Cases Relating to Fisheries Jurisdiction – Contribution to the Procedural Law of the Court with Respect to Provisional Measures, Preliminary Objections and Jurisdiction in case of Default (United Kingdom v. Iceland and Federal Republic of Germany v. Iceland]," *AFDI* 18 (1972): 315–18, 322, http://www.persee.fr/doc/afdi_0066-3085_1972_num_18_1_3855, accessed 7 April 2020.

[179] Fitzmaurice, "The Problem," 114.

[180] ICJ, *Rules of Court (1978) adopted on 14 April 1978 and entered into force on 1 July 1978*, https://www.icj-cij.org/en/rules, accessed 22 March 2020. On the most recent reform of the Rules, see Santiago Torres Bernárdez, "La modification des articles du règlement de la Cour internationale de Justice relatifs aux exceptions préliminaires et aux demandes reconventionnelles [The Modification of the Articles of the Rules of the International Court of Justice on Preliminary Objections and Counterclaims]," *AFDI* 49 (2003): 207–47, https://www.persee.fr/docAsPDF/afdi_0066-3085_2003_num_49_1_3750.pdf, accessed 7 April 2020.

on jurisdiction and admissibility.[181] There was no need to invoke the ICJ practice in the Procedural Order bifurcating the proceedings in the *"Arctic Sunrise" Arbitration*, the only other Annex VII arbitration in which the respondent State also defaulted. The appearing State, the Netherlands, had relayed to the Tribunal its view that Russia's refusal to accept the *Arbitration*, signified in its Note Verbale of 22 October 2013, constituted a plea on jurisdiction.[182] In its *Memorial*, submitted in August 2014, the Netherlands requested that the Tribunal bifurcate the proceedings, in the hope that Russia would reconsider its position and participate in the proceedings.[183] This hope was encouraged by the observation that Russia had initiated proceedings in one case and participated in two proceedings before the ITLOS as well as appeared in one proceeding before the ICJ. It would have been "in line" with its own practice if Russia had appeared before the Annex VII Tribunal in order to challenge its jurisdiction.[184] After consulting Russia on the Netherlands request and failing to elicit a response from it, the *"Arctic Sunrise"* Tribunal decided to bifurcate the proceedings and to rule on the plea on jurisdiction as a preliminary question, but without holding a hearing.[185]

The position of the Philippines in the *South China Sea Arbitration* contrasted with that of the Netherlands in the *"Arctic Sunrise" Arbitration*. In its *Memorial*, the Philippines had not explicitly addressed the issue of bifurcation. Nevertheless, upon its submission, the Philippine Solicitor-General explained to the press the Philippine preference for a single award on both jurisdiction and on the merits, with no bifurcation of the proceedings. The desire to avoid bifurcation was said to be reflected in the structure of the *Memorial*, which tackled jurisdictional issues after—rather than before—discussing the merits. This manner of proceeding was justified on tactical grounds:

181 *South China Sea Arbitration*, Procedural Order No. 4 (21 April 2015), https://pcacases.com/web/sendAttach/1807, accessed 7 April 2020.

182 *The "Arctic Sunrise" Arbitration (Netherlands v. Russia)*, Procedural Order No. 4 (Bifurcation) (21 November 2014), https://pcacases.com/web/sendAttach/1324, accessed 15 January 2020.

183 *The "Arctic Sunrise" Arbitration (Netherlands v. Russia)*, *Memorial of the Kingdom of the Netherlands* (31 August 2014), 23, para. 59, https://pcacases.com/web/sendAttach/1406, accessed 7 April 2020.

184 Ibid., 17–18, paras. 45–48.

185 Ibid., Procedural Order No. 4.

> If you have a very strong case, you do not talk about jurisdiction....You go to [sic] straight to the case....[If] you convince the judges that you're strong on the merits and our claim is just, then the issue of jurisdiction will be folded in as a win on the merits....While ordinarily you go first for the question of jurisdiction, in the particular circumstances of the case, the legal team decided that we propose - and we were allowed – to discuss jurisdiction and merits at the same time.[186]

Responding to an inquiry from the Tribunal following the receipt of China's Position Paper, the Philippines declared that bifurcation would be "neither appropriate or [sic] desirable." It explained that

> [T]he jurisdictional issues in the case between the Philippines and China are plainly interwoven with the merits. The issues raised by the jurisdictional objections identified by China in its Position Paper depend 'in significant measure [on] the same facts and arguments on which the merits of the case depend.' They therefore do not possess an exclusively preliminary character, making bifurcation inappropriate.[187]

For example, the Philippines noted that the exclusion from the Tribunal's jurisdiction of disputes that related to historic bays and titles under Article 298(1) of the Convention would turn on "the scope of the phrase 'historic titles' in Article 298, and... the nature of China's claims," both of which "can only be decided by reference to the substance of China's claim."[188] Similarly, the Philippines commented that questions about Article 297(1), relating to the coastal State's exercise of its sovereign rights or jurisdiction in its exclusive economic zone ("EEZ"), could only be answered, "in light of the specific nature of China's environmentally harmful conduct in the South China Sea."[189] Questions

[186] Esmaquel Paterno II, "PH Faces Major Hurdle in China case," *Rappler*, 12 March 2014, http://www.rappler.com/nation/52764-philippines-china-arbitral-tribunal-jurisdiction, accessed 8 April 2020.

[187] *South China Sea Arbitration*, Procedural Order No. 4, 4.

[188] Philippine Submissions No. 1 and 2 claimed that China's claims to "historic rights" in the South China, embodied in the "nine-dash line," were contrary to the Convention. Award of 12 July 2016, 41, para. 112, B(1) and (2).

[189] Philippine Submissions No. 11 and 12(b) alleged that China had violated its obligations under the Convention to protect and preserve the marine environment in the South China Sea by failing to prevent its fishers from harvesting endangered species and using

about Article 298(1)(b), concerning the exceptions for military activities and for certain law enforcement activities, could only be answered, "in light of the character of China's relevant conduct as either military or non-military in nature."[190] According to the Philippines, such questions could only be assessed in light of the merits of the Philippine claims and consequently lacked an exclusively preliminary nature. As to the "core jurisdictional contentions" in China's Position Paper, the Philippines observed that whether its claims "truly implicate questions of territorial sovereignty and/or maritime delimitation... can only be decided by reference to the nature and substance of the claims of the Philippines on the merits."[191]

A second reason for the Philippine opposition to bifurcation was that it would "needlessly prolong, and increase the costs of, these proceedings when they are already at an advanced stage."[192] If the jurisdictional issues were indeed plainly interwoven with the merits, then a hearing on jurisdiction might simply end up concluding that the preliminary objections could not be decided at that stage and would have to be considered together with the merits, resulting in the prolongation of the proceedings and additional costs.[193] The consideration of costs was all the more crucial for the Philippines, which had to shoulder not only its share of the costs but also that of China. No official figures are available of the actual costs, but one may obtain an idea by consulting the documents of the *"Arctic Sunrise" Arbitration*. Following the constitution of the Tribunal in February 2014 and prior to its first meeting in March 2014, the Netherlands and Russia were each asked to deposit €150,000 as advances for the costs of arbitration. When Russia refused to pay its share,

destructive fishing techniques, as well as by engaging in island-building." Ibid., 41–42, para. 112, B(11) and (12)(b).

190 Under Submission No. 13, the Philippines argued that China had operated its law enforcement vessels in the waters around Scarborough Shoal in a dangerous manner, causing a serious risk of collision with Philippine vessels. Ibid., 42, para. 112, B(13).

191 Ibid., Award on Jurisdiction, 137–38, para. 387. China had argued in the Position Paper that the Philippine Submissions implied or entailed decisions on questions of territorial sovereignty or maritime delimitation, which may be excluded by a State party from compulsory dispute settlement under Article 298(1)(a)(i) of the Convention.

192 Ibid., Procedural Order No. 4, 4.

193 On this point, see counsel for Mauritius in *Chagos Marine Protected Area Arbitration (Mauritius v. United Kingdom)*, Bifurcation Hearing Transcript (11 January 2013), 71–72, https://pcacases.com/web/sendAttach/1564, accessed 14 January 2020.

the Netherlands had to pay the outstanding amount of €150,000.[194] In all, the Netherlands and Russia were requested to make advances on three occasions, and on each occasion, the Netherlands paid for the Russian share.[195] It is not clear whether the amount of the advances was the same on each occasion, but it is clear that the total cost of the *Arbitration* for the Netherlands would have exceeded the cost of the advances, which did not include the costs incurred by the Netherlands for its legal counsel and other matters.

The third reason was the deterioration of the situation in the South China Sea as a result of China's actions:

> [T]he interests of the sound administration of justice would best be served by timely action by the Tribunal and the avoidance of unnecessary delays. The Philippines has previously made known China's increasingly assertive and expansive actions in the South China Sea, including its impeding the resupply of Philippine personnel at Second Thomas Shoal and its undertaking large-scale land reclamation activities with several [sic] environmental consequences. A prompt ruling by the Tribunal would allow future actions and dialogue in the region to take place against the backdrop of an authoritative determination of entitlements and constraints.[196]

The actions of China alluded to by the Philippines were the object of Philippine Submissions No. 14(b) (on the aggravation and extension of the dispute by preventing the rotation and resupply of Philippine personnel stationed at Second Thomas Shoal), No. 11 (on the violation of obligations to protect and preserve the marine environment at Scarborough Shoal and Second Thomas Shoal), and 12(b) (on the violation of duties to protect and preserve the marine environment through occupation and construction activities on Mischief Reef). China's actions had already prompted Philippine expressions of concern to the Tribunal on 18 March and 7 April 2014 (concerning Submission No. 14(b)) and on 30 July 2014 (regarding Submissions No. 11 and 12(b)).[197]

[194] *"Arctic Sunrise" (Kingdom of the Netherlands v. Russian Federation)*, Award on Jurisdiction (26 November 2014), 6, paras. 30–31, https://pcacases.com/web/sendAttach/1325, accessed 8 April 2020.

[195] *The "Arctic Sunrise" Arbitration*, Award on the Merits, 13, para. 69.

[196] *South China Sea Arbitration*, Procedural Order No. 4, 4.

[197] Ibid., Award on Jurisdiction and Admissibility, 18–20, paras. 44, 46, 53.

The first two reasons given by the Philippines to support its opposition to bifurcation were similar to reasons given by States that opposed bifurcation in the *Guyana v. Suriname Arbitration* regarding the delimitation of their maritime boundary (2004–2007) and the *Chagos Marine Protected Area Arbitration* (Mauritius v. UK) concerning the UK's establishment of a Marine Protected Area around the Chagos Archipelago (2010–2015). No default had occurred in either case. In each, the respondent filed preliminary objections and requested a bifurcation of the proceedings. The Rules of Procedure of the *Guyana v. Suriname Arbitration* did not establish a procedure for dealing with a request for bifurcation, but those of the *Chagos Marine Protected Area Arbitration* provided that if the UK wished a preliminary objection to be dealt with as a preliminary matter, it should indicate whether it sought a separate hearing on the question of bifurcation.[198] In other words, a request for bifurcation would not automatically result in a bifurcation of the proceedings but in the holding of a hearing to decide whether the proceedings would be bifurcated. Such "mini-proceedings," as Zhang Xinjung calls them, were indeed held in both cases.[199] In each case, the hearing devoted to the issue of bifurcation lasted for only one day, given that the purpose was not to discuss the issues of jurisdiction and admissibility themselves. In both cases, the reasons adduced against bifurcation were identical to the reasons given by the Philippines. In both cases, the Tribunal rejected the request for bifurcation.

The precedents of these two Annex VII arbitrations cited by the Philippines were not sufficiently convincing to override the ICJ precedent invoked by the Tribunal. In our view, the decisive factor in the Tribunal's reasoning was China's default. In the two arbitrations cited, it was possible to settle the difference of opinion between the parties by holding a hearing to examine the question of whether the proceedings should be bifurcated. In the *South China Sea Arbitration*, China's default made such an approach impossible. A second consideration might have

[198] *Chagos Marine Protected Area Arbitration (Mauritius v. United Kingdom)*, Rules of Procedure (29 March 2012), 6, Art. 11(4), https://pcacases.com/web/sendAttach/1567, accessed 14 January 2020.

[199] Xinjun Zhang, "Bifurcation in Inter-State Cases," *University of Pennsylvania Journal of International Law* 40 (2018–2019): 962, https://scholarship.law.upenn.edu/cgi/viewcontent.cgi?article=1991&context=jil, accessed 24 October 2019. For *Guyana v. Suriname*, see Hearing Transcripts, Day 2 (8 July 2005), https://pcacases.com/web/sendAttach/890, accessed 7 April 2020.

been the sheer number and breadth of issues covered in the Philippine Submissions as well as in China's Position Paper. In the *"Arctic Sunrise" Arbitration*, Russia founded its objection to jurisdiction on a Russian declaration made upon ratification of the Convention, which related to only one provision of the latter, Article 298(1)(b).[200] This fact considerably limited the scope of the matters that the Tribunal had to consider as preliminary questions. This was not the case with China's Position Paper; and even if the Position Paper did not raise preliminary objections to certain Philippine Submissions, such as Nos. 11, 12(b), and 14, referred to above, the Tribunal still was under an obligation to examine possible objections to them.

The bifurcation of the proceedings compelled the Philippines to reverse its position on the Tribunal's jurisdiction and on the admissibility of its claims. At the Hearing on Jurisdiction, the Philippines now argued that there was no need to defer any question of jurisdiction for further consideration with the merits and that all issues of jurisdiction argued during the Hearing "could and should be resolved" at that stage of the proceedings.[201] The Tribunal did not fail to note the inconsistency but considered the latter view to represent the position of the Philippines.[202]

In the organization of the hearing on jurisdiction, the Tribunal had recourse to its procedural powers in order to alleviate some of the practical consequences of default for both the appearing and defaulting States.

2. The Organization of the Hearing on Jurisdiction and Admissibility and the Practical Consequences of Default

The Tribunal accepted several Philippine proposals for the organization of the hearing that were intended to address the practical consequences of China's default for the appearing State. At the same time, the Tribunal, through the exercise of its procedural powers, sought to ensure that China would not be disadvantaged by its default by refusing the Philippine proposal to limit the Hearing's scope and considering objections to a

[200] Note Verbale from the Russian Federation to the PCA dated 27 February 2014, https://pcacases.com/web/sendAttach/1315, accessed 10 March 2020; *"Arctic Sunrise" Arbitration*, Award on Jurisdiction, 8–10, paras. 51–58.

[201] *South China Sea Arbitration*, Hearing on Jurisdiction and Admissibility, Transcript, Day 3 (13 July 2015), 27–28, https://pcacases.com/web/sendAttach/1401, accessed 8 April 2020; Award on Jurisdiction, 138, para. 388.

[202] Ibid., Award on Jurisdiction, 138, para. 389.

jurisdiction that China had not raised; in so doing the Tribunal was acting as China's de facto counsel.

It may be recalled that one of the difficulties identified by the Philippines, like other appearing States in cases before the ICJ, was that it would be "in the position of having to guess what China's arguments might be and formulate arguments for both States."[203] In proceedings in which both parties appear, each would have had the opportunity to become familiar with the other's arguments and evidence by the time of the oral proceedings. Each would then be able to concentrate in its oral arguments on the issues that still divided them[204] and to focus "on those points which have been raised by one party at the stage of written proceedings but which have not so far been adequately addressed by the other, as well as on those which each party wishes to emphasize by way of winding up its arguments."[205] At the ICJ, the parties are urged "not to go over the whole ground covered by the [written] pleadings, or merely repeat the facts and arguments these contain"[206] during the oral hearings. To be sure, China had transmitted a Position Paper to the Tribunal, but the Position and Paper could not be compared to a fully argued Counter-Memorial. In conformity with Article 25(2) of the Rules of Procedure, which will be explained in greater detail in the next Chapter, the Tribunal then requested a supplemental written submission from the Philippines ("*SWSP*"), to address questions that in the Tribunal's view had not been sufficiently canvassed or had not been canvassed at all by the Philippines. Upon receipt of the *SWSP* on 16 March 2015, China was given three months within which to respond. Unsurprisingly, no response was forthcoming. In the absence of comments or observations from China, the Philippines would have been hard-pressed to prepare its oral presentations. During the hearings themselves, China's default meant that the Philippines ran the risk of repeating its arguments in the Hearing's second round when the two parties normally would have responded to each other's initial presentations.

[203] *MP*, 231, vol. I, para. 7.42.

[204] ICJ, *Rules of Court*, Article 60(1).

[205] Ibid., *Practice Directions (as amended on 20 January 2009 and 21 March 2013)*, https://www.icj-cij.org/en/practice-directions, accessed 8 April 2020.

[206] ICJ, *Rules of Court*, Article 60(1).

The Tribunal, basing itself on a series of Philippine proposals and exercising its powers under Article 25(2) of the Rules of Procedure to take whatever steps it may consider necessary to afford each party the full opportunity to present its case, decided that the hearing on jurisdiction and admissibility would consist of two rounds. Two weeks prior to the first round the Tribunal indicated to the Philippines any points or issues that it wished the Philippines especially to address, or on which it considered that there had not been a sufficient argument from it. After the first round of its oral arguments, the Tribunal agreed to consider presenting the Philippines with a further set of questions or topics on which the Philippines could make submissions during a second round.[207]

The Tribunal's positive reception of the Philippine procedural suggestions was remarkable if one recalls that the ICJ has been criticized for its unawareness of or indifference to the practical consequences of default for the appearing State.[208] The Tribunal's questions, transmitted to China and the Philippines in June 2016, undoubtedly assisted the Philippines in identifying the issues "that still divide[d] the Parties" and saved it from the danger of repeating in the oral hearings the facts and arguments that had already been covered in the *Memorial* and the *SWSP*. The Tribunal made clear that this procedure would not prevent it or individual members from raising further questions during the Hearing.[209]

During the first round of the Hearing (7–8 July 2016), the Philippines made its oral statements and responded to the questions raised by the Tribunal two weeks previously as well as to questions by individual judges. On 9 July, the Tribunal met to formulate further questions to be addressed the Philippines, whose team then had three days (including a weekend) in which to prepare its responses. The latter were presented to the Tribunal during the second round. The Tribunal's questions took the place of counter-arguments that the respondent State might have put forward if it had appeared before the Tribunal. In the circumstances of default, the Tribunal was in effect carrying out the critical analysis of Philippine arguments in China's place. Yet the procedure also enabled the

[207] *South China Sea Arbitration*, Procedural Order No. 4, 4. Unfortunately, the text of the Letter is not publicly available.

[208] Fitzmaurice, "The Problem," 91.

[209] *South China Sea Arbitration*, Procedural Order No. 4, 6.

Philippines, through its responses to the Tribunal's questions, to formulate the equivalent of rebuttals of the respondent's arguments that would normally have been delivered in a second round. Evidently, these procedural innovations proved to be satisfactory for the Tribunal and for the Philippines, for they were again implemented during the Hearing on the Merits.

One Philippine proposal that was not accepted by the Tribunal would have limited the Hearing's scope to that of China's Position Paper. The latter, according to the Philippines, did not deny that there existed a dispute over China's claims to historic rights; that China was not claiming "historic titles" over any maritime areas in the South China Sea; that the optional exception for "historic bays and titles" provided for in Article 298(1)(a)(i) of the Convention did not apply to Philippine claims that there was a dispute over the extent of potential entitlements of maritime features; and that the optional exceptions for law enforcement and military activities provided for in Article 298(1)(c) did not apply to Philippine claims.[210] The Tribunal was aware that if it accepted the Philippine proposal, it might not be able to fulfill its obligation under Article 9 of Annex VII to satisfy itself that it had jurisdiction over the dispute. Consequently, the Tribunal ruled that it would consider other possible issues of jurisdiction and admissibility even if they were not raised in China's Position Paper.[211] As a result, the Philippines failed in its effort to exclude several important issues from the Hearing on Jurisdiction. The Tribunal's decision was obviously to the advantage of the defaulting State and increased the burden (not to mention the cost) of preparation for the Hearing on the part of the appearing State.

The Tribunal's interpretation of its duty under Article 9 of Annex VII may be traced to the *Fisheries Jurisdiction Cases* before the ICJ, the first in which the respondent State defaulted throughout the entire proceedings. The Court declared that in examining its own jurisdiction and in fulfillment of its duty under Article 53 of the Statute, it would consider

[210] Ibid., 5.

[211] Ibid., 6, para. 1.4; Hearing on Jurisdiction and Admissibility, Transcript, Day 1 (7 July 2015), 3, https://pcacases.com/web/sendAttach/1399, accessed 19 March 2020.

objections that the defaulting State might raise against the Court's jurisdiction.[212] The Court first examined the Exchange of Notes between the Federal Republic of Germany and Iceland and between the UK and Iceland, concluding that the dispute submitted by the Applicants fell exactly within the terms of the compromissory clause contained in the two Exchanges of Notes. Normally, the text of a treaty would have been an adequate basis for a determination of the Court's jurisdiction. Because of the "particular circumstances of the proceedings "—Iceland's default—the Court not only considered all of Iceland's arguments, it also reconstituted the arguments that Iceland would have presented if it had appeared.[213] It successively reviewed the history of the negotiations; considered the possibility that the negotiations for the Exchanges of Notes took place under some kind of pressure from the UK and the FRG; examined the argument that undertakings for judicial settlement are subject to unilateral denunciation; and analyzed the argument that the agreement was no longer applicable owing to a fundamental change of circumstances.[214]

At the time, the ICJ approach to the question of its jurisdiction in case of default attracted some criticism. According to Favoreu, the Court, in its effort to re-establish the equality of the parties, adopted a more rigorous approach than if Iceland had appeared. He believed that the Court was not obliged to act as if a preliminary objection had been duly filed by Iceland.[215] Fitzmaurice was even more severe, arguing that the Court placed Iceland in a better position than if it had appeared. He feared

212 *Fisheries Jurisdiction (United Kingdom v. Iceland), Jurisdiction of the Court, Judgment, I.C.J. Reports 1973*, 8, para. 12, http://www.icj-cij.org/files/case-related/55/055-19730202-JUD-01-00-BI.pdf, accessed 4 September 2020; *Fisheries Jurisdiction (Federal Republic of Germany v. Iceland), Jurisdiction of the Court, Judgment, I.C.J. Reports 1973*, 54, para. 13, http://www.icj-cij.org/files/case-related/56/056-19730202-JUD-01-00-EN.pdf, accessed 4 September 2020.

213 Louis Favoreu, "L'arrêt de la Cour internationale de Justice dans l'affaire de la compétence en matière de pêcheries (Royaume-Uni c./Islande et Allemagne fédérale c./Islande) [The Judgment of the International Court of Justice in the Case Concerning Fisheries Jurisdiction (United Kingdom v. Iceland and Federal Republic of Germany v. Iceland]," *AFDI* 19 (1973): 276, http://www.persee.fr/doc/afdi_0066-3085_1973_num_19_1_2214, accessed 4 September 2020.

214 *Fisheries Jurisdiction (United Kingdom v. Iceland), Jurisdiction of the Court, Judgment*, 10–21, paras. 20–44; *Fisheries Jurisdiction (Federal Republic of Germany v. Iceland), Jurisdiction of the Court, Judgment*, 56–66, paras. 19–44.

215 Favoreu, "L'arrêt," 276, 278.

that the Court's approach sent the message that the Court would do the defaulting State's work for it and in this way indirectly encouraged further default.[216] Whether or not it was aware of the scholarly criticism, the Court adopted the same approach to examining its jurisdiction in other cases of default. As we have seen, in the *United States Diplomatic and Consular Staff in Tehran Case*, the Court considered the possibility that the creation of a UN fact-finding commission could affect its jurisdiction, a possibility that Iran had never raised in its telegrams to the Court. It may now be taken as a settled practice that in case of default, an international court will consider all possible objections to jurisdiction, including those that the defaulting State might never have formulated if it had appeared. The risk is that this protection of the defaulting State might erode the protection that the appearing State enjoys (or should) enjoy under the Court's rules.[217]

The steps that the *South China Sea* Tribunal took to protect the defaulting State during the Hearing on Jurisdiction were ignored by China and the CSIL. The latter distracts attention from these steps by criticizing another procedural decision of the Tribunal, that which allowed representatives from Indonesia, Japan, Malaysia, Thailand, and Vietnam to attend the Hearing as observers.[218] The attendance of observers could be construed as contrary to China's interests, for two reasons. First, most of the observers were States that had territorial or maritime disputes with China, either in the East China Sea or in the South China Sea. For this reason, China undoubtedly feared that they would not be well-disposed toward China's legal positions in the *South China Sea Arbitration*. Second, their presence at the Hearings implicitly acknowledged and confirmed the legality of the proceedings, contradicting China's official position that initiation by the Philippines of the proceedings was illegal and an abuse of the compulsory dispute settlement procedures of the Convention. The Philippines believed that the observers' presence

216 Fitzmaurice, "The Problem," 108–09, 117.

217 D.P. O'Connell, Fifth Public Sitting, 9 October 1978, *I.C.J. Pleadings*, *Aegean Sea Continental Shelf*, 318, https://www.icj-cij.org/files/case-related/62/062-19781009-ORA-01-00-BI.pdf, accessed 20 March 2020.

218 Award on Jurisdiction, 27, 29–30, paras. 80, 84, 86, Following the precedent of the Hearing on Jurisdiction, representatives from Australia, Indonesia, Japan, Malaysia, Singapore, and Thailand were permitted to attend the Hearing on the Merits as observers. Award of 12 July 2016, 21, 22, 23, 24–25, paras. 61, 63, 65–68, and 70.

> demonstrated the vital importance of these issues to the region, and indeed to the 1982 Convention and the international rule of law. This case is not just between the Philippines and China; it is about everyone who has coasts facing on to the South China Sea. It is about respect for the integrity of the Convention itself.[219]

Careful analysis of the Tribunal's ruling would have revealed that the Tribunal had taken steps to ensure that China, whether it decided to appear before the Tribunal or not, would at the very least have been spared embarrassment. First, the possibility of attendance as observers was limited to States who made a written request to that effect.[220] The Philippines had been of the view that the Hearing should be open to the public.[221] In the Philippine mind, the public probably would have included, in addition to academics and journalists, those who had suffered from the Chinese acts of which the Philippines complained, notably the fishermen who had been prevented from fishing at Mischief Reef since 1995 (Submission No. 8), at Second Thomas Shoal since 1995 (Submission No. 8) and at Scarborough Shoal since 2012 (Submission No. 10), as well as the owners of *M/V Veritas Voyager*, a Singaporean-flagged seismic survey vessel conducting surveys at Reed Bank that was the target of aggressive maneuvers by China Marine Surveillance ("CMS") vessels (Submission No. 8), and perhaps even NGOs.[222] It cannot be excluded that attendance of these non-State actors would have been accompanied by press conferences and demonstrations against China. If anything, the CSIL should have been grateful that the Tribunal restricted the public to State representatives.[223] Second, unlike observers at meetings of international organizations and at international conferences, the observers were not permitted to make statements. The Tribunal explicitly reminded the

[219] *South China Sea Arbitration*, Hearing on Jurisdiction and Admissibility, Transcript, Day 3, 79.

[220] Ibid., Award on Jurisdiction, 25, para. 74.

[221] Ibid., 25, para. 71.

[222] *South China Sea Arbitration*, Award of 12 July 2016, 261–86, 299–318, paras. 649–716, 758–814.

[223] For the Hearing on the Merits, another criterion was adopted: the status of the putative observer as a States party to the Convention. This criterion justified the Tribunal's denial of the US request to attend the Hearing, despite the fact that the Philippines had no objection to the request and indeed, would probably have welcomed US attendance at the Hearing. Award of 12 July 2016, 22–23, paras. 65–68.

observers, almost all of which had territorial and/or maritime disputes with China, that "their role would be to watch and listen, not to make statements."[224]

Notwithstanding these restrictions on the attendance of observers, the CSIL criticized the Tribunal for ignoring China's omnibus objection to all procedural steps, which encompassed provision for the attendance of observers; raising the matter on its own initiative; not offering any reasons for the decision; not offering precedents for the decision; and doing violence to the fundamental principle of party autonomy and party privacy in inter-State arbitral proceedings."[225]

The first three criticisms can be readily dismissed. China's omnibus objection to procedural steps in fact covered the entire *Arbitration*; taking it into account would have paralyzed the proceedings and violated the right of the Philippines to a continuation of the proceedings. It was the Philippines, not the Tribunal, that had raised the issue of the participation of the observers, and the Philippines had given transparency and public access to information as the reasons for its request. The fact that third States, the media, and the public requested copies of documents, beginning with the Rules of Procedure and extending to the Philippine *Memorial*, well before the case was ready for hearing, is ample proof of interest in the proceedings in the region and beyond.[226] For example, Vietnam had requested a copy of the *Memorial* and of Procedural Order No. 3, in which the Tribunal requested further written arguments from the Philippines, shortly after these documents had become available.[227] It is true that neither the Philippines nor the Tribunal offered precedents for the decision, yet this omission did not necessarily mean that the attendance of observers violated some fundamental principle of arbitral practice, let alone a rule of international law.

The CSIL's allegation that there exists a fundamental principle of privacy in arbitral proceedings is more than doubtful. Alexandre Merignhac wrote over 125 years ago that it was for an arbitral tribunal to decide if the proceedings were to take place in public or behind closed doors. Publicity was "undoubtedly" always preferable "in principle," as it

[224] Ibid., Award on Jurisdiction, 27, para. 84.

[225] CSIL, "The South China Sea Arbitration Awards," 629–31, paras. 917, 919, 930.

[226] Ibid., Award on Jurisdiction, 18, para. 41.

[227] Ibid., 19, 22, paras. 47–49, 61–62.

made it possible to monitor the arbitrators' activities. He acknowledged that publicity exposed the tribunal to reactions of public opinion that could interfere with the arbitrators' freedom to decide, particularly if the tribunal met in a major city, and to the risk of disclosures that were unfavorable to one or both of the parties. To avoid public protests, he believed it would be more appropriate to grant access to a narrow audience, such as journalists, diplomats, and international lawyers.[228] Only four years after the publication of Merignhac's book, Article 41 of the Hague Convention of 1899 stipulated that arbitral proceedings "are only public if it be so decided by the Tribunal, with the assent of the parties."[229] The clause makes public proceedings subject to two conditions, the consent of the parties and a decision of the tribunal, but what is important is that the clause did not at all exclude public proceedings. If one examines the *travaux préparatoires* of the Hague Convention of 1899, one finds that the Third Commission of the Hague International Peace Conference adopted this draft article at its 5th meeting (17 July 1899) without discussion or objection.[230] The provision was incorporated as Article 66 in the Hague Convention of 1907.[231] Half a century later, Article 16(1) of the Model Rules on Arbitral Procedure adopted by the UN International Law Commission reproduced this provision.[232] It is inconceivable that the possibility of public proceedings, although subject to very strict conditions, would have been incorporated in any of these international

[228] Mérignhac, *Traité théorique et pratique*, 243–44.

[229] *1899 Convention for the Pacific Settlement of International Disputes*, 11.

[230] *Conférence internationale de la Paix. Sommaire générale. Quatrième partie (Troisième Commission)* [International Peace Conference, General Table of Contents, Fourth Part (Third Commission)], Cinquième séance [5th session] (17 July 1899), 23, in Ministère des Affaires Étrangères [Ministry of Foreign Affairs of the Netherlands], *La conférence internationale de la paix. La Haye, 18 mai-29 juillet 1899* [The International Peace Conference, 18 May-29 July 1899] (New ed.; The Hague: Martinus Nijhoff, 1907), 480, https://ia902705.us.archive.org/0/items/laconfrenceint00inteuoft/laconfrenceint00inteuoft.pdf, accessed 9 April 2020.

[231] *1907 Convention for the Pacific Settlement of International Disputes*, 33.

[232] United Nations International Law Commission, *Model Rules on Arbitral Procedure with a General Commentary, 1958*, in *Yearbook of the International Law Commission 1958*, vol. II, UN Doc. A/CN.4/SER.A/1958/Add.l (New York: United Nations, 1958), 85, https://legal.un.org/docs/?path=../ilc/publications/yearbooks/english/ilc_1958_v2.pdf&lang=EFS, accessed 9 April 2020.

legal instruments had it constituted a breach of a fundamental principle of international law.

The opening to observers of arbitral proceedings, while exceptional, is not wholly unprecedented. Canada and France permitted access of the public to the hearings in the *Filleting within the Gulf of St. Lawrence Case* in June 1986.[233] In the context of Annex VII arbitrations, parties to the protracted *MOX Plant Arbitration*, which was initiated in 2001 by Ireland over the authorization by the UK of the mixed oxide fuel ("MOX") plant located at the Sellafield nuclear facility in the UK, implemented a policy that in one respect was more liberal than that adopted by the *South China Sea* Tribunal. Hearings on the merits and on Ireland's request for provisional measures, held in June 2003, were open to the public, without restriction, subject only to the need to keep certain information confidential.[234] During the Hearing on the Merits (10–13 June 2003), meetings were held in camera at the end of Day 2 and in the middle of the Hearing on Day 3.[235] During the Hearing on Ireland's request for provisional measures (17–21 June 2003), confidential matters were dealt with at the end of Day 5, when the public was asked to leave; in camera sessions were held at the end of the Hearings on Day 6, and at the beginning of the Hearing on Day 8.[236] In the *South China Sea Arbitration*, only States were allowed to attend the Hearings on Jurisdiction

[233] Haritini Dipla, "L'affaire concernant le filetage à l'intérieur du golfe du Saint-Laurent entre le Canada et la France (sentence du 17 juin 1986) [Case Concerning Filleting within the Gulf of St. Lawrence Between Canada and France (Award of 17 June 1986)]," *AFDI* 43 (1986): 239, https://www.persee.fr/issue/afdi_0066-3085_1986_num_32_1, accessed 10 May 2022. The award may be found in *Reports of International Arbitral Awards*, vol. XIX (New York: United Nations, 1990), 225–96, http://legal.un.org/docs/?path=../riaa/cases/vol_XIX/225-296.pdf&lang=O, accessed 10 May 2022.

[234] *MOX Plant Case (Ireland v. United Kingdom)*, Press Release, 2 June 2003, https://pcacases.com/web/sendAttach/871, accessed 9 April 2020; *MOX Plant Case*, Press Release, 17 June 17, 2003, https://pcacases.com/web/sendAttach/872, accessed 9 April 2020.

[235] *MOX Plant Case*, Transcript, Day 2 (June 11, 2003), 45, https://pcacases.com/web/sendAttach/858, accessed 9 April 2020; *MOX Plant Case*, Transcript, Day 3 (June 12, 2003), 32, https://pcacases.com/web/sendAttach/859, accessed 9 April 2020.

[236] Ibid., Transcript, Day 5 (17 June 2003), 9, https://pcacases.com/web/sendAttach/861, accessed 9 April 2020; Transcript, Day 6 (18 June 2003), 28, https://pcacases.com/web/sendAttach/862, accessed 9 April 2020; Transcript, Day 8 (21 June 2003), 16, https://pcacases.com/web/sendAttach/864, accessed 9 April 2020.

and on the Merits as observers. However, none of them was excluded from any part of the sessions on the grounds of confidentiality.

Rather than the CSIL's criticisms of procedures followed during the Hearings on Jurisdiction and on the Merits, which were formulated after the conclusion of the arbitral proceedings, it was China's apprehensions over the Tribunal's decisions on jurisdiction and on the merits that provided the context of press reports, several months after the issuance of the Award on Jurisdiction, that some Chinese academics were exploring the feasibility of exempting China permanently from the jurisdiction of any arbitral tribunal that may be established under the Convention through the denunciation of the latter.

III. To Denounce or Not to Denounce—That Is the Question

In December 2013, Shen Dingli, a professor at Fudan University in Shanghai, reportedly declared at a conference sponsored by a private think tank in Manila that it was a mistake for China to have become a party to the Convention. He was quoted as saying that "we should not have joined" the Convention and that "if China quits [the Convention], it will not be bound by it."[237] By "quitting" the Convention, Shen Dingli was referring to a procedure more formally known as denunciation of or withdrawal from a treaty. Denunciation is defined by the UN as "a procedure initiated unilaterally by a State to terminate its legal engagements under a treaty."[238] The implication of denunciation of the Convention was that China would take itself out of the compulsory dispute settlement procedures of the Convention so that it could no longer be deemed to have accepted arbitration as a dispute settlement procedure and accepted the jurisdiction of any arbitral tribunal that may be established upon another State party's request. Shen Dingli further asserted that "China can quit [the Convention] any time." He gave the usual caveat that his

[237] Ellen Tordesillas, "Would China Withdraw from UNCLOS If UN Court Decides in Favor of PH?" *The Filipino Express*, 16 December 2013, http://www.filipinoexpress.com/ellen-tordesillas/869-would-china-withdraw-from-unclos-if-un-court-decides-in-favor-of-ph, accessed 9 April 2020.

[238] United Nations, *Clauses of Multilateral Treaties: Handbook* (New York: United Nations, 2003), 109, https://treaties.un.org/doc/source/publications/FC/English.pdf, accessed 12 April 2020.

opinion was personal, but as the Filipina journalist reporting the event commented, no Chinese national can speak at an international forum without government permission, leaving the audience to suppose that he had China's tacit approval.[239] At the very least, his remarks could be interpreted as signs of an internal scholarly debate about the possibility of China's denunciation of the Convention.

Shen Dingli's suggestion that China was considering denunciation reminds the observer of the reaction of several States who have responded to the unilateral initiation of proceedings against them before the ICJ by withdrawing their acceptance of the Court's compulsory jurisdiction. Three of these States were defaulting States. Iran denounced its declaration of 1933 on 10 July 1951, five days after the ICJ issued its order on provisional measures in the *Anglo-Iranian Oil Co. Case*.[240] France denounced its declaration on 2 January 1974, approximately six months after the Court's orders on provisional measures, the only State, whether defaulting or not, to do so while proceedings were ongoing.[241] The US withdrew its acceptance of the Court's compulsory jurisdiction on 7 October 1985, approximately 11 months after the Court's judgment on jurisdiction and admissibility and 10 months after withdrawing from the proceedings.[242]

In 2016, a few months after the issuance of the Award on Jurisdiction, the possible withdrawal of China from the Convention resurfaced in Asian publications. Talmon believed that denunciation was a viable option, to prevent other States from allegedly exploiting the Convention's dispute settlement procedures for political purposes.[243] Responding to Talmon,

[239] Tordesillas, "Would China Withdraw."

[240] Rosenne, *The Law and Practice*, vol. II, 789.

[241] Kwiatkowska, "The International Court of Justice," 463.

[242] "United States: Department of State Letter and Statement Concerning Termination of Acceptance of ICJ Compulsory Jurisdiction [7 October 1985]," *International Legal Materials* 24 (1985): 1742–45.

[243] Stefan Talmon, "Denouncing UNCLOS Remains Option for China After Tribunal Ruling," *Global Times*, 3 March 2016, http://www.globaltimes.cn/content/971707.shtml, accessed 9 April 2020.

Davenport and Liu Haiyang cautioned against denunciation.[244] In the end, China refrained from denouncing the Convention.[245]

In the absence of further information, it is impossible to reconstruct the reasoning of Chinese decision-makers, assuming that there was indeed a conscious decision not to denounce the Convention. What can be done here is to explore the reasons why a State party to the Convention that is unhappy with the unilateral initiation of proceedings, unlike States that have accepted the ICJ's compulsory jurisdiction, does not have the option of withdrawing from the Convention's compulsory dispute settlement procedures, unless it denounces the Convention altogether. We shall then examine in greater detail the reasons put forward by the scholars for and against China's denunciation of the Convention.

A. Compulsory Dispute Settlement and Denunciation in the Convention

The Convention differs markedly from other conventions for the codification and progressive development of international law concluded under UN auspices in two significant respects. First, the procedures for compulsory dispute settlement are incorporated in the text of the Convention itself. Second, the Convention provides for the possibility of denunciation by States parties. Given the fact that the compulsory dispute settlement procedures are an integral part of the Convention, a State, such as China, that wishes to remove itself from the jurisdiction of courts and tribunals established under the Convention can only do so by denouncing the Convention.

[244] Tara Davenport, "Why China Shouldn't Denounce UNCLOS," *The Diplomat*, 24 March 2016, https://thediplomat.com/2016/03/why-china-shouldnt-denounce-unclos/, accessed 9 April 2020; Liu Haiyang, "Is Denouncing UNCLOS a Good Option for China?" *Global Times*, 21 April 2016, http://www.globaltimes.cn/content/979454.shtml, accessed 9 April 2020.

[245] At least two observers found it worth noting that China did not withdraw from the Convention. Julian Ku, "The Significance of China's Rejection of the South China Sea Arbitration for Its Approach to International Dispute Settlement and International Law," *Chinese (Taiwan) Yearbook of International Law and Affairs* 34 (2016): 101, and Lorenz Langer, "The South China Sea as a Challenge to International Law and to International Legal Scholarship," *Berkeley Journal of International Law* 36 (2018): 369, https://scholarship.law.berkeley.edu/cgi/viewcontent.cgi?article=1551&context=bjil, accessed 10 April 2020.

1. Compulsory Dispute Settlement as an Integral Part of the Convention

The incorporation of compulsory and binding dispute settlement procedures in the body of the Convention, rather than their incorporation in an optional protocol or the incorporation of non-binding procedures in a multilateral convention, means that any State that becomes a party to the Convention, regardless of the opposition it expressed to them during the negotiation of the Convention, is *ipso facto* bound by them.

Prior to the conclusion of the Convention, conventions for the codification and progressive development of international law concluded under UN auspices adopted different arrangements for compulsory dispute settlement.[246] In the earliest conventions, these procedures were embodied in optional protocols. This was the solution adopted by the four Geneva Conventions on the Law of the Sea of 29 April 1958 (the Convention on the Territorial Sea and the Contiguous Zone,[247] the Convention on the Continental Shelf,[248] the Convention on the High Seas,[249] and the Convention on Fishing and Conservation of the Living Resources of the High Seas[250]), the Vienna Convention on Diplomatic

[246] Unless otherwise indicated, the following paragraph is summarized from Ugo Villani, "Osservazioni sulle soluzione delle controversie nelle Convenzioni di codificazione del diritto internazionale [Observations on Dispute Settlement in Conventions for the Codification of International Law]," in *Le droit international à l'heure de sa codification. Études en l'honneur de Roberto Ago* [International Law at the Time of Its Codification. Studies in Honour of Roberto Ago], vol. II, *Les différends entre États et la responsabilité* [Inter-State Disputes and Responsibility] (Milano: Dott. A. Giuffrè Editore, 1987), 497–508.

[247] Entered into force on 10 September 1964, http://www.gc.noaa.gov/documents/8_1_1958_territorial_sea.pdf, accessed on 10 April 2020.

[248] Entered into force on 10 June 1964, https://legal.un.org/ilc/texts/instruments/english/conventions/8_1_1958_continental_shelf.pdf, accessed 10 April 2020.

[249] Entered into force on 30 September 1962, http://www.gc.noaa.gov/documents/8_1_1958_high_seas.pdf, accessed 10 April 2020.

[250] Entered into force on 20 March 1966, https://www.gc.noaa.gov/documents/8_1_1958_fishing.pdf, accessed 10 April 2020.

Relations of 18 April 1961,[251] the Vienna Convention on Consular Relations of 24 April 1963,[252] and the Convention on Special Missions of 8 December 1969.[253] This system enabled States to ratify the conventions without accepting any system for compulsory dispute settlement. Only States parties that also ratified separately the optional protocols would be bound by them. As Italian scholar Ugo Villani pointed out, this solution, while facilitating ratification of the conventions concerned by a large number of States, carried with it the risk that serious disputes between States that were not parties to the optional protocol would remain unresolved.[254] After 1969, compulsory dispute settlement procedures were incorporated in the text of the treaty itself, with certain variations from one treaty to the next. In the Vienna Convention on the Law of Treaties of 23 May 1969, provision for compulsory dispute settlement, in the form of recourse to the ICJ or conciliation, was made for certain categories of disputes.[255] Under the Vienna Convention on Succession of States in respect of Treaties of 23 August 1978[256] and the Vienna Convention on Succession of States in respect of State Property, Archives and Debts of 8 April 1983,[257] recourse to the ICJ is provided for in the text of the Convention for States that have accepted the ICJ's compulsory jurisdiction. The United Nations Convention on the Law of the Sea of 10 December 1982 differs from these Conventions in that the compulsory dispute settlement procedures are an integral part of the Convention. They may be initiated unilaterally by any State party to the Convention against any other State party to the Convention, and the decisions of the court or tribunal are binding on the two States parties. No separate act

[251] Entered into force on 24 April 1964, https://legal.un.org/ilc/texts/instruments/english/conventions/9_1_1961.pdf, accessed 10 April 2020.

[252] Entered into force on 19 March 1967, https://legal.un.org/ilc/texts/instruments/english/conventions/9_2_1963.pdf, accessed 10 April 2020.

[253] Entered into force on 21 June 1985, https://legal.un.org/ilc/texts/instruments/english/conventions/9_3_1969.pdf, accessed 10 April 2020.

[254] Villani, "Osservazioni," 500.

[255] Entered into force on 27 January 1980, https://legal.un.org/ilc/texts/instruments/english/conventions/1_1_1969.pdf, accessed 10 April 2020.

[256] Entered into force on 6 November 1996, https://legal.un.org/ilc/texts/instruments/english/conventions/3_2_1978.pdf, accessed 10 April 2020.

[257] Not yet in force, https://legal.un.org/ilc/texts/instruments/english/conventions/3_3_1983.pdf, accessed 10 April 2020.

by a State party is required for the compulsory dispute settlement procedures to be applicable to them, although the Convention did provide for a system of automatic limitations to the procedures and optional exclusions from them.

At the Third United Nations Conference on the Law of the Sea ("UNCLOS III"), which drafted the Convention, China was opposed to the consensus on the need for compulsory dispute settlement procedures, which had started to form as early as the second session of UNCLOS III (1974). The reasons for China's opposition were explained when the resulting draft was presented to the plenary in 1975. The first reason was that the super-powers, to protect their vested interests, would allegedly resort to procedures designed to weaken the provisions of the future convention that reflected the interests of developing countries.[258] Interestingly enough, this perspective was not necessarily shared by developing countries themselves. El Salvador, one of the co-chairs of the informal working group on dispute settlement, believed that these procedures would provide small States with powerful means to prevent interference by large States.[259] Second, according to China, unconditional acceptance of the compulsory jurisdiction of an international judicial organ would place that organ above the State and violate State sovereignty. Third, in China's view, "problems within the scope of State sovereignty and exclusive jurisdiction of a sovereign State" should be handled in accordance with that State's laws and regulations. China emphasized that States should settle their disputes through negotiation and consultation. If other States were willing to accept specific provisions on dispute settlement, "those provisions should not be included in the convention itself but should form a separate protocol so that countries could decide for themselves whether to accept it or not."[260] This last view was contrary to the emerging consensus within UNCLOS III. As was explained by El

[258] Mr. Lai Ya-li (China), 60th Plenary meeting, 6 April 1976, A/CONF.62/SR.60, in United Nations, *Third United Nations Conference on the Law of the Sea*, *Official Records*, vol. V, *Summary Records, Plenary, General Committee, First, Second and Third Committees, as well as Documents of the Conference, Fourth Session: New York, 15 March–7 May 1976*, UN Doc. A/CONF.62/[Vol. 5] (New York: UN, 1976), 24, para. 26 ("*UNCLOS III, Official Records*"), https://legal.un.org/docs/?path=../diplomaticconferences/1973_los/docs/english/vol_5/a_conf62_sr60.pdf&lang=E, accessed 10 April 2020.

[259] Nordquist et al., *United Nations Convention on the Law of the Sea 1982*, vol. V, 8.

[260] *UNCLOS III*, *Official Records*, vol. V, 24, para. 28.

Salvador in 1974, an optional protocol was totally inadequate, so that a dispute settlement system had to form an integral part and essential element of the Convention.[261] In plenary sessions, China reiterated that "the submission of a dispute to the compulsory settlement procedure must have the consent of the parties to the dispute."[262] China completely ignored the progress that was being made in informal consultations on the dispute settlement system, in which it apparently did not take part at all.[263]

In the domestic debate on ratification of the Convention, the dispute settlement system was one of the issues that aroused concern in China. Yet it was thought that the Convention's provisions concerning historic waters could be used to strengthen China's rights and interests in the waters adjacent to the Spratly Islands and a whole range of disputes could be excluded from the Convention's dispute settlement procedures.[264] Despite the opposition of China to the principle of compulsory dispute settlement, it became bound by these procedures as soon as it became a party to the Convention. Its opposition to them expressed at UNCLOS III was now of no consequence.

Throughout the *South China Sea Arbitration* China insisted repeatedly on its preference for negotiation and consultation to resolve the disputes with the Philippines. The Tribunal acknowledged that China always insisted on negotiations and had made this preference clear and well known to the Philippines. However, the Tribunal explained that

[261] Nordquist et al., *United Nations Convention on the Law of the Sea 1982*, vol. V, 8.

[262] Mr. Shen Wei-liang (China), 103rd Plenary meeting, 18 May 1978, UN Doc. A/CONF.62/SR.103, in *UNCLOS III*, *Official Records*, vol. IX, *Summary Records, Plenary, General Committee, First, Second and Third Committees, as well as Documents of the Conference, Seventh and Resumed Seventh Session: Geneva, 28 March–19 May 1978; New York, 21 August–15 September* 1978, UN Doc. A/CONF.62/[Vol. 9] (New York: United Nations, 1979). 67, para. 77, https://legal.un.org/docs/?path=../diplomaticconferences/1973_los/docs/english/vol_9/a_conf62_sr103.pdf&lang=E, accessed 10 April 2020.

[263] China is not mentioned at all in accounts of the informal negotiations on dispute settlement. See Nordquist et al., *United Nations Convention on the Law of the Sea 1982*, vol. V, 3–15.

[264] Yann-Huei Song and Zou Keyuan, "Maritime Legislation of Mainland China and Taiwan: Developments, Comparison, Implications, and Potential Challenges for the United States," *Ocean Development and International Law* 31 (2000): 308–09.

> repeated insistence by one party on negotiating indefinitely until an eventual resolution cannot dislodge the "backstop of compulsory, binding procedures" provided by Section 2 of Part XV....One party's preference for one means of dispute settlement, however persistent, cannot imply that if negotiations fail or become futile, the other party has relinquished its right to have recourse to the other means of dispute settlement set out in Section 2 of Part XV.[265]

The dispute settlement procedures being an integral part of the Convention, the option of withdrawing from them while remaining a party to the Convention was not available to China. Iran, France, and the US could remain parties to the ICJ Statute even after withdrawing their acceptance of the Court's compulsory jurisdiction, since compulsory jurisdiction is not an integral element of the Statute. Rather, it requires a separate, optional, act on the part of States parties to the Statute. It would not have been possible for China to remove itself from the system of compulsory dispute settlement incorporated in the Convention without denouncing the Convention in its entirety.

2. The Convention Regime on Denunciation

Two points are relevant to the question of China's possible denunciation of the Convention. First, the Convention contains provisions on denunciation. Second, denunciation may take place at any time, subject only to 12 months' notice, during which the denouncing State remains bound by its obligations under the Convention.

The observation that the Convention contains provisions on denunciation is not a trivial one. The four Geneva Conventions on the Law of the Sea had no such provisions. At the First United Nations Conference on the Law of the Sea ("UNCLOS I," 1958), the desirability of a denunciation clause was discussed within the committees on the continental shelf and on fishing and within the Drafting Committee for all four conventions.[266] The Drafting Committee simply reported that the inclusion of a

[265] *South China Sea Arbitration*, Award on Jurisdiction, 95, para. 247.

[266] The question of denunciation clauses for the four Geneva Conventions on the Law of the Sea has not been discussed in the scholarly literature. It is not mentioned even in passing by Gerald Fitzmaurice, "Some Results of the Geneva Conference on the Law of the Sea. Part I. The Territorial Sea and Contiguous Zone and Related Topics," *International and Comparative Law Quarterly* 8 (1959): 73–121 or by A. Matine-Daftary, "Cours abrégé sur la contribution des conférences de Genève au développement progressif

revision clause in the conventions made unnecessary any clause on denunciation.[267] Within the committee on the continental shelf, those who advocated the insertion of a denunciation clause stressed that the absence of such a clause might create uncertainty, with some States concluding that the Convention would remain in force forever, and others concluding that they needed only to change their mind in order to withdraw from the Convention.[268] It was stressed that the Conference had no right to lay down obligations binding in perpetuity.[269] With great prescience, one delegate declared that in order to avoid difficulties of interpretation, it would be better to be explicit on the matter of denunciation.[270] Opponents of a denunciation clause contended that the task of the Conference was to codify customary law, which by its nature could not be denounced. The Conference did make new law, but this had been adopted by general consent, making it pointless to provide for its denunciation.[271] The debates surrounding the future convention on fishing were somewhat ambiguous. Advocates and opponents of a denunciation clause found justification for their respective positions in the fact that the convention

du droit international de la mer [Abbreviated Course on the Contribution of the Geneva Conferences to the Progressive Development of the Law of the Sea]," *RCADI*, vol. 102 (1961-I), 635–74.

267 *Sixth Report of the Drafting Committee of the Conference: Final Clauses*, UN Doc. A/CONF.13/L.32 (25 April 1958), in *United Nations Conference on the Law of the Sea. Official Records*, vol. II, UN Doc. A/CONF.13/38 (New York: United Nations, 1958), 127 ("*UNCLOS I, Official Records*"), https://legal.un.org/docs/?path=../diplomaticconferences/1958_los/docs/english/vol_2/a_conf_13_l_32.pdf&lang=E, accessed 12 April 2020; Mr. Sole (South Africa), in Summary Record of the 18th Plenary Meeting, 26 April 1958, in *UNCLOS I, Official Records*, vol. II, 56, para. 18, https://legal.un.org/docs/?path=../diplomaticconferences/1958_los/docs/english/vol_2/sr_18.pdf&lang=E, accessed 12 April 2020.

268 Mr. Calero Rodriguês (Brazil), in Summary Record of the 9th Plenary Meeting, 22 April 1958, in *UNCLOS I, Official Records*, vol. II, 19, para. 50, https://legal.un.org/docs/?path=../diplomaticconferences/1958_los/docs/english/vol_2/sr_9.pdf&lang=E, accessed 12 April 2020.

269 Mr. Bartos (Yugoslavia), in Summary Record of the 18th Plenary Meeting, *UNCLOS I, Official Records*, vol. II, p.19, para. 53.

270 Mr. Barros Franco (Chile), in Summary Record of the 9th Plenary Meeting, 22 April 1958, in *UNCLOS I, Official Records*, vol. II, 19, para. 58.

271 Mr. Gros (France), in Summary Record of the 18th Plenary Meeting, *UNCLOS I, Official Records*, vol. II, 56, para. 19.

introduced new law.[272] One opponent remarked in sibylline fashion that the Convention was based on a system of negotiation between States, which should be compulsory; such a system would be undermined if States were able to denounce the Convention.[273] In the end, all proposals for the insertion of a denunciation clause in the four Geneva Conventions were rejected, but with the number of abstentions exceeding the majority votes. Instead, the Conventions incorporated parallel provisions stipulating that any State party to the respective Convention could at any time after the expiration of five years from its entry into force make a. request for revision.[274]

This uneasy compromise was not of much use when in 1971, seven years after the entry into force of the Convention on the Territorial Sea and five years after the entry into force of the Convention on Fishing and the Living Resources of the High Seas, Senegal, which had acceded to the two Conventions in 1961, sought to denounce the two Conventions.[275] The first Convention was criticized for not setting outer limits on the territorial sea, and the second Convention, for not providing for the coastal State's exclusive right to fish in areas of the high seas off its coast. The overall consequence for Senegal was the over-exploitation of the living resources of these areas by an increasing number of vessels from technologically advanced countries. The problem of interpretation that was anticipated in 1958 now arose: did there exist an implicit right of denunciation of a multilateral treaty that did not contain any clause relating to its termination? The UN Secretariat was of the view that in the

[272] Mr. Verzijl (Netherlands) and Mr. Bartos (Yugoslavia), in Summary Record of the 18th Plenary Meeting, *UNCLOS I, Official Records*, vol. II, 58, paras. 58, 60.

[273] Mr. Gros (France), in Summary Record of the 18th Plenary Meeting, *UNCLOS I, Official Records*, vol. II, 57, para. 61. What this system of negotiation consisted of and why it should be compulsory were left unexplained.

[274] J.H.W. Verzijl, "The United Nations Conference on the Law of the Sea, Geneva, 1958," *Netherlands International Law Review* 6 (1959): 7, note 14.

[275] This paragraph is based on Daniel Bardonnet, "La dénonciation par le Gouvernement sénégalais de la Convention sur la mer territoriale et la zone contiguë et de la Convention sur la pêche et la conservation des ressources biologiques de la haute mer, en date du 29 avril 1958 à Genève [The Denunciation by the Senegalese Government of the Convention on the Territorial Sea and the Contiguous Zone and the Convention on Fishing and the Conservation of the Living Resources of the High Seas, concluded on 29 April 1958 at Geneva]," *AFDI* 18 (1972): 123–80, https://www.persee.fr/doc/afdi_0066-3085_1972_num_18_1_1693, accessed 12 April 2020.

absence of such a clause, the matter was subject to general international law, embodied in the Vienna Convention on the Law of Treaties. Article 56(1) of the latter stipulated that a treaty that did not contain any provision regarding its termination and did not provide for denunciation or withdrawal is not subject to denunciation or withdrawal unless the parties intended to admit the possibility of denunciation or withdrawal or a right of denunciation or withdrawal may be implied by the nature of the treaty. The debates in plenary at UNCLOS I make clear that the parties that had rejected the insertion of a denunciation clause in the Geneva Conventions did not intend to admit the possibility of denunciation. Although Senegal was not a party to the Vienna Convention on the Law of Treaties, Article 56 was considered by the UN Secretariat to be declaratory of customary law; making it binding on Senegal. For these reasons, the Secretariat refused to transmit Senegal's denunciation to the States parties to the two Conventions and to register the denunciation. Following Senegal's protest against the Secretariat's position that Article 56 of the Vienna Convention was binding on it, the Secretariat then transmitted the correspondence on the matter to the States parties. Following fresh protests from Senegal, the Secretariat, in another uneasy compromise, allowed Senegal to register the notification of its denunciation itself.

Whether or not the Senegalese denunciation of two Geneva Conventions on the Law of the Sea was in the minds of delegates to UNCLOS III—reference to it does not appear in Senegal's intervention in the plenary meetings[276]—the principle of a denunciation clause began to gain ground in 1979. Several reasons were mentioned in this connection. First, a denunciation clause would increase the chances of the widest possible acceptance of the Convention. Second, given the possibility of a revision of the Convention, a State unable to accept amendments resulting from a revision should not be compelled to remain a party to it. Third, the Convention established an international organization, the International

[276] Mr. Cissé (Senegal), Summary Records of 38th plenary meeting (11 July 1974), *UNCLOS III*, *Official Records*, vol. I, *Summary Records of Plenary Meetings of the First and Second Sessions, and of Meetings of the General Committee, Second Session*, UN Doc. A/CONF.62/[Vol. 1] (New York: United Nations, 1975), 164–65, paras. 90–98, https://legal.un.org/docs/?path=../diplomaticconferences/1973_los/docs/english/vol_1/a_conf62_sr38.pdf&lang=E, accessed 12 April 2020.

Seabed Authority, of which a State could not be expected to be a member in perpetuity.[277]

It is tempting to speculate whether the Convention's drafters would have felt satisfaction that three decades after the conclusion of UNCLOS III in 1982, a State party to the Convention was reported to be considering denunciation of the Convention. Article 317 of the Convention could be thought to facilitate the procedure for a State wishing to denounce the Convention. In the first place, denunciation could take place at any time, by means of notification to the UN Secretary-General. A suggestion made by a Group of Legal Experts in 1979 that no denunciation be permitted during the first five years after the entry into force of the Convention was omitted in the final draft. In this respect, the Convention is more liberal than two other conventions on the law of the sea that has a far more venerable pedigree than the Convention. The Convention on the International Regulations for Preventing Collisions at Sea of 1972 ("COLREGS"), which incorporates the International Regulations for Preventing Collisions at Sea first adopted in 1863, permits denunciation by a State party only after the expiry of five years from the date on which the COLREGS entered into force for that State.[278] The International Convention for the Safety of Life at Sea ("SOLAS") of 1974, the first version of which was adopted in 1914 as a response to the Titanic disaster of 1912, contains an identical provision.[279]

While discussions at UNCLOS III identified several reasons why a State might wish to denounce the Convention, Article 317 does not impose any obligation to provide reasons for the denunciation. If it so chooses, a State party may accompany its notification with reasons, but Article 317(1) of the Convention provides that "[f]ailure to indicate

[277] Nordquist et al., *United Nations Convention on the Law of the Sea 1982*, vol. V, 282.

[278] Article VII(1) of *International Convention on the International Regulations for Preventing Collisions at Sea*, adopted at London on 20 October 1972, entered into force on 15 July 1977, consolidated text as amended in 1981, 1987, 1989, 1993, 2001 and 2007 ("COLREGS 1972"), http://www.ecolregs.com/index.php?option=com_k2&view=itemlist&layout=category&Itemid=505&lang=en, accessed 31 May 2019. In its Submission No. 13, the Philippines alleged that China's dangerous maneuvering of its vessels created the risk of collision with Philippine vessels in 2012, in breach of the COLREGS.

[279] Article XI(1) of *International Convention for the Safety of Life at Sea* (SOLAS 1974), adopted at London on 1 November 1974, entered into force on 25 May 1980, https://www.refworld.org/docid/46920bf32.html, accessed 3 June 2019.

reasons shall not affect the validity of the denunciation." Article 317(1) thus did not take up a suggestion made by the Group of Legal Experts that it be made compulsory to provide reasons for the denunciation. The absence of an obligation to give reasons was buttressed by the confirmation from the President of UNCLOS III that a denunciation would not be subject to challenge through the dispute settlement procedures of the Convention.[280] In this respect, the Convention is similar to the COLREGS and SOLAS.

Denunciation of the Convention does not immediately release the State from its obligations under the Convention. The denunciation will only take effect one year after the receipt of the notification of denunciation by the UN Secretary-General. The Convention, like the COLREGS and SOLAS, allows for the possibility of an extension of the one-year period if the denouncing State so wishes.[281] The requirement that a one-year period elapse before the denunciation takes effect is a standard one and pursues several aims. It will discourage denunciation by a State that has benefited from the application of a treaty from withdrawing from the treaty once it has to fulfill its own obligations.[282] It will discourage denunciation by a State that wishes to avoid responsibility for breaches that it has committed prior to the notice of denunciation. It will discourage denunciation followed by an immediate breach of obligations under the treaty that the State has just denounced.[283] If necessary, it will allow sufficient time for negotiations between the denouncing State and the other parties to the treaty. Should negotiations fail, the period will permit the other parties to the treaty to take any measures necessary to enable them to address the consequences of the denunciation.[284]

[280] Nordquist et al., *United Nations Convention on the Law of the Sea 1982*, vol. V, 283–84.

[281] COLREGS 1972, Article VII(3); SOLAS 1974, Article XI(3).

[282] Laurence R. Helfer, "Exiting Custom: Analogies to Treaty Withdrawals," *Duke Journal of Comparative and International Law* 21 (2010): 67, https://scholarship.law.duke.edu/cgi/viewcontent.cgi?article=2909&context=faculty_scholarship, accessed 12 April 2020.

[283] Ibid., "Terminating Treaties," in Duncan B. Hollis (ed.), *The Oxford Guide to Treaties* (Oxford: Oxford University Press, 2012), 641, https://scholarship.law.duke.edu/cgi/viewcontent.cgi?article=5338&context=faculty_scholarship, accessed 10 April 2020.

[284] Sir Francis Vallat (United Kingdom), 59th meeting of the Committee of the Whole, 8 May 1968, UN Doc. A/CONF.39/C.1/SR.59 in *United Nations Conference on the Law of Treaties. First session Vienna, 26 March–24 May 1968. Official*

After the one-year period has elapsed, the State that has denounced the Convention must still comply with the financial and contractual obligations that accrued while it was a Party to the Convention. Moreover, denunciation does not affect any right, obligation, or legal situation of that State created through the implementation of the Convention prior to the date when the denunciation takes effect. Finally, denunciation would not affect the duty of the denouncing State to fulfill any obligation embodied in the Convention to which it is subject under customary international law.

These provisions must be integrated into the calculations of the State that is considering whether to denounce the Convention or not.

B. The Lesser of Two Evils?

Advocates and opponents of China's denunciation of the Convention agreed that any decision should be the result of a legal and political cost–benefit analysis.[285] In the legal analysis, the balance appeared to be slightly tilted toward remaining a State party. In contrast, a political analysis would have yielded no benefits for denunciation.

1. The Legal Consequences of Denunciation

Denunciation would protect China from recourse by other States to compulsory dispute settlement, with the proviso that such protection would only become effective a year after the denunciation. It could be argued that China would be able to enjoy the benefits of the Convention under customary law. However, as a non-party, China would not be able to participate in the shaping of the future law of the sea and might encounter difficulties in obtaining recognition for its claim to an extended continental shelf.

From Talmon's perspective, the beneficial consequences of denunciation were twofold. First, it would allegedly offer protection against attempts by Vietnam, Indonesia, or Malaysia, with which China also had territorial and maritime disputes in the South China Sea, to follow the Philippine example and to invoke the Convention's compulsory dispute

Records, vol. I, UN Doc. A/CONF.39/11/ (New York: United Nations, 1969), 339, para. 2, https://legal.un.org/docs/?path=../diplomaticconferences/1968_lot/docs/english/sess_1.pdf&lang=EF, accessed 13 April 2020.

[285] Talmon, "Denouncing UNCLOS."

mechanisms to settle their disputes with China. Second, China would allegedly continue to enjoy many of the rights of States parties to the Convention without bearing the burden of the obligations it imposed on them. The reason for this was that such rights, e.g., the sovereign rights of the coastal State in its EEZ and over the continental shelf, were already part of customary law; the exceptions would be Parts XII (on protection and preservation of the marine environment), XIV (on the transfer of technology) and XV (dispute settlement). Talmon admitted that denunciation would not release China from the obligations that accrued to it while it was a State party to the Convention.[286] In particular, China would still be bound by any decisions of the Arbitral Tribunal, even after it denounced the Convention.[287]

Davenport warned against the argument that denunciation would protect China from claims by Vietnam, Indonesia, or Malaysia in the South China Sea and by Japan in the East China Sea. She argued that nothing would stop any of these States from initiating an arbitration against China within the one-year notification period, which would offer them the final opportunity to bring China before an international tribunal. Davenport fortified her warning by referring to the experience of Colombia following its denunciation of the Pact of Bogotá of 30 April 1948.[288] The Pact, a multilateral treaty concluded under the auspices of the Organization of American States ("OAS"), had been the legal basis for the proceedings instituted by Nicaragua against Colombia at the ICJ in 2001, concerning sovereignty over several islands and keys as well as the delimitation of their respective EEZs and continental shelves in the western Caribbean Sea.[289] The eleven-year judicial saga culminated in a delimitation that was harshly criticized in Colombia for being difficult to foresee and to implement, creating problems, breaking with precedent, not being in conformity with geographical reality, applying equity in excessively flexible fashion, and applying proportionality in inflexible

[286] Ibid.

[287] Davenport, "Why China Shouldn't Denounce UNCLOS."

[288] Ibid. *American Treaty on Pacific Settlement (Pact of Bogota)*, signed at Bogotá, 30 April 1948, entered into force on 6 May 1949, https://www.oas.org/sap/peacefund/resolutions/Pact_of_Bogot%C3%A1.pdf, accessed 15 April 2020.

[289] *Territorial and Maritime Dispute (Nicaragua v. Colombia), Preliminary Objections, Judgment*, *I.C.J. Reports 2007*, 875–76, para. 142, https://www.icj-cij.org/files/case-related/124/124-20071213-JUD-01-00-BI.pdf, accessed 13 April 2020.

fashion.[290] On 29 November 2012, 10 days after the ICJ judgment, Colombia denounced the Pact of Bogotá, with the aim of preventing the filing of further territorial and maritime claims by Nicaragua and other States.[291] As the denunciation would take effect only one year after the notification, Colombian scholars warned that it would not have a retroactive effect and that during the one-year period, Nicaragua could still file cases against Colombia with the ICJ over such matters as the recognition of Nicaragua's rights over its extended continental shelf and Colombia's blocking of the exercise of Nicaragua's rights in the Nicaraguan EEZ that had been recognized by the ICJ judgment.[292] This is exactly what Nicaragua did: the case on the first matter was filed on 16 September 2013, and the case on the second, on 26 November 2013, just one

[290] Marco Gerardo Monroy Cabra, "Análisis de la posición jurídica de Colombia ante la Corte de La Haya [Analysis of Colombia's Legal Position before the ICJ]," in Carlos Holmes Trujillo García and María Lucía Torres Villarreal (eds.), *Contribución de la Universidad del Rosario al debate sobre el fallo de La Haya: Análisis del caso Nicaragua vs. Colombia* [Contribution of the Universidad del Rosario to the Debate on the ICJ Judgment: Analysis of the Nicaragua vs. Colombia Case] (Bogotá: Editorial Universidad del Rosario, 2013), 24, https://pure.urosario.edu.co/ws/portalfiles/portal/21996451/pi_Contribucion_UR_fallo_Haya_final.pdf, accessed 13 April 2020.

[291] Andrés Sarmiento Lamus, "Impacto e implementación en Colombia de la decisión de fondo de la Corte Internacional de Justicia en el diferendo territorial y marítimo (Nicaragua c. Colombia) [Impact and Implementation in Colombia of the Decision on the Merits of the International Court of Justice in the Territorial and Maritime Dispute (Nicaragua v. Colombia)]," *Anuario mexicano de derecho internacional* [Mexican Yearbook of International Law] 16 (2016): 413, http://www.scielo.org.mx/scielo.php?script=sci_abstract&pid=S1870-46542016000100401&lng=en&nrm=iso&tlng=fr, accessed 15 April 2020.

[292] Andrea Mateus Rugeles, "Denuncia del Pacto de Bogotá: Implicaciones jurídicas para Colombia [Denunciation of the Pact of Bogotá: Legal Implications for Colombia]," in Carlos Holmes Trujillo García and María Lucía Torres Villarreal (eds.), *Contribución de la Universidad del Rosario al debate sobre el fallo de La Haya: Análisis del caso Nicaragua vs. Colombia* [Contribution of the Universidad del Rosario to the Debate on the ICJ Judgment Analysis of the Nicaragua vs. Colombia Case] (Bogotá: Editorial Universidad del Rosario, 2013), 10, https://pure.urosario.edu.co/ws/portalfiles/portal/21996451/pi_Contribucion_UR_fallo_Haya_final.pdf, accessed 13 April 2020.

day before the expiry of the one-year notification period.[293] Colombia's denunciation merely triggered the filing of further cases against it. Similarly, China's denunciation of the Convention could have triggered a rush to file cases against China and fulfilled the Philippine hope that the *South China Sea Arbitration* would encourage other littoral States to have recourse to the Convention's dispute settlement mechanism to resolve their disputes with China.[294]

The argument that China would enjoy the same rights as do States parties because these rights were now part of customary law encompasses a broad range of issues. It is obvious that the argument can have no relevance for the exploration and exploitation of the resources of the international seabed area beyond national jurisdiction ("the Area"), the regime for which was established only by Part XI of the Convention. Consequently, as Talmon admits, China's energy companies would be excluded, once China ceased to be a party to the Convention, from activities in the Area, unless these companies were registered with and sponsored by another State party to the Convention.[295] It is impossible to deal at any length with such a complex issue in this limited context. The following discussion will concentrate on two issues that illustrate the difficulties created by reliance on customary law to guarantee the enjoyment of rights under the Convention.

The first is a general problem confronting non-States parties like the US. To begin with, certain regimes were created by the Convention and are consequently not (yet) part of customary law. For a naval power like the US and for an aspiring naval power like China, the two most important are transit passage in straits used for international navigation (Article 38 of the Convention) and archipelagic sealane passage (Article 53 of

[293] Nicaragua, *Application Instituting Proceedings* (16 September 2013), *Question of the Delimitation of the Continental Shelf Between Nicaragua and Colombia beyond 200 nautical miles from the Nicaraguan Coast (Nicaragua v. Colombia)*, https://www.icj-cij.org/files/case-related/154/17532.pdf, accessed 13 April 2020; Nicaragua, *Application Instituting Proceedings* (26 November 2013), *Alleged Violations of Sovereign Rights and Maritime Spaces in the Caribbean Sea (Nicaragua v. Colombia)*, https://www.icj-cij.org/en/case/155/institution-proceedings, accessed 13 April 2020.

[294] *South China Sea Arbitration*, Hearing on the Merits and Remaining Issues of Jurisdiction and Admissibility, Final Transcript, Day 4 (30 November 2015), 191–92, https://pcacases.com/web/sendAttach/1550, accessed 16 April 2020.

[295] Talmon, "Denouncing UNCLOS."

the Convention).[296] These obligations imposed on coastal States and archipelagic States are crucial for the innocent passage of foreign vessels, including warships, and foreign aircraft in waters that used to be part of the high seas and that are now enclosed as a result of the creation of the regimes of the EEZ and of archipelagic States. These passage rights may only be claimed by States parties to the Convention vis-à-vis other States parties to the Convention. As regards those regimes that are undoubtedly part of customary law—those applicable to the EEZ and the continental shelf—it would be a mistake to assume that customary law is static. A practice that denies passage rights, which is at present considered a breach of customary law, might be transformed into a new customary rule if States parties to the Convention follow the practice and fulfill the conditions for the formation of a customary rule. States that are not parties to the Convention would not possess the same ability to influence the development of a customary rule.[297] China could not fulfill its aim of encouraging States parties to the Convention to acquiesce to Chinese authority over contested space and contribute to the formation of new norms specific to China's littoral space.[298]

The second problem that would confront China if it withdrew from the Convention is more specific, relating to claims over an extended continental shelf (i.e., beyond the 200-nautical mile limit). The resource potential contained in the extended continental shelf regions of the world is held in iron-manganese nodules and crusts, which contain manganese,

[296] William Schachte, "Protecting and Enhancing US National Security: The Reality of the Operational Aspects of UNCLOS," in Myron H. Nordquist et al. (eds.), *The Law of the Sea Convention: US Accession and Globalization* (Leiden: Martinus Nijhoff Publishers, 2012), 90.

[297] Ibid.; see also David A. Balton, "UNCLOS: The Stakes for America," Michael J. Mattler, "UNCLOS: The Stakes for America," and Nanette DeRenzi, "Protecting and Enhancing US National Security," in Myron H. Nordquist et al. (eds.), *The Law of the Sea Convention: US Accession and Globalization* (Leiden: Martinus Nijhoff Publishers, 2012), 45, 59, 94, 95.

[298] Isaac B. Kardon, "China's Maritime Interests and the Law of the Sea: Domesticating Public International Law," in John Garrick and Yan Chang Bennett (eds.), *China's Socialist Rule of Law Reforms Under Xi Jinping* (Milton Park, Abingdon, Oxon: Routledge, 2016), 180.

copper, nickel, cobalt, oil, gas, and gas hydrates.[299] Gas hydrates are ice-like crystalline minerals that form when low molecular weight gas (such as methane, ethane, or carbon dioxide) combines with water and freezes into a solid under low temperature and moderate pressure conditions. Gas hydrate deposits may contain roughly twice the carbon contained in all reserves of coal, oil, and conventional natural gas combined, making them a potentially valuable energy resource.[300] The Convention permits coastal States to claim a continental shelf beyond 200 nautical miles, extending to the outer edge of the continental margin.[301] The outer edge of the continental margin is to be established by a coastal State by either a line delineated "by reference to the outermost fixed points at each of which the thickness of sedimentary rocks is at least 1 per cent of the shortest distance from such point to the foot of the continental slope" or by a line delineated "by reference to fixed points not more than 60 nautical miles from the foot of the continental slope."[302] To prevent the extended continental shelf from encroaching even further on the Area, the outer limits of the continental shelf are set at either 350 nautical miles from the baselines of the territorial sea or at 100 nautical miles from the 2,500-meter isobath (a line connecting the depth of 2,500 meters).[303] A coastal State must submit information on the outer limits of its continental shelf to a body established by the Convention, the Commission on the Limits of the Continental Shelf ("CLCS"), which makes recommendations to the coastal State on the establishment of the outer limits. The limits established by a coastal State on the basis of the CLCS recommendations will be final and binding.[304]

For a non-party to the Convention, the first question is whether it has the right to claim an extended continental shelf under customary

[299] Bramley J. Murton, "A Global Review of Non-Living Resources on the Extended Continental Shelf," *Revista Brasileira de Geofísica* [Brazilian Journal of Geophysics] 18 (2000): 301, http://www.scielo.br/scielo.php?pid=S0102-261X2000000300007&script=sci_arttext&tlng=es, accessed 15 April 2020.

[300] US Department of Commerce, National Oceanic and Atmospheric Administration, Office of Ocean Exploration and Research, *What Are Gas Hydrates?* https://oceanexplorer.noaa.gov/facts/hydrates.html, accessed 14 April 2020.

[301] Convention, Article 76(1).

[302] Ibid., Article 76(4)(i) and (ii).

[303] Ibid., Article 76(6).

[304] Ibid., Article 76(8).

law. Judicial and scholarly opinion provides an affirmative answer.[305] Had China denounced the Convention, it would have been able to maintain its claim to an extended continental shelf.[306] It is less certain whether there are criteria under customary law distinct from those laid down in Article 76 for determining whether or not a State's continental margin extends beyond 200 nautical miles from the baseline,[307] and whether there is anything under customary law that would make the outer limits set by a State not a party to the Convention binding and final, distinct from the recommendations of the CLCS.[308] Negative answers to both questions are implicit in the arguments of advocates of US accession to the Convention that stress that unless the US becomes a party to the Convention, it cannot submit data on its extended continental shelf and that without CLCS recommendation, the US will not be able to obtain international recognition for US control of the resources on the extended continental shelf.[309] Davenport points out that some international judicial decisions make clear that a submission to the CLCS can strengthen a State's claim to an extended continental shelf.[310]

China had already devoted ten years to collecting data on its extended continental shelf before submitting preliminary findings to the CLCS in

305 Bjarni Már Magnússon, "Can the United States Establish the Outer Limits of Its Extended Continental Shelf Under International Law?" *Ocean Development and International Law* 48 (2017): 7–8.

306 Talmon, "Denouncing UNCLOS."

307 *Question of the Delimitation of the Continental Shelf Between Nicaragua and Colombia beyond 200 Nautical Miles from the Nicaraguan Coast (Nicaragua v. Colombia), Preliminary Objections, Judgment*, Separate opinion of Judge Greenwood, *I.C.J. Reports 2016*, 185, para. 19, https://www.icj-cij.org/files/case-related/154/154-20160317-JUD-01-03-BI.pdf, accessed 15 April 2020; Tullio Treves, "La limite extérieure du plateau continental: Évolution récente de la pratique [The Outer Limit of the Continental Shelf: The Recent Evolution of Practice]," *AFDI* 35 (1989): 724–35, www.persee.fr/web/revues/home/prescript/article/afdi_0066-3085_1989_num_35_1_2929, accessed 15 April 2020.

308 Magnússon, "Can the United States Establish," 6.

309 Lisa Murkowski, "US Interests in Prompt Adherence to the Law of the Sea Convention," and R. Bruce Josten, "US LOS Ratification: A Potential Resource Bonanza for US Industry," in Myron H. Nordquist et al. (eds.), *The Law of the Sea Convention: US Accession and Globalization* (Leiden: Martinus Nijhoff Publishers, 2012), 22–23, 74; Balton, "UNCLOS: The Stakes for America," 46.

310 Davenport, "Why China Shouldn't Denounce UNCLOS."

May 2009, followed by partial submissions in 2012 and 2013.[311] Consideration of China's claim has already been deferred as a result of protests from Japan and the Republic of Korea. It is difficult to imagine what alternative mechanisms or procedures for securing international recognition of its claim under customary international law would be available to China once it had denounced the Convention[312]; it is not difficult to imagine how Japan and the Republic of Korea would have exploited China's denunciation of the Convention in order to contest China's claim.

If the legal consequences of denunciation already weighed in favor of remaining a party to the Convention, an analysis of its political consequences would almost certainly have tipped the balance against denunciation.

2. The Political Consequences of Denunciation

The political consequences of denunciation would have been uniformly negative, given the symbolic value of the Convention in China's foreign policy and the context in which it would have taken place.

UNCLOS III was the first major multilateral conference for the codification and progressive development of international law in which the People's Republic of China participated since it replaced Taiwan (Republic of China) as China's representative at the UN in 1971.[313] It was Taiwan that had been invited to UNCLOS I (1958) and the

[311] Ibid.; James Manicom, "China's Claims to an Extended Continental Shelf in the East China Sea: Meaning and Implications," *China Brief* 9 (9 July 2009): 9, https://jamestown.org/wp-content/uploads/2009/07/cb_009_23.pdf?x73233, accessed 15 April 2020; United Nations Convention on the Law of the Sea, Commission on the Limits of the Continental Shelf, *Progress of Work in the Commission on the Limits of the Continental Shelf, Thirty-second session (New York, 15 July-30 August 2013), Statement by the Chair* (24 September 2013), 2, 12–13, paras. 3, 59–61, UN Doc. CLCS/80, https://undocs.org/en/clcs/80, accessed 15 April 2020.

[312] Davenport, "Why China Shouldn't Denounce UNCLOS."

[313] In 1971, the UN General Assembly adopted resolution 2758, by a vote of 76 for, 35 against, with 17 abstentions. The second paragraph of the preamble declared that the representatives of the government of the People's Republic of China are "the only lawful representatives of China to the United Nations." Accordingly, the General Assembly decided "to restore all its rights to the People's Republic of China," to recognize "the representatives of its government as the only legitimate representatives of China to the UN," and "to expel forthwith the representatives of Chiang Kai-shek from the place which they unlawfully occupy at the United Nations and in all the organizations related to it." UN General Assembly Resolution 2758 (XXVI), "Restoration of the Lawful Rights of the People's Republic of China in the United Nations," UN Doc. A/RES/2758

Second United Nations Conference on the Law of the Sea ("UNCLOS II," 1960), as well as the diplomatic conferences that negotiated the Vienna Conventions on Diplomatic Relations (1961), on Consular Relations (1963) and on the Law of Treaties (1968–1969) under UN auspices. It was Taiwan that had represented the whole of China at the diplomatic conferences that revised the COLREGS (1948 and 1960) and SOLAS (1948 and 1960), under the auspices of the Intergovernmental Maritime Consultative Organization ("IMCO," now International Maritime Organization, "IMO"). The Convention was therefore the first major multilateral treaty that the People's Republic of China concluded as the legitimate representative of China at the UN.[314] Chinese scholars disagree on the extent of China's participation at UNCLOS III: some claim that China participated actively in the negotiations, while others admit that China's proposals were very often broad policy outlines or general principles rather than specific regulations.[315]

China's participation at UNCLOS III was noteworthy for China's identification with the Third World. China described itself as a "developing socialist state belonging to the Third World" or simply as a "Third World State."[316] For China, the basic contradiction underlying UNCLOS III was the opposition between the Third World States and the two Superpowers. The Third World States were said to be striving to change the outdated legal regime of the seas based on colonialism, imperialism,

(XXVI)(25 October 1971) http://www.un.org/en/ga/search/view_doc.asp?symbol=A/RES/2758(XXVI), accessed 14 April 2020.

[314] Isaac B. Kardon, "China Can Say No: Analyzing China's Rejection of the South China Sea Arbitration toward a New Era of International Law with Chinese Characteristics," *University of Pennsylvania Asian Law Review* 13 (2018): 4, https://scholarship.law.upenn.edu/cgi/viewcontent.cgi?article=1037&context=alr, accessed 14 April 2020. Kardon says it was China's first multilateral treaty "as a UN member state." Strictly speaking, China has always been a UN member State. The question between 1945 and 1971 at the UN was whether the Republic of China or the People's Republic of China should occupy the seat of China at the UN.

[315] The first view is expressed by Liu Haiyang, "Is Denouncing UNCLOS," the second by Gao Zhiguo, "China and the Law of the Sea," in Myron H. Nordquist et al. (eds.), *Freedom of Seas, Passage Rights and the 1982 Law of the Sea Convention* (Leiden: Martinus Nijhoff Publishers, 2009), 276.

[316] Mr. Chai Shu-fan (China) in 25th plenary meeting (2 July 1974), UN Doc. A/CONF.62/SR.25, in *UNCLOS III, Official Records*, vol. I, 81, para. 19; Mr. Ling Ching (China), in 28th plenary meeting (3 July 1974), UN Doc. A/CONF.62/SR.25, in *UNCLOS III, Official Records*, vol. I, 109, para. 77.

and hegemony, to safeguard their maritime rights and interests, and to establish a fair and reasonable new law of the sea; for them, the formulation of a new convention was an important element of the struggle to establish a new international economic order. The two Superpowers were accused of seeking to maintain their position of hegemony, clinging to the outdated legal regime of the sea, and being unwilling to relinquish their control and monopoly of the seas and oceans.[317] China stressed that unity among developing countries was essential for UNCLOS III to make progress. It accused the two Superpowers of seeking to undermine their unity, whereas China firmly supported the developing countries' proposals. China emphasized the enormous efforts by developing countries to formulate a new convention acceptable to all States and hailed its adoption as a "first step towards the establishment of a new legal order of the sea."[318] In the twenty-first century, Chinese scholars continue to consider the adoption of the Convention as a victory of the Third World in their long-term struggle for maritime rights and against the maritime hegemony of the two Superpowers and as part of the establishment of a new international economic order.[319]

Since China's accession to the Convention in 1996, China has claimed that it has played an increasingly important role in the law of the sea.[320]

[317] Mr. Lin Ching (China), 76th plenary meeting (17 September 1976), A/CONF.62/SR.76, in *UNCLOS III*, *Official Records*, vol. VI, *Summary Records, Plenary, General Committee, First, Second and Third Committees, as well as Documents of the Conference, Fifth Session: New York, 2 August–17 September 1976*, UN Doc. A/CONF.62/[Vol. 6] (New York: United Nations, 1976), 26, paras. 59, 61, 62, https://legal.un.org/docs/?path=../diplomaticconferences/1973_los/docs/english/vol_6/a_conf62_sr76.pdf&lang=E, accessed 10 April 2020; Mr. Shen Chi-Ching (China), 78th plenary meeting (28 June 1977), UN Doc. A/CONF.62/SR.78, in *UNCLOS III*, *Official Records*, vol. VII, *Summary Records and Documents, Sixth Session, New York, 23 May–15 July 1977*, UN Doc. A/CONF/.62/[Vol. 7] (New York: United Nations, 1977), 8, para. 15, https://legal.un.org/docs/?path=../diplomaticconferences/1973_los/docs/english/vol_7/a_conf62_sr78.pdf&lang=E, accessed 16 April 2020.

[318] Mr. Shen Weiliang (China), 182nd Plenary meeting (30 April 1982), UN DOC. A/CONF.62/SR.182 in *UNCLOS III*, *Official Records*, vol. XVI, *Summary Records, Plenary, First and Second Committees, as well as Documents of the Conference, Eleventh Session, New York, 8 March–30 April 1982*, UN Doc. A/CONF.62/[Vol. 16] (New York: United Nations, 1984), 161, para. 121, https://legal.un.org/docs/?path=../diplomaticconferences/1973_los/docs/english/vol_16/a_conf62_sr182.pdf&lang=E, accessed 16 April 2020.

[319] Gao Zhiguo, "China and the Law of the Sea," 276–77.

[320] This paragraph is based on ibid., 294–95.

It asserts that it has contributed to bringing the Convention into force and full operation, although it is not clear what exactly such a contribution entailed. Overall, China views the Convention favorably. It seeks to modify provisions of the Convention that it considers weak or imperfect, such as the passage of foreign warships in the territorial sea.[321] China considers it an achievement that it is incorporating many Convention provisions in its domestic law.

China's rosy self-image would have been severely undermined had China denounced the Convention, particularly since denunciation would have taken place as a response to what China perceived as unfavorable awards in the *South China Sea Arbitration*. Chinese scholar Liu Haiyang believed that the Philippines and the US would exploit the denunciation to "defame China in every way they can."[322] In his view, while China's non-participation in and non-acceptance of the *Arbitration* was a legal choice under the Convention and international law, the denunciation would "make China seem in the wrong and may be taken as a sign that China is facing a setback as a result of losing the case."[323] This reasoning is not easy to understand. A rejection of China's legal theses by the Arbitral Tribunal would signify without room for doubt a finding that China was indeed "in the wrong" and would certainly represent a "setback" for China's legal position. There would have been no need for denunciation to produce such effects. More plausible is the argument that denunciation might raise concerns among other States regarding China's general attitude toward international law and create fears that China might also denounce other treaties in the event of decisions that it deemed unfavorable to it.[324] Denunciation would have made it much more difficult to believe the reassurances offered by scholars such as Julian Ku that China's conduct in the *South China Sea Arbitration* would not be repeated in other fora for dispute settlement, particularly at the World Trade Organization ("WTO").[325]

[321] Mr. Shen Weiliang (China), 182nd Plenary meeting (30 April 1982), UN DOC. A/CONF.62/SR.182 in *UNCLOS III*, *Official Records*, vol. XVI, 161–62, para. 122.

[322] Liu Haiyang, "Is Denouncing UNCLOS."

[323] Ibid.

[324] Ibid.

[325] Ku, "The Significance," 102.

Davenport added that denunciation would undermine the already fragile belief in China's claim that its rise would be "peaceful." Certainly, it would damage trust and confidence in China among the littoral States, damaging the prospects for bilateral negotiations on the South China Sea disputes that China tirelessly and relentlessly called for.[326] China's denunciation of the Convention would not be seen in the same light as the US refusal to accede to the Convention. As Davenport explains convincingly, US refusal to become a party to the Convention is tolerated because the US generally complied with the provisions of the Convention.[327] In contrast, a denunciation by China would take place following a decision by an international tribunal that China had breached international law and would with reason be seen as flouting international law.

It has been established that China's default in the *South China Sea Arbitration* did not alter its status as a party to the case, did not deprive the Tribunal of the power to determine its own jurisdiction, and did not relieve China of the duty to comply with the decisions of the Tribunal. The remaining Chapters of the book will analyze how the Tribunal exercised its procedural powers in order to alleviate the practical difficulties created by China's default and to acquire knowledge of the facts in the *South China Sea Arbitration*.

References

1899 Convention for the Pacific Settlement of International Disputes, https://pca-cpa.org/wp-content/uploads/sites/6/2016/01/1899-Convention-for-the-Pacific-Settlement-of-International-Disputes.pdf, accessed 3 April 2020.

1907 Convention for the Pacific Settlement of International Disputes, https://pca-cpa.org/wp-content/uploads/sites/6/2016/01/1907-Convention-for-the-Pacific-Settlement-of-International-Disputes.pdf, accessed 3 April 2020.

Aegean Sea Continental Shelf (Greece v. Turkey). Interim Protection. Order of 11 September 1976. I.C.J. Reports 1976, pp. 3–14, http://www.icj-cij.org/files/case-related/62/062-19760911-ORD-01-00-BI.pdf, accessed 3 April 2020.

———. Separate Opinion of Judge Tarazi. *I.C.J. Reports 1976*, pp. 31–34, https://www.icj-cij.org/files/case-related/62/062-19760911-ORD-01-08-BI.pdf, accessed 3 April 2020.

[326] Davenport, "Why China Shouldn't Denounce UNCLOS."

[327] Ibid.

Aerial incident of March 10th, 1953 (United States of America v. Czechoslovakia). United States. *Application Instituting Proceedings* (22 March 1955). *I.C.J. Pleadings, Aerial incident of March 10th, 1953*, pp. 8–26, https://www.icj-cij.org/files/case-related/25/025-19550322-APP-1-00-BI.pdf, accessed 5 April 2020.

———. *Order of March14, 1956: I.C.J. Reports 1956*, pp. 6–8, https://www.icj-cij.org/files/case-related/25/025-19560314-ORD-01-00-BI.pdf, accessed 5 April 2020.

Alleged Violations of Sovereign Rights and Maritime Spaces in the Caribbean Sea (Nicaragua v. Colombia). Nicaragua. *Application Instituting Proceedings* (26 November 2013), https://www.icj-cij.org/en/case/155/institution-proceedings, accessed 13 April 2020.

American Treaty on Pacific Settlement (Pact of Bogota). Signed at Bogotá, 30 April 1948. Entered into force on 6 May 1949, https://www.oas.org/sap/peacefund/resolutions/Pact_of_Bogot%C3%A1.pdf, accessed 15 April 2020.

Anglo-Iranian Oil Co. (United Kingdom v. Iran). Communication from the Minister of Foreign Affairs of Iran to the President of the International Court of Justice, dated 29 June 1951, with Three Annexes. *I.C.J. Pleadings, Anglo-Iranian Oil Co. Case*, 672–98, https://www.icj-cij.org/files/case-related/16/8987.pdf, accessed 19 March 2020.

———. *(Jurisdiction). Judgment of July 22, 1952: I.C.J. Reports 1952*, 93–115, https://www.icj-cij.org/files/case-related/16/016-19520722-JUD-01-00-BI.pdf, accessed 19 March 2020

———. "Observations préliminaires: Refus du Gouvernement impérial de reconnaître la compétence de la Cour [Preliminary Observations: Refusal by the Imperial Government to Accept the Jurisdiction of the Court] (4 February 1952)." *I.C.J. Pleadings, Anglo-Iranian Oil Co. Case*, 281–319, https://www.icj-cij.org/files/case-related/16/10980.pdf, accessed 6 April 2020

———. Oral Proceedings. *I.C.J. Pleadings, Anglo-Iranian Oil Co. Case*, 424–669, https://www.icj-cij.org/files/case-related/16/016-19510630-ORA-01-00-BI.pdf, accessed 8 January 2020.

———. *Order of July 5th, 1951: I.C.J. Reports 1951*, 100–01, https://www.icj-cij.org/files/case-related/16/016-19510705-ORD-01-00-BI.pdf, accessed 6 April 2020.

Antarctica Case (United Kingdom v. Argentina). United Kingdom. *Application Instituting Proceedings* (4 May 1955). *I.C.J. Pleadings. Antarctica Cases*, 8–47, https://www.icj-cij.org/files/case-related/26/026-in19550504-APP-1-00-BI.pdf, accessed 5 April 2020.

———. *Order of March 16th, 1956: I.C.J. Reports 1956*, 12–14, https://www.icj-cij.org/files/case-related/26/026-19560316-ORD-01-00-BI.pdf, accessed 5 April 2020.

Antarctica Case (United Kingdom v. Chile). United Kingdom. *Application Instituting Proceedings* (4 May 1955). *I.C.J. Pleadings, Antarctica Cases*, 48–77, https://www.icj-cij.org/files/case-related/27/027-19550504-APP-1-00-BI.pdf, accessed 5 April 2020.

———. *Order of March 16th, 1956: I.C.J. Reports 1956*, 15–17, https://www.icj-cij.org/files/case-related/27/027-19560316-ORD-01-00-BI.pdf, accessed 5 April 2020.

Arangio-Ruiz, Gaetano. "Non-Appearance Before the International Court of Justice. Final Report." *Annuaire de l'Institut de droit international* [Yearbook of the Institute of International Law]. Session de Bâle [Basel Session], 64-I (1991), 280–339, http://www.gaetanoarangioruiz.it/publications/non-appearance-before-the-international-court-of-justice/, accessed 13 October 2019.

———. "Non-Appearance Before the International Court of Justice. Preliminary Report." *Annuaire de l'Institut de droit international* [Yearbook of the Institute of International Law]. Session de Bâle [Basel Session], 64-I (1991), 193–279, http://www.gaetanoarangioruiz.it/publications/non-appearance-before-the-international-court-of-justice/, accessed 13 October 2019.

———. "Notes on Non-Appearance Before the International Court of Justice." *Le droit international à l'heure de sa codification. Études en l'honneur de Roberto Ago* [International Law at the Time of Its Codification. Studies in Honour of Roberto Ago]. Vol. II. *Les différends entre États et la responsabilité* [Inter-State Disputes and Responsibility], 3–48. Milano: Dott. A. Giuffrè Editore, 1987.

"Arctic Sunrise" Arbitration (Kingdom of the Netherlands v. Russian Federation). Award on Jurisdiction (26 November 2014), https://pcacases.com/web/sendAttach/1325, accessed 8 April 2020.

———. Award on the Merits (14 August 2015), https://pcacases.com/web/sendAttach/1438, accessed 17 March 2020.

———. *Memorial of the Kingdom of the Netherlands* (31 August 2014), https://pcacases.com/web/sendAttach/1406, accessed 7 April 2020.

———. Note Verbale from the Russian Federation to the PCA dated 27 February 2014, https://pcacases.com/web/sendAttach/1315, accessed 10 March 2020.

———. Procedural Order No. 4 (Bifurcation) (21 November 2014), https://pcacases.com/web/sendAttach/1324accessed 15 January 2020.

"Arctic Sunrise" (Kingdom of the Netherlands v. Russian Federation). Provisional Measures. Order of 22 November 2013. Joint Separate Opinion of Judges Wolfrum and Kelly. *ITLOS Reports 2013*, 256–61, https://www.itlos.org/fileadmin/itlos/documents/cases/case_no.22/published/C22_Wolfrum_Kelly_221113.pdf, accessed 16 March 2020.

Balch, Thomas. *The Alabama Arbitration*. Philadelphia: Allen, Lane & Scott, 1900, https://archive.org/details/alabamaarbitrat00balcgoog, accessed 3 April 2020.
Balton, David A. "UNCLOS: The Stakes for America." *The Law of the Sea Convention: US Accession and Globalization*, 44–47. Eds. Myron H. Nordquist et al. Leiden: Martinus Nijhoff Publishers, 2012.
Bardonnet, Daniel. "La dénonciation par le Gouvernement sénégalais de la Convention sur la mer territoriale et la zone contiguë et de la Convention sur la pêche et la conservation des ressources biologiques de la haute mer, en date du 29 avril 1958 à Genève [The Denunciation by the Senegalese Government of the Convention on the Territorial Sea and the Contiguous Zone and the Convention on Fishing and the Conservation of the Living Resources of the High Seas, concluded on 29 April 1958 at Geneva]." *Annuaire français de droit international* [French Yearbook of International Law] 18 (1972): 123–80, https://www.persee.fr/doc/afdi_0066-3085_1972_num_18_1_1693, accessed 12 April 2020.
Bedjaoui, Mohammed, and Fatsah Ouguergouz. "Le forum prorogatum devant la Cour Internationale de Justice: Les ressources d'une institution ou la face cachée du consensualisme [Forum Prorogatum Before the International Court of Justice: The Resources of an Institution or the Hidden Face of Consensualism]." *African Yearbook of International Law* 5 (1997): 91–114.
Bowett, D.W. "Contemporary Developments in Legal Techniques in the Settlement of Disputes." *Recueil des cours de l'Académie de droit international de La Haye* [Collected Courses of the Hague Academy of International Law]. Vol. 180 (1983-II), 169–235.
Chagos Marine Protected Area Arbitration (Mauritius v. United Kingdom). Bifurcation Hearing Transcript (11 January 2013), https://pcacases.com/web/sendAttach/1564, accessed 14 January 2020.
———. Rules of Procedure (29 March 2012), https://pcacases.com/web/sendAttach/1567, accessed 14 January 2020.
Chang Yen-Chiang. "China's Non-Participation Approach Toward the South China Sea Arbitration." *Chinese (Taiwan) Yearbook of International Law and Affairs* 34 (2016): 56–72.
China, People's Republic of. Ministry of Foreign Affairs. *Briefing by Xu Hong, Director-General of the Department of Treaty and Law on the South China Sea Arbitration Initiated by the Philippines 2016/05/12*, https://www.fmprc.gov.cn/nanhai/eng/wjbxw_1/t1364804.htm, accessed 16 January 2020.
———. *Foreign Ministry Spokesperson Hua Chunying's Remarks on the Philippines' Efforts in Pushing for the Establishment of the Arbitral Tribunal in Relation to the Disputes Between China and the Philippines in the South China Sea* (26 April 2013), https://www.fmprc.gov.cn/mfa_eng/xwfw_665399/s2510_665401/2535_665405/t1035577.shtml, accessed 10 March 2020.

Chinese Society of International Law. "The South China Sea Arbitration Awards: A Critical Study." *Chinese Journal of International Law* 17 (2018): 207–748.
———. "The Tribunal's Award in the 'South China Sea Arbitration' Initiated by the Philippines Is Null and Void." *Chinese Journal of International Law* 15 (2016): 457–87.
Colliard, Claude-Albert. "La Non-comparution [Non-Appearance]." *La juridiction internationale permanente* [Permanent International Jurisdiction], 167–90. Société française pour le droit international [French Society for International Law]. Colloque de Lyon [Lyons Colloquium]. Paris: Éditions A. Pedone, 1987.
Convention for the Establishment of a Central American Court of Justice. American Journal of International Law 2, No. 1/2, *Supplement: Official Documents* (1908): 231–43.
Convention on the Continental Shelf. Done at Geneva on 29 April 1958. Entered into force on 10 June 1964, https://legal.un.org/ilc/texts/instruments/english/conventions/8_1_1958_continental_shelf.pdf, accessed 10 April 2020.
Convention on Fishing and Conservation of the Living Resources of the High Seas. Done at Geneva on 29 April 1958. Entered into force on 20 March 1966, https://www.gc.noaa.gov/documents/8_1_1958_fishing.pdf, accessed 10 April 2020.
Convention on the High Seas. Done at Geneva on 29 April 1958. Entered into force on 30 September 1962, http://www.gc.noaa.gov/documents/8_1_1958_high_seas.pdf, accessed 10 April 2020.
Convention on Special Missions. Done at New York on 8 December 1969. Entered into force on 21 June 1985, https://legal.un.org/ilc/texts/instruments/english/conventions/9_3_1969.pdf, accessed 10 April 2020.
Convention on the Territorial Sea and the Contiguous Zone. Done at Geneva on 29 April 1958. Entered into force on 10 September 1964, http://www.gc.noaa.gov/documents/8_1_1958_territorial_sea.pdf, accessed on 10 April 2020.
Corfu Channel Case. Judgment of December 15th 1949: I.C.J. Reports 1949, 244–65, http://www.icj-cij.org/files/case-related/1/001-19491215-JUD-01-00-BI.pdf, accessed 30 March 2020.
———. Oral Proceedings (Second Part). *I.C.J. Pleadings, Corfu Channel Case*. Vol. IV, 7–699, https://www.icj-cij.org/files/case-related/1/001-19491117-ORA-01-00-BI.pdf, accessed 8 January 2020.
———. United Kingdom. *Application Instituting Proceedings* (13 May 1947). *I.C.J. Pleadings, Corfu Channel Case*. Vol. I, 8–17, https://www.icj-cij.org/files/case-related/1/1499.pdf, accessed 27 March 2020.
Cot, Jean-Pierre. "Affaire des Essais nucléaires (Australie c. France et Nouvelle-Zélande c. France). Demandes en indication de mesures conservatoires. Ordonnances du 22 juin 1973 [The Nuclear Tests Cases (Australia v. France

and New-Zealand v. France). Requests for the Indication of Provisional Measures. Orders of 22 June 1973]." *Annuaire français de droit international* [French Yearbook of International Law] 19 (1973): 252–71, http://www.persee.fr/doc/afdi_0066-3085_1973_num_19_1_2213, accessed 1 April 2020.

Davenport, Tara. "Why China Shouldn't Denounce UNCLOS." *The Diplomat*, 24 March 2016, https://thediplomat.com/2016/03/why-china-shouldnt-denounce-unclos/, accessed 9 April 2020.

DeRenzi, Nanette. "Protecting and Enhancing US National Security." *The Law of the Sea Convention: US Accession and Globalization*, 86–92. Eds. Myron H. Nordquist et al. Leiden: Martinus Nijhoff Publishers, 2012.

Dipla, Haritini. "L'affaire concernant le filetage à l'intérieur du golfe du Saint-Laurent entre le Canada et la France (sentence du 17 juin 1986) [Case Concerning Filleting within the Gulf of St. Lawrence Between Canada and France (Award of 17 June 1986)]." *Annuaire français de droit international* [French Yearbook of International Law] 43 (1986): 239–58, https://www.persee.fr/issue/afdi_0066-3085_1986_num_32_1, accessed 10 May 2022.

Elias, Taslim O. *The International Court of Justice and Some Contemporary Problems. Essays on International Law*. Dordrecht: Springer Science+Business Media, 1983.

Elkind, Jerome B. "Normative Surrender." *Michigan Journal of International Law* 9 (1988): 263–90, https://repository.law.umich.edu/cgi/viewcontent.cgi?article=1758&context=mjil, accessed 26 March 2020.

Esmaquel, Paterno II. "PH Faces Major Hurdle in China Case." *Rappler*, 12 March 2014, http://www.rappler.com/nation/52764-philippines-china-arbitral-tribunal-jurisdiction, accessed 8 April 2020.

Favoreu, Louis. "L'arrêt de la Cour internationale de Justice dans l'affaire de la compétence en matière de pêcheries (Royaume-Uni c./Islande et Allemagne fédérale c./Islande) [The Judgment of the International Court of Justice in the Case Concerning Fisheries Jurisdiction (United Kingdom v. Iceland and Federal Republic of Germany v. Iceland]." *Annuaire français de droit international* [French Yearbook of International Law] 19 (1973): 272–89, http://www.persee.fr/doc/afdi_0066-3085_1973_num_19_1_2214, accessed 4 September 2020.

———. "Les arrêts de la Cour Internationale de Justice relatifs à la compétence en matière de pêcheries (Royaume-Uni c/ Islande et République fédérale d'Allemagne c. Islande — Arrêts du 25 juillet 1974) [The Judgments of the International Court of Justice on Fisheries Jurisdiction (United Kingdom v. Iceland and Federal Republic of Germany v. Iceland – Judgments of 25 July 1974]." *Annuaire français de droit international* [French Yearbook of International Law] 20 (1974): 253–85, http://www.persee.fr/doc/afdi_0066-3085_1974_num_20_1_2271, accessed 17 March 2020.

———. "Les ordonnances des 17 et 18 août 1972 dans les affaires relatives à la compétence en matière de pêcheries - Contribution au droit procédural de la Cour en matière de mesures conservatoires, exceptions préliminaires et compétence en cas de défaut (Royaume-Uni c. Islande et République fédérale d'Allemagne c. Islande) [The Orders of 17 and 18 August 1972 in the Cases Relating to Fisheries Jurisdiction – Contribution to the Procedural Law of the Court with Respect to Provisional Measures, Preliminary Objections and Jurisdiction in Case of Default (United Kingdom v. Iceland and Federal Republic of Germany v. Iceland)." *Annuaire français de droit international* [French Yearbook of International Law] 18 (1972): 291–322, http://www.persee.fr/doc/afdi_0066-3085_1972_num_18_1_3855, accessed 7 April 2020.

Filleting within the Gulf of St. Lawrence Between Canada and France. Award of 17 June 1986. *Reports of International Arbitral Awards*. Vol. XIX, 225–96. New York: United Nations, 1990, http://legal.un.org/docs/?path=../riaa/cases/vol_XIX/225-296.pdf&lang=O, accessed 10 May 2022.

Fisheries Jurisdiction (Federal Republic of Germany v. Iceland). Jurisdiction of the Court. Judgment. I.C.J. Reports 1973, 49–67, http://www.icj-cij.org/files/case-related/56/056-19730202-JUD-01-00-EN.pdf, accessed 4 September 2020.

———. *Order of 18 August 1972. I.C.J. Reports 1972*, 188–90, https://www.icj-cij.org/files/case-related/56/056-19720818-ORD-01-00-BI.pdf, accessed 7 April 2020.

———. *Merits. Judgment. I.C.J. Reports 1974*, 175–216, http://www.icj-cij.org/files/case-related/56/056-19740725-JUD-01-00-BI.pdf, accessed 17 March 2020.

———. Oral Proceedings on the Request for the Indication of Interim Measures of Protection. *I.C.J. Pleadings, Fisheries Jurisdiction*. Vol. II, 41–61, https://www.icj-cij.org/files/case-related/56/056-19720802-ORA-01-00-BI.pdf, accessed 29 March 2020.

Fisheries Jurisdiction (United Kingdom v. Iceland). Jurisdiction of the Court. Judgment. I.C.J. Reports 1973, 3–23, http://www.icj-cij.org/files/case-related/55/055-19730202-JUD-01-00-BI.pdf, accessed 4 September 2020.

———. *Order of 18 August 1972. I.C.J. Reports 1972*, 181–83, https://www.icj-cij.org/files/case-related/55/055-19720818-ORD-01-00-BI.pdf, accessed 7 April 1972; accessed 7 April 2020.

———. *Merits. Judgment. I.C.J. Reports 1974*, 3–44, https://www.icj-cij.org/files/case-related/55/055-19740725-JUD-01-00-BI.pdf, accessed 17 March 2020.

———. Dissenting Opinion of Judge Gros. *I.C.J. Reports 1974*, 126–49, https://www.icj-cij.org/files/case-related/55/055-19740725-JUD-01-08-BI.pdf, accessed 11 August 2019.

———. Dissenting Opinion of Judge Onyeama. *I.C.J. Reports 1974*, 164–73, https://www.icj-cij.org/files/case-related/55/055-19740725-JUD-01-10-BI.pdf, accessed 1 April 2020.

———. Oral Proceedings on Interim Measures of Protection. *I.C.J. Pleadings, Fisheries Jurisdiction*. Vol. I, 91–120, https://www.icj-cij.org/files/case-related/55/055-19720801-ORA-01-00-BI.pdf, accessed 29 March 2020.

———. Oral Proceedings on the Jurisdiction of the Court. *I.C.J. Pleadings, Fisheries Jurisdiction*. Vol. II, 241–63, https://www.icj-cij.org/files/case-related/55/055-19730105-ORA-01-00-BI.pdf, accessed 7 October 2019.

———. Oral Proceedings on the Merits. *I.C.J. Pleadings, Fisheries Jurisdiction*. Vol. I, 436–518, http://www.icj-cij.org/files/case-related/55/055-19740325-ORA-01-00-BI.pdf, accessed 22 April 2020.

Fitzmaurice, Gerald. "The Problem of the 'Non-Appearing' Defendant Government." *British Yearbook of International Law* 51 (1980): 89–122.

———. "Some Results of the Geneva Conference on the Law of the Sea. Part I. The Territorial Sea and Contiguous Zone and Related Topics." *International and Comparative Law Quarterly* 8 (1959): 73–121.

Gao Zhiguo. "China and the Law of the Sea." *Freedom of Seas, Passage Rights and the 1982 Law of the Sea Convention*, 265–96. Eds. Myron H. Nordquist et al. Leiden: Martinus Nijhoff Publishers, 2009.

Goldmann, Matthias. "International Courts and Tribunals, Non-Appearance." *Max Planck Encyclopedia of Public International Law* (2006).

Goy, Raymond. "Le règlement de l'affaire des pêcheries islandaises [The Settlement of the Icelandic Fisheries Case]." *Revue générale de droit international public* [General Journal of Public International Law] 82 (1978): 434–536.

Grant, John P., and J. Craig Barker. *Parry & Grant Encyclopaedic Dictionary of International Law*, 3rd ed. Oxford: Oxford University Press, 2009.

Guyana v. Suriname. Hearing Transcripts, Day 2 (8 July 2005), https://pcacases.com/web/sendAttach/890, accessed 7 April 2020.

Helfer, Laurence R. "Exiting Custom: Analogies to Treaty Withdrawals." *Duke Journal of Comparative and International Law* 21 (2010): 65–80, https://scholarship.law.duke.edu/cgi/viewcontent.cgi?article=2909&context=faculty_scholarship, accessed 12 April 2020.

———. "Terminating Treaties." *The Oxford Guide to Treaties*, 634–50. Ed. Duncan B. Hollis. Oxford: Oxford University Press, 2012, https://scholarship.law.duke.edu/cgi/viewcontent.cgi?article=5338&context=faculty_scholarship, accessed 10 April 2020.

Institut de droit international [Institute of International Law]. Session de Bâle [Basel Session]. *Non-Appearance Before the International Court of Justice* (1991), https://www.idi-iil.org/app/uploads/2017/06/1991_bal_01_en.pdf, accessed 16 March 2020.

International Convention on the International Regulations for Preventing Collisions at Sea. Adopted at London on 20 October 1972. Entered into force 15 July 1977, consolidated text as amended in 1981, 1987, 1989, 1993, 2001 and 2007, http://www.ecolregs.com/index.php?option=com_k2&view=itemlist&layout=category&Itemid=505&lang=en, accessed 31 May 2019.

International Convention for the Safety of Life at Sea (SOLAS 1974). Adopted at London on 1 November 1974. Entered into force on 25 May 1980, https://www.refworld.org/docid/46920bf32.html, accessed 3 June 2019.

International Court of Justice. *The International Court of Justice Handbook*. The Hague: International Court of Justice, 2019, https://www.icj-cij.org/files/publications/handbook-of-the-court-en.pdf, accessed 7 September 2020.

———. *Practice Directions (as amended on 20 January 2009 and 21 March 2013)*, https://www.icj-cij.org/en/practice-directions, accessed 8 April 2020.

———. *Rules of Court (1978) adopted on 14 April 1978 and entered into force on 1 July 1978*, https://www.icj-cij.org/en/rules, accessed 22 March 2020.

———. *Statute*, http://www.icj-cij.org/en/statute, accessed 10 March 2020.

Josten, R. Bruce. "US LOS Ratification: A Potential Resource Bonanza for US Industry." *The Law of the Sea Convention: US Accession and Globalization*, 72–75. Eds. Myron H. Nordquist et al. Leiden: Martinus Nijhoff Publishers, 2012.

Juste Ruiz, José. "Mootness in International Adjudication: The Nuclear Tests Cases." *German Yearbook of International Law* 20 (1977): 358–74.

Kardon, Isaac B. "China Can Say No: Analyzing China's Rejection of the South China Sea Arbitration. Toward a New Era of International Law with Chinese Characteristics." *University of Pennsylvania Asian Law Review* 13 (2018): 1–46, https://scholarship.law.upenn.edu/cgi/viewcontent.cgi?article=1037&context=alr, accessed 14 April 2020.

———. "China's Maritime Interests and the Law of the Sea: Domesticating Public International Law." *China's Socialist Rule of Law Reforms Under Xi Jinping*, 179–96. Eds. John Garrick and Yan Chang Bennett. Milton Park, Abingdon, Oxon: Routledge, 2016.

Ku, Julian. "The Significance of China's Rejection of the South China Sea Arbitration for Its Approach to International Dispute Settlement and International Law." *Chinese (Taiwan) Yearbook of International Law and Affairs* 34 (2016): 73–103.

Kwiatkowska, Barbara. "The International Court of Justice and the Law of the Sea. Some Reflections." *Theory of International Law at the Threshold of the 21st Century. Essays in Honor of Krzysztof Skubiszewski*, 439–85. Ed. Jerzy Makarczyk. The Hague: Kluwer Law International, 1996.

Lacharrière, Guy de. "Commentaires sur la position juridique de la France à l'égard de la licéité de ses expériences nucléaires [Commentaries on the Legal Position of France with Respect to the Legality of Its Nuclear Tests].” *Annuaire français de droit international* [French Yearbook of International Law] 19 (1973): 235–51, http://www.persee.fr/doc/afdi_0066-3085_1973_num_19_1_2212, accessed 2 April 2020.

Langavant, Emmanuel, and Olivier Pirotte. “L’affaire des pêcheries islandaises. L’arrêt de la cour internationale de justice du 25 juillet 1974 [The Icelandic Fisheries Case. The Judgment of the International Court of Justice of 25 July 1974].” *Revue générale de droit international public* [General Journal of Public International Law] 80 (1976): 55–103.

Langer, Lorenz. “The South China Sea as a Challenge to International Law and to International Legal Scholarship.” *Berkeley Journal of International Law* 36 (2018): 362–95, https://scholarship.law.berkeley.edu/cgi/viewcontent.cgi?article=1551&context=bjil, accessed 10 April 2020.

Lapradelle, Albert Geouffre de, and Nicolas Politis (eds.). *Recueil des arbitrages internationaux* [Collection of International Arbitrations]. Vol. I. *1798–1855*. Paris: A. Pedone Éditeur, 1905, https://ia600309.us.archive.org/19/items/recueildesarbit01lapr/recueildesarbit01lapr.pdf, accessed 26 March 2020.

———. *Recueil des arbitrages internationaux* [Collection of International Arbitrations]. Vol. II. *1856–1872*. Paris: A. Pedone Éditeur, 1923, https://ia802607.us.archive.org/3/items/recueildesarbitr02lapruoft/recueildesarbitr02lapruoft.pdf, accessed 26 March 2020.

Liu Haiyang. “Is Denouncing UNCLOS a Good Option for China?” *Global Times*, 21 April 2016, http://www.globaltimes.cn/content/979454.shtml, accessed 9 April 2020.

McWhinney, Edward. “International Law-making and the Judicial Process: The World Court and the French Nuclear Tests Case.” *Syracuse Journal of International Law and Commerce* 3 (1975): 9–46, https://surface.syr.edu/cgi/viewcontent.cgi?article=1033&context=jilc, accessed 1 April 2020.

Magnússon, Bjarni Már. “Can the United States Establish the Outer Limits of Its Extended Continental Shelf Under International Law?” *Ocean Development and International Law* 48 (2017): 1–16.

Mangoldt, Hans von. “Versäumnisverfahren in der internationalen (Schieds)Gerichtsbarkeit und souveräne Gleichheit [Default Procedures in International Arbitration and Adjudication and Sovereign Equality].” *Völkerrecht als Rechtsordnung, internationale Gerichtsbarkeit, Menschenrechte. Festschrift für Hermann Mosler* [International Law as a Legal Order, International Adjudication, Human Rights. Festschrift for Hermann Mosler], 503–29. Ed. Rudolf Bernhardt. Berlin: Springer Verlag, 1983.

Manicom, James. “China’s Claims to an Extended Continental Shelf in the East China Sea: Meaning and Implications.” *China Brief* 9 (9 July 2009): 9–11, https://jamestown.org/wp-content/uploads/2009/07/cb_009_23.pdf?x73233, accessed 15 April 2020.

Martens, Fedor Fedorovich. *Traité de droit international* [A Treatise on International Law]. Vol. III. Translated from Russian by Alfred Léo. Paris: Chevalier-Marescq et Cie. Successeurs, 1887, https://ia800902.us.archive.org/32/items/traitddroitint00martgoog/traitdedroitint00martgoog.pdf, accessed 13 January 2020.

Martin, Pierre-Marie. "L'affaire de la compétence en matière de pêcheries (les arrêts de la C.I.J. du 2 février 1973) [The Fisheries Jurisdiction Cases (The I.C.J. Judgments of 2 February 1973)]." *Revue générale de droit international public* [General Journal of Public International Law] 78 (1974): 435–58.

Mateus Rugeles, Andrea. "Denuncia del Pacto de Bogotá: Implicaciones jurídicas para Colombia [Denunciation of the Pact of Bogotá: Legal Implications for Colombia]." *Contribución de la Universidad del Rosario al debate sobre el fallo de La Haya: Análisis del caso Nicaragua vs. Colombia* [Contribution of the Universidad del Rosario to the Debate on the ICJ Judgment: Analysis of the Nicaragua vs. Colombia Case], 1–22. Eds. Carlos Holmes Trujillo García and María Lucía Torres Villarreal. Bogotá: Editorial Universidad del Rosario, 2013, https://pure.urosario.edu.co/ws/portalfiles/portal/21996451/pi_Contribucion_UR_fallo_Haya_final.pdf, accessed 13 April 2020.

Matine-Daftary, A. "Cours abrégé sur la contribution des conférences de Genève au développement progressif du droit international de la mer [Abbreviated Course on the Contribution of the Geneva Conferences to the Progressive Development of the International Law of the Sea]." *Recueil des cours de l'Académie de droit international de La Haye* [Collected Courses of the Hague Academy of International Law]. Vol. 102 (1961-I), 635–74.

Mattler, Michael J. "UNCLOS: The Stakes for America." *The Law of the Sea Convention: US Accession and Globalization*, 57–62. Eds. Myron H. Nordquist et al. Leiden: Martinus Nijhoff Publishers, 2012.

"Memorandum para ser transmitido au Senado da Cidade Libre de Hamburgo, para se encarregar da arbitragem relativamente à reclamação dos Sres Yuille, Shortridge e Cia [Memorandum to Be Transmitted to the Senate of the Free City of Hamburg, to Take Charge of the Arbitration Relating to the Claim of Messrs. Yuille, Shortridge and Co.] [8 March 1861]." *Pasicrisie internationale 1794–1900. Histoire documentaire des arbitrages internationaux* [Compendium of International Caselaw 1794–1900. A Documentary History of International Arbitrations], 377–78. Ed. Henri La Fontaine. Berne: Imprimerie Stampfli & Cie, 1902, https://ia600205.us.archive.org/9/items/pasicrisieinter00fontgoog/pasicrisieinter00fontgoog.pdf, accessed 11 March 2020.

Mérignhac, Alexandre. *Traité théorique et pratique de l'arbitrage international: le rôle du droit dans le fonctionnement actuel de l'institution et dans ses destinées futures* [A Theoretical and Practical Treatise on International Arbitration: The Role of Law in the Present Operation of the Institution and in Its Future

Destiny]. Paris: Librairie du Recueil général des Lois et des arrêts et du Journal du Palais, 1895, https://ia601407.us.archive.org/14/items/traitthoriqueet00mrgoog/traitthoriqueet00mrgoog.pdf, accessed 3 April 2020.

Military and Paramilitary Activities in and Against Nicaragua (Nicaragua v. United States of America). Merits. Judgment. I.C.J. Reports 1986, 14–150, http://www.icj-cij.org/files/case-related/70/070-19860627-JUD-01-00-BI.pdf, accessed 17 March 2020.

———. *Judgment*. Dissenting Opinion of Judge Schwebel. *I.C.J. Reports 1986*, 259–527, http://www.icj-cij.org/files/case-related/70/070-19860627-JUD-01-09-BI.pdf, accessed 31 March 2020.

———. Oral Hearings on the Merits. *I.C.J. Pleadings, Military and Paramilitary Activities in and Against Nicaragua*. Vol. V, 3–241, https://www.icj-cij.org/files/case-related/70/070-19850912-ORA-01-00-BI.pdf, accessed 17 March 2020.

Ministère des Affaires Étrangères [Ministry of Foreign Affairs of the Netherlands]. *La Conférence internationale de la paix. La Haye, 18 mai-29 juillet 1899* [The International Peace Conference, 18 May-29 July 1899], new ed. The Hague: Martinus Nijhoff, 1907, https://ia902705.us.archive.org/0/items/laconfrenceint00inteuoft/laconfrenceint00inteuoft.pdf, accessed 9 April 2020.

Monroy Cabra, Marco Gerardo. "Análisis de la posición jurídica de Colombia ante la Corte de La Haya [Analysis of Colombia's Legal Position before the ICJ]." *Contribución de la Universidad del Rosario al debate sobre el fallo de La Haya: Análisis del caso Nicaragua vs. Colombia* [Contribution of the Universidad del Rosario to the Debate on the ICJ Judgment: Analysis of the Nicaragua vs. Colombia Case], 23–30. Eds. Carlos Holmes Trujillo García and María Lucía Torres Villarreal. Bogotá: Editorial Universidad del Rosario, 2013, https://pure.urosario.edu.co/ws/portalfiles/portal/21996451/pi_Contribucion_UR_fallo_Haya_final.pdf, accessed 13 April 2020.

Moore, John Bassett. *History and Digest of the International Arbitrations to Which the United States Has Been a Party*. Vol. III. Washington, D.C.: Government Printing Office, 1898, https://ia800204.us.archive.org/18/items/historyanddiges01moorgoog/historyanddiges01moorgoog.pdf, accessed 2 April 2020.

———. *The United States and International* Arbitration. Boston: The American Peace Society, 1896.

Mosler, Hermann. "Nichtteilnahme einer Partei am Verfahren vor dem Internationalen Gerichtshof [Non-Participation of a Party in Proceedings before the International Court of Justice]." *Staatsrecht – Völkerrecht – Europarecht. Festschrift für Hans-Jürgen Schlochauer* [Constitutional Law – International Law - European Law. Festschrift for Hans-Jürgen Schlochauer], 439–56. Ed. Ingo von Münch. Berlin:Walter de Gruyter, 1981.

MOX Plant Case (Ireland v. United Kingdom). Press Release (2 June 2003), https://pcacases.com/web/sendAttach/871, accessed 9 April 2020.

———. Press Release (17 June 2003), https://pcacases.com/web/sendAttach/872, accessed 9 April 2020.

———. Transcript, Day 2 (11 June 2003), https://pcacases.com/web/sendAttach/858, accessed 9 April 2020.

———. Transcript, Day 3 (12 June 2003), https://pcacases.com/web/sendAttach/859, accessed 9 April 2020.

———. Transcript, Day 5 (17 June 2003), https://pcacases.com/web/sendAttach/861, accessed 9 April 2020.

———. Transcript, Day 6 (18 June 2003), https://pcacases.com/web/sendAttach/862, accessed 9 April 2020.

———. Transcript, Day 8 (21 June 2003), https://pcacases.com/web/sendAttach/864, accessed 9 April 2020.

Muller, Wim. "China's Missed Opportunity in South China Sea Arbitration." *chathamhouse.org* (19 March 2015), https://www.chathamhouse.org/expert/comment/china-s-missed-opportunity-south-china-sea-arbitration, accessed 13 March 2020.

Murkowski, Lisa. "US Interests in Prompt Adherence to the Law of the Sea Convention." *The Law of the Sea Convention: US Accession and Globalization*, 19–23. Eds. Myron H. Nordquist et al. Leiden: Martinus Nijhoff Publishers, 2012.

Murton, Bramley J. "A Global Review of Non-Living Resources on the Extended Continental Shelf." *Revista Brasileira de Geofísica* [Brazilian Journal of Geophysics] 18 (2000): 281–306, http://www.scielo.br/scielo.php?pid=S0102-261X2000000300007&script=sci_arttext&tlng=es, accessed 15 April 2020.

Nordquist, Myron H. et al. (eds.), *United Nations Convention on the Law of the Sea 1982*. Vol. V. *Settlement of Disputes, General and Final Provisions and Related Annexes and Resolutions*. Leiden: Brill, 1989.

Nottebohm Case (Preliminary Objection). Judgment of November 18th, 1953: I.C.J. Reports 1953, 111–25, https://www.icj-cij.org/files/case-related/18/018-19531118-JUD-01-00-BI.pdf, accessed 30 March 2020.

———. Oral Arguments concerning the Preliminary Objection. *I.C.J. Pleadings, Nottebohm Case*, 10–29, https://www.icj-cij.org/files/case-related/18/018-19531110-ORA-01-00-BI.pdf, accessed 8 January 2020.

Nuclear Tests (Australia v. France). Interim Protection. Order of 22 June 1973. I.C.J. Reports 1973, 99–110, http://www.icj-cij.org/files/case-related/58/058-19730622-ORD-01-00-BI.pdf, accessed 3 April 2020

———. Dissenting Opinion of Judge Sir Garfield Barwick. *I.C.J. Reports 1974*, 391–455, http://www.icj-cij.org/files/case-related/58/058-19741220-JUD-01-09-BI.pdf, accessed 1 April 2020.

———. *Judgment. I.C.J. Reports 1974*, 253–74, https://www.icj-cij.org/files/case-related/58/058-19741220-JUD-01-00-BI.pdf, accessed 1 April 2020.

———. Oral Arguments on Jurisdiction and Admissibility. *I.C.J. Pleadings, Nuclear Tests*. Vol. II, 383–527, https://www.icj-cij.org/files/case-related/58/058-19740704-ORA-01-00-BI.pdf, accessed 30 March 2020.

Nuclear Tests (New Zealand v. France). Interim Protection. Order of 22 June 1973. I. C.J. Reports 1973, 135–47, https://www.icj-cij.org/files/case-related/59/059-19730622 ORD-01-00-BI.pdf, accessed 3 April 2020.

———. *Judgment. I.C.J. Reports 1974*, 457–78, https://www.icj-cij.org/files/case-related/59/059-19741220-JUD-01-00-BI.pdf, accessed 19 March 2020.

———. Oral Proceedings on the Request for the Indication of Interim Measures of Protection. *I.C.J. Pleadings, Nuclear Tests*. Vol. II, 97–142, https://www.icj-cij.org/files/case-related/59/059-19730524-ORA-01-00-BI.pdf, accessed 30 March 2020.

Nussbaum, Arthur. "The Arbitration Between the Lena Goldfields, Ltd. and the Soviet Government." *Cornell Law Quarterly* 36 (1950/1951): 31–53, https://scholarship.law.cornell.edu/cgi/viewcontent.cgi?article=1582&context=clr accessed 2 January 2020.

Permanent Court of International Justice. Advisory Committee of Jurists. *Procès-verbaux of the Proceedings of the Committee, June 16th–July 24th, 1920, with Annexes*. The Hague: Van Langenhuysen Frères, 1920, https://ia600900.us.archive.org/6/items/procsverbauxof00leaguoft/procsverbauxof00leaguoft.pdf, accessed 26 March 2020.

Question of the Delimitation of the Continental Shelf Between Nicaragua and Colombia beyond 200 nautical miles from the Nicaraguan Coast (Nicaragua v. Colombia). Nicaragua. *Application Instituting Proceedings* (16 September 2013), https://www.icj-cij.org/files/case-related/154/17532.pdf, accessed 13 April 2020.

———. *Preliminary Objections. Judgment*. Separate Opinion of Judge Greenwood. *I.C.J. Reports 2016*, 177–86, https://www.icj-cij.org/files/case-related/154/154-20160317-JUD-01-03-BI.pdf, accessed 15 April 2020.

Rosenne, Shabtai. "The General List of the International Court of Justice." *Theory of International Law at the Threshold of the 21st Century. Essays in Honor of Krzysztof Skubiszewski*, 805–16. Ed. Jerzy Makarczyk. The Hague: Kluwer Law International, 1996.

———. "The Reconceptualization of Objections in the International Court of Justice." *Comunicazioni e studi* [Communications and Studies] 14 (1975): 735–61.

———, with the assistance of Yaël Ronen. *The Law and Practice of the International Court 1990–2005*. Leiden: Martinus Nijhoff Publishers, 2006.

St. J. Macdonald, R., and Barbara Hough. "The *Nuclear Tests* Case Revisited." *German Yearbook of International Law* 20 (1977): 337–57.

Sarmiento Lamus, Andrés. "Impacto e implementación en Colombia de la decisión de fondo de la Corte Internacional de Justicia en el diferendo territorial y marítimo (Nicaragua c. Colombia) [Impact and Implementation in Colombia of the Decision on the Merits of the International Court of Justice in the Territorial and Maritime Dispute (Nicaragua v. Colombia)]." *Anuario mexicano de derecho internacional* [Mexican Yearbook of International Law] 16 (2016): 401–23, http://www.scielo.org.mx/scielo.php?script=sci_abstract&pid=S1870-46542016000100401&lng=en&nrm=iso&tlng=fr, accessed 15 April 2020.

Schachte, William. "Protecting and Enhancing US National Security: The Reality of the Operational Aspects of UNCLOS." *The Law of the Sea Convention: US Accession and Globalization*, 86–92. Eds. Myron H. Nordquist et al. Leiden: Martinus Nijhoff Publishers, 2012.

Scott, James Brown. "The Closing of the Central American Court of Justice." *American Journal of International Law* 12 (1918): 380–82.

———. *The Proceedings of the Hague Peace Conferences. Translation of the Official Texts. The Conference of 1899.* New York: Oxford University Press, 1920, https://ia802604.us.archive.org/18/items/proceedingshagu02scotgoog/proceedingshagu02scotgoog.pdf, accessed 3 April 2020.

———. *The Project of a Permanent Court of International Justice and Resolutions of the Advisory Committee of Jurists. Report and Commentary.* Washington, D.C.: Carnegie Endowment for International Peace, Division of International Law, 1920, https://ia800205.us.archive.org/12/items/cu31924016941142/cu31924016941142.pdf, accessed 26 March 2020.

Shihata, Ibrahim F.I. *The Power of the International Court to Determine Its Own Jurisdiction: Compétence de la Compétence.* Dordrecht: Springer Science+Business Media, 1965.

Sinclair, Ian. "Some Procedural Aspects of Recent International Litigation." *International and Comparative Law Quarterly* 30 (1981): 338–57.

Song, Yann-Huei, and Zou Keyuan. "Maritime Legislation of Mainland China and Taiwan: Developments, Comparison, Implications, and Potential Challenges for the United States." *Ocean Development and International Law* 31 (2000): 303–45.

South China Sea Arbitration. Award on Jurisdiction and Admissibility (29 October 2015), https://pcacases.com/web/sendAttach/2579, accessed 10 March 2020.

———. Award of 12 July 2016, https://pcacases.com/web/sendAttach/2086, accessed 10 March 2020.

———. Hearing on Jurisdiction and Admissibility. Transcript, Day 1 (7 July 2015), https://pcacases.com/web/sendAttach/1399, accessed 19 March 2020.
———. Transcript, Day 3 (13 July 2015), https://pcacases.com/web/sendAttach/1401, accessed 8 April 2020.
———. Hearing on the Merits and Remaining Issues of Jurisdiction and Admissibility. Transcript, Day 4 (30 November 2015), https://pcacases.com/web/sendAttach/1550, accessed 16 April 2020.
———. *Memorial of the Philippines* (30 March 2014). Vol. I, https://files.pca-cpa.org/pcadocs/Memorial%20of%20the%20Philippines%20Volume%20I.pdf, accessed 23 April 2020.
———. Vol. V. Annexes, https://files.pca-cpa.org/pcadocs/The%20Philippines%27%20Memorial%20-%20Volume%20V%20%28Annexes%20103-157%29.pdf, accessed 23 March 2020.
———. Annex 144. Association of Southeast Asian Nations, Declaration on the Conduct of the Parties in South China Sea (4 November 2002), 321–25.
———. Procedural Order No. 4 (21 April 2015), https://pcacases.com/web/sendAttach/1807, accessed 7 April 2020.
———. Rules of Procedure (27 August 2013), https://pcacases.com/web/sendAttach/233, accessed 5 April 2020.
———. *Supplemental Written Submission of the Philippines* (16 March 2015). Vol. VIII. Annexes, https://files.pca-cpa.org/pcadocs/The%20Philippines%27%20Supplemental%20Written%20Submission%20-%20Volume%20VIII%20%28Annexes%20466-499%29.pdf, accessed 10 March 2020.
———. Annex 467. People's Republic of China, Position Paper of the Government of the People's Republic of China on the Matter of Jurisdiction in the South China Sea Arbitration Initiated by the Republic of the Philippines (7 December 2014), 9–33.
Sur, Serge. "Les affaires des essais nucléaires (Australie c. France, Nouvelle Zélande c. France), C.I.J. – arrêts du 20 décembre 1974 [The Nuclear Tests Cases (Australia v. France, New Zealand v. France), I.C.J. – Judgments of 20 December 1974]." *Revue générale de droit international public* [General Journal of Public International Law] 79 (1975): 972–1022.
Talmon, Stefan. "Denouncing UNCLOS Remains Option for China After Tribunal Ruling." *Global Times*, 3 March 2016, http://www.globaltimes.cn/content/971707.shtml, accessed 9 April 2020.
———. *The South China Sea Arbitration: Is There a Case to Answer?* Bonn: Universität Bonn, Institute for Public International Law, 2014, https://papers.ssrn.com/sol3/papers.cfm?abstract_id=2393025, accessed 13 March 2020.

Territorial and Maritime Dispute (Nicaragua v. Colombia). Preliminary Objections. Judgment. I.C.J. Reports 2007, 832–77, https://www.icj-cij.org/files/case-related/124/124-20071213-JUD-01-00-BI.pdf, accessed 13 April 2020.

"Text of US Statement on Withdrawal from Case before the World Court." *New York Times*, 19 January 1985, http://www.nytimes.com/1985/01/19/world/text-of-us-statement-on-withdrawal-from-case-before-the-world-court.html?pagewanted=all&pagewanted=print, accessed 13 March 2020.

Thierry, Hubert. "Les arrêts du 20 décembre 1974 et les relations de la France avec la Cour internationale de justice [The Judgments of 20 December 1974 and French Relations with the International Court of Justice]." *Annuaire français de droit international* [French Yearbook of International Law] 20 (1974): 286–98, http://www.persee.fr/doc/afdi_0066-3085_1974_num_20_1_2272, accessed 1 April 2020.

Thirlway, Hugh. "The Law and Procedure of the International Court of Justice 1960–1989. Part Twelve." *British Yearbook of International Law* 71 (2000): 1–63.

———. "'Normative Surrender' and the 'Duty' to Appear Before the International Court of Justice: A Reply." *Michigan Journal of International Law* 11 (1990): 912–25, https://repository.law.umich.edu/cgi/viewcontent.cgi?article=1670&context=mjil, accessed 27 March 2020.

Thirlway, H.W.A. *Non-Appearance Before the International Court of Justice.* Cambridge: Cambridge University Press, 1985.

Tordesillas, Ellen. "Would China Withdraw from UNCLOS If UN Court Decides in Favor of PH?" *The Filipino Express*, 16 December 2013, http://www.filipinoexpress.com/ellen-tordesillas/869-would-china-withdraw-from-unclos-if-un-court-decides-in-favor-of-ph, accessed 9 April 2020.

Torres Bernárdez, Santiago. "La modification des articles du règlement de la Cour internationale de Justice relatifs aux exceptions préliminaires et aux demandes reconventionnelles [The Modification of the Articles of the Rules of the International Court of Justice on Preliminary Objections and Counterclaims]." *Annuaire français de droit international* [French Yearbook of International Law] 49 (2003): 207–47, https://www.persee.fr/docAsPDF/afdi_0066-3085_2003_num_49_1_3750.pdf, accessed 7 April 2020.

———. "Non-Appearance Before the International Court of Justice." *Annuaire de l'Institut de droit international* [Yearbook of the Institute of International Law]. Session de Bâle [Basel Session], 64-I (1991), 348–70, http://www.gaetanoarangioruiz.it/publications/non-appearance-before-the-international-court-of-justice/, accessed 13 October 2019.

Treatment in Hungary of Aircraft of United States of America (United States of America v. Hungarian People's Republic). United States. *Application Instituting Proceedings* (3 March 1954). *I.C.J. Pleadings*, *Treatment in Hungary of Aircraft of United States of America*, 8–41, https://www.icj-cij.org/files/case-related/22/022-19540303-APP-1-00-BI.pdf, accessed 5 April 2020.

———. *Order of July 12, 1954: I.C.J. Reports 1954*, 99–101, https://www.icj-cij.org/files/case-related/22/022-19540712-ORD-01-00-BI.pdf, accessed 5 April 2020.

Treatment in Hungary of Aircraft of United States of America (United States of America v. Union of Soviet Socialist Republics). United States. *Application Instituting Proceedings* (3 March 1954). *I.C.J. Pleadings*, *Treatment in Hungary of Aircraft of United States of America*, 42–64, https://www.icj-cij.org/files/case-related/23/023-19540303-APP-1-00-BI.pdf, accessed 5 April 2020.

———. *Order of July 12, 1954: I.C.J. Reports 1954*, 103–05, https://www.icj-cij.org/files/case-related/23/023-19540712-ORD-01-00-BI.pdf, accessed 5 April 2020.

Treves, Tullio. "La limite extérieure du plateau continental: Evolution récente de la pratique [The Outer Limit of the Continental Shelf: The Recent Evolution of Practice]." *Annuaire français de droit international* [French Yearbook of International Law] 35 (1989): 724–35, www.persee.fr/web/revues/home/prescript/article/afdi_0066-3085_1989_num_35_1_2929, accessed 15 April 2020.

Trial of Pakistani Prisoners of War (Pakistan v. India). Pakistan. *Application Instituting Proceedings* (1 May 1973). *I.C.J. Pleadings*, *Trial of Pakistani Prisoners of War*, 4–6, https://www.icj-cij.org/files/case-related/60/9461.pdf, accessed 27 March 2020.

———. Oral Arguments. *I.C.J. Pleadings*, *Trial of Pakistani Prisoners of War*, 21–107, http://www.icj-cij.org/files/case-related/60/060-19730504-ORA-01-00-BI.pdf, accessed 4 March 2018.

"United States: Department of State Letter and Statement Concerning Termination of Acceptance of ICJ Compulsory Jurisdiction [7 October 1985]." *International Legal Materials* 24 (1985): 1742–45.

United Nations. *Commentary on the Draft Convention on Arbitral Procedure Adopted by the International Law Commission at its Fifth Session, prepared by the Secretariat*. New York: United Nations, 1955, https://legal.un.org/ilc/documentation/english/a_cn4_92.pdf, accessed 26 March 2020.

———. *Final Clauses of Multilateral Treaties: Handbook*. New York: United Nations, 2003, https://treaties.un.org/doc/source/publications/FC/English.pdf, accessed 12 April 2020.

———. *Third United Nations Conference on the Law of the Sea Official Records*. Vol. I. *Summary Records of Plenary Meetings of the First and Second Sessions, and of Meetings of the General Committee, Second Session*. UN Doc. A/CONF.62/[Vol. 1]. New York: United Nations 1975.

———. *Official Records*. Vol. V. *Summary Records, Plenary, General Committee, First, Second and Third Committees, as well as Documents of the Conference, Fourth Session: New York, 15 March–7 May 1976*. UN Doc. A/CONF.62/[Vol.5]. New York: United Nations, 1976.
———. *Official Records*. Vol. VI. *Summary Records, Plenary, General Committee, First, Second and Third Committees, as well as Documents of the Conference, Fifth Session: New York, 2 August–17 September 1976*. UN Doc. A/CONF.62/[Vol. 6]. New York: United Nations, 1976.
———. *Official Records*. Vol. VII. *Summary Records and Documents, Sixth Session: New York, 23 May–15 July 1977*. UN Doc. A/CONF/.62/[Vol. 7]. New York: United Nations, 1977.
———. *Official Records*. Vol. IX. *Summary Records, Plenary, General Committee, First, Second and Third Committees, as well as Documents of the Conference, Seventh and Resumed Seventh Session: Geneva, 28 March–19 May 1978; New York, 21 August–15 September 1978*. UN Doc. A/CONF.62/[Vol. 9]. New York: United Nations, 1979.
———. *Official Records*. Vol. XVI. *Summary Records, Plenary, First and Second Committees, as well as Documents of the Conference, Eleventh Session, New York, 8 March–30 April 1982*. UN Doc. A/CONF.62/[Vol. 16]. New York: United Nations, 1984.
———. *United Nations Conference on the Law of the Sea. Official Records*. Vol. II. UN Doc. A/CONF.13/38. New York: United Nations, 1958, https://legal.un.org/docs/?path=../diplomaticconferences/1958_los/docs/english/vol_2/a_conf_13_l_32.pdf&lang=E, accessed 12 April 2020
———. *United Nations Convention on the Law of the Sea*. Concluded at Montego Bay on 10 December 1982. Entered into force on 16 November 1994, http://www.un.org/Depts/los/convention_agreements/texts/unclos/closindx.htm, accessed 21 March 2019.
———. *United Nations Conference on the Law of Treaties. First Session Vienna, 26 March–24 May 1968. Official Records*. New York: United Nations, 1969.
———. Division for Ocean Affairs and the Law of the Sea. *Annex VI. Statute of the International Tribunal for the Law of the Sea*, http://www.un.org/depts/los/convention_agreements/texts/unclos/annex6.htm, accessed 11 March 2020.
———. *Annex VII. Arbitration*, http://www.un.org/depts/los/convention_agreements/texts/unclos/annex7.htm, accessed 10 March 2020.
———. General Assembly Resolution 2758 (XXVI). "Restoration of the Lawful Rights of the People's Republic of China in the United Nations." UN Doc. A/RES/2758 (XXVI)(25 October 1971). http://www.un.org/en/ga/search/view_doc.asp?symbol=A/RES/2758(XXVI), accessed 14 April 2020.
———. International Law Commission. *Model Rules on Arbitral Procedure with a General Commentary, 1958. Yearbook of the International Law Commission*

1958. Vol. II. UN Doc. A/CN.4/SER.A/1958/Add.l. New York: United Nations, 1958, https://legal.un.org/docs/?path=../ilc/publications/yearbooks/english/ilc_1958_v2.pdf&lang=EFS, accessed 9 April 2020.

United Nations Convention on the Law of the Sea. Commission on the Limits of the Continental Shelf. *Progress of Work in the Commission on the Limits of the Continental Shelf*, *Thirty-Second Session (New York, 15 July–30 August 2013). Statement by the Chair* (24 September 2013). UN Doc. CLCS/80, https://undocs.org/en/clcs/80, accessed 15 April 2020.

United States Diplomatic and Consular Staff in Tehran. Judgment. I.C.J. Reports 1980, 3–48, https://www.icj-cij.org/files/case-related/64/064-19800524-JUD-01-00-BI.pdf, accessed 11 October 2019.

United States. Department of Commerce. National Oceanic and Atmospheric Administration. Office of Ocean Exploration and Research. *What Are Gas Hydrates?* https://oceanexplorer.noaa.gov/facts/hydrates.html, accessed 14 April 2020.

———. Department of State. Office of the Historian. *John Jay's Treaty 1794–95*, https://history.state.gov/milestones/1784-1800/jay-treaty, accessed 2 April 2020.

———. Foreign Service Institute. *The Alabama Claims, 1862–1872* (2017), https://history.state.gov/milestones/1861-1865/alabama, accessed 2 April 2020.

Verzijl, J.H.W. "The United Nations Conference on the Law of the Sea, Geneva, 1958." *Netherlands International Law Review* 6 (1959): 1–14.

Vienna Convention on Consular Relations. Done at Vienna on 24 April 1963. Entered into force on 19 March 1967, https://legal.un.org/ilc/texts/instruments/english/conventions/9_2_1963.pdf, accessed 10 April 2020.

Vienna Convention on Diplomatic Relations. Done at Vienna on 18 April 1961. Entered into force on 24 April 1964, https://legal.un.org/ilc/texts/instruments/english/conventions/9_1_1961.pdf, accessed 10 April 2020.

Vienna Convention on the Law of Treaties. Done at Vienna on 23 May 1969. Entered into force on 27 January 1980, https://legal.un.org/ilc/texts/instruments/english/conventions/1_1_1969.pdf, accessed 10 April 2020.

Vienna Convention on Succession of States in respect of State Property, Archives and Debts. Done at Vienna on 8 April 1983, Not yet in force, https://legal.un.org/ilc/texts/instruments/english/conventions/3_3_1983.pdf, accessed 10 April 2020.

Vienna Convention on Succession of States in respect of Treaties. Done at Vienna on 23 August 1978. Entered into force on 6 November 1996, https://legal.un.org/ilc/texts/instruments/english/conventions/3_2_1978.pdf, accessed 10 April 2020.

Villani, Ugo. "Osservazioni sulle soluzione delle controversie nelle Convenzioni di codificazione del diritto internazionale [Observations on Dispute Settlement in Conventions for the Codification of International Law]." *Le droit international à l'heure de sa codification. Études en l'honneur de Roberto Ago* [International Law at the Time of Its Codification. Studies in Honour of Roberto Ago]. Vol. II. *Les différends entre États et la responsabilité* [Inter-State Disputes and Responsibility], 497–521. Milano: Dott. A. Giuffrè Editore, 1987.

Wentker, Alexander. *Nichtteilnahme als Grenzphänomen zwischenstaatlicher Gerichts- und Schiedsverfahren – die Fälle South China Sea und "Arctic Sunrise"* [Non-Participation in Inter-State Proceedings Before International Tribunals – the South China Sea and "Arctic Sunrise" Cases]. Heidelberg: Max Planck Institute for Comparative Public Law and International Law, 2018, https://papers.ssrn.com/sol3/papers.cfm?abstract_id=3248261, accessed 17 March 2020.

Yee, Sienho. "Forum Prorogatum in the International Court." *German Yearbook of International Law* 42 (1999): 147–91.

Zhang Xinjun. "Bifurcation in Inter-State Cases." *University of Pennsylvania Journal of International Law* 40 (2018–2019): 937–88, https://scholarship.law.upenn.edu/cgi/viewcontent.cgi?article=1991&context=jil, accessed 24 October 2019.

CHAPTER 3

The Defaulting State and Fact-Finding in the *South China Sea Arbitration*

Article 9 of Annex VII of the United Nations Convention on the Law of the Sea ("the Convention") imposes a heavy duty on an arbitral tribunal in the event of one party's default: "Before making its award, the arbitral tribunal must satisfy itself not only that it has jurisdiction over the dispute but also that the claim is well founded in fact and law."[1] The *South China Sea* Tribunal acknowledged that China's non-participation imposed "a special responsibility on the Tribunal," as there was no system of default judgment under the Convention.[2]

Two particular difficulties for an international court arising from default had been identified by the 1991 resolution on "Non-appearance Before the International Court of Justice ("ICJ")" of the *Institut de droit international* (Institute of International Law, "IDI"): the full implementation of the equality of the parties and the acquisition by the Court of knowledge of the facts relevant to decision-making on provisional

[1] United Nations Division for Ocean Affairs and the Law of the Sea, *Annex VII. Arbitration* ("*Annex VII*"), http://www.un.org/depts/los/convention_agreements/texts/unclos/annex7.htm, accessed 10 March 2020; *United Nations Convention on the Law of the Sea*, concluded at Montego Bay on 10 December 1982, entered into force on 16 November 1994 ("Convention"), http://www.un.org/Depts/los/convention_agreements/texts/unclos/closindx.htm, accessed 21 March 2020.

[2] *South China Sea Arbitration*, Award of 12 July 2016, 49, para. 129, https://pcacases.com/web/sendAttach/2086, accessed 10 March 2020.

A. C. Robles Jr., *The Defaulting State and the South China Sea Arbitration*, https://doi.org/10.1007/978-981-19-6394-0_3

measures, preliminary objections, and the merits.[3] It comes as no surprise that the IDI highlighted these two difficulties. In cases of default, an international court's efforts to comply with its obligations might upset the equality of the parties. The risk arises because in cases of default, the adversarial element, through which each party brings to the court's attention evidence and legal arguments favorable to its position and unfavorable to that of its adversary, disappears.[4] The court's efforts to reestablish the equality of the parties might penalize one or the other party. This risk is particularly acute when the international court must undertake fact-finding. Default deprives the international tribunal of "the benefit of the defaulting party's complete and fully argued statement regarding the facts"[5] and "the assistance that evidence and arguments from the non-appearing party could have provided it in its decision-making."[6] In such circumstances, the ICJ has declared that it was obliged by the Statute "to employ whatever means and resources may enable

[3] Institut de droit international [Institute of International Law, "IDI"], Session de Bâle [Basel Session], *Non-appearance Before the International Court of Justice* (1991), 2, https://www.idi-iil.org/app/uploads/2017/06/1991_bal_01_en.pdf, accessed 16 March 2020.

[4] Richard M. Mosk, "The Role of Facts in International Dispute Resolution," *Recueil des Cours de l'Académie de droit international de La Haye* [Collected Courses of the Hague Academy of International Law], vol. 304 (2003-IV), 59–60 ("*RCADI*").

[5] *Military and Paramilitary Activities in and against Nicaragua (Nicaragua v. United States of America), Merits, Judgment, I.C.J. Reports 1986*, 38, para. 56, http://www.icj-cij.org/files/case-related/70/070-19860627-JUD-01-00-BI.pdf, accessed 17 March 2020.

[6] *Fisheries Jurisdiction (United Kingdom v. Iceland), Merits, Judgment, I.C.J. Reports 1974*, 9, para. 17, https://www.icj-cij.org/files/case-related/55/055-19740725-JUD-01-00-BI.pdf, accessed 17 March 2020; *Fisheries Jurisdiction (Federal Republic of Germany v. Iceland), Merits, Judgment, I.C.J. Reports 1974*, 181, para.17, http://www.icj-cij.org/files/case-related/56/056-19740725-JUD-01-00-BI.pdf, accessed 17 March 2020; *Nuclear Tests (Australia v. France), Judgment, I.C.J. Reports 1974*, 257, para. 15, http://www.icj-cij.org/files/case-related/58/058-19741220-JUD-01-00-BI.pdf, accessed 17 March 2020; *Nuclear Tests (New Zealand v. France), Judgment, I.C.J. Reports 1974*, 461, para. 15, http://www.icj-cij.org/files/case-related/59/059-19741220-JUD-01-00-BI.pdf, accessed 17 March 2020; *Aegean Sea Continental Shelf, Judgment, I.C.J. Reports 1978*, 7–8, para. 15, http://www.icj-cij.org/files/case-related/62/062-19781219-JUD-01-00-BI.pdf, accessed 17 March 2020; *United States Diplomatic and Consular Staff in Tehran, Judgment, I.C.J. Reports 1980*, 18, para. 33, https://www.icj-cij.org/files/case-related/64/064-19800524-JUD-01-00-BI.pdf, accessed 17 March 2020; *"Arctic Sunrise" Arbitration (Kingdom of The Netherlands v. Russian Federation)*, Award on the Merits (14 August 2015), 4, para. 19, https://pcacases.com/web/sendAttach/1438, accessed 17 March 2020.

it to satisfy itself whether the submissions of the applicant State are well-founded in fact and law."[7]

International courts possess a broad range of powers that enable them to acquire knowledge of the facts on provisional measures, preliminary objections, and the merits. They may request that the parties furnish documents and information at their disposal prior to, during, and after the oral proceedings; request information from third parties, such as international organizations; refer technical issues to experts; call witnesses of their own; carry out site visits; and take judicial notice of notorious facts (i.e., without requiring the party that seeks to rely on them to provide proof of the facts).[8] Indeed, the problem, according to some authors, is not so much the availability of the powers but the reluctance of international courts to make use of them in seeking facts.[9] When both parties to a case are appearing before the court, there is no obligation for an international court to have recourse to such powers. Cases of default seem to provide a justification and an opportunity for a court's more active role, particularly in fact-finding, and thus for more extensive use of the court's powers.[10] Nevertheless, the ICJ has emphasized that the equality of the parties must remain its basic principle—neither party must be placed at a disadvantage.[11]

The IDI's stress on difficulties in fact-finding, with the implication that fact-finding can raise more serious problems than the question of the applicable law, reflects the assumption that the court knows the law (*jura*

[7] *Nicaragua*, *Merits*, *Judgment*, 40, para. 59.

[8] Chittharanjan F. Amerasinghe, *Evidence in International Litigation* (Leiden: Martinus Nijhoff Publishers, 2005), 152–61; Rüdiger Wolfrum, "Taking and Assessing Evidence in International Adjudication," in Tafsir Malick Ndiaye et al. (eds.), *Law of the Sea, Environmental Law and Settlement of Disputes: Liber Amicorum Judge Thomas A. Mensah* (Leiden: Martinus Nijhoff Publishers, 2007), 352; Christian J. Tams and James G. Devaney, "Article 49," in Andreas Zimmerman et al. (eds.), *The Statute of the International Court of Justice: A Commentary* (3rd ed.; Oxford: Oxford University Press, 2019), 1417–19, 1421. Wolfrum was a member and Mensah the President of the *South China Sea* Tribunal.

[9] Mosk, "The Role of Facts," 46–47.

[10] Wolfrum, "Taking and Assessing Evidence," 343–44. Alexander Wentker, *Nichtteilnahme als Grenzphänomen zwischenstaatlicher Gerichts- und Schiedsverfahren—die Fälle South China Sea und Arctic Sunrise* [Non-participation in Inter-State Proceedings Before International Tribunals—The South China Sea and Arctic Sunrise Cases] (Heidelberg: Max Planck Institute for Comparative Public Law and International Law, 2018), 51, https://papers.ssrn.com/sol3/papers.cfm?abstract_id=3248261, accessed 17 March 2020.

[11] *Nicaragua*, *Merits*, *Judgment*, 26, para. 31.

novit curia).[12] Notwithstanding this assumption, individual ICJ judges have occasionally complained that the Court has erroneously interpreted a defaulting State's legal position and in so doing penalized that State. In the *Fisheries Jurisdiction Cases*, Judge Gros objected to the Court's reference to conservation of Icelandic fishery resources because in his view, Iceland's commitments in its agreements with the UK and the Federal Republic of Germany were limited to the extension of the fishing zone.[13] At the other extreme is the opinion that the appearing State should, in effect, be penalized, by means of the court acting as the counsel of the defaulting State. This view, expressed by an ICJ judge, requires that the Court assume that the defaulting State is right, not wrong, until the appearing State has proven the defaulting State to be wrong.[14] In effect, default would supply the defaulting State with the most competent counsel possible—the Court itself.[15]

Needless to say, the conception of the Court's role as counsel for the defaulting State was not accepted by the appearing State in the case concerned, Nicaragua. As the latter pointed out, this conception would accord more rights to the defaulting State than to the appearing State, shift the burden of proof to the latter, and prevent it from expressing itself freely out of respect for the Court. Nicaragua protested that the Statute's provisions on default did not mean that the Court was to supply the pleadings that the defaulting party might have made or introduce

[12] Hermann Mosler, "Nichtteilnahme einer Partei am Verfahren vor dem Internationalen Gerichtshof [Non-participation of a Party in Proceedings Before the International Court of Justice]," in Ingo von Münch (ed.), *Staatsrecht—Völkerrecht—Europarecht. Festschrift für Hans-Jürgen Schlochauer* [Constitutional Law—International Law—European Law. Festschrift for Hans-Jürgen Schlochauer] (Berlin: Walter de Gruyter, 1981), 455.

[13] *Fisheries Jurisdiction (United Kingdom v. Iceland), Merits, Judgment*, Dissenting Opinion of Judge Gros, *I.C.J. Reports 1974*, 128–29, https://www.icj-cij.org/files/case-related/55/055-19740725-JUD-01-08-BI.pdf, accessed 21 April 2020.

[14] *Nicaragua, Merits, Judgment*, Dissenting Opinion of Judge Schwebel, *I.C.J. Reports 1986*, 319, para. 123, http://www.icj-cij.org/files/case-related/70/070-19860627-JUD-01-09-BI.pdf, accessed 31 March 2020.

[15] Joe Verhoeven, "Le droit, le juge et la violence (les arrêts Nicaragua c. États-Unis) [The Law, the Judge and Violence (The *Nicaragua v. United States* Judgments)]," *Revue générale de droit International public* [General Journal of Public International Law] 91 (1987): 1197 ("*RGDIP*").

factual materials on the record that had not been subject to the appearing State's scrutiny.[16]

A former ICJ President has argued convincingly that an international court must strike a balance between the two parties in a case of default in the following fashion. It must take the place of the defaulting State by obtaining the required factual information and undertaking the analysis of the appearing State's evidence and legal arguments that the defaulting State would have carried out had it appeared. The court should not, however, act as the counsel of the defaulting State, by carrying out fact-finding and making legal arguments on its behalf. The court should not put the appearing State in a situation in which it would have to imagine the defaulting State's arguments and respond to them.[17]

Under the Rules of Procedure of the *South China Sea Arbitration*, the Tribunal was authorized to "take all appropriate measures in order to establish the facts."[18] Such measures included site visits and the appointment of independent experts.[19] In the event of default, the Tribunal was empowered to request supplemental written arguments from the appearing party, to pose questions to it on specific issues that in the Tribunal's view had not been adequately canvassed or had not been canvassed at all in the *Memorial*, and to take any measures that it deemed necessary "to afford to each of the Parties a full opportunity to present

[16] *I.C.J. Pleadings, Military and Paramilitary Activities in and against Nicaragua (Nicaragua v. United States of America)*, Vol. V, Oral Arguments on the Merits, Public Sitting of 20 September 1985, 238, https://www.icj-cij.org/files/case-related/70/070 19850912-ORA-01-00-BI.pdf, accessed 17 March 2020. On this point, see Hans von Mangoldt, "Versäumnisverfahren in der internationalen (Schieds)Gerichtsbarkeit und souveräne Gleichheit [Default Procedures in International Arbitration and Adjudication and Sovereign Equality]," in Rudolf Bernhardt (ed.), *Völkerrecht als Rechtsordnung, internationale Gerichtsbarkeit, Menschenrechte. Festschrift für Hermann Mosler* [International Law as a Legal Order, International Adjudication, Human Rights. Festschrift for Hermann Mosler] (Berlin: Springer Verlag, 1983), 524.

[17] Mohammed Bedjaoui, "L'égalité des États dans le procès international, un mythe [Equality of States in International Judicial Proceedings, A Myth?]?" in *Le procès international* [International Judicial Proceedings]. *Liber Amicorum Jean-Pierre Cot* (Bruxelles: Établissements Émile Bruylant, 2009), 22–23; James Gerard Devaney, *Fact-Finding Before the International Court of Justice* (Cambridge: Cambridge University Press, 2016), 117.

[18] *South China Sea Arbitration*, Rules of Procedure (27 August 2013), Article 22(2), 10, https://pcacases.com/web/sendAttach/233, accessed 11 May 2020.

[19] Ibid., Articles 22(2) and 24, 10, 11.

its case."[20] As we shall see in this Chapter, the Tribunal exercised all of its powers, and in so doing, acted in practice as counsel for the defaulting party, as the lead counsel for the Philippines freely admitted. The Tribunal not only took into account China's Position Paper on the jurisdiction of the Tribunal; it also attempted to develop arguments on jurisdiction and on the merits that China might have made if it had fully participated.[21] Neither the legal team nor the Philippines held this against the Tribunal. Indeed, from the appearing party's perspective, the Tribunal's efforts meant that it had "left no stone unturned"[22] in responding to the challenges created by China's default. In the words of a Chinese scholar, the Tribunal sought to reduce the impact of China's default and to ensure the proper administration of justice.[23]

In this Chapter, fact-finding will be broadly understood to include the effort to ascertain the defaulting State's legal arguments. The first part will examine the way in which the Tribunal dealt with the defaulting State's informal communications and public statements, which took the place of its formal submissions, and mitigated the impact of default for the appearing State by allowing it to make a supplemental submission. In this manner, the Tribunal exercised its powers to acquire knowledge of the facts in such a way as to fulfill its obligation under Annex VII of the Convention. In this respect the Tribunal's approach did not differ from that of the ICJ. The second part will discuss an additional burden imposed on the Tribunal by the attempt of non-parties to the case to make submissions to it as self-proclaimed or de facto *amicus curiae* ("friends of the court"). The Tribunal did not use its procedural powers to make any formal decision regarding the admissibility of such submissions, but it did not dismiss them outright. On the contrary, it took into consideration submissions of two of the three entities claiming to be *amici curiae*. The

[20] Ibid., Article 25(2), 12.

[21] Paul S. Reichler, quoted in Julie Makinen, "U.S. Lawyer Who Led Philippines' Case Says Beijing's Boycott Made His Job Harder in South China Sea Arguments," *Los Angeles Times*, 12 July 2016, https://www.latimes.com/world/asia/la-fg-south-china-sea-lawyer-20160712-snap-story.html, accessed 21 April 2020.

[22] *South China Sea Arbitration*, Hearing on Jurisdiction and Admissibility, Transcript, Day 3 (13 July 2015), 79, https://pcacases.com/web/sendAttach/1401, accessed 8 April 2020.

[23] Liao Shiping, "Fact-Finding in Non-appearance Before International Courts and Tribunals," unpublished ms., Beijing Normal University, 2018, 40, https://ssrn.com/abstract=3187971, accessed 22 March 2020.

three entities' contribution to the Tribunal's fact-finding will be assessed on the basis of criteria identified in the rules and caselaw of investor-State arbitration. After the discussion of what might be considered submissions from the parties and non-parties to the *Arbitration*, the third part will discuss the Tribunal's exercise of its powers to put oral questions, to appoint independent experts, and to take all appropriate measures in order to establish the facts, with a view to fulfilling its duty under Article 9 of Annex VII of the Convention.

I. The "Submissions" of the Parties in the Context of Default

Defaulting States are rarely able to hold fast to their resolution to remain completely aloof from proceedings initiated against them. They often transmit informal communications to the international court concerned and make public statements relating to the proceedings. Fitzmaurice believes that such conduct is not only insincere, it also contradicts the assertion frequently made by defaulting States that the ICJ manifestly lacks jurisdiction. If the lack of jurisdiction were manifest, then surely there would be no need to demonstrate it.[24] More importantly, this practice threatens the equality of the parties. As the Philippines pointed out, China, while refusing to participate in the proceedings, could not be prevented from informally presenting information on questions of fact or law arising in the *Arbitration*.[25] In contrast, the appearing party is bound

[24] Gerald Fitzmaurice, "The Problem of the 'Non-appearing' Defendant Government," *British Yearbook of International Law* 51 (1980): 91 ("*BYIL*"). Fitzmaurice compares them to actors saying their lines in the wings rather than on stage (90). Highet describes them as phantom opponents. Keith Highet, "Nonappearance and Disappearance Before the international Court of Justice," *American Journal of International Law* 81 (1987): 244 ("*AJIL*").

[25] *South China Sea Arbitration*, *Memorial of the Philippines* (30 March 2014), vol. I, 130, para. 7.41 ("*MP*"), https://files.pca-cpa.org/pcadocs/Memorial%20of%20the%20Philippines%20Volume%20I.pdf, accessed 23 April 2020. Spijkers misunderstands this and thinks that the Philippines was actually encouraging China to continue issuing statements and keep publishing on the proceedings. The context excludes this interpretation of the Philippine statement. Otto Spijkers, "Non-participation in Arbitral Proceedings Under Annex VII United Nations Convention on the Law of the Sea: *Arctic Sunrise* and *South China Sea* Compared," in Angela Del Vecchio and Roberto Virzo (eds.), *Interpretations of the United Nations Convention on the Law of the Sea by International Courts and Tribunals* (Cham, Switzerland: Springer International Publishing, 2019), 181.

by the conditions set by rules of procedure, notably time limits, for the submission of pleadings.

Yet defaulting States' practice of transmitting informal communications and making public statements on the proceedings may mitigate one of the disadvantages of default for the appearing State and the international court concerned, who would otherwise be deprived of evidence and legal arguments from the defaulting State. Of course, such informal communications and public statements can hardly be considered the equivalent of fully argued pleadings. This imposes on the appearing State the additional burden of having to reconstruct the defaulting State's arguments, the better to refute them. Once again, default results in a disadvantage for the appearing State.

The *South China Sea Arbitration* is remarkable for acknowledging the practical difficulties created by default for the appearing State and seeking to alleviate them by inviting the Philippines to make a supplemental submission on matters that in the Tribunal's view had not been sufficiently canvassed or had not been canvassed at all by the Philippines in its *Memorial*.

A. The Defaulting State's Informal Communications

Communications from the defaulting State that are transmitted to the ICJ in a form and manner not in conformity with the terms, conditions, and deadlines normally imposed on parties by its Rules of Court are deemed "informal," "irregular," or "extra-procedural."[26] Despite the proclaimed determination not to participate in the judicial proceedings initiated against it, it is a common practice for defaulting States to submit

[26] In the ICJ context, informal or irregular communications are defined as those that are submitted at times that according to the ICJ Statute and Rules of Court are not at the disposal of the defaulting State and are submitted not by that party's agent but through diplomatic channels. Shabtai Rosenne, "The Reconceptualization of Objections in the International Court of Justice," *Comunicazioni e studi* [Communications and Studies] 14 (1975): 756; Gaetano Arangio-Ruiz, "Notes on Non-appearance Before the International Court of Justice," in *Le droit international à l'heure de sa codification. Études en l'honneur de Roberto Ago* [International Law at the Time of Its Codification. Studies in Honour of Roberto Ago], vol. II, *Les différends entre États et la responsabilité* [Inter-State Disputes and Responsibility] (Milano: Dott. A. Giuffrè Editore, 1987), 5.

to the ICJ letters and documents "in ways and by means not contemplated by the Rules of Court."[27] The volume of informal communications may vary, from the two telegrams having nearly identical content sent by Iran in December 1979 and March 1980 to the ICJ in *United States Diplomatic and Consular Staff in Tehran* to the two letters and four telegrams sent by Iceland to the ICJ between May and December 1972 in the *Fisheries Jurisdiction Cases*.[28] Appearing States have on occasion expressed their frustration with such a practice. In the *Aegean Sea Continental Shelf Case*, initiated in 1976 by Greece against Turkey over a dispute concerning the delimitation of their respective continental shelves, Greece described the attitude of Turkey, which had sent two letters to the ICJ denying jurisdiction, as one of "semi-default": Turkey had felt entitled not to appear, but submitted documents to justify the Court's lack of jurisdiction.[29] As a result, Turkey was neither totally present nor totally absent in the proceedings.[30] The tone of scholarly commentary on informal communications is markedly more hostile. The defaulting State is charged with making a de facto appearance, indirectly defending its case by "unorthodox, backstairs or sideward methods" while technically still not appearing; this enables it to continue to assert that it is not a party to the case.[31] A widespread view is that the practice of informal communications places the defaulting State in almost as good a position as if it had actually appeared, thus upsetting the equality of the parties.[32]

Informal communications do create procedural difficulties for the appearing party and the international court. They may nonetheless be useful in communicating legal arguments and the associated evidence to

[27] *Nicaragua, Merits, Judgment*, 25, para. 31.

[28] Pierre-Marie Martin, "L'affaire de la compétence en matière de pêcheries (les arrêts de la C.I.J. du 2 février 1973) [The Fisheries Jurisdiction Cases (The I.C.J. Judgments of 2 February 1973)]," *RGDIP* 78 (1974): 446. The text of the two Iranian telegrams is to be found in *United States Diplomatic and Consular Staff in Tehran*, 10, para. 9. The text of the Icelandic letters and telegrams is not publicly available.

[29] Mr. De Visscher, Oral Arguments on Jurisdiction, Sixth Public Sitting (12 October 1978), *I.C.J. Pleadings, Aegean Sea Continental Shelf (Greece v. Turkey)*, 386 (translated from the French), https://www.icj-cij.org/files/case-related/62/062-19781009-ORA-01-00-BI.pdf, accessed 20 March 2020.

[30] Mr. Weil, Oral Arguments on Jurisdiction, Eighth Public Sitting (10 October 1978), *I.C.J. Pleadings, Aegean Sea Continental Shelf*, 348 (translated from the French).

[31] Fitzmaurice, "The Problem," 89.

[32] Arangio-Ruiz, "Notes," 5.

the court. In the *South China Sea Arbitration*, China's informal communications proved valuable mainly in informing the Philippines and the Tribunal of China's legal arguments against jurisdiction. After the issuance of the Award on Jurisdiction and Admissibility, China's informal communications for the most part restated China's objections to the Tribunal's jurisdiction; as such, they were much less useful to the Philippines and the Tribunal in the merits phase of the proceedings.

1. Informal Communications in Lieu of Pleadings

Informal communications pose dilemmas for the appearing State, but the ICJ has adopted the view that its duty under Article 53 of its Statute requires it to take them into account.

From the appearing State's perspective, informal communications are objectionable because they do not conform to the time limits set by the ICJ and their contents do not amount to complete pleadings. In proceedings in which both parties appear, time limits are set by the Court for the submission of the applicant State's *Memorial*, to be followed by the respondent State's *Counter-Memorial*. The defaulting State that transmits informal communications ignores these time limits, sometimes transmitting them at a very late stage of the proceedings and making it difficult, if not practically impossible, for the appearing State to prepare responses to them.

As defaulting States deny the jurisdiction of the international court, informal communications are often sent in the initial phases of the proceedings. In the *Trial of Pakistani Prisoners of War Case*, initiated by Pakistan against India on 11 May 1973, India set out its objections to the Court's jurisdiction in two letters dated 23 and 25 May 1973. To give Pakistan the time to consider them, a hearing on Pakistan's request for provisional measures that was originally set for 29 May was postponed to 4 June 1973.[33] On the afternoon of the hearing's first day, the Court received another letter from India. Pakistan's exasperated representative observed that the cycle could go on indefinitely if India

[33] *Affaire relative au Procès de prisonniers de guerre pakistanais* [Trial of Pakistani Prisoners of War Case], I.C.J. Press Release 1973/14 (25 May 1973) (French version only), https://www.icj-cij.org/files/case-related/60/11572.pdf, accessed 22 April 2020; *Affaire relative au procès de prisonniers de guerre pakistanais—Report de l'ouverture des audiences* [Trial of Pakistani Prisoners of War Case—Postponement of the Opening of the Sittings], Press Release 1973/16 (28 May 1973) (French version only), https://www.icj-cij.org/files/case-related/60/11578.pdf, 22 April 2020.

commented on any observations that he made during the Hearing, which comments would be followed by a Pakistani reply, in turn prompting an Indian rejoinder.[34] India's litigation strategy undermined the equality of the parties, because Pakistan was obliged to follow the procedure laid down by the Statute and the Rules of Court, it was given only one night in which to prepare its response to a document that had surely taken India more than a night to prepare, and it was obliged to deal with issues of jurisdiction at the stage of provisional measures. In effect, Pakistan was penalized as a result of India's default. India's litigation strategy also hindered the proper administration of justice by the Court. India's piecemeal submission of arguments followed by successive Pakistani replies would have made it difficult for the Court to determine the appropriate moment in which to close a phase of the proceedings.[35]

In the *Aegean Sea Continental Shelf Case*, a 10,000-word informal communication transmitted to the Court by Turkey on the morning of 10 October 1978, the second day of the hearing on jurisdiction, was probably intended to afford the appearing party as little time as possible to deal with Turkey's arguments.[36] It seems, though, that the Court did not take this communication into account in its decision.[37] In contrast, in the *Nicaragua Case*, the Court, without giving notice to Nicaragua, explicitly took into account in its decision-making a document forwarded to the Court by the US on the second day of the Hearing on the Merits. Nicaragua had urged the Court to disregard the document, which would never have been allowed had the two parties to the case been present. The Court justified its action by the special circumstances of the case, i.e., US

[34] Mr. Bakhtiar, Oral Arguments, Request for the Indication of Interim Measures of Protection, Second Public Sitting (5 June 1973), *I.C.J. Pleadings, Trial of Pakistani Prisoners of War (Pakistan v. India)*, 56, http://www.icj-cij.org/files/case-related/60/060-19730504-ORA-01-00-BI.pdf, accessed 22 April 2020.

[35] Pierre-Michel Eisemann, "Les effets de la non-comparution devant la Cour internationale de Justice [The Effects of Non-appearance Before the International Court of Justice]," *Annuaire français de droit international* [French Yearbook of International Law] 19 (1973): 361, 365 ("*AFDI*"), https://www.persee.fr/docAsPDF/afdi_0066-3085_1973_num_19_1_2217.pdf, accessed 23 March 2020.

[36] Ian Sinclair, "Some Procedural Aspects of Recent International Litigation," *International and Comparative Law Quarterly* 30 (1981): 349 ("*ICLQ*").

[37] There is only one reference to it in the entire judgment. *Aegean Sea Continental Shelf*, *Judgment*, 14, para. 7.

default.[38] The US litigation strategy upset the equality of the parties, as did the Court's treatment of the document.[39]

Informal communications submitted after the formal closure of proceedings are rare, but they will not create difficulties for the appearing State if an international court decides to ignore them. Should the court wish to take them into account, it should give the appearing party the opportunity to comment on them, in order not to undermine the equality of the parties.[40] In the *"Arctic Sunrise" Arbitration*, Russia transmitted to another arbitral tribunal instituted under Annex VII of the Convention a Position Paper in August 2015, six months after the Hearing on the Merits. After informing the Netherlands, the Tribunal decided not to take it into account and gave three reasons for its refusal: the Position Paper was brought to its attention at a late stage; Russia had denied that it was a formal submission; and the issues raised in the Position Paper were fully addressed in the Award, which was issued a week after the Tribunal's receipt of the Position Paper. The Tribunal's attitude is all the more comprehensible when we consider that throughout the proceedings, Russia had been given 15 days after the Netherlands submission of each written pleading within which to indicate whether it intended to respond. If it did have such an intention, it was granted six months within which to submit its response. At no point had Russia given any indication of its

[38] *Nicaragua, Merits, Judgment*, 44, para. 73.

[39] Paul S. Reichler and Yuri B. Parkhomenko, "*Nicaragua v. United States* and Matters of Evidence Before the International Court of Justice," in Edgardo Sobenes Obregón and Benjamin Samson (eds.), *Nicaragua Before the International Court of Justice. Impacts on International Law* (Cham, Switzerland: Springer International Publishing AG, 2018), 49. Ian Brownlie described the ICJ's action as "obviously wrong." Observations of Mr. I. Brownlie (18 October 1990), in Gaetano Arangio-Ruiz, "Non-appearance Before the International Court of Justice. Final Report," *Annuaire de l'Institut de droit international* [Yearbook of the Institute of International Law], Session de Bâle [Basel Session], 64-I (1991), 344 ("Non-appearance Final Report"), http://www.gaetanoarangioruiz.it/publications/non-appearance-before-the-international-court-of-justice/, accessed 13 October 2019; Pierre-Michel Eisemann, "L'arrêt de la CIJ dans l'affaire des activités militaires et paramilitaires au Nicaragua et contre celui-ci (Nicaragua c. Etats-Unis) fond arrêt du 27 juin 1986 [The Judgment of the ICJ in the Military and Paramilitary Activities in and against Nicaragua Case (Nicaragua v. United States), Merits, Judgment of 27 June 1986]," *AFDI* 32 (1986): 161, http://www.persee.fr/doc/afdi_0066-3085_1986_num_32_1_2714, accessed 22 April 2020.

[40] D.W. Bowett, "Contemporary Developments in Legal Techniques in the Settlement of Disputes," *RCADI*, vol. 180 (1983-II), 210.

intention to make any submission.[41] The Tribunal's treatment of Russia's informal communication obviated any difficulties it might have otherwise created for the Netherlands.

If informal communications set out arguments and evidence from the defaulting State without being formal pleadings, the appearing State must decide whether to respond to them. Occasionally the appearing State objects to the admissibility of informal communications. In the *Trial of Pakistani Prisoners of War Case*, Indian letters that objected to the Court's jurisdiction were a distraction from Pakistan's request for provisional measures.[42] In the *Nuclear Tests Cases*, Australia objected in the provisional measures phase to the Court's taking notice of French communications that had been transmitted outside the Court's established procedures and for this reason could be considered irregular.[43] In *United States Diplomatic and Consular Staff in Tehran*, the United States did not wish the Court to consider two Iranian telegrams that accused the US of intervening in Iranian domestic affairs for twenty-five years.[44] Other considerations militate in favor of a response by the appearing State. To be sure, informal communications put it at a procedural disadvantage. At the same time, they could mitigate difficulties that default creates for it, by giving it the opportunity to become acquainted with the legal arguments of the defaulting State. These arguments, although presented only in outline form and with little or no evidence, may be arguments that the court might wish to consider, so that it would be unwise for the appearing State to ignore them.[45]

A cursory examination of the proceedings of several cases reveals that appearing States have expressed dissatisfaction with the fact that informal

[41] *The Arctic Sunrise Arbitration*, Award on the Merits, 7, 8, 9, 12–13, paras. 40, 45, 51, 52, 68.

[42] Mr. Bakhtiar, Oral Arguments, Request for the Indication of Interim Measures of Protection, Second Public Sitting (5 June 1973), *I.C.J. Pleadings*, *Trial of Pakistani Prisoners of War*, 56.

[43] Argument of Senator Murphy, First Public Sitting (21 May 1973), Oral Arguments on the Request for Indication of Interim Measures of Protection, *I.C.J. Pleadings*, *Nuclear Tests Cases*, vol. I, 183, http://www.icj-cij.org/files/case-related/58/058-19730521-ORA-01-00-BI.pdf, accessed 8 September 2020.

[44] Mr. Schwebel, Oral Arguments, Third Public Sitting (18 March 1980), *I.C.J. Pleadings*, *United States Diplomatic and Consular Staff in Tehran*, 277, https://www.icj-cij.org/files/case-related/64/064-19800318-ORA-01-00-BI.pdf, accessed 22 April 2020.

[45] Sinclair, "Some Procedural Aspects," 353.

communications are in no way comparable to formal pleadings. In the *Trial of Pakistani Prisoners of War Case*, Pakistan declared that India's successive letters to the Court could not be equated with a completed *Counter-Memorial*, making it difficult for Pakistan to prepare a considered reply.[46] A *Counter-Memorial* would have included India's submissions, its legal arguments, and the supporting factual evidence. In the *Fisheries Jurisdiction Cases*, Iceland's failure to present a coherent statement of its claim had entailed considerable difficulties for the UK. In the UK view, it was incumbent on Iceland to prove its claim, as it was the party that was challenging the law by extending its exclusive fishing zone to 50 nautical miles.[47] In *United States Diplomatic and Consular Staff*, the US fear was that Iran's two succinct telegrams to the Court would not be sufficient to prove the existence of a dispute over the interpretation and application of the Vienna Conventions on Diplomatic Relations and on Consular Relations. The US was compelled to insist that despite the absence of a series of formal diplomatic exchanges between the two States, Iran was aware of, rejected, and refused to negotiate US claims.[48]

As for the attitude of the ICJ itself, it has never rejected informal communications from a defaulting State. It seems that it was only in the *Nuclear Tests Cases* that consideration of the defaulting State's informal communications was delayed. Judge Gros, a French national, objected to the Court's failure to decide whether the French document was a pleading in the case which should have been taken into account on a footing of equality with Australia's observations.[49] Fitzmaurice believed that to obviate the disadvantages for the appearing State of the practice of

[46] Mr. Bakhtiar, Second Public Sitting, *I.C.J. Pleadings*, *Trial of Pakistani Prisoners of War*, 56.

[47] Right Hon. Samuel Silkin, Fifth Public Sitting (25 March 1974), Oral Proceedings on the Merits, *I.C.J. Pleadings, Fisheries Jurisdiction*, vol. I, 440, 461, http://www.icj-cij.org/files/case-related/55/055-19740325-ORA-01-00-BI.pdf, accessed 22 April 2020.

[48] Mr. Schwebel, Third Public Sitting, *I.C.J. Pleadings, United States Diplomatic and Consular Staff in Tehran*, 277; Vincent Coussirat-Coustère, "L'arrêt de la Cour internationale de Justice sur le personnel diplomatique américain à Téhéran [The Judgment of the International Court of Justice on American Diplomatic Staff in Teheran]," *AFDI* 26 (1980): 210, https://www.persee.fr/docAsPDF/afdi_0066-3085_1980_num_26_1_2388.pdf, accessed 20 March 2020.

[49] *Nuclear Tests (Australia v. France), Interim Protection, Order of 22 June 1973, I.C.J. Reports 1973*, Dissenting Opinion of Judge Gros, 117, https://www.icj-cij.org/en/case/58/orders, accessed 9 August 2019.

informal communications, the Court should not take cognizance of such communications.[50] The Court has never adopted this approach. As Judge Gros pointed out, this would be tantamount to penalizing the defaulting State for its default.[51] For the Court, consideration of informal communications was a duty under Article 53 of the Statute. The Court's attitude was probably most clearly expressed in the *Aegean Sea Continental Shelf Case*. The defaulting State, Turkey, had referred in a letter to the ICJ to a right conferred to it by the General Act for the Pacific Settlement of International Disputes of 1928 to invoke a reservation that Greece had made to the General Act upon Greek accession in 1931 and that excluded disputes relating to the territorial status of Greece. The latter argued that the reservation should not be considered by the Court because Turkey had not raised the issue of its effect as a preliminary objection in conformity with the Rules of Court and had thus not "enforced" the reservation in conformity with the General Act. In the Court's view, the formal statement by Turkey, made in response to a Court communication, constituted an enforcement of the reservation; it would not be fulfilling its duty under the Statute if it left out of consideration a reservation that had been properly brought to its attention earlier in the proceedings.[52] Whatever the possible disadvantages that consideration of informal communications causes to the appearing State, it cannot be denied that they reduce the risk of a court delivering a judgment in ignorance of the defaulting State's legal arguments and the associated factual evidence.[53]

[50] Fitzmaurice, "The Problem," 117.

[51] *Nuclear Tests (Australia v. France), Interim Protection, Order*, Dissenting Opinion of Judge Gros, 118.

[52] *Aegean Sea Continental Shelf*, *Judgment*, 19, 20, paras. 43, 47. The Court's treatment of Turkey's communication came in for considerable scholarly criticism. Mario Bettati, "L'affaire du plateau continental de la Mer Egée devant la Cour internationale de Justice — Compétence (arrêt du 19 décembre 1978) [The Case of the Aegean Sea Continental Shelf Before the International Court of Justice – Jurisdiction (Judgment of 19 December 1978)]," *AFDI* 24 (1978): 317–18, http://www.persee.fr/doc/afdi_0066-3085_1978_num_24_1_2099, accessed 8 September 2020; Karin Oellers-Frahm, "Die Entscheidung des Internationalen Gerichtshofes im griechisch-türkischen Streit um die Festlandsockel in der Äegaeis [The Judgment of the International Court of Justice in the Greco-Turkish Dispute on the Continental Self in the Aegean]," *Archiv des Völkerrechts* [Archive of International Law] 18 (1980): 392.

[53] H.W.A. Thirlway, *Non-appearance Before the International Court of Justice* (Cambridge: Cambridge University Press, 1985), 168.

The importance of informal communications is such that the ICJ sometimes seemed to attach significance to the absence of communications from the defaulting State.[54] In *United States Diplomatic and Consular Staff in Tehran*, Iran had claimed that the fate of the hostages was a marginal or secondary aspect of an overall problem, that of 25 years of US interference in Iranian domestic politics. The Court observed that Iran had not explained why the violation of diplomatic and consular law manifested in the hostage-taking could not be examined separately from the overall problem of Iran–US relations and had not explained or defined the legal or factual connection between the hostage-taking and the overall problem. In the absence of further explanation from Iran, the Court decided that it could continue to hear the case.[55]

After this survey of the treatment by international courts of informal communications from defaulting States, it is now possible to discuss the treatment by the *South China Sea* Tribunal of China's informal communications.

2. China's Informal Communications in the South China Sea Arbitration

Like other defaulting States before the ICJ, China was unable to adhere to its resolution not to participate in the arbitral proceedings. Informal communications were essential elements in China's litigation strategy, enabling it to reap the benefits of participation while it continued to deny that it was a party to the case. Unlike Iceland in the *Fisheries Jurisdiction Cases* and Iran in the *United States Diplomatic and Consular Staff in Tehran* case, China sent letters and communications to the Tribunal until practically the conclusion of the proceedings. Almost all of these communications had identical content—China's objections to the Tribunal's jurisdiction. Consequently, China's informal communications served to inform the Philippines and the Tribunal of China's legal arguments only in the jurisdictional phase; its other informal communications were by definition of little utility in the merits phase of the proceedings.

China's first communication to the Tribunal on 29 July 2013, following its initial meeting, reiterated China's non-acceptance of the

[54] Ibid., 127–28, 147–48.

[55] *United States Diplomatic and Consular Staff in Tehran, Judgment*, 20, paras. 37–38.

Arbitration.[56] The next and most important communication from China was a Position Paper, which was transmitted to the Tribunal on 8 December 2014, one week before the expiry of the time limit for the submission of China's *Counter-Memorial.*[57] On 6 February 2015, in response to a request for comments on procedural matters such as the bifurcation of proceedings and the appointment of an expert hydrographer, China wrote to the Tribunal declaring its omnibus objection to all procedural steps that would require some kind of response from China.[58] On 1 July 2015, a few days before the Hearing on Jurisdiction, China wrote again to the Tribunal to remind it of its Position Paper and to express its refusal of any arbitral arrangements, including the hearing procedures.[59] On 20 May 2016, nearly six months after the closure of the oral proceedings, China transmitted a Foreign Ministry statement urging all sides (who remained unidentified) to encourage the Philippines to settle the dispute through negotiations.[60] On 3 June 2016, China transmitted a Foreign Ministry statement on the maritime feature known as Itu Aba in the Spratly Islands.[61] On 8 June 2016, another Chinese letter

[56] *South China Sea Arbitration*, Award on Jurisdiction and Admissibility (29 October 2015), 17, para. 37 ("Award on Jurisdiction"), https://pcacases.com/web/sendAttach/2579, accessed 10 March 2020.

[57] Ibid., *Supplemental Written Submission of the Philippines* (16 March 2015), Annex 467, People's Republic of China, Position Paper of the Government of the People's Republic of China on the Matter of Jurisdiction in the South China Sea Arbitration Initiated by the Republic of the Philippines (7 December 2014), vol. VIII, 32, para. 92 ("*SWSP*"), https://files.pca-cpa.org/pcadocs/The%20Philippines%27%20Supplemental%20Written%20Submission%20-%20Volume%20VIII%20%28Annexes%20466-499%29.pdf, accessed 10 March 2020; Award on Jurisdiction, 20, 21, paras. 53, 55, 56.

[58] Ibid., Annex 470, Letter from H.E. Ambassador Chen Xu, Embassy of the People's Republic of China in The Hague, to H.E. Judge Thomas A. Mensah (6 February 2015), vol. VIII, 73–84; Award on Jurisdiction, 22, paras. 60, 64.

[59] *South China Sea Arbitration, The Philippines' Annexes Cited During Hearing on Jurisdiction (Annexes 574–583)* (13 July 2015), Annex 574, Letter from H.E. Chen Xu, Ambassador of the People's Republic of China to the Kingdom of The Netherlands, to H.E. Judge Thomas A. Mensah (1 July 2015), 1–3, https://files.pca-cpa.org/pcadocs/Annexes%20cited%20during%20Hearing%20on%20Jurisdiction%20%28Annexes%20574-583%29.pdf, accessed 24 April 2020; Award on Jurisdiction, 27, para. 84.

[60] Award on Jurisdiction, 34, para. 97.

[61] Ibid., 35, para. 100.

reiterated China's arguments against jurisdiction.[62] In a final letter on 10 June 2016, China transmitted the CSIL statement criticizing the Award on Jurisdiction.[63]

The Position Paper served to inform the Philippines and the Tribunal of China's legal arguments on jurisdiction and admissibility. A Chinese scholar has described it as "the most authoritative and comprehensive statement" by China on the jurisdiction of the Tribunal.[64] It could not be considered as the equivalent of a *Counter-Memorial*,[65] because it deliberately avoided touching on the merits of the Philippine Submissions and it did not comply with the requirement that all documentary, witness, expert, and other evidence upon which the party relied be submitted together with the written submissions.[66] China would have been well within its rights to file a preliminary objection by the date set for the filing of its *Counter-Memorial*. The problem was that China's Position Paper simultaneously sought to prevent the proceedings from continuing and denied that China was under an obligation to comply with any Award of the Tribunal. One could say that this combined statement of preliminary objection and announcement of non-compliance amounted to more than a formal preliminary objection.[67]

While the defaulting State sought a procedural advantage for itself through this informal communication, the Philippines nevertheless welcomed the Position Paper as "significant and helpful."[68] Counsel for the Philippines gave both political and legal reasons for the Philippine attitude. The political reason: "China obviously felt pressured to demonstrate to the international community – and the arbitral tribunal itself…that it

[62] Ibid., 36, para. 102.

[63] Ibid., para. 103.

[64] Qiang Ye, "Does China's Position Paper on the South China Sea Arbitration Constitute a Preliminary Objection?" in Shicun Wu and Keyuan Zou (eds.), *Arbitration Concerning the South China Sea: Philippines Versus China* (London: Routledge, 2016), 92.

[65] Ibid., 95.

[66] *South China Sea Arbitration*, Rules of Procedure, Article 18(1), 8.

[67] Professor O'Connell, Oral Arguments on Jurisdiction, Fifth Public Sitting (9 October 1978), *I.C.J. Pleadings*, *Aegean Sea Continental Shelf Case*, 318-19.

[68] *SWSP*, vol. I, 123, para. 26.2, https://files.pca-cpa.org/pcadocs/Supplemental%20Written%20Submission%20Volume%20I.pdf, accessed 23 April 2020.

is not an outlaw nation disrespectful of international law."[69] The legal reason:

> China has made it easier for both the arbitral tribunal and the Philippines to do their jobs. The arbitral tribunal will now be fully apprised of China's arguments on jurisdiction, instead of having to guess what they might have been. And the Philippines will now have concrete targets to aim at (and demolish) in future written and oral proceedings.[70]

What the Philippines opposed was the Tribunal's proposal to bifurcate the proceedings. When it seemed that bifurcation was inevitable, the Philippines attempted, as we have seen in Chapter 2, to limit the scope of the Hearing on Jurisdiction to the objections that China had stated in the Position Paper.[71] In a Letter to the Tribunal dated 23 June 2015, a month prior to the Hearing on Jurisdiction, the Philippines reiterated the view that any issue of jurisdiction or admissibility could be waived by virtue of its non-inclusion in the Position Paper.[72] A precedent for limiting the scope of the hearing on jurisdiction and admissibility to the Position Paper was offered by the proceedings in the *"Arctic Sunrise" Arbitration*, in which the Tribunal referred to Russia's Note Verbale as a plea on jurisdiction, addressed the plea, and rejected it.[73]

The Tribunal, in deciding bifurcation, did not agree to the Philippine proposal to circumscribe the scope of the Hearing on Jurisdiction. In the Tribunal's view, its duty under Article 9 of Annex VII required that it consider other issues of jurisdiction and admissibility that had not been discussed in China's Position Paper.[74] This is another sense in which the appearing State is disadvantaged by default and the Tribunal is acting

[69] Paul Reichler Statement, quoted in Ayee Macaraig, "PH Lawyer: We Can 'Demolish' China's Arguments," *Rappler*, 21 January 2015, https://www.rappler.com/nation/78464-reichler-statement-scs-developments, accessed 23 April 2020.

[70] Ibid.

[71] *SWSP*, vol. I, 123–24, paras. 26.2, 26.3, 26.4, Letter of 16 March 2015 to the Tribunal, quoted in *South China Sea Arbitration*, Procedural Order No. 4 (21 April 2015), 5, https://pcacases.com/web/sendAttach/1807, accessed 7 April 2020.

[72] Hearing on Jurisdiction, Transcript, Day 2 (8 July 2015), 74, https://pcacases.com/web/sendAttach/1400, accessed 16 March 2020.

[73] *SWSP*, vol. I, 123–24, paras. 26.2, 26.3, 26.4; Letter of 16 March 2015 to the Tribunal.

[74] Procedural Order No. 4, 6, para. 1.4.

as counsel of the defaulting State. In proceedings in which both parties appear, the jurisdictional phase is limited to the preliminary objections raised by the respondent State. An international court would not on its own seek other possible grounds for preliminary objections. In cases of default, the court feels compelled to examine all possible objections to its jurisdiction and to the admissibility of the applicant's claims. Long before the wave of defaults of the 1970s and the 1980s, Judge Lauterpacht had already warned that the ICJ could not fulfill its duty in case of default by "ignoring possibly decisive objections for the mere reason that the interested party [i.e., the defaulting State] has not put them forward."[75] By considering all possible issues of jurisdiction and admissibility, including those that China had not raised or perhaps even imagined, the Tribunal was in effect acting as China's counsel.

In the merits phase of the proceedings, the Philippines and the Tribunal, like other appearing States and the ICJ in other cases, did not have a fully argued *Counter-Memorial* before them. The only informal communication from China that put forward arguments on the merits was the letter of 3 June 2016, on the status of Itu Aba as a maritime feature in the Spratly Islands, transmitted to the Tribunal more than six months after the closure of the oral proceedings. It inevitably brings to mind D.W. Bowett's observation that the worst feature of informal communications is that they are usually submitted at a very late stage, compelling the appearing State to answer them at very short notice. An even more serious objection may be raised against communications that are received after the formal closure of the oral proceedings. They entail the risk that the court or tribunal's decision may be influenced by arguments to which the appearing State has not had the opportunity to reply, in violation of the principle of the equality of the parties.[76] The only way that the international court or tribunal can avoid penalizing the appearing State would involve forwarding the correspondence to it and soliciting its comments on the issues raised in these communications.

China's letter of 3 June 2016 declared that "China has, based on the Nansha Islands as a whole, territorial sea, exclusive economic zone and

[75] Hersch Lauterpacht, *The Development of International Law by the International Court* (New York: Frederick A. Praeger Publishers, 1958), 255–56, footnote 42; Thirlway, *Non-appearance*, 121.

[76] Bowett, "Contemporary Developments," 210.

continental shelf."[77] The Tribunal interpreted this as an assertion that the Spratly Islands could be enclosed within a system of archipelagic baselines, making China in effect an archipelagic State under the Convention. This is not the place to rehearse the Tribunal's discussion of the issue. Suffice it to say that the Tribunal concluded that "China...is constituted principally by territory on the mainland of Asia and cannot meet the definition of an archipelagic State."[78] For this reason, the Spratly Islands could not be enclosed within a system of archipelagic straight lines and could not be considered as having the right to maritime entitlements "as a whole." It is necessary to point this out, because one commentator has remarked that the Tribunal made a finding on the status of China as an archipelagic State when it was not called upon to do so.[79] A careful reading of the Award reveals that if China had not written to the Tribunal, the Philippines would not have been given the opportunity to contradict China's thesis and the Tribunal would not have had the occasion to make a pronouncement on the issue. The letter of 3 June 2016 appears to be an attempt to delay the conclusion of the proceedings, by forcing the Tribunal to examine China's statement on the status of Itu Aba. In proceedings in which two States appear, such late submissions would never have been permitted, unless the Tribunal had made arrangements for the receipt of such submissions after the closure of the oral proceedings.[80] The procedural disadvantage that the Philippines might

[77] Quoted in Award of 12 July 2016, 35, para. 100.

[78] Award of 12 July 2016, 235, para. 571.

[79] Julian Ku, "Short, Quick Take on the Philippines' Sweeping Victory in the South China Sea Arbitration," *Lawfare*, 12 July 2016, https://www.lawfareblog.com/short-quick-take-philippines-sweeping-victory-south-china-sea-arbitration, accessed 23 April 2020. The misunderstanding is explicable because the commentary was published on the day the Award was issued and it was perhaps not possible to go through the fine print of the 479-page Award.

[80] In the *Fisheries Jurisdiction Cases*, the ICJ did not declare at the closure of the oral hearings that further communications would not be possible. Transcripts of the hearings and copies of the responses of the appearing States were sent to Iceland. Had Iceland responded to these documents, the Tribunal would have been obliged to reopen the hearings. Louis Favoreu, "Les arrêts de la Cour Internationale de Justice relatifs à la compétence en matière de pêcheries (Royaume-Uni c/ Islande et République fédérale d'Allemagne c. Islande — Arrêts du 25 juillet 1974) [The Judgments of the International Court of Justice on Fisheries Jurisdiction (United Kingdom v. Iceland and Federal Republic of Germany v. Iceland – Judgments of 25 July 1974]," *AFDI* 20 (1974): 258,

have suffered from the receipt of this letter was mitigated to the extent that the Tribunal transmitted it to the Philippines for its comments.[81]

The other three letters transmitted to the Tribunal several months after the closure of the oral proceedings merely repeated China's objections to the Tribunal jurisdiction, offered no assistance to the Tribunal's deliberations, and were not taken into consideration by the Tribunal. Given these circumstances, it does not seem that Yoshifumi Tanaka's concern that the Philippines was disadvantaged by China's default is entirely justified.[82] Chapter 5 will attempt to explain China's unrelenting reiteration of its objections to jurisdiction as conduct consistent with the conduct of State and party authorities in China toward courts and judicial proceedings. In one instance, the Tribunal seemed to have attached significance to the absence of informal communications from China. When examining the Philippine allegation that China had violated its obligations to protect and preserve the marine environment through its island-building in the South China Sea, and in particular, that China had failed to carry out an environmental impact assessment ("EIA"), the Tribunal directly asked China, by means of letters dated 5 February and 15 March 2016, for a copy of any EIA that it had prepared. In the absence of a response, the Tribunal observed that in the past, China, despite its non-participation, had found occasions and means to communicate statements by its officials or by others writing in line with China's interests. The Tribunal believed that had China wished to draw attention to the existence of an EIA and its content, China would surely have done so. China's silence implied that it had not carried out an EIA. It should be pointed out in passing that the absence of an EIA was not the basis of the Tribunal's finding that China had breached the Convention; rather it was the failure to communicate any EIA to an international organization.[83]

http://www.persee.fr/doc/afdi_0066-3085_1974_num_20_1_2271, accessed 17 March 2020.

[81] Award of 12 July 2016, 36, para. 108.

[82] Yoshifumi Tanaka, *The South China Sea Arbitration: Towards an International Legal Order in the Oceans* (Oxford: Hart Publishing, 2019), 28.

[83] Award of 12 July 2016, 396–97, para. 991; Chinese Society of International Law ("CSIL"), "The South China Sea Arbitration Awards: A Critical Study," *Chinese Journal of International Law* 17 (2018): 592, para. 820.

The Tribunal's observation of China's practice was an astute one, for China had not hesitated on other occasions to express its views on the proceedings and related issues through public statements.

B. The Defaulting State's Public Statements

Public statements will be understood here to refer only to statements actually made by the defaulting State, rather than any information or material in the public domain concerning the case or matters related to the case. The strictures on informal communications to the Tribunal apply with equal force to public statements by the defaulting State, with the added disadvantage that the latter are not even addressed to the international court or tribunal concerned.[84] The ICJ justifies the recourse to such public statements by affirming that in cases of default, "it is especially incumbent upon [the Court] to satisfy itself that it is in possession of all the available facts."[85] One might add that public statements, like informal communications, may provide information on the defaulting State's legal arguments. In the *South China Sea Arbitration*, China's public statements provided some information to the Philippines and the Tribunal on China's legal positions as regards only a handful of Philippine submissions. The Tribunal treated public statements in the same way that it did informal communications, in fulfillment of its duty under Article 9 of Annex VII of the Convention.

1. Public Statements in Lieu of Pleadings

Defaulting States occasionally make official statements that directly address issues raised in the proceedings to which they are parties. Even when they do not, it is still possible to find public statements concerning issues related to the dispute, published prior to or during the proceedings.

In the *Nuclear Tests Cases*, France was not content to transmit to the Court its objections to jurisdiction.[86] As the proceedings were ongoing,

[84] *Nicaragua*, *Merits*, *Judgment*, Dissenting Opinion of Judge Schwebel, 308, para. 124.

[85] *Nuclear Tests (Australia v. France)*, *Judgment*, 263, para. 31.

[86] "L'ambassadeur de France aux Pays-Bas au Greffier [The French Ambassador to The Netherlands to the Registrar] (16 May 1973)," *I.C.J. Pleadings*, *Nuclear Tests (Australia v. France)*, vol. I, 347–57, https://www.icj-cij.org/files/case-related/58/11007.pdf, accessed 24 April 2020.

it published a *Livre Blanc* (White Paper), which presented French arguments on jurisdiction and on the merits. The section on jurisdiction was quite brief, reprising arguments already discussed in detail in an informal communication to the Court. This section was still valuable, given that the contents of its correspondence with the Court were published only after the proceedings had been concluded. In the French view, the Court manifestly lacked jurisdiction to hear the case because France had explicitly excluded disputes concerning activities related to national defense from its acceptance of the Court's compulsory jurisdiction; no adverse conclusion concerning French consent to the jurisdiction of the Court could be drawn from the General Act for the Pacific Settlement of Disputes of 1928; and the dispute was not legal in nature.[87] The sections on the legal and scientific merits of the claims by Australia and New Zealand were more substantial. First, France sought to demonstrate that its atmospheric nuclear tests in the South Pacific did not cause any damage to populations and to flora and fauna. On the scientific issues, it pointed out that French tests represented only 5% of all tests by the five nuclear States; that the testing technique used generated infinitely small particles that rose to very high altitudes and were dispersed by the wind; that the sites chosen were uninhabited, inaccessible, rarely visited by shipping and air lines, and at least 4000 kilometers away from major cities in Australia and New Zealand; and that the radiation doses generated were much smaller than the doses resulting from natural and artificial radiation.[88] On the legal issues, France observed that Australia and New Zealand recognized the legality of atmospheric nuclear testing carried out by the US and the UK; that no new norm of international law had evolved making it possible to assess French nuclear tests on the basis of rules different from those applied to earlier nuclear tests; that the law of international responsibility as applied to the protection of the environment did not provide any basis for the claims of Australia and New Zealand; and that the law of the sea had not been modified as regards the creation of danger

[87] *République française* [French Republic], *Comité interministériel pour l'information* [Interministerial Committee for Information], *Livre Blanc sur les expériences nucléaires* [White Paper on Nuclear Tests] (1973), 23–24, http://www.moruroa.org/medias/pdf/Livre%20Blanc.pdf, accessed 21 July 2019.

[88] Ibid., 3–10.

zones since the time that the US and the UK had carried out their nuclear tests.[89]

According to a distinguished commentator, the White Paper filled a gap created by French default. It was analogous to an extended written brief concerning the formal legal issues and was the clearest and most formal statement of legal arguments and evidence by any of the parties. The critique of the double standards of Australia and New Zealand seemed particularly convincing.[90] In the end, the Court had no opportunity to pronounce on its jurisdiction, much less on the merits, as it ruled that French announcements of the cessation of atmospheric nuclear testing meant that the dispute no longer existed.

In *United States Diplomatic and Consular Staff in Tehran*, Iran had explained its objections to the ICJ's jurisdiction in two telegrams, after which there was no further communication from Iran. The difficulties facing the United States and the Court were aggravated by the fact that the position of the Iranian government on the hostage-taking was not expressed in a single document. It had to be deduced by the Court from approximately 40 speeches delivered by or interviews of Iranian religious leaders and their family members, ministers, leaders of student associations, and even anonymous students during the hostage crisis.[91] On the basis of these numerous statements, the Court concluded that the taking of the hostages by the students, who had no official status as agents or organs of the Iranian State, was not imputable to Iran. However, official approval of the hostage-taking transformed the continuing occupation of the Embassy and the detention of the hostages into acts of the Iranian State.[92]

In the *Nicaragua Case*, no US counter-memorial on the merits was before the Court. That said, many of the US legal arguments on the

[89] Ibid., 13–21.

[90] Edward McWhinney, "International Law-making and the Judicial Process: The World Court and the French Nuclear Tests Case," *Syracuse Journal of International Law and Commerce* 3 (1975): 18, 42, https://surface.syr.edu/cgi/viewcontent.cgi?article=1033&context=jilc, accessed 26 April 2020.

[91] See Annexes 2–41 and 47 in *Memorial of the Government of the United States of America* (12 January 1980), *I.C.J. Pleadings*, *United States Diplomatic and Consular Staff in Tehran*, 73–98, 105, https://www.icj-cij.org/files/case-related/64/9551.pdf, accessed 24 April 1980.

[92] *United States Diplomatic and Consular Staff in Tehran, Judgment*, 29–30, 32–33, paras. 58–59, 73–74.

merits and some of the factual evidence supporting them had been presented in summary form in its *Counter-Memorial* on jurisdiction and in the publication that it forwarded to the Court on the second day of the Hearing on the Merits.[93] The appearing State was able to furnish the ICJ with a wide variety of public statements attributable to the US to support its case, published prior to and during the proceedings.[94] One set consisted of statements by US President Reagan and senior officials of his administration. A statement made at a press conference of the President was interpreted by the ICJ as an admission that the US had something to do with an attack on the Nicaraguan port of Corinto on 10 October 1983 but not necessarily that US personnel were directly involved.[95] A report of the Intelligence Committee of the US House of Representatives revealed in 1983 that funding had been approved for a program of covert actions against Nicaragua.[96] Members of the US Congress informed the press that the President had approved a CIA plan for the mining of Nicaraguan ports.[97] At the UN Security Council, the US admitted in 1982 that the US undertook the high-altitude overflights for reconnaissance purposes of which Nicaragua complained.[98] The US Central Intelligence Agency supplied in 1983 a manual entitled *Psychological Operations in Guerrilla Warfare* that contained a section on "Implicit and Explicit Terror." The manual declared that "it should be necessary…to fire on a citizen who was trying to leave the town."[99] Despite the US withdrawal from the proceedings, the large number of official declarations, interviews with US officials, press reports of official declarations, official documents, and other documents facilitated the Court's fact-finding.[100]

[93] *Counter-Memorial of the United States of America* (17 August 1984), *I.C.J. Pleadings, Military and Paramilitary Activities in and against Nicaragua*, vol. IV, 56–68, paras. 189–225, https://www.icj-cij.org/files/case-related/70/9627.pdf, accessed 26 April 2020.

[94] Such statements may be found in the *Memorial of Nicaragua (Merits), I.C.J. Pleadings, Military and Paramilitary Activities in and against Nicaragua*, vol. IV, 164–293, https://www.icj-cij.org/files/case-related/70/9619.pdf, accessed 24 April 2020.

[95] *Nicaragua, Merits, Judgment*, 49, para. 83.

[96] Ibid., 55, para. 95.

[97] Ibid., 47, para. 78.

[98] Ibid., 51, para. 88.

[99] Ibid., 66, para. 118.

[100] Eisemann, "L'arrêt," 188.

The quantity of factual material and the circumstances of the case, including US "disappearance," were such that the Court set guidelines for itself in evaluating the evidence. The most important guidelines required the Court to give weight to statements by State representatives that are unfavorable to the State they represent; to give little or no weight to self-serving declarations, statements, or testimony by State officials; to give weight to statements by disinterested parties; not to treat opinions as evidence; not to treat as evidence reports in press articles or books; and to adopt a cautious approach to what passes for public knowledge. These guidelines proved useful not just in the case but also in subsequent cases involving hotly disputed and complex facts in which both parties appeared before the Court.[101]

Most of China's public statements in the *South China Sea Arbitration* fell in the category of self-serving declarations, statements, or testimony by State officials, but the Tribunal did not necessarily disregard them.

2. China's Public Statements in the South China Sea Arbitration

In the *South China Sea Arbitration*, the Philippines could not find any Chinese White Paper, publications of government agencies, or interviews of non-State actors that were available to appearing States in other cases of default. Most Chinese statements on the *Arbitration*, which were issued mainly by the Foreign Ministry, provided little information to the Philippines and the Tribunal on China's legal positions and arguments. A handful of public statements that were the exceptions did not necessarily redound to China's benefit.

China's default meant that the task of collecting its public statements, which should have been its responsibility, fell to the Philippines. It should be noted, however, that the Tribunal searched for and found a number of public statements on its own initiative. These were China's statements at the 15th session of the International Seabed Authority in 2009[102]; an interview on 27 May 2015 by a staff member of the Chinese Embassy in Canada on the subject of China's construction activities in the

[101] Paul S. Reichler, "The Impact of the Nicaragua Case on Matters of Evidence and Fact-Finding," *Leiden Journal of International Law* 25 (March 2012): 149–56. Reichler was counsel for Nicaragua in the *Nicaragua Case* and for the Philippines in the *South China Sea Arbitration*.

[102] Award of 12 July 2016, 199, notes 496–97.

Spratly Islands[103]; a Foreign Ministry statement of 21 December 2015 on the publication of the transcript of the Hearing of the Merits[104]; a Foreign Ministry statement on 6 May 2016, declaring that in its construction activities on the Spratly Islands, China followed the principle of conducting the green project, took the approach of "natural simulation," and adopted dynamic protection measures[105]; and a Foreign Ministry "Briefing on the South China Sea Arbitration Initiated by the Philippines," of June 2016, nearly six months after the closure of the oral proceedings on the merits.[106] The significance of all but the last document will be discussed below. An explanation for the restatement of China's position on the Tribunal's jurisdiction given in the Briefing at such a late stage in the proceedings will be attempted in Chapter 5. It is not clear from the Award of 12 July 2016 whether the text of the Briefing was transmitted to the Philippines for comments. It is possible that for the Tribunal, there was no need to do so, in view of the fact that the Briefing restated China's well-known views.

The bulk of the public statements assembled by the Philippines consisted of responses of Foreign Ministry spokespersons to questions put to them by journalists during daily press conferences.[107] The constraints dictated by the format are evident: responses were brief; by definition

[103] *Philippines' Annexes Cited During the Merits Hearing* (30 November 2015) ("*PAMH*"), Annex 820, Embassy of the People's Republic of China in Canada, An Interview on China's Construction Activities on the Nansha Islands and Reefs (27 May 2015), 5–9, https://files.pca-cpa.org/pcadocs/Annexes%20cited%20during%20Hearing%20on%20Jurisdiction%20%28Annexes%20574-583%29.pdf, accessed 24 April 2020; *South China Sea Arbitration*, Hearing on the Merits and Remaining Issues of Jurisdiction and Admissibility, Transcript, Day 4 (30 November 2015), 82–83, https://pcacases.com/web/sendAttach/1550, accessed 16 April 2020.

[104] Ministry of Foreign Affairs, People's Republic of China, *Foreign Ministry Spokesperson Hong Lei's Regular Press Conference* (21 December 2015), http://www.fmprc.gov.cn/mfa_eng/xwfw_665399/s2510_665401/t1326449.shtml, accessed 3 May 2020; quoted in Award of 12 July 2016, 28, para. 82.

[105] Award of 12 July 2016, 365–66, para. 920.

[106] Ibid., 28, 32–34, paras. 82, 96.

[107] See the following in *MP*, vol. V, https://files.pca-cpa.org/pcadocs/The%20Philippines%27%20Memorial%20-%20Volume%20V%20%28Annexes%20103-157%29.pdf, accessed 23 March 2020:

1. Annex 124, Ministry of Foreign Affairs of the People's Republic of China, Foreign Ministry Spokesperson Hong Lei's Regular Press Conference on February 19, 2013 (20 February 2013), 161–65;

they could not provide detailed evidence; they varied little from one press conference to the next; and with the exceptions that will be noted below,

2. Annex 125, Ministry of Foreign Affairs of the People's Republic of China, Foreign Ministry Spokesperson Hong Lei's Regular Press Conference on February 20, 2013 (21 February 2013), 167–69;
3. Annex 127, Ministry of Foreign Affairs of the People's Republic of China, Foreign Ministry Spokesperson Hua Chunying's Remarks on the Philippines' Efforts in Pushing for the Establishment of the Arbitral Tribunal in Relation to the Disputes Between China and the Philippines in the South China Sea (26 April 2013), 181–84;
4. Annex 131, Ministry of Foreign Affairs of the People's Republic of China, Foreign Ministry Spokesperson Hong Lei's Statement Regarding Comments by an Official of the United States Department of State on the South China Sea (8 February 2014), 203–05.

See the following in *South China Sea Arbitration*, *Written Responses of the Philippines to the Tribunal's 13 July 2015 Questions* (23 July 2015) ("*WRPTQ*"), vol. II, https://files.pca-cpa.org/pcadocs/The%20Philippines%27%20Written%20Responses%20to%20the%20Tribunal%27s%2013%20July%202015%20Questions%20-%20Volume%20II%20%28Annexes%20584-606%29.pdf, accessed 27 April 2020:

1. Annex 584, Ministry of Foreign Affairs of the People's Republic of China, Foreign Ministry Spokesperson Hong Lei's Regular Press Conference on May 22, 2013 (22 May 2013), 1–4;
2. Annex 585, Ministry of Foreign Affairs of the People's Republic of China, Foreign Ministry Spokesperson Hua Chunying's Regular Press Conference on June 16, 2014 (16 June 2014), 5–9;
3. Annex 586, Ministry of Foreign Affairs of the People's Republic of China, Foreign Ministry Spokesperson Hong Lei's Regular Press Conference on February 27, 2015 (27 February 2015), 11–16;
4. Annex 587, Ministry of Foreign Affairs of the People's Republic of China, Foreign Ministry Spokesperson Hong Lei's Regular Press Conference on April 15, 2015 (15 April 2015), 17–20;
5. Annex 588, Ministry of Foreign Affairs of the People's Republic of China, Foreign Ministry Spokesperson Hong Lei's Regular Press Conference on April 17, 2015 (17 April 2015), 21–24;
6. Annex 589, Ministry of Foreign Affairs of the People's Republic of China, Foreign Ministry Spokesperson Hong Lei's Regular Press Conference on April 27, 2015 (27 April 2015), 27–31;
7. Annex 590, Ministry of Foreign Affairs of the People's Republic of China, Foreign Ministry Spokesperson Hua Chunying's Regular Press Conference on May 27, 2015 (27 May 2015), 33–37.

See the following in *South China Sea Arbitration*, *Supplemental Documents of the Philippines* (19 November 2015) ("*SDP*"), vol. I, https://files.pca-cpa.org/pcadocs/The%20Philippines%27%20Supplemental%20Documents%20-%20Volume%20I%20%28Annexes%20607-667%29.pdf, accessed 27 April 2020:

they added little to what was already known about China's legal positions and arguments. The spokespersons tirelessly repeated that China's

1. Annex 619, Ministry of Foreign Affairs of the People's Republic of China, Foreign Ministry Spokesperson Hua Chunying's Regular Press Conference on September 9, 2014 (9 September 2014), 137–42;
2. Annex 620, Ministry of Foreign Affairs of the People's Republic of China, Foreign Ministry Spokesperson Hong Lei's Regular Press Conference on December 9, 2014 (9 December 2014), 143–46;
3. Annex 621, Ministry of Foreign Affairs of the People's Republic of China, Foreign Ministry Spokesperson Hong Lei's Remarks on Vietnam's Statement on the Chinese Government's Position Paper on Rejecting the Jurisdiction of the Arbitral Tribunal Established at the Request of the Philippines for the South China Sea Arbitration (12 December 2014), 147–49;
4. Annex 623, Ministry of Foreign Affairs of the People's Republic of China, Foreign Ministry Spokesperson Hong Lei's Regular Press Conference on March 11, 2015 (11 March 2015), 161–64;
5. Annex 624, Ministry of Foreign Affairs of the People's Republic of China, Foreign Ministry Spokesperson Hua Chunying's Regular Press Conference on April 9, 2015 (9 April 2015), 165–70;
6. Annex 625, Ministry of Foreign Affairs of the People's Republic of China, Foreign Ministry Spokesperson Hong Lei's Regular Press Conference on April 28, 2015 (28 April 2015), 171–76;
7. Annex 626, Ministry of Foreign Affairs of the People's Republic of China, Foreign Ministry Spokesperson Hua Chunying's Remarks on US Defense Secretary Carter's Speech Relating to the Issue of the South China Sea at the Shangri-La Dialogue (30 May 2015), 177–80;
8. Annex 627, Ministry of Foreign Affairs of the People's Republic of China, Foreign Ministry Spokesperson Hong Lei's Regular Press Conference on June 9, 2015 (9 June 2015), 181–86;
9. Annex 628, Ministry of Foreign Affairs of the People's Republic of China, Foreign Ministry Spokesperson Hua Chunying's Remarks on the Philippines' Playing up and Airing of a Documentary on the South China Sea Issue (29 June 2015), 187–90;
10. Annex 629, Ministry of Foreign Affairs of the People's Republic of China, Foreign Ministry Spokesperson Hua Chunying's Regular Press Conference on July 8, 2015 (8 July 2015), 191–96;
11. Annex 630, Ministry of Foreign Affairs of the People's Republic of China, Foreign Ministry Spokesperson Hua Chunying's Remarks on the Philippines' Reinforcing a Military Vessel Illegally "Grounded" on China's Ren'ai Jiao (15 July 2015), 197–201;
12. Annex 635, Ministry of Foreign Affairs of the People's Republic of China, Foreign Ministry Spokesperson Hua Chunying's Remarks on the Release of the Transcript of the Oral Hearing on Jurisdiction by the South China Sea Arbitral Tribunal Established at the Request of the Philippines (24 Aug. 2015), 223–27;
13. Annex 638, Ministry of Foreign Affairs of the People's Republic of China, Foreign Ministry Spokesperson Hong Lei's Regular Press Conference on September 29, 2015 (29 September 2015), 241–46;

sovereignty over the Spratly Islands and adjacent waters was indisputable; that its sovereignty and its claims to relevant rights had been formed in the course of history; and that they were backed with abundant historical

14. Annex 639, Ministry of Foreign Affairs of the People's Republic of China, Foreign Ministry Spokesperson Hong Lei's Regular Press Conference on September 29, 2015 (29 September 2015), 247–50;
15. Annex 643, Ministry of Foreign Affairs of the People's Republic of China, Foreign Ministry Spokesperson Lu Kang's Regular Press Conference on October 27, 2015 (27 October 2015), 265–70;
16. Annex 644, Ministry of Foreign Affairs of the People's Republic of China, Foreign Ministry Spokesperson Lu Kang's Remarks on USS Lassen's Entry into Waters near Relevant Islands and Reefs of China's Nansha Islands (27 October 2015), 271–74;
17. Annex 645, Ministry of Foreign Affairs of the People's Republic of China, Vice Foreign Minister Zhang Yesui Makes Stern Representations to US over US Naval Vessel's Entry into Waters near Relevant Islands and Reefs of China's Nansha Islands (27 October 2015), 275–78;
18. Annex 646, Ministry of Foreign Affairs of the People's Republic of China, Foreign Ministry Spokesperson Lu Kang's Regular Press Conference on October 28, 2015 (28 October 2015), 279–82;
19. Annex 647, Ministry of Foreign Affairs of the People's Republic of China, Foreign Ministry Spokesperson Lu Kang's Regular Press Conference on October 29, 2015 (29 October 2015), 283–86;
20. Annex 648, People's Republic of China, Ministry of National Defense, Defense Ministry's Regular Press Conference on October 29 (29 October 2015), 287–92;
21. Annex 649, Ministry of Foreign Affairs of the People's Republic of China, Statement of the Ministry of Foreign Affairs of the People's Republic of China on the Award on Jurisdiction and Admissibility of the South China Sea Arbitration by the Arbitral Tribunal Established at the Request of the Republic of the Philippines (30 October 2015), 293–96;
22. Annex 650, Ministry of Foreign Affairs of the People's Republic of China, Foreign Ministry Spokesperson Lu Kang's Regular Press Conference on October 30, 2015 (30 October 2015), 297–301;
23. Annex 651, Ministry of Foreign Affairs of the People's Republic of China, Foreign Ministry Spokesperson Hua Chunying's Regular Press Conference on November 2, 2015 (2 November 2015), 302–04;
24. Annex 652, Ministry of Foreign Affairs of the People's Republic of China, Foreign Ministry Spokesperson Hua Chunying's Regular Press Conference on November 3, 2015 (3 November 2015), 305–10;
25. Annex 653, Ministry of Foreign Affairs of the People's Republic of China, Foreign Ministry Spokesperson Hua Chunying's Regular Press Conference on November 5, 2015 (5 November 2015), 311–14;
26. Annex 654, Ministry of Foreign Affairs of the People's Republic of China, Foreign Ministry Spokesperson Hong Lei's Regular Press Conference on November 10, 2015 (10 November 2015), 315–18.

and jurisprudential evidence. These statements were no different from the statements that were already available on the Foreign Ministry website prior to the initiation of the *Arbitration*, and like the latter, were not backed up with the kind of legal arguments and factual evidence that are expected of formal pleadings. Needless to say, these statements were hardly relevant to the *Arbitration*, which did not aim to settle questions of sovereignty, despite China's claims to the contrary.

At several important points in the arbitral proceedings, the Foreign Ministry issued official statements. On 24 August 2015, it published remarks on the release of the transcript of the Hearing on Jurisdiction.[108] On 30 October 2015, it issued a statement on the Award on Jurisdiction and Admissibility.[109] Finally, on 21 December 2015, it published a statement on the publication of the transcript of the Hearing on the Merits.[110] All of these statements, which were duly noted by the Tribunal, merely reprised China's position on jurisdiction. If we examine only these statements, one can hardly confirm the widespread impression that China made great efforts to make known its legal arguments and the factual evidence to support them. China's statements bear no comparison to the *Livre Blanc* (White Paper) published by France on the occasion of the *Nuclear Tests Cases*. China was, of course, only being consistent with the litigation strategy it had already announced in the Position Paper: it would not comment on the merits of any of the Philippine claims.

A handful of China's public statements did shed new light on China's legal positions concerning several Philippine claims. On 27 October 2015, China's Vice Foreign Minister stated that China

> respects and safeguards the freedom of navigation and overflight in the South China Sea to which all countries are entitled under international law . ... There has been and will be no obstruction to navigation and overflight freedom in the South China Sea.[111]

This statement was repeated by the Foreign Ministry spokesperson on 3 November 2015, who added that no problems were encountered by

[108] *SDP*, Annex 635, 17–18, para. 53.

[109] Ibid., Annex 649; Award of 12 July 2016, 20–21, para. 61.

[110] Award of 12 July 2016, 28, para. 82.

[111] *SDP*, Annex 645.

100,000 ships from around the world sailing safely and freely through the South China Sea every year.[112] These and other statements stressing that the freedom of navigation and freedom of overflight in the South China Sea were not impaired were key to determining whether China's claim to historic rights was equivalent to a claim to historic title and hence to sovereignty over the sea areas enclosed within the "nine-dash line," which the Philippines had asked the Tribunal to declare as incompatible with the Convention in its Submissions No. 1 and 2. Freedom of navigation and freedom of overflight are freedoms of the high seas, which are not subject to national jurisdiction. In the territorial sea, which is a belt of sea adjacent to the land territory of a coastal State and over which it exercises sovereignty up to a maximum of 12 nautical miles from the baselines drawn along the coast, there is neither freedom of navigation (beyond a right of innocent of passage) nor freedom of overflight.[113] Hence, China's statement indicated that its claim to "historic rights" did not claim sovereignty over the waters of the South China Sea within the "nine-dash line." This being the case, the optional exception to jurisdiction over disputes concerning "historic bays and titles," which had been incorporated in a declaration made by China in 2006, was not applicable, enabling the Tribunal to exercise jurisdiction over Submissions No. 1 and 2 and to examine the merits of the latter.

Another set of public statements proved to be relevant for the Tribunal's examination of Philippine Submissions No. 11 and 12(b), which claimed, among others, that China's island-building in the South China Sea violated China's obligations to protect and preserve the marine environment. In a series of virtually identical statements, the Foreign Ministry spokesperson had declared that China's construction activities were well within its sovereignty, lawful, justified, reasonable, and therefore beyond reproach.[114] A notable exception was a statement made on 9 April 2015, in which the Foreign Ministry Spokesperson claimed that China's construction projects on the islands and reefs had gone through scientific assessments and rigorous tests.[115] This statement was

[112] *SDP*, Annex 651.

[113] Convention, Articles 2, 3, 17–20.

[114] See for example in *WRPTQ*, vol. I, Annexes 585, 586, and 588; see also in *SDP*, vol. I, Annexes 619 and 627.

[115] *SDP*, vol. I, Annex 624.

unaccompanied by any evidence and would never have been acceptable in proceedings in which both parties appeared. Yet it could be interpreted to mean that China had carried out an EIA prior to undertaking construction, as required by Article 206 of the Convention. As a result, during the Hearing on the Merits, the Tribunal, exercising its power to put questions to the parties and to request additional information from them, asked the Philippines if it was aware of statements by Chinese experts that contradicted Philippine claims regarding the environmental impact of China's construction activities in the Spratly Islands. With only the weekend between the two rounds of the Hearing available to it for research, the Philippines still managed to find a statement by China's State Oceanic Administration ("SOA") entitled "Construction Work at Nansha Reefs Will Not Harm Oceanic Ecosystems."[116] This 500-word statement was rightly described by counsel for the Philippines as nothing more than a pseudo-evaluation. EIAs prepared for other environmental projects and submitted to the ICJ take up volumes.[117] The 500-word SOA statement would never have been acceptable in proceedings in which two parties appeared, but the Tribunal could not be certain that it was not backed up by an EIA. As we shall see in Chapter 4, this was one of the considerations for the Tribunal's decision to appoint independent experts.

In relation to the environmental impact of China's construction activities on one reef in particular, Mischief Reef, which was the object of Philippine Submission No. 12(b), the Tribunal had to determine whether the activities were military in character. Had this been the case, the optional exception concerning military activities would have barred the Tribunal's jurisdiction.[118] Fortunately for the Philippines, China's President Xi Jinping had declared during a state visit to the US that China's construction activities "do not target or impact any country, and China does not intend to pursue militarization."[119] This statement by the head of State was taken as authoritative by the Tribunal, which concluded

[116] *PAMH*, Annex 821, China State Oceanic Administration, "Construction Work at Nansha Reefs Will Not Harm Oceanic Ecosystems" (18 June 2015), 11–14, https://files.pca-cpa.org/pcadocs/The%20Philippines%27%20Annexes%20cited%20during%20Merits%20Hearing%20%28Annexes%20820-859%29.pdf, accessed 27 April 2020.

[117] Hearing on the Merits, Transcript, Day 4, 184–86.

[118] Convention, Article 298(1)(b).

[119] *SDP*, Annex 664, United States, The White House, Office of the Press Secretary, Press Release: Remarks by President Obama and President Xi of the People's Republic of

that the optional exception for military activities was not applicable to Philippine Submission No. 12(b) and that it had jurisdiction to entertain it.

The last set of public statements that were made by China and that assisted the Tribunal in understanding China's legal positions was made in multilateral settings. A statement made at a meeting of States parties of the Convention in 2014 reiterated that China's construction activities in the Spratly Islands were civilian in character, rendering the exception for military activities inapplicable.[120] Earlier statements in other multilateral settings were also consulted by the Tribunal. Diplomatic communications that had been made to the UN Secretary-General in response to submissions by Malaysia and Vietnam to the Commission on the Limits of the Continental Shelf ("CLCS") in 2009 and that claimed historic rights in the South China Sea within the "nine-dash line" were central to the consideration of Philippine Submissions No. 1 and 2, even if they did not clarify the nature of the historic rights claimed by China.[121] Other diplomatic communications to the UN Secretary-General,[122] statements

China in Joint Press Conference (25 September 2015), vol. I, 481–97, quoted in Award of 12 July 2016, 412, para. 1027.

[120] *SDP*, Annex 618, Permanent Mission of the People's Republic of China to the United Nations, Statement by Ambassador Wang Min at the 24th Meeting of the UNCLOS States Parties Under the Agenda Item "Report of the Secretary General Under Article 319 of UNCLOS" (13 June 2014), vol. I, 133–36. This Annex was erroneously identified as Annex 624 in the Award of 12 July 2016, 372, note 1090.

[121] *MP*, Annex 191, *Note Verbale* from the Permanent Mission of the People's Republic of China to the United Nations to the Secretary-General of the United Nations, No. CML/17/2009 (7 May 2009) and Annex 192, *Note Verbale* from the Permanent Mission of the People's Republic of China to the United Nations to the Secretary-General of the United Nations, No. CML/18/2009 (7 May 2009), vol. VI, 283–88, 289–94, https://files.pca-cpa.org/pcadocs/The%20Philippines%27%20Memorial%20-%20Volume%20VI%20%28Annexes%20158-221%29.pdf, accessed 27 April 2020.

[122] *MP*, Annex 228, Japan, Submission to the United Nations Commission on the Limits of the Continental Shelf (27 December 2013), vol. VII, 127–206, https://files.pca-cpa.org/pcadocs/The%20Philippines%27%20Memorial%20-%20Volume%20VII%20%28Annexes%20222-255%29.pdf, accessed 27 March 2019; *MP*, Annex 189, *Note Verbale* from the Permanent Mission of the People's Republic of China to the United Nations to the Secretary-General of the United Nations, No. CML/2/2009 (6 February 2009), vol. VI, 275–28, https://files.pca-cpa.org/pcadocs/The%20Philippines%27%20Memorial%20-%20Volume%20VI%20%28Annexes%20158-221%29.pdf, accessed 27 April 2020; Award of 12 July 2016, 197, paras. 451–52.

at the meeting of the States parties of the Convention,[123] and statements at the 15th Session of the International Seabed Authority, an international organization established by the Convention,[124] were prompted by Japan's submission to the CLCS, also in 2009, which claimed an extended continental shelf from Oki-no-tori-shima, a small atoll in the western Pacific Ocean between Okinawa and the Northern Mariana Islands. China objected to Japan's submission on the ground that the atoll was a rock within the meaning of Article 121(3), i.e., it was an island with no human habitation and economic life of its own and as such did not enjoy entitlement to an exclusive economic zone and continental shelf. The Tribunal considered these statements as expressions of China's position regarding Article 121(3) of the Convention, which laid down the definition of a rock as a special type of island. An understanding of China's position on the matter was essential to the consideration of Philippine Submissions No. 3 and 7, which requested that the Tribunal rule that Scarborough Shoal, Johnson Reef, Cuarteron Reef, and Fiery Cross were rocks within the meaning of Article 121(3) of the Convention.

For the most part, China's legal positions on Philippine claims were established by the Tribunal from the dozens of confidential diplomatic communications between the Philippines and China that were declassified by the Philippines for purposes of the proceedings. Still the Philippines was conscious that the absence of adversarial proceedings would create difficulties for it in the presentation of its case. The Tribunal's response to this concern was a novel procedure that involved the submission of supplemental pleadings by the appearing State.

C. The Appearing State's Supplemental Submission

Article 25(2) of the *South China Sea Arbitration*'s Rules of Procedure specifies two measures that a Tribunal must take in the event that one

[123] *SDP*, Annex 668, *Note Verbale* from the Permanent Mission of the People's Republic of China to the United Nations to the Secretary-General of the United Nations (21 May 2009), reprinted in UN Convention on the Law of the Sea, Meeting of States Parties, Proposal for the inclusion of a supplementary item in the agenda of the nineteenth Meeting of States Parties, UN Doc. SPLOS/196 (22 May 2009), 1–4, https://files.pca-cpa.org/pcadocs/The%20Philippines%27%20Supplemental%20Documents%20-%20Volume%20II%20%28Annexes%20608-709%29.pdf, accessed 7 April 2019; Award of 12 July 2016, 198, paras. 454–55.

[124] Award of 12 July 2016, 197–99, paras. 451–58.

party does not appear or fails to defend its case: the Tribunal must either request that the appearing State submit written arguments or put questions to it. These powers can arguably be derived from the Tribunal's power "at any time during the arbitral proceedings [to] require the Parties to produce documents, exhibits or other evidence within such a period of time as the Arbitral Tribunal shall determine."[125] That said, the powers granted under Article 25(2) are specific to cases of default and limit the submissions to "specific issues which the Arbitral Tribunal considers have not been canvassed, or have been inadequately canvassed, in the pleadings submitted by the appearing Party." Within three months of the Tribunal's request, the appearing State had to make a supplemental submission on the issues identified by the Tribunal. The defaulting State would then have three months within which to submit its comments on the supplemental submission.[126] To appreciate the innovative character of this procedure, one must explain the dilemmas of the appearing State to which it seeks to respond. This procedure was implemented systematically in the jurisdictional and merits phases of the proceedings in the *South China Sea Arbitration*.

1. The Dilemmas of the Appearing State

In its *Memorial* the Philippines recalled one consequence of the principle of the equality of the parties: non-appearance by one party should not disadvantage either the non-appearing State or the appearing State. In its view it was the Philippines that was disadvantaged by China's non-appearance: "[t]he Philippines is in the position of having to guess what China's arguments might be and formulate arguments for both States."[127] The procedure institutionalized in Article 25(2) of the Rules of Procedure had already been requested by some appearing States in other cases and had been proposed by scholars nearly thirty years before.

Appearing States in cases before the ICJ are aware of the Court's duty under Article 53 of the Statute. In the absence of adversarial proceedings, they have adopted a litigation strategy that presents fully to the Court the

125 *South China Sea Arbitration*, Rules of Procedure, Article 22(4), 10.

126 Ibid., Article 25(2), 12.

127 *MP*, vol. I, 231, para. 7.42.

arguments advanced by the defaulting State in its informal communications, "unsupported though they may be."[128] They have accepted that it is their duty "to see that all necessary materials, whether they tell for or against [the appearing party] are put before the Court," "to indicate various arguments that might have been advanced against [the appearing party] at this lectern," and "to assist the Court by examining possible arguments that [the defaulting State] might adduce if [it] were here."[129] In the *Fisheries Jurisdiction Case*, the UK had examined, as possible legal bases for Iceland's claim to a 50-nautical mile exclusive fisheries zone, the concept of patrimonial sea, which originated in Latin America, and that of permanent sovereignty over natural resources, asserted primarily by developing countries. Neither concept had been put forward by Iceland itself.[130]

This litigation strategy generates fresh difficulties for the appearing State. The practical difficulties were discussed by Greece in the *Aegean Sea Continental Shelf* Case. Greece had sought to found the jurisdiction of the Court on the General Act for the Pacific Settlement of International Disputes of 1928.[131] Turkey, in its informal communications, argued that the General Act was no longer in force. If it had appeared before the Court, its *Counter-Memorial* should have borne the burden of proving that contention. Greece would not have been obliged to present an entire section of its *Memorial* arguing that the General Act was in force. Rather this section would have been included in its refutation of the Turkish thesis. Turkey's default compelled Greece to put in the *Memorial*, anticipating Turkey's default, material that should not have appeared before

[128] Sir Peter Rawlinson, Oral Arguments on the Jurisdiction of the Court, Third Public Sitting (5 January 1973), *I.C.J. Pleadings*, *Fisheries Jurisdiction (United Kingdom v. Iceland)*, vol. I, 246.

[129] Rt. Hon. Samuel Silkin, Oral Arguments on the Merits, Fifth Public Sitting (25 March 1974), *I.C.J. Pleadings, Fisheries Jurisdiction (United Kingdom v. Iceland)*, vol. I, 441, 461.

[130] Ibid., 464.

[131] *General Act of Arbitration (Pacific Settlement of International Disputes)*, done at Geneva on 26 September 1928 and entered into force on 16 August 1929, League of Nations, *Treaty Series*, vol. 93, 343, https://treaties.un.org/doc/Publication/UNTS/LON/Volume%2093/v93.pdf, accessed 28 April 2020.

the Greek Reply to a Turkish *Counter-Memorial*. This gave the impression that Greece was setting out to prove something rather than to refute its opposite.[132]

Greece explained in general terms the difficulties confronting the appearing State. It would have to satisfy the Court without the benefit of hearing arguments that the defaulting State might have made and it had to determine how far to proceed in refuting objections that have not been publicly expressed by the defaulting State but that may or may not be entertained by the Court.[133] The exercise seemed to be paradoxical, in that the appearing State would have to imagine, the better to refute them subsequently, arguments that the defaulting State could have put forward.[134] There is, of course, the risk that the appearing State would not successfully imagine the arguments that the defaulting State could have put forward. Australia probably had this risk in mind when it requested in the *Nuclear Tests Case* that in the event the ICJ felt that Australia had not adequately dealt with a point that the Court found relevant to its decision, the Court should inform Australia of it and enable Australia to make further written submissions or to provide explanations at the oral hearing.[135] Greece requested in the *Aegean Sea Continental Shelf Case* that if the Court considered that there were any question that it should address, the Court should indicate it to Greece to enable the latter to put forward arguments on the matter. Otherwise "issues never canvassed in open court might prevail" in the Court's deliberation.[136]

In the *Nuclear Tests Cases*, the Court ignored the appearing State's request.[137] It may be recalled that the Court had declared, on the basis of

[132] Professor O'Connell, Oral Arguments on Jurisdiction, Sixth Public Sitting (10 October 1978), *I.C.J. Pleadings*, *Aegean Sea Continental Shelf Case*, 340.

[133] Ibid., 5th Public Sitting (9 October 1978), *I.C.J. Pleadings*, *Aegean Sea Continental Shelf Case*, 318.

[134] Mr. De Visscher, Oral Arguments on Jurisdiction, Sixth Public Sitting (12 October 1978), *I.C.J. Pleadings*, *Aegean Sea Continental Shelf*, 348 (translated from the French); Bowett, "Contemporary Developments," 209.

[135] *Memorial on Jurisdiction and Admissibility submitted by the Government of Australia* (23 November 1973), *I.C.J. Pleadings*, *Nuclear Tests Cases (Australia v. France)*, vol. I, 249, 250, paras. 8, 9, http://www.icj-cij.org/files/case-related/58/9443.pdf, accessed 28 April 2020.

[136] Professor O'Connell, Fifth Public Sitting (9 October 1978), *I.C.J. Pleadings*, *Aegean Sea Continental Shelf Case*, 320.

[137] Sinclair, "Some Procedural Aspects," 347.

French leaders' statements made after the closure of the oral proceedings on jurisdiction that France would cease atmospheric nuclear testing, that the claims of Australia and New Zealand no longer had any object and had refused to give a judgment.[138] This judgment was severely criticized within and outside the Court, for it had been issued at the conclusion of proceedings on jurisdiction and admissibility, which had been argued at length in the written and oral proceedings and which should have been the object of the decision. The Court had not given any indication to the two States that it was considering whether the dispute still had any object and that it would take into account unilateral French declarations. It had not given them the opportunity to submit oral or written arguments on the new issue and the new materials.[139]

Thirlway disagrees with these States' understanding of their difficulties. He suggests that the problem arises not so much from default but from the reluctance of judges or the Court to indicate their line of thought, obliging the appearing State to imagine every conceivable argument.[140] To this one might respond that the judges are tacitly formulating arguments on behalf of the defaulting State, arguments that might not occur to the appearing State. Fortunately, the consensus on the procedural steps to be taken to mitigate the difficulties encountered by the appearing

[138] *Nuclear Tests (Australia v. France), Judgment*, 263, 267, 270, 271, 272, paras. 30, 41, 52, 59, 52, https://www.icj-cij.org/files/case-related/58/058-19741220-JUD-01-00-BI.pdf, accessed 1 April 2020; *Nuclear Tests (New Zealand v. France), Judgment*, 467, 475, 477, 478, paras. 31, 44, 62, 65, https://www.icj-cij.org/files/case-related/59/059-19741220-JUD-01-00-BI.pdf, accessed 19 March 2020.

[139] *Nuclear Tests (Australia v. France), Judgment*, Dissenting Opinion of Judge Sir Garfield Barwick, *I.C.J. Reports 1974*, 391–92, http://www.icj-cij.org/files/case-related/58/058-19741220-JUD-01-09-BI.pdf, accessed 1 April 2020; Serge Sur, "Les affaires des essais nucléaires (Australie c. France, Nouvelle Zélande c. France), C.I.J. – arrêts du 20 décembre 1974 [The Nuclear Tests Cases (Australia v. France, New Zealand v. France), I.C.J. – Judgments of 20 December 1974]," *RGDIP* 79 (1975): 978; R. St. J. Macdonald and Barbara Hough, "The Nuclear Tests Case Revisited," *German Yearbook of International Law* 20 (1977): 354, 357 ("*GYIL*"); José Juste Ruiz, "Mootness in International Adjudication: The Nuclear Tests Cases," *GYIL* 20 (1977): 365; Sinclair, "Some Procedural Aspects," 348, 356; and Taslim O. Elias, *The International Court of Justice and Some Contemporary Problems: Essays on International Law* (Dordrecht: Springer Science+Business Media, 1983), 105. The French declarations were made on 16 August 1974 by the Minister of Defence, on 25 September 1974 by the Minister for Foreign Affairs at the United Nations General Assembly, and on 11 October 1974 by the Minister of Defense.

[140] Thirlway, *Non-appearance*, 150, 163.

State makes it unnecessary to resolve this point. In 1981, Sinclair had already urged the adoption by the Court of a strategy that would ensure that appearing States are not disadvantaged in the manner described by Australia and Greece. In this strategy, the ICJ would play a more active role by inviting arguments from the appearing State(s) on issues that the Court may feel tempted to take into account on its own initiative and that have not been canvassed or have not been adequately canvassed in written or oral pleadings.[141] A few years later, Bowett expressed the view that such a procedure would also be useful in proceedings in which both parties appear.[142] Thirlway endorsed Sinclair's proposal in 1985, affirming that it would reestablish equality between the parties (appearing and defaulting) and would remove any ground for complaints of disadvantage by the appearing State.[143] Arangio-Ruiz observed in 1987 that there could be no legal objection to Sinclair's suggestion and that the power to implement it would fall within the ICJ's power to regulate its proceedings.[144] The scholarly seal of approval of this procedure was given by the IDI, whose 1991 resolution on non-appearance before the ICJ urged that the ICJ "invite argument from the appearing party on specific issues which the Court considers have not been canvassed or have been inadequately canvassed in the written or oral pleadings."[145]

With the "disappearance" of the phenomenon of default before international courts in the following two decades, there was no opportunity to implement this procedure, which is rarely mentioned in the scholarly literature.[146] The first occasion on which the procedure was put to the test was the *South China Sea Arbitration*, followed shortly after by the *"Arctic Sunrise" Arbitration*, both proceedings under Annex VII of the Convention.[147]

[141] Sinclair, "Some Procedural Aspects," 356.

[142] Bowett, "Contemporary Developments," 201.

[143] Thirlway, *Non-appearance*, 174, 178.

[144] Arangio-Ruiz, "Notes," 33.

[145] IDI, *Non-appearance Before the International Court of Justice*, Article 3(a).

[146] The exception is Judith Levine and Garth L. Schofield, "Navigating Uncharted Procedural Waters in a Rising Sea of Cases at the Permanent Court of Arbitration," in Stephen Minas and H. Jordan Diamond (eds.), *Stress Testing the Law of the Sea: Dispute Resolution, Disasters and Emerging Challenges* (Leiden: Brill Nijhoff, 2018), 109.

[147] *The "Arctic Sunrise" Arbitration (Netherlands v. Russia)*, Rules of Procedure (17 March 2014), Article 25(2), 12, https://pcacases.com/web/sendAttach/1317, accessed

Without denying the innovative character of the procedure, one can argue that it is a logical extension of the power of an international court or tribunal to "at any time prior to or during the hearing indicate any points or issues to which it would like the parties specially to address themselves, or on which it considers that there has been sufficient argument."[148] In practice, the ICJ has rarely made use of this power.[149] The ITLOS, which possesses the power under Article 76(1) of its Rules "at any time prior to or during the hearing [to] indicate any points or issues which it would like the parties specially to address, or on which it considers that there has been sufficient argument"[150] has regularly exercised this power.[151] Indeed ITLOS judgments make clear the occasions in which the ITLOS has indicated to the parties the points or issues that it wanted them specially to address.[152]

The distinct contribution of the *South China Sea Arbitration* has been to adapt this procedure to the context of default, recommended by the IDI as a means of alleviating some of the disadvantages experienced by appearing parties and reestablishing the equality of the parties.

29 April 2020. Coincidentally the president of both Tribunals was Judge Thomas A. Mensah.

[148] ICJ, *Rules of Court, adopted on 14 April 1978 and entered into force on 1 July 1978*, Article 62(1), https://www.icj-cij.org/en/rules, accessed 22 March 2020.

[149] Shabtai Rosenne with the assistance of Yaël Ronen, *The Law and Practice of the International Court 1990–2005* (4th ed.; Leiden: Martinus Nijhoff Publishers, 2006), vol. III, *Procedure*, 1299–1300.

[150] *Rules of the Tribunal (ITLOS/8), as adopted on 28 October 1997 and amended on 15 March 2001, 21 September 2001, 17 March 2009 and 25 September 2018*, https://www.itlos.org/fileadmin/itlos/documents/basic_texts/Itlos_8_E_25.09.18.pdf, accessed 29 April 2020.

[151] Amerasinghe, *Evidence*, 15.

[152] See, for example, *The M/V "SAIGA" (No. 2) Case (Saint Vincent and the Grenadines v. Guinea)*, Judgment of 1 July 1999, 19, para. 19, https://www.itlos.org/fileadmin/itlos/documents/cases/case_no_2/published/C2-J-1_Jul_99.pdf, accessed 27 June 2018. *Southern Bluefin Tuna Cases (New Zealand v. Japan; Australia v. Japan), Provisional Measures, Order of 27 August 1999, ITLOS Reports 1999*, 283, para. 19, https://www.itlos.org/fileadmin/itlos/documents/cases/case_no_3_4/published/C34-O-27_aug_99.pdf, accessed 27 January 2020.

2. The Application of Article 25(2) of the Rules of Procedure of the South China Sea Arbitration

Article 25(2) was applied when China failed to submit a Counter-Memorial by the time limit of 15 December 2014. The Tribunal then requested that the Philippines make a supplementary written submission within three months, on the basis of 16 questions set by the Tribunal relating to admissibility, jurisdiction, and the merits; China was given three months within which to respond.[153] Following receipt of the *Supplemental Written Submission* ("*SWSP*") and its 10 volumes of annexes, the Tribunal decided to bifurcate the proceedings.[154] The Philippines then suggested, without specifically invoking Article 25(2), that a month prior to the Hearing on Jurisdiction, the Tribunal indicate any points or issues that it would like the Philippines specially to address, or on which it considered that there had been an insufficient argument.[155] The Tribunal responded by sending to the Philippines and China on 23 June 2015 a list of issues for the Philippines to address during the Hearing; answers to these questions were provided during the Hearings.[156] The same procedure was adopted prior to the Hearing on the Merits. On 10 November 2016, approximately two weeks prior to the Hearing on the Merits, the Tribunal provided an "Annex of Issues the Philippines May Wish to Present" as guidance for the Hearing.[157] The Annex has not been published, making it impossible to determine whether the Tribunal invoked Article 25(2) as the basis for its request. The Philippines provided answers orally during the Hearings to the questions raised in the Annex. The operation of this procedure has been misunderstood as penalizing the Philippines. It is not necessary to agree with this interpretation to realize that in practice, the Tribunal was acting as the de facto counsel of China.

Novelty might go some way to explaining the misunderstanding of the procedure. Spijkers seems to be under the impression that the Philippines was penalized during the proceedings for China's default. He reminds us that the Tribunal itself clearly stated that non-appearance did not

[153] Award on Jurisdiction, 21, paras. 58–59.

[154] Ibid., 23, para. 68.

[155] *South China Sea Arbitration*, Procedural Order No. 4, 4.

[156] Ibid., 6, para. 1.6; Award on Jurisdiction, 24, 26, paras. 68, 78.

[157] Award of 12 July 2016, 21, para. 63.

operate "to change the burden of proof or to raise or lower the standard of proof normally expected of a party to make out its claims or defenses."[158] Concretely, he believes that the Tribunal should not have assumed the burden of proof on behalf of China and, as a corollary, the Philippines should not have been compelled to provide more evidence and clarifications. He believes that this is exactly what happened: "The Tribunal constantly asked the Philippines to produce more evidence, to provide more witnesses, to give more elaborate argumentation, etc." The paradoxical consequence was that China was allegedly rewarded for its default.[159] Spijkers concluded that the Tribunal should have adopted a tougher attitude toward China, by declaring that default was contrary to good faith and by "going a bit more in the direction of pronouncing a kind of default judgment."[160]

It is undeniable that the Philippines had to make a supplemental written submission and answer questions formulated by the Tribunal prior to the two Hearings, answered oral questions raised during the actual Hearings, and submitted a volume of annexes prior to the Hearing on Jurisdiction and five volumes of annexes prior to the Hearing on the Merits. This observation does not authorize the conclusion that the Philippines was being penalized for China's default or that the Tribunal was contradicting itself. In the first place, the obligation imposed on the Philippines to make a supplemental written submission and to answer questions transmitted to it prior to the two Hearings was in application of Article 25(2) of the Rules of Procedure, which in turn had been formulated in response to a concern expressed by the Philippines that it would have to imagine China's arguments before refuting them. In the second place, it is questionable whether the Philippines had assumed a heavier burden than would have been the case if China had formally participated in the proceedings. A *Counter-Memorial* from China might have easily triggered a second round of written pleadings. In a sense, the *SWSP* took the place of a Philippine reply to counter-arguments, with the difference that the counter-arguments that should have been presented by the opposing party in a *Counter-Memorial* were replaced by questions that

[158] Ibid., 50, para. 131.

[159] Spijkers, "Non-participation," 186.

[160] Ibid., 187. It is not clear what he understands by "going a bit more in the direction of pronouncing a kind of default judgment."

were formulated by the Tribunal prior to the two Hearings. The written questions transmitted to the Philippines during the two Hearings replaced the arguments that the respondent State should have presented during the first round of the oral hearings, during which only the issues that still divide the parties were to be discussed. Once the non-punitive character of the obligation on the Philippines to make a supplemental submission and to answer written questions from the Tribunal is accepted, it is no longer necessary to deal with the issue whether the Tribunal should have adopted a tougher attitude toward China, except to say that that course of action is prohibited by Article 9 of Annex VII of the Convention and that it would have provided more solid ground for Chinese accusations of bias on the part of the Tribunal.

The scope of the *SWSP* was broad, encompassing issues of jurisdiction, admissibility, and the merits. It is true that China's Position Paper did not express any opinions on the merits of the Philippine claims, but the Philippine *Memorial* covered all these issues and by the time the request for further written argument was issued, China had already received a copy of the *Memorial*. Moreover, at that time, the Tribunal had not yet decided to bifurcate the proceedings. The scope was also broad because the Tribunal requested Philippine comments on public statements made not just by Chinese government officials but also by "others."[161] The unidentified "others" could refer to Chinese scholars or scholars explicitly writing on behalf of China.[162] The Philippines was not entirely relieved of the duty to imagine China's arguments, as the Tribunal instructed it to consider any objections to jurisdiction or admissibility that could be reasonably expected to be raised, whether or not these objections had been raised by China.[163] One gets the impression, though, that the Tribunal left little to the Philippine imagination. The Annex to the Tribunal's letter of 23 June identified 38 issues set out in eight categories, which the

[161] Award of 12 July 2016, 21, para. 59.

[162] An example of a publication falling in the latter category is Stefan Talmon and Bing Bing Jia (eds.), *The South China Sea Arbitration: A Chinese Perspective* (Oxford: Hart Publishing, 2014). In the Preface (vi), the editors presented the book "as a kind of amicus curiae brief advancing possible legal arguments *on behalf of* the absent respondent (italics supplied)." They feared that as a result of China's default, its voice would not be heard in the proceedings.

[163] Hearing on Jurisdiction, Transcript, Day 2, 131.

Philippines found to be extremely useful.[164] The scope of the Tribunal's questions was such that the *SWSP* was nearly as long as the *Memorial* and the annexes to the *SWSP* filled more volumes than the annexes to the *Memorial*.

A perusal of the *SWSP* and the transcripts of the two Hearings, from which one may deduce the text of the Tribunal's questions, justifies the conclusion that in practice the Tribunal was acting as China's counsel in the proceedings. One set of questions was undoubtedly inspired by China's Position Paper. For instance, the first question addressed by the *SWSP* took as its point of departure the Position Paper's contention that through the Declaration on the Conduct of the Parties in the South China Sea ("DOC") adopted by the Association of Southeast Asian Nations ("ASEAN") and China in 2002, ASEAN member States and China had undertaken to resolve their territorial and jurisdictional disputes through friendly consultations and negotiation by the States directly concerned, excluding recourse to compulsory dispute settlement.[165] The Tribunal asked the Philippines whether the DOC constituted an agreement that excluded recourse to compulsory dispute settlement.[166] Similarly, the origins of Questions 3, 6, 7, 8, and 12 may be traced to the Position Paper.[167] A second set of questions was formulated by the Tribunal on its own initiative. In other words, the Tribunal was seeking to place itself in China's shoes and attempting to imagine objections that China would have raised had it appeared. For instance, the Tribunal asked the Philippines to clarify the relationship between an alleged violation of the Convention on Biological Diversity ("CBD") and the Convention.[168] Philippine allegations of China's violation of its obligation to protect and preserve the marine environment had not elicited any response or comment from China in the Position Paper. The rationale for the

[164] Ibid.

[165] Position Paper, 28, para. 54. *MP*, vol. V, Annex 144, Association of Southeast Asian Nations, Declaration on the Conduct of Parties in South China Sea (4 November 2002), 321–24, https://files.pca-cpa.org/pcadocs/The%20Philippines%27%20Memorial%20-%20Volume%20V%20%28Annexes%20103-157%29.pdf, accessed 23 March 2020.

[166] *SWSP*, vol. I, 3–5.

[167] Ibid., 11–14, 23–25, 27–35, 37–41, and 59–61.

[168] Ibid., 55–58. *Convention on Biological Diversity* (CBD), signed at Rio de Janeiro on 5 June 1992, entered into force on 29 December 1993, https://www.cbd.int/doc/legal/cbd-en.pdf, accessed 29 April 2020.

Tribunal's question was the Philippine claim in the *Memorial* that China's construction activities in the Spratly Islands constituted violations of the CBD.[169] The implication was that if the Philippines alleged a violation of the CBD, it might first have to attempt dispute settlement under the CBD before having recourse to arbitration under Annex VII of the Convention. A close reading of the transcripts of the two Hearings discloses a similar pattern: one set of questions was prompted by China's known positions, a second set was formulated by the Tribunal itself, attempting to imagine China's questions if China had appeared before it. No protest was forthcoming from the Philippines over the Tribunal's conduct as China's de facto counsel. After all, the procedure had been set in place in response to the Philippine account of the practical difficulties that China's default created for it.

Consideration of the defaulting State's informal communications and public statements as well as the request for a supplemental written submission from the appearing State were measures that the Tribunal had to take in response to China's default. The Tribunal also had to deal with unexpected attempts by non-parties to the *Arbitration* to present submissions to it as self-proclaimed *amici curiae*.

II. Submissions of *Amici Curiae* as Surrogates for the Defaulting State

An *amicus curiae* has been defined as "a nonparty to the dispute," who as "a friend, offers to provide the court or tribunal its special perspectives, arguments, or expertise on the dispute, usually in the form of a written *amicus curiae* brief or submission."[170] The participation of *amicus curiae* in judicial proceedings is recognized in common law jurisdictions and is increasingly accepted, whether formally or informally, in civil law jurisdictions. A number of international courts and adjudicatory bodies, such as the European Court of Human Rights ("ECtHR"), the Interamerican Court of Human Rights ("IACtHR"), and North America Free Trade

[169] *MP*, vol. I, 190–92, paras. 6.82–6.89.

[170] *Aguas Provinciales de Santa Fe S.A., Suez, Sociedad General de Aguas de Barcelona S.A. and InterAguas Servicios Integrales del Agua S.A. v. Argentine Republic* (ICSID Case No. ARB/03/17), Order in Response to a Petition for Participation as Amicus Curiae (17 March 2006), 5, para. 9, https://www.italaw.com/sites/default/files/case-documents/ita0803.pdf, accessed 30 April 2020.

Agreement ("NAFTA") Chapter 11 Tribunals, also accept *amicus curiae* briefs.[171] At the international level, the participation of *amicus curiae* is justified on various grounds: it opens up international courts to the recipients of decisions, brings civil society closer to distant international disputes, provides standing to otherwise excluded stakeholders, enhances transparency, brings forward bribery or corruption issues, improves the quality of the award(s), gives legitimacy to international courts, and democratizes international law.[172]

The rationale for *amicus curiae* participation in the *South China Sea Arbitration* seems to have been first put forward by Talmon, who went so far as to argue that in the event of default a tribunal had a duty to accept or solicit *amicus curiae* briefs to obtain a more complete picture of the procedural or substantive issues.[173] Talmon and Chinese scholar Bing Bing Gia edited a book, which they presented "as a kind of amicus curiae brief advancing possible legal arguments on behalf of the absent respondent." They feared that as a result of China's default, its voice would not be heard in the proceedings.[174] This was a novel argument for *amicus curiae* participation and one that was easy to counter. For its voice to be heard, all China had to do was to appear before the Arbitral Tribunal. Appearance would have obviated the need for surrogates to take up the cudgels for it, as if it were a helpless victim.

The Rules of Procedure of the *South China Sea Arbitration*, like the Statute and Rules of the ITLOS, Annex VII of the Convention, and the Rules of Procedure of other arbitrations under Annex VII of the Convention, do not contain any provisions specifically relating to the admission of *amicus curiae* submissions. The ITLOS Rules do provide for

[171] Steven Kochevar, "Amici Curiae in Civil Law Jurisdictions," *Yale Law Journal* 122 (2013): 1656, 1659–63, http://www.yalelawjournal.org/pdf/1158_hvj33ruz.pdf, accessed 30 April 2020.

[172] Luigi Crema, "Testing *Amici Curiae* in International Law: Rules and Practice," *Italian Yearbook of International Law* 22 (2013): 95; Eugenia Levine, "Amicus Curiae in International Investment Arbitration: The Implications of an Increase in Third-Party Participation," *Berkeley Journal of International Law* 29 (2011): 217, https://pdfs.semanticscholar.org/d6e6/9224c67a9828ed4b999d0ddc0edac2a8eaad.pdf?_ga=2.78278035.622179642.1588227597-515656435.1588227597, accessed 30 April 2020.

[173] Stefan Talmon, *The South China Sea Arbitration: Is There a Case to Answer?* (Bonn: Universität Bonn, Institute for Public International Law, 2014), 7, https://papers.ssrn.com/sol3/papers.cfm?abstract_id=2393025, accessed 13 March 2020.

[174] Talmon and Jia, *The South China Sea Arbitration*, vi.

the possibility that an intergovernmental organization may furnish information to it, either upon the Tribunal's request or on its own initiative, in a contentious case.[175] In advisory proceedings of the ITLOS Seabed Disputes Chamber, intergovernmental organizations may be invited by the Chamber to furnish information to it.[176] Despite the limitation of this possibility to intergovernmental organizations, Greenpeace International and the World Wide Fund for Nature ("WWF") requested authorization to present a brief as *amici curiae* in an ITLOS advisory procedure in 2010. The ITLOS President decided that their submissions would not be included in the case file but that they would be transmitted to the States parties to the Convention and would be posted on a separate section of the ITLOS website.[177] Three years later, Greenpeace International requested authorization to submit an *amicus curiae* brief in the proceedings for the request on provisional measures in the *"Arctic Sunrise" Case*. Greenpeace, which operated the *Arctic Sunrise*, was undoubtedly in a position to furnish information to the ITLOS on the circumstances of the boarding and detention of the vessel and its crew by Russia. As the text of the request is not publicly available, it is not clear on what legal grounds the request was founded. The Netherlands had no objection, but the ITLOS refused to grant the request. The day following the ITLOS order, Russia, in its objection to the request, explicitly cited the fact that Greenpeace was not an intergovernmental organization.[178] Unlike in the advisory proceedings, the Greenpeace submission was not posted on the ITLOS website.

In the *South China Sea Arbitration* it was suggested that a legal basis for the admission of *amicus curiae* submissions could be found either in Article 5 of Annex VII, which empowers a tribunal to determine its

[175] ITLOS, *Rules of the Tribunal*, Article 84, 33.

[176] Ibid., Article 133, 50.

[177] *Responsibilities and Obligations of States with respect to Activities in the Area, Advisory Opinion, ITLOS Reports 2011*, 19, para. 13, https://www.itlos.org/fileadmin/itlos/documents/cases/case_no_17/17_adv_op_010211_en.pdf, accessed 30 April 2020. See Statement of Stichting Greenpeace Council (Greenpeace International) and the World Wide Fund for Nature (13 August 2010), https://www.itlos.org/fileadmin/itlos/documents/cases/case_no_17/Statement_Greenpeace_WWF.pdf, accessed 30 April 2020.

[178] *"Arctic Sunrise" (Kingdom of The Netherlands v. Russian Federation), Provisional Measures, Order of 22 November 2013, ITLOS Reports 2013*, 234, paras. 15–19, https://www.itlos.org/fileadmin/itlos/documents/cases/case_no.22/published/C22_Order_221113.pdf, accessed 30 April 2020.

own procedure, provided that each party is assured the full opportunity to be heard,[179]or in Article 10(1) of the Rules of Procedure, which authorizes the Tribunal to conduct the arbitration "in such manner as it considers appropriate."[180] Apparently, neither provision was invoked by the Tribunal when it solicited the views of the Philippines and China on 16 December 2014 on the possibility of admitting submissions from *amici curiae*. As already mentioned in Chapter 1, China expressed its firm opposition to such a possibility.[181] One might ask whether the Tribunal had in mind a submission from Vietnam, which by that time had already written twice to the Tribunal. In April 2014, when requesting copies of all pleadings and annexes, Vietnam had declared that its legal rights and interests could be affected by the *Arbitration*.[182] In December 2014, Vietnam requested that the Tribunal give due regard to Vietnam's legal rights and interests, protested against China's claim to historic rights, rejected that claim, and supported the Tribunal's jurisdiction to apply the Convention. Rather than an *amicus curiae* submission, Vietnam had in mind the possibility of intervention.[183] In the end, no application to intervene was received from Vietnam.[184]

Two non-parties to the dispute explicitly requested and claimed the status of *amici curiae*—the Chinese (Taiwan) Society of International Law ("C(T)SIL"), in March 2016, and the Asia–Pacific Institute of International Law ("APIIL"), in June 2016.[185] One is surprised to note that China did not reiterate its "firm opposition" to the participation of *amicus*

[179] Talmon, *The South China Sea Arbitration*, 7.

[180] Chang Yen-Chiang, "How Does the [sic] Amicus Curiae Submission Affect a Tribunal [sic] Decision?" *Leiden Journal of International Law* 30 (2017): 656.

[181] Award on Jurisdiction, 22, 23, paras. 63, 64.

[182] Ibid., 19, para. 47.

[183] Ibid., 20, para. 54.

[184] For the Tribunal's treatment of communications from Vietnam, see Tanaka, *The South China Sea Arbitration*, 27–28.

[185] *Amicus Curiae Submission by the Chinese (Taiwan) Society of International Law to the PCA in the Matter of the Arbitration Between the Republic of the Philippines and the People's Republic of China* (25 March 2016) ("C(T)SIL"), http://csil.org.tw/home/wp-content/uploads/2016/03/SCSTF-Amicus-Curiae-Brief-final.pdf, accessed 30 April 2020; Asia–Pacific Institute of International Law, *Amicus Curiae Brief to the Arbitral Tribunal on the South China Sea Arbitration* (6 June 2016) ("APIIL"), http://www.fredkan.com/mavista/upload/File/APIIL%20Amicus%20curiae%20brief%20&%20Appendix%20(1).pdf, accessed 21 January 2020.

curiae on either occasion. To these two one might add Taiwan, which did not apply for participation as *amicus curiae*. Initially, Taiwan was said to have considered the possibility of intervention as a third party, but this was ruled out, because of Taiwan's "unique and complicated political status," i.e., it is not recognized as a State by most States and it is not a party to the Convention. Taiwan is reported to have applied to send representatives to the Hearing on Jurisdiction, a request that was denied by the Tribunal, allegedly on the advice of both the Philippines and China.[186] Interest in the *Arbitration* heightened in Taiwan after the release on 21 December 2015 of the transcript of the Hearing on the Merits, during which the Philippines had presented arguments in support of the view that Itu Aba, a maritime feature occupied by Taiwan, was a rock within the meaning of Article 121(3) of the Convention.[187] In 2016, Taiwan responded with a series of statements that came to the Tribunal's attention: a press release from the Taiwanese Foreign Ministry on 23 January; remarks from Taiwan's President on 28 January; a Position Paper on Taiwan's South China Sea Policy on 21 March; further remarks from the Taiwanese President on 23 March; and the *amicus curiae* brief of the C(T)SIL, also on 23 March.[188] Again, one must note that China did not object to the Tribunal's taking notice of the materials from Taiwan or to

[186] Yann-huei Song, "Taiwan's Response to the Philippines-PRC South China Sea Arbitration," *Asian Maritime Transparency Initiative*, 15 July 2015, https://amti.csis.org/taiwans-response-to-the-philippines-prc-south-china-sea-arbitration/, accessed 30 April 2020.

[187] Wei-chin Lee, "Taiwan, the South China Sea Dispute, and the 2016 Arbitration Decision," *Journal of Chinese Political Science* 22 (2017): 238.

[188] *South China Sea Arbitration, Responses of the Philippines to the Tribunal's 5 February 2016 Request for Comments (Annexes 864–892)* (11 March 2016) ("*RTRC*"), Annex 875, Ministry of Foreign Affairs of the Republic of China (Taiwan), "Taiping Island Is an Island, Not a Rock, and the ROC Possesses Full Rights Associated with an Exclusive Economic Zone and Continental Shelf in Accordance with UNCLOS" (23 January 2016), 216–52; Annex 876, Office of the President of the Taiwan Authority of China, "Remarks by President Ma on Taiping Island" (28 January 2016), 253–51, https://files.pca-cpa.org/pcadocs/The%20Philippines%27%20Written%20Responses%20%2811%20March%202016%29%20%28Annexes%20864-892%29.pdf, accessed 30 April 2020; Republic of China (Taiwan), *Position Paper on ROC South China Sea Policy* (21 March 2016), http://multilingual.mofa.gov.tw/web/web_UTF-8/South/Position%20Paper%20on%20ROC%20South%20China%20Sea%20Policy.pdf, accessed 4 May 2020; Republic of China, Mainland Affairs Council, *President Ma's Remarks at International Press Conference regarding Taiping Island in Nansha Islands* (23 March 2016), https://www.mac.gov.tw/en/News_Content.aspx?n=FE07F9DA122E29D4&sms=3A4E63FA5107487D&s=F3B2B90AA560D22F, accessed 4 May 2020.

its request for comments from China and the Philippines on these documents.[189] In March 2016, the Philippines submitted a 26-page response to the first two documents from Taiwan, accompanied by 15 annexes on Itu Aba totaling 170 pages, including two expert reports on groundwater resources and soil resources in Itu Aba.[190] This was followed five weeks later by a 40-page response to the second set of documents from Taiwan, accompanied by another 21 annexes, including two further expert reports on soil resources and groundwater resources on Itu Aba, totaling 239 pages.[191] The fact that the Tribunal sought comments from the Philippines and China on the materials from Taiwan and that the Tribunal considered these materials together with the Philippine responses in its deliberations has convinced some commentators that Taiwan became a respondent or a de facto party, at least on certain matters.[192] In our view, this is going too far. One can hardly conceive of a party that did not receive copies of the pleadings of the Philippines or the transcript of the Hearings at the same time as China or was not allowed to appear before the Tribunal or to rebut the Philippine responses. Taiwan's role in the *Arbitration* is more appropriately compared to that of an *amicus curiae*.

The Tribunal did not use any of its procedural powers to make a formal decision on the status of any of the three non-parties to the dispute as *amicus curiae*. The following paragraphs are justified by the fact that two of the three explicitly claimed such a status and the third may be considered a de facto *amicus curiae*. More importantly, they will seek

[189] Award of 12 July 2016, 31, para. 89.

[190] *RTRC*, 17–42, paras. 43–115, https://pcacases.com/web/sendAttach/1849, accessed 30 April 2020; *RTRC (Annexes 864–892)*, Annexes 878–92, 264–441, https://files.pca-cpa.org/pcadocs/The%20Philippines%27%20Written%20Responses%20%2811%20March%202016%29%20%28Annexes%20864-892%29.pdf, accessed 30 April 2020.

[191] *South China Sea Arbitration, Responses of the Philippines to the Tribunal's 1 April 2016 Request for Comments on Additional Materials Regarding the Status of Itu* (25 April 2016), https://pcacases.com/web/sendAttach/1850, accessed 30 April 2020 ("*RTRC Itu Aba*"); *RTRC Itu Aba (Annexes 893–913)*, https://pcacases.com/web/sendAttach/1850, accessed 30 April 2020.

[192] Michael Sheng-ti Gau, "The Sino-Philippine Arbitration on the South China Sea Disputes and the Taiwan Factor," *Journal of East Asia and International Law* 9 (2016): 496; Anne Hsiu-An Hsiao, "The South China Sea Arbitration and Taiwan's Claim: Legal and Political Implications," *Journal of Chinese Political Science* 22 (2017): 225.

to assess the contribution of these three entities to the Tribunal's fact-finding. This assessment, which has never been undertaken, will be based not on the two criteria identified by the IDI, the equality of the parties and the acquisition of knowledge of the facts, but on criteria that may be derived from the rules and the caselaw of investor-State arbitration. The reason is that investor-State investment tribunals have on multiple occasions had to respond to requests for *amicus curiae* participation, enabling them to identify criteria that may be relevant, *mutatis mutandis*, to inter-State arbitration. The NAFTA rules and practice are relevant because they were groundbreaking, but they bound only the three parties to NAFTA. The advantage of the rules and practice of the International Centre for the Settlement of Investment Disputes ("ICSID"), which developed a few years later, is that they are applicable to all States members of the World Bank that ratify it. These criteria are the identity and interest of the party identifying itself as *amicus curiae*; assistance that the *amicus curiae* could provide the court or tribunal; and the impact of the submission of the *amicus curiae* on the proceedings. The criterion specific to investor-State arbitrations is the interest and identity of the prospective *amicus curiae*. The second and third criteria correspond approximately to the two criteria or difficulties identified by the IDI, acquisition of knowledge of the facts and the equality of the parties. It could be plausibly argued that under the criteria identified by investor-State tribunals and the IDI, *amici curiae* must be able to provide assistance to the court or tribunal's decision-making and their participation in the proceedings must not prejudice either party or disrupt the proceedings. The following discussion will hopefully make clear why prospective *amici curiae* must not only have an interest in the proceedings but must also be independent from the parties to the dispute.

A. The Interest of the Amicus Curiae *in the Proceedings and Its Independence*

Interest of the applicant for *amicus curiae* status in the proceedings is a requirement of NAFTA and ICSID rules; in practice a number of tribunals also consider independence. The three non-parties that claimed the status of *amicus curiae* in the *South China Sea Arbitration* seemed to satisfy these criteria to varying degrees.

1. An Overview of NAFTA and ICSID Rules and Practice

NAFTA and ICSID rules and practice impose varying requirements that applicants for *amicus curiae* status must satisfy if they wish to demonstrate their interest in the proceedings and their independence.

The NAFTA Free Trade Commission, which consisted of ministerial representatives of the three NAFTA parties (Canada, Mexico, and the US), adopted in 2003 a statement on the participation of non-disputing parties, the term used in the NAFTA context to refer to *amici curiae*.[193] To be granted permission to make a written submission to a tribunal, a non-disputing party had to disclose its membership and legal status (e.g., company, trade association, or other nongovernmental organization), its general objectives, the nature of its activities, and any parent organization (including any organization that directly or indirectly controls the applicant); any affiliation, direct, or indirect, with any disputing party; any government, person or organization that has provided any financial or other assistance in preparing the submission; and the nature of the interest that the applicant has in the arbitration.[194] This statement was adopted two years after a NAFTA Tribunal allowed three NGOs to submit *amicus curiae* briefs for the first time. The Tribunal had been established upon the request of a Canadian manufacturer of methanol, an ingredient in a gasoline additive that was allegedly banned in California for political reasons.[195]

[193] The following paragraphs draw heavily on Farouk El-Hosseny and Ezequiel H. Vetulli, "Amicus Acceptance and Relevance: The Distinctive Example of Philip Morris v. Uruguay," *Netherlands International Law Review* 64 (2017): 73–94.

[194] NAFTA Free Trade Commission, *Statement on Non-disputing Party Participation* (7 October 2003), B.2(c) to (f) ("*FTC Statement*"), http://www.sice.oas.org/tpd/nafta/commission/nondispute_e.pdf, accessed 1 May 2020. NAFTA was replaced by the United States–Mexico–Canada Agreement (USMCA), which entered into force on 1 July 2020.

[195] *Methanex Corporation v. United States*, Decision of the Tribunal on Petitions from Third Persons to Intervene as Amici Curiae of 15 January 2001, https://www.italaw.com/sites/default/files/case-documents/ita0517_0.pdf, accessed 1 May 2020. For an overview of the Decision, see Patrick Dumberry, "The Admissibility of *Amicus Curiae* Briefs by NGOs in Investors-States Arbitration: The Precedent Set by the Methanex Case in the Context of NAFTA Chapter 11 Proceedings," *Non-state Actors and International Law* 1 (2001): 201–14, and Howard Mann, "Opening the Doors, At Least a Little: Comment on the Amicus Decision in Methanex v. United States," *Review of European Community and International Environmental Law* 10 (2001): 241–44. For an overview of the case, see Howard Mann, "Methanex v. United States," *Investment Treaty News* (18 October 2018), https://www.iisd.org/itn/2018/10/18/methanex-v-united-states/, accessed 1 May 2020.

Three years after the adoption of the NAFTA statement, the ICSID amended its Arbitration Rules to grant arbitral tribunals authority to accept *amicus curiae* briefs. The ICSID was established by the Convention for the Settlement of Investment Disputes ("ICSID Convention") to provide facilities for conciliation and arbitration between States parties to the ICSID Convention, which at present number 157, and investors of other States parties. The ICSID Convention applies to disputes that States parties and investors have agreed to submit to it.[196] Such consent is given by States parties through bilateral investment treaties. Under the 2006 Arbitration Rules, a person or entity that is not a party to an investor-State dispute and that wishes to make a submission to a tribunal established under the ICSID Convention must demonstrate, among others, that it would address a matter within the scope of the dispute and that it has a significant interest in the proceedings.[197] The Arbitration Rules were amended a year after an arbitral tribunal acceded to a petition submitted by NGOs for participation as *amicus curiae*. The conditions that the Tribunal had established for the admissibility of their petition related to their expertise, their independence vis-à-vis the disputing parties, and their experience.[198]

As the ICSID Arbitration Rules do not explicitly require independence, the application of the criterion varies among tribunals. In 2006 a foundation and three individuals filed a petition for *amici* status in the case instituted by Suez, Sociedad General de Aguas de Barcelona S.A., and InterAguas Servicios Integrales del Agua S.A. against Argentina over the failure, as a result of emergency measures taken by the latter during its financial crisis in 2001, of a company that had a 30-year concession contract with Argentina to provide public water and sewage services. The Tribunal ruled that the foundation had failed to provide information on

[196] *Convention on the Settlement of Investment Disputes Between States and Nationals of Other States*, done at Washington, D.C., and entered into force on 14 October 1966 Articles 1(2), 25(1), https://icsid.worldbank.org/en/Documents/resources/2006%20CRR_English-final.pdf, accessed 1 May 2020.

[197] *Rules of Procedure for Arbitration Proceedings (Arbitration Rules)*, Article 37(2)(b) and (c), ("ICSID Arbitration Rules"), https://icsid.worldbank.org/en/Documents/resources/2006%20CRR_English-final.pdf, accessed 1 May 2020.

[198] *Suez, Sociedad General de Aguas de Barcelona, S.A. and Vivendi Universal, S.A. v. Argentine Republic*, ICSID Case No. ARB/03/19, Order in response to a Petition for Participation as Amicus Curiae (12 February 2007), https://www.italaw.com/sites/default/files/case-documents/ita0815.pdf, accessed 1 May 2020.

the nature and size of its membership, the qualifications of its leadership, the expertise of its staff, and the activities in which it had engaged. The individuals, who had merely indicated that they supported themselves from the exercise of their professions, had failed to provide information on the nature of their professional and financial relationships with either of the parties.[199]

In 2010, an application to file *amicus curiae* submissions under Article 37(2) of the ICSID Arbitration Rules was made by the World Health Organization ("WHO"), the Secretariat of the Framework Convention on Tobacco Control ("FCTC") and the Pan American Health Organization ("PAHO") in the proceedings initiated by the tobacco company Philip Morris against Uruguay in 2010 over the tobacco control measures enacted by the latter. The Uruguayan measures prohibited manufacturers from selling multiple varieties of their brand and required health warnings to be printed on 80 % of the area of cigarette packages.[200] Philip Morris challenged the independence of the three organizations, but the Tribunal did not address the company's arguments on this point in its decision.[201] The scope of the criteria of independence and interest in the proceedings was clarified by a decision of the same Arbitral Tribunal to refuse two further requests to file submissions. The Avaaz Foundation had justified its request on the grounds of its "unique composition." The *Philip Morris* Tribunal ruled that the allegedly unique composition was insufficient to consider that the Foundation's participation would be relevant to the case. The request of the Inter-American Association of Intellectual Property ("ASIPI") was denied because of doubts about its independence. It turned out that one of the counsel of Philip Morris

[199] *Suez, Sociedad General de Aguas de Barcelona S.A., and InterAguas Servicios Integrales del Agua S.A. v. The Argentine Republic*, ICSID Case No. ARB/03/17, Order in Response to a Petition for Participation as Amicus Curiae, 12, para. 30; Florian Grisel and Jorge E. Viñuales, "L'amicus curiae dans l'arbitrage d'investissement [Amicus curiae in Investment Arbitration]," *ICSID Review* 22 (2007): 420.

[200] Stefanie Schacherer, "Philip Morris v. Uruguay," *Investment Treaty News*, 18 October 2018, https://www.iisd.org/itn/2018/10/18/philip-morris-v-uruguay/, accessed 1 May 2020.

[201] *Philip Morris Brands Sàrl, Philip Morris Products S.A. and Abal Hermanos S.A. v. Oriental Republic of Uruguay*, ICSID Case No. ARB/10/7, Procedural Order No. 3 (17 February 2015) ("*Philip Morris v. Uruguay*"), https://www.italaw.com/sites/default/files/case-documents/italaw4161.pdf, accessed 23 January 2020.

was a member of its board.[202] Another tribunal, established to settle a dispute over the expropriation by Zimbabwe in 2005 of land owned by German-Swiss investors, ruled that "apparent independence" from the parties was implicit in Rule 37(2) of the ICSID Arbitration Rules and denied the request of an NGO and four indigenous communities to file *amicus curiae* submissions on the grounds that they were not independent from the government of Zimbabwe.[203] Whether this award will set a precedent is controversial, for it did not provide a definition of "apparent" or "independence." Without definitions, a non-disputing party cannot be sure that even a remote or tenuous connection with a party might be grounds for denying their participation in the arbitration. If the reason for lack of independence is conflict with the interests of one of the parties, this might perhaps be inevitable, given that the non-disputing party is required to have a "significant interest" in the proceedings.[204]

Despite the apparent differences, it can be plausibly argued that the two sets of criteria converge around two requirements. First, the applicant for *amicus curiae* status must establish its interest in the proceedings. Under NAFTA rules and practice, the applicant must explain its general objectives, the nature of its activities, and the nature of its interest in the proceedings; under ICSID rules and practice, the applicant must demonstrate its expertise and experience. Second, the applicant must establish its independence vis-à-vis the parties. In the NAFTA framework, independence is indirectly demonstrated by disclosure of the membership, the identity of parent organization, if any, the affiliation with any disputing party, and any assistance received in the preparation of the submission. Though ICSID rules and practice are somewhat vague on the criteria

[202] Ibid.

[203] *Bernhard von Pezold and Others v. Republic of Zimbabwe*, ICSID Case No. ARB/10/15, Procedural Order No. 2 (26 June 2012), 18, para. 56, https://www.italaw.com/sites/default/files/case-documents/ita1044.pdf, accessed 1 May 2020; Jacob Greenberg, "ICSID Tribunal Orders Zimbabwe to Return Expropriated Farms. Bernhard von Pezold and Others v. Zimbabwe, ICSID Case No. ARB/10/15," *Investment Treaty News*, 16 May 2016, https://www.iisd.org/itn/2016/05/16/icsid-tribunal-orders-zimbabwe-to-return-expropriated-farms-bernhard-von-pezold-and-others-v-zimbabwe-icsid-case-no-arb-10-15-jacob-greenberg/, accessed 1 May 2020.

[204] Lucas Bastin, "*Amici Curiae* in Investor-State Arbitration: Eight Recent Trends," *Arbitration International* 30 (2014): 138–40; Thomas Leary, "Non-disputing Parties and Human Rights in Investor-State Arbitration," *Journal of World Investment and Trade* 18 (2017): 1070–71.

for determination of independence, it is clear that links with one of the parties, whether the investor or the State, will cast doubt on the independence of the applicant. It is these two criteria that may be applied to de facto or self-proclaimed *amici curiae* in the *South China Sea Arbitration.*

2. *The Interest of the De Facto or Self-Proclaimed* Amici Curiae *in the* South China Sea Arbitration *and Their Independence*

Taiwan and the C(T)SIL took care to circumscribe their interest in the proceedings to the status of Itu Aba. In contrast, the APIIL proclaimed a broad interest—integrity of the dispute settlement system of the Convention. If independence from one of the parties is agreed to be a requirement for an *amicus curiae*, there will probably be a consensus that the first two enjoyed independence from China; the status of the APIIL was uncertain, if not questionable.

In theory the overlap between the interest of China and Taiwan in the proceedings was substantial, if not total. It was the Republic of China that published in 1948 the first map with the "nine-dash line." Following the establishment of the People's Republic of China in 1949, the latter inherited the "nine-dash line" claim from Taiwan; inevitably its presentation of the historical evidence relies on Taiwan's efforts prior to 1949.[205] The Hearing on the Merits made it evident that the interest of Taiwan and the C(T)SIL in the proceedings lay not in the explanation of China's claim to historic rights based on the "nine-dash line," but in the determination of the status of Itu Aba. The Tribunal did not at all examine Taiwan's actions in the 1990s when it was evaluating the nature and scope of China's claim to historic rights within the "nine-dash line."[206] The importance of Itu Aba for Taiwan is obvious. Since 1956, Taiwan has controlled Itu Aba, on which it has stationed its Coast Guard and from which it regularly patrols the South China Sea.[207] Taiwan's Foreign Ministry accused the Philippines of distorting the facts and misinterpreting the law to argue that Itu Aba was a rock and not an island, and that it therefore should not have

[205] Lynn Kuok, *Tides of Change: Taiwan's Evolving Position in the South China Sea and Why Other Actors Should Take Notice* (Washington, D.C.: Center for East Asia Policy Studies, Brookings Institution, 2015), 1–2, https://www.brookings.edu/wp-content/uploads/2016/06/taiwan-south-china-sea-kuok-paper.pdf, accessed 15 March 2020; Hsiao, "The South China Sea Arbitration," 215; Wei-chin Lee, "Taiwan," 231, 233.

[206] Hsiao, "The South China Sea Arbitration," 219.

[207] Kuok, *Tides*, 2.

any maritime entitlements beyond 12 nautical miles.[208] The interest of the C(T)SIL also lay in the status of Itu Aba, which had allegedly been described in an inaccurate or misleading fashion by the Philippines.[209] The aim of the statements of Taiwan and of the C(T)SIL was to demonstrate that Itu Aba could sustain human habitation and economic life of its own, met the criteria of an island as defined in Article 121 of the Convention, and enjoyed full rights associated with a territorial sea, a contiguous zone, an exclusive economic zone ("EEZ"), and a continental shelf.

The proclaimed interest of the APIIL in the *Arbitration*, expressed eight months after the issuance of the Award on Jurisdiction and seven months after the closure of the oral proceedings, was the exercise by the Tribunal of its jurisdiction over issues that allegedly lay outside its jurisdiction and were not justiciable through arbitration under Annex VII of the Convention. More generally (and more vaguely), the APIIL claimed that it wished "to protect the credibility and integrity of the Tribunal and UNCLOS arbitral process."[210]

Any attempt to apply the criterion of independence to these three entities is bound to raise thorny issues for all three entities. An inquiry into the affiliation of Taiwan with one of the parties can become an inquiry into the status of Taiwan as an independent State under international law. This is not the place to rehearse the entire debate on the issue. Suffice it to say that in response to a question during the Hearing on the Merits whether the Philippines, whose analysis of the early claim of historic rights focused on Taiwanese records, could distinguish between China and Taiwan, the Philippines reaffirmed that there was only one China; that since 1949 the People's Republic of China spoke for or on behalf of China; that the actions of the predecessor government, including those of the Republic of China, were attributable to China; and that the actions of the Taiwan

[208] *RTRC*, Annex 875, vol. II, 217.

[209] C(T)SIL, 6, paras. 15–16.

[210] APIIL, 2, para. 3.

authorities since 1949 were not per se attributable to China.[211] Subsequently the Philippines described Taiwan succinctly as a "non-State and non-party to UNCLOS."[212]

The other NAFTA criterion on independence directs us to the question whether the *amicus curiae* received any assistance, financial or material, from any other entity in the preparation of its brief. There is no evidence that Taiwan received any assistance of any type from China in the preparation of its arguments. During the arbitral proceedings, a few Chinese statements acknowledged an interest common to China and Taiwan. In July 2015, the Foreign Ministry, in response to a question concerning a statement made by the President of Taiwan that after World War II, China had resumed sovereignty over the islands in the South China Sea according to international legal documents, declared that Chinese people on both sides of the Taiwan Straits had the responsibility and the obligation to jointly safeguard their territorial sovereignty and maritime rights and interests.[213] This statement was repeated upon the release of the transcript of the Hearing on Jurisdiction.[214] The Philippines for its part emphasized that the interests of China and Taiwan were aligned in seeking the maximum possible entitlements for Itu Aba and other maritime features in the South China Sea.[215] It is another matter entirely whether there was actual collaboration between China and Taiwan in the preparation of Taiwan's statements on Itu Aba. A more interesting question stems from China's failure to object to the Tribunal's admission of the materials from Taiwan, when it had expressed its "firm opposition" to participation by *amicus curiae*. In general, China is cautious about the involvement in South China Sea issues of Taiwan, which is excluded from regional negotiations and regional forums. China's attitude on the matter is a function of overall cross-Strait relations.[216] We can do no more than allude here to the argument that between 2008 and 2016, the

[211] *South China Sea Arbitration*, Hearing on the Merits, Transcript, Day 2 (25 November 2015), 6, https://pcacases.com/web/sendAttach/1548, accessed 27 April 2020.

[212] *RTRC Itu Aba*, 46, para. 111.

[213] *SDP*, Annex 629.

[214] Ibid., Annex 650.

[215] *RTRC*, 20, para. 52.

[216] Kuok, *Tides*, 2.

position of the Taiwanese government, which embraced the consensus that there was only one China and defended Taiwanese sovereignty and maritime rights in the South China Sea, was welcomed by China, which for this reason tolerated Taiwan's initiatives.[217] In other words, in the arbitral proceedings, China's attitude toward Taiwan's participation was permissive.

The C(T)SIL described itself as an independent non-profit academic institution. It is part of the network of the International Law Association ("ILA"), hosts international conferences, and publishes scholarly works.[218] Its independence from one of the parties to the *Arbitration* can be taken for granted. Questions were raised about its independence from the Taiwanese government, with which it appears to have close ties. Its submissions appeared to have official endorsement and they were introduced at a press conference by the Taiwanese President.[219] That said, its dependence on the Taiwanese government would have mattered less than its independence from China.

The most intriguing entity is the APIIL. It was established on 19 April 2016 as an independent non-profit NGO under Hong Kong laws. Its mission was said to be to promote and uphold international law "as a system for peaceful resolution of international conflict through the rule of law and to promote peace and development among and within national states in a globalized world." Its members were said to be academics and practitioners "with expertise and interest in international law operating in different countries and jurisdictions."[220] The APIIL's statements, without further evidence, would not have satisfied the NAFTA requirement that the applicant must disclose its membership, the nature of its activities, relations with any parent organization, affiliation with any of the parties, or assistance received in the preparation of its submission. The APIIL's statements were not supported by information on the size of the membership, the qualifications of its leadership, the expertise of staff,

[217] Hsiao, "The South China Sea Arbitration," 223; Wei-chin Lee, "Taiwan," 235.

[218] C(T)SIL, 4, paras. 12–14.

[219] Gau, "The Sino-Philippine Arbitration," 492; Greg Torode and J.R. Wu, "Taiwan Enters South China Sea Legal Fray, As Group Seeks to Sway International Court," *Reuters*, 10 May 2016, http://www.reuters.com/article/us-southchinasea-taiwan/taiwan-enters-south-china-sea-legal-fray-as-group-seeks-to-sway-international-court-idUSKCN0Y02LD, accessed 3 May 2020.

[220] APIIL, 1, para. 2.

and the activities in which it had engaged, information that an ICSID Tribunal deemed necessary in order to judge the independence of the putative *amicus curiae*.[221] In spite of its grandiloquent aims, the existence of APIIL seemed to be shadowy at best. It was established only two months prior to the drafting of the *amicus curiae* brief that it wished to submit to the Tribunal. It had no track record of international legal practice, had no website or public contact information, and did not make available the names of its members, except for those of the four signatories of the brief.[222] According to a report from China, its chair, Daniel Fung, was at the time a delegate to the Chinese People's Political Consultative Conference ("CPPCC") in Beijing, an advisory body in which the dominant organization is the Chinese Communist Party ("CCP"). The APIIL Chair is also a founding governor of the China–US Exchange Foundation, which is said to be financed among others, by Chinese state-owned enterprises ("SOEs") and the People's Liberation Army's ("PLA") Academy of Military Science.[223] The APIIL's existence also seems to be ephemeral, as it does not seem to have shown any sign of life since the publication of its *amicus curiae* brief. Given these circumstances, one is apt to wonder whether the APIIL was established for the sole purpose of submitting the brief. Moreover, if the information regarding the ties of its chair with Beijing is accurate, then its degree of independence from one of the parties to the *Arbitration* is questionable, at best.

While the criterion of independence is not accepted by all investor-State tribunals as a basis for evaluating the participation of *amici curiae*, all agree on the central importance of the possible assistance that *amici curiae* could render to an arbitral tribunal.

[221] *Suez, Sociedad General de Aguas de Barcelona S.A., and InterAguas Servicios Integrales del Agua S.A. v. The Argentine Republic*, 12, para. 30.

[222] These were Daniel R. Fung, Prof. John Anthony Carty, Prof. Natalie Klein, and Kaiser Leung.

[223] Mark C. Eades, "Shell Game: China Plays Legal Trick to Delay Ruling," *Foreign Policy*, 24 June 2016, China, https://foreignpolicyblogs.com/2016/06/24/china-legal-trick-south-sea-ruling/, accessed 3 May 2020. Eades, who possesses competence in the Chinese language, is a writer for the Foreign Policy Association, a non-profit organization with headquarters in New York City, and is based in Shanghai.

B. The Assistance Provided by Amici Curiae *to the Arbitral Tribunal*

The assistance provided by *amici curiae* is not necessarily that of a neutral observer. It is now accepted at the domestic level and by some international courts that a "friend of the court" can be a "friend of a party." In the *South China Sea Arbitration*, the arguments and evidence put forward by Taiwan, the C(T)SIL, and the APIIL uniformly supported Chinese positions.

1. "Friends of the Court" or "Friends of a Party"?

In the US, it is now accepted that an *amicus curiae* can be a friend of one of the parties to a case. At the international level, the role of the *amicus curiae* may vary, depending on the tribunal, between that of a "friend of the court" or a "friend of a party."

The origins of the *amicus curiae* can be traced back to Roman law, under which a judge, particularly if acting alone, would call upon some lawyer to assist with his counsel.[224] The figure of the *amicus curiae* was incorporated into English law in the early fifteenth century. At first only barristers were allowed to act as *amici*; later, permission was given to any bystander. The *amicus curiae* gave information to assist the court on some matter of law in regard to which the court was doubtful or mistaken. The assistance given by bystanders consisted of bringing up cases not known to the judge; calling attention to manifest errors, appropriate statutes in force, or the death of a party; and informing the court of Parliament's interest in passing legislation.[225] By the first half of the eighteenth century, it was accepted that an *amicus curiae* was no longer precluded from commitment to a case. In practice the *amicus* acted directly and officially as counsel for one who was not formally party to a case.[226] In the US, the evolution was marked by a shift from neutrality to advocacy. In the nineteenth century, outsiders were allowed to intervene where injustice would be caused by lack of representation. Initially the *amicus curiae*

224 John Bouvier, *Bouvier's Law Dictionary and Concise Encyclopedia*, vol. I (Kansas City, MO: Vernon Law Book Company, 1914), 188, https://ia800201.us.archive.org/3/items/cu31924022836229/cu31924022836229.pdf, accessed 3 May 2020.

225 Samuel Krislov, "The Amicus Curiae Brief: From Friendship to Advocacy," *Yale Law Journal* 72 (1963): 695.

226 Ibid., 697.

was a device used to protect governmental interests, especially in connection with grants of land. The right of participation was gradually expanded to private litigants. By the 1930s, *amici curiae* had become active participants in a struggle among interest groups and they were of increasing significance in the outcome of cases.[227] They are no longer friends of the court; rather they are friends of a party.[228] The *amicus curiae* is a means for the US Supreme Court to gain information from political groups, to foster third-party involvement through the encouragement of group representation, and occasionally, to champion the Court's point of view.[229]

At the international level, the possibility of *amicus curiae* participation has been restricted to proceedings before human rights courts, international criminal tribunals, and investor-State tribunals. The nature and the conditions of their participation vary from one tribunal to the next. Their potential contribution or assistance to the court or tribunal concerned, which is usually formulated in general terms (e.g., "the proper administration of justice" or "the proper determination of a case") varies between that of a neutral "friend of the court" or a "friend of a party." The European Convention on Human Rights ("ECHR") does not explicitly use the term "*amicus curiae*," preferring to use the expression "third-party intervention." Article 36(2) of the ECHR provides that the President of the ECtHR may, "in the interest of the proper administration of justice," invite any State party to the Convention which is not a party to the proceedings or any person concerned who is not the applicant to submit written comments or take part in hearings.[230] Submissions that are authorized are forwarded to the parties to the case, who have the right to reply to the written submissions in writing or exceptionally at the hearing.[231] The purposes of third-party intervention are not identified in the ECHR. In practice, third parties are of two types. The first corresponds to *amicus*

[227] Ibid., 699, 703.

[228] Ibid., 704.

[229] Ibid., 720.

[230] Council of Europe, European Court of Human Rights, *European Convention on Human Rights*, Article 36(2), 22, https://www.echr.coe.int/Documents/Convention_ENG.pdf, accessed 23 December 2019.

[231] European Court of Human Rights, Registry of the Court, *Rules of Court* (Strasburg: Registry of the Court, 2019), Rule 43, 22–23, https://www.echr.coe.int/Documents/Rules_Court_ENG.pdf, accessed 1 May 2020.

curiae in the strict sense of the expression. They aim to enlighten the ECtHR by submitting studies to it on points of fact or law, and in particular, studies in comparative law and, in this manner, to influence the ECtHR caselaw, for the benefit of the interests that they defend. An example of such a group is the Voluntary Euthanasia Society. The second type consists of individuals who have a direct and personal stake in the case, arising from the decision in the domestic trial. These are individuals whose interests are opposed to those of the applicant filing a case with the ECtHR.[232] Third parties influence ECtHR decisions by informing the ECtHR of the existence of State practice favorable to enhanced protection of human rights; by providing it with the inspiration for judicial decisions borrowed from another system; and by setting out the terms of philosophical debates on ethical questions.[233]

International criminal tribunals have often used *amici curiae* to assist them in augmenting legal argumentation on issues of considerable importance to the accused or to a chamber.[234] The use of *amicus curiae* at all stages of the proceedings, "for the proper determination of a case," is explicitly provided for in Rule 103 of the International Criminal Court ("ICC").[235] *Amici curiae* have been allowed to file briefs on three issues: the requisite mental element for military commanders, liability for failure to punish as applied to non-State actors ("NSAs"), and causation as an element of superior responsibility. In these roles, the *amicus curiae* does seem to be a "friend of the court." On one occasion, though, an *amicus curiae* was also appointed as de facto counsel for a defendant who had

232 Ludovic Hennebel, "Le rôle des *amici curiae* devant la Cour européenne des droits de l'homme [The Role of *amici curiae* Before the European Court of Human Rights]," *Revue trimestrielle des droits de l'homme* [Trimestral Journal of Human Rights] 71 (2007): 653–55.

233 Ibid., 658–65. For the role of *amici curiae* in the Inter-American system, see Francisco Rivera Juaristi, "The Amicus Curiae in the Inter-American Court of Human Rights (1982–2013)," unpublished ms., Santa Clara University, 1 August 2014, https://papers.ssrn.com/sol3/papers.cfm?abstract_id=2488073, accessed 4 May 2020.

234 This paragraph draws heavily on Gideon Boas et al., *International Criminal Law Practitioner Library*, vol. III, *International Criminal Procedure* (Cambridge: Cambridge University Press, 2011), 166–70.

235 International Criminal Court, *Rules of Procedure and Evidence*, ICC Doc. 10ICC-ASP/1/3 (2002), Rule 103(1), 39, https://www.icc-cpi.int/iccdocs/pids/legal-texts/rulesprocedureevidenceeng.pdf, accessed 4 May 2020.

been allowed to defend himself.[236] The *amicus curiae* in this context seemed to be a "friend of a party" and a "friend of the court" at the same time. The Rules of Procedure of the International Criminal Tribunal for the Former Yugoslavia ("ICTY"), the International Criminal Tribunal for Rwanda ("ICTR"), and the Special Court for Sierra Leone ("SCSL") contain identical provisions authorizing their trial or appeals chambers to invite or grant leave to a State, organization, or a person to appear before the chamber and to make submissions on any issue specified by the chamber.[237] In these contexts, the role of the *amicus curiae* appears to be closer to that of a "friend of the court." The ICTY and the ICTR have used this power in a wide range of circumstances relating to both substantive and procedural issues; the SCSL invited an *amicus curiae* to make a submission on the immunity of a former Liberian President from the exercise of the SCSL's jurisdiction.[238]

The rules applicable to the participation of *amicus curiae* in investor-State arbitration still seem to imply that the *amicus curiae* should be a friend of the Court, rather than a friend of a party, and should not replicate the positions of a party.[239] Under the ICSID Amended Arbitration Rules, the *amicus curiae* may be authorized if it would assist the tribunal "in the determination of a factual or legal issue related to the proceeding by bringing a perspective, particular knowledge or insight that is different from that of the disputing parties" and would address a matter within the scope of the dispute.[240] In the *Philip Morris v. Uruguay Arbitration*, the

[236] Boas et al., *International Criminal Law Practitioner Library*, vol. III, 168–70.

[237] International Criminal Tribunal for the Former Yugoslavia, *Rules of Procedure and Evidence*, Rule 74, 74, UN Doc. IT/32/Rev.50 (8 July 2015), https://www.icty.org/x/file/Legal%20Library/Rules_procedure_evidence/IT032Rev50_en.pdf, accessed 4 May 2020; International Criminal Tribunal for Rwanda, *Rules of Procedure and Evidence* (13 May 2015), Rule 74, 87, https://unictr.irmct.org/sites/unictr.org/files/legal-library/150513-rpe-en-fr.pdf, accessed 4 May 2020. Special Court for Sierra Leone, *Rules of Procedure and Evidence* (4 December 2013), Rule 74, 41, http://www.rscsl.org/Documents/RSCSL-Rules.pdf, accessed 4 May 2020.

[238] Boas et al., *International Criminal Law Practitioner Library*, vol. III, 166–68.

[239] Crema, "Testing *Amici Curiae*," 114.

[240] ICSID Amended Arbitration Rules, 37(2)(a) and (b). The United Nations Commission for International Trade Law ("UNCITRAL") Rules on Transparency in Treaty-based investor-State Arbitration, Article 4(3)(a) and (b) contain identical provisions. *UNCITRAL Rules on Transparency in Treaty-based investor-State Arbitration* (1 April 2014), 8–9, https://www.uncitral.org/pdf/english/texts/arbitration/rules-on-transparency/Rules-on-Transparency-E.pdf, accessed 4 May 2020.

WHO and the Secretariat of the FCTC argued in their application for *amicus curiae* status that they would assist the Tribunal, in particular "by providing evidence of the relationship between large graphic health warnings, bans on misleading branding and the protection of public health," "providing facts concerning tobacco control globally and the regulatory environment" in Uruguay, and bringing perspective, knowledge, and insight distinct from those of the parties.[241] The Tribunal agreed with the two organizations that they would be able to bring perspective, knowledge, or insight distinct from that of the disputing parties,

> considering that WHO is in a unique position to provide information on tobacco control globally as the directing and coordinating authority on international health work and that WHO FCTC is the entity established by the [FCTC] with the mandate to coordinate activities to assist parties in implementation of the WHO FCTC obligations.[242]

The submissions of the two international organizations proved to be crucial in the establishment of the facts of the case, such as the health effects of tobacco consumption, and in the Tribunal's legal analysis of the measures taken by Uruguay as reasonable, effective, and evidence-based.[243]

Having clarified the nature of assistance that an *amicus curiae* may provide to an international court, we may now turn to the issue of the assistance that Taiwan, the C(T)SIL, and the APIIL were in a position to provide to the *South China Sea* Tribunal.

2. The Assistance of the De Facto or Self-Proclaimed Amici Curiae *in the* South China Sea Arbitration

There is no doubt that in the *South China Sea Arbitration*, Taiwan and the C(T)SIL, which claimed to provide assistance in determining the status of Itu Aba, and the APIIL, which claimed to provide assistance in determining the Tribunal's jurisdiction, were all acting as "friends of

[241] *Philip Morris v. Uruguay*, Procedural Order No. 3, 2, para. 7. The FCTC was adopted by the World Health Assembly on 21 May 2003 and entered into force on 27 February 2005. The text of the Convention is available at https://apps.who.int/iris/rest/bitstreams/50793/retrieve, accessed 12 May 2022.

[242] Ibid., 6, para. 24.

[243] El-Hosseny and Vetulli, "Amicus Acceptance and Relevance," 90–91.

China." A close examination of the submissions of Taiwan, the C(T)SIL, and the APIIL will reveal the limits of the contribution that they could have made to the Tribunal's decision-making.

The "perspective, knowledge or insight" that Taiwan and C(T)SIL could bring to the proceedings related to the determination of the status of Itu Aba as a fully entitled island—a naturally formed area of land, permanently above water at high tide, entitled to a territorial sea, EEZ, and continental shelf—or as a rock within the meaning of Article 121(3) of the Convention—an island with no human habitation or economic life of its own, without entitlement to an EEZ and continental shelf. Like China, Taiwan and the C(T)SIL defended the thesis that Itu Aba was entitled to an EEZ and a continental shelf.

As has already been mentioned, the Tribunal did not use any of its procedural powers to grant formally the status of *amicus curiae* to any of the three entities. What it did was to transmit the submissions of Taiwan, and the C(T)SIL to the Philippines and China. Obviously, it was only China's default that created interest on the part of the Philippines and the Tribunal in the "perspective, particular knowledge and insight" that the Taiwanese entities could bring to the proceedings. Once the Taiwanese statements were communicated to the Philippines, they were exposed to the risks and perils of the adversarial process.

The C(T)SIL statement claimed that it was in a position to facilitate a more comprehensive study of Itu Aba from scientific, historical, cultural, and legal perspectives. To this end, it offered to arrange a site visit for the Tribunal members.[244] Observers believed that Taiwan, having occupied Itu Aba since 1956, was in the best position to provide evidence of its status.[245] Taiwan's statements sought to demonstrate that Itu Aba had enough fresh water to sustain human habitation; that it had soil suitable for agriculture; and that it had a history of human habitation and economic life of its own. The evidence that Taiwan marshalled in support of these theses was said to be significantly different from the information provided by the Philippines and to have helped the Tribunal acquire a balanced approach to determining the status of Itu Aba, preventing it

[244] C(T)SIL, 5, paras. 16–17.

[245] Kuok, *Tides*, 19.

from relying only on the submissions of the Philippines.[246] One commentator could not help proudly announcing that Taiwan's statements had been prepared by "heavyweight experts" on international law.[247]

The Philippines recognized that the materials from Taiwan were intended to be a legal pleading and constituted an explicit attempt to rebut the Philippine contention that Itu Aba was a "rock" within the meaning of Article 121(3) of the Convention. In the Philippine view, Taiwan's assertions about Itu Aba could not withstand scrutiny.[248] The Tribunal summarized the critical remarks of the Philippines on specific pieces of evidence furnished by Taiwan and the C(T)SIL to prove that Itu Abu possessed sufficient fresh water and soil resources to sustain human habitation and had a long-standing history of human habitation.[249] Here attention will be paid to the methodological errors committed by the Taiwanese in the presentation of their evidence. For the sake of brevity, only one or two examples will be given of each error; many more can be found in the responses of the Philippines to the Taiwanese materials.

First, the Taiwanese materials did not cite any evidence of any kind to support many assertions. Two examples of unsupported assertions were the statement made by the Taiwanese President that Itu Aba had a rich supply of groundwater and the C(T)SIL statement that agricultural production could supply food for hundreds of people.[250] Second, the C(T)SIL did not provide the sources of its statements as exhibits, as would have been required of a formal pleading. For example, the C(T)SIL claimed that evidence of human activity was provided in fishermen's diaries going back to the Sung (960–1279) and Ming (1368–1644) dynasties. The Philippines responded that the references could not have been to Itu Aba, since they described a foothold for sailors beginning their voyage to the South China Sea. Itu Aba, which is 540 nautical miles from China, is too far away as the starting point of a journey.[251] Third, the evidence provided by different Taiwanese sources contradicted each other. For instance, the Foreign Ministry claimed that operational

[246] Chang Yen-Chiang, "How," 660.

[247] Gau, "The Sino-Philippine Arbitration," 496.

[248] *RTRC*, 19, para. 48.

[249] Award of 12 July 2016, 190–93, paras. 432–40.

[250] Ibid., 19, para. 50; *RTRC Itu Aba*, 31, para. 78.

[251] *RTRC Itu Aba*, 5, para. 12.

groundwater wells provided sufficient drinking water on Itu Aba, but the C(S)IL admitted that only Well No. 5 produced fresh water. Unfortunately for Taiwan and the C(T)SIL, a 1994 Taiwanese study observed that the underground water was salty and unsuitable for drinking.[252] The evidence provided by this last source was particularly valuable, in view of the Taiwanese President's attack on the Philippines for allegedly ignoring it intentionally and concealing it to mislead the judges. The Philippines duly expressed its gratitude to Taiwan for bringing the document to its attention.[253] Fourth, the evidence was misleading. To prove human habitation on Itu Aba, the C(T)SIL mentioned a gravestone that dated to the Qing dynasty (1644–1912). As the Philippines explained, if there had been human habitation on Itu Aba, there should have been a graveyard, not a solitary headstone. The lone grave marker confirmed that Itu Aba was uninhabited.[254] Fifth, and perhaps most seriously, the evidence submitted was deliberately incomplete. An exhibit attached by the C(T)SIL to its statement reported a 1919 visit to Itu Aba. The exhibit did not quote that part of the report that said that there were no humans, no other animals or birds on Itu Aba, other than wild mice.[255] A news article attached to the C(T)SIL statement contained a second-hand reference to pepper, pumpkin, and nipa growing well on Itu Aba. That part of the article which stated that "in terms of agriculture and forestry there was almost nothing worth looking at" was left out in the translation supplied by the C(T)SIL.[256] The latter probably had not anticipated that the Philippines would track the original documents in Asian archives or obtain full translations of the partially translated documents.[257] In retrospect, these serious methodological errors, though not noted by the Tribunal in the Award of 12 July 2016, could not but diminish considerably the "perspective, particular knowledge and insight" from Taiwan that could assist the decision-making of the Tribunal, which placed no reliance at all

[252] Ibid., 19, para. 46.

[253] Ibid.

[254] Ibid., 5, para. 14.

[255] Ibid., para. 16.

[256] Ibid., 37, para. 91.

[257] Ibid., 1, para. 5. It is puzzling that a paper that was prepared by what Gau ("The Sino-Philippine Arbitration," 496) called "heavyweight experts" in international law contains such grave methodological errors.

on the materials provided by Taiwan when assessing the status of Itu Aba as an island or a rock.[258] The critical remarks of the Philippines probably confirmed in the Tribunal's mind that direct observations of the maritime features in the Spratly Islands were impossible where human modifications have obscured the original status of a feature.[259]

The "perspective, knowledge or insight" that the APIIL claimed to contribute focused on jurisdiction and the justiciability of the disputes. The APIIL did not hesitate to affirm that its brief was "not about whether the Philippines or China is right."[260] Yet half of its self-proclaimed *amicus curiae* brief dealt with alleged factual and legal errors existing in the Award on Jurisdiction, which had been issued eight months prior to the preparation of the APIIL brief. Its "perspective, particular knowledge or insight," which endorsed the arguments set forth in China's Position Paper or by Chinese scholars, was in reality not distinct from that of one of the parties. Notwithstanding its protestations to the contrary, it was clear that in the APIIL's view, China was right.

The value of the "perspective, particular knowledge or insight" that the APIIL could bring to the proceedings was more than doubtful. In the first half of its brief, the APIIL merely restated China's objections to jurisdiction: the dispute submitted by the Philippines to arbitration could not be characterized as relating to the interpretation or application of the Convention given that sovereignty over the maritime features listed in the Philippine submissions was undetermined; maritime entitlements could not be determined without a knowledge of the ownership of a maritime feature; Philippine submissions relating to the determination of entitlements of maritime features in the South China Sea amounted to the exercise of maritime delimitation; and Chinese actions in preventing fishing by Philippine nationals in the waters of the South China Sea could be considered as law enforcement activities against illegal fishing.[261]

The other half of the APIIL brief, on the justiciability of the South China Sea disputes, did represent "perspective, particular knowledge

258 Award of 12 July 2016, 238–54, paras. 580–626.

259 Ibid., 138, para. 321.

260 Shi Jiangtao, "Legal Challenge May Delay Court Rulings on Claims in the South China Sea," *South China Morning Post*, 20 June 2016, https://www.scmp.com/news/china/diplomacy-defence/article/1977758/legal-challenge-may-delay-court-rulings-claims-south, accessed 5 May 2020.

261 APIIL, 9, 13–14, 15, paras. 15–16, 29, 35.

or insight" different from that of the parties, but one is hard put to determine how this could have assisted the Tribunal in its decision-making.[262] The general issue of justiciability was said to be that the dispute, involving intertwined questions of history and international politics, was not amenable to arbitration.[263] The APIIL came close to an ad hominem argument when it questioned the "subtlety, depth and competence" of the international judicial profession to adjudicate historically complex and politically sensitive questions.[264] Even assuming that the Tribunal had jurisdiction, the APIIL believed it should decline to rule on the merits of the Philippine submissions, on the grounds that the *Arbitration* could not permanently settle the real issues in dispute between the Philippines and China. "If each party could carry on as before, then the arbitration process is rendered an exercise in futility."[265] The APIIL appeared to be arguing that China's non-compliance with any eventual award would mean that there would be no point in the whole exercise—an argument that seems strange, at the very least, coming from an organization that claimed to be concerned about the "credibility and integrity of the Tribunal and arbitration under the Convention."

The APIIL then went on to identify numerous individual issues of justiciability. First, the Tribunal did not have sufficient material before it to form an effective or comprehensive judgment.[266] The reply to this is that in that case, the Tribunal would simply reject Philippine submissions. Second, other States that claimed or de facto possessed maritime features were not parties to the *Arbitration*.[267] This argument had been disposed of by the Tribunal in its Award on Jurisdiction.[268] Third, the APIIL cited difficulties in comparing incomplete Chinese, French, British, and other

[262] The idea that the South China Sea disputes are not justiciable is particularly associated with one of the signatories of the brief. See Anthony Carty, "The South China Sea Disputes Are Not Yet Justiciable," in Shicun Wu and Keyuan Zou (eds.), *Arbitration Concerning the South China Sea: Philippines Versus China* (London: Routledge, 2016), 23–51.

[263] APIIL, 16, para. 38.

[264] Ibid., 17, para. 40.

[265] Ibid., 17, para. 38.

[266] Ibid., 19, para. 48.

[267] Ibid.

[268] Award on Jurisdiction, 71–74, paras. 179–88.

national archives in the region.[269] Fourth, the APIIL claimed that the historical narrative revealed largely contested facts concerning the history of the dispute raised by the Philippines.[270] Again, one can argue that if the last two statements were true, then the Tribunal would simply reject Philippine submissions. Finally, the APIIL doubted whether Article 121 of the Convention, dealing with islands and rocks, was justiciable.[271] The APIIL contended that underlying the conflicts over the interpretation of Article 121 was the wisdom of the Convention itself, which attached so much significance to the principle that claims to the sea and its resources follow from such a vague concept as land.[272] To solve the South China Sea disputes, the APIIL called for a vast research program involving the archives of all the major States that have exercised power in the region in the last 150 years[273] and the revision of the Convention, authority for which proposal was derived from a lone (Taiwanese) scholar.[274]

One could hardly expect the Tribunal to consider as assistance to its decision-making the "perspective, particular knowledge or insight" that rehashed arguments of one of the parties on jurisdiction, a matter that had already been settled eight months previously, and that called on it to terminate the proceedings because it was not qualified to rule on the issues, China would not comply with the Award, archival research covering 150 years had yet to be carried out, and the Convention needed revision. The Tribunal did not specifically name the APIIL, referring instead to "unsolicited statements and commentaries from Chinese associations and organisations pertaining to issues covered in Award on Jurisdiction." Two reasons that it gave for not asking the Philippines to comment on these statements and commentaries, as it had done for the statements from Taiwan and the C(T)SIL, were to be expected in the light of the contents of the APIIL brief: they were concerned with matters of jurisdiction already decided by the Tribunal and they did not offer to assist the Tribunal on the merits of the Philippine claims.[275] Given these two

[269] APIIL, 19, para. 48.

[270] Ibid., 20, para. 49.

[271] Ibid., para. 51.

[272] Ibid., para. 53.

[273] Ibid., 23, para. 57.

[274] Ibid., para. 52.

[275] Award of 12 July 2016, 37, para. 104.

circumstances, asking the Philippines to comment on the APIIL's statement and granting the APIIL the procedural rights that it claimed would have adversely affected the orderly conduct of the proceedings.

C. *The Orderly Conduct of Arbitral Proceedings and* Amici Curiae

NAFTA and ICSID tribunals require two other essential conditions before permitting *amicus curiae* participation: their participation should not disrupt the proceedings and that neither disputing party should be unduly burdened or unfairly prejudiced by such submissions. In the *South China Sea Arbitration*, the Philippines accepted the burden, the prejudice, and the disruption entailed by the Tribunal's request that it respond to the materials from Taiwan; the Tribunal probably disregarded the APIIL paper because it would have disrupted the proceedings.

1. An Overview of NAFTA and ICSID Rules and Practice

NAFTA and ICSID rules and practice are broadly consistent, seeking to prevent *amicus curiae* participation from disrupting arbitral proceedings or from constituting an undue burden or unfairly prejudicing one of the parties.

The NAFTA FTA Statement on non-disputing party participation requires an arbitral tribunal to ensure that "(a) any non-disputing party submission avoids disrupting the proceedings; and (b) neither disputing party is unduly burdened or unfairly prejudiced by such submissions."[276] The Statement stipulates two ways of avoiding the disruption of the proceedings and unduly burdening the parties. First, granting *amicus curiae* status does not require the Tribunal to address the *amicus* submission. Second, granting permission to make an *amicus* submission does not entitle the *amicus* to make further submissions, which will require a new request for permission.[277]

The rationale for these procedural conditions may in part be traced to specific objections raised by Methanex Corporation to the requests for *amicus curiae* participation in the *Methanex v. United States Arbitration*. The disruption of the proceedings was not explicitly raised by Methanex, but the latter did refer to the risk that a favorable decision by the Tribunal

[276] *FTC Statement*, Section B.7(a) and (b).

[277] Ibid., Section B.(9).

might set a precedent, encouraging other groups to seek to appear as *amici curiae*.[278] Methanex identified an increase in the costs of the proceedings as the burden represented by *amicus curiae* participation if it would have to respond to their submissions.[279] The *Methanex* Tribunal acknowledged the prejudice that Methanex might suffer from participation by *amici curiae*, who would be more likely to counter the position of Methanex and to support that of the US.[280] These objections did not dissuade the *Methanex* Tribunal from granting permission to *amicus curiae* to make written submissions. The *Methanex* Tribunal agreed that a burden could be added if Methanex and the US sought to respond to the *amici* submissions. In its view, however, the risk of the additional burden was inherent in every adversarial procedure that admitted presentations by *amici*. The Tribunal pointed out that at least initially, the burden would be shared by both parties. The Tribunal did not believe that the burden would be inevitably excessive, for it could set limitations to the submissions and it would not allow witnesses to present evidence, obviating the need for cross-examination.[281] The Tribunal declared itself willing to provide Methanex procedural protection against the risk of being unfairly prejudiced by *amici* submissions that opposed its position, although the Tribunal did not specify what such protection might consist of.[282]

Like the FTC Statement, the ICSID Arbitration Rules stipulate that

> The Tribunal shall ensure that the non-disputing party submission does not disrupt the proceeding or unduly burden or unfairly prejudice either party, and that both parties are given an opportunity to present their observations on the non-disputing party submission.[283]

Commentaries and caselaw give a clearer idea of the nature of disruption that *amicus* participation might cause. Proceedings might be disrupted if a Tribunal is overwhelmed with requests for participation as *amici curiae*, particularly if the subject matter of the arbitration is of

[278] *Methanex v. United States*, Decision, 8, para. 15.

[279] Ibid., para. 14.

[280] Ibid., 22, para. 50.

[281] Ibid., 16, para. 36.

[282] Ibid., 22, para. 50.

[283] ICSID Arbitration Rules, Article 37(2), 117.

strong public interest.[284] The untimely submission of requests for participation might also be a source of disruption of proceedings as well as a burden to the parties. Five NGOs filed a petition for *amicus curiae* status on 1 December 2006 in a case instituted by Suez, Sociedad General de Aguas de Barcelona S.A., and Vivendi Universal against Argentina over a number of Argentine actions and omissions related to the country's financial crisis, which allegedly derailed a 30-year concession to operate water and waste-water services in and around Buenos Aires and destroyed the value of the companies' investment.[285] The three companies contended that the petition had been filed too late and that its timing was likely to cause disruption of the proceedings. The *Suez* Tribunal disagreed, pointing out that it had authorized the submission of requests for *amicus curiae* participation only after the issuance of its Award on Jurisdiction on 3 August 2006. Although it was four months after the latter date that the organizations submitted their applications for *amicus curiae* status, the Tribunal believed that consideration of the petition would not impede the progress of the case. There was sufficient time to receive the submissions well before the time limit for the submission of the memorials, set for August 2007, and beginning of the hearings, scheduled in October 2007. It would therefore be possible to integrate "the *amicus* process into the general course of the arbitration." It would also be possible to avoid burdening the parties by setting time limits that avoided conflicts with other deadlines as well as by setting limits on the length of the *amicus* submissions and requiring that the submissions not include annexes.[286]

In the *Biwater Gauff (Tanzania) Ltd v. Tanzania Case*, which was filed by the company for the termination of a contract to implement a project to develop Tanzania's water and sewer infrastructure and services project, five NGOs submitted a request for *amicus curiae* status in

[284] Aurélia Antonietti, "The 2006 Amendments to the ICSID Rules and Regulations and the Additional Facility Rules," *ICSID Review* 21 (2006): 436; Nicolette Butler, "Non-disputing Party Participation in ICSID Disputes: *Faux Amici*?" *Netherlands International Law Review* 66 (2019): 148.

[285] For a background on the case, see Lise Johnson, "Argentina on the Hook for Breach of Fair and Equitable Treatment. Suez, Sociedad General de Aguas de Barcelona S.A., and Vivendi Universal v. Argentine Republic (ICSID Case No. ARB/03/19)," *Investment Treaty News*, 23 September 2010, https://www.iisd.org/itn/2010/09/23/awards-and-decisions/, accessed 8 May 2020.

[286] *Suez, Sociedad General de Aguas de Barcelona, S.A. and Vivendi Universal, S.A. v. Argentine Republic*, ICSID Case No. ARB/03/19, Order, 11, para. 11.

November 2006. Biwater objected that the petition was filed at a very late date, considering that the existence of the proceedings had been public knowledge since August 2005, the issue of *amicus* had been raised at the first procedural meeting, and the hearings were set to begin in April 2007. In Biwater's view, adding the petitioners to the proceedings would place "intolerable strain on an already tight timetable."[287] The Tribunal, which expressed sympathy with Biwater's concern, did not dismiss the request for *amicus curiae* status and instead established a two stage process to reduce the burden on the parties. In the first stage, the petitioners would file a single submission, without any evidence or documentation; the parties would then have three weeks to decide whether to address the petition and to inform each other whether each would address the petition during the hearing. In the second stage, the Tribunal would issue directions following the hearing for responses if any party wished to respond to the petition and for further submissions from the petitioners, if necessary.[288] The risk of unfair prejudice to the parties, particularly to Biwater, would be reduced to some extent through the possibility given to the parties of presenting observations on the *amicus* submissions.

Several procedural decisions of the Tribunal in the *Philip Morris v. Uruguay Case* shed further light on the means to avoid disruption of the proceedings and undue burden or unfair prejudice to the parties. As may be recalled, the first requests for *amicus curiae* status were filed by two international organizations, the WHO and the FCTC Secretariat.[289] Philip Morris objected that the proposed *amicus curiae* brief would unduly burden the parties. Philip Morris claimed that it had already been compelled to review a large volume of documents that in its view were unrelated to the issues in the *Arbitration*, to which the brief would add even more unrelated information.[290] Uruguay disagreed, citing several

[287] *Biwater Gauff (Tanzania) Ltd. v. United Republic of Tanzania*, ICSID Case No. ARB/05/22, Procedural Order No. 5 (2 February 2007), 11, para. 36, https://www.italaw.com/sites/default/files/case-documents/ita0091_0.pdf, accessed 7 May 2020.

[288] Ibid., 18–19, para. 60; Eduardo Savarese, "Amicus Curiae Participation in Investor-State Arbitral Proceedings," *Italian Yearbook of International Law* 17 (2007): 110.

[289] A similar request was subsequently filed by the Pan American Health Organization ("PAHO"). The Tribunal also granted it permission to file an *amicus curiae* brief. *Philip Morris v. Uruguay*, Award, 8 July 2016, 8, paras. 40–42, https://www.italaw.com/sites/default/files/case-documents/italaw7417.pdf, accessed 1 May 2020.

[290] Ibid., Procedural Order No. 3, 4, para. 16.

reasons. First, the WHO and the FCTC Secretariat only requested permission to present a written submission, which they had already provided together with their request. Second, enough time remained before the time limit for the submission of the parties' second round of pleadings. Finally, the WHO and the FCTC did not request permission to attend the hearings, obviating the need to make special arrangements for them.[291] The Tribunal did not directly address the parties' observations, but did take several measures in order to reduce the burden on the parties. A time limit of 30 days was set for the submission of the *amicus* brief, which was not to be accompanied by documents or evidence. The Tribunal also reserved the right to order the two organizations to reimburse or pay costs if either party requested the reimbursement of costs incurred in responding to the *amicus* submissions.[292]

Two NGOs, the Avaaz Foundation and the ASIPI, also filed separate requests for *amicus curiae* status. Among the reasons that the Tribunal adduced for refusing to grant the requests was their untimely character. The request of Avaaz was submitted late in the proceedings, when Philip Morris had already submitted all of its written pleadings, consisting of the *Memorial on the Merits* and the *Reply on the Merits*. In these circumstances, the Avaaz Foundation's participation would disrupt the proceedings and unfairly prejudice one of the parties.[293] The ASIPI request had also been filed late in the proceedings—one month before the hearing on the merits, to be exact. For the Tribunal, the ASIPI request would disrupt the proceedings and unduly burden and unfairly prejudice the parties, who were in the process of preparing for the hearing on the merits.[294]

Notwithstanding the absence of a formal decision on the admission of *amicus curiae* submissions, it is still possible to assess the burden and unfair prejudice that they could have caused to the Philippines as well as the disruption of the proceedings that they could have entailed.

[291] Ibid., 5, para. 20.

[292] Ibid., 8, para. 31.

[293] Ibid., Award, 8 July 2016, 10, para. 52.

[294] Ibid., Procedural Order No. 3, 10–11, para. 55; Sophie Lamb et al., "Recent Developments in the Law and Practice of Amicus Briefs in Investor-State Arbitration," *Indian Journal of Arbitration Law* 5 (2017): 83–84, http://ijal.in/sites/default/files/IJAL%20Volume%205_Issue%202_Sophie%20Lamb%20et%20al.pdf, accessed 5 May 2020.

2. The Burden and Unfair Prejudice to the Philippines and the Disruption of the Proceedings in the South China Sea Arbitration

The Philippines accepted the burden, the unfair prejudice, and the disruption of the proceedings arising from the submissions of Taiwan and the C(T)SIL, with a view to alleviating some of the practical difficulties caused by China's default. Fortunately, the Philippines was not required to respond to the APIIL statement, as the Tribunal's handling of the latter frustrated an attempt to disrupt the proceedings.

The burden and unfair prejudice to the Philippines resulted not so much from the fact that the Taiwanese materials objectively supported the position of China—in investor-State arbitration, *amicus curiae* submissions by NGOs almost always support the State against the foreign investor[295]—but from the fact that the Taiwanese materials were not subject to any time limits or other procedural conditions. As we have seen above, time limits and the need to request permission for each submission are among the means of reducing the burden and unfair prejudice to the parties arising from *amicus* submissions. Requests for *amicus curiae* status have been refused for being submitted a month before the hearing on the merits. In the *South China Sea Arbitration*, the Taiwanese and C(T)SIL materials were brought to the Tribunal's attention after the closure of the oral proceedings, when the Tribunal was already engaged in its deliberation.[296] The Taiwanese materials first came to the attention of the Tribunal in February 2016, three months after the Hearing on the Merits. Given that Taiwan was not a party to the *Arbitration* and that the written and oral proceedings had already been concluded, the Tribunal would have been well within its rights to refuse to consider the Taiwanese and C(T)SIL submissions. Yet the Tribunal, which was aware that the Taiwanese and C(T)SIL materials could provide insights into China's position on the status of Itu Aba, requested a Philippine response. After the Philippines had submitted its response to the Tribunal in March 2016, the second set of materials from Taiwan prompted another request from the Tribunal in the same month, obliging the Philippines to respond within a month. It is doubtful that an investor-State tribunal would have been willing to accommodate two successive rounds of submissions from

[295] El-Hosseny and Vetulli, "Amicus Acceptance and Relevance," 79.

[296] *RTRC Itu Aba*, 3, para. 6.

amici curiae that had not been approved or solicited and had been communicated to it three or four months after the closure of the oral hearings. Such submissions would undoubtedly have been considered as disrupting the proceedings and imposing a burden on or causing unfair prejudice to one of the parties. In this case, the burden or prejudice was even greater, in that only one party was appearing before the Tribunal, with no expectation that the defaulting party would take the trouble to respond to the Taiwanese materials.

It could be argued in defense of Taiwan and the C(T)SIL that they had only realized the importance of the status of Itu Aba in December 2015, following the publication of the Hearing transcripts. It would have been impossible for them to prepare a response before that date. To this one can respond that neither Taiwan nor the C(T)SIL were (or could have been) parties to the case and as such did not have the right to make submissions to the Tribunal in any case. The Philippines, which would have been fully justified in requesting that the Tribunal disregard the Taiwanese and C(T)SIL materials, did not do so, because it was aware of the "exceptional difficulties" that China's default had caused for the Tribunal.[297] The Philippines admitted that the coincidence of Chinese and Taiwanese interests in maximum entitlements for maritime features in the South China Sea would make it useful to consider the legal arguments and evidence from Taiwan.

The condition imposed by a number of Tribunals that *amicus* submissions should not include annexes and documentation is not relevant in this situation, in which the *amicus* was in practice filing a pleading on behalf of a (defaulting) party. The C(T)SIL did attempt to replicate the format of pleadings by attaching annexes and documents to its brief. Regrettably, the C(T)SIL's presentation of its evidence was methodologically flawed, as we have already seen. For this reason, responding to the materials submitted not only by the C(T)SIL but also by Taiwan imposed a heavier burden on the Philippines than would have been the case for a properly documented *Counter-Memorial*. There would have been no need for the Philippines to commission fresh translations of documents or to research original documents in various archives if the C(T)SIL had provided complete translations and annexed documents to its statement, as would have been required of a *Counter-Memorial*. After having been

[297] Ibid., para. 8.

compelled to respond to the second set of Taiwanese materials and finding that they did not present solid or reliable factual evidence, or indeed, any evidence, the Philippines visibly lost its patience and declared that the time for further submissions was over and that no further attempts by Taiwan to influence the Tribunal's deliberations should be entertained.[298]

The burden or unfair prejudice to the Philippines and the disruption of the proceedings resulting from the participation of APIIL would have been much greater. As has already been mentioned, the APIIL transmitted its statement challenging the jurisdiction of the Tribunal in June 2016, eight months after the issuance of the Award on Jurisdiction and seven months after the Hearing on the Merits. As if this were not enough, the APIIL sought the reopening of the oral hearings to enable it to present its arguments.[299] Most applicants for *amicus curiae* status in investor-State arbitrations have requested permission to attend oral hearings. No such request has ever been granted. Here a self-proclaimed *amicus curiae*, whose independence from one of the parties and whose potential assistance to the Tribunal were doubtful at best, was demanding that the Tribunal reopen oral hearings simply to accommodate it. It was certainly a demand, because its putative chair declared to the Chinese news agency that "the PCA [sic] has the responsibility to respond to the brief."[300] Whether or not the APIIL was expecting a favorable response to its demand, examination of its paper and possibly, transmission to the Philippines for comments would certainly have delayed the proceedings. That the aim pursued by the APIIL was to delay the issuance of the Award on the merits is confirmed by reports of a belief among legal scholars in China that the APIIL action would delay or postpone the award of the Tribunal on the merits.[301] The APIIL would have prepared its statement shortly before the Philippine presidential elections of May 2016, which

[298] Ibid., 56, para. 112.

[299] APIIL, 2, para. 4.

[300] Xinhua, "HK Legal Organ Queries PCA's Arbitration Jurisdiction over South China Sea Disputes," *Europe China Daily*, 17 June 2016, http://europe.chinadaily.com.cn/world/2016-06/17/content_25739694.htm, accessed 10 May 2020. The references to the PCA in the article are likely to generate doubts in readers' minds over the expertise of the APIIL in international law. As any undergraduate who has taken a course in international law knows, the PCA is not a court. In the *South China Sea Arbitration*, the PCA was the Registry for the Arbitral Tribunal constituted under Annex VII of the Convention.

[301] Shi Jiangtao, "Legal Challenge;" Eades, "Shell Game."

could have given China hope that a new administration would change course. The link with the Chinese government is suggested by the extensive press coverage of the APIIL statement, which was presented as a major legal development in the proceedings[302]—a misleading assessment, if ever there was one. It is likely that the Tribunal did devote just enough time to the APIIL submission to determine that it raised jurisdictional issues that had already been settled by its Award on Jurisdiction and that it did not offer to assist it in its decision-making on the merits. It is equally likely that the paper was transmitted to the Philippines. This time, though, the Tribunal did not ask the Philippines for a response, in this manner minimizing the burden and unfair prejudice to the Philippines and the disruption to the proceedings.

Consideration of informal communications, of public statements, of supplemental submissions, and of submissions from self-proclaimed or de facto *amici curiae* constitutes an exercise of a tribunal's fact-finding powers unique to cases of default. The *South China Sea* Tribunal's exercise of an international court's ordinary fact-finding powers was also decisively conditioned by China's default.

III. The Tribunal's Exercise of Its Other Fact-Finding Powers

Under the Rules of Procedure of the *South China Sea Arbitration*, the Tribunal possessed two other fact-finding powers, powers that have also been granted to other arbitral tribunals established under Annex VII of the Convention: the general power to "take all appropriate measures in order to establish the facts"[303] and the power to appoint independent

[302] Eades, "Shell Game."

[303] *South China Sea Arbitration*, Rules of Procedure, Article 10(1), 5; *MOX Plant Case (Ireland v. United Kingdom)*, Rules of Procedure (25 October 2001), Article 12(2), 8, https://pcacases.com/web/sendAttach/848, accessed 12 May 2020; *Guyana v. Suriname*, Rules of Procedure (24 February 2004), Article 11(2), 5, http://www.pcacases.com/web/sendAttach/882, accessed 11 May 2020; *Bay of Bengal Maritime Boundary Arbitration Between Bangladesh and India*, Rules of Procedure (08 October

experts.[304] One power that has been omitted in all the Rules of Procedure that are publicly available is the power to put questions to the parties, witnesses, and experts during the oral proceedings. In contrast, the Statute of ITLOS, which after all is also a tribunal established under the Convention, specifically provides that the Tribunal "may, during the hearing, put questions to the agents, counsel and advocates, and may ask them for explanations" and that "[q]uestions may be put to them [witnesses and experts] by the President of the Tribunal and by the judges."[305] Obviously, the omission of comparable provisions in the Rules of Procedure of Annex VII tribunals does not deprive these tribunals of the power to put questions to the parties, witnesses, and experts during the hearings. This power is an inherent power of international courts and tribunals, recognized in Article 47 of the Convention for the Pacific

2009), Article 12(3), 8, http://www.pcacases.com/web/sendAttach/375, accessed 11 May 2020; *Chagos Marine Protected Area Arbitration (Mauritius v. United Kingdom)*, Rules of Procedure (29 March 2012), Article 12(2), 7, https://pcacases.com/web/sendAttach/1567, accessed 14 January 2020; *The ARA Libertad Arbitration (Argentina v. Ghana)*, Rules of Procedure (31 July 2013), Article 15(2), 8, https://pcacases.com/web/sendAttach/427, accessed 12 May 2020; *The Atlanto-Scandian Herring Arbitration (The Kingdom of Denmark in respect of the Faroe Islands v. The European Union)*, Rules of Procedure (15 March 2014), Article 15(2), 9, https://pcacases.com/web/sendAttach/305; and *"Arctic Sunrise" Arbitration*, Rules of Procedure, Article 22(2), 10, all accessed 12 May 2020.

304 *South China Sea Arbitration*, Rules of Procedure, Article 24, 11; *Barbados v. Trinidad and Tobago*, Rules of Procedure (23 August 2004), Article 12(4), 5, https://pcacases.com/web/sendAttach/1062, accessed 11 May 2020; *Guyana v. Suriname*, Rules of Procedure, Article 11(3), 5; *Bay of Bengal Maritime Boundary Arbitration*, Rules of Procedure, Article 12(4), 8; *Chagos Marine Protected Area Arbitration*, Rules of Procedure, Article 12(4), 7; *The ARA Libertad Arbitration*, Rules of Procedure (31 July 2013), Article 19, 9; *The Atlanto-Scandian Herring Arbitration*, Rules of Procedure, Article 19, 10; *"Arctic Sunrise" Arbitration*, Rules of Procedure, Article 24, 11–12. Article 11(2) of the Rules of Procedure of *Barbados v. Trinidad and Tobago* (5), contains a slightly different formulation:

> The Tribunal may at any time call upon the parties to produce such evidence or to give such explanations as the Tribunal considers necessary for the elucidation of any aspect of the matters in issue, or may itself seek other information for this purpose, in which case it shall notify the Parties.

305 *Rules of the Tribunal* (ITLOS/8), Articles 76(2) and 80, 28, 30. The difference is that the ITLOS is a permanent tribunal, whose Statute is in Annex VI of the Convention.

Settlement of International Disputes of 1899, Article 72 of the Convention for the Pacific Settlement of International Disputes of 1907, Article 51 of the PCIJ Statute (referring to witnesses), Article 51 of the ICJ Statute (referring to witnesses and experts), and Article 61(2) of the ICJ Rules of Court (referring to agents, counsel, and advocates of the parties).[306] An international court would not be worth the name if it did not possess the power to put questions to the parties, witnesses, and experts during oral hearings.

Confronted by the default of one of the parties, the *South China Sea* Tribunal made extensive use of all these powers in undertaking fact-finding. The following discussion of the exercise of the power to put questions will be limited to the questions to the parties; the impact on the proceedings of the questions to the experts will be reserved for the following Chapter. The exercise of the power to appoint independent experts will be confined to procedural questions around the appointment of independent experts and the evaluation of expert evidence. The proper role of experts in international adjudication, their independence and impartiality, and the Tribunal's assessment of expert evidence will also be examined in greater detail in the following Chapter. The last section of this Chapter will discuss the Tribunal's action to obtain evidence on its own initiative, in exercise of its power to take all appropriate measures in order to establish the facts.

A. *The Power to Put Questions to the Parties During Oral Proceedings*

For several structural reasons, international courts make sparing use of the power to put questions to the parties to a dispute during oral hearings. The default of a party in the *South China Sea Arbitration* accounts for the important role played by questions to the appearing party during the oral proceedings in the Tribunal's fact-finding, the Tribunal's questions in effect replacing counter-arguments or rebuttals of the Philippine arguments by the defaulting State.

306 *1899 Convention for the Pacific Settlement of International Disputes*, https://pca-cpa.org/wp-content/uploads/sites/6/2016/01/1899-Convention-for-the-Pacific-Settlement-of-International-Disputes.pdf, accessed 3 April 2020; *1907 Convention for the Pacific Settlement of International Disputes*, https://pca-cpa.org/wp-content/uploads/sites/6/2016/01/1907-Convention-for-the-Pacific-Settlement-of-International-Disputes.pdf, accessed 3 April 2020.

1. The Power to Put Questions During Oral Proceedings and Default
It has been observed by international judges themselves that questions tend to be relatively few in oral proceedings before international courts.[307] This phenomenon may be attributed to the structural context of such proceedings. It is mainly in cases of default that questions assume greater importance during oral proceedings.

The paucity of questions has been attributed by a former ICJ President to the need to show respect for sovereign States, which have consented to appear before the court or tribunal and may withdraw from the proceedings, or worse, from the system of judicial settlement, to express their dissatisfaction.[308] An equally important factor, if not more so, is the organization of the proceedings. For permanent international courts, the size of the court—15 members in the case of the ICJ and 21 members in the case of the ITLOS—may make oral questioning of counsel during their presentations impractical.[309] Some judges may be reluctant to ask questions, which could give the impression that they have formed or are forming a particular line of thought.[310] The conditions in which parties present their pleadings also hinder the free exchange with judges. Oral pleadings are set speeches prepared in advance by counsel under the supervision of the respective parties. In view of the high stakes, the latter are reluctant to allow counsel full freedom to answer questions spontaneously, without clearing the response with the party.

International courts have devised procedural strategies to enable them to exercise their power to put questions with minimal disruption to the proceedings. Questions are put to counsel at the end of a presentation or

[307] Stephen M. Schwebel, "Three Cases of Fact-Finding by the International Court of Justice," in Stephen M. Schwebel, *Justice in International Law: Selected Writings* (Cambridge: Cambridge University Press, 1994), 125; see also Joseph Akl, "L'amélioration des méthodes de travail du Tribunal international du droit de la mer [The Improvement of the Working Methods of the International Tribunal for the Law of the Sea]," *The Contribution of the International Tribunal for the Law of the Sea to the Rule of Law: 1996–2016* (Leiden: Brill/Nijhoff, 2018), 234.

[308] Schwebel, "Three Cases," 128.

[309] Arthur Watts, "Enhancing the Effectiveness of Procedures of International Dispute Settlement," *Max Planck Yearbook of United Nations Law*, 5 (2001): 26, https://www.mpil.de/en/pub/publications/periodic-publications/max-planck-yearbook/volume-5.cfm, accessed 12 May 2020.

[310] Schwebel, "Three Cases," 127.

before a break in the proceedings. Answers are usually not required immediately—the parties are given time in which to prepare their response. This enables counsel to consult with and seek the approval of the party. The reply will usually be given in writing.[311] At the ITLOS, questions of individual judges are first discussed in deliberations before or during oral proceedings, after which they may be included in the Tribunal's questions to the parties.[312] Annex VII arbitral tribunals have devised a broad range of strategies for putting their questions to the parties. The *Barbados v. Trinidad and Tobago* Tribunal formulated four questions that were transmitted to the parties at the conclusion of the first round of the oral hearings, to be answered during the second round of the proceedings.[313] The *Bay of Bengal* Tribunal transmitted its questions in writing to the parties approximately a week prior to the opening of the oral proceedings.[314] Finally, one of the members of the *Chagos Marine Protected Area* Tribunal transmitted his questions in writing to the parties at the opening of the oral proceedings.[315]

From the very first case of complete default of the respondent in the 1970s, the greater willingness on the part of ICJ judges to put questions to the appearing party during oral proceedings was already perceptible.[316] When formulating their questions, the judges served as de facto counsel for the defaulting party. Two examples should suffice to illustrate the point.[317] In the *United States Diplomatic and Consular Staff in Tehran Case*, we may recall that Iran denied the ICJ's jurisdiction, on the grounds that the hostage-taking was a "secondary" or "marginal"

[311] Watts, "Enhancing," 26; Tams and Devaney, "Article 49," 1419.

[312] David Anderson, "Article 76," in P. Chandrasekhara Rao and Philippe Gautier (eds.), *The Rules of the International Tribunal for the Law of the Sea: A Commentary* (Leiden: Martinus Nijhoff Publishers, 2006), 218.

[313] *Barbados v. Trinidad and Tobago*, Transcript, Day 5 (24 October 2005), 110, https://pcacases.com/web/sendAttach/1104, accessed 10 May 2020.

[314] *Bay of Bengal Maritime Boundary Arbitration*, Hearing Transcript, Day 1 (9 December 2013), 94, https://pcacases.com/web/sendAttach/388, accessed 11 May 2020.

[315] *Chagos Marine Protected Area Arbitration*, Hearing Transcript, Day 2 (23 April 2014), 8, https://pcacases.com/web/sendAttach/1572, accessed 12 May 2020.

[316] Favoreu, "Les arrêts," 267.

[317] The role of questions in the *Fisheries Jurisdiction Cases* will be discussed in the following subsection.

aspect of the larger problem of US intervention in Iranian domestic affairs over 25 years. The US argued that Iranian grievances were not relevant to the proceedings and should not be allowed to interfere with US claims.[318] Notwithstanding the rebuttal, Judge Gros asked the US to respond to the allegation that the US Embassy in Tehran was a center for espionage; to identify the legal bases for the US rejection of the Iranian thesis that the dispute concerned fundamentally US attitude toward Iran prior to the hostage-taking; and to specify the grievances that Iran could submit to a UN Commission of Inquiry.[319] Judge Morozov and the Court as a whole asked the US questions that Iran itself had not (and by the very nature of things) could not have presented. Judge Morozov asked the US to explain why it wasted one month in pursuing its defense by asking the Court twice to postpone the fixing of a date for the opening of the oral proceedings.[320] For its part, the Court asked, among others, whether the establishment or the work of the UN Commission of Inquiry affected the Court's jurisdiction to continue the proceedings or their admissibility.[321] For a French commentator, the US responses to these and other questions largely compensated for the absence of Iran.[322] At the same time, the questions highlighted the inequality between the parties created by Iran's default and the Court's acting as Iran's de facto legal counsel. The appearing party was compelled to answer questions that should have been addressed to Iran (e.g., Judge Gros's question on the grievances that Iran could submit to the UN Commission of Inquiry) or that could undermine its legal position (e.g., the Court's question on the effect of the

[318] Mr. Owen, Third Public Sitting (18 March 1980), Minutes of the Public Sittings held from 18 to 20 March and on 24 May 1980, *I.C.J. Pleadings*, *United States Diplomatic and Consular Staff in Tehran*, 266, https://www.icj-cij.org/files/case-related/64/064-19800318-ORA-01-00-BI.pdf, accessed 11 October 2019.

[319] Question de M. Gros [Question of Mr. Gros], Third Public Sitting; Question de M. Gros [Question of Mr. Gros], Fifth Public Sitting, 20 March 1980, *I.C.J. Pleadings*, *United States Diplomatic and Consular Staff in Tehran*, 268, 312.

[320] Question by Judge Morozov, Third Public Sitting, *I.C.J. Pleadings*, *United States Diplomatic and Consular Staff in Tehran*, 298.

[321] President Sir Humphrey Waldock, Third Public Sitting, *I.C.J. Pleadings*, *United States Diplomatic and Consular Staff in Tehran*, 254.

[322] Coussirat-Coustère, "L'arrêt," 203.

Commission of Inquiry on its jurisdiction). The defaulting party was, by definition, exposed to no such risks.[323]

During the oral proceedings on the merits in the *Nicaragua Case*, most of the judges' questions were directed to witnesses that Nicaragua had called to testify rather than to Nicaragua. In the absence of the US, the examination of the witnesses by Nicaragua could not be followed by cross-examination by the US, but it seems that the judge of US nationality, Judge Schwebel, thought that it was his duty to carry out the cross-examination on behalf of the US.[324] Performance of such a duty would be consistent with his conception of the role of the Court as counsel for the defaulting party.[325] It would explain the very large number of questions that he put to the witnesses and to the counsel of Nicaragua.[326] It would also explain the manner in which he put his questions, characterized as rapid, abrupt, and clearly intended to get the witnesses to contradict themselves or to react to a US publication that only he possessed.[327] Finally, it would explain the content of his questions, which assumed that Nicaragua was guilty of the acts of which it was accused by the US. For example, on being told by a witness that a defector who had recanted his testimony against Nicaragua was living in Nicaragua, Judge Schwebel responded sarcastically: "He wasn't shot on the spot? He showed no signs of torture? He walked away as a free man?"[328] Referring to kidnapping carried out by El Salvadoran insurgents, Judge Schwebel prefaced his question to a witness about alleged Nicaraguan responsibility for such acts with the following statement: "Let us assume, for the purpose of this question, two facts. First, that the leadership of the El Salvadoran insurgents operates from Nicaragua; and second, that arms have been shipped through Nicaragua

[323] Ibid.

[324] Eisemann, "L'arrêt," 162.

[325] *Nicaragua, Merits, Judgment*, Dissenting Opinion of Judge Schwebel, 319, para. 125.

[326] *I.C.J. Pleadings, Military and Paramilitary Activities in and against Nicaragua (Nicaragua v. United States of America)*, vol. V, 30–34 (Public Sitting of 12 September 1985), 46–48 (13 September 1985), 59–68, 78–79 (16 September 1985), 91–92, 99–102 (17 September 1985), 123 (18 September 1985) and 140–45 (19 September 1985).

[327] Eisemann, "L'arrêt," 162.

[328] Nineteenth Public Sitting (16 September 1985), *I.C.J. Pleadings, Military and Paramilitary Activities in and against Nicaragua*, vol. V, 68.

to Salvadoran insurgents."[329] Questions of this type, which were far from isolated instances, upset the equality of the parties, to the detriment of the appearing State.[330] Fortunately, this conduct was attributable to an individual judge and not to the Court as a whole.

The conduct of the Tribunal and its members in the *South China Sea Arbitration* demonstrates that it is possible to put questions on behalf of the defaulting State without assuming that the appearing State is in the wrong.

2. Questions During Oral Proceedings in the South China Sea Arbitration

In some respects, the procedure for putting questions during oral proceedings in the *South China Sea Arbitration* did not change substantially when compared with the procedure followed during proceedings in which both parties appear before the court. During presentations by the Philippines, judges rarely interrupted; questions were put at the end of presentations or at a convenient moment in the sessions. One may surmise that the large number of questions put to the Philippines is in part attributable to the smaller size of the Arbitral Tribunal compared to that of the ICJ or ITLOS. This smaller size is apparently more conductive to the formulation of questions, as a cursory survey of the proceedings of arbitral tribunals demonstrates and as the judges themselves testify.[331] But the procedures for adopting the questions were adapted to the context of default, and the scope of the questions, particularly during the second rounds of both Hearings, proves that the Tribunal was indeed acting as China's de facto counsel.

One procedure for putting questions was derived from Article 25(2). It may be recalled that Article 25(2) authorized the Tribunal to request a supplemental written submission from the appearing State or to put questions to the latter on issues that had not been canvassed or had been inadequately canvassed in its pleadings. In practice the Tribunal had recourse to both procedures. The Philippines was not only requested to make a Supplemental Written Submission; the Tribunal also posed a

[329] Ibid., 79.

[330] Eisemann, "L'arrêt," 162.

[331] See for example, *Bay of Bengal Maritime Boundary Arbitration*, Hearing Transcript, Day 1, 10.

series of questions to the Philippines, approximately a month prior to each Hearings, questions that the Philippines was to address during the Hearings themselves. The Philippines proceeded to answer these questions in the first round of each Hearing.[332] As we have seen, some Annex VII arbitral tribunals or individual members of these tribunals communicated their questions in writing to the parties prior to or at the opening of the oral hearings. The procedure under Article 25(2) is innovative in that it was adopted in the context of default in response to concerns expressed by the appearing party.

Another procedural innovation was implemented by the Tribunal, upon the request made by the Philippines prior to the Hearing on Jurisdiction. The Tribunal agreed that following the first round of presentations, it would meet to determine whether it wished to put to the Philippines a final set of questions, or topics on which it wanted further submissions.[333] The rationale for this procedure was identical to that for the adoption of the special procedure under Article 25(2) of the Rules of Procedure: to enable the Philippines to make submissions on matters that in the Tribunal's view had not been sufficiently canvassed or had not at all been canvassed by the Philippines and in so doing, to alleviate the difficulties created by default for the appearing State. At its meeting, held after the first round of pleadings during the Hearing on Jurisdiction, the Tribunal formulated six questions, which were transmitted to the Philippines on the next day. Following a weekend of preparation, the Philippines responded to the questions in the second round of pleadings on the Hearing's last day; it was also permitted to provide written answers within a week. It is interesting to note that copies of the questions were provided not just to China but also to the observer States.[334] The same

[332] *South China Sea Arbitration*, Hearing on Jurisdiction, Transcript, Day 1 (7 July 2015), 47, 66–67, 82, 84, 85, 90, https://pcacases.com/web/sendAttach/1399, accessed 19 March 2020; Transcript, Day 2, 14, 23, 25, 32, 55-56, 117, 133, 145-46, 146–48; Hearing on the Merits, Transcript, Day 1 (24 November 2015), 98, https://pcacases.com/web/sendAttach/1547, accessed 19 March 2020; Transcript, Day 2 (25 November 2015), 13–14, 15, 32–33, 34, 34–35, 35–36, 37, 38, 39, 42, 43, 45, 47, 48, 55–56, 69, 70, 81, 88, 96, 134, 136, 145–46, 155, 156, 159, 160, 161, 164, 171, 172, 174, 185, 186, 188, 188–89, 213, https://pcacases.com/web/sendAttach/1548, accessed 27 April 2020; Transcript, Day 3 (26 November 2015), 18–19, 29, 34, 46, https://pcacases.com/web/sendAttach/1549, accessed 13 October 2019.

[333] *South China Sea Arbitration*, Procedural Order No. 4, 4.

[334] Hearing on Jurisdiction, Transcript, Day 3, 1, 81.

procedure was followed during the Hearing on the Merits, except that the number of questions was much higher (25 for counsel, and 34 for the two experts).

The practice of formulating questions after the first round of oral pleadings, to be addressed by the parties in the second round, is not entirely new. At the ICJ, the practice has developed of putting questions to parties at the end of the first round of oral pleadings.[335] As we have seen, one or two Annex VIII arbitral tribunals also adopted the same practice. The procedure adopted in the *South China Sea Arbitration* is novel in that it was adopted in the context of default in response to concerns expressed by the appearing party and it was systematically followed in both the jurisdiction and merits phases of the proceedings.

The first part of this Chapter has already given the reader an idea of the scope of the questions put to the Philippines under Article 25(2) of the Rules of Procedure, answers to which were provided in writing and orally during the two Hearings. The following observations will concentrate on the questions put to the Philippines during the second round of oral pleadings. A few questions referred to issues that China had raised in the Position Paper and in its public statements. For example, the Tribunal asked the Philippines whether it had undertaken an obligation under the 2002 DOC signed by ASEAN and China to resolve their territorial and maritime disputes exclusively by negotiation, as China asserted.[336] The question whether there existed a legal dispute between China and the Philippines with respect to each of the Philippine submissions seems to have been inspired by the view of a German scholar who had argued against the Tribunal's jurisdiction.[337] By the time of the Hearing on Jurisdiction, the Tribunal had already extracted as many questions as it could from China's Position Paper. Consequently, most of the questions put to the Philippines in the second round of oral pleadings, during both Hearings, were questions that the Tribunal had formulated on the assumption that China could have formulated them if it had been present. In other words, the Tribunal was acting as China's de facto counsel.

A couple of examples taken from the second round of each Hearing should suffice to prove the point. On the last day of the Hearing on

[335] Rosenne, *The Law and Practice*, vol. III, 1299.

[336] Hearing on Jurisdiction, Transcript, Day 3, 29, 59.

[337] Ibid., Day 2, 133; Talmon, *The South China Sea Arbitration*, 14–17.

Jurisdiction, the Tribunal, which had to determine whether the optional exception to jurisdiction for military activities applied to China's construction activities in the Spratly Islands, asked the Philippines whether a military activity ceased to be military if it concurrently served non-military purposes.[338] The context for this question was China's oft-repeated assertion that the purpose of the construction activities was civilian, e.g., disaster management. No argument of this kind had been made in China's Position Paper.

For the second round of the Hearing on the Merits, China's Position Paper, which had deliberately avoided discussing the merits of Philippine claims, was not of much use to the Tribunal in formulating questions to be answered by the Philippines. Practically all of the 25 questions put to the Philippines, not to mention the 34 questions put to the experts, in the second round of pleadings were questions formulated by the Tribunal on behalf of China and, in one instance, on behalf of Taiwan. The question relating to Itu Aba was particularly complex, consisting of nearly 1,000 words and separated into six parts. Each part quoted a scientific or legal article on the Spratly Islands or on Itu Abu that suggested that there could be fresh water on Itu Aba, or there could be soil in which food-producing plants might be able to grow. The Philippines was then asked to comment on these statements.[339] The question whether the Philippines was aware of any Chinese statement that contradicted the Philippine assessment of the environmental impact of China's construction activities in the Spratly Islands compelled the Philippines to research over a weekend China's official pronouncements. The Philippines failed to find an EIA; instead, it found a 500-word article by China's State Oceanic Administration ("SOA").[340] The admission in 2018 by the CSIL that China had not undertaken an EIA prior to undertaking construction activities in the Spratly Islands is eloquent proof of the thoroughness of the Philippine research. The irony is that the Philippine research would have served to bolster China's legal contentions if China had indeed carried out an EIA.

This is the appropriate moment to dismiss the criticism directed by the CSIL at the Tribunal, on the grounds that it had "improperly allowed

338 Hearing on Jurisdiction, Transcript, Day 2, 53.

339 Hearing on the Merits, Transcript, Day 3, 14–15.

340 *PAMH*, Annex 821.

the Philippines, many times to submit supplemental evidential materials well beyond reasonable time limits."[341] The CSIL reminds us that for the proper administration of justice, international courts do not generally admit new evidence produced by the parties after the written proceedings are closed. It cites Article 52 of the ICJ Statute and Article 56 of the ICJ Rules of Court, which prohibit the presentation of new evidence after the closure of written proceedings, unless the other party agrees, or the Court considers it necessary in exceptional circumstances. The purposes of these rules are to prevent the party wishing to submit the new documents from springing a surprise on the ICJ and the other party and from prolonging the proceedings.[342] The CSIL acknowledges that under Article 22(4) of the Rules of Procedure of the *South China Sea Arbitration*, the Tribunal was empowered, at any time, to require the parties to produce documents, exhibits, or other evidence but argues that this provision did not allow the Tribunal to deviate from the Convention and general principles of international law. The CSIL objected that the Tribunal permitted, and even requested, the Philippines, to submit supplementary evidence beyond 16 June 2015, the time limit for China's reply to the *SWSP*, which the CSIL considered to be the date of the closure of the written proceedings. It charged the Tribunal with disregarding fairness and impartiality and acting arbitrarily.[343]

The flaw in the CSIL's critique lies in its grudging admission, expressed in five words ("and even requested the Philippines") and never repeated, that the documents were requested by the Tribunal. These were the *Philippines' Annexes cited during Hearing on Jurisdiction*; four volumes of *The Philippines' Supplemental Documents*, submitted prior to the Hearing on the Merits; two volumes of *The Philippines' Annexes cited during Merits Hearing*; and *The Philippines' Written Responses to the Tribunal's November 2015 Question*. All these volumes accompanied responses to

[341] CSIL, "The South China Sea Arbitration Awards," 635.

[342] Rosenne, *The Law and Practice*, vol. III, 1278; James Brown Scott (ed.), *The Project of a Permanent Court of International Justice and Resolutions of the Advisory Committee of Jurists. Report and Commentary* (Washington, D.C.: Carnegie Endowment for International Peace, Division of International Law, 1920), 145–46, https://ia800205.us.archive.org/12/items/cu31924016941142/cu31924016941142.pdf, accessed 18 May 2020.

[343] CSIL, "The South China Sea Arbitration Awards," 635–36, paras. 934, 937, 938–40.

questions put to the Philippines by the Tribunal, prior to and during the two Hearings. They were not documents and evidence spontaneously submitted by the Philippines and permitted by the Tribunal without any decision as to their admissibility. It is hardly an uncommon occurrence, and it can scarcely be objectionable, that when a party answers a question, it supplies documents in support of its answer. A situation of this type was succinctly described by the President of the *Bay of Bengal* Tribunal, responding to a query from one party whether the Tribunal was requesting that the parties seek new evidence in order to answer a question. The President said that since the question raised new issues, the Tribunal did not exclude the possibility that new evidence would be submitted. In his view, such new evidence would be requested evidence.[344] In the *South China Sea Arbitration*, the documents and evidence submitted by the Philippines in the above list clearly fall in the category of "requested evidence."[345]

It should be pointed out that none of the procedural rights of the defaulting State was violated. China received copies of all the materials submitted by the Philippines prior to and during the Hearings as well the daily transcripts of the Hearings. Following the Hearings, China was given the opportunity to comment on the transcripts, which recorded the Philippine responses to the questions put to it prior to and during the Hearings, on the written responses submitted by the Philippines after the Hearings, or on anything that was said during the Hearings.[346] China could have taken advantage of the opportunities afforded to it to raise objections to any of these materials. It chose not to make its views known on any of these matters. The CSIL cannot now invoke fairness and impartiality to criticize the Tribunal, as if the questions had been put to the

[344] *Bay of Bengal Maritime Boundary Arbitration*, Hearing Transcript, Day 4 (13 December 2013), 348, https://pcacases.com/web/sendAttach/391, accessed 11 May 2020.

[345] This explanation is also relevant for Philippine submissions in response to requests for comments on the documents from Taiwan and the C(T)SIL (11 March and 25 April 2016), on the coral reef experts' report (26 April 2016), on the British archival materials (28 April 2016), and on the French archival materials (28 April 2016).

[346] Hearing on Jurisdiction, Transcript, Day 3, 82; Hearing on the Merits, Transcript, Day 4, 206. Needless to say, China was also given the same opportunities as the Philippines to respond to the materials from Taiwan, to the reports of the coral reef and navigational safety experts, and to the UK and French archival materials. China received copies of all the Philippine responses to all these materials.

Philippines and the documents and evidence submitted to the Tribunal behind China's back.

When we turn to the Tribunal's exercise of its power to appoint independent experts, we realize that once more, China neglected to take advantage of the opportunities afforded to it by the Rules of Procedure to communicate its views on procedural decisions made by the Arbitral Tribunal.

B. The Tribunal's Power to Appoint Independent Experts

As mentioned above, the Tribunal's rationale for engaging independent experts and the Tribunal's evaluation of the expert evidence demand a separate chapter. This section will confine itself to the discussion of the procedures for the appointment of independent experts and for the evaluation of their reports by the parties and by the Tribunal. This discussion might appear superfluous had not the CSIL complained that the Tribunal did not disclose the basis on which the coral reef experts were selected and that the coral reef experts' report was not subjected to any rigorous examination by the Tribunal. For some unexplained reason, the CSIL referred exclusively to the coral reef experts, but we may assume that the critique also applies to the expert hydrographer and the navigational safety expert. These critiques ignore the fact that the Rules of Procedure provided procedures for China and the Philippines to express their views on the Tribunal's appointment of the experts, and in particular their qualifications, independence, and impartiality. The CSIL also neglects the fact that the Rules of Procedure did not leave the evaluation of the experts' reports entirely to the Tribunal and provided mechanisms for the parties to evaluate them.

1. The Procedures for the Appointment of Independent Experts

The CSIL found it objectionable that the Tribunal did not disclose the basis or the procedures for selection of the independent experts.[347] It approvingly cites WTO practice, under which the parties are consulted prior to the appointment of experts and specialized international organizations are requested to provide lists of potential experts. The CSIL also refers to Annex VIII of the Convention, under which experts are

[347] CSIL, "The South China Sea Arbitration Awards," 637, para. 944.

to be selected from lists in four fields maintained by specialized international organizations. It recognizes that no such provisions are to be found in Annex VII, but asserts that the procedures for the selection of experts provide for recourse to specialized international organizations.[348] It seems that for the CSIL, Annex VII should first be amended to require recourse to specialized international organizations before any experts can be appointed at all. More importantly, the CSIL fails to realize that the *South China Sea* Tribunal, like Annex VII arbitral tribunals that appointed experts, did seek the views of the parties on the appointment of independent experts and gave them the opportunity to challenge the qualifications, impartiality, and independence of the experts.

The first step taken by the *South China Sea* Tribunal was to seek the views of the Philippines and China on the desirability of appointing experts, a step that was only implicit in the Rules of Procedure. This was the first opportunity for China to express its objections to the appointment of the experts. China believed that its omnibus objection to any and all procedural steps in the *Arbitration*, including the holding of the *Arbitration* itself, dispensed it from the need to object to this particular procedural step.[349] A party's failure to object at this point and to provide specific reasons for the objection would already have deprived it of the right to object *ex post facto* to the appointment of independent experts in proceedings in which both parties appeared before a tribunal. As for the Philippines, when asked by the Tribunal in December 2014 about the utility and timing of the appointment of an expert hydrographer, it believed that it would be "desirable" for the Tribunal to appoint "as soon as convenient a 'knowledgeable, independent, and impartial hydrographer' from whose input 'many issues in dispute... would benefit significantly'."[350] The Philippines went further and indicated the desired qualifications of the expert hydrographer.

Under Article 24(1) of the Rules of Procedure of the *South China Sea Arbitration*, the next steps involved communication of the expert's terms of reference to the parties, the submission by the candidate of a description of his or her qualifications, and a statement of his or her impartiality and independence, and the communication of the candidate's declaration

[348] Ibid., 638, para. 947.

[349] Ibid., 639, para. 947.

[350] Award of 12 July 2016, 18, para. 55.

and statement to the parties.[351] Upon being informed in August 2015 of the name of the proposed expert hydrographer and provided with his terms of reference, curriculum vitae, and declaration of impartiality and independence, the Philippines proposed that the terms of reference make it clear that it was for the Tribunal, and not for the expert, to make any determination as to legal questions, in particular questions on the status of maritime features as islands or rocks under Article 121(3) of the Convention.[352] The Tribunal accepted the clarification.

It seems that when the Tribunal decided in February and April 2016 to appoint coral reef experts and a navigational safety expert, the Tribunal communicated their terms of reference, curriculum vitae, and statements of impartiality and independence at the same time to the parties.[353] This accelerated procedure may be justified by the circumstances—the appointments were made after the closure of the oral proceedings and the Tribunal was already undertaking its deliberation. Nevertheless, there is little doubt that had they chosen to do so, China or the Philippines could not have been stopped from objecting to the appointment of the experts, their terms of reference, their qualifications, and their declaration of independence and impartiality. On these later occasions, the Philippines approved the proposed appointments and made no comments on the experts' terms of reference, qualifications, and declarations of independence and impartiality. On no occasion did China raise objections. The brief explanation of these procedures belies the CSIL's assertion that the procedures for appointment of experts lacked transparency. The CSIL's charge that China was not consulted in the appointment of the independent experts is totally untrue. The CSIL's unfavorable comparison of the Tribunal's practice with that of the WTO, whose panels are said to hear the parties' views on necessity, manner, and other requirements prior to the appointment of the experts, is wholly unjustified.[354]

[351] Identical provisions are to be found in Article 19(1) and (5) of the Rules of Procedure of the *ARA Libertad Arbitration*, in Article 24(1) and (2) of the Rules of Procedure of the *"Arctic Sunrise" Arbitration*, and in Article 19(1) of the Rules of Procedure of the *Antlanto-Scandian Herring Arbitration*. Article 11(3) of the Rules of Procedure of *Guyana v. Suriname* provides only for the communication of the terms of reference to the parties.

[352] Award of 12 July 2016, 19, para. 58.

[353] Ibid., 30–31, paras. 84, 85, 86, 90.

[354] CSIL, "The South China Sea Arbitration Awards," 638, para. 947.

Had there been any questions from the parties regarding the candidates' qualifications, impartiality, and independence, an innovative procedure established by the Rules of Procedure of the *South China Sea Arbitration*, like those of the *ARA Libertad Arbitration*, *"Arctic Sunrise" Arbitration*, and the *Atlanto-Scandian Herring Arbitration*, would have been set in motion. This procedure was absent in the Rules of Procedure of earlier arbitrations under Annex VII of the Convention. Under the Rules of Procedure of the *South China Sea Arbitration*, a party that had any objections to the qualifications, impartiality, or independence of the proposed expert had to inform the Tribunal within a period to be indicated by the Tribunal. The latter would then be under a duty to decide promptly whether to accept any such objection. As there have so far been no challenges to the appointments of experts by Annex VII tribunals, it is not clear what procedure was to be followed by the Tribunal in case objections were raised. Once an expert was appointed, parties could no longer object to his or her qualifications, impartiality, or independence, unless the party became aware of reasons for the objection only after the appointment had been made. The Philippines raised no objections to the qualifications, impartiality, and independence of all the experts proposed by the Tribunal. China did not respond to the Tribunal's repeated requests for comments. In view of this circumstance, there is no reason to take seriously the CSIL's objections to the qualifications, independence, and impartiality of the independent experts once the arbitral proceedings had been completed. To do otherwise would be to grant it more rights than those enjoyed by the appearing State, whose silence at this stage would have barred it from raising objections once the appointment had been made and *a fortiori*, after the arbitral proceedings had been concluded.

Ironically, the Rules of Court of the ICJ, whose practice in *not* appointing experts is the CSIL's model, do not contain any provisions that require it to consult the parties on the appointment of experts and that give the parties the opportunity to object to their qualifications, impartiality, and independence. It is only logical to suppose that the procedures adopted by Annex VII tribunals for the appointment of independent experts, which were similar to those of the *South China*

Sea Arbitration, explain the absence of challenge to the qualifications, independence, or impartiality of the independent experts.[355]

The Rules of Procedure of the *South China Sea Arbitration* are also remarkable for introducing procedures for the evaluation of and possible challenges to the reports of the independent experts.

2. The Procedures for the Evaluation by the Parties of the Independent Experts' Reports

The Rules of Procedure of the *South China Sea Arbitration*, like those of the *ARA Libertad Arbitration*, *"Arctic Sunrise" Arbitration*, and the *Atlanto-Scandian Herring Arbitration*, provided for a two-stage procedure for the parties' evaluation of the opinion of independent experts. Transmittal of the independent experts' opinions and the responses of the parties might facilitate the emergence of a consensus among them. If a consensus failed to emerge, a hearing would be organized during which the parties could question the independent experts and present their own experts. The aim of both stages was to facilitate the emergence of a consensus among the independent experts and the parties on the technical issues dealt with by the independent experts.

Independent experts are appointed to provide expert opinions to a court or tribunal. Their opinion may confirm the expert opinions of one or both parties, or it may offer an opinion different from both. In either scenario, it stands to reason that the parties must be informed of the contents of the expert opinion. Under the Rules of Procedure of the *South China Sea Arbitration*, independent experts' reports were to be transmitted to the parties to give them the opportunity to express their opinions on and objections to the reports.[356] It may be assumed that the parties would then ask their respective experts to evaluate the independent experts' reports. This way of proceeding could identify areas of agreement and disagreement among the independent experts and the parties' experts. If the parties' evaluations of the experts' reports revealed large areas of agreement among the parties' experts and the independent experts, the consensus could assist the Tribunal in its own evaluation

[355] An expert hydrographer was appointed in *Barbados v. Trinidad and Tobago*, a legal expert in *Guyane v. Suriname*, and two experts to assess the reparations due to The Netherlands in the *"Arctic Sunrise" Arbitration*.

[356] Rules of Procedure, Article 24(4), 12.

of the technical issues that were the subject matter of the independent experts' report and provide a sound basis for the Tribunal's decision.

In the *South China Sea Arbitration*, the Tribunal transmitted to the Philippines and China the reports of the coral reef experts and the navigational safety expert. The Philippines had no objections to the reports, because they largely confirmed the conclusions of its own experts. China did not respond to the Tribunal's requests for comments. Yet after the conclusion of the arbitral proceedings, the CSIL cast doubt on the validity of the opinion of the coral reef experts, alleging the hasty manner in which the report was produced.[357] Objections of this type do not deserve to be taken seriously. Otherwise, China would be granted more rights than the appearing State, whose failure to respond to a request for comments would have barred it from subsequently challenging the expert opinion.

The Rules of Procedure in the *South China Sea Arbitration* are remarkable for anticipating a scenario in which a consensus failed to emerge between the experts of one or both of the parties, on the one hand, and the independent experts, on the other.[358] Had a party objected to the independent experts' findings, there would have been a second stage involving the organization of a hearing, upon the request of a party. But it was not just the parties that had the right to request the organization of a hearing. The Tribunal could on its own initiative convene such a hearing. The reason is that for a Tribunal, disagreements between experts would obviously be of no assistance to it in reaching a decision. Faced with a disagreement among experts, the Tribunal could conceivably consider it necessary to hold a hearing, for the purposes of promoting a consensus among the experts or at least narrowing the disagreements among them. The independent experts and the parties would have participated in the hearing, which would have been conducted following the procedure for the examination and cross-examination of experts and witnesses presented by the parties. The parties and their experts would have had the opportunity to examine and cross-examine the independent experts as well as to present their own expert witnesses to testify on the issues that divided the parties and the independent experts. This type of experts' meetings has been widely proposed as a means of reducing, if not entirely eliminating,

[357] CSIL, "The South China Sea Arbitration Awards," 638, para. 947.

[358] Rules of Procedure, Article 24(5), 11.

disagreements among experts. Any agreement that emerged among the experts could serve as the basis for the Tribunal's decision-making.

This second stage is inspired by the WTO practice of organizing oral consultations called "joint meetings," in which the panel hearing a dispute, the independent experts, the parties to the dispute, and the parties' experts participate.[359] The independent experts make statements in which they put forward their primary arguments, outline the main differences between their views and those of the parties' experts, react to the parties' comments on their written opinions, and give oral answers to questions put to them in writing prior to the meeting. The parties then follow up any points made by the experts. A major part of the meetings is devoted to questioning of the independent experts by the parties. The parties' experts may make occasional interventions. At the conclusion of the meeting, the independent experts make closing statements to consider the points they deem the most important. The joint meetings make it possible to explain the concepts, principles, and methods that underlie scientific arguments, improving the understanding of technical issues for all the participants in the meetings.

By providing for the possibility of a second stage inspired by WTO practice, the Rules of Procedure of the *South China Sea Arbitration*, like those of the *ARA Libertad Arbitration*, *"Arctic Sunrise" Arbitration*, and the *Atlanto-Scandian Herring Arbitration*, introduced a major innovation in the practice of international courts. There was no occasion to implement the innovative procedure, given the lack of objections from the Philippines and China's failure to comment on the independent experts' reports. In any event, this recapitulation of the procedures for evaluation by the parties of the expert opinions demonstrates that China was afforded all possible opportunities to object to the independent experts' reports. Its failure to raise objections when given the opportunity to do so deprives it of the right to object to the expert opinions long after the conclusion of the arbitral proceedings.

The only remaining task for this Chapter is the discussion of the Tribunal's exercise of its power to take all appropriate measures in order to establish the facts.

[359] This paragraph is summarized from Caroline E. Foster, *Science and the Precautionary Principle in International Courts and Tribunals: Expert Evidence, Burden of Proof and Finality* (Cambridge: Cambridge University Press, 2011), 116–19.

C. The Tribunal's Exercise of Its Power to Take All Appropriate Measures in Order to Establish the Facts

In the months following the closure of the oral proceedings, the Tribunal in the *South China Sea Arbitration* undertook several fact-finding initiatives that can be justified primarily on the basis of the Tribunal's power to take all appropriate measures in order to establish the facts under Article 22(2) of the Rules of Procedure.[360] As part of its deliberations on the environmental impact of China's island-building activities in the Spratly Islands, the Tribunal did an independent search for Chinese official publications that could have a Hearing on the issues. It found twelve such publications, which it transmitted to China and the Philippines in

[360] Award of 12 July 2016, 29, para. 84.

February 2016 for their comments.[361] This first initiative has gone largely unnoticed by observers.[362] The two subsequent initiatives have attracted more attention, since they formed the basis for the Tribunal's conclusions concerning the status of Itu Abu and other maritime features in the

[361] Ibid., para. 84(a). Two of the documents were compiled by the Philippines in *PAMH*: Annex 820, 5–9, and Annex 821, Statement of the State Oceanic Administration dated 18 June 2015, 11–14. The others were compiled in *RTRC (Annexes 864–892)* (3 March 2016):

1. Annex 864, China State Oceanic Administration, The Guidance for the Assessment of Coastal Marine Ecosystem Health, Marine Industry Standards of the People's Republic of China, No. HY/T 087-2005 (2005), 5–7;
2. Annex 865, China State Oceanic Administration, "2012 Communique [sic] on Marine Environment of China, Part 2: Marine Biodiversity and Ecological Conditions" (1 April 2013), 8–21;
3. Annex 866, China State Oceanic Administration, Code of Practice for Marine Monitoring Technology, Part 5: Marine Ecology, Marine Industry Standards of the People's Republic of China, No. HY/T 147.5-2013 (25 April 2013), 22–24;
4. Annex 867, China State Oceanic Administration, "2013 Communique [sic] on Marine Environment of China, Part 2: Conditions of Marine Ecology" (25 March 2014), 25–36;
5. Annex 868, China State Oceanic Administration, Technical Guidelines for Environmental Impact Assessment of Marine Engineering, National Standards of the People's Republic of China, No. GB/T 19485-2014 (1 April 2014), 37–128;
6. Annex 869, China State Oceanic Administration, South China Sea Branch, "Communique [sic] on the Oceanic Conditions of the South China Seas Region in 2013" (14 August 2014), 129–59;
7. Annex 870, China State Oceanic Administration, "2014 Communique [sic] on Marine Environment of China, Part 2: Conditions of Marine Ecology" (16 March 2015), 160–70;
8. Annex 871, China State Oceanic Administration, South China Sea Branch, "Communique [sic] on the Oceanic Conditions of the South China Sea Region in 2014" (28 May 2015), 171–200;
9. Annex 872, China State Ocean Administration, "Construction Activities at Nansha Reefs Did Not Affect the Coral Reef Ecosystem" (10 June 2015), 201–08, https://files.pca-cpa.org/pcadocs/The%20Philippines%27%20Written%20Responses%20%2811%20March%202016%29%20%28Annexes%20864-892%29.pdf, accessed 3 May 2020.

[362] See *RTRC*, 10–16, paras. 17–42. There is no mention of it in Tara Davenport, "Procedural Issues Arising from China's Non-participation in the *South China Sea Arbitration*," in S. Jayakumar et al. (eds.) *The South China Sea Arbitration: The Legal Dimension* (Cheltenham: Edward Elgar Publishing, 2018), 65–98, or in Jacqueline Joyce F. Espenilla, "Judicial Fact-Finding Initiatives in the *South China Sea Arbitration*," *Asian Journal of International Law* 9 (2019): 20–30.

South China Sea as islands, rocks (islands not entitled to an EEZ and a continental shelf), or low-tide elevations. The Tribunal sought from the UK Hydrographic Office ("UKHO") hydrographic surveys on the South China Sea carried out by the UK Royal Navy and by the Imperial Japanese Navy prior to 1945 and gave the Philippines and China three weeks in April 2016 in which to respond to them.[363] The Tribunal then obtained documents from the *Bibliothèque Nationale de France* (the National Library of France) and from the *Archives Nationales d'Outre-Mer* (the National Overseas Archives), which were transmitted to China and the Philippines in May 2016, barely a month after the submission of the Philippine response on the UKHO materials.[364] The last two independent initiatives (but not the first) provoked the wrath of the CSIL, which charged the Tribunal not only with improperly allowing the Philippines to submit supplemental evidence well beyond written time limits, but also with taking over the burden of proof from the Philippines.[365] The following paragraphs will argue first, that while independent fact-finding by courts is usually limited, cases of default provide a rationale for independent fact-finding, and second, that in the *South China Sea Arbitration*, the Tribunal undertook the first initiative because it was attempting to compensate for China's failure to transmit an EIA to it, and the second and third initiatives, because the Tribunal was pursuing a line of inquiry that did not correspond to the approaches of the Philippines, China, or Taiwan.

1. Independent Fact-Finding by International Courts and Default

While the active role of international courts in fact-finding is well-established in their statutes or rules, there is doubt about the extent

[363] Award of 12 July 2016, 30–31, para. 89(a); *Responses of the Philippines to the Tribunal's 1 April 2016 Request for Comments on Materials from the Archives of the United Kingdom Hydrographic Office* (28 April 2016) ("*RTRC UKHO*"), https://pcacases.com/web/sendAttach/1851, accessed 15 May 2020. The documents are not publicly available, but they are identified in the footnotes of *RTRC UKHO*.

[364] Award of 12 July 2016, 35, para. 99; *Responses of the Philippines to the Tribunal's 26 May 2016 Request for Comments on Materials from the French Archives* (3 June 2016) ("*RTRC French Archival Materials*"), https://pcacases.com/web/sendAttach/1852, accessed 15 May 2020. The documents are listed in the footnotes of the *RTRC French Archival Materials*. Most of the documents obtained from the *Bibliothèque Nationale de France* are accessible to anyone, as the author can testify.

[365] CSIL, "The South China Sea Arbitration Awards," 632, para. 924.

of independent fact-finding that is permitted. Cases of default seem to provide a rationale for fact-finding on its own initiative by an international court.

In the practice of arbitral tribunals since the nineteenth century, their very broad fact-finding powers was already recognized.[366] In the twentieth century, the statutes of some of the most important permanent tribunals, the PCIJ, the ICJ, and the ITLOS, conferred on them the general power to "make all arrangements connected with the taking of evidence."[367] Further provisions of the Statutes or the Rules of these courts specify these arrangements. They enable the court concerned to call upon the parties to produce any document or to supply any explanations, or in the case of the ICJ and the ITLOS, it may itself seek information for this purpose; to entrust any individual or entity with an inquiry or expert opinion; to carry out site visits; to indicate at any time prior to or during the hearing any points or issues to which it would like the parties specially to address themselves, or on which it considers that there has been sufficient argument; to put questions during the hearings to the agents, counsel, advocates, witnesses, and experts; to call during the hearings witnesses and expert on its own initiative; and to request international organizations for information relevant to cases before it.[368]

Whether the scope of international courts' broad powers in matters of evidence, and in particular, the power to seek information on its own or to call during hearings witnesses and experts on its own initiative, encompasses the power to investigate facts on their own initiative is less clear. It is a well-established principle that the burden of proving the facts that a party relies on to support its claim falls on that party; international courts decide cases on the basis of evidence submitted by the parties. A court that attempted to find evidence on its own initiative, which might be in favor of one party or the other, would upset the equality of the parties

[366] Jean-Charles Witenberg, "La théorie des preuves devant les juridictions internationales [The Theory of Evidence Before International Jurisdictions]," *RCADI*, vol. 56 (1936-II), 52.

[367] PCIJ, *Statute*, Article 48, *Statute and Rules of Court*, 1st Edition, Series D. No. 1 (1926), https://www.icj-cij.org/files/permanent-court-of-international-justice/serie_D/D_01_1e_edition.pdf, accessed 3 April 2020; ICJ, *Statute*, Article 48; ITLOS, *Statute*, Article 27.

[368] PCIJ, *Statute*, Articles 49, 50, 51; ICJ, *Statute*, Articles 34, 50, 51, 66; ICJ, *Rules of Court*, Articles 61(1), 61(2) 62(1), 66 69(1); ITLOS, *Rules of the Tribunal*, Articles 57(2), 76(1), 76(2) 77(1), 77(2), 82.

as well as endanger its independence and impartiality.[369] Amerasinghe stresses that in order to preserve impartiality, a judge is not expected to acquire and adduce evidence for or against one of the parties.[370] Implicit recognition of such risks may perhaps be found in the practice of the ICJ, which has never exercised the power to seek evidence on its own or to call witnesses or experts during hearings on its own initiative.

An international court that sought to seek evidence on its own initiative would in all likelihood find that most, if not all, of the evidence, is in the hands of the States parties. The court would be handicapped in its search by the lack of its own investigative body that could act in the territories of States parties to the dispute or of third States.[371] This is not the least of the paradoxes of international justice: No link matching the link between the judiciary and the executive power in domestic legal systems corresponds to the breadth and the gravity of its task.[372]

Thirlway and Devaney have raised the question whether default authorizes an international court to undertake an independent investigation of the facts and evidence.[373] Devaney has identified two apparently contradictory approaches of the ICJ to the question.[374] In the *Corfu Channel Case*, the very first case of default, it stated that Article 53 of the Statute did not compel it to examine the accuracy of the appearing party's submissions in all their details, which might prove impossible in practice.[375] This statement, which was quoted in *United States Diplomatic and Consular Staff in Tehran* and in the *Nicaragua* judgment on the merits, suggests

[369] Amerasinghe, *Evidence*, 148; Markus Benzing, *Das Beweisrecht vor internationalen Gerichten und Schiedsgerichten in zwischenstaatlichen Streitigkeiten* [The Law of Evidence Before International Courts and Arbitral Tribunals in Inter-State Disputes] (Heidelberg: Springer, 2010), 135; W.F. Foster, "Fact Finding and the World Court," *Canadian Yearbook of International Law* 7 (1969): 160.

[370] Amerasinghe, *Evidence*, 34.

[371] Benzing, *Das Beweisrecht*, 21.

[372] Paul Reuter, "La responsabilité internationale: Problèmes choisis (1955–56) [International Responsibility: Selected Problems]," in Paul Reuter, *Le développement de l'ordre juridique international* [The Development of the International Legal Order] (Paris: Éditions Economica, 1995), 520; Benzing, *Das Beweisrecht*, 74.

[373] Thirlway, *Non-appearance*, 123; Devaney, *Fact-Finding*, 117.

[374] This paragraph is based on Devaney, *Fact-finding*, 117.

[375] *Corfu Channel Case, Judgment of December 15th 1949: I.C.J. Reports 1949*, 248, http://www.icj-cij.org/files/case-related/1/001-19491215-JUD-01-00-BI.pdf, accessed 30 March 2020.

that the ICJ did not have to undertake additional fact-finding in order to fulfill its duty under Article 53.[376] In the former case, the Court did not examine more closely the Iranian claim that the hostage problem was a marginal part of an overall problem of US intervention in Iranian domestic affairs for 25 years.[377] A quarter of a century after the decision in the *Corfu Channel Case*, the Court declared in the *Nuclear Tests Cases* that in cases of default, it was "especially incumbent upon the Court to satisfy itself that it is in possession of all the available facts."[378] This statement was reaffirmed in the *Nicaragua Case*, when the Court declared that it was not bound to confine its consideration to the material submitted to it by the appearing State.[379] These later statements suggest that default places a greater fact-finding burden on the Court. In the *Nuclear Tests Cases*, the Court took into consideration public statements made by high officials of the defaulting State after the closure of the oral proceedings. In the *Nicaragua Case* it drew on the material in the public domain, most of which had been submitted by Nicaragua together with its Memorial.[380] In the latter case, Judge Oda warned that Article 53 of the Statute did not mean that the Court was required to establish the facts on its own on behalf of the defaulting State.[381]

In the *South China Sea Arbitration*, the Tribunal did attempt to establish the facts on its own on behalf of the defaulting State, but it also did so in pursuit of a line of inquiry on the status of maritime features that diverged from those of the Philippines, China, and Taiwan.

[376] *United States Diplomatic and Consular Staff in Tehran*, 9, para. 11; *Nicaragua, Merits, Judgment*, 25, para. 30.

[377] Elias, *The International Court of Justice*, 66.

[378] *Nuclear Tests Case (Australia v. France)*, 263–64, paras. 31, 32; *Nuclear Tests Case (New Zealand v. France)*, 468, para 32.

[379] *Nicaragua, Merits, Judgment*, 25, para. 30.

[380] The list of the Nicaraguan materials is annexed to the *Memorial of Nicaragua*, and most are reproduced in *I.C.J. Pleadings, Military and Paramilitary Activities in and against Nicaragua*, vol. V, XII–XIV, 135–458.

[381] *Nicaragua, Merits, Judgment*, Dissenting Opinion of Judge Oda, 245, para. 69, http://www.icj-cij.org/files/case-related/70/070-19860627-JUD-01-08-BI.pdf, accessed 17 May 2020.

2. *The Tribunal's Independent Fact-Finding in the* South China Sea Arbitration

The Tribunal's independent fact-finding in the *South China Sea Arbitration* pursued two aims: it sought to compensate for China's failure to submit an EIA to it, and it sought evidence for its independent line of inquiry relating to the status of maritime features in the South China Sea.

The Tribunal's fact-finding on behalf of China stemmed from the Philippine Submissions No. 11 and 12(b) that China's island-building in the Spratly Islands had violated China's duty under the Convention to preserve and protect the marine environment. The Philippines had presented satellite images of the construction activities at different points in time and submitted two expert reports on the damage to coral reefs as fragile marine ecosystems. Philippine efforts to prove its case were hampered by the inability to investigate conditions on the ground. The Philippines was unable to send scientists to report on these conditions, nor were there any independent observers on which to draw. Its approach relied on drawing "obvious inferences" about the harm that large-scale construction activities cause to fragile coral reefs.[382] The Tribunal, which was not satisfied by this approach, took two steps to assist its fact-finding. Between the two rounds of the Hearing on the Merits, it asked the Philippines whether it was aware of any Chinese statement that contradicted the Philippine assessment of the impact of China's construction activities on the marine environment. As we have seen, it was this question that compelled the Philippines to search for and locate a 500-word SOA statement. Second, approximately two months after the oral hearings, the Tribunal, in addition to asking China if it had carried out an EIA and deciding to appoint the first coral reef expert, took the initiative to search for Chinese materials.[383]

Clearly, had China appeared in the proceedings, or had it responded to the Tribunal's inquiry whether it had carried out an EIA, there would have been no need for the Tribunal to search for Chinese materials that could have been the equivalent of an EIA. For the Tribunal, the alternative to undertaking its own fact-finding and appointing independent experts would have been to adopt the approach described by the ICJ in the *Corfu Channel Case*—acknowledge that it was impossible to prove

[382] Hearing on the Merits, Transcript, Day 4, 19–20.

[383] Award of 12 July 2016, 29, para. 84(a).

the accuracy of all of the details of the Philippine claims and accept them, based on the satellite images and the reports of the Philippine-appointed experts. Such a solution would have left doubt whether China had actually conducted an EIA and would have raised the question whether the Tribunal was fulfilling its duty under Article 9 of Annex VII to satisfy itself that the Philippine claims were well founded in fact. To dispel any doubt and to fulfill its duty under Article 9 of Annex VII, the Tribunal decided to search for Chinese materials on its own. It was not inevitable that the Tribunal's independent fact-finding would place China at a disadvantage, as a Chinese author seems to suggest.[384] Before undertaking its research, the Tribunal could not have been confident that it would not find a Chinese EIA, the discovery of which would have seriously undermined Philippine arguments. As things stood, none of the documents that the Tribunal found on its own amounted, either individually or in aggregate, to an EIA, allowing the Philippines and the Tribunal to conclude that China had violated its obligation to carry out an EIA under Article 206 of the Convention.[385] The thoroughness of the Tribunal's independent fact-finding was confirmed when the CSIL admitted in 2018 that China had not conducted an EIA.[386]

The Tribunal's other fact-finding initiatives were not undertaken on behalf of either China or the Philippines, but in pursuit of an approach to the determination of the status of maritime features that differed markedly from the approaches of China, Taiwan, and the Philippines. It was not inevitable that the outcome of the Tribunal's independent fact-finding on the status of maritime features in the Spratly Islands would confirm the two sets of Philippine submissions. Submissions No. 4 and 6 claimed that Second Thomas Shoal, Mischief Reef, Subi Reef, McKennan Reef (including Hughes Reef), and Gaven Reef, were low-tide elevations—features that were exposed at low tide but covered with water at high tide and as such did not generate entitlements to a territorial sea, EEZ, and continental shelf.[387] Submissions No. 3 and 7 claimed that Scarborough Shoal, Johnson Reef, Cuarteron Reef, and Fiery Cross Reef were "rocks"

[384] Liao Shiping, "Fact-Finding," 17–18. Liao Shiping's statement seems to be based on a misunderstanding of Thirlway, *Non-appearance*, 123.

[385] See the Philippine evaluation of these documents in *RTRC*, 10–16, paras. 17–42.

[386] CSIL, "The South China Sea Arbitration Awards," 592, para. 820.

[387] Convention, Article 13.

within the meaning of Article 121(3) of the Convention—islands with no human habitation or economic life of their own. China, in contrast, claimed that the Spratly Islands as a whole were entitled to an EEZ and a continental shelf. Taiwan argued that Itu Aba was a fully entitled island, possessing an EEZ and a continental shelf.

The Tribunal first set about determining whether all these features were low-tide elevations or high-tide elevations. After having identified the high-tide elevations, it then proceeded to determine whether they were islands or rocks within the meaning of Article 121(3) of the Convention. The Tribunal also examined six other islands in the Spratly Islands (Itu Aba, Thitu, West York Island, Spratly Island, North-East Cay, and South-Est Cay) that were not identified in the Philippine Submissions. The reason for this was that their entitlement (or lack of it) to an EEZ and a continental shelf could decisively influence a Tribunal decision on the Philippine claims that China had prevented it from exercising its sovereign rights over living and non-living resources in the Philippine EEZ and continental shelf and that China had failed to prevent its nationals from exploiting the living resources of the Philippine EEZ.

To determine the status of the maritime features identified in its Submissions as low-tide elevations, islands, or rocks, the Philippines had marshalled evidence from satellite imagery and published nautical charts of the Philippines, China, Malaysia, Vietnam, the US, and the UK. Prior to the Hearing on the Merits the Tribunal had already put questions to the Philippines that in retrospect provided clues to the different approach that it would eventually adopt. This approach also differed from the approach dependent on direct observation of contemporary conditions that was adopted by Taiwan a few months after the Hearing on the Merits to prove that Itu Aba was an island entitled to an EEZ and a continental shelf. In particular, the Tribunal had asked the Philippines whether it had sought hydrographic survey plans undertaken by the UK in the nineteenth century and Japan in the period leading up to World War II. The Philippines had not done so, in view of the "absolute consistency" of the charts and the satellite data.[388]

[388] Hearing on the Merits, Transcript, Day 2, 38; Award of 12 July 2016, 142, para. 331.

In the Award of 12 July 2016, the Tribunal explained the technical reasons for its skepticism regarding satellite imagery.[389] Without explicitly citing Taiwan, it also rejected the approach relying on direct observation to determine the original status of a maritime feature, the reason being that many maritime features in the South China Sea had been subject to substantial human modification. Islands were defined by Article 121(1) of the Convention as "naturally formed" areas of land. It followed that human activity could not change a low-tide elevation into an island,[390] and for that matter, a rock into an island. Such transformations were precisely the object of Chinese and Taiwanese activities in the Spratly Islands. The Tribunal stressed the value for determining the status of features that were remote, subject to the demands of competing States, and carefully surveyed infrequently, of original survey data, prepared by individuals with direct experience and knowledge of the area. This approach was already implicit in the question to the Philippines referred to above.[391] The Philippines failed to realize that the Tribunal was suggesting a different approach and, as a result, it did not undertake any search for original survey data. The Philippine failure compelled the Tribunal to seek independently materials derived from UK and Japanese surveys and from French archival sources, several months after the oral proceedings.[392] As mentioned above, the Tribunal then transmitted these materials to the Philippines and China for their comments. The Philippine responses to the UKHO and French archival materials are among the submissions that the CSIL criticized for allegedly having been permitted after the submission of the *SWSP*.[393] Clearly, the Philippine responses were requested by the Tribunal, not submissions spontaneously made by the Philippines and permitted by the Tribunal, without a decision as to their admissibility. There could be no question of the Tribunal not admitting them. As was probably to be expected by this stage of the

[389] Award of 12 July 2016, 138–40, paras. 322–26. This critique will be discussed in greater detail in the next Chapter.

[390] Ibid., 131–32, para. 306.

[391] The text of the question is not available. One may only deduce that the question had been put to the Philippines by reading the transcript of the Hearing on the Merits. Hearing on the Merits, Transcript, Day 2, 38.

[392] Award of 12 July 2016, 142, para. 331.

[393] CSIL, "The South China Sea Arbitration Awards," 635–36, paras. 934, 937, 938–40.

proceedings, China did not comment on the UK and French archival materials, on which the Tribunal drew for most of its conclusions on the status of maritime features.[394]

The CSIL charged the Tribunal with contravening the basic requirement of the burden of proof, by virtue of which it is the duty of a party to produce the evidence that proves its claim. It accused the Tribunal of abusing its discretion by taking the initiative to seek evidence on its own, taking over the burden of proof that should have been borne by the Philippines, and deciding, based on this evidence, in favor of the Philippines. In its view, if the evidence provided by the Philippines carried no weight, the Tribunal should have decided that the Philippine Submissions were not founded in fact and rejected them.[395] The charge that the Tribunal decided in favor of the Philippines is the easiest to refute. The Tribunal did agree with the Philippines that Mischief Reef, Second Thomas Shoal, and Subi Reef are low-tide elevations (Submission No. 4) and that Scarborough Shoal, Johnson Reef, Cuarteron Reef, and Fiery Cross Reef are rocks, i.e., islands without human habitation and economic life of their own (Submissions No. 3 and 7), as are all the high-tide features in the Spratly Islands, including Itu Abu. As for Gaven Reef (North) and McKennan Reef, the Tribunal declared them to be high-tide features, contrary to the Philippine claim that they were low-tide elevations (Submission No. 6).[396]

The CSIL's first two charges and its conclusion fundamentally misunderstand the context of the Tribunal's independent fact-finding. The Tribunal could have rejected the Philippine submissions without further ado if—and only if—it adopted the same logic underlying the Philippine approach and agreed that satellite imagery and published nautical charts were reliable bases for making determinations on the status of maritime features and it had at its disposal satellite imagery and published charts that contradicted the Philippine claims. Similarly, it could have rejected the Taiwanese arguments outright if it had agreed that direct observation of the contemporary state of a maritime feature was a reliable basis for determining the status of Itu Aba and that it had at its disposal information about Itu Aba's contemporary state that contradicted the

[394] Award of 12 July 2016 142, para. 331.

[395] CSIL, "The South China Sea Arbitration Awards," 632, 634, paras. 923, 924, 931, 932, 933.

[396] Award of 12 July 2016, 154–55, 157–64, paras. 352–54, 359–66.

Taiwanese claims. The Tribunal did not dismiss without further ado the Philippine and Taiwanese arguments because it was following a distinct line of inquiry, one that stressed the importance of original survey data, prepared by individuals with direct experience and knowledge of the area. Through its questions put to the Philippines prior to the Hearing on the Merits, the Tribunal had already suggested that the Philippines investigate such survey data. This suggestion was not picked up by the Philippines, which believed that the satellite imagery and the published nautical charts were more than sufficient to prove its case. Had the Tribunal pursued its independent line of inquiry during the deliberations and rejected the Philippine Submissions on the basis of this line of inquiry, without giving the Philippines the opportunity to make submissions relating to the new materials and the Tribunal's different approach to the issues, the procedural rights of the Philippines would have been violated and the decision would have been a great surprise to the Philippines. It was only proper that the Philippines be informed of the distinct line of inquiry that the Tribunal was following and that it be given the opportunity to make submissions concerning the new materials and the new line of inquiry. Needless to say, China was also informed of this line of inquiry, received copies of the UK and French archival materials, and was given the opportunity to respond to the materials found by the Tribunal—facts that the CSIL conveniently neglected to mention. Lastly, the risk of the Tribunal assuming the burden of proof for the Philippines, a concern also shared by Davenport,[397] was minimal, for it could not have known beforehand whether these materials would confirm the Philippine claims or not. A priori there would have been at least an equal probability that the materials would prove China's and Taiwan's claims.

We may understand the situation better by referring to two ICJ cases of default in which the ICJ adopted lines of inquiry that were distinct from those advocated or pleaded by the parties and that became the basis of its decision. In the *Fisheries Jurisdiction Cases*, the UK and the Federal Republic of Germany ("FRG") had asked the ICJ to declare that Iceland's 50-nautical mile exclusive fisheries zone was without foundation in international law and was invalid, that the exclusive fisheries zone was not opposable to them, and that Iceland was not entitled unilaterally to exclude their fishing vessels from the areas beyond the limits that they had agreed to in a 1961 Exchange of Notes with Iceland and to

[397] Davenport, "Procedural Issues," 97.

impose restrictions on their fishing vessels in such areas.[398] The Court's judgments declared that the exclusive fisheries zone was not opposable to the UK and to the FRG and that Iceland was not entitled unilaterally to exclude their fishing vessels from the areas beyond the agreed limits and to impose restrictions on their fishing vessels in such areas, but the Court did not declare that Iceland's 50-nautical mile exclusive fisheries zone was contrary to international law, as the two States had requested.[399] Several judges criticized the Court for not answering the first question whether Iceland's 50-nautical mile exclusive fisheries zone was contrary to international law.[400] The omission would not have surprised the UK, at least: during the oral proceedings on the merits, one judge had asked it whether the Court could rule on its second and third submissions without ruling on the first. The UK answered in the affirmative.[401] It was the FRG, to whom the same question had not been put, that had cause to be surprised.

In the *Nuclear Tests Cases* both appearing States were caught unawares by the Court's decision. Both had been instructed to submit arguments on jurisdiction and admissibility and had argued at length on these matters in the oral proceedings. Both had the right to expect that the Court's decision would deal with jurisdiction and admissibility.[402] Instead, the Court's decision declared that their claims no longer had any object and that as a result, the Court was not called upon to give a decision.[403] The Court found support for its decision in French public

[398] This paragraph relies heavily on Favoreu, "Les arrêts," 261–62.

[399] *Fisheries Jurisdiction (United Kingdom v. Iceland), Merits, Judgment*, 34, para. 79; *Fisheries Jurisdiction (Federal Republic of Germany v. Iceland), Merits, Judgment*, 205, para.77.

[400] *Fisheries Jurisdiction (United Kingdom v. Iceland), Merits, Judgment*, Dissenting Opinion of Judge Petrén, 151, http://www.icj-cij.org/files/case-related/55/055-19740725-JUD-01-09-BI.pdf, accessed 18 May 2020; Dissenting Opinion of Judge Gros, 128, para. 5; Dissenting Opinion of Judge Onyeama, 165, 171, paras. 1, 16, https://www.icj-cij.org/files/case-related/55/055-19740725-JUD-01-10-BI.pdf, accessed 1 April 2020.

[401] Rt. Hon. Samuel Silkin, Oral Arguments on the Merits, Fifth Public Sitting (25 March 1974), *I.C.J. Pleadings, Fisheries Jurisdiction (United Kingdom v. Iceland)*, vol. I, 45; Argument of Mr. Slynn, Sixth Public Sitting (29 March 1974), 488.

[402] Even a French author concedes this point. Sur, "Les affaires des essais nucléaires," 978.

[403] *Nuclear Tests (Australia v. France), Judgment*, 272, para. 62; *Nuclear Tests (New Zealand v. France), Judgment*, 478, para. 65.

statements, many of them made after the closure of the oral proceedings, which the Court interpreted to mean that France had made a unilateral commitment to cease atmospheric nuclear testing. One cannot but agree with critics that the Court should have informed the appearing States that it had introduced new materials into the proceedings and that it was pursuing a separate, different, and new line of inquiry after the closure of the oral proceedings. Following the Court's instructions, Australia and New Zealand had first presented arguments on jurisdiction and admissibility. By definition, they could not have made submissions and presented arguments during the oral hearings on the French statements, which had been made after the closure of the oral proceedings, and on the new question that the Court was considering during its deliberations. Respect for the procedural rights of Australia and New Zealand would have demanded that they be given the opportunity to present arguments on the French documents and on the different line of inquiry that the Court was pursuing, if necessary, by reopening the oral proceedings.[404]

In the *Fisheries Jurisdiction Cases*, the Court had given an indication to at least one of the appearing States that it was considering a different approach to the latter's submissions; unfortunately, it failed to give the same indication to the other appearing State. Given the nature of the submission concerned, no fact-finding on the part of the Court was required. In the *Nuclear Tests Cases* the Court had taken notice of public statements made by the defaulting State after the closure of the oral proceedings, an act that was tantamount to independent fact-finding. Regrettably, it did not give an indication to the appearing States that it had done so and that it was considering a new line of inquiry. Like the ICJ in the *Fisheries Jurisdiction Cases*, the Tribunal in the *South China Sea Arbitration* realized that a different approach to the assessment of the Philippine claims was necessary and gave an intimation to the parties—the appearing and the defaulting States—that it was adopting a new approach. Unlike the ICJ in these cases, it was compelled to undertake independent fact-finding, by reason of the inability or unwillingness of the appearing State to search for the surveys of the British and Japanese navies. Unlike the ICJ in the *Nuclear Tests Cases*, the Tribunal informed the appearing

404 *Nuclear Tests (Australia v. France), Judgment*, Dissenting Opinion of Judge Sir Garfield Barwick, 391–92; St. J. Macdonald and Hough, "The Nuclear Tests Case Revisited," 354, 357; Juste Ruiz, "Mootness," 365; Sinclair, "Some Procedural Aspects," 348; Elias, *The International Court of Justice*, 105, 117; Thirlway, *Non-appearance*, 152, 178.

and defaulting States of its independent fact-finding and gave them the opportunity to present arguments on the new materials. Seen in this light, the conduct of the Tribunal in the *South China Sea Arbitration* appears exemplary.

The recourse of the Tribunal to independent experts also provides a model to other international courts and tribunals, to which we now turn.

References

1899 Convention for the Pacific Settlement of International Disputes, https://pca-cpa.org/wp-content/uploads/sites/6/2016/01/1899-Convention-for-the-Pacific-Settlement-of-International-Disputes.pdf, accessed 3 April 2020.

1907 Convention for the Pacific Settlement of International Disputes, https://pca-cpa.org/wp-content/uploads/sites/6/2016/01/1907-Convention-for-the-Pacific-Settlement-of-International-Disputes.pdf, accessed 3 April 2020.

Aegean Sea Continental Shelf. Judgment. I.C.J. Reports 1978, 3–45, http://www.icj-cij.org/files/case-related/62/062-19781219-JUD-01-00-BI.pdf, accessed 17 March 2020.

———. Oral Arguments on Jurisdiction. *I.C.J. Pleadings*, *Aegean Sea Continental Shelf (Greece v. Turkey)*, 293–498, https://www.icj-cij.org/files/case-related/62/062-19781009-ORA-01-00-BI.pdf, accessed 20 March 2020.

Aguas Provinciales de Santa Fe S.A., Suez, Sociedad General de Aguas de Barcelona S.A. and InterAguas Servicios Integrales del Agua S.A. v. Argentine Republic. ICSID Case No. ARB/03/17. Order in Response to a Petition for Participation as Amicus Curiae (17 March 2006), https://www.italaw.com/sites/default/files/case-documents/ita0803.pdf, accessed 30 April 2020.

Akl, Joseph. "L'amélioration des méthodes de travail du Tribunal international du droit de la mer [The Improvement of the Working Methods of the International Tribunal for the Law of the Sea]." *The Contribution of the International Tribunal for the Law of the Sea to the Rule of Law: 1996–2016*, 230–39. Leiden: Brill/Nijhoff, 2018.

Amerasinghe, Chittaranjan F. *Evidence in International Litigation*. Leiden: Martinus Nijhoff Publishers, 2005.

Anderson, David. "Article 76." *The Rules of the International Tribunal for the Law of the Sea: A Commentary*, 217–18. Eds. P. Chandrasekhara Rao and Philippe Gautier. Leiden: Martinus Nijhoff Publishers, 2006.

Antonietti, Aurélia. "The 2006 Amendments to the ICSID Rules and Regulations and the Additional Facility Rules." *ICSID Review* 21 (2006): 427–48.

The ARA Libertad Arbitration (Argentina v. Ghana). Rules of Procedure (31 July 2013), https://pcacases.com/web/sendAttach/427, accessed 12 May 2020.

Arangio-Ruiz, Gaetano. "Non-appearance Before the International Court of Justice. Final Report." *Annuaire de l'Institut de droit international* [Yearbook of the Institute of International Law]. Session de Bâle [Basel Session], 64-I (1991), 280–339, http://www.gaetanoarangioruiz.it/publications/non-appearance-before-the-international-court-of-justice/, accessed 13 October 2019.

———. "Notes on Non-appearance Before the International Court of Justice." *Le droit international à l'heure de sa codification. Études en l'honneur de Roberto Ago* [International Law at the Time of Its Codification. Studies in Honour of Roberto Ago]. Vol. II. *Les différends entre États et la responsabilité* [Inter-State Disputes and Responsibility], 3–48. Milano: Dott. A. Giuffrè Editore, 1987.

"Arctic Sunrise" (Kingdom of The Netherlands v. Russian Federation). Provisional Measures. Order of 22 November 2013. ITLOS Reports 2013, 230–53, https://www.itlos.org/fileadmin/itlos/documents/cases/case_no.22/published/C22_Order_221113.pdf, accessed 30 April 2020.

"Arctic Sunrise" Arbitration (Kingdom of The Netherlands v. Russian Federation). Award on the Merits (14 August 2015), https://pcacases.com/web/sendAttach/1438, accessed 17 March 2020.

———. Rules of Procedure (17 March 2014), https://pcacases.com/web/sendAttach/1317, accessed 29 April 2020.

Asia-Pacific Institute of International Law. *Amicus Curiae Brief to the Arbitral Tribunal on the South China Sea Arbitration* (6 June 2016), http://www.fredkan.com/mavista/upload/File/APIIL%20Amicus%20curiae%20brief%20&%20Appendix%20(1).pdf, accessed 21 January 2020.

The Atlanto-Scandian Herring Arbitration (The Kingdom of Denmark in respect of the Faroe Islands v. The European Union). Rules of Procedure (15 March 2014), https://pcacases.com/web/sendAttach/305, accessed 12 May 2020.

Barbados v. Trinidad and Tobago. Rules of Procedure (23 August 2004), https://pcacases.com/web/sendAttach/1062, accessed 11 May 2020.

———. Transcript, Day 5 (24 October 2005), https://pcacases.com/web/sendAttach/1104, accessed 10 May 2020.

Bastin, Lucas. "*Amici Curiae* in Investor-State Arbitration: Eight Recent Trends." *Arbitration International* 30 (2014): 125–44.

Bay of Bengal Maritime Boundary Arbitration Between Bangladesh and India. Hearing Transcript, Day 1 (9 December 2013), https://pcacases.com/web/sendAttach/388, accessed 11 May 2020.

———. Hearing Transcript, Day 4 (13 December 2013), https://pcacases.com/web/sendAttach/391, accessed 11 May 2020.

———. Rules of Procedure (08 October 2009), http://www.pcacases.com/web/sendAttach/375, accessed 11 May 2020.

Bedjaoui, Mohammed. "L'égalité des États dans le procès international, un mythe [Equality of States in International Judicial Proceedings, A Myth?]?"

Le procès international [International Judicial Proceedings]. *Liber Amicorum Jean-Pierre Cot*, 1–27. Bruxelles: Établissements Émile Bruylant, 2009.

Bennouna, Mohamed. "Experts Before the International Court of Justice: What For?" *Journal of International Dispute Settlement* 9 (2018): 345–51.

Benzing, Markus. *Das Beweisrecht vor internationalen Gerichten und Schiedsgerichten in zwischenstaatlichen Streitigkeiten* [The Law of Evidence Before International Courts and Arbitral Tribunals in Inter-State Disputes]. Heidelberg: Springer, 2010.

Bernhard von Pezold and Others v. Republic of Zimbabwe. ICSID Case No. ARB/10/15. Procedural Order No. 2 (26 June 2012), https://www.italaw.com/sites/default/files/case-documents/ita1044.pdf, accessed 1 May 2020.

Bettati, Mario. "L'affaire du plateau continental de la Mer Egée devant la Cour internationale de Justice — Compétence (arrêt du 19 décembre 1978) [The Case of the Aegean Sea Continental Shelf Before the International Court of Justice – Jurisdiction (Judgment of 19 December 1978)]." *Annuaire français de droit international* [French Yearbook of International Law] 24 (1978): 303–20, http://www.persee.fr/doc/afdi_0066-3085_1978_num_24_1_2099, accessed 8 September 2020.

Biwater Gauff (Tanzania) Ltd. v. United Republic of Tanzania. ICSID Case No. ARB/05/22. Procedural Order No. 5 (2 February 2007), https://www.italaw.com/sites/default/files/case-documents/ita0091_0.pdf. accessed 7 May 2020.

Boas, Gideon et al. *International Criminal Law Practitioner Library*. Vol. III. *International Criminal Procedure*. Cambridge: Cambridge University Press, 2011.

Bouvier, John. *Bouvier's Law Dictionary and Concise Encyclopedia*. Vol. I. Kansas City, MO: Vernon Law Book Company, 1914, https://ia800201.us.archive.org/3/items/cu31924022836229/cu31924022836229.pdf, accessed 3 May 2020.

Bowett, D.W. "Contemporary Developments in Legal Techniques in the Settlement of Disputes." *Recueil des Cours de l'Académie de droit international de La Haye* [Collected Courses of the Hague Academy of International Law]. Vol. 180 (1983-II), 169–235.

Butler, Nicolette. "Non-disputing Party Participation in ICSID Disputes: *Faux Amici*?" *Netherlands International Law Review* 66 (2019): 143–78.

Carty, Anthony. "The South China Sea Disputes Are Not Yet Justiciable." *Arbitration Concerning the South China Sea: Philippines Versus China*, 23–51. Eds. Shicun Wu and Keyuan Zou. London: Routledge, 2016.

Chagos Marine Protected Area Arbitration (Mauritius v. United Kingdom). Hearing Transcript, Day 2 (23 April 2014), https://pcacases.com/web/sendAttach/1572, accessed 12 May 2020.

———. Rules of Procedure (29 March 2012), https://pcacases.com/web/sendAttach/1567, accessed 14 January 2020.

Chang Yen-Chiang. "How Does the [sic] Amicus Curiae Submission Affect a Tribunal [sic] Decision?" *Leiden Journal of International Law* 30 (2017): 647–60.

China, People's Republic of. Ministry of Foreign Affairs. *Foreign Ministry Spokesperson Hong Lei's Regular Press Conference* (21 December 2015), http://www.fmprc.gov.cn/mfa_eng/xwfw_665399/s2510_665401/t1326449.shtml, accessed 3 May 2020.

Chinese Society of International Law. "The South China Sea Arbitration Awards: A Critical Study." *Chinese Journal of International Law* 17 (2018): 207–748.

Chinese (Taiwan) Society of International Law. *Amicus Curiae Submission by the Chinese (Taiwan) Society of International Law to the PCA in the Matter of the Arbitration Between the Republic of the Philippines and the People's Republic of China* (25 March 2016), http://csil.org.tw/home/wp-content/uploads/2016/03/SCSTF-Amicus-Curiae-Brief-final.pdf, accessed 30 April 2020.

Convention on Biological Diversity (CBD). Signed at Rio de Janeiro on 5 June 1992. Entered into force on 29 December 1993, https://www.cbd.int/doc/legal/cbd-en.pdf, accessed 29 April 2020.

Convention on the Settlement of Investment Disputes Between States and Nationals of Other States. Done at Washington, D.C. Entered into force on 14 October 1966, https://icsid.worldbank.org/en/Documents/resources/2006%20CRR_English-final.pdf, accessed 1 May 2020.

———. *Rules of Procedure for Arbitration Proceedings (Arbitration Rules)*, https://icsid.worldbank.org/en/Documents/resources/2006%20CRR_English-final.pdf, accessed 1 May 2020.

Corfu Channel Case. Judgment of December 15th 1949: I.C.J. Reports 1949, 244–65, http://www.icj-cij.org/files/case-related/1/001-19491215-JUD-01-00-BI.pdf, accessed 30 March 2020.

Council of Europe. European Court of Human Rights. *European Convention on Human Rights*, https://www.echr.coe.int/Documents/Convention_ENG.pdf, accessed 23 December 2019.

Coussirat-Coustère, Vincent. "L'arrêt de la Cour internationale de Justice sur le personnel diplomatique américain à Téhéran [The Judgment of the International Court of Justice on American Diplomatic Staff in Teheran]." *Annuaire français de droit international* [French Yearbook of International Law] 26 (1980): 201–24, https://www.persee.fr/doc/afdi_0066-3085_1980_num_26_1_2388, accessed 20 March 2020.

Crema, Luigi. "Testing *Amici Curiae* in International Law: Rules and Practice." *Italian Yearbook of International Law* 22 (2013): 91–132.

Davenport, Tara. "Procedural Issues Arising from China's Non-participation in the *South China Sea Arbitration*." *The South China Sea Arbitration: The*

Legal Dimension, 65–98. Eds. S. Jayakumar et al. Cheltenham: Edward Elgar Publishing, 2018.

Devaney, James Gerard. *Fact-Finding Before the International Court of Justice*. Cambridge: Cambridge University Press, 2016.

Dumberry, Patrick. "The Admissibility of *Amicus Curiae* Briefs by NGOs in Investors-States Arbitration: The Precedent Set by the Methanex Case in the Context of NAFTA Chapter 11 Proceedings." *Non-state Actors and International Law* 1 (2001): 201–14.

Eades, Mark C. "Shell Game: China Plays Legal Trick to Delay Ruling." *Foreign Policy*, 24 June 2016, https://foreignpolicyblogs.com/2016/06/24/china-legal-trick-south-sea-ruling/, accessed 3 May 2020.

Eisemann, Pierre-Michel. "L'arrêt de la CIJ dans l'affaire des activités militaires et paramilitaires au Nicaragua et contre celui-ci (Nicaragua c. Etats-Unis) (fond) arrêt du 27 juin 1986 [The Judgment of the ICJ in the Military and Paramilitary Activities in and against Nicaragua Case (Nicaragua v. United States), Merits, Judgment of 27 June 1986]." *Annuaire français de droit international* [French Yearbook of International Law] 32 (1986): 153–91, http://www.persee.fr/doc/afdi_0066-3085_1986_num_32_1_2714, accessed 22 April 2020.

———. "Les effets de la non-comparution devant la Cour internationale de Justice [The Effects of Non-appearance Before the International Court of Justice]." *Annuaire français de droit international* [French Yearbook of International Law] 19 (1973): 351–75, https://www.persee.fr/docAsPDF/afdi_0066-3085_1973_num_19_1_2217.pdf, accessed 23 March 2020.

El-Hosseny Farouk, and Ezequiel H. Vetulli. "Amicus Acceptance and Relevance: The Distinctive Example of Philip Morris v. Uruguay." *Netherlands International Law Review* 64 (2017): 73–94.

Elias, Taslim O. *The International Court of Justice and Some Contemporary Problems. Essays on International Law*. Dordrecht: Springer Science+Business Media, 1983.

Espenilla, Jacqueline Joyce F. "Judicial Fact-Finding Initiatives in the *South China Sea Arbitration*." *Asian Journal of International Law* 9 (2019): 20–30.

European Court of Human Rights. Registry of the Court. *Rules of Court*. Strasburg: Registry of the Court, 2019, https://www.echr.coe.int/Documents/Rules_Court_ENG.pdf, accessed 1 May 2020.

Favoreu, Louis. "Les arrêts de la Cour Internationale de Justice relatifs à la compétence en matière de pêcheries (Royaume-Uni c/ Islande et République fédérale d'Allemagne c. Islande — Arrêts du 25 juillet 1974) [The Judgments of the International Court of Justice on Fisheries Jurisdiction (United Kingdom v. Iceland and Federal Republic of Germany v. Iceland – Judgments of 25 July 1974]." *Annuaire français de droit international* [French Yearbook of International Law] 20 (1974): 253–85, http://www.persee.fr/doc/afdi_0066-3085_1974_num_20_1_2271, accessed 17 March 2020.

Fisheries Jurisdiction (Federal Republic of Germany v. Iceland). Merits. Judgment. I.C.J. Reports 1974, 175–216, http://www.icj-cij.org/files/case-related/56/056-19740725-JUD-01-00-BI.pdf, accessed 17 March 2020.

Fisheries Jurisdiction (United Kingdom v. Iceland). Merits. Judgment. I.C.J. Reports 1974, 3–44, https://www.icj-cij.org/files/case-related/55/055-19740725-JUD-01-00-BI.pdf, accessed 17 March 2020.

———. Dissenting Opinion of Judge Gros. *I.C.J. Reports 1974*, 126–49, https://www.icj-cij.org/files/case-related/55/055-19740725-JUD-01-08-BI.pdf, accessed 11 August 2019.

———. Dissenting Opinion of Judge Onyeama. *I.C.J. Reports 1974*, 164–73, https://www.icj-cij.org/files/case-related/55/055-19740725-JUD-01-10-BI.pdf, accessed 1 April 2020.

———. Dissenting Opinion of Judge Petrén. *I.C.J. Reports 1974*, 150–63, http://www.icj-cij.org/files/case-related/55/055-19740725-JUD-01-09-BI.pdf, accessed 18 May 2020.

———. Oral Arguments on the Jurisdiction of the Court. *I.C.J. Pleadings, Fisheries Jurisdiction (United Kingdom v. Iceland)*. Vol. I, 241–63, https://www.icj-cij.org/files/case-related/55/055-19730105-ORA-01-00-BI.pdf, accessed 7 October 2019.

———. Oral Proceedings on the Merits. *I.C.J. Pleadings, Fisheries Jurisdiction*. Vol. I, 436–518, http://www.icj-cij.org/files/case-related/55/055-19740325-ORA-01-00-BI.pdf, accessed 22 April 2020.

Fitzmaurice, Gerald. "The Problem of the 'Non-appearing' Defendant Government." *British Yearbook of International Law* 51 (1980): 89–122.

Foster, Caroline E. *Science and the Precautionary Principle in International Courts and Tribunals: Expert Evidence, Burden of Proof and Finality*. Cambridge: Cambridge University Press, 2011.

Foster, W.F. "Fact Finding and the World Court." *Canadian Yearbook of International Law* 7 (1969): 150–91.

Framework Convention on Tobacco Control. Done at Geneva on 21 May 2003. Entered into force on 27 February 2005, https://apps.who.int/iris/rest/bitstreams/50793/retrieve, accessed 12 May 2022

Gau, Michael Sheng-ti. "The Sino-Philippine Arbitration on the South China Sea Disputes and the Taiwan Factor." *Journal of East Asia and International Law* 9 (2016): 479–96.

Greenberg, Jacob. "ICSID Tribunal Orders Zimbabwe to Return Expropriated Farms. Bernhard von Pezold and others v. Zimbabwe, ICSID Case No.

ARB/10/15." *Investment Treaty News*, 16 May 2016, https://www.iisd.org/itn/2016/05/16/icsid-tribunal-orders-zimbabwe-to-return-expropriated-farms-bernhard-von-pezold-and-others-v-zimbabwe-icsid-case-no-arb-10-15-jacob-greenberg/, accessed 1 May 2020.

Grisel, Florian, and Jorge E. Viñuales. "L'amicus curiae dans l'arbitrage d'investissement [Amicus curiae in Investment Arbitration]." *ICSID Review* 22 (2007): 380–432.

Guyana v. Suriname. Rules of Procedure (24 February 2004), http://www.pcacases.com/web/sendAttach/882, accessed 11 May 2020.

Hennebel, Ludovic. "Le rôle des *amici curiae* devant la Cour européenne des droits de l'homme [The Role of *amici curiae* Before the European Court of Human Rights]." *Revue trimestrielle des droits de l'homme* [Trimestral Journal of Human Rights] 71 (2007): 641–68.

Highet, Keith. "Nonappearance and Disappearance Before the international Court of Justice." *American Journal of International Law* 81 (1987): 237–54.

Hsiao, Anne Hsiu-An. "The South China Sea Arbitration and Taiwan's Claim: Legal and Political Implications." *Journal of Chinese Political Science* 22 (2017): 211–28.

Institut de droit international [Institute of International Law]. Session de Bâle [Basel Session]. *Non-appearance Before the International Court of Justice* (1991), https://www.idi-iil.org/app/uploads/2017/06/1991_bal_01_en.pdf, accessed 16 March 2020.

International Court of Justice. *Rules of Court, adopted on 14 April 1978 and entered into force on 1 July 1978*, https://www.icj-cij.org/en/rules, accessed 22 March 2020.

International Criminal Court. *Rules of Procedure and Evidence.* ICC Doc. 10ICC-ASP/1/3 (2002), https://www.icc-cpi.int/iccdocs/pids/legal-texts/rulesprocedureevidenceeng.pdf, accessed 4 May 2020.

International Criminal Tribunal for the Former Yugoslavia. *Rules of Procedure and Evidence.* UN Doc. IT/32/Rev.50 (8 July 2015), https://www.icty.org/x/file/Legal%20Library/Rules_procedure_evidence/IT032Rev50_en.pdf, accessed 4 May 2020.

International Criminal Tribunal for Rwanda. *Rules of Procedure and Evidence* (13 May 2015), https://unictr.irmct.org/sites/unictr.org/files/legal-library/150513-rpe-en-fr.pdf, accessed 4 May 2020.

International Tribunal for the Law of the Sea. *Rules of the Tribunal (ITLOS/8), as adopted on 28 October 1997 and amended on 15 March 2001, 21 September 2001, 17 March 2009 and 25 September 2018*, https://www.itlos.org/fileadmin/itlos/documents/basic_texts/Itlos_8_E_25.09.18.pdf, accessed 29 April 2020.

Johnson, Lise. "Argentina on the Hook for Breach of Fair and Equitable Treatment. Suez, Sociedad General de Aguas de Barcelona S.A., and Vivendi Universal v. Argentine Republic (ICSID Case No. ARB/03/19)." *Investment Treaty News*, 23 September 2010, https://www.iisd.org/itn/2010/09/23/awards-and-decisions/, accessed 8 May 2020.

Juste Ruiz, José. "Mootness in International Adjudication: The Nuclear Tests Cases." *German Yearbook of International Law* 20 (1977): 358–74.

Kochevar, Steven. "Amici Curiae in Civil Law Jurisdictions." *Yale Law Journal* 122 (2013): 1652–69, http://www.yalelawjournal.org/pdf/1158_hvj33ruz.pdf, accessed 30 April 2020.

Krislov, Samuel. "The Amicus Curiae Brief: From Friendship to Advocacy." *Yale Law Journal* 72 (1963): 694–721.

Ku, Julian. "Short, Quick Take on the Philippines' Sweeping Victory in the South China Sea Arbitration." *Lawfare*, 12 July 2016, https://www.lawfareblog.com/short-quick-take-philippines-sweeping-victory-south-china-sea-arbitration, accessed 23 April 2020.

Kuok, Lynn. *Tides of Change: Taiwan's Evolving Position in the South China Sea and Why Other Actors Should Take Notice*. Washington, D.C.: Center for East Asia Policy Studies, Brookings Institution, 2015, https://www.brookings.edu/wp-content/uploads/2016/06/taiwan-south-china-sea-kuok-paper.pdf, accessed 15 March 2020.

Lamb, Sophie et al. "Recent Developments in the Law and Practice of Amicus Briefs in Investor-State Arbitration." *Indian Journal of Arbitration Law* 5 (2017): 72–92, http://ijal.in/sites/default/files/IJAL%20Volume%205_Issue%202_Sophie%20Lamb%20et%20al.pdf, accessed 5 May 2020.

Lauterpacht, Hersch. *The Development of International Law by the International Court*. New York: Frederick A. Praeger Publishers, 1958.

Leary, Thomas. "Non-disputing Parties and Human Rights in Investor-State Arbitration." *Journal of World Investment and Trade* 18 (2017): 1062–72.

Lee, Wei-chin. "Taiwan, the South China Sea Dispute, and the 2016 Arbitration Decision." *Journal of Chinese Political Science* 22 (2017): 229–50.

Levine, Eugenia. "Amicus Curiae in International Investment Arbitration: The Implications of an Increase in Third-Party Participation." *Berkeley Journal of International Law* 29 (2011): 200–24, https://pdfs.semanticscholar.org/d6e6/9224c67a9828ed4b999d0ddc0edac2a8eaad.pdf?_ga=2.78278035.622179642.1588227597-515656435.1588227597, accessed 30 April 2020.

Levine, Judith, and Garth L. Schofield. "Navigating Uncharted Procedural Waters in a Rising Sea of Cases at the Permanent Court of Arbitration." *Stress Testing the Law of the Sea: Dispute Resolution, Disasters and Emerging Challenges*, 95–149. Eds. Stephen Minas and H. Jordan Diamond. Leiden: Brill Nijhoff, 2018.

Liao Shiping. "Fact-Finding in Non-appearance Before International Courts and Tribunals." Unpublished ms., Beijing Normal University, 2018, https://ssrn.com/abstract=3187971, accessed 22 March 2020.

Macaraig, Ayee. "PH Lawyer: We Can 'Demolish' China's Arguments." *Rappler*, 21 January 2015, https://www.rappler.com/nation/78464-reichler-statement-scs-developments, accessed 23 April 2020.

McWhinney, Edward. "International Law-Making and the Judicial Process: The World Court and the French Nuclear Tests Case." *Syracuse Journal of International Law and Commerce* 3 (1975): 9–46, https://surface.syr.edu/cgi/viewcontent.cgi?article=1033&context=jilc, accessed 1 April 2020.

Makinen, Julie. "U.S. Lawyer Who Led Philippines' Case Says Beijing's Boycott Made His Job Harder in South China Sea Arguments." *Los Angeles Times*, 12 July 2016, https://www.latimes.com/world/asia/la-fg-south-china-sea-lawyer-20160712-snap-story.html, accessed 21 April 2020.

Mann, Howard. "Methanex v. United States." *Investment Treaty News*, 18 October 2018, https://www.iisd.org/itn/2018/10/18/methanex-v-united-states/, accessed 1 May 2020.

———. "Opening the Doors, at Least a Little: Comment on the Amicus Decision in Methanex v. United States." *Review of European Community and International Environmental Law* 10 (2001): 241–44.

Martin, Pierre-Marie. "L'affaire de la compétence en matière de pêcheries (les arrêts de la C.I.J. du 2 février 1973) [The Fisheries Jurisdiction Cases (The I.C.J. Judgments of 2 February 1973)]." *Revue générale de droit international public* [General Journal of Public International Law] 78 (1974): 435–58.

Methanex Corporation v. United States. Decision of the Tribunal on Petitions from Third Persons to Intervene as Amici Curiae of 15 January 2001, https://www.italaw.com/sites/default/files/case-documents/ita0517_0.pdf, accessed 1 May 2020.

Military and Paramilitary Activities in and against Nicaragua (Nicaragua v. United States of America). Jurisdiction of the Court and Admissibility of the Application. Counter-Memorial of the United States of America (17 August 1984). *I.C.J. Pleadings, Military and Paramilitary Activities in and against Nicaragua*. Vol. II. https://www.icj-cij.org/files/case-related/70/9627.pdf, accessed 26 April 2020.

———. *Memorial of Nicaragua (Merits). I.C.J. Pleadings, Military and Paramilitary Activities in and against Nicaragua*. Vol. IV, https://www.icj-cij.org/files/case-related/70/9619.pdf, accessed 24 April 2020.

———. *Merits. Judgment. I.C.J. Reports 1986*, 14–150, http://www.icj-cij.org/files/case-related/70/070-19860627-JUD-01-00-BI.pdf, accessed 17 March 2020.

———. Dissenting Opinion of Judge Oda. *I.C.J. Reports 1986*, 212–58, http://www.icj-cij.org/files/case-related/70/070-19860627-JUD-01-08-BI.pdf, accessed 17 May 2020.

———. Dissenting Opinion of Judge Schwebel. *I.C.J. Reports 1986*, 259–527, http://www.icj-cij.org/files/case-related/70/070-19860627-JUD-01-09-BI.pdf, accessed 31 March 2020.

———. Oral Hearings on the Merits. *I.C.J. Pleadings, Military and Paramilitary Activities in and against Nicaragua*. Vol. V, 3–241, https://www.icj-cij.org/files/case-related/70/070-19850912-ORA-01-00-BI.pdf, accessed 17 March 2020.

Mosk, Richard M. "The Role of Facts in International Dispute Resolution." *Recueil des cours de l'Académie de droit international de La Haye* [Collected Courses of the Hague Academy of International Law]. Vol. 304 (2003-IV), 9–179.

Mosler, Hermann. "Nichtteilnahme einer Partei am Verfahren vor dem Internationalen Gerichtshof [Non-participation of a Party in Proceedings Before the International Court of Justice]." *Staatsrecht – Völkerrecht – Europarecht. Festschrift für Hans-Jürgen Schlochauer* [Constitutional Law – International Law – European Law. Festschrift for Hans-Jürgen Schlochauer], 439–56. Ed. Ingo von Münch. Berlin: Walter de Gruyter, 1981.

MOX Plant Case (Ireland v. United Kingdom). Rules of Procedure (25 October 2001), https://pcacases.com/web/sendAttach/848, accessed 12 May 2020.

The M/V "SAIGA" (No. 2) Case (Saint Vincent and the Grenadines v. Guinea). Judgment of 1 July 1999, 10–76, https://www.itlos.org/fileadmin/itlos/documents/cases/case_no_2/published/C2-J-1_Jul_99.pdf, accessed 27 January 2020.

NAFTA Free Trade Commission. *Statement on Non-disputing Party Participation* (7 October 2003), http://www.sice.oas.org/tpd/nafta/commission/nondispute_e.pdf, accessed 1 May 2020.

Nuclear Tests (Australia v. France). Judgment. I.C.J. Reports 1974, 253–74, https://www.icj-cij.org/files/case-related/58/058-19741220-JUD-01-00-BI.pdf, accessed 1 April 2020.

———. Dissenting Opinion of Judge Sir Garfield Barwick. *I.C.J. Reports 1974*, 391–455, http://www.icj-cij.org/files/case-related/58/058-19741220-JUD-01-09-BI.pdf, accessed 1 April 2020.

———. "L'ambassadeur de France aux Pays-Bas au Greffier [The French Ambassador to The Netherlands to the Registrar] (16 May 1973)." *I.C.J. Pleadings, Nuclear Tests (Australia v. France)*. Vol. I, 347–57, https://www.icj-cij.org/files/case-related/58/11007.pdf, accessed 24 April 2020.

———. *Memorial on Jurisdiction and Admissibility submitted by the Government of Australia* (23 November 1973). *I.C.J. Pleadings, Nuclear Tests Cases*

(Australia v. France). Vol. I, 249–380, http://www.icj-cij.org/files/case-related/58/9443.pdf, accessed 28 April 2020.

Nuclear Tests (New Zealand v. France). Judgment. I.C.J. Reports 1974, 457–78, https://www.icj-cij.org/files/case-related/59/059-19741220-JUD-01-00-BI.pdf, accessed 19 March 2020.

Oellers-Frahm, Karin. "Die Entscheidung des Internationalen Gerichtshofes im griechisch-türkischen Streit um die Festlandsockel in der Äegaeis [The Judgment of the International Court of Justice in the Greco-Turkish Dispute on the Continental Self in the Aegean]." *Archiv des Völkerrechts* [Archive of International Law] 18 (1980): 377–92.

Permanent Court of International Justice. *Statute and Rules of Court*, 1st Edition. Series D. No. 1 (1926), https://www.icj-cij.org/files/permanent-court-of-international-justice/serie_D/D_01_1e_edition.pdf, accessed 3 April 2020.

Philip Morris Brands Sàrl, Philip Morris Products S.A. and Abal Hermanos S.A. v. Oriental Republic of Uruguay. ICSID Case No. ARB/10/7. Award (8 July 2016), https://www.italaw.com/sites/default/files/case-documents/italaw7417.pdf, accessed 1 May 2020.

———. Procedural Order No. 3 (17 February 2015), https://www.italaw.com/sites/default/files/case-documents/italaw4161.pdf, accessed 23 January 2020.

Reichler, Paul S., and Yuri B. Parkhomenko. "*Nicaragua v. United States* and Matters of Evidence Before the International Court of Justice." *Nicaragua Before the International Court of Justice. Impacts on International Law*, 43–58. Eds. Edgardo Sobenes Obregón and Benjamin Samson. Cham, Switzerland: Springer International Publishing AG, 2018.

Republic of China (Taiwan). *Position Paper on ROC South China Sea Policy* (21 March 2016), http://multilingual.mofa.gov.tw/web/web_UTF-8/South/Position%20Paper%20on%20ROC%20South%20China%20Sea%20Policy.pdf, accessed 4 May 2020.

———. Mainland Affairs Council. *President Ma's Remarks at International Press Conference regarding Taiping Island in Nansha Islands* (23 March 2016), https://www.mac.gov.tw/en/News_Content.aspx?n=FE07F9DA122E29D4&sms=3A4E63FA5107487D&s=F3B2B90AA560D22F, accessed 4 May 2020.

République française [French Republic]. *Comité interministériel pour l'information* [Interministerial Committee for Information]. *Livre Blanc sur les expériences nucléaires* [White Paper on Nuclear Tests] (1973), http://www.moruroa.org/medias/pdf/Livre%20Blanc.pdf, accessed 21 July 2019.

Responsibilities and Obligations of States with respect to Activities in the Area. Advisory Opinion. ITLOS Reports 2011, 10–78, https://www.itlos.org/fileadmin/itlos/documents/cases/case_no_17/17_adv_op_010211_en.pdf, accessed 30 April 2020.

———. Statement of Stichting Greenpeace Council (Greenpeace International) and the World Wide Fund for Nature (13 August 2010), https://www.itlos.org/fileadmin/itlos/documents/cases/case_no_17/Statement_Greenpeace_WWF.pdf, accessed 30 April 2020.

Reuter, Paul. *Le développement de l'ordre juridique international* [The Development of the International Legal Order]. Paris: Éditions Economica, 1995.

Riddell, Anna, and Brendan Plant. *Evidence Before the International Court of Justice*. London: British Institute of International and Comparative Law, 2009.

Rivera Juaristi, Francisco. "The Amicus Curiae in the Inter-American Court of Human Rights (1982–2013)." Unpublished ms., Santa Clara University, 1 August 2014, https://papers.ssrn.com/sol3/papers.cfm?abstract_id=2488073, accessed 4 May 2020.

Rosenne, Shabtai. "The Reconceptualization of Objections in the International Court of Justice." *Comunicazioni e studi* [Communications and Studies] 14 (1975): 735–62.

——— with the assistance of Yaël Ronen. *The Law and Practice of the International Court 1920–2005*. Leiden: Martinus Nijhoff Publishers, 2006.

Savarese, Eduardo. "Amicus Curiae Participation in Investor-State Arbitral Proceedings." *Italian Yearbook of International Law* 17 (2007): 99–121.

Schacherer, Stefanie. "Philip Morris v. Uruguay." *Investment Treaty News*, 18 October 2018, https://www.iisd.org/itn/2018/10/18/philip-morris-v-uruguay/, accessed 1 May 2020.

Shi Jiangtao. "Legal Challenge May Delay Court Rulings on Claims in the South China Sea." *South China Morning Post*, 20 June 2016, https://www.scmp.com/news/china/diplomacy-defence/article/1977758/legal-challenge-may-delay-court-rulings-claims-south, accessed 5 May 2020.

Schwebel, Stephen M. *Justice in International Law: Selected Writings*. Cambridge: Cambridge University Press, 1994.

Scott, James Brown. *The Project of a Permanent Court of International Justice and Resolutions of the Advisory Committee of Jurists. Report and Commentary*. Washington, D.C.: Carnegie Endowment for International Peace, Division of International Law, 1920, https://ia800205.us.archive.org/12/items/cu31924016941142/cu31924016941142.pdf, accessed 26 March 2020.

Sinclair, Ian. "Some Procedural Aspects of Recent International Litigation." *International and Comparative Law Quarterly* 30 (1981): 338–57.

Song, Yann-huei. "Taiwan's Response to the Philippines-PRC South China Sea Arbitration." *Asian Maritime Transparency Initiative*, 15 July 2015, https://amti.csis.org/taiwans-response-to-the-philippines-prc-south-china-sea-arbitration/, accessed 30 April 2020.

South China Sea Arbitration. Award on Jurisdiction and Admissibility (29 October 2015), https://pcacases.com/web/sendAttach/2579, accessed 10 March 2020.

———. Hearing on Jurisdiction. Transcript, Day 1 (7 July 2015), https://pcacases.com/web/sendAttach/1399, accessed 19 March 2020.

———. Transcript, Day 2 (8 July 2015), https://pcacases.com/web/sendAttach/1400, accessed 16 March 2020.

———. Transcript, Day 3 (13 July 2015), https://pcacases.com/web/sendAttach/1401, accessed 8 April 2020.

———. Hearing on the Merits and Remaining Issues of Jurisdiction and Admissibility. Transcript, Day 1 (24 November 2015), https://pcacases.com/web/sendAttach/1547, accessed 19 March 2020.

———. Transcript, Day 2 (25 November 2015), https://pcacases.com/web/sendAttach/1548, accessed 27 April 2020.

———. Transcript, Day 3 (26 November 2015), https://pcacases.com/web/sendAttach/1549, accessed 13 October 2019.

———. Transcript, Day 4 (30 November 2015), https://pcacases.com/web/sendAttach/1550, accessed 16 April 2020.

———. *Memorial of the Philippines*. Vol. I (30 March 2014), https://files.pca-cpa.org/pcadocs/Memorial%20of%20the%20Philippines%20Volume%20I.pdf, accessed 27 March 2019.

———. Vol. V. Annexes (30 March 2014), https://files.pca-cpa.org/pcadocs/The%20Philippines%27%20Memorial%20-%20Volume%20V%20%28Annexes%20103-157%29.pdf, accessed 23 March 2020.

———. Annex 124. Ministry of Foreign Affairs of the People's Republic of China, Foreign Ministry Spokesperson Hong Lei's Regular Press Conference on February 19, 2013 (20 February 2013), 161–65.

———. Annex 125. Ministry of Foreign Affairs of the People's Republic of China, Foreign Ministry Spokesperson Hong Lei's Regular Press Conference on February 20, 2013 (21 February 2013), 167–69.

———. Annex 127. Ministry of Foreign Affairs of the People's Republic of China, Foreign Ministry Spokesperson Hua Chunying's Remarks on the Philippines' Efforts in Pushing for the Establishment of the Arbitral Tribunal in Relation to the Disputes Between China and the Philippines in the South China Sea (26 April 2013), 181–84.

———. Annex 131. Ministry of Foreign Affairs of the People's Republic of China, Foreign Ministry Spokesperson Hong Lei's Statement Regarding

Comments by an Official of the United States Department of State on the South China Sea (8 February 2014), 203–05.
———. Annex 144. Association of Southeast Asian Nations, Declaration on the Conduct of Parties in South China Sea (4 November 2002), 321–24.
———. Vol. VI. Annexes (30 March 2014), https://files.pca-cpa.org/pcadocs/The%20Philippines%27%20Memorial%20-%20Volume%20VI%20%28Annexes%20158-221%29.pdf, accessed 27 April 2020.
———. Annex 189. *Note Verbale* from the Permanent Mission of the People's Republic of China to the United Nations to the Secretary-General of the United Nations, No. CML/2/2009 (6 February 2009), 275–78.
———. Annex 191. *Note Verbale* from the Permanent Mission of the People's Republic of China to the United Nations to the Secretary-General of the United Nations, No. CML/17/2009 (7 May 2009), 283–88.
———. Annex 192. *Note Verbale* from the Permanent Mission of the People's Republic of China to the United Nations to the Secretary-General of the United Nations, No. CML/18/2009 (7 May 2009), 289–94.
———. Annexes. Vol. VII, https://files.pca-cpa.org/pcadocs/The%20Philippines%27%20Memorial%20-%20Volume%20VII%20%28Annexes%20222-255%29.pdf, accessed 27 March 2019.
———. Annex 228. Japan, Submission to the United Nations Commission on the Limits of the Continental Shelf (27 December 2013), 127–206.
———. Procedural Order No. 4 (21 April 2015), https://pcacases.com/web/sendAttach/1807, accessed 7 April 2020.
———. *The Philippines' Annexes Cited During Hearing on Jurisdiction (Annexes 574–583)* (13 July 2015), https://files.pca-cpa.org/pcadocs/Annexes%20cited%20during%20Hearing%20on%20Jurisdiction%20%28Annexes%20574-583%29.pdf, accessed 21 April 2020.
———. Annex 574. Letter from H.E. Chen Xu, Ambassador of the People's Republic of China to the Kingdom of The Netherlands, to H.E. Judge Thomas A. Mensah (1 July 2015), 1–3.
———. *The Philippines' Annexes Cited During Merits Hearing* (30 November 2015), https://files.pca-cpa.org/pcadocs/Annexes%20cited%20during%20Hearing%20on%20Jurisdiction%20%28Annexes%20574-583%29.pdf, accessed 24 April 2020.
———. Annex 820. Embassy of the People's Republic of China in Canada, An Interview on China's Construction Activities on the Nansha Islands and Reefs (27 May 2015), 5–9.
———. Annex 821. China State Oceanic Administration, "Construction Work at Nansha Reefs Will Not Harm Oceanic Ecosystems" (18 June 2015), 11–14.

———. *Responses of the Philippines to the Tribunal's 5 February 2016 Request for Comments (Annexes 864–892)* (11 March 2016), https://files.pca-cpa.org/pcadocs/The%20Philippines%27%20Written%20Responses%20%2811%20March%202016%29%20%28Annexes%20864-892%29.pdf, accessed 30 April 2020.
———. Annex 864. China State Oceanic Administration, The Guidance for the Assessment of Coastal Marine Ecosystem Health, Marine Industry Standards of the People's Republic of China, No. HY/T 087-2005 (2005), 5–7.
———. Annex 865. China State Oceanic Administration, "2012 Communique [sic] on Marine Environment of China, Part 2: Marine Biodiversity and Ecological Conditions" (1 April 2013), 8–21.
———. Annex 866. China State Oceanic Administration, Code of Practice for Marine Monitoring Technology, Part 5: Marine Ecology, Marine Industry Standards of the People's Republic of China, No. HY/T 147.5-2013 (25 April 2013), 22–24.
———. Annex 867. China State Oceanic Administration, "2013 Communique [sic] on Marine Environment of China, Part 2: Conditions of Marine Ecology" (25 March 2014), 25–36.
———. Annex 868. China State Oceanic Administration, Technical Guidelines for Environmental Impact Assessment of Marine Engineering, National Standards of the People's Republic of China, No. GB/T 19485-2014 (1 April 2014), 37–128.
———. Annex 869. China State Oceanic Administration, South China Sea Branch, "Communique [sic] on the Oceanic Conditions of the South China Seas Region in 2013" (14 August 2014), 129–59.
———. Annex 870. China State Oceanic Administration, "2014 Communique [sic] on Marine Environment of China, Part 2: Conditions of Marine Ecology" (16 March 2015), 160–70.
———. Annex 871. China State Oceanic Administration, South China Sea Branch, "Communique [sic] on the Oceanic Conditions of the South China Sea Region in 2014" (28 May 2015), 171–200.
———. Annex 872. China State Ocean Administration, "Construction Activities at Nansha Reefs Did Not Affect the Coral Reef Ecosystem" (10 June 2015), 201–08.
———. Annex 875. Ministry of Foreign Affairs of the Republic of China (Taiwan), "Taiping Island Is an Island, Not a Rock, and the ROC Possesses Full Rights Associated with an Exclusive Economic Zone and Continental Shelf in Accordance with UNCLOS" (23 January 2016), 216–52.
———. Annex 876. Office of the President of the Taiwan Authority of China, "Remarks by President Ma on Taiping Island" (28 January 2016), 253–61.
———. *Responses of the Philippines to the Tribunal's 1 April 2016 Request for Comments on Additional Materials Regarding the Status of Itu Aba* (25

April 2016), https://pcacases.com/web/sendAttach/1850, accessed 30 April 2020.

———. *Responses of the Philippines to the Tribunal's 1 April 2016 Request for Comments on Materials from the Archives of the United Kingdom Hydrographic Office* (28 April 2016), https://pcacases.com/web/sendAttach/1851, accessed 15 May 2020.

———. *Responses of the Philippines to the Tribunal's 26 May 2016 Request for Comments on Materials from the French Archives* (3 June 2016), https://pcacases.com/web/sendAttach/1852, accessed 15 May 2020.

———. Rules of Procedure (27 August 2013), https://pcacases.com/web/sendAttach/233, accessed 5 April 2020.

———. *Supplemental Documents of the Philippines*. Vol. I (19 November 2015), https://files.pca-cpa.org/pcadocs/The%20Philippines%27%20Supplemental%20Documents%20-%20Volume%20I%20%28Annexes%20607-667%29.pdf, accessed 27 April 2020.

———. Annex 618. Permanent Mission of the People's Republic of China to the United Nations, Statement by Ambassador Wang Min at the 24th Meeting of the UNCLOS States Parties Under the Agenda Item "Report of the Secretary-General Under Article 319 of UNCLOS" (13 June 2014), 133–36.

———. Annex 619. Ministry of Foreign Affairs of the People's Republic of China, Foreign Ministry Spokesperson Hua Chunying's Regular Press Conference on September 9, 2014 (9 September 2014), 137–42.

———. Annex 620. Ministry of Foreign Affairs of the People's Republic of China, Foreign Ministry Spokesperson Hong Lei's Regular Press Conference on December 9, 2014 (9 December 2014), 143–46.

———. Annex 621. Ministry of Foreign Affairs of the People's Republic of China, Foreign Ministry Spokesperson Hong Lei's Remarks on Vietnam's Statement on the Chinese Government's Position Paper on Rejecting the Jurisdiction of the Arbitral Tribunal Established at the Request of the Philippines for the South China Sea Arbitration (12 December 2014), 147–49.

———. Annex 623. Ministry of Foreign Affairs of the People's Republic of China, Foreign Ministry Spokesperson Hong Lei's Regular Press Conference on March 11, 2015 (11 March 2015), 161–64.

———. Annex 624. Ministry of Foreign Affairs of the People's Republic of China, Foreign Ministry Spokesperson Hua Chunying's Regular Press Conference on April 9, 2015 (9 Apr. 2015), 165–70.

———. Annex 625. Ministry of Foreign Affairs of the People's Republic of China, Foreign Ministry Spokesperson Hong Lei's Regular Press Conference on April 28, 2015 (28 Apr. 2015), 171–76.

———. Annex 626. Ministry of Foreign Affairs of the People's Republic of China, Foreign Ministry Spokesperson Hua Chunying's Remarks on US

Defense Secretary Carter's Speech Relating to the Issue of the South China Sea at the Shangri-La Dialogue (30 May 2015), 177–80.

———. Annex 627. Ministry of Foreign Affairs of the People's Republic of China, Foreign Ministry Spokesperson Hong Lei's Regular Press Conference on June 9, 2015 (9 June 2015), 181–86.

———. Annex 628. Ministry of Foreign Affairs of the People's Republic of China, Foreign Ministry Spokesperson Hua Chunying's Remarks on the Philippines' Playing up and Airing of a Documentary on the South China Sea Issue (29 June 2015), 187–90.

———. Annex 629. Ministry of Foreign Affairs of the People's Republic of China, Foreign Ministry Spokesperson Hua Chunying's Regular Press Conference on July 8, 2015 (8 July 2015), 191–96.

———. Annex 630. Ministry of Foreign Affairs of the People's Republic of China, Foreign Ministry Spokesperson Hua Chunying's Remarks on the Philippines' Reinforcing a Military Vessel Illegally "Grounded" on China's Ren'ai Jiao (15 July 2015), 197–201.

———. Annex 635. Ministry of Foreign Affairs of the People's Republic of China, Foreign Ministry Spokesperson Hua Chunying's Remarks on the Release of the Transcript of the Oral Hearing on Jurisdiction by the South China Sea Arbitral Tribunal Established at the Request of the Philippines (24 August 2015), 223–27.

———. Annex 638. Ministry of Foreign Affairs of the People's Republic of China, Foreign Ministry Spokesperson Hong Lei's Regular Press Conference on September 29, 2015 (29 September 2015), 241–46.

———. Annex 639. of Foreign Affairs of the People's Republic of China, Foreign Ministry Spokesperson Hong Lei's Regular Press Conference on September 29, 2015 (29 September 2015), 247–50.

———. Annex 643. Ministry of Foreign Affairs of the People's Republic of China, Foreign Ministry Spokesperson Lu Kang's Regular Press Conference on October 27, 2015 (27 October 2015), 265–70.

———. Annex 644. Ministry of Foreign Affairs of the People's Republic of China, Foreign Ministry Spokesperson Lu Kang's Remarks on USS Lassen's Entry into Waters Near Relevant Islands and Reefs of China's Nansha Islands (27 October 2015), 271–74.

———. Annex 645. Ministry of Foreign Affairs of the People's Republic of China, Vice Foreign Minister Zhang Yesui Makes Stern Representations to US over US Naval Vessel's Entry into Waters Near Relevant Islands and Reefs of China's Nansha Islands (27 October 2015). 275–78.

———. Annex 646. Ministry of Foreign Affairs of the People's Republic of China, Foreign Ministry Spokesperson Lu Kang's Regular Press Conference on October 28, 2015 (28 October 2015), 279–82.

———. Annex 647. Ministry of Foreign Affairs of the People's Republic of China, Foreign Ministry Spokesperson Lu Kang's Regular Press Conference on October 29, 2015 (29 October 2015), 283–86.
———. Annex 648. People's Republic of China, Ministry of National Defense, Defense Ministry's Regular Press Conference on October 29 (29 October 2015), 287–92.
———. Annex 649. Ministry of Foreign Affairs of the People's Republic of China, Statement of the Ministry of Foreign Affairs of the People's Republic of China on the Award on Jurisdiction and Admissibility of the South China Sea Arbitration by the Arbitral Tribunal Established at the Request of the Republic of the Philippines (30 October 2015), 293–96.
———. Annex 650. Ministry of Foreign Affairs of the People's Republic of China, Foreign Ministry Spokesperson Lu Kang's Regular Press Conference on October 30, 2015 (30 October 2015), 297–301.
———. Annex 651. Ministry of Foreign Affairs of the People's Republic of China, Foreign Ministry Spokesperson Hua Chunying's Regular Press Conference on November 2, 2015 (2 November 2015), 302–04.
———. Annex 652. Ministry of Foreign Affairs of the People's Republic of China, Foreign Ministry Spokesperson Hua Chunying's Regular Press Conference on November 3, 2015 (3 November 2015), 305–10.
———. Annex 653. Ministry of Foreign Affairs of the People's Republic of China, Foreign Ministry Spokesperson Hua Chunying's Regular Press Conference on November 5, 2015 (5 November 2015), 311–14.
———. Annex 654. Ministry of Foreign Affairs of the People's Republic of China, Foreign Ministry Spokesperson Hong Lei's Regular Press Conference on November 10, 2015 (10 November 2015), 315–18.
———. Annex 664. United States, The White House, Office of the Press Secretary, Press Release: Remarks by President Obama and President Xi of the People's Republic of China in Joint Press Conference (25 September 2015), 481–97.
———. Vol. II, https://files.pca-cpa.org/pcadocs/The%20Philippines%27%20Supplemental%20Documents%20-%20Volume%20II%20%28Annexes%20608-709%29.pdf, accessed 7 April 2019.
———. Annex 668. *Note Verbale* from the Permanent Mission of the People's Republic of China to the United Nations to the Secretary-General of the United Nations (21 May 2009), reprinted in UN Convention on the Law of the Sea, Meeting of States Parties, Proposal for the inclusion of a supplementary item in the agenda of the nineteenth Meeting of States Parties, U.N. Doc. SPLOS/196 (22 May 2009), 1–4.
———. *Supplemental Written Submission of the Philippines*. Vol. I (16 March 2015), https://files.pca-cpa.org/pcadocs/Supplemental%20Written%20Submission%20Volume%20I.pdf, accessed 23 April 2020.

———. Vol. VIII. Annexes (16 March 2015), https://files.pca-cpa.org/pcadocs/The%20Philippines%27%20Supplemental%20Written%20Submission%20-%20Volume%20VIII%20%28Annexes%20466-499%29.pdf, accessed 10 March 2020.

———. Annex 467. People's Republic of China, Position Paper of the Government of the People's Republic of China on the Matter of Jurisdiction in the South China Sea Arbitration Initiated by the Republic of the Philippines (7 December 2014), 19–34.

———. Annex 470. Letter from H.E. Ambassador Chen Xu, Embassy of the People's Republic of China in The Hague, to H.E. Judge Thomas A. Mensah (6 February 2015), 73–84.

———. *Written Responses of the Philippines to the Tribunal's 13 July 2015 Questions*. Vol. II. Annexes (23 July 2015), https://files.pca-cpa.org/pcadocs/The%20Philippines%27%20Written%20Responses%20to%20the%20Tribunal%27s%2013%20July%202015%20Questions%20-%20Volume%20II%20%28Annexes%20584-606%29.pdf, accessed 27 April 2020.

———. Annex 584. Ministry of Foreign Affairs of the People's Republic of China, Foreign Ministry Spokesperson Hong Lei's Regular Press Conference on May 22, 2013 (22 May 2013), 1–4.

———. Annex 585. Ministry of Foreign Affairs of the People's Republic of China, Foreign Ministry Spokesperson Hua Chunying's Regular Press Conference on June 16, 2014 (16 June 2014), 5–9.

———. Annex 586. Ministry of Foreign Affairs of the People's Republic of China, Foreign Ministry Spokesperson Hong Lei's Regular Press Conference on February 27, 2015 (27 February 2015), 11–16.

———. Annex 587. Ministry of Foreign Affairs of the People's Republic of China, Foreign Ministry Spokesperson Hong Lei's Regular Press Conference on April 15, 2015 (15 April 2015), 17–20.

———. Annex 588. Ministry of Foreign Affairs of the People's Republic of China, Foreign Ministry Spokesperson Hong Lei's Regular Press Conference on April 17, 2015 (17 April 2015), 21–24.

———. Annex 589. Ministry of Foreign Affairs of the People's Republic of China, Foreign Ministry Spokesperson Hong Lei's Regular Press Conference on April 27, 2015 (27 April 2015), 27–30.

———. Annex 590. Ministry of Foreign Affairs of the People's Republic of China, Foreign Ministry Spokesperson Hua Chunying's Regular Press Conference on May 27, 2015 (27 May 2015), 33–37.

Southern Bluefin Tuna Cases (New Zealand v. Japan; Australia v. Japan). Provisional Measures. Order of 27 August 1999. ITLOS Reports 1999, 280–301, https://www.itlos.org/fileadmin/itlos/documents/cases/case_no_3_4/published/C34-O-27_aug_99.pdf, accessed 27 January 2020.

Special Court for Sierra Leone. *Rules of Procedure and Evidence* (4 December 2013), http://www.rscsl.org/Documents/RSCSL-Rules.pdf, accessed 4 May 2020.

Spijkers, Otto. "Non-participation in Arbitral Proceedings Under Annex VII United Nations Convention on the Law of the Sea: '*Arctic Sunrise*' and *South China Sea* Compared." *Interpretations of the United Nations Convention on the Law of the Sea by International Courts and Tribunals*, 171–90. Eds. Angela Del Vecchio and Roberto Virzo. Cham, Switzerland: Springer International Publishing, 2019.

Suez, Sociedad General de Aguas de Barcelona S.A., and InterAguas Servicios Integrales del Agua S.A. v. The Argentine Republic. ICSID Case No. ARB/03/17. Order in Response to a Petition for Participation as Amicus Curiae (17 March 2006), https://www.italaw.com/sites/default/files/case-documents/ita0803.pdf, accessed 21 July 2020.

Suez, Sociedad General de Aguas de Barcelona, S.A. and Vivendi Universal, S.A. v. Argentine Republic. ICSID Case No. ARB/03/19. Order in response to a Petition for Participation as Amicus Curiae (12 February 2007), https://www.italaw.com/sites/default/files/case-documents/ita0815.pdf, accessed 1 May 2020.

Talmon, Stefan. *The South China Sea Arbitration: Is There a Case to Answer?* Bonn: Universität Bonn, Institute for Public International Law, 2014, https://papers.ssrn.com/sol3/papers.cfm?abstract_id=2393025, accessed 13 March 2020.

———, and Bing Bing Jia (eds.). *The South China Sea Arbitration: A Chinese Perspective.* Oxford: Hart Publishing, 2014.

Tams, Christian J., and James G. Devaney. "Article 49." *The Statute of the International Court of Justice: A Commentary*, 3rd ed., 1115–26. Eds. Andreas Zimmermann et al. Oxford: Oxford University Press, 2019.

Tanaka, Yoshifumi. *The South China Sea Arbitration: Towards an International Legal Order in the Oceans* Oxford: Hart Publishing, 2019.

Thirlway, H.W.A. *Non-appearance Before the International Court of Justice.* Cambridge: Cambridge University Press, 1985.

Torode, Greg, and J.R. Wu. "Taiwan Enters South China Sea Legal Fray, As Group Seeks to Sway International Court." *Reuters*, 10 May 2016, http://www.reuters.com/article/us-southchinasea-taiwan/taiwan-enters-south-china-sea-legal-fray-as-group-seeks-to-sway-international-court-idUSKCN0Y02LD, accessed 3 May 2020.

Trial of Pakistani Prisoners of War (Pakistan v. India). Pakistan. *Affaire relative au Procès de prisonniers de guerre pakistanais* [Trial of Pakistani Prisoners of War Case]. I.C.J. Press Release 1973/14 (25 May 1973), https://www.icj-cij.org/files/case-related/60/11572.pdf, accessed 22 April 2020.

———. *Affaire relative au procès de prisonniers de guerre pakistanais – Report de l'ouverture des audiences* [Trial of Pakistani Prisoners of War Case – Postponement of the Opening of the Sittings]. Press Release 1973/16 (28 May 1973), https://www.icj-cij.org/files/case-related/60/11578.pdf, 22 April 2020.

———. Pakistan. *Application Instituting Proceedings*, 1 May 1973. *I.C.J. Pleadings. Trial of Pakistani Prisoners of War*, 4–6, https://www.icj-cij.org/files/case-related/60/9461.pdf, accessed 27 March 2020.

———. Oral Arguments. Request for the Indication of Interim Measures of Protection. *I.C.J. Pleadings, Trial of Pakistani Prisoners of War*, 21–107, http://www.icj-cij.org/files/case-related/60/060-19730504-ORA-01-00-BI.pdf, accessed 4 March 2018.

United Nations Commission for International Trade Law. *UNCITRAL Rules on Transparency in Treaty-Based Investor-State Arbitration* (1 April 2014), https://www.uncitral.org/pdf/english/texts/arbitration/rules-on-transparency/Rules-on-Transparency-E.pdf, accessed 4 May 2020.

United Nations Convention on the Law of the Sea. Concluded at Montego Bay on 10 December 1982. Entered into force on 16 November 1994, http://www.un.org/Depts/los/convention_agreements/texts/unclos/closindx.htm, accessed 21 March 2019.

United Nations. Division for Ocean Affairs and the Law of the Sea. *Annex VII. Arbitration*, http://www.un.org/depts/los/convention_agreements/texts/unclos/annex7.htm, accessed 10 March 2020.

United States Diplomatic and Consular Staff in Tehran (United States of America v. Iran). Judgment. I.C.J. Reports 1980, 3–48, https://www.icj-cij.org/files/case-related/64/064-19800524-JUD-01-00-BI.pdf, accessed 11 October 2019.

———. *Memorial of the Government of the United States of America* (12 January 1980). *I.C.J. Pleadings, United States Diplomatic and Consular Staff in Tehran (United States v. Iran)*, 143–247, https://www.icj-cij.org/files/case-related/64/9551.pdf, accessed 24 April 1980.

———. Oral Arguments. *I.C.J. Pleadings, United States Diplomatic and Consular Staff in Tehran*, 251–323, https://www.icj-cij.org/files/case-related/64/064-19800318-ORA-01-00-BI.pdf, accessed 22 April 2020.

Verhoeven, Joe. "Le droit, le juge et la violence (les arrêts *Nicaragua c. États-Unis)* [The Law, the Judge and Violence (The *Nicaragua v. United States* Judgments)]." *Revue générale de droit international public* [General Journal of Public International Law] 91 (1987): 1159–1239.

von Mangoldt, Hans. "Versäumnisverfahren in der internationalen (Schieds)Gerichtsbarkeit und souveräne Gleichheit [Default Procedures in International Arbitration and Adjudication and Sovereign Equality]." *Völkerrecht als Rechtsordnung, internationale Gerichtsbarkeit, Menschenrechte.*

Festschrift für Hermann Mosler [International Law as a Legal Order, International Adjudication, Human Rights. Festschrift for Hermann Mosler], 503–29. Ed. Rudolf Bernhardt. Berlin: Springer Verlag, 1983.

Watts, Arthur. "Enhancing the Effectiveness of Procedures of International Dispute Settlement." *Max Planck Yearbook of United Nations Law* 5 (2001): 21–40.

Wentker, Alexander. *Nichtteilnahme als Grenzphänomen zwischenstaatlicher Gerichts- und Schiedsverfahren – die Fälle South China Sea und "Arctic Sunrise"* [Non-participation in Inter-State Proceedings Before International Tribunals – the South China Sea and "Arctic Sunrise" Cases]. Heidelberg: Max Planck Institute for Comparative Public Law and International Law, 2018, https://papers.ssrn.com/sol3/papers.cfm?abstract_id=3248261, accessed 17 March 2020.

Witenberg, Jean-Charles. "La théorie des preuves devant les juridictions internationales [The Theory of Evidence Before International Jurisdictions]." *Recueil des Cours de l'Académie de droit international de La Haye* [Collected Courses of the Hague Academy of International Law]. Vol. 56 (1936-II), 1–106.

Wolfrum, Rüdiger. "Taking and Assessing Evidence in International Adjudication." *Law of the Sea, Environmental Law and Settlement of Disputes. Liber Amicorum Judge Thomas A. Mensah*, 341–57. Eds. Tafsir Malick Ndiaye and Rüdiger Wolfrum. Leiden: Martinus Nijhoff Publishers, 2007.

Xinhua. "HK Legal Organ Queries PCA's Arbitration Jurisdiction over South China Sea Disputes." *Europe China Daily*, 17 June 2016, http://europe.chinadaily.com.cn/world/2016-06/17/content_25739694.htm, accessed 10 May 2020.

Ye Qiang. "Does China's Position Paper on the South China Sea Arbitration Constitute a Preliminary Objection?" *Arbitration Concerning the South China Sea: Philippines Versus China*, 91–104. Eds. Shicun Wu and Keyuan Zou. London: Routledge, 2016.

CHAPTER 4

The Defaulting State and the Experts in the *South China Sea Arbitration*

Fact-finding is one of the greatest challenges confronting an international court in a situation of default.[1] In the *South China Sea Arbitration*, the difficulties in fact-finding were magnified considerably by the complex scientific and technical evidence that the Philippines provided in support of Submissions No. 4, 6, 11, 12(b), and 13. One only has to glance at the content of some of the evidence to become convinced of this.

To prove that Mischief Reef, Second Thomas Shoal, Subi Reef, Gaven Reef, and McKennan Reef (including Hughes Reef) were low-tide elevations, which are surrounded by and are above water at low tide but submerged at high tide (Submissions No. 4 and 6),[2] the Philippine *Memorial* provided two sets of satellite images for each. For example, one image of Mischief Reef was shown in Band 1 (blue-green), corresponding to shorter wavelength light (0.45–0.52 μm) that penetrates

[1] *Institut de droit international* [Institute of International Law], Session de Bâle [Basel Session], *Non-Appearance Before the International Court of Justice* (1991), https://www.idi-iil.org/app/uploads/2017/06/1991_bal_01_en.pdf, accessed 16 March 2020.

[2] *United Nations Convention on the Law of the Sea* ("Convention"), Article 13(1), http://www.un.org/depts/los/convention_agreements/texts/unclos/unclos_e.pdf, accessed 19 May 2020. For the text of the Philippine submissions, see *South China Sea Arbitration*, Award of 12 July 2016, 41–43, para. 112, https://pcacases.com/web/sendAttach/2086, accessed 19 May 2020.

A. C. Robles Jr., *The Defaulting State and the South China Sea Arbitration*, https://doi.org/10.1007/978-981-19-6394-0_4

water better than other bands.[3] In that image, its underwater contours were evident. The second image was in Band 4 (near infrared), corresponding to longer wavelengths (0.76–0.90 μm) that are almost entirely absorbed by water. Only features above water are visible in Band 4, which allegedly makes clear that there was no evidence of any above-water features at Mischief Reef.[4] Satellite imagery was also included in an expert report on the geographical characteristics and status of 49 maritime features in the South China Sea submitted by the Philippines; one of the report's authors, Dr. Clive Schofield, was presented by the Philippines for examination during the Hearing on the Merits.[5]

To support its claim that the harvesting by Chinese fishers of endangered species and China's island-building in the South China Sea harmed the marine environment (Submissions No. 11 and 12(b)), the Philippines submitted evidence that extraction of corals, an endangered species, reduces the structural complexity of reefs, affecting the reef's ability to support fishes and other animals, and that the island-building resulted in significant damage to the habitats of vulnerable species.[6] This and other evidence were presented in two reports by two coral reef experts, Professors Kent E. Carpenter and Loke Ming Chou, with the first author being presented for examination during the Hearing on the Merits.[7] Finally, to

[3] The symbol "μm" refers to a micrometer, defined as one-millionth of a meter (10^{-6} meter). It was formerly referred to as "micron." *Larousse Dictionary of Science and Technology* (Edinburgh: Larousse plc, 1995), 700.

[4] *South China Sea Arbitration, Memorial of the Philippines* (30 March 2014), vol. I, 134, para. 5.64. ("*MP*"), https://files.pca-cpa.org/pcadocs/Memorial%20of%20the%20Philippines%20Volume%20I.pdf, accessed 23 April 2020. For the descriptions of all the features, see 132–36, paras. 5.59–5.73. The images themselves are in volume II of the *Memorial*, which is not available on the website of the Permanent Court of Arbitration ("PCA"), the Registry in the case.

[5] *South China Sea Arbitration, Supplemental Written Submission of the Philippines* (16 March 2015), Annex 513, C. Schofield et al., An Appraisal of the Geographical Characteristics and Status of Certain Insular Features in the South China Sea (March 2015), vol. IX, 143–245 ("*SWSP*"), https://files.pca-cpa.org/pcadocs/The%20Philippines%27%20Supplemental%20Written%20Submission%20-%20Volume%20IX%20%28Annexes%20500-521%29.pdf, accessed 19 May 2020.

[6] *MP*, vol. I, 203, para. 6.116.

[7] Ibid., Annex 240, E. Carpenter, Ph.D., Eastern South China Sea Environmental Disturbances and Irresponsible Fishing Practices and their Effects on Coral Reefs and

support its claim that China's law enforcement vessels caused serious risk of collision to Philippine vessels navigating around Scarborough Shoal in April and May 2012 (Submission No. 13), the Philippines cited as an example of a dangerous maneuver a Chinese vessel's attempt at a distance of less than 100 meters to cross the port bow of a Philippine vessel. The latter was only able to avoid a collision by increasing its speed to 20 knots and altering course to starboard.[8]

In proceedings in which both parties appear, an international court can count on the assistance of the parties' experts in assessing complex scientific and technical evidence. Even then, the assistance might not be all that helpful if equally qualified experts presented diametrically opposed conclusions. The possibility that scientific experts of comparable qualification, presented as impartial and independent, and presumed to be presenting evidence in good faith, nevertheless contradict each other, had already been observed in the award in the *Trail Smelter Arbitration* in the 1930s.[9] One source of disagreements may lie in the difference in paradigms that structure the work of scientists, as pointed out by Thomas Kuhn. Nevertheless, scientists who share paradigms may still disagree with each other on such matters as the facts that the paradigm has shown to be particularly revealing of the nature of things, the application of the paradigm to new areas, and the solution of problems that the paradigm is

Fisheries (22 March 2014), vol. VII, 389–437 ("First Carpenter Report"), https://files.pca-cpa.org/pcadocs/The%20Philippines%27%20Memorial%20-%20Volume%20VII%20%28Annexes%20222-255%29.pdf, accessed 19 May 2020; *Supplemental Documents of the Philippines* (19 November 2015) ("*SDP*"), Annex 699, K.E. Carpenter and L.M. Chou, Environmental Consequences of Land Reclamation Activities on Various Reefs in the South China Sea (14 November 2015), vol. II, 235–93 ("Second Carpenter Report"), https://files.pca-cpa.org/pcadocs/The%20Philippines%27%20Supplemental%20Documents%20-%20Volume%20II%20%28Annexes%20608-709%29.pdf, accessed 19 May 2020; *The Philippines' Annexes Cited During the Merits Hearing* (30 November 2015), Annex 850, John McManus, "Offshore Coral Reef Damage, Overfishing and Paths to Peace in the South China Sea," 578–608 ("*PAMH*"), https://files.pca-cpa.org/pcadocs/The%20Philippines%27%20Annexes%20cited%20during%20Merits%20Hearing%20%28Annexes%20820-859%29.pdf, accessed 19 May 2020.

[8] *MP*, vol. I, 203, 209, 212–13, paras. 6.116. 6.129, 6.145.

[9] *Trail Smelter Case (United States, Canada)*, Awards of 16 April 1938 and 11 March 1941, *Reports of International Arbitral Awards* ("*RIAA*"), vol. III (New York: United Nations, 2006), 1922, https://legal.un.org/riaa/cases/vol_III/1905-1982.pdf, accessed 11 October 2020.

unable to resolve.[10] A survey of domestic caselaw in major Western States seemed to confirm Kuhn's theoretical propositions. It found that the major sources of disagreement among scientists were the theoretical or methodological framework to be applied to base facts in order to address the question; the base facts that are relevant to providing an answer; the competing versions of base facts; and the application of a selected set of generalizations to a selected set of base facts.[11]

The appointment by an international court of its own experts as a solution to "the battle of the experts" is increasingly advocated by some judges[12] and many scholars,[13] a solution that has been the exception rather than the rule in the practice of the International Court of Justice ("ICJ").[14] In the event of default, an international court would be hard-pressed to evaluate on its own the complex scientific and technical

[10] Thomas Kuhn, *The Structure of Scientific Revolutions* (2nd ed., enlarged; Chicago: The University of Chicago Press, 1970), 77–92.

[11] Déirdre Dwyer, *The Judicial Assessment of Expert Evidence* (Cambridge: Cambridge University Press, 2009), 136–37.

[12] *Pulp Mills on the River Uruguay (Argentina v. Uruguay), Judgment, I.C.J. Reports 2010*, Joint Dissenting Opinion of Judges Al-Khasawneh and Simma, 108–20, http://www.icj-cij.org/files/case-related/135/135-20100420-JUD-01-01-BI.pdf, accessed 13 September 2020; Bruno Simma, "The International Court of Justice and Scientific Expertise," *Proceedings of the Annual Meeting (American Society of International Law)* 106 (28 March 2012): 230–33; Giorgio Gaja, "Assessing Expert Evidence in the ICJ," *The Law and Practice of International Courts and Tribunals* 15 (2015): 409–18 ("*LPICT*"). Gaja was also an ICJ member at the time of writing.

[13] The scholarly literature on the subject is voluminous. For a sampling, see Jean D'Aspremont and Makane Moïse Mbengue. "Strategies of Engagement with Scientific Fact-finding in International Adjudication," *Journal of International Dispute Settlement* 5 (2014): 240–72 ("*JIDS*"); Caroline E. Foster, "New Clothes for the Emperor? Consultation of Experts by the International Court of Justice," *JIDS* 5 (2014): 139–73; Brendan Gogarty, "Conceptions and (Mis)conceptions of Science in International Treaties: The ICJ Whaling Case in Context," *Yearbook of Polar Law* 7 (2015): 607–22; Brendan Gogarty and Peter Lawrence. "The ICJ *Whaling* Case: Missed Opportunity to Advance the Rule of Law in resolving Science-related Disputes in Global Commons?" *Heidelberg Journal of International Law* 77 (2017): 261–98; Guillaume Gros, "The ICJ's Handling of Science in the *Whaling in the Antarctic* Case: A Whale of a Case?" *JIDS* 6 (2015): 578–620; Lucas Carlos Lima, "The Evidential Weight of Experts before the ICJ: Reflections on the *Whaling in the Antarctic* Case," *JIDS* 6 (2015): 621–35; and Anna Riddell and Brendan Plant, *Evidence Before the International Court of Justice* (London: British Institute of International and Comparative Law, 2009), 329–58.

[14] Mohamed Bennouna, "Experts Before the International Court of Justice: What for?" *JIDS* 9 (2018): 348; Joan E. Donoghue, "Expert Scientific Evidence in a Broader

evidence presented by the appearing party. In this situation, the utility of court-appointed experts is more readily recognized even by judges who are otherwise reluctant to support the appointment of independent experts.[15] The *South China Sea* Tribunal explicitly attributed its appointment of independent experts to China's default, which required it to be vigilant in determining whether Philippine claims were well founded in fact and in law and consequently, to test the evidence provided by the Philippines and to augment the record.[16] In all, the Tribunal appointed five independent experts. An expert hydrographer, Grant Boyes, an Australian national, was appointed in August 2015, to assist the Tribunal in reviewing and analyzing geographic and hydrographic information, photographs, satellite imagery, and other technical data.[17] A coral reef expert, Dr. Sebastian Ferse, a German national, was appointed in February 2016, followed by the appointment of two other coral reef experts, Professor Peter Mumby and Dr. Selina Ward, both Australian nationals, in April 2016, to determine whether Chinese island-building had detrimental effects on coral reef systems and how long such effects would last.[18] A navigational safety expert, Captain Gurpreet Singh Singhota, a UK national, was appointed in March 2016 to assist the Tribunal in determining whether the navigational safety provisions covered by the Convention had been violated.[19] The Tribunal's recourse to the assistance of independent experts has been rightly identified as a unique, if not innovative, element in the Tribunal's approach to fact-finding in the *South China Sea Arbitration*.[20]

Context," *JIDS* 9 (2018): 379–87. At the time of writing, both authors were ICJ members.

[15] Bennouna, "Experts," 350.

[16] Award of 12 July 2016, 5, 50, 52, paras. 16, 132, 136, https://pcacases.com/web/sendAttach/2086, accessed 10 March 2020. A German scholar who argued that the Tribunal lacked jurisdiction admitted the legitimacy of the Tribunal's recourse to experts in case of doubt about the facts. Stefan Talmon, *The South China Sea Arbitration: Is There a Case to Answer?* (Bonn: Universität Bonn, Institute for Public International Law, 2014), 8, https://papers.ssrn.com/sol3/papers.cfm?abstract_id=2393025, accessed 13 March 2020.

[17] Award of 12 July 2016, 19, 51, paras. 58, 133.

[18] Ibid., 30, 31, 52, paras. 85, 90. 136.

[19] Ibid., 29, 30, paras. 84(c), 85.

[20] Laurence Boisson de Chazournes and Guillaume Yvan Jean Gros, "L'expert et le Tribunal international du droit de la mer [The Expert and the International Tribunal for

In its post-litigation critiques of the two Awards, the Chinese Society of International Law ("CSIL") denied the need for independent experts by contrasting the Tribunal's appointment of five experts with the caution of the ICJ, which has appointed experts only twice in 70 years.[21] The CSIL did not explain how the Tribunal should have assessed the complex scientific and technical evidence submitted by the Philippines,[22] nor did it analyze that evidence or the evidence presented by the independent experts. Instead, the CSIL and other Chinese scholars attacked both the experts presented by the Philippines and the independent experts for their lack of independence and impartiality. The criticism against Schofield for providing expert testimony on the status of Itu Aba that allegedly contradicted his previous writings implied that he tailored his evidence to the needs of the case.[23] Such was also the implication of the criticism directed against Carpenter and Chou, for preparing reports after the proceedings had been initiated,[24] and against the coral reef experts appointed

the Law of the Sea]," in Guillaume Le Floch (ed.), *Les 20 ans du Tribunal international du droit de la mer* [Twenty Years of the International Tribunal for the Law of the Sea] (Paris: Éditions A. Pedone, 2018), 182; Tara Davenport, "Procedural Issues Arising from China's Non-Participation in the *South China Sea Arbitration*," in S. Jayakumar et al. (eds.), *The South China Sea Arbitration: The Legal Dimension* (Cheltenham: Edward Elgar Publishing, 2018), 95; Jacqueline Joyce F. Espenilla, "Judicial Fact-Finding Initiatives in the *South China Sea Arbitration*," *Asian Journal of International Law* 9 (2019): 21; Makane Moïse Mbengue, "The South China Sea Arbitration Innovation in Marine Environmental Fact-Finding and Due Diligence Obligations," *ASIL* [American Society of International Law] *Unbound* (12 December 2016): 285–89; and Harry Ormsby, "Judicial Fact-finding and the South China Sea Arbitration," *Kluwer Arbitration Blog*, 6 September 2016, http://kluwerarbitrationblog.com/2016/09/06/judicial-fact-finding-and-the-south-china-sea-arbitration/, accessed 11 September 2020. As will be noted later, several of these authors have advanced interpretations of the experts' role(s) in the *South China Sea Arbitration* that are questionable.

[21] Chinese Society of International Law ("CSIL"), "The South China Sea Arbitration Awards: A Critical Study." *Chinese Journal of International Law* 17 (2018): 637, para. 941 ("*CJIL*").

[22] The CSIL probably did not want the Tribunal to evaluate the evidence and for that matter, to conduct the proceedings at all.

[23] He Tiantian, "Commentary on Award on Jurisdiction and Admissibility of the Philippines-Instituted Arbitration Under Annex VII to the UNCLOS: A Discussion on Fact-Finding and Evidence," *Chinese Journal of Global Governance* 2 (2016): 122; CSIL, "The South China Sea Arbitration Awards," 532, 536, paras. 677, 683.

[24] CSIL, "The South China Sea Arbitration Awards," 532, 536, paras. 677, 683.

by the Tribunal, for allegedly producing a report favorable to the Philippines in 17 days.[25] The CSIL, which had failed to examine the contents of the experts' reports, nevertheless managed to accuse the Tribunal of not subjecting the reports of the coral reef experts (and presumably the reports of the other experts) to any "rigorous examination" or "prudent evaluation."[26]

We have already explained in Chapter 3 the procedures for the appointment of the independent experts, for challenging their competence, independence, and impartiality, and for challenging the independent experts' reports. In proceedings in which both parties appear, a party that failed to have recourse to these procedures would be deemed to have waived its right to object to them subsequently, and *a fortiori* after the conclusion of the proceedings. Challenges of the latter type are clearly motivated by dissatisfaction with a court's decisions and cannot be taken seriously. The CSIL, speaking on behalf of China, should have known this. Strictly speaking, therefore, the discussion could stop here. Several reasons argue in favor of a detailed examination of the CSIL's allegations. First, it will preempt charges of hiding beyond legal technicalities and of attempting to disguise the inability to respond to the charges. Second, it will provide an opportunity to examine the contribution of all the experts, and not just the handful that Chinese scholars single out for condemnation, to fact-finding in the *South China Sea Arbitration*. This exercise is all the more necessary because the only other author who has undertaken it did not fully comprehend the role of the expert hydrographer and did not base the assessment of the contributions of the coral reef experts and the navigational safety experts on a reading of the expert reports.[27] Third, the evaluation of the independence and impartiality of party-appointed experts and independent experts will hopefully make a contribution to the lively scholarly debate of the last two decades on these issues.

The first part of this Chapter argues that the United Nations Convention on the Law of the Sea ("Convention") provides in certain instances for an active role for experts in the interpretation and application of the Convention. Judicial decision-making and the practice of arbitral tribunals constituted under Annex VII of the Convention bear witness to this active

[25] Ibid., 638, para. 947.

[26] Ibid., para. 946.

[27] Espenilla, "Judicial Fact-Finding Initiatives."

role. In view of the attack by the CSIL and Chinese scholars on the independence and impartiality of the experts appointed by the Philippines and the experts appointed by the Tribunal, the second part will draw on the scholarly literature to carry out its own assessment of the independence and impartiality of both categories of experts. Given the failure of the CSIL and Chinese scholars as well as non-Chinese scholars to analyze the expert evidence and the Tribunal's analysis of such evidence, the third, fourth, and fifth parts will summarize the expert evidence submitted by the Philippines, the reports submitted by the independent experts, and the Tribunal's assessment of the evidence submitted by the two categories of experts concerning the status of maritime features, the harm to the marine environment caused by China's island-building in the South China Sea, and navigational safety. The third section will demonstrate that the Tribunal did not simply adopt the expert report submitted by the Philippines on the status of maritime features. Rather it submitted it to critical analysis, with the assistance of the expert hydrographer. The fourth and fifth parts will show that to assess the evidence on harm to the marine environment resulting from China's island-building in the South China Sea and the dangerous behavior of China's official vessels in the waters around Scarborough Shoal, the Tribunal undertook a two-stage analysis. It first subjected the expert evidence submitted by the Philippines to critical analysis, with the assistance of the independent experts, before subjecting the evidence presented by the independent experts to critical analysis.

It should be noted at the outset that there is no formal definition of expert in general international law.[28] As suggested by Savadogo, a legal definition may be found in Article 1(1) of the Headquarters Agreement of the International Tribunal for the Law of the Sea ("ITLOS") with the Federal Republic of Germany, under the terms of which an "expert" is "a person called at the instance of a party to a dispute or at the instance of the Tribunal to present testimony in the form of expert opinions,

[28] Louis Savadogo, "Le recours des juridictions internationales à des experts [The Recourse of International Jurisdictions to Experts]," *Annuaire français de droit international* [French Yearbook of International Law] 50 (2004): 232 ("*AFDI*"), https://www.persee.fr/docAsPDF/afdi_0066-3085_2004_num_50_1_3795.pdf, accessed 21 May 2020; Markus Benzing, *Das Beweisrecht vor internationalen Gerichten und Schiedsgerichten in zwischenstaatlichen Streitigkeiten* [The Law of Evidence before International Courts and Arbitral Tribunals in Inter-State Disputes] (Heidelberg: Springer, 2010), 355.

based on special knowledge, skills, experience or training."[29] A definition put forward by Argentina in the *Pulp Mills Case* against Uruguay describes an expert as "a person chosen for his/her technical knowledge and who, in legal proceedings, may be asked: (1) by a Party or court to shed light on certain matters in dispute...(b) by a Party, to be a member of its delegation and to participate in the hearings."[30] An expert differs from a witness in that the former gives his/her opinion on what he or she sincerely believes, on the basis of his/her special knowledge or experience, while the latter speaks of facts within his/her personal knowledge.[31]

Scholarly definitions emphasize that an expert is an independent and objective individual or organization with a unique knowledge of the facts falling within this expertise that is relevant to the resolution of a dispute before a court.[32] Expert evidence is said to provide a degree of objectivity unmatched by conventional (factual) evidence, one reason for this being that expert evidence is testable.[33] It is accepted and expected that States parties to a case before an international court will seek the assistance of experts in all fields, and not just in the natural sciences, in preparing their written submissions and oral pleadings.[34] For their part, international

[29] Savadogo, "Le recours," 232; *Agreement Between the International Tribunal for the Law of the Sea and the Government of the Federal Republic of Germany regarding the Headquarters of the Tribunal and Exchange of Notes*, 14 December 2004, 5, https://www.itlos.org/fileadmin/itlos/documents/basic_texts/headquarters_agreement_eofn_eng.pdf, accessed 21 May 2020.

[30] Jean Salmon (ed.), *Dictionnaire de droit international public* [Dictionary of Public International Law] (Bruxelles: Établissements Émile Bruylant, 2001), 283, quoted by Philippe Sands, counsel for Argentina, ICJ, *Pulp Mills on the River Uruguay (Argentina v. Uruguay)*, Verbatim record 2009/21 (29 September 2009), 14, note 25 ("*Pulp Mills*, Verbatim Record"), https://www.icj-cij.org/files/case-related/135/135-20090929-ORA-01-01-BI.pdf, accessed 21 May 2020.

[31] Christian J. Tams, "Article 51," in Andreas Zimmermann et al. (eds.), *The Statute of the International Court of Justice A Commentary* (3rd ed.; Oxford University Press, 2019), 1443; Shabtai Rosenne, with the assistance of Yaël Ronen, *The Law and Practice of the International Court 1990–2005*, vol. III, *Procedure* (4th ed.; Leiden: Martinus Nijhoff Publishers, 2006), 1308; Riddell and Plant, *Evidence*, 343.

[32] Isabelle Van Damme, "The Assessment of Expert Evidence in International Adjudication," *JIDS* 9 (2018): 402.

[33] Artur Appazov, *Expert Evidence and International Criminal Justice* (Cham, Switzerland: Springer International Publishing AG Switzerland, 2016), 85.

[34] In international commercial arbitration, the selection of expert witnesses is said to be the most important decision made by a party's counsel after the selection of arbitrators.

courts and tribunals must correctly appreciate the scientific and technical facts.[35] To this end, they are authorized by their statutes to entrust an individual or entity with an expert report. The ICJ has explained, without making a distinction between experts appointed by the parties to a case and experts appointed by the Court, that the purpose of expert opinion is "to assist it in giving judgment on issues submitted to it."[36] Whether or not they appoint their own experts, international courts or tribunals are faced with the task of evaluating the opinions of experts. If the courts or tribunals have confidence in their ability to evaluate expert evidence, they may not find it essential to engage independent experts in the first place.

The framework of the Convention and the practice of other Annex VII tribunals will enable us to understand that contrary to the practice of the ICJ, experts are intended to play a role, and do play a role, in the interpretation and application of the Convention.

I. The Role of Experts in the Interpretation and Application of the Convention

The CSIL, by contrasting the *South China Sea* Tribunal's appointment of five independent experts with the ICJ's cautious attitude, seems to assume that ICJ practice is a rule of international law binding on other international courts and tribunals. The practice of the ICJ, which is as well known for rejecting requests from a party to appoint an expert as for rarely making use of its power to appoint experts,[37] is just that—a practice. It can hardly be imposed on parties to the Convention, several

Margaret L. Moses, *The Principles and Practice of International Commercial Arbitration* (Cambridge: Cambridge University Press, 2008), 76.

[35] "[T]he decisions and conclusions of the Court largely depend on a correct appreciation of the scientific and technical facts." *Pulp Mills on the River Uruguay (Argentina v. Uruguay), Judgment, I.C.J. Reports 2010*, Declaration of Judge Yusuf, 217, para. 6, https://www.icj-cij.org/files/case-related/135/135-20100420-JUD-01-05-BI.pdf, accessed 21 May 2020.

[36] *Application for Revision and Interpretation of the Judgment of 24 February 1982 in the Case concerning the Continental Shelf (Tunisia/Libyan Arab Jamahiriya) (Tunisia v. Libyan Arab Jamahiriya), Judgment, I.C.J. Reports 1985*, 228, para. 65, https://www.icj-cij.org/files/case-related/71/071-19851210-JUD-01-00-BI.pdf, accessed 21 May 2020.

[37] Christian J. Tams, "Article 50," in Andreas Zimmermann et al. (eds.), *The Statute of the International Court of Justice A Commentary* (3rd ed.; Oxford University Press, 2019), 1291.

provisions of which institutionalize the role of experts in compulsory dispute settlement entailing binding decisions. Outside of the areas in which the Convention explicitly provides for the participation of experts, several arbitral tribunals established under Annex VII of the Convention to settle maritime delimitation disputes have developed a practice of engaging an expert hydrographer; in one instance, a tribunal also had recourse to assistance provided by a legal expert.

A. Experts and Compulsory Dispute Settlement Under the Convention

Experts may participate in compulsory dispute settlement as members of any court or tribunal having jurisdiction under the Convention, without the right to vote, or as members of an arbitral tribunal under Annex VIII of the Convention on special arbitration.

1. Experts Under Article 289 of the Convention

Article 289 lists the conditions in which experts may participate in a court or tribunal having jurisdiction under the Convention, which may be the ICJ, the ITLOS, an arbitral tribunal under Annex VII of the Convention, or an arbitral tribunal under Annex VIII of the Convention (although this last seems unlikely). An understanding of Article 289 is essential for assessing the innovative character of the *South China Sea* Tribunal's appointment of experts, which did not go as far as applying Article 289.

Under Article 289, the dispute submitted to the court or tribunal must involve scientific or technical matters. No definition is provided of such matters.[38] Presumably it is for the court and the parties, who must consult each other prior to the appointment of the experts, to decide what constitutes scientific or technical matters. In the minds of the Convention's drafters, the purpose of experts' participation would be to ensure that the decision of the court or tribunal does not contain technical errors.[39] Article 289 implicitly recognizes that judges and arbitrators are not familiar with scientific or technical matters; it also reflects the view

[38] Tullio Treves, "Article 289. Experts," in Alexander Proelss et al. (eds.), *United Nations Convention on the Law of the Sea 1982: A Commentary* (München: C.H. Beck, 2017), 1865.

[39] Myron H. Nordquist et al., *United Nations Convention on the Law of the Sea 1982: A Commentary*, vol. V, *Settlement of Disputes, General and Final Provisions and Related Annexes and Resolutions* (Leiden: Brill, 1989), 51.

of the then Socialist States of Eastern Europe that law of the sea disputes were (or would be) generally scientific or technical in nature.[40]

The qualifications of the experts are not enumerated in Article 289. Instead, they are to be found in Article 2(3) of Annex VIII of the Convention, which stipulates the drawing up of lists from which members of special arbitral tribunals under that Annex and experts under Article 289 must preferably be chosen. The experts must be persons whose competence in the legal, scientific, or technical aspects of the respective field is established and generally recognized and who enjoy the highest reputation for fairness and integrity.

The procedures for the selection of the experts are fairly simple. A party to the dispute may request the appointment of experts, or a court or tribunal may decide to do so on its own initiative. The only condition is that there must be consultation between the court or tribunal and the parties to the dispute (and not just the party who made the request). The Rules of the ITLOS provide for a situation in which States parties to a dispute submitted to it request the appointment of experts under Article 289. Under Article 15(1) of the ITLOS Rules, the request for the selection of experts must be made by the closure of the written proceedings.[41] Experts will be selected by the ITLOS upon the proposal of its President, who is required to consult the parties for this purpose. Like ITLOS members, experts are required to be independent, to enjoy the highest reputation for fairness, competence, and integrity, and to make a solemn declaration before assuming their duties.

The experts appointed under Article 289 will sit with the other members of the court or the tribunal, but they will not have the right to vote. It is expected that experts' participation in the court's deliberation will minimize one of the risks for a court that appoints independent experts—that of delegating its decision to experts—presumably because in this situation the experts are already members of the court.[42] Experts under Article 289 should not be confused with experts that present their opinions to the court on behalf of one or the other party. The latter type of expert is chosen exclusively by a party to the dispute. They may

[40] Treves, "Article 289," 1864.

[41] Ibid., 1865.

[42] Alan Boyle and James Harrison, "Judicial Settlement of International Environmental Disputes: Current Problems," *JIDS* 4 (2013): 272; Bennouna, "Experts," 348–49.

be cross-examined by counsel for and contradicted by experts of the other party; they do not have the right to sit with the judges. Experts under Article 289 are analogous to the "assessors" described in Article 30 (2) of the ICJ Statute. Despite the similarity, a proposal to replace the term "experts" with "assessors" failed to gain approval at the Third United Nations Conference on the Law of the Sea ("UNCLOS III," 1973–1982), which drafted the Convention.[43]

Having explained Article 289 and keeping in mind the procedures followed by the *South China Sea* Tribunal when appointing the expert hydrographer, the coral reef experts, and the navigational safety expert, one may cast doubt on recent commentaries that suggest that the *South China Sea Arbitration* was the first case in which Article 289 was utilized. Espenilla prefaces her discussion of the role of independent experts with a summary of Article 289, implying that the latter was the basis for the Tribunal's appointment of independent experts.[44] She forgets that nowhere did the Tribunal invoke Article 289. She also overlooked the fact that if Article 289 had been applied, one important condition laid down in that Article had not been fulfilled: the experts appointed by the Tribunal, despite their outstanding qualifications, were not on the lists of experts maintained under Annex VIII of the Convention. Finally, the participation of the coral reef experts and the navigational safety expert did not correspond to that envisaged in Article 289: they did not sit with the Tribunal during its deliberations. The role of the expert hydrographer was more ambiguous, as we shall see below, yet the fact remains that he was not appointed under Article 289 of the Convention.

Boisson de Chazournes and Gros also imply that Article 289 was applied by the Tribunal when they asserted that it appointed an "assessor."[45] Quite apart from the fact that they used a term that does not appear in Article 289 (or in the Convention, for that matter), Boisson de Chazournes and Gros ignored the Tribunal's account of its own procedure. Nowhere in the two Awards is Article 289 invoked. Moreover, Boisson de Chazournes and Gros failed to identify the "assessor" in question. The "assessor" appears, in their view, to be an individual, who is to

[43] Nordquist et al., *United Nations Convention on the Law of the Sea 1982: A Commentary*, vol. V, 51.

[44] Espenilla, "Judicial Fact-Finding Initiatives," 25.

[45] Boisson de Chazournes and Gros, "L'expert," 182.

be distinguished from a "group of experts" and an "individual expert," the latter being appointed by the Tribunal. As the only experts who can be deemed to constitute a group were the coral reef experts, the assessor that they had in mind could either be the expert hydrographer or the navigational safety expert. Boisson de Chazournes and Gros give us no further clues as to the identity of the "assessor," and, more importantly, to the contribution of the "assessor" to the Tribunal's fact-finding. To sum up, there is no cause yet to revise commentaries of the Convention that observe that Article 289 has never been utilized.[46]

Annex VIII of the Convention reflects legal recognition of the important role of experts in the settlement of disputes in a number of functional fields.

2. Experts and Special Arbitration Under Annex VIII of the Convention

Annex VIII, which has been described by a delegate to UNCLOS III as one of the most original creations of the Convention,[47] differs from Annex VII, and indeed from other compulsory dispute settlement procedures under the Convention, in that it identifies four functional fields in which arbitration by experts is possible, and it provides explicitly for the possibility of fact-finding by experts.

Special arbitration is a compulsory dispute settlement procedure that a State party to the Convention may accept by unilateral declaration at any time for the settlement of disputes with another State having accepted the same procedure in the areas of fisheries, the protection and preservation of the marine environment, marine scientific research, or navigation, including pollution from vessels and by dumping. Compulsory dispute settlement relating to the conservation of fisheries resources of the high seas had been entrusted by the Geneva Convention on Fishing and Conservation of the Living Resources of the High Seas, 1958, to a commission consisting of "well-qualified persons being nationals of States not involved in the dispute and specializing in legal, administrative or

[46] Treves, "Article 289," 1866.

[47] Raymond Ranjeva, "Le règlement des différends [Dispute Settlement]," in René-Jean Dupuy and Daniel Vignes (eds.), *Traité du nouveau droit de la mer* [Treatise on the New Law of the Sea] (Paris: Éditions Economica, 1985), 1162.

scientific questions relating to fisheries."[48] To fisheries, Annex VIII added the three other functional fields.

Following the functional logic, the members of an Annex VIII tribunal, normally consisting of five members, will be preferably chosen from lists of experts in the four fields that are to be drawn up and maintained by the competent international organization in that field: in the field of fisheries, by the Food and Agriculture Organization of the United Nations ("FAO"), in the field of protection and preservation of the marine environment, by the United Nations Environment Programme ("UNEP"), in the field of marine scientific research, by the Intergovernmental Oceanographic Commission ("IOC"); and in the field of navigation, including pollution from vessels and by dumping, by the International Maritime Organization ("IMO"). Each State Party to the Convention is entitled to nominate two experts in each field whose competence in the legal, scientific, or technical aspects of such field is established and generally recognized and who enjoy the highest reputation for fairness and integrity.[49] This last requirement is identical to that applicable to members of the ITLOS and of arbitral tribunals under Annex VII of the Convention.

By definition, decisions of special arbitral tribunals under Annex VIII, like those of the other compulsory dispute settlement procedures under

[48] *Convention on Fishing and Conservation of the Living Resources of the High Seas*, done at Geneva on 29 April 1958, entered into force on 20 March 1966, Articles 4–9, https://www.gc.noaa.gov/documents/8_1_1958_fishing.pdf, accessed 10 April 2020. This mechanism has never been utilized to settle a concrete dispute.

[49] United Nations Division for Ocean Affairs and the Law of the Sea, *Annex VIII, Special Arbitration*, Article 2(2) and (3), https://www.un.org/depts/los/convention_agreements/texts/unclos/annex8.htm, accessed 22 May 2020. See the *List of Experts in the Field of Fisheries Maintained by the Food and Agriculture Organization of the United Nations (Communicated on 12 January 2017)*, https://www.un.org/Depts/los/settlement_of_disputes/expertsunclosVIIIjan2017fao.pdf, accessed 5 February 2020; *List of Experts in the Field of Marine Scientific Research Maintained by the Intergovernmental Oceanographic Commission of UNESCO (as at 28 January 2016)*, https://www.un.org/Depts/los/settlement_of_disputes/expertsunclosVIII_iocunesco.pdf, accessed 5 February 2020; *List of Experts in the Field of Navigation, including Pollution from Vessels and by Dumping, Maintained by the International Maritime Organization (as at 8 April 2019)*, https://www.un.org/Depts/los/settlement_of_disputes/expertsunclosVIIIimo2019.pdf, accessed 5 February 2020; *List of Experts in the Field of Protection and Preservation of the Marine Environment Maintained by the United Nations Environment Programme (Communicated on 8 November 2002)*, https://www.un.org/Depts/los/settlement_of_disputes/expertsunclosVIIInov2002unep.pdf, accessed 5 February 2020.

the Convention, are binding. More noteworthy is the possibility that if the parties to the dispute so request, a special arbitral tribunal may carry out an inquiry to establish the facts giving rise to the dispute. The resulting findings of fact will be considered conclusive for the parties.[50] Underlying the special arbitral tribunal's fact-finding function is the idea that in certain circumstances, facts may be the most in dispute, rather than the overarching legal positions.[51] The parties may go further and request that the special arbitral tribunal formulate recommendations that will serve as a basis for a review of the issues that have given rise to the dispute, hopefully enabling the parties to undertake further negotiations.[52]

Annex VIII has been chosen as a compulsory dispute settlement mechanism by a limited number of States, none of whom has to date had recourse to it.[53] Nevertheless the survey of Annex VIII, as well as that of Article 289, serves to demonstrate that the excessive caution that the CSIL praises in ICJ practice as regards the role of experts in dispute settlement is alien to the Convention. This observation is confirmed by the practice of arbitral tribunals established under Annex VII of the Convention.

B. Experts in the Practice of Annex VII Arbitral Tribunals

We have already seen in Chapter 3 that the Rules of Procedure of most Annex VII arbitral tribunals contain provisions relating to the appointment of independent experts and the assessment of independent experts' reports by the parties. Arbitral tribunals that have settled maritime delimitation disputes have appointed expert hydrographers[54]; in one instance, a tribunal also appointed a legal expert.

[50] *Annex VIII*, Articles 5(1) and (2).

[51] Richard Caddell, "Annex VIII. Special Arbitration," in Alexander Proelss et al. (eds.), *United Nations Convention on the Law of the Sea 1982: A Commentary* (München: C.H. Beck, 2017), 2492.

[52] Ranjeva, "Le règlement des différends," 1163.

[53] See the list in United Nations Treaty Collection, *Law of the Sea, United Nations Convention on the Law of the Sea Montego Bay, 10 December 1982* (2020), https://treaties.un.org/Pages/ViewDetailsIII.aspx?src=TREATY&mtdsg_no=XXI-6&chapter=21&Temp=mtdsg3&clang=_en, accessed 22 May 2020.

[54] At the time of writing (2020), three maritime delimitation disputes have been submitted to arbitration under Annex VII of the Convention (*Barbados v. Trinidad and*

1. The Role of the Expert Hydrographer

A basic understanding of the scope of hydrography will shed light on the assistance that an expert hydrographer provided to several arbitral tribunals established under Annex VII of the Convention.

Hydrography has been defined by the International Hydrographic Organization ("IHO") as

> [t]hat branch of applied sciences which deals with the measurement and description of the features of the seas and coastal areas for the primary purpose of navigation and all other marine purposes and activities, including inter alia: offshore activities, research, protection of the environment and prediction services.[55]

Hydrography deals with all those operations necessary to determine the configuration of the ocean/sea floor. Hydrographers measure the depth of the seafloor, tides, currents, gravity, magnetic field strength, and the physical, chemical, and structural properties of the water column and the seabed. A hydrographic survey entails the collection by systematic surveys at sea and along the coast of geo-referenced data relating to coastal morphology, including infrastructure for maritime navigation (aids to navigation and port configuration); the depth of water, including all hazards to navigation and items pertinent to other marine activities; the composition of the seabed; tides, tidal streams, and currents; and the physical and chemical properties of the water column.[56]

Tobago, 2004–2006, https://pca-cpa.org/en/cases/104/; *Guyana v. Suriname*, 2004–2007, https://pca-cpa.org/en/cases/9/; and *Bay of Bengal Maritime Boundary Arbitration Between Bangladesh and India*, 2009–2014, https://pca-cpa.org/en/cases/18/) and three to the ITLOS (*Delimitation of the Maritime Boundary Between Bangladesh and Myanmar in the Bay of Bengal (Bangladesh/Myanmar)*, 2009–2012, https://www.itlos.org/cases/list-of-cases/case-no-16/; *Delimitation of the Maritime Boundary Between Ghana and Côte d'Ivoire in the Atlantic Ocean (Ghana/Côte d'Ivoire)*, 2014–2017, https://www.itlos.org/cases/list-of-cases/case-no-23/; and *Delimitation of the Maritime Boundary between Mauritius and Maldives in the Indian Ocean (Mauritius/Maldives)*, 2019–), all accessed 22 May 2020.

55 International Oceanographic Commission ("IOC"), International Hydrographic Organization ("IHO"), and International Association of Geodesy ('IAG"), *A Manual of Technical Aspects of the United Nations Convention on the Law of the Sea—1982* (Monaco: International Hydrographic Bureau, 2006), Chapter 1-7, https://www.gc.noaa.gov/documents/gcil_iho_tech_aspects_los.pdf, accessed 24 May 2020.

56 Ibid. The water column is a vertical continuum of water from sea surface to sea-bed. International Hydrographic Organization ("IHO"), *Hydrographic Dictionary*, Part I, vol.

Closely related to hydrography are two other sciences: geodesy and marine geoscience. Geodesy is the science of measurement and mapping of the earth's surface. It includes the determination of the earth's external gravity field as well as the surface of the ocean floor.[57] Marine geoscience is the study of the material that comprises the coastal zone, the seabed, and sub-sea structures and of the processes that affect that material. It is concerned with the composition and distribution of sedimentary and non-sedimentary material, as well as the mechanisms of their emplacement. Its investigative mechanisms include direct sampling and measurement and remote sensing observations (transmission of acoustic signals and measurement of terrestrial gravity and magnetic fields) for determining the physical and chemical characteristics of structures that cannot be directly accessed. The findings of marine geoscience help explain the shape and variability of the shoreline and of the seabed.[58]

The assistance of an expert hydrographer is necessary in maritime delimitation cases where the tribunal is requested to "describe the course of the maritime boundary in terms of geodetic lines connecting geographic coordinates of points."[59] As explained by the hydrographer who acted as expert in the three maritime delimitation cases submitted to arbitration under Annex VII of the Convention, geographic coordinates need to be referred to a geodetic datum, just as a "dollar" needs to be defined as "American," "Canadian," or "Jamaican." Lines need to be defined as "geodesic" (the technically correct name for a "great circle") or as a rhumb line (or loxodrome—a line of constant angle from North), or a circular arc of a defined radius about a defined point, from a defined point in a clockwise or anti-clockwise direction and usually ending at a defined point.[60] In the *South China Sea Arbitration*, the appointment

I, *English* (5th ed.; Monaco: IHO, 1994), 268, http://hd.iho.int/en/index.php/International_nautical_mile, accessed 19 May 2020.

[57] IOC, IHO, and IAG, *A Manual*, Chapter 1-7 – 1-8.

[58] Wolfgang Torge, *Geodesy* (2nd ed.; Berlin: Walter de Gruyter, 1991), 1.

[59] *Treaty Between the Government of Canada and the Government of the United States of America to Submit to Binding Dispute Settlement the Delimitation of the Maritime Boundary in the Gulf of Maine Area* (25 November 1981), Article II, para. 2, in *I.C.J. Pleadings Delimitation of the Maritime Boundary in the Gulf of Maine Area (Canada/United States)*, vol. I, 10, https://www.icj-cij.org/files/case-related/67/9595.pdf, accessed 24 May 2020.

[60] David H. Gray, "Technical Standards for Judicial Decisions and Experts Appointed by Courts," paper presented at the 7th IHO-IAG-ABLOS [Advisory Board on the Law of

of an expert hydrographer was fully justified, in spite of the fact that the Arbitral Tribunal had not been requested to undertake maritime delimitation, because the Philippines relied heavily on satellite imagery as evidence for the status of Mischief Reef, Second Thomas Shoal, Subi Reef, Gaven Reef, and McKennan Reef (including Hughes Reef) as low-tide elevations (above water at low tide and below water at high tide).

The *Guyana v. Suriname Arbitration* relating to the delimitation of the two States' maritime boundaries offers an excellent example of the way in which recourse to expert assistance contributed to fully resolving the dispute in a scientifically sound way.[61] The Tribunal appointed an expert hydrographer to clarify the technical and scientific details of the dispute. His functions, which were to be performed according to international and geodetic standards, were to assist the Tribunal in the drawing and explanation of the maritime boundary line(s) in a technically precise manner and to assist it in the preparation of the Award.[62] During the oral hearings, the expert hydrographer met separately with the experts of the two parties to discuss a list of technical questions. During the meeting, he was able to put questions to the parties, who in turn put questions to him.[63] After the closure of the oral proceedings, the expert provided valuable assistance to the Tribunal during its deliberations. When it appeared that a Marker "B" would be crucial in the drawing of the maritime boundary, the hydrographer requested that the parties provide the positions of Marker "B" as well as other points in the 1960 Survey within the geographic area of Corentyn River, their geodetic datum, and the World

the Sea] Conference, Monaco, 3–5 October 2012, 2, 8, https://www.iho.int/mtg_docs/com_wg/ABLOS/ABLOS_Conf8/ABLOS8_Abstracts_Programme_v9.2.pdf, accessed 8 July 2017.

61 Riddell and Plant, *Evidence*, 353.

62 *Guyana v. Suriname*, Award of the Arbitral Tribunal (17 September 2007), 22, para. 108, https://pcacases.com/web/sendAttach/902, accessed 24 May 2020.

63 Ibid., Hearing Transcripts, vol. 1 (7 December 2006), 140–41, https://pcacases.com/web/sendAttach/891, accessed 24 May 2020; Hearing Transcripts, vol. 2 (8 December 2006), 152–54, 305, https://pcacases.com/web/sendAttach/892, accessed 24 May 2020; Hearing Transcripts, vol. 7 (15 December 2006), 88, https://pcacases.com/web/sendAttach/897, accessed 24 May 2020; Philippe Sands, "Science and International Litigation," in Denis Alland et al. (eds.), *Unité et diversité du droit international. Écrits en l'honneur du professeur Pierre-Marie Dupuy* [Unity and Diversity of International Law. Essays in Honour of Professor Pierre-Marie Dupuy] (Leiden: Martinus Nijhoff Publishers, 2014), 895.

Geodetic Survey ("WGS")-84 datum position of these points. The hydrographer noticed that Guyana, in its response, had provided coordinates of Marker "A" that did not correspond to those provided by Guyana in its own *Memorial*. Guyana acknowledged the mistake and explained that the difference in coordinates was due to the rounding off of their values. Suriname was unable to find any information in response to the hydrographer's request, contested the use of WGS-84 coordinates for Marker "A" as provided by Guyana, and urged the Tribunal to use the astronomical coordinates previously used by both States. Guyana then rejected the proposal to use astronomical coordinates, arguing that these were inaccurate and represented a difference of over 411 meters with the WGS-84 coordinates. In view of the disagreement—one that the Tribunal on its own was scarcely in a position to resolve—the Tribunal ordered the hydrographer to make a site visit to Guyana to inspect what Guyana alleged to be Marker "B" and to gather data relating to the issues raised by the two States. The expert's report of the site visit was transmitted to the parties for their comments. Suriname suggested a clarification, which Guyana accepted. The coordinates identified by the hydrographer were accepted by the two parties and the Tribunal.[64]

The hydrographer's assistance did not end there. When each party provided its computed results of the provisional equidistance line based on the basepoints that the Tribunal indicated, certain points were not equidistant from the basepoints. Furthermore, neither party computed the equidistant line using all the basepoints accepted by the Tribunal. The hydrographer therefore had to recompute the turning points on the equidistance line provided by both parties. A technical annex drafted by the hydrographer supplied the technical analysis of the data.[65] Understandably, the Award has been praised for being based on a sound understanding and acknowledgment of the technical points in dispute.[66]

The *Guyana v. Suriname case* also demonstrates that recourse to a legal expert may be essential to resolve procedural questions.

[64] *Guyana v. Suriname*, Corrected Report on Site Visit (30 July 2007), https://pcacases.com/web/sendAttach/901, accessed 24 May 2020: *Guyana v. Suriname*, Award, 22–25, paras. 110–126.

[65] *Guyana v. Suriname*, Award, 128, para. 397.

[66] Riddell and Plant, *Evidence*, 356.

2. The Role of the Legal Expert

The principle of *jura novit curia* (the judge knows the law) means that any assistance that an independent expert may provide to the court should relate to fact-finding and not to the ascertainment of international law. Judges take pains to stress that expert opinion on legal questions is (or should) in principle be excluded.[67] The operation of the principle is qualified in the case of law of limited geographical scope, such as domestic law and regional law, with which an international court is not presumed to be familiar.[68] In the *Guyane v. Suriname Case*, the Tribunal had recourse to the assistance of an expert who combined competence in international law and linguistic competence to assist it in resolving a problem relating to access to documents that threatened to upset the equality of the parties.

When preparing its *Memorial*, Guyana realized that it needed access to files in the archives of the Ministry of Foreign Affairs of the Netherlands, the former colonial power in Suriname.[69] The latter objected, on the grounds that the records covered many sensitive subjects, among which were Suriname's national security and territorial disputes. Suriname also explained that access to records concerning ongoing international boundary disputes was restricted by Dutch policy. Guyana then requested that the Tribunal order Suriname to withdraw its objection to Guyana's access to the documents. The Tribunal, stressing the importance of the equality of arms and good faith cooperation in international legal proceedings, first asked Guyana to submit a list of documents in the Dutch archives that it was seeking to access, with an explanation of their relevance to the dispute. Guyana's problem was that it could not identify the documents precisely without access to the files. After consulting the parties, the Tribunal then decided not to consider any document taken from a file in the Dutch archives to which Guyana had been denied access. This decision placed the two parties in a situation of equality but

[67] "Le droit comme norme et son interpretation ne peut faire l'objet d'une expertise [law as norm and its interpretation may not be the object of expert opinion]," *Différend Industrie Vicentine Elettro-Meccaniche (I.V.E.M.)* —Décision n° 183 du 7 mars 1955 [Industrie Vicentine Elettro-Meccaniche (I.V.E.M. Dispute. Decision No. 183] (7 March 1955)," *RIAA*, vol. XIII (New York: United Nations, 2006), 369, http://legal.un.org/docs/?path=../riaa/cases/vol_XIII/325-381.pdf&lang=O, accessed 23 July 2020.

[68] D'Aspremont and Mbengue, "Strategies," 243.

[69] This paragraph and the following are summarized from *Guyana v. Suriname*, Award, 3–19, paras. 11–62.

would have also handicapped Suriname's ability to present its case to the Tribunal.

At the same time, the Tribunal decided to appoint a Dutch-speaking independent expert who was charged with two tasks. First, the expert, a Belgian international law professor, would review files that Suriname had already introduced or would introduce and examine Suriname's proposal to remove or redact parts of the file or documents. Second, he would examine Guyana's request that Suriname disclose files or documents that were identified with reasonable specificity and that were in the possession or under the control of the Netherlands as well as any request from Suriname to remove or redact documents or files. The Tribunal set guidelines to enable the expert to distinguish between files and documents relating to the maritime boundary dispute before it, on the one hand, and files and documents relating to the two parties' land boundary or disputes with third States, on the other.

To safeguard the parties' procedural rights, the Tribunal took steps with which we are already familiar. Prior to appointment, it sought the parties' views on the expert's terms of reference. The expert was required to sign a confidentiality undertaking and a declaration of independence and impartiality. The Tribunal transmitted copies of his report to Guyana and Suriname for their responses. It was only after receiving these comments that the Tribunal made its decisions on the expert's recommendations, which concerned Suriname's proposals for redaction of documents that had been or would be submitted. In the process, Suriname also requested documents from Guyana, which the latter transmitted to Suriname. To sum up, the Tribunal's decision to appoint an independent expert made it possible to resolve a procedural difficulty that could have prevented both parties from presenting fully their respective case and become a major obstacle to the conduct of the proceedings.

An assessment of the assistance provided by the experts in the *South China Sea Arbitration* requires an evaluation of their independence and impartiality.

II. The Independence and Impartiality of the Experts in the *South China Sea Arbitration*

Experts must provide guarantees of independence and impartiality, whether they are appointed by States or by an international court. Otherwise their opinions will be of little value.

Assumptions as to the content of independence and impartiality underlie the post-*Arbitration* attacks of CSIL and Chinese scholars on some of the experts appointed by the Philippines and some of the experts appointed by the Tribunal. The attack on Schofield for allegedly presenting an expert opinion that contradicted his earlier views assumes that experts should not change their views. The criticism of Carpenter and Loke Ming Chou's reports for being prepared while proceedings were ongoing presupposes that only expert reports prepared prior to judicial proceedings are impartial. The objection to the preparation of the coral reef experts' report in three weeks presumes that it should take a long time for experts to prepare a report. The present part explores the related concepts of independence and impartiality of both party-appointed experts and experts appointed by a court (also known as "independent experts") as a precondition for the assessment of the independence and impartiality of both categories of experts on the status of maritime features, on coral reefs, and on navigational safety in the *South China Sea Arbitration*.

A. Conceptions of Independence and Impartiality

An effort must first be made to distinguish the related concepts of independence and impartiality. Then the procedures that international courts and tribunals employ to ascertain the independence and impartiality of party-appointed experts and independent experts will be discussed.

1. The Scope of the Independence and Impartiality of Experts

The scholarly literature focuses on the independence and impartiality of party-appointed experts. This focus may be the product of the assumption that court-appointed experts are by definition independent and impartial and the limited recourse of most international courts to the appointment of experts. Interestingly enough, scholarly definitions distinguish between independence and impartiality of party-appointed experts, while the actors in international adjudication—States, judges, registries, counsel, and the experts themselves—tend to conflate these concepts.

A scholarly definition of independence refers to "the fact that a person-...does not depend on any authority other than their [sic] own...or at the very least does not depend on the State in whose territory they perform their duties."[70] Analyses of the roles of court-appointed experts at the national level define their independence in relation to the parties. At the international level, an expert who is an employee of the State that appoints him/her cannot be independent, as the State could influence his/her views.[71] In the *Whaling in the Antarctic Case*, in which Australia alleged that Japan's large-scale program of whaling violated the International Convention for the Regulation of Whaling, one author of an Australian "scientific report" annexed to Australia's *Memorial* was the chief scientist of Australia's Antarctic program.[72] Despite his qualifications as a scientist, identifying him as an expert would have made him vulnerable to the charge of lack of independence as an employee of the Australian government. Australia wisely refrained from calling the report an "expert opinion" and did not present the author as an expert witness for examination during the oral proceedings. Instead, the chief scientist formed part of the delegation that presented oral arguments on Australia's behalf to the ICJ. As such, he would have been expected to put forward the best possible argument for Australia.[73]

Lack of independence can produce partiality or bias, but there may be other sources of bias.[74] The sources of bias may be personal, intellectual, and financial. Bias may be personal if the expert feels sympathy with the party that retains him/her and feels pressure to stay on that party's side. Personal bias may be conscious if the expert adapts his/her opinion so that it favors one party; it may be unconscious, leading the expert to make mistakes in following the scientific method. The source of bias might be financial. After all, the expert is paid for and acting on behalf of the party that appoints him/her. As a result of this "commissioning

[70] Salmon, *Dictionnaire*, 283, quoted in *Pulp Mills*, Verbatim Record 2009/21, 14, note 26.

[71] *Pulp Mills*, Verbatim Record, CR 2009/21, 22–27, paras. 20–25.

[72] *Whaling in the Antarctic (Australia v. Japan: New Zealand intervening)*, *Memorial of Australia* (9 May 2011), Appendix 1, W. de la Mare, N. Kelly, D. Peel, Antarctic Baleen Whale Populations, April 2011, 282–333, https://www.icj-cij.org/files/case-related/148/17382.pdf, accessed 28 May 2020; Lima, "The Evidential Weight," 630.

[73] Arthur Watts, "Enhancing the Effectiveness of Procedures of International Dispute Settlement," *Max Planck Yearbook of United Nations Law* 5 (2001): 29, https://www.mpil.de/en/pub/publications/periodic-publications/max-planck-yearbook/volume-5.cfm, accessed 12 May 2020.

[74] The following discussion is based on Appazov, *Expert Evidence*, 14–15, 68, 69, 74, 77, 176; Dwyer, *The Judicial Assessment*, 163, 166, 176, 177.

bias," the expert may be strongly influenced by the client's interest.[75] The expert might also be concerned about the prospects for future employment. The source of bias might be intellectual, if the expert feels that his/her professional reputation is at stake and depends on the outcome of the case.

Parties to a case are aware that an expert must be or perceived to be impartial, but this does not stop them from engaging in "expert shopping," with the aim of identifying an expert whom they can expect to give a favorable opinion. In this way the party can use an expert who genuinely holds the opinion that the party represents, and the expert can maintain his/her integrity during the proceedings. The "hired gun" expert is one who is associated with certain positions and is hired by parties seeking to establish that position.[76] A party might go further and openly pressure the expert to adapt his/her report to the party's requirements.[77] Experts may be able to resist such pressures on the basis of codes of conduct governing their profession or simply out of concern for their reputation, preventing them from behaving in ways that would prejudice their standing in the profession.[78] Analyses of the role of court-appointed experts at the national level admit that court-appointed experts are not necessarily exempt from bias. Like the experts appointed by the parties, court-appointed experts may share the views of one of the parties to the case, hold biases that are different from those of both parties, have unconscious biases, or share widely held attitudes in the scientific community.[79]

Mégret clarifies the notion of impartiality and provides us some bases for challenging the impartiality of experts. In his view, impartiality consists of the absence of prior emotional attachment to a case, approaching a

[75] Oren Perez, "Judicial Strategies for Reviewing Conflicting Expert Evidence: Biases, Heuristics, and Higher-order Evidence," *American Journal of Comparative Law* 64 (2016): 77.

[76] Evan Bell, "Judicial Assessment of Expert Evidence," *Judicial Studies Institute Journal* 2 (2010): 55, https://www.ijsj.ie/assets/uploads/documents/pdfs/2010-Edition-02/article/judicial-assessment-of-expert-evidence.pdf, accessed 7 November 2019.

[77] Appazov, *Expert Evidence*, 76, 176; Dwyer, *The Judicial Assessment*, 177.

[78] Kate Parlett, "Parties' Engagement with Experts in International Litigation," *JIDS* 9 (2018): 451; Caroline E. Foster, *Science and the Precautionary Principle in International Courts and Tribunals: Expert Evidence, Burden of Proof and Finality* (Cambridge: Cambridge University Press, 2011), 98.

[79] Appazov, *Expert Evidence*, 15, 83.

case free of obvious ethnic, racial, and religious biases, and the ability to approach issues with a fresh mind. One may gauge an expert's impartiality on the basis of positions that they have occupied, declarations that they have made as academics, or specific engagement with some of the cases or situations in which they are involved.[80] Of particular interest here are past declarations as a source of bias, given that Chinese scholars criticized one of the experts appointed by the Philippines for allegedly adopting views during the arbitral proceedings that were different from those he expressed in his academic writings. To determine whether past declarations demonstrate bias, Mégret identifies four factors to be taken into account: the fact that the opinion is actually expressed, the form of the opinion and the forum in which it is expressed, the substance of the opinion, and the context. The context may be further analyzed in terms of a series of dichotomies, the second element of which affords some presumption that the opinion expressed in the past declaration is strongly held and is a potential source of bias: unrelated/related, general/specific, old/recent, relative/absolute, consensual/polemical, legal/factual, official/personal capacity, expert/activist, and private/public.[81]

Scholarly definitions of and distinctions between independence and impartiality are not as clear-cut in the minds of the actors in international adjudication. The debate between Argentina and Uruguay on the independence of experts during the oral proceedings of the *Pulp Mills on the River Uruguay Case* at the ICJ provides ample proof of this lack of clarity. Argentina had alleged that Uruguay violated the Statute of the River Uruguay by authorizing and constructing two pulp mills on the River Uruguay, which had harmful effects on the quality of the waters of the River Uruguay and on the areas affected by it. Uruguay believed that an expert who is retained by one of the parties is, by definition, not independent: "there is, and can be no such thing, as an independent expert." It believed that an expert's report, prepared to support a party's claim, should be treated with caution. In Uruguay's view, only the expert evaluations and statements issued by competent international organizations and

[80] Frédéric Mégret, "International Judges and Experts' Impartiality and the Problem of Past Declarations," *LPICT* 10 (2011): 33.

[81] Ibid., 48–66.

the expert reports issued by independent consultants engaged by international organizations could be independent reports.[82] Argentina argued that an expert who is not a State employee and who has no personal interest in the outcome of the dispute may be properly considered independent. Often these experts are respected senior academics, who would not wish to compromise their international reputations by tailoring their evidence to the needs of a particular State or case.[83] In its Judgment, the ICJ did not express a view on the two competing conceptions.[84] The point here is that if we keep in mind the distinctions made above between independence and impartiality, we realize that both States were in reality debating the impartiality of experts, which they incorporated in the concept of independence.

Further evidence that the other main actors in international judicial proceedings—judges, registry staff, counsel, and experts—conflate independence and impartiality is found in a survey of 62 respondents carried out by a team from the University of Geneva. While all actors claim that they value the independence and impartiality of experts, they use the two terms interchangeably and no clear definition of either concept exists in the minds of most of them.[85] ICJ judges and registry staff consider that there is a greater need for objectivity on the part of court-appointed experts. Party-appointed experts who have appeared before the ICJ consider impartiality synonymous with independence. They see themselves as "independent" as long as they are stating what they believe to be true and are not being dishonest in supporting the party appointing them. This conception of independence does not exclude the possibility of selecting among several scientific interpretations that which is most favorable to the appointing State, as long as that interpretation is scientifically reliable. The party-appointed experts believe that they are able to

[82] *Pulp Mills*, Verbatim Record, CR 2009/19 (24 September 2009), 33–34, paras. 2–3, http://www.icj-cij.org/files/case-related/135/135-20090924-ORA-01-00-BI.pdf, accessed 26 May 2020.

[83] Ibid., CR 2009/21, 22–27, paras. 20–25.

[84] *Pulp Mills on the River Uruguay (Argentina v. Uruguay), Judgment, I.C.J. Reports 2010*, 172, para. 68, http://www.icj-cij.org/files/case-related/135/135-20100420-JUD-01-00-BI.pdf, accessed 26 May 2020.

[85] Laurence Boisson de Chazournes et al., "One Size Does Not Fit All—Uses of Experts before International Courts and Tribunals: An Insight into the [sic] Practice," *JIDS* 9 (2018): 481–85.

maintain their "independence" even if they meet with the legal teams of the party that appointed them, as long as the purpose is to discuss scientific issues and the expert is not made aware of the party's legal strategy until the oral hearings.[86] For party-appointed experts who have appeared before the ITLOS, only the court-appointed expert is expected to be independent. In their view, appointment by a party entails supporting the party's claim. This conception of the expert's duty toward a party is tempered somewhat by recognition of the need for honesty in technical matters. This group of party-appointed experts placed greater emphasis on the notion of credibility, without having a clear definition of the notion.[87] It is somewhat ironic that party-appointed experts who have appeared before the ICJ simultaneously believe that they can maintain their independence and/or impartiality and suspect that court-appointed experts may inadvertently bring to bear their background and prejudices on their assessment.[88]

Whenever a party-appointed expert is asked to present oral testimony to a court, the process of examination may be utilized to determine his/her independence and impartiality.

2. The Procedures for Determining the Independence and Impartiality of Experts

A State may take steps, or more precisely, refrain from taking certain steps, if it wishes to ensure the (perception of) independence, understood as absence of dependence on the authority of the State, and impartiality, understood as the absence of bias, of the experts that it appoints. It will not hire its own nationals or State officials as experts. It will not inform the expert of its legal strategy while the expert is preparing his/her report. The expert presented by Australia during the oral proceedings of the *Whaling in the Antarctic Case* wrote afterward that he was able to observe Australia's strategy only during the oral proceedings.[89] A State will not give any instructions to the expert and will not give any guidance

[86] Ibid., 484.

[87] Ibid., 491–92.

[88] Ibid., 485.

[89] Marc Mangel, "Whales, Science, and Scientific Whaling in the International Court of Justice," *PNAS* [Proceedings of the National Academy of Sciences], 113 (20 December 2016): 14523, https://www.pnas.org/content/pnas/113/51/14523.full.pdf, accessed 25 May 2020.

as to the choice of methods or principles in support of scientific arguments or any indication concerning the range or depth of the scientific evidence to be provided in court, as the expert called by Japan in the *Whaling in the Antarctic Case* testified.[90] Any such measures are entirely at the discretion of the State appointing the expert. In contrast, international courts rely on institutional procedures in order to assess the independence and impartiality of party-appointed experts, the most important of which is cross-examination during the oral proceedings. Separate procedures have had to be established for determining the independence and impartiality of court-appointed experts upon their appointment and upon the submission of their reports, an area in which Annex VII tribunals have played a pioneering role.

The main function of the system of examination of party-appointed experts, like that of witnesses, is to obtain the specialized knowledge and the sincere beliefs of the expert and to enable their veracity and credibility to be challenged and tested.[91] The expert is first examined by the party that has called him/her (examination in chief), then by the opposing party (cross-examination), and possibly by the first party again (re-examination), after which the judges may put their own questions to the expert. Depending on the court's discretion, the expert's written report may replace the examination in chief. At the ICJ and at the ITLOS, the party appointed expert, before testifying, makes a solemn declaration, under the terms of which he/she "will speak the truth, the whole truth, and nothing but the truth" and his/her statement will be in accordance with his/her sincere belief.[92] The requirement of a solemn declaration is

[90] *Whaling in the Antarctic*, Lars Walløe, *Scientific Review of Issues Raised by the Memorial of Australia, Including its Two Appendices* (9 April 2013), http://www.icj-cij.org/files/case-related/148/17418.pdf, accessed 26 May 2020.

[91] Rosenne, *The Law and Practice*, vol. III, 1308.

[92] ICJ, *Rules of Court, adopted on 14 April 1978 and entered into force on 1 July 1978*, Article 64(b), https://www.icj-cij.org/en/rules, accessed 22 March 2020; ITLOS, *Rules of the Tribunal* (ITLOS/8), *as adopted on 28 October 1997 and amended on 15 March 2001, 21 September 2001, 17 March 2009 and 25 September 2018*, Article 79(b), 32, https://www.itlos.org/fileadmin/itlos/documents/basic_texts/Itlos_8_E_25.09.18.pdf, accessed 29 April 2020.

intended to underline that unlike counsel, a party-appointed expert owes a duty to the court.[93]

The survey carried out by the University of Geneva team reveals that ICJ and ITLOS members, the Registries of both tribunals, and counsel consider that cross-examination is the best means of revealing the expert's independence together with the inherent scientific quality of expert opinions.[94] Party-appointed experts are somewhat less enthusiastic. They stress the need for greater guidance from the two courts, without which cross-examination would in their view not be an efficient procedure enabling the court to make use of expert knowledge.[95]

The way in which cross-examination by the opposing party and questioning by the judges may enable a court to determine the independence and impartiality of a party-appointed expert is illustrated in the *Whaling in the Antarctic Case*. The expert presented for examination by Japan was compelled to admit that he had received one of the highest honors conferred by Japan on foreigners in the field of fisheries; that he had participated in the review of the predecessor of the program that the ICJ was reviewing to determine whether Japan was carrying out whaling for purposes of scientific research; that he was one of the unidentified co-authors of the studies that reviewed the first program; and that for these reasons, he had a personal stake in the outcome of the case. Counsel for Australia argued that the expert was in reality presenting evidence as an advocate and not as an expert and urged him to withdraw the claim that he was an independent expert witness. Little wonder that at one point the expert implied that he was being subjected to harassment by counsel for Australia.[96]

If cross-examination cast doubt on the expert's independence, some of the expert's own declarations tended to affirm his impartiality, but

[93] *Pulp Mills*, *Judgment*, Separate Opinion of Judge Greenwood, 231, para. 27, https://www.icj-cij.org/files/case-related/135/135-20100420-JUD-01-06-BI.pdf, accessed 26 May 2020.

[94] Boisson de Chazournes et al., "One Size," 487, 489, 491.

[95] Ibid., 487, 491.

[96] *Whaling in the Antarctic (Australia v. Japan, New Zealand Intervening)*, Verbatim Record, CR 2013/14 (3 July 2013), 24, 25, 31, 35, https://www.icj-cij.org/files/case-related/148/148-20130703-ORA-02-00-BI.pdf, accessed 26 May 2020. One commentator described the cross-examination of the expert as "harsh." Gros. "The ICJ's Handling," 584, 585.

in a way that was prejudicial to the party that had called him. In his report, he had already criticized aspects of Japan's program of scientific whaling. In particular, he believed that Japanese scientists had not given completely transparent explanations of the way that sample sizes of the whales harvested for scientific research were calculated and determined. He was under the impression that sample sizes were influenced by funding considerations.[97] During the oral proceedings, a question raised by a judge as to whether he was referring to sample sizes of mink whales highlighted the expert's criticism of Japan's program.[98] The expert volunteered the opinion that Japan's proposal regarding fin whales was not very well-conceived, because the main part of the fin whale population was located outside the area where Japan's program of scientific whaling was to be carried out.[99] Needless to say, an expert opinion and expert testimony that criticizes the position of the party appointing him/her enjoy a high degree of credibility. It is doubtless for this reason that the expert's remarks critical of Japan's research programs were explicitly referred to by the Court in its Judgment.[100]

Cross-examination by the parties is in theory limited to party-appointed experts. International courts have developed distinct procedures for determining the independence and impartiality of court-appointed experts, procedures that do not make hard-and-fast distinctions between independence and impartiality. The unique feature of these procedures is that they are carried out in two stages: prior to or upon the appointment of the experts, and upon the submission of the expert report. Prior to appointment the assessment of independence and impartiality will be based on the qualifications and the professional experience of the expert. Upon submission of the expert report, the contents of the report will give the parties an indication of the independence and impartiality of the court-appointed experts.

The practice of the *Guyana v. Suriname Arbitration* seems to have offered a precedent for other tribunals established under Annex VII of the Convention and for the ICJ itself. As we have seen in the previous

97 Walløe, *Scientific Review*.

98 *Whaling in the Antarctic*, Verbatim Record, CR 2013/14, 49.

99 Ibid., 47.

100 *Whaling in the Antarctic (Australia v. Japan: New Zealand Intervening), Judgment, I.C.J. Reports 2014*, 275, 280, paras. 159, 180, http://www.icj-cij.org/files/case-related/148/148-20140331-JUD-01-00-BI.pdf, accessed 26 May 2020.

Chapter, the *South China Sea* Tribunal adopted similar procedures—prior to the appointment of the experts, it transmitted to the Philippines and China the qualifications, the declaration of independence and impartiality, and the terms of reference of the experts.[101] One innovation introduced by the *South China Sea* Tribunal, which devoted detailed provisions on experts appointed by the Tribunal, was terminological. Whereas the Rules of Procedure of earlier or even contemporaneous arbitrations under Annex VII (*Barbados v. Trinidad and Tobago*, *Guyana v. Suriname*, *Bay of Bengal*, *Chagos Marine Protected Area*, and *ARA Libertad*) had referred to the experts appointed by the respective Tribunal simply as "experts," the experts appointed by the Tribunal in the *South China Sea Arbitration* are qualified as "independent experts."[102] The qualification implies that they are independent in relation to both the parties and the Tribunal, in the sense of not being subject to their control. Another innovation explicitly provided for the possibility of objections by China or the Philippines to the qualifications, independence, and impartiality of the experts, with an obligation imposed on the Tribunal to decide promptly on the objection. The Rules of Procedure went further and allowed China or the Philippines the right to object after the appointment of the expert and while the proceedings are ongoing, provided that the reasons for the objection became known to China or the Philippines only after the appointment had been made.

A further opportunity for the parties to ascertain the independence and impartiality of the court-appointed experts arises once the expert's report has been submitted. If the contents of the report show signs of the preparation of the report under the authority of other actors or signs of bias, a party or the parties may raise objections and make suggestions for modification. Once again, the Tribunal in the *South China Sea Arbitration* introduced a procedural innovation. Anticipating a situation in which one or both parties objected strongly to the experts' report, or in which for other reasons the Tribunal considers it necessary, a hearing could have been organized during which the parties could have put questions to the experts and presented their own expert witnesses to testify on the points

[101] Award of 12 July 2016, 19, 30, 31, paras. 58, 85, 90.

[102] *South China Sea Arbitration*, Rules of Procedure (27 August 2013), Article 24(2), 11, https://pcacases.com/web/sendAttach/233, accessed 11 May 2020.

of disagreement with the experts.[103] This procedure, had it been implemented, would have in practice subjected the independent experts to a process very similar to the cross-examination of party-appointed experts.

It is ironic that the CSIL should characterize the *South China Sea* Tribunal's appointment of independent experts as "obviously flawed," on the basis of a comparison with the practice of the ICJ over 70 years.[104] On the contrary, it is the ICJ practice that is "obviously flawed." In 70 years, the ICJ has officially appointed experts only twice. The reality, already noted more than 25 years ago by a former ICJ President, is that the ICJ has a habit of employing experts in all fields—cartography, hydrography, geography, linguistics, and even law—to assist it in understanding issues in particular cases, without informing the parties to the case.[105] The ICJ's practice of engaging "*experts fantômes* (ghost experts)," as they were somewhat mockingly described by two judges,[106] deprives the parties of the opportunity to inspect their qualifications and challenge their independence and impartiality. The parties would not have enough information to enable them to request such an opportunity, given that they were not informed of the hiring of experts in the first place. Judges have strenuously defended the practice of hiring "ghost experts," because the advice they provide, for example on the precise geographic coordinates clearly identified by the Court or on the drawing of a chart comprising these points, allegedly does not affect the content of the Court's decision.[107] The survey carried out by the University of Geneva team makes it clear that judges' defense of the practice has not convinced party-appointed experts and legal counsel of its wisdom.[108]

The CSIL would have had the *South China Sea* Tribunal imitate the opaque practice of the ICJ. The record shows that it was the ICJ that adopted the practice of Annex VII arbitral tribunals. This much became

[103] Ibid., Article 24(5), 11.

[104] CSIL, "The South China Sea Arbitration Awards," 637.

[105] Sir Robert Jennings, "International Lawyers and the Progressive Development of International Law," in Makarczyk (ed.), *Theory of International Law at the Threshold of the 21st Century. Essays in Honour of Krzysztof Skubiszewski* (The Hague: Kluwer Law International, 1996), 415.

[106] *Pulp Mills, Judgment*, Joint Dissenting Opinion of Judges Al-Khasawneh and Simma, 113, para. 14.

[107] Gaja, "Assessing," 414.

[108] Boisson de Chazournes et al., "One Size," 487.

clear in 2016, when the ICJ decided to appoint, half a century after appointing its first independent experts, two experts in the *Maritime Delimitation Case in the Caribbean Sea and the Pacific Ocean (Costa Rica v. Nicaragua)*. The ICJ sought the parties' views on the subject of the expert opinion, the number and mode of appointment of the experts, and the procedure to be followed, after which it decided to engage two experts. Following the precedent of the *Guyana v. Suriname Arbitration* and other arbitrations under Annex VII of the Convention, each of the two experts was required to declare, "upon my honour and conscience, that I will perform my duties as expert honourably and faithfully, impartially and conscientiously..." The declaration of independence and impartiality fills a gap in the ICJ Statute, which contains no reference to the independence and impartiality of experts appointed by the Court.[109] The ICJ ruled that the expert report would be transmitted to Costa Rica and Nicaragua for their responses. The Court did not go as far as the *South China Sea* Tribunal, which had provided for the possibility of a separate hearing in case of serious disagreements between the parties and the experts, but it did require that the experts attend the oral proceedings in order to answer questions from the parties.[110]

After having explored the scope of independence and impartiality of experts in general, we may now attempt an assessment of the independence and impartiality of the party-appointed experts and the independent experts in the *South China Sea Arbitration*.

B. The Assessment of the Independence and Impartiality of the Experts in the South China Sea Arbitration

The discussion will cover all the authors of the expert reports submitted by the Philippines and all of the experts appointed by the Tribunal, for it is safe to assume that the CSIL and Chinese scholars wished to tar them all with the same brush.

109 Parlett, "Parties' Engagement," 441.

110 *Maritime Delimitation in the Caribbean Sea and the Pacific Ocean (Costa Rica v. Nicaragua), Order of 31 May 2016, I.C.J. Reports 2016*, 236, 238, paras. 4, 10(3), 10(7), 10(8), https://www.icj-cij.org/files/case-related/157/157-20160531-ORD-01-00-BI.pdf, accessed 27 May 2020.

1. The Party-Appointed Experts

If independence is understood to mean lack of dependence on any authority other than one's own, then the authors of the three expert reports submitted by the Philippines were independent. None was in the same situation as the Australian scientist who co-authored one of the scientific reports submitted by Australia together with its *Memorial*. When presenting two of them to the Arbitral Tribunal for examination, the Philippines declared that they were independent, in the sense that their statements were based on their own views and expertise.[111] The following paragraphs will therefore concentrate on the issue of impartiality. All of the experts presented by the Philippines may be judged to be free of "commissioning bias," when we evaluate their qualifications and expertise as well as the contents of their report.

Two of the three belong to the category of senior academics who would not jeopardize their international reputations by tailoring their expert opinions to the needs of a case. The first author of the report on the status of maritime features in the South China Sea, Professor Clive Schofield, who was also presented by the Philippines as an expert witness, is a geographer who has provided technical advice and support to States engaged in boundary negotiations and in cases before the ICJ. To cite just one example, he was a scientific and technical adviser to the Nigerian delegation in the oral proceedings at the ICJ in the *Land and Maritime Boundary Between Cameroon and Nigeria Case*.[112] Professor Victor Prescott had also served as an expert witness in cases before the ICJ and the US Supreme Court. The third author, Robert van de Poll designed, created, and developed the CARIS LOTS (Law of the Sea) software, which allows States to construct, manage, maintain, and update a coastal State's baseline model as well as to address all aspects of Article 76

[111] *South China Sea Arbitration*, Hearing on the Merits and Remaining Issues of Jurisdiction and Admissibility, Transcript, Day 2 (25 November 2015), 2–10 ("Hearing on the Merits"), https://pcacases.com/web/sendAttach/1548, accessed 27 April 2020; Transcript, Day 3 (26 November 2015), 48, https://pcacases.com/web/sendAttach/1549, accessed 13 October 2019.

[112] *Land and Maritime Boundary Between Cameroon and Nigeria (Cameroon v. Nigeria: Equatorial Guinea intervening), Judgment*, *I.C.J. Reports 2002*, 303, http://www.icj-cij.org/files/case-related/94/094-20021010-JUD-01-00-BI.pdf, accessed 22 July 2020.

of the Convention on the continental shelf.[113] At the time of the preparation of the expert report for the *South China Sea Arbitration*, he had been involved in three-fourths of all extended continental shelf submissions made until 2015 to the United Nations Commission on the Limits of the Continental Shelf ("CLCS").[114] Experts having this type of professional experience would not risk international reputations by tailoring their expert opinions to the needs of the State that retained them.[115]

The qualifications and experience of the two coral reef experts also offer no grounds for impeaching their impartiality. The expert who was presented by the Philippines for examination, Dr. Kent E. Carpenter, has had significant and extensive research experience on coral reefs in the Philippines, first as a Peace Corps volunteer for three years (1975–1978), as a post-doctoral student (1985–1987) and as a Fulbright Visiting Professor (2011). He has collaborated on numerous research projects with Filipino scientists and speaks Tagalog, one of the major Philippine languages.[116] That having been said, he had significant international experience beyond that acquired in the Philippines: as a research scientist at the Kuwaiti Institute for Scientific Research for three years (1987–1990); as a Senior Fishery Resources Officer at the UN FAO (1991–1996); and as manager (since 2005) of the Marine Biodiversity Unit and Global Marine Species Assessment of an international NGO, the International Union for the Conservation of Nature ("IUCN"). Unlike the expert called by Japan in the *Whaling in the Antarctic* case, Carpenter supplied all the information regarding his ties with the State that had appointed him as expert in an attachment to his expert opinion.

Carpenter's co-author in the second report, Dr. Loke Ming Chou, can also be put in the category of senior academics with international reputations. He was professor of Biological Sciences at the National University of Singapore for 37 years (1977–2014), a member of the Scientific

[113] CARIS, *CARIS LOTS Article 76, Product Overview* (Fredericton, New Brunswick: CARIS, 2017), http://www.caris.com/products/lots/overview.cfm, accessed 4 September 2017; CARIS, *LOTS Brochure* (Fredericton, New Brunswick: CARIS, 2017), http://www.caris.cm/downloads/brochures/lots-en.pdf, accessed 4 September 2017.

[114] *SWSP*, Annex 513, vol. IX, 241–43.

[115] *Pulp Mills*, Verbatim Record, CR 2009/21, 22–27.

[116] First Carpenter Report, 420–37; *South China Sea Arbitration*, Hearing on the Merits, Transcript, Day 3, 48.

and Technical Advisory Committee of the Global Coral Reef Monitoring Network ("GCRMN") of the International Coral Reef Initiative ("ICRI") for 16 years (1996–2012), and Committee chair (2003–2005). He has been a member of the Asia Environmental Council Executive Board since 1998, a member of the Joint Group of Experts on the Scientific Aspects of Marine Environmental Protection ("GESAMP") since April 2010, and a member of the roster of experts of the Asia–Pacific Economic Cooperation Marine Resource Conservation Working Group since November 2010. He served as advisor or expert to regional projects, such as the UNEP South China Sea Project (2002–2009) and the Global Environmental Finance—United Nations Development Programme ("GEF/UNDP") Partnerships in Environmental Management for the Seas of East Asia.[117]

The qualifications and experience of the navigational safety expert, Professor Craig Allen, offer solid guarantees of impartiality. He is a lawyer as well as a holder of a US merchant marine license as master of ocean-going vessels. He had nearly 20 years of service with the US Coast Guard (1975–1995), during which he performed, executed, and/or supervised more than 1000 collision avoidance maneuvers in various capacities, including operations officer, navigator, and commanding officer, on Coast Guard vessels. He also conducted over 100 investigations into vessel casualties and oil spills. He is the author of *Farwell's Rules of the Nautical Road* (2004), the leading book on the International Convention on the International Regulations for Preventing Collisions at Sea ("COLREGS, 1972") in the US.[118] The COLREGS are the collision regulations that Chinese vessels violated in 2012 in the waters around Scarborough Shoal, according to Philippine Submission No. 13. One might add that he provided his expert opinion pro bono, as he has done for several national and international litigation support projects.

[117] Second Carpenter Report, 241–42.

[118] Adopted at London on 20 October 1972, entered into force on 15 July 1977; consolidated text as amended in 1981, 1987, 1989, 1993, 2001 and 2007, http://www.ecolregs.com/index.php?option=com_k2&view=itemlist&layout=category&Itemid=505&lang=en, accessed 31 May 2019; *MP*, Annex 239, Opinion of Craig H. Allen, Judson Falknor Professor of Law, University of Washington (19 March 2014), vol. VII, 373, 380–87, https://files.pca-cpa.org/pcadocs/The%20Philippines%27%20Memorial%20-%20Volume%20VII%20%28Annexes%20222-255%29.pdf, accessed 19 May 2020.

Beyond their qualifications and expertise, it is the content of the experts' report that is likely to provide evidence of impartiality. As the third, fourth, and fifth parts of this Chapter will examine in detail the expert evidence, attention at this stage will be centered on the experts who were criticized by the CSIL for partiality. The most serious charge was raised against the first author of the report on the status of maritime features in the South China Sea, which was submitted by the Philippines in response to three requests from the Tribunal for information on the status as submerged feature, low-tide elevation, rock, or island of any maritime feature claimed by China that could potentially give rise to an EEZ or a continental shelf; historical, anthropological, geographic, and hydrographic information on eleven maritime features in the Spratly Islands; and geographic and hydrographic information regarding Macclesfield Bank as well as any other technical data relevant to the assessment of its status as a submerged feature, low-tide elevation, rock, or island.[119] In fact, the scope of the expert report was much broader, as it covered a total of 49 maritime features in the South China Sea. Guarantees of the independence and impartiality of the experts are to be found in their professional and academic background. Their assessments of the status of two maritime features, which differed from those of the Philippines, together with their evaluation of the limitations of satellite imagery, are manifestations of their impartiality.

One may find the most convincing evidence of the three experts' impartiality, understood as absence of bias, in the expert report. They agreed with the Philippines on the status of 47 of the 49 maritime features that they examined, but their views on two maritime features, Central London Reef and Erica Reef, contradicted those of the Philippines. The Philippines, drawing on nautical charts and sailing directions, concluded that both were low-tide elevations, which would not be entitled to a territorial sea. In contrast, the three experts were of the view that both could be considered as high-tide elevations, which would be entitled to a twelve-mile territorial sea. The bases of their conclusion for Central London Reef were sailing directions that indicated the presence of a sandbank that covers at high tide on that reef, and for Erica Reef, satellite imagery

[119] *SWSP*, vol. I, 116–17, https://files.pca-cpa.org/pcadocs/Supplemental%20Written%20Submission%20Volume%20I.pdf, accessed 28 May 2020.

that suggested the presence of drying areas that may be elevated above high water.[120]

The expert report, in explaining its research approach, drew up a balance sheet of the advantages and the limitations of satellite imagery that was more measured than the Philippine assessment. One can understand the Philippine decision to rely heavily on satellite imagery, which avoids sensitive issues of territorial sovereignty that other methods of obtaining information may generate.[121] China would surely have objected to ship surveys in the territorial sea of the Spratly Islands or to aerial surveys that would have involved overflight of the reefs where China was carrying out island-building. During the Hearing on the Merits, the Philippines declared that "[t]he satellite imagery, including the EOMAP analysis of each of the features, consistently, completely and without the slightest ambiguity" demonstrated that all five features in Submissions No. 4 and 6 were covered by water at high tide.[122] The experts' report did give the highest value to the satellite images in degree of accuracy of the different data sources:

> Satellite imagery proved to be especially valuable in the appraisal and classification of features....Satellite imagery acquired and analysed for the present report has proved to be invaluable in enhancing understanding of the geographical characteristics of the insular features under discussion.[123]

Yet the experts did not fail to identify some of the limitations of satellite imagery. In their view, there was no substitute for on-the-ground field mapping. Satellite imagery was valuable when it was problematic or impossible to undertake field surveys. They gave one example of the limitations of satellite imagery: a part of a feature that remained above high water could escape detection through analysis of satellite images if it were very small. They pointed out that this might be the case for 17 features at Scarborough Shoal and the Spratly Islands that consisted

[120] *SWSP*, vol. I, 118–19.

[121] Youna Lyons, "Prospects for Satellite Imagery of Insular Features and Surrounding Marine Habitats in the South China Sea," *Marine Policy* 45 (2014): 147.

[122] *South China Sea Arbitration*, Hearing on the Merits Transcript, Day 2 (25 November 2015), 35, https://pcacases.com/web/sendAttach/1548, accessed 27 April 2020.

[123] *SWSP*, Annex 513, vol. IX, 159.

predominantly of reefs and shoals and were reported as being submerged or awash at high tide but with individual or small groups of rocks or very small islets being visible at high water. If any part of the feature that remained above water were very small, even the best resolution satellite imagery would prove inconclusive in confirming that fact.[124] They emphasized that they did not use satellite imagery in isolation; it was complemented by other sources of hydrographic and other geographic information, including nautical charts and sailing directions.[125]

It was Schofield's testimony on the status of Itu Aba that has attracted criticism that he is not "independent"—the more accurate word would be "impartial." Chinese scholar He Tiantian contends that Schofield changed his views on Itu Aba's legal status for purposes of the proceedings. He cites a 1996 article co-authored by Schofield in which it was acknowledged that Itu Abu was inhabited since 1956 and a 2014 co-authored article in which it was stated that "it can be argued in good faith that the islands we have identified are not 'rocks which cannot sustain human habitation or economic life of their own' within the meaning of Article 121(3)."[126] The CSIL called attention to a 2005 article co-authored by Schofield, which declared that "it is reasonable to assume that the rocks and the drying reefs can sustain an economic life of their own in the context of Article 121(3) of UNCLOS." The CSIL then added in a faux-solemn tone that "for reasons unknown to us, Schofield testified as an expert witness against his own opinion."[127]

The possible contradiction in Schofield's views had not escaped the attention of the Tribunal, which did not hesitate to ask him whether his position on Itu Aba Island had evolved and changed over time. In the expert report, he and his co-authors had classified Itu Aba as a rock within the meaning of Article 121(3). He responded that he had not changed his position on Itu Aba's status as an island, because Itu Aba met the requirements for an island laid down in Article 121(1) of the Convention—it is a naturally formed area of land surrounded by water and above

[124] Ibid., 214.

[125] Ibid., 159.

[126] Robert C. Beckman and Clive H. Schofield, "Defining EEZ Claims from Islands: A Potential South China Sea Change," *The International Journal of Marine and Coastal Law* 29 (2014): 210; He Tiantian, "Commentary," 123.

[127] CSIL, "The South China Sea Arbitration Awards," 532, para. 677.

water at high tide. He had written in 2013 that Itu Aba "may conceivably" be considered an island entitled to an EEZ and a continental shelf because at the time reports on Itu Aba were mixed. He pointed out that the arbitral proceedings gave him the opportunity to fully examine the facts and to review material that was not available to him in 2013, after which review he had arrived at the firm belief that Itu Aba was a rock within the meaning of Article 121(3) of the Convention. The Tribunal also asked him why he had written that Article 121(3) was ambiguous. He replied that it was subject to interpretation and that to his knowledge, no court or tribunal had provided a definitive interpretation of the provision.[128]

A change of position, if indeed there was one, is not necessarily a sign of partiality or bias. As we have seen above, Mégret has argued convincingly that impartiality entails, among others, the ability to approach issues with a "fresh mind," which in turn entails the willingness to consider all elements in as rational and dispassionate way as possible. From this perspective, a change in position may be considered as a sign of impartiality.[129] The "absolute/relative" dichotomy is relevant for assessing Schofield's past declaration that Itu Aba was an island rather than a rock. Following Mégret's approach, we can say that the expression of the opinion by Schofield in cautious, hypothetical terms suggested that he needed to know more and that he was speaking on the basis of facts as they appeared at the time when he was writing. The engagement of Schofield as an expert in the *South China Sea Arbitration* gave him the opportunity to examine evidence to which he had not had access at the time he was writing his previous opinion. This evidence now served as the basis of the firm belief that Itu Aba was a rock. From this perspective, a change of opinion is not a sign of partiality but a sign of impartiality. On the contrary, it is the unwillingness to change opinion that is a sign of bias.[130]

The CSIL was unable to highlight any manifestations of bias in the contents of the reports of the coral reef experts and the navigational safety expert. As regards the former, Chinese scholar He Tiantian was only able

[128] *South China Sea Arbitration*, Hearing on the Merits, Transcript, Day 4 (30 November 2015), 50–51, https://pcacases.com/web/sendAttach/1550, accessed 16 April 2020.

[129] Mégret, "International Judges," 44.

[130] Ibid., 53.

to make an insinuation of commissioning bias (although he did not use the expression), on the grounds that their reports were prepared for the purposes of the case, while the arbitral proceedings were ongoing. He Tiantian cites an ICJ statement that the Court "will treat with caution evidentiary materials prepared for this case."[131] It is not at all clear that the application of this principle is evidence of a commissioning bias. First, the ICJ has not declared that this principle also applies to expert evidence.[132] Second, the ICJ does not question the relevance and reliability of expert reports submitted to it simply because they were "specially prepared" for a case. In the *Pulp Mills Case*, one or the other of the parties were able to submit scientific and technical reports that were prepared by international organizations on Uruguay's pulp mill projects well before proceedings were initiated. Not all States are so lucky as to have such reports at their disposal when international legal proceedings are initiated. In the event reports of this kind were unavailable, an international court could hardly disregard expert reports prepared for purposes of a case by the parties. The alternative would mean not having any expert report at all. As for the navigational safety expert, neither the CSIL nor individual Chinese scholars were able to find so much as insinuations of bias.

Having dismissed possible objections to the independence and impartiality of the party-appointed experts, we may now turn to those directed at the Tribunal-appointed experts, which are even less consequential.

2. The Independent Experts

The independence and impartiality of the independent experts may be assessed on the basis of their qualifications and experience at the time of their appointment and of the contents of their reports, at the time of their submission to the Tribunal and the parties. The latter assessment will be reserved for the succeeding parts of this chapter, simply because in the eyes of the CSIL, the support offered by the reports for Philippine claims was *ipso facto* evidence of bias and the alleged bias was allegedly not corrected through critical analyses of the reports by the Tribunal. This

[131] *Armed Activities on the Territory of the Congo (Democratic Republic of the Congo v. Uganda), Judgment, I.C.J. Reports 2005*, 201, para. 61, https://www.icj-cij.org/files/case-related/116/116-20051219-JUD-01-00-BI.pdf, accessed 27 May 2020; He Tiantian, "Commentary," 122.

[132] Lima, "The Evidential Weight," 627.

section will limit itself to the assessment of the independence and impartiality of the independent experts that the parties and the Tribunal could have undertaken at the time of their appointment. Particular attention will be paid to the CSIL's criticism of the coral reef experts for preparation of a report in 17 days and for not being Asian.[133]

The qualifications of the expert hydrographer were disclosed to the Philippines and China but were not posted on the PCA website. A quick online search discloses that Grant Boyes has advised and assisted 20 countries and several territories in the Pacific and South East Asian region on various aspects of maritime boundaries and offshore limits, including the negotiation of maritime delimitations. In a career spanning over 30 years, he spent ten years as Maritime Boundaries Coordinator with the South Pacific Forum Fisheries Agency and eight as a private consultant.[134] He has co-authored scholarly papers on such topics as Australia's approach to using remotely sensed data to determine territorial sea baselines,[135] establishing an Australian marine spatial data infrastructure,[136] and the universal digital marine cadaster.[137]

The navigational safety expert's qualifications were attached to his expert report. Captain Gurpreet S. Singhota had 14 years of seagoing experience, including six years as commander on a super tanker, a bulk carrier, and a chemical tanker and other types of vessels. Among his achievements in a 26-year career at the IMO (1987–2013), he assisted in the preparation of amendments to the COLREGS, 1972 and in the revision of Chapter V (Safety of Navigation) of the International Convention for the Safety of Life at Sea, 1974 ("SOLAS 1974"). In view of Captain Singhota's professional experience as a commander of several

[133] CSIL, "The South China Sea Arbitration Awards," 627, para. 910.

[134] 6th IHO-IAG ABLOS Conference, International Hydrographic Bureau, Monaco, 25–27 October 2010, https://legacy.iho.int/mtg_docs/com_wg/ABLOS/ABLOS_Conf6/S4P1-B.pdf, accessed 29 May 2020.

[135] Co-authored with Colin French, Mark Alcock, Phil Symonds and Bill Hirst, 6th IHO-IAG-ABLOS Conference, Monaco, 25–28 October 2010, https://www.iho.int/mtg_docs/com_wg/ABLOS/ABLOS_Conf6.htm, accessed 8 July 2017.

[136] Co-authored with Mark Alcock and Matthew McGregor, 7th ABLOS Conference, Monaco, 3–5 October 2012, https://www.iho.int/mtg_docs/com_wg/ABLOS/ABLOS_Conf8/ABLOS8_Abstracts_Programme_v9.2.pdf, accessed 8 July 2017.

[137] Co-authored with Mark Alcock and Matthew McGregor, 8th ABLOS Conference, Monaco, 20–22 October 2015, https://www.iho.int/mtg_docs/com_wg/ABLOS/ABLOS_Conf8/ABLOS8_Abstracts_Programme_v9.2.pdf, accessed 8 July 2017.

types of vessels and as an international civil servant concentrating on the COLREGS and SOLAS, he was obviously ideally placed to assess whether the maneuvers of Chinese vessels constituted violations of the COLREGS. His report ("Singhota Report"), submitted in April 2016, was not annexed to the Award of 12 July 2016, but was posted on the PCA website after the Award of 12 July 2016 had been issued.[138]

As for the coral reef experts, the CSIL implied that the expert report was biased because it was prepared within 17 days, calculated from the time of appointment of Professor Mumby and Dr. Ward, to the time of submission of the report. The CSIL professed to be astonished that the three experts could complete their report on such complex issues in a very short span of time, denounced the hasty manner in which the report was produced, and objected that none of them was Asian.[139] The CSIL should have taken the time to examine the three coral reef experts' qualifications, which are attached to their expert report. Had it taken the trouble to do so, it would have realized that the three coral reef experts are all experts on the recovery of coral reefs, with decades of cumulative research experience spanning not just Southeast Asia, but also the Pacific, the Middle East, and Africa.

Dr. Sebastian Ferse, who taught tropical aquatic ecology at the University of Bremen in Germany, already had over 10 years of research experience as a coral reef ecologist in Southeast Asia (particularly Indonesia), the Pacific Islands, East Africa, and the Red Sea. Prior to his appointment, his research had focused largely on coral reef restoration and ecological functioning, in particular the roles of reef fishes and their link to the reef habitat. He coordinated a joint Indonesian-German research project addressing pollution impacts on coastal systems and coral reefs in Jakarta Bay and offshore islands; at the time of the *Arbitration* he was leader of an interdisciplinary working group that addressed the resilience of coral reef social-ecological coral reef systems in Melanesia and of a research project assessing anthropogenic influences on reef ecology in Indonesia.[140] Peter

[138] Captain Gupreet S. Singhota, *Report of the International Navigational Safety Expert Appointed by the Permanent Court of Arbitration [sic], The Hague, The Netherlands*, 15 April 2016, 2, para. 2 ("Singhota Report"), https://pcacases.com/web/sendAttach/1810, accessed 29 May 2020.

[139] CSIL, "The South China Sea Arbitration Awards," 635, para. 947.

[140] *Assessment of the Potential Environmental Consequences of Construction Activities on Seven Reefs in the Spratly Islands in the South China Sea. Expert Report of Dr. rer. nat.*

Mumby was a professor of coral reef ecology at the University of Queensland, Australia. For his doctorate degree, he developed new ways to use satellite and airborne imagery to evaluate the health of coral reefs. Professor Mumby had been adviser to a number of governments on coral reef and fisheries policy, including Australia, Belize, the Bahamas, Bonaire, the Maldives, and Indonesia; adviser to the UNDP on coastal management, the UNEP on reef resilience, and UNESCO on marine ecosystem; and chair of a remote sensing working group for the World Bank. At the time of his appointment, he was Chief Scientist of the World Bank/GEF Capturing Coral Reef Ecosystem Services Project.[141] Dr. Selina Ward was a coral biologist working as a Senior Lecturer in the School of Biological Sciences at the University of Queensland, Australia. Her research focused on the responses of corals to environmental stress including elevated nutrients, mechanical damage, and elements of climate change such as ocean acidification and temperature elevations. Dr. Ward was a former president of the Australian Coral Reef Society, the Program and Partnerships manager for the International River symposium for eleven years, and a board member of the International River Foundation.[142]

Having dismissed any possible challenges to the independence and impartiality of the party-appointed experts and the independent experts, we may now examine in greater detail the complex scientific and technical evidence submitted by the Philippines, the reports of the independent experts, and the Tribunal's evaluation of the expert evidence submitted by the two categories of experts in the areas of the status of features, the harm to the marine environment caused by China's island-building, and navigational safety.

III. The Assessment of the Scientific and Technical Evidence on the Status of Maritime Features

An international court that appoints its own experts to resolve fact-finding difficulties arising from conflicting expert opinions or from default

Sebastian C.A. Ferse, Professor Peter Mumby, PhD and Dr. Selina Ward, PhD (26 April 2016), 4–5 ("Ferse Report"), https://pcacases.com/web/sendAttach/1809, accessed 29 May 2020.

[141] Ibid., 5.

[142] Ibid., 5–6.

may find that the independent experts provide yet another interpretation of the scientific evidence that is as plausible as those presented by the two parties or by the appearing party (in the event of default). In these circumstances, the court would find itself back at square one.[143] The question is then how the court can know whether to accept the opinion of the court-appointed expert or not, if it appointed an expert precisely because it cannot accurately determine facts that require specialized knowledge.[144] Simply deferring to the court-appointed experts could entail loss of control over them[145] Refusing to adopt the expert's opinion would require justification.

Could the strategies and techniques used by judges, domestic or international, to assess expert evidence without the assistance of court-appointed experts be useful?[146] On one point judges and scholars agree: the opinions of court-appointed experts are not binding on them. As a judge ad hoc in the *Corfu Channel Case* put it, "[a]ccording to a general rule of procedure, the Court is not bound by the opinion of experts. The Court may accept or reject it; but it must always give sufficient reasons."[147] Similarly, a Franco-Italian Conciliation Commission, established under the Peace Treaty with Italy of 10 February 1947 to settle disputes relating, among others, to restitution of property taken by Italy from Allied countries during World War II, declared in 1955 that "expert opinion is not binding on the Conciliation Commission."[148] Scholars emphasize that courts that appoint experts do not *ipso facto* delegate

[143] Cymie Payne, "Mastering the Evidence: Improving Fact-Finding by International Courts," *Environmental Law* 41 (2011): 1195.

[144] Dwyer, *The Judicial Assessment*, 3.

[145] Appazov, *Expert Evidence*, 7, 63.

[146] Bell, "Judicial Assessment," 55–96; Perez, "Judicial Strategies," 75–120; Donoghue, "Expert Scientific Evidence," 379–87; Gaja, "Assessing," 409–18.

[147] *Corfu Channel Case, Judgment of December 15th 1949: I.C.J. Reports 1949*, Dissenting opinion by Judge ad hoc Ečer, 253, http://www.icj-cij.org/files/case-related/1/001-19491215-JUD-01-01-BI.pdf, accessed 1 June 2020; Bennouna, "Experts," 345; Riddell and Plant, *Evidence*, 330.

[148] *Différend Industrie Vicentine Elettro-meccaniche (I.V.E.M.), Décision N° 183 du 7 mars 1955*, 369; *Treaty of Peace with Italy*, signed at Paris 10 February 1947, https://www.loc.gov/law/help/us-treaties/bevans/m-ust000004-0311.pdf, accessed 1 June 2020; Daniel-Henri Vignes, "La Commission de conciliation franco-italienne [The Franco-Italian Conciliation Commission]," *AFDI* 1 (1955): 212–17, http://www.persee.fr/doc/afdi_0066-3085_1955_num_1_1_1162, accessed 1 June 2020.

decision-making to the experts: "judges decide cases, experts do not."[149] Judges insist that it is courts that interpret legal, terms, categorize legally the factual issues, and assess the burden of proof.[150]

That having been said, it has been observed that on the rare occasions when they have appointed experts, international courts have tended to give greater weight to the opinions of these experts than to those of party-appointed experts and that they tended to adopt the reports of court-appointed experts as a whole.[151] The manner in which the experts prepared the report may be one reason for this attitude. In the *Corfu Channel Case* Judgment on the merits, the ICJ gave great weight to the opinion of naval experts who conducted a site visit to Albania and Yugoslavia because they had carried out their task "in a manner giving every guarantee of correct and impartial information."[152] The substantive contents of the report may also provide reasons for the court's adoption of the expert report. The Franco-Italian Commission declared that it had no reason not to adopt the report of its expert unless the expert's line of argument contradicted the facts as they appeared on the record, well-known facts, legal provisions, or the rules of logic.[153]

No such statements of principle are to be found in the *South China Sea* Awards. It is possible to comprehend the way(s) in which the Tribunal assessed the complex scientific and technical evidence submitted by the

[149] Bell, "Judicial Assessment," 93; Tullio Scovazzi, "Between Law and Science: Some Considerations Inspired by the *Whaling in the Antarctic* Judgment," *Questions of International Law* 14 (2015): 16, http://www.qil-qdi.org/wp-content/uploads/2015/04/03_Whaling-Case_SCOVAZZI_FIN_REV.pdf, accessed 1 June 2020.

[150] *Pulp Mills*, *Judgment*, Joint Dissenting Opinion of Judges Al-Khasawneh and Simma, 113, para. 12; *Pulp Mills*, *Judgment*, Declaration of Judge Yusuf, 209, para. 10; Riddell and Plant, *Evidence*, 329.

[151] Benzing, *Das Beweisrecht*, 173, 561.

[152] *Corfu Channel Case*, *Judgment of April 9th, 1949*: *I.C.J. Reports 1949*, 22, http://www.icj-cij.org/files/case-related/1/001-19490409-JUD-01-00-BI.pdf, accessed 1 June 2020.

[153] *Différend I.V.E.M.*, 369; *Différend Héritiers de S.A.R. Mgr le Duc de Guise — Décision n⁰ 162 du 20 novembre 1953* [Dispute concerning the Heirs of H.R.H. The Duke of Guise – Decision No. 162 of 20 November 1953]," *RIAA*, vol. XIII (New York: United Nations, 1964), 168, para. 2, https://legal.un.org/riaa/cases/vol_XIII/150-170_Heritiers.pdf, accessed 1 June 2020; Savadogo, "Le recours," 252; Benzing, *Das Beweisrecht*, 172.

Philippines and the independent experts' report by careful reading of the expert reports and the Award of 12 July 2016.

On the status of maritime features, the Philippines submitted an expert report, one of whose authors was presented for examination by the Tribunal, and a scientific and technical report, on which the expert had to answer questions during the oral proceedings.[154] These reports and the Tribunal's analysis, which was in all likelihood attributable to the expert hydrographer, have been passed over in silence by practically all commentators. The highly technical nature of the discussions on satellite imagery in the reports and in the Award of 12 July 2016 may have discouraged any attempts to analyze the expert evidence submitted by the Philippines and the expert advice received by the Tribunal. The neglect is unfortunate, for the *South China Sea Arbitration* appears to be the first occasion in which an international court, with expert assistance, has engaged in a detailed assessment of the value of satellite imagery as evidence. In the *Pulp Mills Case*, Argentina and Uruguay both presented satellite images to the ICJ in support of their conflicting assessments of the responsibility for algal bloom of discharges from a pulp mill authorized by Uruguay.[155] The Court did not analyze the satellite imagery and dismissed the evidence presented by Argentina with the statement that it had not been established to its satisfaction that the algal bloom episode referred to by Argentina was caused by discharges from the pulp mill authorized by Uruguay.[156] That approach to scientific and technical evidence contrasts sharply with that of the *South China Sea* Tribunal, which undertook a detailed analysis of the evidence based on satellite

[154] *SWSP*, Annex 513, vol. IX, 143–245; *SDP*, Annex 807, EOMAP GmbH & Co, Satellite Derived Bathymetry for Selected Features in the South China Sea (18 November 2015), vol. V, 8–27, http://www.pcacases.com/pcadocs/The%20Philippines%27%20Supplemental%20Documents%20-%20Volume%20III%20%28Annexes%20710-756%29.pdf, accessed 2 June 2020.

[155] *Pulp Mills Case*, Verbatim Record, CR 2009/14 (16 September 2009), 44 para. 15, http://www.icj-cij.org/files/case-related/135/135-20090916-ORA-01-00-BI.pdf, accessed 2 June 2020; *Pulp Mills Case*, Verbatim Record, CR 2009/16 (21 September 2009), 61–63, paras. 59–60, http://www.icj-cij.org/files/case-related/135/135-20090921-ORA-01-00-BI.pdf, accessed 2 June 2020; Verbatim Record, CR 2009/20 (28 September 2009), 46–47, paras. 10–14, http://www.icj-cij.org/files/case-related/135/135-20090928-ORA-01-00-BI.pdf, accessed 2 June 2020.

[156] *Pulp Mills*, *Judgment*, 96–97, paras. 248–50.

imagery and satellite-derived bathymetry submitted by the Philippines. And it was right to do so. One can readily imagine that a judgment in which the Tribunal simply declared that the evidence derived from satellite imagery and satellite-derived bathymetry was not satisfactory without further explanation would not been convincing and would have come as a surprise to the Philippines.

A second reason for analyzing the complex scientific and technical evidence submitted by the Philippines and the Tribunal's analysis thereof is that it was the assessment of the limitations of satellite imagery that provided the rationale for the Tribunal's decision to consult different British and French archival materials. Failure to analyze the complex scientific and technical evidence submitted by the Philippines and the Tribunal's assessment of the latter can only lead to an underestimation, if not a negative assessment, of the role played by the expert hydrographer. It creates the impression that the only specific advice he provided was confirmation that information on the historical and modern observation of tidal ranges in the Spratly Islands all appear to be consistent with each other.[157] Espenilla assumes quite rightly that some consultation must have occurred between the Tribunal and the hydrographer, but believes that the lack of transparency as regards his contribution made him an "*expert fantôme* (ghost expert)."[158] Assessments of this kind may be understandable in the absence of an expert report attached to the Award of 12 July 2016. Nevertheless, it is possible to identify the impact of the expert hydrographer's advice through a careful reading of the Award. It cannot be excluded that it was not deemed necessary to attach an expert or technical report to the Award to avoid a simple repetition of the advice that was already incorporated in the body of the Award. In its assessment of the value of satellite imagery and of satellite-derived bathymetry presented by the Philippines as evidence, the Tribunal completely adopted the opinion of its expert hydrographer.

157 Davenport, "Procedural Issues," 92; Espenilla, "Judicial Fact-Finding Initiatives," 25; Award of 12 July 2016, 137, para. 317.

158 Espenilla, "Judicial Fact-Finding Initiatives," 25.

A. The Scientific and Technical Evidence Submitted by the Philippines

In support of its claim that Mischief Reef, Second Thomas Shoal, Subi Reef, Gaven Reef, and McKennan Reef (including Hughes Reef) are low-tide elevations (Submissions No. 4 and 6), the Philippines submitted satellite imagery that had been generated by two different remote sensing systems: Landsat and DigitalGlobe.[159] As mentioned previously, it produced two sets of images for each feature. The Band 1 (blue-green) images correspond to shorter wavelengths of 0.45–0.52 μm, which can penetrate water.[160] In Band 1, the underwater contours of the feature are visible. Band 4 (infrared) images correspond to longer wavelengths of 0.76–0.90 μm, which are almost entirely absorbed by water. In Band 4, there are no features above water.[161] A footnote explained that "multi-band imagery is multispectral, meaning that it is collected from several parts of the electromagnetic spectrum (the entire range of light radiation), from gamma rays to radio waves, including X-rays, microwaves and visible light."[162] During the Hearing on the Merits, the expert clarified that the satellite imagery allowed for multispectral image analysis, which involves different red, green, and blue (R + G + B) band combinations from within the satellite image. This technique makes it possible to more easily distinguish between features that are above water and those that are entirely submerged, by maximizing or minimizing the degree of penetration of the water column in the image presented.[163] In response to the Tribunal's questions put to it prior to the Hearing on the Merits, the Philippines added bathymetric models, generated through a process called satellite-derived bathymetry. All purported to show that the five features named in Submissions No. 4 and 6 were below water at high tide. In the absence of more detailed technical reports either from the Philippines or from the experts, an attempt will be made here to provide a simple technical background on satellite imagery and satellite-derived

[159] The images are reproduced in volume II of the *Memorial*, which is unfortunately not publicly available.

[160] A micrometer (μm) is a measure of length equal to 10^{-6} meters.

[161] *MP*, vol. I, 132, 37, paras. 5.59–5.73.

[162] Ibid., 133, footnote 473.

[163] Hearing on the Merits, Transcript, Day 3, 7.

bathymetry, in the hope that it will make the expert's subsequent discussion with the Tribunal and the Tribunal's critique of satellite imagery more comprehensible, or at least less opaque.

1. Satellite Imagery and Remote Sensing Systems

While the Philippines acquired modern high-resolution satellite imagery, it may have neglected its potential limitations.

UN General Assembly Resolution 41/65 defines remote sensing (also known as "earth observation") as

> the sensing of the Earth's surface from space by making use of the properties of electromagnetic waves emitted, refracted or diffracted by the sensed objects, for the purpose of improving natural resources management, land use and the protection of the environment.[164]

As indicated by this definition, waves or particles constitute the form taken by electromagnetic radiation, or energy emitted by objects on the earth's surface. Remote sensing is based on the detection of electromagnetic radiation, which consists of an electric field and a magnetic field and is emitted or reflected by objects on the Earth's surface. The wavelength of electromagnetic radiation, the length of one wave cycle, measured as the distance between successive wave crests, is important for remote sensing. The wavelength of electromagnetic spectrum varies across a spectrum ranging from the shorter wave lengths (gamma rays, with wavelengths shorter than 10^{-10} meters, and X-rays, with wavelengths ranging from 10^{-8} to 10^{-12} meters) at one extreme to radio waves (wavelength from 1 to 10^3 meters) at the other. This constitutes the electromagnetic spectrum to which the Philippines referred in its *Memorial*. The regions of the electromagnetic spectrum that are useful for remote sensing are the ultraviolet portion (wavelength 10^{-9} to 10^{-5} meters), the visible portion

164 United Nations General Assembly, Resolution 41/65, Principles Relating to Remote Sensing of the Earth from Space, Annex, Principle 1, Doc. A/RES/41/65 (3 December 1986), https://digitallibrary.un.org/record/126423?ln=en, accessed 2 June 2020. A standard text defines "remote sensing" as "the practice of deriving information about the Earth's land and water surfaces using images acquired from an overhead perspective, using electromagnetic radiation in one or more regions of the electromagnetic spectrum, reflected or emitted from the Earth's surface." James B. Campbell and Randolph H. Wynne, *Introduction to Remote Sensing* (5th ed.; New York: The Guilford Press, 2011), 6.

(wavelength 0.4 to 0.7×10^{-6} meters, with the shortest visible wavelength being violet and the longest being red, while blue, green, yellow, and orange fall in between), and the infrared region (wavelengths 0.7 to 100×10^{-6} meters).[165]

Remote sensing measures the radiation that is reflected from objects (targets) that are on the earth's surface and that are illuminated by electromagnetic energy from the sun, which emits energy at every wavelength. Different objects absorb and reflect different wavelengths, which are in different portions of the electromagnetic spectrum. For example, chlorophyll in leaves strongly absorbs radiation in the red and blue wavelengths and reflects green wavelengths. In the summer, when the chlorophyll content is at its maximum, leaves appear greenest. In the autumn, when there is less chlorophyll, there is less absorption and more reflection of red wavelengths, so that leaves appear red or yellow.[166]

After energy has been scattered by or emitted from the target, a sensor, which is "remote" because it is not in contact with the target, collects and records the electromagnetic radiation. The record of the amount of energy collected by the sensor from a narrow wavelength range is stored in a channel or band. For example, Band 4 measures the intensity of near infrared (IR) energy reflected. The data stored is represented as one of the three primary colors, red, blue, and green, so-called because no single one can be created from the other two and all other colors can be formed by combining B, G, and R.[167] Colors are assigned to certain bands because the human eye is not sensitive to ultraviolet or infrared red light. Colors from the visible portion of the electromagnetic spectrum—red, green, and blue—are used to build a composite image from remote sensing data that makes sense to human eyes.[168]

Sensors are sensitive to certain spectral bands. Sensors like panchromatic cameras, radar sensors, or laser scanners only measure in one specific

[165] Natural Resources Canada, *Fundamentals of Remote Sensing* (Ottawa: Canada Centre for Remote Sensing, 2016), 9–12, http://www.nrcan.gc.ca/sites/www.nrcan.gc.ca/files/earthsciences/pdf/resource/tutor/fundam/pdf/fundamentals_e.pdf, accessed 2 June 2020.

[166] Ibid., 116–17.

[167] Ibid., 6. For further information, see Table 4.1.

[168] United States Geological Survey ("USGS"), *Landsat - Earth Observation Satellites*, Fact Sheet 3015–3081 (November 2015), 1, http://pubs.usgs.gov/fs/2015/3081/fs20153081.pdf, accessed 3 June 2020.

Table 4.1 Landsat Thematic Mapper (TM) and Enhanced Thematic Mapper plus (ETM) + bands

Band	*Name*	*Bandwidth (µm)**	*Spatial resolution*	
1	Blue	0.45–0.515	30 m	This short wavelength of light penetrates clear water better than other bands It is often the band of choice for monitoring aquatic ecosystems (mapping sediments in water, coral reef habitats) Illuminates material in shadows Absorbed by chlorophyll, so plants do not show up very brightly in this band Useful for soil/vegetable discrimination, forest-type mapping, identifying man-made features
2	Green	0.525–0.605	30 m	Penetrates clear water fairly well Gives excellent contrast between clear and turbid water Helps find oil on the surface of the water and vegetation Reflects more green light than any other visible color Man-made features are still visible
3	Red	0.63–0.69	30 m	Limited water penetration Since vegetation absorbs nearly all red light (it is sometimes called the chlorophyll absorption band) this band can be useful for distinguishing between vegetation and soil and monitoring vegetation health Useful for identifying vegetation types, soils and urban (city and town) features
4	Near Infrared	0.75–0.90	30 m	Since water absorbs nearly all light at this wavelength, water bodies appear very dark This contrasts with the bright reflectance for soil and vegetation, so it is a good band for defining water/land interface (boundaries of bodies of water) Very good at detecting and analyzing vegetation

(continued)

Table 4.1 (continued)

Band	*Name*	*Bandwidth (μm)**	*Spatial resolution*	
5	Shortwave Infrared-1	1.55–1.75	30 m	Limited cloud penetration Very sensitive to moisture, useful for measuring moisture content of soil and vegetation Provides good contrast between different types of vegetation Helps differentiate between soil and clouds
6	Thermal Infrared	10.4–12	60 m (Landsat 7) 120 m (Landsat 4 &5	Useful to observe temperature and its effects, e.g., daily and seasonal variations Useful to identify some vegetation density, cover type and moisture Helps to locate geothermal activity Primarily used for geological applications
7	Shortwave Infrared-2	2.08–2.35	30 m	Limited cloud penetration Provides good contrast between different types of vegetation Useful for measuring moisture content of soil and vegetation Helps differentiate between snow and clouds Particularly helpful for discriminating among different types of rock formations
8	Panchromatic	0.52–0.9	15 m	Only Landsat 7 has a 15-m panchromatic "sharpening band" It has 15-m resolution used to "sharpen" images

*1 μm = 10^{-6} meters

Sources

iGETT (Integrated Geospatial Education and Technology Training), 2013. ***Landsat Spectral Bands***. Remote Sensing in 2012. Corpus Christi, TX: Del Mar College, 2013, http://igett.delmar.edu/Resources/Remote%20Sensing%20Technology%20Training/Landsat_bands-sm.pdf, accessed 11 March 2016

NASA Goddard Space Flight Center. Landsat 7 Education and Outreach, 2011. ***Landsat Spectral Band***. Virginia Community College System. Geospatial Extension Program. Department of Forest Resources and Environmental Conservation. Geospatial Institute 2011. Blacksburg, VA May 21-26, 2011, http://gep.frec.vt.edu/VCCS/materials/2011/Day4/Handouts/Landsat%20Spectral%20Bands.pdf, accessed 11 March 2016

University of California Berkeley College of Natural Resources. Geospatial Innovation Facility. Center for Biodiversity and Conservation, n.d. ***Landsat Spectral Band Information***, http://gif.berkeley.edu/documents/Landsat%20Band%20Information.pdf, accessed 11 March 2016

band. Multispectral scanners (MSS), like the primary sensor on board Landsat 1 (1972), Landsat 2 (1975), and Landsat 3 (1978), measure in several spectral bands at the same time. The reflected radiation is recorded simultaneously in different wavelength bands. Sensing simultaneously in several spectral bands makes it possible to relate properties that show up well in specific spectral bands.[169]

An image is any pictorial representation used to detect and record electromagnetic energy. It is divided into tiny squares called pixels (picture elements), each of which is assigned a digital number representing its relative brightness (reflected light energy). The size of the pixel corresponds to the "spatial resolution" of the sensor, which determines the smallest object detectable. "30-meter data" would refer to data in a matrix or grid of elements measuring 30 meters × 30 meters.[170] For a homogeneous feature to be detected, its size has to be equal to or larger than the size of the area on the ground viewed (resolution cell). If a feature is smaller than the resolution cell, it may not be detectable. In fine or high-resolution images, small objects can be detected.[171]

The Philippines acquired most of its satellite imagery from Landsat, the first satellite to acquire space-based images of the Earth's land surface. Landsat was launched as Earth Resources Technology Satellite ("ERTS-1") in 1972 by the US Departments of the Interior and Agriculture and the National Aeronautics and Space Administration ("NASA") and later renamed Landsat 1. The imagery acquired by the Philippines was of several types and drawn from differing timeframes with a range of resolutions. These included Landsat Thematic Mapper4 ("TM4," "Landsat 4"), launched in 1982 and ended in 1993; TM5 ("Landsat 5"), launched in 1984 and ended in 2011, at 30.0- and 28.5-meter ground resolution imagery; Landsat TM7 ("Landsat 7"), launched in 2000 and ended in 2006, at 14.25-meter ground resolution imagery; and TM8 ("Landsat 8"), launched in 2010 and ended in 2014, at 14.25-meter ground resolution imagery.[172] The TM sensor collected data in six spectral bands.

169 Klaus Tempfli et al. (eds.), *Principles of Remote Sensing. An Introductory Textbook* (Enschide, The Netherlands: The International Institute for Geo-Information Science and Earth Observation, 2009), 89.

170 Woody Turner et al., "Remote Sensing for Biodiversity Science and Conservation," *Trends in Ecology and Evolution*, 18 (June 2003): 307.

171 Natural Resources Canada, *Fundamentals*, 39–40.

172 *SWSP*, Annex 513, vol. IX, 158.

Landsat 7 carries the enhanced Thematic Mapper Plus ("ETM+"), which collects data in eight spectral bands.[173] The latter system includes digital elevation modelling ("DEM") capability for topography (elevation) and bathymetry (water depths). The Philippines used the DEM component of Landsat 8 to conduct a three-dimensional advanced mapping and image analysis exercise. This precision mapping technique was used to produce optically derived bathymetry.[174]

Modern high-resolution satellite imagery ranging from 0.5- to 1.0-meter ground resolution was acquired by the Philippines from DigitalGlobe.[175] DigitalGlobe's Standard Imagery products use several satellites, which include QuickBird, GeoEye-1, WorldView-1, WorldView-2, and WorldView-3. The images are described as high-resolution (30, 40, 50, and 60 centimeters); panchromatic, natural color, color infrared or 4-band pan-sharpened; and 1.6 to 2.4 meters multispectral.[176]

The limitations of satellite imagery are recognized by scientists from NASA, which manages Landsat. They caution us that remote sensing products should not be taken at face value and stress the "tremendous importance" of getting information to validate what remote sensing data appear to be telling the user. Atmospheric phenomena, mechanical problems with the sensor, and numerous other effects might distort one's view.[177] Similarly, the London Institute of Space Policy and Law emphasizes that "ground-truth evidence"—samples or records of on-site observation—is indispensable. Evidence of this type may help to distinguish cannabis from other crops.[178] Perhaps even more importantly,

[173] See Table 4.1.

[174] Hearing on the Merits, Transcript, Day 3, 8.

[175] *SWSP*, Annex 513, vol. IX, 158.

[176] DigitalGlobe, *Data Sheet Information Products, Standard Imagery* (Westminster, CO: DigitalGlobe, 7 October 2016), https://dg-cms-uploads-production.s3.amazonaws.com/uploads/document/file/21/Standard_Imagery_DS_10-7-16.pdf, accessed 3 June 2020.

[177] Turner et al., "Remote Sensing," 312.

[178] London Institute of Space Policy and Law, *Evidence from Space. Study for the European Space Agency on Use of Space-derived Earth Observation Information as Evidence in Judicial and Administrative Proceedings as Part of its Series of Studies in Support of Actions to Integrate New Developments in the Current EO Services*, Doc. ESA-ISPAL.76/Final (London: London Institute of Space Policy and Law, 2012), 10, 20, https://www.space-institute.org/app/uploads/1342722048_Evidence_from_Space_25_June_2012_-_No_Cover_zip.pdf, accessed 4 June 2020.

if remote sensing data is to be submitted as evidence to a court, it will require expert evidence on the system employed, the methods of processing of the data, and the interpretation of the information.[179] The digital nature of remote sensing data involves the translation of observed facts into digital data and from digital data back to intelligible information.[180] The data requires processing; interpretation is necessary to attribute specific meaning to the sensed data.[181] Testimony on these matters will have to be provided by an expert witness, whether he/she be the instrument designer, the expert on data treatment, or the interpreter of the resultant information.[182]

For the Hearing on the Merits, the Philippines complemented these satellite images with bathymetric models obtained through satellite-derived bathymetry.

2. Satellite-Derived Bathymetry and Bathymetric Models

The Philippines submitted bathymetric models for a whole range of features in the Spratly Islands, derived from high-resolution satellite images by the German company EOMAP. Bathymetric models of each of the five features were established at Lowest Astronomical Tide, Highest Astronomical Tide, and Mean High Water.[183] Each model recorded satellite sensor data (e.g., WorldView 2), spectral bands, spatial resolution, and the date of recording. To take the example of Subi Reef, EOMAP analysis showed that parts of the reef encircling the lagoon were above water at Lowest Astronomical Tide (in orange in the image). At Mean High Water, no part of Subi Reef was above water (the parts of the reef encircling the lagoon were all in blue). On this basis, the Philippines concluded that Subi Reef was a low-tide elevation. The Philippines argued that EOMAP's

[179] Ibid., 19.

[180] Ibid., 24, 27.

[181] Ibid., 281.

[182] Ibid., 281, 284.

[183] "Highest Astronomical Tide" refers to the highest tidal level which can be predicted to occur under average meteorological conditions and under any combination of astronomical conditions. "Lowest Astronomical Tide" refers to the lowest tide level which can be predicted to occur under average meteorological conditions and under any combination of astronomical conditions. "Mean High Water" (M.H.W.) refers to the average height of all high waters at a place over a 19-year period. IHO, *Hydrographic Dictionary*, Part I, vol. I, 104, 135, 144; *SDP*, Annex 807, vol. VI, 8–27.

analysis confirmed that like Subi Reef, the other four features named in its submissions (Mischief Reef, Second Thomas Shoal, McKennan Reef, and Gaven Reef) were below water at high tide.[184] While bathymetric models seemed to offer advantages in calculating depths in the shallow waters of the South China Sea, EOMAP itself recognized the possible limitations of satellite-derived bathymetry.

Bathymetry is the study of the "beds" or "floors" of water bodies, including the ocean, rivers, streams, and lakes. It covers the measurement of the ocean's depth relative to sea level and "submarine topography," or the depths and shapes of underwater terrain.[185] Water depth can be measured by instruments carried on vessels, especially by acoustic (sonar) instruments that measure depths directly below the vessel.[186] However, very shallow areas, such as flat reefs, are generally not covered because they cannot be safely explored by survey boats,[187] and because it is expensive and time-consuming to do so. Airborne operations can complement traditional sonar surveys and can be used to map very shallow waters and surface areas, but their cost restricts their use to specific areas.[188] Hence, bathymetry is especially important near coastlines, harbors, shoals, and banks, not only because shallow water can present hazards to navigation but also because sedimentation, erosion, and scouring of channels can alter underwater topography rapidly.

Empirical or mechanistic models are used to derive water depth from remote sensing data.[189] This method is based on the optical properties of the water column. The intensity of radiation decreases exponentially with depth, so that brightness decreases as depth increases. Dark values suggest

[184] Hearing on the Merits, Transcript (Day 2), 26–32. The bathymetric analyses of Subi Reef are in *SDP*, Annex 807, 24–27.

[185] US Department of Commerce, National Oceanic and Atmospheric Administration, National Ocean Service, *What is Bathymetry?* (Silver Spring, MD: National Ocean Service, 6 July 2017), https://oceanservice.noaa.gov/facts/bathymetry.html, accessed 3 June 2020.

[186] Campbell and Wynne, *Introduction to Remote Sensing*, 558.

[187] Franck Magron, "Shallow Water Bathymetry," *SPC* [Secretariat of the Pacific Community] *Newsletter*, 120 (January/March 2007): 44.

[188] Ibid.

[189] Amitansu Pattanaik et al., "Estimation of Shallow Water Bathymetry using IRS-Multispectral Imagery of Odisha Coast, India," *Aquatic Procedia* 4 (2015): 174, https://www.sciencedirect.com/science/article/pii/S2214241X15000255, accessed 3 June 2020.

that the bottom is deep, beyond the 20-meter range, while bright values suggest that the bottom is near the surface.[190]

Many authors argue that bathymetry approaches involving satellite imagery data are fast and economically advantageous solutions to automatic water depth calculation in shallow water. They use available images and the images themselves have a very large footprint compared with airborne and ship surveys, which are more localized. EOMAP explains that its satellite-derived bathymetric models rely on satellite sensors that detect sunlight reflected from the surface and algorithms that use this sunlight information to calculate the depth of the water column as well as the seafloor reflectance of color.[191] The methods of deriving the depth from satellite data are empirical methods and physics-based methods.[192] EOMAP explains that satellite-image technologies constituted a rapid and cost-effective solution to the problem of providing shallow-water bathymetry for the South China Sea, where the islands are several kilometers away from the nearest coast, they are surrounded by water deeper than 1000 meters, the areas are disputed territory, and the data about underwater topography are outdated or inaccessible.[193]

EOMAP acknowledged the possible limitations of satellite-derived bathymetry. The main problem is that the atmospheric column above the water column contains particles that also absorb light. The resultant signal contains depth information but is mixed with other components. The accuracy of depth as determined through this method is far less than that of sonar or airborne operations. As it is dependent on the clarity of the water, satellite-derived bathymetry only retrieves depths down to approximately 30 meters. Therefore, it will often require some

[190] Campbell and Wynne, *Introduction to Remote Sensing*, 560.

[191] Reflectance refers to the ratio of light given off by an object to the amount of light striking the object, expressed as percentage. IHO, *Hydrographic Dictionary*, Part I, vol. I, 197.

[192] EOMAP, *EOMAP Satellite Derived Bathymetry White Paper* (Seefeld, Germany: EOMAP, 10 April 2014), 1, 2, http://www.eomap.com/exchange/pdf/EOMAP_Bathy_20140410.pdf, accessed 3 June 2020.

[193] Ibid., *EOMAP Provides Bathymetry for South China Sea* (Seefeld, Germany: EOMAP, 16 June 2015), http://www.eomap.com/eomap-provides-bathymetry-for-south-china-sea/, accessed 3 June 2020.

kind of area-specific calibration, using ground-truth data and atmospheric correction to normalize data.[194]

Having in mind these basic ideas of remote sensing and satellite-derived bathymetry, we are now in a better position to understand the Tribunal's critical analysis of the expert and scientific evidence submitted by the Philippines.

B. The Tribunal's Critical Analysis of the Scientific and Technical Evidence Submitted by the Philippines

Two preliminary observations are in order. First, during the first round of the Hearing on the Merits, Professor Schofield summarized the results of the expert report that he prepared with two co-authors.[195] As the Rules of Procedure indicated, the written report constituted the examination in chief (examination by the party that called him). Schofield would have been subject to cross-examination by China if it had appeared. In China's absence, the Tribunal put questions to the expert between the Hearing's first and second rounds, following the procedure suggested by the Philippines to the Tribunal prior to the Hearing on Jurisdiction. The expert then had to respond to the questions—twelve in all, of which six referred to satellite imagery and the bathymetric models—during the Hearing's second round.[196]

Second, careful reading of the questions and the Tribunal's analysis incorporated in the Award of 12 July 2016 will convince the observer that it was the expert hydrographer who formulated the questions and undertook the analysis of the expert's responses. The non-attribution of the questions and the analysis to the expert hydrographer, which prompted Espenilla's not entirely accurate characterization of the expert hydrographer as a "phantom expert," must be taken as a sign that the Tribunal assumed ultimate responsibility for them. In other words, the Tribunal adopted the opinions of its expert, but it was the Tribunal that made the final determination on the status of the features, as specified by the Philippines in the expert hydrographer's terms of reference. The

[194] Magron, "Shallow Water Bathymetry," 46.

[195] Hearing on the Merits, Transcript, Day 3, 4–10.

[196] Ibid., Day 4, 52–62.

Tribunal's analysis of the limitations of satellite imagery and satellite-derived bathymetry concerned the spatial resolution of the remote sensing systems and the vertical accuracy of the imagery.

1. The Spatial Resolution of Remote Sensing Systems

The two issues of concern to the Tribunal were the limitations of the spatial resolution of Landsat images and the methods used to correct these limitations.

Schofield was asked to identify which satellite imagery was high-resolution and low-resolution. He explained that the resolution of Landsat TM7 and TM8 imagery was at the lower end of the scale, at ±30 meters. These low-resolution images were complemented by high-resolution images of 0.5 meters and 1.85 meters resolution from WorldView 1 and WorldView 2 imagery, with accuracy of ±2.0 meters.[197] The Tribunal pointed out in the Award of 12 July 2016 that the 30-meter ground resolution of Landsat 4 and 5 images meant that each pixel was equivalent to a square of 30 meters on each side and that the Landsat 7 and 8 images have the same 30-meter ground resolution for spectral bands as Landsat 4 and 5. Small rocks or coral boulders on a reef platform that may be a meter or less across still reach above water at high tide, in which case they could be properly considered as islands.[198] Yet they would not be captured by satellite imagery.

The Tribunal asked Schofield if the Red–Green–Blue Bands included the use of the panchromatic band, which could have improved the spatial resolution of multispectral images. A black and white (panchromatic) band in Landsat 7 and 8 has a ground resolution of 15 meters, which could have been utilized for purposes of sharpening images.[199] A panchromatic sensor consists of a single band detector sensitive to radiation within a wide spectral range covering the visible as well as the infrared wavelengths. If the wavelength range lies within the visible range, the resulting image will appear as a black and white photo taken from

[197] Hearing on the Merits, Transcript, Day 4, 58.

[198] Award of 12 July 2016, 138, para. 323.

[199] The following paragraph draws heavily on Kidiyo Kpalma et al., "Recent Trends in Satellite Image Pan-sharpening Techniques," paper presented at the 1st International Conference on Electrical, Electronic and Computing Engineering, June 2014, Vrniacka Banja, Serbia, https://hal.archives-ouvertes.fr/hal-01116094/document, accessed 3 June 2020.

space. Panchromatic images always have greater resolution than multispectral images from the same satellite, because much more energy per unit area is gathered by a panchromatic area with its wide bandwidth. The sensor of a multispectral imaging system is obtained from a set of multiband sensors. The recorded radiation of a multispectral imaging system is within a narrow range of wavelengths for each band. Both brightness and spectral (color) information on the targets are available on the resulting image, but multispectral images have low resolution. Pansharpening (or panchromatic sharpening) fuses panchromatic and multispectral images to create a single high spectral and spatial high-resolution image by using suitable algorithms.[200] Pansharpening combines the best of both worlds: it increases spatial resolution while simultaneously preserving spectral information in a multispectral image.[201]

Schofield admitted that he and his colleagues did not carry out pansharpening because the multispectral analysis that they did undertake used a different combination of Red–Green–Blue of the six available bands that are provided by the satellite image.[202] The Tribunal observed that even had they undertaken pansharpening, the maximum resolution that could be derived from satellite imagery was still only 15 meters. The small rock or coral boulder on a reef platform that was one meter or less across but above water at high tide would still have remained undetected. In the Tribunal's view, the maximum resolution of 15 meters was insufficient to establish the presence or absence of features above water at high tide.[203] The WorldView family of satellites provided higher-resolution imagery, but this was used for features that other evidence already suggested were above water at high tide. High-resolution satellite imagery was not used for spectral analysis to detect whether low-tide elevations were submerged at high water.[204]

The Tribunal also asked Schofield whether orthorectification, which had not at all been mentioned in the experts' report, had been supplied by

[200] Ibid.

[201] Ibid.

[202] Hearing on the Merits, Transcript, Day 4, 55.

[203] Award of 12 July 2016, 138, para. 323.

[204] High water is the maximum height reached by a rising tide. Aaron L. Shalowitz and Michael W. Reed, *Shore and Sea Boundaries*, vol. I (Washington, D.C.: U.S. Department of Commerce, Coast and Geodetic Survey, 1962), 293.

the imagery provider and if so, what process had been used.[205] Orthorectification is necessary when there is distortion across the image caused by distortions from the sensor and the earth's terrain. For example, since satellite imagery can be collected by scanning side to side along a path, this movement while collecting the image means that a spatially adjacent part of an image may have been collected from a nonadjacent part of the sensor. By orthorectifying an image, the distortions are geometrically removed, creating a planimetric image at every location with consistent scale across all parts of the image.[206] Schofield answered that the images were orthorectified exports from the satellite-image provider and were then georectified to be accurate to various resulting pixel resolutions for those used in the expert report. All the images thus had an accuracy of ±2.0 meters.[207]

The Tribunal pointed out in its Award of 12 July 2016 a difficulty with the experts' approach that the latter apparently had not identified: the time of image capture generally did not align with either high water or low water,[208] i.e., the data were not recorded at either high water or low water. The precise tidal conditions prevailing at the time an image was captured could only be estimated, but the estimates could be confirmed only by observations on the ground.[209] The implication was that if one

[205] Hearing on the Merits, Transcript, Day 4, 57.

[206] ESRI, *Fundamentals of Orthorectifying a Raster Dataset* (Redlands, CA: ESRI, 2016), https://desktop.arcgis.com/en/arcmap/10.3/manage-data/raster-and-images/fundamentals-of-orthorectifying-a-raster-dataset.htm, accessed 3 June 2020. Planimetry refers to the measurement of plane surfaces. A planimetric image presents only the horizontal positions for the features represented; distinguished from a topographic image by the omission of relief in measurable form. IHO, *Hydrographic Dictionary*, Part I, vol. I, 142, 179.

[207] Hearing on the Merits, Transcript, Day 4, 57. Georectification refers to the removal of geometric distortions between sets of data points, most often the removal of terrain, platform, and sensor-induced distortions from remote sensing imagery. C.D. Lippitt, "Georeferencing and Georectification," in John P. Wilson (ed.), *The Geographic Information Science & Technology Body of Knowledge (3rd Quarter 2020 Edition)* (Ithaca, N.Y.: University Consortium for Geographic Information Science, 2020), https://doi.org/10.22224/gistbok/2020.3.3, https://gistbok.ucgis.org/bok-topics/georeferencing-and-georectification, accessed 9 October 2020.

[208] Low water is the minimum height reached by a falling tide. Shalowitz and Reed, *Shore*, vol. I, 299.

[209] Award of 12 July 2016, 139, para. 324.

cannot determine whether an image was taken at high tide or low tide, it is not possible to confirm whether a feature is submerged at high tide.

The Tribunal, undoubtedly following the advice of the expert hydrographer, also expressed concerns about the vertical accuracy of the imagery and the vertical error associated with bathymetric models.

2. The Vertical Accuracy of Imagery and the Vertical Error of Bathymetric Models

The Tribunal's questions on vertical accuracy referred to Landsat and DigitalGlobe imagery. The Tribunal's questions on the vertical accuracy of bathymetric models were directed at EOMAP's bathymetric models.

Determining vertical and horizontal accuracy, as explained by DigitalGlobe, is an exercise in measuring geolocation accuracy. Geolocation accuracy is determined by comparing a known, surveyed location (typically a ground control point, "GCP"), to the corresponding photo-identifiable feature in an image product. For an individual control point, the geolocation error is measured by calculating the difference between the observed location in the product and the known, surveyed location. Vertical accuracy is measured using DigitalGlobe's Basic Stereo product, which delivers two images with 100% overlap over the aera of interest ("AOI"). For vertical accuracy, the pixel locations corresponding to a GCP for each image of a stereo pair are combined to determine the estimated height. A vertical error relative to the known height is then measured. For a set of control points in the stereo pair, the LE90 accuracy is then calculated. LE90 is the 90th percentile linear error, meaning that a minimum of 90% of vertical errors fall within the stated LE90 value.[210]

Schofield explained that for Landsat TM7 imagery, vertical accuracy was better than ±15 meters root mean square error (RMSE) and of the order of ±12 meters with respect to Landsat TM8 imagery. RMSE is a measure of total error defined as the square root of the sum of

[210] DigitalGlobe, *Base Product Series FAQ* (Westminster, CO: DigitalGlobe, 2017), 1, https://www.c-agg.org/wp-content/uploads/DigitalGlobe-Base-Product-FAQ.pdf, accessed 3 June 2020; DigitalGlobe, *Accuracy of World View Products*, White Paper Accuracy 5/16 (Westminster, CO: DigitalGlobe, 16 May 2016), 4, 8, https://dg-cms-uploads-production.s3.amazonaws.com/uploads/document/file/38/DG_ACCURACY_WP_V3.pdf, accessed 3 June 2020.

the variance and the square of the bias.[211] RMSE, which is a measure of the differences between predicted or calculated values and actual or observed/measured value, is an indicator of the accuracy of the spatial analysis and/or remote sensing. The RMSE aggregates each individual difference between the calculated and actual value, called a residual, into a single measure. Schofield recognized that the degree of potential error was "obviously substantial."[212]

With respect to the higher-resolution DigitalGlobe imagery from WorldView1 and 2 satellites, Schofield informed the Tribunal that the estimated vertical error was 1.7 meters.[213] The vertical accuracy related to EOMAP's analysis was in the range of 0.5 meters, with a CE90 degree of confidence; that is, a circular error at 90% confidence in terms of spatial location error.[214] CE90 is the circular error at the 90th percentile. This means that a minimum of 90% of the points measured has a horizontal error less than the stated CE90 value.[215] To Schofield's estimates, the Tribunal added an error of ±25% of water depth. For WorldView Satellites, the further error was less, at ±10% of water depth.[216]

In its Award the Tribunal criticized the lack of explanation of the vertical accuracy of EOMAP'S models. It also pointed out that the tidal datum used for determining high-tide features was the Highest Astronomical Tide, which is normally used to determine clearances for vessels (the minimum vertical or horizontal space available for passage). Hence it was inappropriate for categorization of maritime features.[217] The final limitation was that EOMAP had not (and in the Tribunal's view could

[211] Organisation for Economic Co-operation and Development ("OECD"), *Glossary of Statistical Terms* (Paris: OECD, July 2005), https://stats.oecd.org/glossary/detail.asp?ID=6660, accessed 3 June 2020.

[212] Hearing on the Merits, Transcript, Day 4, 55–56.

[213] Ibid.

[214] DigitalGlobe, *Base Product Series FAQ*, 4.

[215] Ibid.

[216] Award of 12 July 2016, 139, para. 324.

[217] Ibid. A tidal datum, or simply datum, is any numerical or geometrical quantity or set of such quantities that may serve as a reference or base for other quantities. In geodesy a datum is defined by a set of parameters specifying the reference surface or the reference coordinate system. Therefore, two types of datums are required: a horizontal datum that forms the basis for computations of horizontal control surveys in which the curvature of the earth is considered, and a vertical datum to which elevations are referred. IHO, *Hydrographic Dictionary*, Part I, vol. I, 59.

not have) presented imagery of the features that was actually captured during the tidal conditions presented. The EOMAP imagery presented images of each maritime feature at Highest Astronomical Tide, Lowest Astronomical Tide, and Mean High Water. Schofield explained that the tidal assessment model used to determine Lowest Astronomical Tide was obtained from the UK Hydrographic Office ("UKHO"), which provided a model of nearby tidal stations. The nearest such station in the Spratly Islands was North Danger Reef. EOMAP then used spatial interpolation techniques from this station in order to create the tidal model. EOMAP interpolated all the tidal values for specific dates and times of satellite-image acquisition. It was precisely the fact that EOMAP used imagery captured at one point in time and then extrapolated the results for other tidal conditions on the basis of a model of tidal conditions at the time the image was captured that the Tribunal found problematic. In the Tribunal's view, the accuracy of the presentation of any particular tidal state depended entirely on EOMAP's model of the tidal state on the feature at the precise moment the image was captured. EOMAP did not explain the way this calculation was done and did not recognize that the tidal range on the particular day that satellite images were taken would have been affected by atmospheric conditions, adding a further degree of error into the calculation.[218]

Little wonder that the Tribunal qualified the satellite imagery submitted by the Philippines as "poor" and "imprecise." Schofield had disagreed, pointing out that the satellite images had far higher scale than that of the largest scale nautical charting of the South China Sea. He did admit that especially small features, such as isolated rocks and pinnacles, or coral heads that are barely above the high-tide mark, might still not be discernible even using the highest-resolution satellite imagery. This limitation could not be underestimated if it is recalled that Article 121 of the Convention does not specify any minimum size for an island.[219] While the Tribunal did not accept the degree of accuracy or certainty that the Philippines gave to satellite imagery,[220] it did identify three conditions in which satellite imagery would be useful for proving the existence or non-existence of large sand cays where the area clearly covers (is submerged)

[218] Award of 12 July 2016, 139, para. 324.

[219] Hearing on the Merits, Transcript, Day 3, 9.

[220] Award of 12 July 2016, 138, para. 322.

in water across a series of images.[221] The first is that very high-resolution stereoscopic imagery must be used.[222] Stereoscopic imagery had not been mentioned at all in the Philippine submissions, in the experts' report, in the expert's testimony, or in the Tribunal's questions to the expert. One may find explanations in the literature produced by DigitalGlobe, which explains that in stereoscopic imagery collection, the satellite sensor acquires two images of the same location taken from different angles. In DigitalGlobe's stereoscopic imagery, the images are taken by the same satellite about 45–90 seconds apart. The satellite takes a shot of the location of interest, after which it continues traveling along its orbit for a short time, and then rotates the camera to point back toward the same location to collect the second image. This is called in-track stereo. A stereoscopic pair can also be acquired in cross-track stereo mode, when the satellite completes at least one orbit between the two image collections.[223] The second and third conditions are that the imagery must be taken at or near high tide and that in-person observation of tidal conditions must be taken at a nearby location.[224] States that wish to submit to an international court satellite imagery as evidence of the status of maritime features would do well to take note of the conditions enumerated briefly by the Tribunal.

This analysis of the limitations of satellite imagery and satellite-derived bathymetry, which undoubtedly drew on the opinion of the expert hydrographer, convinced the Tribunal of the need for a different approach to the determination of the status of maritime features. As this approach was already discussed in the previous Chapter, it will not be discussed further. We shall now turn to the analysis of the consequences of China's island-building for fragile ecosystems in the South China.

221 A cay, also spelled key, is a small, low island, usually sandy, situated on a coral reef platform. Sand cays are usually built on the edge of the coral platform, opposite the direction from which the prevailing winds blow. The Editors of Encyclopaedia Britannica, "Cay," *Encyclopaedia Britannica* (2020), https://www.britannica.com/science/atoll, accessed 9 October 2020.

222 Award of 12 July 2016, 140, para. 326.

223 University of Minnesota, Polar Geospatial Center, *Introduction to Stereoscopic Imagery. Collection Mode* (St. Paul, MN: Polar Geospatial Center, University of Minnesota College of Science and Engineering, 23 February 2017), https://www.pgc.umn.edu/guides/stereo-derived-elevation-models/introduction-to-stereoscopic-imagery/?print=pdf, accessed 4 June 2020.

224 Award of 12 July 2016, 140, para. 326.

On these issues, the degree of consensus was much higher among the experts.

IV. The Assessment of the Scientific and Technical Evidence on the Harm to the Marine Environment Caused by China's Island-Building

The Tribunal's decisions on the harm to the marine environment caused by China's island-building have attracted considerable scholarly attention.[225] To avoid repetition, this Part will approach the scientific and technical evidence emphasizing the procedures followed by the Tribunal to assess it.

The Philippines submitted two expert reports, the first as an annex to its *Memorial* ("First Carpenter Report") and the second in response to questions put to it by the Tribunal prior to the Hearing on the Merits ("Second Carpenter Report").[226] The Philippines also submitted a conference paper by Professor John McManus ("McManus Report"), another coral reef expert.[227] The McManus Report, though not described as an "expert report," was occasionally quoted by the Tribunal; it assumed an important role in the assessment of the scientific and technical evidence by the independent experts and through this, that of the Tribunal. The

[225] Chie Kojima, "South China Sea Arbitration and Protection of the Marine Environment: Evolution of UNCLOS Part XII through Interpretation and the Duty to Cooperate," *Asian Yearbook of International Law* 21 (2015): 166–80; Mbengue, "The South China Sea Arbitration," 285–89; Nilufer Oral, "The South China Sea Arbitral Award, Part XII of UNCLOS and the Protection and Preservation of the Marine Environment," in S. Jayakumar et al. (eds.), *The South China Sea Arbitration: The Legal Dimension* (Cheltenham: Edward Elgar 2018), 223–46; Ilias Plakokefalos, "Environmental Law Aspects of the South China Sea Arbitration Award," paper presented at the Symposium on the South China Sea Award, Netherlands Institute for the Law of the Sea, Utrecht Centre for Oceans Water and Sustainability Law, School of Law, Utrecht University, 7 December 2016, https://papers.ssrn.com/sol3/papers.cfm?abstract_id=2880624, accessed 5 June 2020; Alfredo C. Robles, Jr., *Endangered Species and Fragile Ecosystems in the South China Sea: The Philippines v. China Arbitration* (Singapore: Palgrave-Macmillan, 2020); Tim Stephens, "The Collateral Damage from China's 'Great Wall of Sand': The Environmental Dimensions of the South China Sea Case," *Australian Yearbook of International Law* 24 (2017): 41–56; and Yoshifumi Tanaka, "The South China Sea Arbitration: Environmental Obligations under the Law of the Sea Convention," *Review of European, Comparative and International Environmental Law* 27 (2018): 90–96.

[226] *MP*, Annex 240, vol. VII, 389–437; *SDP*, Annex 699, vol. II, 237–93.

[227] *PAMH*, Annex 850, 578–608.

Tribunal undertook its assessment in two stages. After assessing on its own the scientific and technical evidence submitted by the Philippines, the Tribunal assessed it with the assistance of independent experts.

A. The Tribunal's Assessment of the Scientific and Technical Evidence Submitted by the Philippines

Professor Carpenter summarized the two Carpenter Reports during the first round of the Hearing on the Merits and answered questions from the Tribunal during the second round. Undoubtedly, the assessment of the environmental impacts of China's island-building was handicapped by the absence of official Chinese (counter) assessments, let alone Environmental Impact Assessments ("EIAs"). To compensate for China's absence in the proceedings, the Tribunal, as already mentioned in the previous Chapter, undertook its own research for Chinese statements that could pass for expert or scientific reports after the closure of the oral proceedings.

1. The Tribunal's Examination of the Expert Witness

The Tribunal's examination of the expert witness paid particular attention to the harmful effects on the marine environment of China's island-building and the reliability of the methodology employed by Carpenter and his colleague to arrive at their conclusions.

The First Carpenter Report concentrated on the harmful environmental consequences of the harvesting by Chinese fishermen of vulnerable and endangered species, such as giant clams, corals, and sharks, from Scarborough Shoal and Second Thomas Shoal and their use of dynamite and cyanide in fishing. Although Questions 3, 4, 7, 10, 11, 19, and 20 (out of 22 questions put to Professor Carpenter) sought clarifications on these activities, the Tribunal seems not to have experienced any difficulty accepting Carpenter's expert opinion on these matters.[228] This is indirectly confirmed by the fact that the Tribunal did not deem it necessary to appoint an expert on fisheries after the closure of the oral proceedings. The coverage in the First Carpenter Report of China's island-building, which was only noticeable on Mischief Reef and McKennan Reef, as well as its environmental consequences on coral reefs, was limited. One possible explanation for this is that China had just began its island-building at the time the First Carpenter Report was being prepared. That

[228] Hearing on the Merits, Transcript, Day 4, 144–46, 150–51, 158–60.

Report was based on aerial photographs, the source of which was not clearly identified.[229]

By the time of the Hearing on the Merits in November 2015, China's island-building had expanded considerably to cover seven reefs. Understandably, the Second Carpenter Report was almost entirely devoted to the harmful effects of the expanded program of island-building. The number of questions put to Carpenter on these issues—15 in all—is eloquent proof of the degree of scrutiny that the Tribunal brought to bear on the Second Carpenter Report. Apart from the questions on the mechanisms of harm, two sets of questions were crucial for the Tribunal's decision-making. First, the Tribunal wished to know whether the ecosystem around Scarborough Shoal and Second Thomas Shoal was a rare and fragile ecosystem; whether Professor Carpenter was aware of ecosystems in oceans similar to them; and how he would compare the endurance of reefs and species in the South China Sea to that of other ecosystems in oceans. The expert replied that the South China Sea reefs represent an assemblage of species found in no other oceanic reefs in the world and that Scarborough Shoal and Second Thomas Shoal belonged to one of the most fragile marine ecosystems in the world.[230] Next, the Tribunal inquired whether China had taken all the necessary measures to prevent harm to the South China Sea, and what measures could be taken to encourage recovery of the coral reefs. Carpenter suggested dismantling of the artificial islands in such a way that sediments are discharged into deep water, where they would do less environmental harm than on the reefs, and reinforcing the islands so that the sedimentation plumes would not leak from the islands. That said, he concurred with McManus that the reefs may not recover for decades and that the reefs with extensive island-building would never be the same.[231]

The scope of these two sets of questions largely coincides with that of Article 194 (5) of the Convention, which requires that States take measures necessary to protect and preserve rare or fragile ecosystems. One might ask whether in so doing the Tribunal was running the risk of delegating decision-making on the Philippine claims to the expert. Yet it is difficult to see how the Tribunal could have formulated the questions differently. Article 194 (5), like many rules of international environmental

[229] *MP*, Annex 240, vol. VII, 404–06, 408–10.

[230] Hearing on the Merits, Transcript, Day 4, 154–55.

[231] Ibid., 155–57.

law, requires States to behave in certain ways, rather than imposing on them the obligation to achieve certain outcomes. Such rules, which are formulated having in mind scientific uncertainties, inevitably blur the distinction between fact and law and require the participation of experts in the interpretation of the rules.[232]

The other major concern of the Tribunal was the experts' degree of confidence in the accuracy of their understanding of the scope and nature of China's island-building, in view of the fact that they cited secondary sources, among which there were online sources.[233] Carpenter explained that the methodological approach consisted of three elements. The first, satellite imagery, obtained through the Asian Maritime Transparency Institute ("AMTI") from DigitalGlobe, was very clear. Second, online sources confirmed the interpretation derived from satellite imagery. The third source was the independent scientific evaluation of Professor McManus, who had calculated from satellite imagery that China's island-building had completely destroyed 12.82 square kilometers of coral reefs.[234] This figure was close to Carpenter's own Geographic Information Systems ("GIS") calculation of 13.62 square kilometers.[235] Carpenter declared that the satellite imagery provided "absolutely no evidence...that any effective measures had been taken to preserve the ecological environment [sic]. Instead, full-scale dredging went ahead, with the obvious catastrophic effect on the coral reef."[236] Carpenter laid great stress on the fact that Chinese claims concerning measures that it allegedly took to prevent harm to the coral reefs were in contradiction with the state of scientific knowledge on these questions. The effects of dredging on coral reefs are very well understood by scientists and well-documented in the scientific literature. As Carpenter emphasized, China's assertions were "contrary to everything that we know about coral reef ecology and conservation."[237]

[232] Foster, *Science*, 6–7.

[233] Hearing on the Merits, Transcript, Day 4, 147.

[234] McManus Report, 602.

[235] The satellite images of the reefs are to be found in the Second Carpenter Report: Fiery Cross Reef (249, 259–61), Mischief Reef (250- 254–55), Subi Reef (251, 252, 255), Cuarteron Reef (253, 257, 258), and Johnson Reef (256).

[236] Hearing on the Merits, Transcript, Day 4, 148.

[237] Ibid., 149.

China's default prevented the Tribunal from acquiring the certainty that China's statements were not backed up by some type of scientific report. In view of this uncertainty, the Tribunal took two steps following the closure of the oral proceedings: it simultaneously made an independent search for Chinese statements that could have been equivalent to a scientific report and it appointed its own coral reef experts. The independent experts' report will be discussed in the following section. The following remarks will be directed to the twelve Chinese statements that the Tribunal found in the course of its research and that were transmitted in February 2016 by the Tribunal to the Philippines and China for comments.

2. The Tribunal's Search for Scientific and Technical Evidence from China

The statements were of different types. Two were made by officials of China's Foreign Ministry.[238] Three were communiqués on the marine environment published in 2012, 2013, and 2014 by China's State Oceanic Administration ("SOA").[239] Two were communiqués of the SOA's South China Sea Branch.[240] Two were SOA statements on China's

[238] Regular Press Conference of Foreign Ministry Spokesperson Hua Chunying, dated 9 April 2015 and Interview with Mr. Ouyang Yujing, Director-General of the Department of Boundary and Ocean Affairs of the Ministry of Foreign Affairs of the People's Republic of China, dated 27 May 2015, cited in *South China Sea Arbitration*, *Responses of the Philippines to the Tribunal's 5 February 2016 Request for Comments* (11 March 2016), 1–6, paras. 3–11 ("*RTRC*"), https://pcacases.com/web/sendAttach/1849, accessed 7 July 2020.

[239] See the following in *RTRC (Annexes 864–892)* (3 March 2016):

1. Annex 865, China State Oceanic Administration, "2012 Communique [sic] on Marine Environment of China, Part 2: Marine Biodiversity and Ecological Conditions" (1 April 2013), 8–21;
2. Annex 867, China State Oceanic Administration, "2013 Communique [sic] on Marine Environment of China, Part 2: Conditions of Marine Ecology" (25 March 2014), 25–36; and
3. Annex 870, China State Oceanic Administration, "2014 Communique [sic] on Marine Environment of China, Part 2: Conditions of Marine Ecology" (16 March 2015), 160–70, https://files.pca-cpa.org/pcadocs/The%20Philippines%27%20Written%20Responses%20%2811%20March%202016%29%20%28Annexes%20864-892%29.pdf, accessed 3 May 2020.

[240] See the following in *RTRC (Annexes 864–892)*:

island-building in the Spratly Islands.[241] The last three documents were SOA technical guidelines for the evaluation of the health of coastal marine ecosystems, monitoring of the marine environment, and the EIA of marine engineering.[242] It was the Philippines rather than the experts appointed by the Philippines that responded to the 12 documents located by the Tribunal. On the basis of Philippine comments and its own analysis, the Tribunal realized that only four documents were relevant to its decision-making.

The Philippines did not have any difficulty in demonstrating that the 12 statements, whether individually or as a group, could in no way be considered the equivalent of a scientific report, comparable to the two Carpenter Reports and the McManus Report, or of an EIA.

1. Annex 869, China State Oceanic Administration, South China Sea Branch, "Communique [sic] on the Oceanic Conditions of the South China Seas Region in 2013" (14 August 2014), 129–59, and
2. Annex 871, China State Oceanic Administration, South China Sea Branch, "Communique [sic] on the Oceanic Conditions of the South China Sea Region in 2014" (28 May 2015), 171–200.

241 *PAMH*, Annex 821, China State Oceanic Administration, "Construction Work at Nansha Reefs Will Not Harm Oceanic Ecosystems" (18 June 2015), 11–14; *RTRC (Annexes 864–892)*, Annex 872, China State Oceanic Administration, "Construction Activities at Nansha Reefs Did Not Affect the Coral Reef Ecosystem" (10 June 2015), 201–08, https://files.pca-cpa.org/pcadocs/The%20Philippines%27%20Written%20Responses%20%2811%20March%202016%29%20%28Annexes%20864-892%29.pdf, all accessed 3 May 2020.

242 See the following in *RTRC (Annexes 864–892)*:

1. Annex 864, China State Oceanic Administration, The Guidance for the Assessment of Coastal Marine Ecosystem Health, Marine Industry Standards of the People's Republic of China, No. HY/T 087-2005 (2005), 5–7;
2. Annex 866, China State Oceanic Administration, Code of Practice for Marine Monitoring Technology, Part 5: Marine Ecology, Marine Industry Standards of the People's Republic of China, No. HY/T 147.5-2013 (25 April 2013), 22–24; and
3. Annex 868, China State Oceanic Administration, Technical Guidelines for Environmental Impact Assessment of Marine Engineering, National Standards of the People's Republic of China, No. GB/T 19485-2014 (1 April 2014), 37–128, https://files.pca-cpa.org/pcadocs/The%20Philippines%27%20Written%20Responses%20%2811%20March%202016%29%20%28Annexes%20864-892%29.pdf, all accessed 3 May 2020.

The two statements made by Foreign Ministry Officials did not provide any evidence to back up China's claim that it had carried out science-based assessment, taken into full account ecological preservation or fishery protection, followed strict environmental standards or requirements, adopted any effective measures to preserve the environment, or specify its efforts of ecological monitoring and preservation.[243] The three communiqués on the marine environment published in 2012, 2013, and 2014 concerned the general conditions of China's marine environment, focused largely on waters close to the mainland and Hainan Island, and did not address the ecological conditions of the marine islands in the southern part of the South China Sea.[244] The two communiqués of the SOA's South China Sea Branch did not provide information about marine ecosystems where China had been carrying out artificial island-building or the impacts of China's island-building.[245] The two SOA statements on China's island-building in the Spratly Islands were not supported by evidence and were in many cases thoroughly contradicted by the scientific and technical evidence that the Philippines had presented.[246] The last three documents were technical guidelines for the evaluation of the health of coastal marine ecosystems, monitoring of the marine environment, and the EIA of marine engineering. None provided any evidence that the guidelines had been followed in the maritime areas where island-building had taken place.[247]

On the basis of Philippine comments and its own analysis, the Tribunal realized that most of these documents did not represent scientific and technical reports on China's island-building in the South China Sea. Only the two statements made by Foreign Ministry officials and the two SOA statements that directly addressed the issue of the environmental consequences of China's island-building were specifically referred to in the Award of 12 July 2016 as statements of China's position on issues raised in the expert and scientific reports submitted by the Philippines and in the expert testimony before the Tribunal. The contents of the eight other

[243] *RTRC,* 1–6, paras. 3–11.

[244] Ibid., 6–8, paras. 17–20.

[245] Ibid., 8–9, paras. 22–24.

[246] Ibid., 10–15, paras. 27–38.

[247] Ibid., 15–16, paras. 39–41.

statements were not analyzed by the Tribunal in the Award of 12 July 2016.[248]

If we examine the chronology of the appointment of the independent coral reef experts, it becomes clear that the Tribunal did not wait for the Philippine comments on these 12 documents before deciding to appoint the first of the three experts who assisted it in assessing the scientific and technical evidence submitted by the Philippines.

B. The Tribunal's Assessment, with Expert Assistance, of the Scientific and Technical Evidence Submitted by the Philippines

One finds an explanation of the Tribunal's approach to the evaluation of the experts' opinion in the following passage:

> Based on the compelling evidence, expert reports, and critical assessment of Chinese claims described above, the Tribunal has no doubt that China's artificial island-building activities on the seven reefs in the Spratly Islands have caused devastating and long-lasting damage to the marine environment.[249]

The compelling evidence of China's island-building seems to refer to that submitted by the Philippines on the progress of China's island-building between 2013 and 2015.[250] The reference to expert opinions makes no distinction between those submitted by the Philippines and that of the independent experts, which apparently had equal weight in the Tribunal's view. It seems, though, that the Tribunal attached great weight to the report of the independent experts ("Ferse Report"). The passage quoted above also indicates that contrary to the charge of the CSIL, the Tribunal subjected the experts' reports to critical assessment.

1. The Tribunal's Adoption of the Independent Experts' Report

The Terms of Reference of the three independent experts' work implicitly recognized that it would be subject to the same constraint as that of the

[248] Award of 12 July 2016, 364–69, paras. 916–24.

[249] Ibid., 394, para. 983.

[250] Ibid., 329–55, paras. 852–90.

experts appointed by the Philippines—the impossibility of a site visit. The three experts were to assist the Tribunal by

> [1] examining and analysing the record submitted by the Philippines on the issue of environmental harm to coral reefs as a result of island building activities at Cuarteron Reef, Fiery Cross Reef, Gaven Reef, Johnson Reef, Hughes Reef, Mischief Reef, and Subi Reef; [2] assessing the accuracy and certainty of the scientific conclusions drawn by the Philippines and its experts; [3] reporting on the condition of the coral reefs at Cuarteron Reef, Fiery Cross Reef, Gaven Reef, Johnson Reef, Hughes Reef, Mischief Reef, and Subi Reef prior to the commencement of Chinese construction activities, and the extent to which any likely harm to the reef systems can be attributed to such activities; [4] reporting on the nature and extent of the possible harm to coral reefs as a result of China's construction activities, as those activities are described in the record or in other publicly available sources; [5] reporting on the broader impacts of China's construction activities on the marine ecosystem in and around the South China Sea and on fisheries resources; and [6] reporting on the anticipated duration of likely harm to coral reefs and the prospects and likely rate at which the coral reefs in question will rejuvenate.[251]

When evaluating the adverse environmental impacts of China's island-building on coral reefs and the prospects for their recovery, the Tribunal drew its conclusions mainly from the Ferse report. Another tangible manifestation of the Tribunal's approach to the independent experts' opinion is its acceptance of satellite imagery when it was consulted by the independent experts.

The Tribunal described the conclusions of the Ferse Report on China's island-building as "unequivocal."[252] The unprecedented impact on the reefs involved the direct destruction of the reefs subjected to direct land reclamation, loss of complex structure built up over centuries of reefs subjected to dredging in order to create landfill, severe coral mortality on reefs affected by the associated sedimentation and nutrient release, severely diminished capacity for ongoing carbonate production on several reefs, and impaired capacity to keep up with increasing sea level rise.[253] The Tribunal also quoted extensively from the Ferse Report on the extent

[251] Ferse Report, 7.

[252] Award of 12 July 2016, 389, para. 978.

[253] Ferse Report, 3; Award of 12 July 2016, 389, para. 978.

and likely duration of the harm. The independent experts anticipated that the harm caused by direct burial of reef habitat and areas affected by dredging would be near-permanent. Furthermore, recovery from harm resulting from removal of major geomorphological structures would not be likely on ecological time scales. Harm to areas affected by smothering of sediments and increased turbidity would endure for decades within lagoons and for weeks or months on the outer reef slopes. The independent experts stressed that island-building has reduced the productivity and complexity of the reefs, the nursery habitat for fish species, and their ability to replenish the fisheries of littoral States.[254] The Ferse Report was also the basis for the Tribunal's critique of the two SOA statements, which had claimed that China had taken effective mitigation measures and that construction did not damage the environment on the reefs. In response to these implausible statements, the Ferse Report had stated that they are "contradicted by the facts" and that they were "largely in disagreement with the available information."[255]

In their assessment of the state of the coral reefs before China initiated extensive island-building in 2013, Ferse and his colleagues consulted analysis based on satellite imagery for Cuarteron Reef, Fiery Cross Reef, Hughes Reef, and Mischief Reef.[256] The independent experts' estimate that island-building had destroyed up to 60% of the shallow reef habitat of the affected reefs and their estimates of the increase in land area in each reef were calculated from a 2016 study by Mora, Caldewell, Bierkeland, and McManus on Chinese dredging in the South China Sea, which used Landsat 8 satellite imagery.[257] The satellite images had been taken at intervals of several weeks and the data had been interpolated, so that the information provided did not exactly show the beginning and the end of dredging. What the data did was to indicate the main periods of land accretion.[258] In these images, only land above sea level is visible in the short-wave infrared band (Landsat Band 6), while land above sea level and natural reef areas (e.g., coral reefs and submerged natural sandbars) are both visible in the red optical band (Landsat Band 4). By subtracting

[254] Ferse Report, 42–46; Award of 12 July 2016, 390, para. 979.

[255] Ferse Report, 2, 48; Award of 12 July 2016, 982, para. 391.

[256] Ferse Report, 17, 18, 19.

[257] Ibid., 1, 32–35.

[258] Ibid., 30.

the size of visible areas in Landsat Band 6 from the size of visible areas in Landsat Band 4, Mora et al. had been able to quantify the total size of natural reef areas; the area of reclamation is the size of visible areas in Landsat Band 6.[259] It may be presumed that as the purpose of the satellite imagery was not to determine the legal status of the maritime features in question, the Tribunal, which must have been advised on this matter by the expert hydrographer, was satisfied with its use in this different context.

If one now turns to the Tribunal's examination of other effects of China's construction activities, one finds references to the experts' use of satellite imagery without further comment from the Tribunal. The Ferse Report refuted, with the assistance of evidence from satellite and aerial imagery, the SOA's claims that construction had tried to avoid the spawning periods of certain fish categories, had avoided fine sand going into the reclamation areas to maintain the water quality of coral reef areas, had left unaffected photosynthesis of corals, and had effects that were "partial, temporary, controllable and recoverable."[260]

One should not deduce from the Tribunal's adoption of the Ferse Report's conclusions that the independent experts' overall assessment differed significantly from that of the experts appointed by the Philippines. On the contrary, the Ferse Report concluded that on the whole, the Carpenter Reports were generally accurate descriptions of the impacts construction, despite occasional under- or over-estimation of the damage.[261] The Tribunal agreed that the Ferse Report largely confirmed the conclusions of the First and Second Carpenter Reports.[262] One may find striking illustration of the complementary nature of the experts' reports in the clarification sought by Professor Ferse and his colleagues, through the Tribunal, from McManus, whose academic paper had estimated that China was responsible for more than 90% of the overall damage from dredging and filling among offshore coral reefs in the South China Sea.[263] The independent experts wished to know the proportions

[259] Camilo Mora et al., "Dredging in the Spratly Islands: Gaining Land but Losing Reefs," *PLoS Biology* 14: 31002422 (31 March 2016): 2–4.

[260] Ferse Report, 53, 57; Award of 12 July 2016, 391–93, paras. 982, 982(b), 982(c), 982(e).

[261] Ferse Report, 4.

[262] Award of 12 July 2016, 390, para. 980.

[263] McManus Report, 601.

of reef damage that McManus would assign to dredging and to clam shell extraction. In a letter and a new paper submitted to the Tribunal through the Philippines, McManus estimated that China was responsible for at least 39 square kilometers of damage from shallow dredging and 69 square kilometers of damage from the harvesting of giant clams using propellers. The ratio of shallow dredging to clam harvest damage was 0.57:1.[264] This response prompted Professor Carpenter to make a further declaration, submitted to the Tribunal through the Philippines, that it corroborated and reinforced the conclusions he expressed in his testimony.[265]

The final step in the Tribunal's fact-finding was the critical assessment of the independent experts' report.

2. The Tribunal's Critical Assessment of the Independent Experts' Report

It may be recalled that international courts do not consider expert opinion binding on them and stress that they do not delegate decision-making to court-appointed experts. In the CSIL's view, this understanding of the limits of expert opinion was violated by the Tribunal, which the CSIL accused of not subjecting the Ferse Report to rigorous examination or evaluation.[266] Had the CSIL taken the trouble to read the expert reports submitted by both categories of experts as well as the Award of 12 July 2016, it would have realized that it was the Tribunal that provided the key concepts that served as a framework for analysis and that it refrained from reference to scientific issues that were disputed among the experts.

The first key concept that the Tribunal had to define was "ecosystem." Article 194(5) of the Convention refers to rare or fragile ecosystems, a concept that is left undefined, as the Tribunal pointed out.[267] The Philippines in its written and oral pleadings had defined coral reefs as ecosystems and described the ecological goods and services that they provide, without

[264] Letter dated 22 April 2016 from John McManus, https://pcacases.com/web/sendAttach/1917, accessed 9 June 2020.

[265] Declaration of Prof. Kent E. Carpenter, Ph.D., 24 April 2016, https://pcacases.com/web/sendAttach/1917, accessed 9 June 2020.

[266] CSIL, "The South China Sea Arbitration Awards," 638, para. 946.

[267] Award of 12 July 2016, 376, para. 945.

citing a formal definition of ecosystem.[268] A scientific article annexed to the Philippine *Memorial* defined an ecosystem as a relatively discrete unit of nature; as the study of processes within these entities; and as the application of principles derived from ecosystem ecology to achieve certain management goals.[269] Rather than making a choice from different scientific definitions, the Tribunal adopted an internationally accepted one, provided in a legally binding instrument, the Convention on Biological Diversity of 1992 ("CBD"). The CBD's Article 2 defines an ecosystem as "a dynamic complex of plant, animal and micro-organism communities and their non-living environment acting as a functional unit."[270] The definition of the concepts of "rare" and "fragile" ecosystems and "vulnerable" or "threatened" species was the object of questions put to Professor Carpenter during the Hearing on the Merits.[271] On the basis of the CBD definition of ecosystem, the expert reports, and the expert testimony of

[268] *MP*, Annex 262, F. Moberg and C. Folke, "Ecological Goods and Services of Coral Reef Ecosystems", *Ecological Economics* 29, No. 2 (1999), vol. VIII, 229–34, http://www.pcacases.com/pcadocs/The%20Philippines%27%20Memorial%20-%20Volume%20VIII%20%28Annexes%20256-275%29.pdf, accessed 9 June 2020; Hearing on the Merits, Transcript, Day 3, 15–17.

[269] John M. Blair et al., "Ecosystems as Functional Units in Nature," *Natural Resources & Environment* 14 (Winter 2000): 150.

[270] *Convention on Biological Diversity*, done at Rio de Janeiro on 5 June 1992, entered into force on 29 December 1993, https://www.cbd.int/doc/legal/cbd-en.pdf, accessed 9 June 2020; Award of 12 July 2016, 376, para. 945.

[271] The CBD Conference of the Parties understands that an area is fragile if it contains a high proportion of species that are highly susceptible to degradation or depletion by human activity or by natural events or with slow recovery. A species is vulnerable if it is a species of low fecundity, slow growth, long time to sexual maturity, and longevity. Conference of the Parties to the CBD, Ninth Meeting, Decision IX/20, Marine and Coastal Biodiversity, Doc. UNEP/CBD/COP/DEC/IX/20 (9 October 2008), Annex 1, 7, https://www.cbd.int/doc/decisions/cop-09/cop-09-dec-20-en.pdf, accessed 9 June 2020. An ecosystem is defined as "rare" by the IMO as part of its Guidelines for the Identification and Designation of Particularly Sensitive Sea Areas, if it only occurs in a few locations or has been seriously depleted across its range. An area is fragile if it is highly susceptible to degradation by natural events or by activities of people. IMO Assembly, 24th session, A24/Res. 982, *Resolution 982 adopted on 1 December 20005. Revised Guidelines for the Identification and Designation of Particularly Sensitive Sea Areas*, http://www.imo.org/en/KnowledgeCentre/IndexofIMOResolutions/Assembly/Documents/A.982(24).pdf, accessed 9 June 2020.

Professor Carpenter, the Tribunal had no doubt that the marine environment where China's island-building took place constituted "rare or fragile ecosystems."[272]

The other key concepts identified by the Tribunal constituted a veritable framework for the analysis of the Ferse Report. Close reading of the independent experts' reveals that they reviewed the two Carpenter Reports and all Chinese statements in succession, statement by statement. This presentation made it difficult to obtain an overall view of Chinese claims. Instead of merely reproducing the Ferse Report's critical comments, the Tribunal identified the categories into which the environmental effects of China's island-building were to be classified. It is worth stressing this point, which becomes obvious only when one compares the format of the Ferse Report and that of the Award of 12 July 2016. Without such a comparison, one gets the mistaken impression that the point-by-point refutation of the Chinese statements was purely and simply adopted by the Tribunal.[273]

There were nine such categories identified by the Tribunal: replenishment, timing of works, water quality, restoration and transplantation, impact on reef structure, impact on reef health, selection of sites containing dead coral, and the use of "nature simulation" method and recovery. The categories may be described as purely empirical for several reasons. They were not derived from general scientific principles. They appear to be applicable only to coral reefs, making it uncertain whether some or all of the categories, such as "use of nature simulation method," could be applied to other ecosystems or habitats. There appears to be some overlap between some of the categories ("impact on reef structure" and "restoration and transplantation"). Most importantly, the Tribunal did not specify degrees of harm to the coral reefs in particular or to the marine environment in general. The harmful effects were to be determined by the scientists themselves.

It was within this framework that the Tribunal adopted the conclusions of the Ferse Report, which settled the most striking disagreements between the two Carpenter Reports and the McManus report, on the one hand, and the SOA statements, on the other. Two examples should suffice to illustrate the point. The Second Carpenter Report had stated

[272] Award of 12 July 2016, 376, para. 945.

[273] Espenilla, "Judicial Fact-Finding Initiatives," 27, creates this impression.

that corals dredged for landfill materials were destroyed. Those that were not destroyed were smothered, as their feeding and respiration valves were clogged and they were prevented from getting enough sunlight to enable the microalgae that they house to photosynthesize.[274] In contrast, a SOA statement claimed that China had adopted a "natural simulation" method.[275] Under the heading "use of the natural simulation method," the Tribunal cited the Ferse Report's conclusion that the construction process, rather than simulating the natural process of island development, increased the erosion of the reefs by shifting the balance between carbonate accretion and erosion, and thus increased the risk of drowning the reef as sea levels continue to rise.[276] At the Hearing on the Merits, Professor Carpenter had testified that China's actions had caused grave harm to the marine environment of the South China Sea and that the potentially irreversible damage to the reef system of the Spratly Islands would have serious repercussions for the highly interconnected and interdependent ecosystem of the South China Sea.[277] On the contrary, the SOA had asserted that the ecological impact of the construction was partial, temporary, controllable, and recoverable.[278] Under the heading of "recovery," the Tribunal cited the Ferse Report's conclusion that for large areas of reef affected, recovery was unlikely or would take decades or centuries.[279] One reason for the Tribunal's apparently greater reliance on the Ferse Report may be the fact that some of the Chinese statements that the Ferse Report analyzed had not been available to Carpenter and Loke Ming Chou at the time that they prepared their report. As we may recall, these statements, together with those of Chinese Foreign Ministry Officials, had been found by the Tribunal in the course of the independent research that it undertook after the closure of the oral proceedings. It is possible that one explanation for the Tribunal's adoption of the Ferse Report is that it analyzed Chinese statements of which Professors Carpenter and Chou could not have been aware.

[274] Second Carpenter Report, 250.

[275] *SDP*, Annex 821, 11–14.

[276] Ferse Report, 56; Award of as July 2016, 393, para. 982(g).

[277] Hearing on the Merits, Transcript, Day 3, 54.

[278] *PAMH*, Annex 808, 14.

[279] Ferse Report, 57; Award of 12 July 2016, 394, para. 982(i).

Further evidence of the Tribunal's critical evaluation of the two sets of expert reports may be found in the Tribunal's attitude toward scientific disagreements, which implicitly admitted that in the absence of scientific consensus among the experts, the Tribunal was not in a position to resolve these disagreements.[280] The Tribunal's attitude may only be deduced from a close reading of all the experts' reports, for the Tribunal did not explicitly identify the disagreements before making a declaration that it would not address them. The Tribunal's silence on the matter is undoubtedly due to the fact that the resolution of the disagreements was not necessary for it to reach a decision. Nevertheless it is worthwhile analyzing the Tribunal's attitude, for it provides evidence that the Tribunal critically evaluated the evidence submitted by the two sets of experts. The two most important issues on which the experts disagreed related to reef interconnectivity and phase shifts.

Reef (inter)connectivity has been defined as the flux of larvae between reef locations, creating a network of interconnected reefs. In this sense reef connectivity is synonymous with larval dispersal (the spread of larvae from spawning site to settlement site) and natal dispersal (the process of moving away from the birthplace). Reef connectivity could also refer to the flux of water mass (oceanographic interconnectivity), transporting sediments, particulate or dissolved organic and inorganic matter, trace metals and/or pollutants from reef to reef. Reef population connectivity refers to the exchange of individuals among subpopulations during any stage of their life history.[281]

The Second Carpenter Report had contended that the Spratly reefs are highly interconnected and play key roles in maintaining and replenishing regional biodiversity, as larvae originating from the Spratly Islands are spread by currents across the central South China Sea as well as to the western shore of the islands of Palawan and Luzon in the Philippines and beyond into the seas of the Philippines. Carpenter and Loke Ming Chou affirmed that the Spratly Islands are likely an important source of larvae for the hard coral *acropora millepora* for reefs in Palawan. In a reef

[280] *Trail Smelter Case (United States, Canada)*, Awards of 16 April 1938 and 11 March 1941, RIAA, vol. III (New York: United Nations, 2006), 1922, https://legal.un.org/riaa/cases/vol_III/1905-1982.pdf, accessed 11 October 2020.

[281] Claire Paris-Limouzy, "Reef Interconnectivity/Larval Dispersal," in David Hopley (ed.), *Encyclopedia of Modern Coral Reefs: Structure, Form and Process* (Dordrecht: Springer Netherlands, 2011), 881.

system like this, the loss or degradation of even one reef creates a gap in the overall connectivity of all the reefs in the Spratlys as well as the other reefs in the South China Sea.[282] Environmental damage to the Spratlys reefs that reduces the parent population of fishes, corals, and other marine plants and animals will influence the number of recruits of these animals to the Philippine archipelago, damaging the ability of coral reefs and other marine communities to recover from disturbances within the Philippine archipelago and the sustainability of fisheries.[283]

The Ferse Report expressed reservations about the postulated effects of China's island-building on connectivity, due to the paucity of scientific field studies on connectivity in the Spratly Islands. The independent experts were able to identify only two modeling studies on this point, and in their view, both suffered from serious methodological limitations. The most important seemed to be that the scale of the oceanographic models—approximately five-kilometer grid cells—was too coarse to represent larval dispersal adequately. While it is true that some fish species have very limited larval dispersal, others have dispersal that exceeds 100 kilometers, as predicted by one of the two studies. In the three independent experts' opinion, the extent and detailed patterns of connectivity between the seven affected reefs and other reefs of the Spratly Islands are difficult to ascertain without extensive genetic studies and are likely to vary for species with different duration of the larval stage and larval ecology. The Second Carpenter Report's assertion that "the degradation of even one reef creates a gap in the overall connectivity of all the reefs in the Spratlys" and leads to "the collapse of connectivity" seemed to the independent experts to be very strong statements. They did not doubt that the degradation of the seven reefs would have significant effects on larval and population dynamics throughout the Spratly Islands and very likely beyond, but they stressed that the extent of effects was difficult to ascertain based on the existing scientific information.[284]

The second major area of disagreement between the experts appointed by the Philippines and the independent experts concerned the idea of

[282] Second Carpenter Report, 265.

[283] First Carpenter Report, 400–01.

[284] Ferse Report, 37–38, 43, 44–45.

coral-algal phase-shifts, which refer to the shift from coral to algal dominance on reefs.[285] Crucial to the understanding of the phase shift is the process of nitrogen fixation. The latter refers to any natural or industrial process that causes free nitrogen (N_2), which is a relatively inert gas plentiful in air, to combine chemically with other elements to form more reactive nitrogen compounds, such as ammonia, nitrates, or nitrites. Significant amounts of nitrogen are fixed as ammonia, nitrites, and nitrates by soil microorganisms. The symbiotic nitrogen fixing bacteria invade the root hairs of host plants, where they multiply and stimulate the formation of root nodules, enlargements of plant cells, and bacteria in intimate association. Within the nodules, the bacteria convert the nitrogen to ammonia, which the host plant utilizes for its development.[286]

The Second Carpenter Report explained that corals contribute to nitrogen fixation by converting dissolved nitrogen gases in the water to ammonious ions and other derivatives that are essential for the synthesis of biological molecules in all organisms. Degradation of reefs negatively impacts nitrogen fixation by corals, which controls algal growth. When less nitrogen is fixed by corals, it becomes more available to algae, causing the larger and fleshy macroalgae to proliferate. The quick growth and biomass increase of the macroalgae smother the reef-building corals and seagrasses as well as facilitate the spread of coral disease. The macroalgae shade and deprive corals and seagrasses of sunlight and colonize the space available for coral larvae and seagrass seeds to establish. The result is a phase-shift toward an algae-dominated habitat, which supports less diversity and is ecologically less vibrant than a coral reef. Beyond a certain threshold, it is almost impossible for an ecosystem to revert to a coral-dominated system.[287]

The independent experts were of the view that the anticipation of a phase-shift to seaweed (algal) dominance was not well-justified. They shared the view that reefs can become locked into undesirable states, but they pointed out that there was no evidence that seaweeds had overtaken the reefs of the Spratly Islands and that there was scant evidence

[285] John W. McManus et al., "Coral Reef Fishing and Coral-algal Phase Shifts: Implications for Global Reef Status," *ICES Journal of Marine Science* 57 (2000): 574.

[286] The Editors of Encyclopaedia Britannica, "Nitrogen Fixation: Chemical Reaction," *Encyclopædia Britannica* (2020), https://www.britannica.com/science/nitrogen-fixation, accessed 10 June 2020.

[287] Second Carpenter Report, 267.

of the state of the reefs after China's island-building. They observed that in general, Indo-Pacific ocean reefs rarely exhibited shifts toward fleshy algal dominance except when there is intensive fishing or profound physical damage from typhoons. In the latter circumstance, nutrient released from the reef matrix may help sustain seaweed blooms. In their opinion, it was feasible but uncertain that dredging could cause local seaweed blooms that slow or prevent coral recovery.[288]

The Tribunal's awareness of the importance of a shift from coral-based to an algal-based community is highlighted in two questions it put to Professor Carpenter during the Hearing on the Merits.[289] In our view, the absence of allusions to such a phenomenon in the Award of 12 July 2016, apart from the summary of the Carpenter Reports, is indicative of the Tribunal's decision not to take a position on the issue in the absence of a consensus among the experts. Notwithstanding this cautious attitude, the Tribunal was able to reach the conclusion, based on other grounds, that China's island-building had caused harm to the marine environment.

In contrast to the two previous instances, there was practically no disagreement between the expert appointed by the Philippines and the expert appointed by the Tribunal that the dangerous maneuvers of Chinese vessels violated the COLREGS.

V. The Assessment of the Technical Evidence on Navigational Safety

The Tribunal's decision on Philippine Submission No. 13 has been neglected by many commentators.[290] This neglect is to be regretted, because the COLREGS, 1972 play a central role in ensuring the safety of maritime navigation[291] and because the *South China Sea Arbitration* seems to be the first occasion in which they have been invoked as the legal basis for a decision on an inter-State claim concerning (near-)collision of vessels. For our purposes, the decision is equally interesting for the fact

[288] Ferse Report, 45.

[289] Hearing on the Merits, Transcript, Day 4, 160–62.

[290] The exception is Alfredo C. Robles, Jr., *Vessel Collisions in the Law of the Sea: The South China Sea Arbitration* (Singapore: Palgrave-Macmillan, 2022).

[291] Tullio Treves, "La navigation [Navigation]," in René-Jean Dupuy and Daniel Vignes (eds.), *Traité du Nouveau droit de la mer* [Treatise on the New Law of the Sea] (Paris: Éditions Économica, 1985), 728.

that expert opinions on an international convention were submitted by the Philippines and by a Tribunal-appointed expert, apparently in contradiction with the idea that expert opinion on legal questions is (or should) in principle be excluded.[292] Doubtless one reason, if not the main reason, for the recourse to expert opinion is that the COLREGS are based on the practice of mariners and are addressed primarily to them. As such they may not necessarily be immediately comprehensible to specialists of international law or the law of the sea. This circumstance makes it all the more imperative that we examine the Tribunal's analysis of the expert opinion submitted by the Philippines, with the assistance of independent experts.

A. The Technical Evidence Submitted by the Philippines

The expert appointed by the Philippines, Professor Craig Allen, was not charged with any fact-finding tasks. The Philippine account of the incidents that occurred in the waters around Scarborough Shoal on 28 April and 26 May 2012 was uncontested, not because China failed to appear before the Tribunal, but because China, from the first moment that the Philippines protested over the conduct of the Chinese vessels, did not contest it. The mandate entrusted to Allen by the Philippines was to

> examine the circumstances surrounding the April 28 and May 26, 2012 encounters between public vessels of the Peoples' Republic of China (PRC) and the Republic of the Philippines (RP), with a view toward assessing the vessels' compliance with the 1972 Convention on the Prevention of Collisions (COLREGS 1972) and other applicable international law.[293]

In his opinion, the expert identified the specific rules of the COLREGS that were applicable to the two incidents and examined the possible exceptions to the application of those rules.

1. Identification of the Applicable Rules of the COLREGS, 1972

The two reports from Philippine government agencies reviewed by Allen provide detailed accounts of the incidents but they did not invoke the COLREGS, much less any COLREGS rules that were violated by the

[292] *Différend I.V.E.M.—Décisions n°s 125 et 183*, 369.

[293] *MP*, Annex 239, vol. VII, 374.

Chinese vessels' conduct.[294] If the documents of the *Arbitration* are anything to go by, it was the Allen Opinion that identified the applicable rules of the COLREGS.

A quick summary of the two incidents is in order. At 9:00 AM on 28 April 2012, the Chinese vessel FLEC (Fisheries Law Enforcement Command) 310 approached the Philippine vessel BRP ("*Barko ng Republika ng Pilipinas*," Vessel of the Republic of the Philippines) *Pampanga*, which was stationary, from port to almost dead ahead at a distance of 500 yards and a speed of 20.3 knots.[295] A quarter of an hour later, FLEC 310 approached another Philippine vessel, BRP *EDSA II*, which was due to relieve BRP *Pampanga* in the task of maritime patrol and law enforcement. FLEC 310 passed from starboard quarter to the port side of the ship at a distance of 200 yards and a speed of 20.6 knots.[296] The maneuver created two-meter-high waves in the wake of FLEC 310, battering two Philippine rubber boats that were transferring personnel.[297] In a confidential report, BRP *Pampanga*'s Commanding Officer characterized the behavior of the Chinese vessels as bullying and as a violation of the "International Code of Conduct"; by the latter he probably had in mind the COLREGS.[298]

[294] *MP*, Annex 78, Report from Commanding Officer, SARV-003, Philippine Coast Guard, to Commander, Coast Guard District Northwestern Luzon, Philippine Coast Guard (28 April 2012), 147–58, and Annex 82, Report from Angelito A. Arunco et al., FRPLEU-QRT [Fisheries Resource Protection and Law Enforcement Unit/Quick Response Team] Officers, Bureau of Fisheries and Aquatic Resources, Republic of the Philippines, to Director, Bureau of Fisheries and Aquatic Resources, Republic of the Philippines (28 May 2012), vol. IV, 147–58, 163–95, http://www.pcacases.com/pcadocs/The%20Philippines%27%20Memorial%20-%20Volume%20IV%20%28Annexes%2061-102%29.pdf, accessed 11 June 2020.

[295] "Port," as a direction, is equivalent to "left hand" when facing forward. "Dead ahead" means "exactly ahead on the ship's fore and aft line." A knot is a nautical unit of velocity representing a speed of 6080 feet per hour, equivalent to 101.3 ft. per minute and 1.69 feet per second, and nearly equal to -5 metres per second. The knot is the only unit of velocity in existence. The name is derived from the knots in the common log line. C.W.T. Layton et al., *Dictionary of Nautical Words and Terms* (2nd ed.; Glasgow: Brown Ferguson & Son Ltd., Naval Publishers, 1982), 292, 119, 216.

[296] "Starboard" is the direction equivalent to "right hand" when facing forward. Layton et al., *Dictionary*, 371, 292.

[297] *MP*, Annex 78, vol. IV, 155–58; Award of 12 July 2016, 418, paras. 1047–50.

[298] *MP*, Annex 78, vol. IV, 156.

On 26 May 2012, Philippine vessel MCS (Monitoring, Control and Surveillance) 3008, which was to resupply Philippine vessel BRP *Corregidor* at Scarborough Shoal, was approached by Chinese vessel CMS (China Marine Surveillance) 71, which increased its speed and attempted to cross the port bow of MCS 3008 at less than 100 yards. When the latter increased speed, altered course to starboard, and passed to the rear of CMS 71 to avoid a collision, CMS 71 again swung to its starboard and attempted to cross the starboard bow of MCS 3008. After the latter had executed another maneuver to avoid a collision, it was approached by FLEC 303, which aimed to cross its starboard bow. MCS 3008 increased speed to 22 knots, swerved toward the rear of FLEC 303, and continued toward BRP *Corregidor*. MCS 3008 was pursued by FLEC 303, CMS 71, and CMS 84. When MCS 3008 pulled away from BRP *Corregidor*, CMS 84 again began to chase it, with the aim of crossing through its bow. As MCS 3008 approached the lagoon of Scarborough Shoal, FLEC 303 at a distance of 50 yards altered course to cross to its starboard bow and when it was dead ahead of MCS 3008, it established a blocking position. CMS 71 moved fast toward MCS3 3008 but was able to approach it only at a distance of 70 yards because of the latter's speed. Near the entrance of the basin of Scarborough Shoal, MCS 3008, faced with mooring lines planted by Chinese fishing vessels, maneuvered backwards to avoid the lines. In order to enter the basin, MCS 3008 increased speed, maneuvered hard to starboard, and swerved toward FLEC 306, which went all engines back, determined to ram it. MCS 3008 increased speed, maneuvered left to dodge FLEC, and was finally able to enter the Shoal's basin.[299]

From these accounts, Allen had to determine which rules the Chinese vessels had violated. The Convention on the International Regulations for Preventing Collisions at Sea is quite brief, consisting of eight articles on general obligations, territorial application, procedures for revision

[299] *MP*, Annex 82, vol. IV, 204–06; Award of as July 2016, 418–21, paras. 1050–58. "All engines back" is the command given if both port and starboard engines are to be used and the direction is "back." U.S. Naval Institute, *Chapter 7*, *Navigation*, https://www.usni.org/search?f%5B0%5D=bundle_type%3Abook&f%5B1%5D=bundle_type%3Aperson&search_api_fulltext=&sort_by=search_api_relevance&sort_order=DESC&f%5B0%5D=bundle_type%3Abook&f%5B1%5D=bundle_type%3Aperson&page=427, accessed 14 September 2020.

and amendments and the final provisions.[300] It is the annexed International Regulations for Preventing Collisions at Sea that are relevant for the analysis of the two incidents. The International Regulations consist of 38 rules divided into five parts (A-general, B-steering and sailing rules, C-lights and shapes, D-sound and light signals, and E-exemptions), with four further annexes (on the positioning and technical details of lights and shapes, additional signals for fishing vessel fishing in close proximity, technical details of sound signal appliances, and distress signals). The steering and sailing rules are further subdivided into three sections—conduct of vessels in any condition of visibility (Rules 4–10), conduct of vessels in sight of one another (Rules 11–18), and conduct of vessels in restricted visibility (Rule 19).

In Allen's view, the first Rule that the Chinese vessels violated was the good seamanship rule, which is embodied in Rule 2 (a) in Part A and requires all vessels to take such precautions as are required by the ordinary practice of seamen.[301] For Allen, intentionally endangering another vessel through high-speed blocking or harassment maneuvers, which occurred on both dates, constituted flagrant disregard of good seamanship. Next, the expert determined that the Philippine and Chinese vessels were in sight of one another. Accordingly, the applicable rules were the Steering and Sailing Rules in Section B.1 (rules for vessels in any condition of visibility, Rules 4–10) and Section B.2 (rules for vessels in sight of one another, including Rules 11–18). Rules 6, 8, 15, and 16 of Section B

[300] *COLREGS—International Regulations for Preventing Collisions at Sea*, done at London on 20 October 1972, entered into force on 15 July 1977 www.mar.ist.utl.pt/mventura/Projecto-Navios-I/IMO-Conventions (copies)/COLREG-1972.pdf, accessed 11 June 2020.

[301] Rule 2 (Responsibility) reads as follows:

> (a) Nothing in these Rules shall exonerate any vessel, or the owner, master or crew thereof, from the consequences of any neglect to comply with these Rules or of the neglect of any precautions which may be required by the ordinary practice of seamen, or by the special circumstances of the case.
>
> (b) In construing and complying with these Rules due regard shall be had to all dangers of navigation and collision and to any special circumstances, including the limitations of the vessels involved, which may make a departure from these Rules necessary to avoid immediate danger.

were violated by the Chinese vessels. Rule 6 requires vessels to proceed all times at safe speed.[302] Rule 8 imposes a duty to take action to avoid collision that shall be such as to result in passing at a safe distance.[303] Allen acknowledged that the COLREGS do not define "safe distance," the determination of which is context-specific. Nevertheless, it must be large enough to leave a margin for error and to allow for the unexpected. On 28 April, FLEC 310 failed to take positive action to avoid collision. In the May incident, CMS 71, FLEC 303, and FLEC 306 violated Rule 8 by failing to take timely and positive action to pass MCS 3008 at a safe distance. Rule 15 prescribes the conduct of vessels in a crossing situation.[304] In that situation, the Chinese vessels that had the Philippine vessels on their starboard side had a duty to keep out of the way of the latter. In May 2012, CMS 71 as the give-way vessel was required to avoid crossing ahead of MCS 3008. In the April incident, FLEC 310 violated

[302] The first paragraph of Rule 6 (Safe speed) reads as follows:

Every vessel shall at all times proceed at a safe speed so that she can take proper and effective action to avoid a collision and be stopped within a distance appropriate to the prevailing circumstances and conditions.

[303] The relevant paragraphs of Rule 8 (Action to avoid a collision) are the following:

> (a) Any action taken to avoid collision shall be taken in accordance with the Rules of this Part and shall, if the circumstances of the case admit, be positive, made in ample time and with due regard to the observance of good seamanship.
>
> (d) Action taken to avoid a collision with another vessel shall be such as to result in passing at a safe distance. The effectiveness of the action shall be carefully checked until the other vessel is finally past and clear.

[304] The text of Rule 15 (Crossing situation) is as follows:

> When two power-driven vessels are crossing so as to involve risk of collision, the vessel which has the other on her own starboard side shall keep out of the way and shall, if the circumstances of the case admit, avoid crossing ahead of the other vessel.

the requirement of Rule 16 to "take early and substantial action to keep clear."[305]

The expert appointed by the Philippines also had to address China's arguments that implied that the COLREGS were not applicable in the two incidents.

2. The Inapplicability of the Exceptions to the Application of the COLREGS, 1972

Contrary to its responses to charges that it violated the COLREGS on previous occasions,[306] China did not contest the Philippine account of the facts. Responding to a Philippine protest over the incident of 28 April 2012,[307] China had declared that

> various jurisdiction measures adopted by the Chinese government over Huangyan Island [Scarborough Shoal] and its waters, and activities by Chinese ships, including government public service ships and fishing boats, in Huangyan Island and its waters are completely within China's sovereignty.[308]

This statement could be interpreted to mean that in China's view the COLREGS did not apply in waters under its sovereignty, or alternatively,

[305] Allen Opinion, 376–78. Rule 16 (Action by give-way vessel) reads as follows: "Every vessel which is directed to keep out of the way of another vessel shall, as far as possible, take early and substantial action to keep well clear."

[306] Jonathan G. Odom, "The True 'Lies' of the Impeccable Incident: What Really Happened, Who Disregarded International Law, and Why Every Nation (Outside of China) Should Be Concerned," *Michigan State University College of Law Journal of International Law* 18 (2010): 411–52, https://digitalcommons.law.msu.edu/cgi/viewcontent.cgi?article=1025&context=ilr, accessed 11 June 2020.

[307] *MP*, Annex 209, *Note Verbale* from the Department of Foreign Affairs of the Philippines to the Embassy of the People's Republic of China in Manila, No. 12-1222 (30 April 2012), vol. VI, 393–96. https://files.pca-cpa.org/pcadocs/The%20Philippines%27%20Memorial%20-%20Volume%20VI%20%28Annexes%20158-221%29.pdf, accessed 11 June 2020.

[308] *MP*, Annex 211, *Note Verbale* from the Embassy of the People's Republic of China in Manila to the Department of Foreign Affairs of the Republic of the Philippines, No. (12) PG-239 (25 May 2012), vol. VI, 401–04, https://files.pca-cpa.org/pcadocs/The%20Philippines%27%20Memorial%20-%20Volume%20VI%20%28Annexes%20158-221%29.pdf, accessed 11 June 2020; Award of as July 2016, 426–28, paras. 1076–80.

that the COLREGS did not apply to "government public service ships." Allen's expert opinion refuted both interpretations.

First, under Rule 1(a), the COLREGS apply to vessels on the high seas and all waters connected with it that are navigable by seagoing vessels. Consequently, the incidents of April and May 2012 occurred in waters to which the COLREGS apply.[309] It would not matter if China were the sovereign over Scarborough Shoal and the incidents occurred in what would have been China's territorial sea. It should be added that this interpretation is shared by standard commentaries on the COLREGS.[310]

Second, under the same rule, the COLREGS apply to all vessels. Government-owned or -operated vessels are required to observe the COLREGS, even if they are engaged in non-commercial services and are immune from the jurisdiction of other States. Rule 1(c) includes some distinction between public and non-public vessels. Rule 3(g) provides for limited accommodation for them when they are engaged in such activities as mine clearance, aircraft launch and recovery, and underway replenishment operations. Otherwise, public vessels, like the Chinese vessels involved in the incidents, are required to comply with the COLREGS.[311]

China's response to the Philippine protest implied that public vessels engaged in law enforcement activities are exempt from the duty to comply with the COLREGS. Having performed, executed, and/or supervised more than a thousand collision avoidance maneuvers and conducted over a hundred investigations into vessel casualties and oil spills, Allen was aware that occasionally there is a tension between the COLREGS and the operational requirements of public vessels engaged in constabulary operations. The US Coast Guard approaches vessels to identify them and determine their flag and the nature of their operations, and if necessary, to intercept them in order to carry out law enforcement boarding. Yet the Coast Guard's mission does not excuse it from compliance with the COLREGS.

[309] Allen Opinion, 375.

[310] Reginald Godfrey Marsden, *A Treatise on the Law of Collisions at Sea* (London: Stevens and Sons, 1880), 134, https://ia800205.us.archive.org/26/items/cu31924022403897/cu31924022403897.pdf, accessed 11 June 2020; Christopher B. Llana and George P. Wisneskey, *Handbook of the Nautical Rules of the Road: A Convenient Take-Along Guide for Sail and Power Boaters* (3rd. ed., 2009 [online]), 66, http://navruleshandbook.com/Rule1.html, accessed 29 June 2018.

[311] Allen Opinion, 376; Hearing on the Merits, Transcript, Day 3, 60.

This is made clear by Rule 2 (b), which permits departure from the COLREGS only when necessary to "avoid immediate danger" of collision. In the US, courts strictly construe the "special circumstances" rule. Departure from the rules is limited to situations involving "an immediate danger, perfectly clear; and departure from the rules must be no more than necessary."[312] Other authoritative commentators concur that the "special circumstances" rule does not give any vessel the right to take action contrary to the COLREGS even when it is considered advantageous to do so.[313] Allen concludes that arguments that government-owned or -operated vessels can ignore the COLREGS with impunity when engaged in constabulary operations found no support in the COLREGS or the caselaw.[314]

It would not be unreasonable to assume that the opinion of the author of one of the standard texts on the COLREGS in the US is authoritative. Yet the Tribunal, as part of its efforts to satisfy itself that the Philippine claims were well founded in fact and in law, appointed an independent expert on navigational safety.

B. The Assessment by the Tribunal, with Expert Assistance, of the Expert Evidence Submitted by the Philippines on Navigational Safety

The Singhota Report largely concurred with the Allen Opinion. The consensus embodied in the two reports served as the basis for the Tribunal's own analysis of the evidence submitted by both experts.

1. The Assessment by the Independent Expert of the Expert Evidence Submitted by the Philippines

The Singhota Report agreed with the Allen Opinion that the two incidents occurred when the Chinese and Philippine vessels were in sight of one another; that the applicable rules of the COLREGS were Rules 2, 6, 8, 15, and 16; that the COLREGS do not define "safe distance"; that the Chinese vessels violated Rules 2, 6, 8, and 16 on 28 April 2012; and that

312 Ibid., 378.

313 A.N. Cockcroft and J.N.F. Lameijer, *Guide to the Collision Avoidance Rules—International Regulations for Preventing Collisions at Sea, 7th Edition Incorporating the 1981, 1987, 1989, 1993, 2001 and 2007 Amendments* (Langford Lane, Kidlington, Oxford: Butterworth and Heinemann, 2012), 4.

314 Allen Opinion, 378; Hearing on the Merits, Transcript, Day 3, 62.

the violations during both incidents were intentional. There is a slight difference of emphasis in their application of the Rules to the near collisions in May 2012. The Allen Opinion affirmed that CMS 71, FLEC 303, and FLEC 306 violated Rules 2, 6, 8, 15, and 16, whereas the Singhota Report stressed the breaches of Rules 2, 6, 8, and 15. The Singhota Report proved to be valuable to the Tribunal for providing the correct information on the status of the Philippines as a party to the COLREGS and for its account of the incidents.

In its *Memorial*, the Philippines assumed that it was a party to the COLREGS at the time of the two incidents. According to the Philippines, it had acceded on 15 December 1981 to the COLREGS, which had allegedly entered into force for it on 15 March 1982.[315] In reality, the Philippines acceded to the COLREGS only on 10 June 2013, nearly six months after the date of initiation of the *Arbitration*, 22 January 2013.[316] The treaty to which the Philippines had acceded in 1980 was SOLAS 1974,[317] which the Philippines had inexplicably confused with the COLREGS in the *Memorial*. Presumably by the time of the Hearing on the Merits in November 2015, the Philippines had discovered this error, which would explain why at the Hearing, the Philippines did not reiterate its claim that it was a party to the COLREGS at the time of the two incidents.[318] It was Captain Singhota, a former official of the IMO, the depositary of the COLREGS, who correctly pointed out that the COLREGS, 1972 entered into force for the Philippines on 10 June 2013.[319] The Tribunal duly recorded this fact in its Award. The Tribunal

[315] *MP*, vol. I, 208, para. 6.132.

[316] IMO, *Status of Conventions—Comprehensive Information including Signatories, Contracting States, Declarations, Reservations, Objections and Amendments* (London: IMO, 2020), 97, http://www.imo.org/en/About/Conventions/StatusOfConventions/Documents/Status%20-%202020%20May.pdf, accessed 12 June 2020.

[317] *International Convention for the Safety of Life at Sea (SOLAS 1974)*, done at London, 1 November 1974, entered into force on 25 May 1980, https://www.refworld.org/docid/46920bf32.html, accessed 12 June 2020.

[318] If one examines the chronology, one may assume that the Philippines discovered its error sometime between 22 January 2013, the date of initiation of the *Arbitration*, and 10 June 2013, when it finally acceded to the COLREGS. But then one is hard put to explain why the *Memorial*, which was submitted to the Tribunal on 30 March 2014, reproduced the error. Perhaps this error may be the result of miscommunication between the Philippines and the foreign lawyers who drafted the *Memorial*.

[319] Singhota Report, 2, para. 3.

decided that despite the fact that the Philippines did not become party to the COLREGS until 2013, the COLREGS were binding on China and the Philippines at the time of the two incidents by virtue of Article 94 of the Convention, which incorporated the COLREGS into the latter.[320]

The Singhota Report's presentation of the two incidents differed from that of the Allen Report. The latter organized its account on the basis of the Rules that had been breached and then illustrated the breaches of the rule concerned in the two incidents. This presentation allowed the Allen Opinion to notice a pattern: the Chinese vessels grew more reckless with each new incident.[321] The Singhota Report organized its account on the basis of the incident and then explained the Rules that had been breached in the incident. In this manner, the Singhota Report was able to explain the risk of collision associated with each violation of a Rule. To take the example of the near collisions in April 2012: the high-speed maneuvering by FLEC 310 and its veering away at an unsafe distance were incompatible with Rule 2(b) because a momentary decision-making lapse on the part of the bridge team engine or steering gear failure would have inevitably resulted in a catastrophic collision. The high-speed passes of FLEC 310, which did not observe the requirement of safe speed in Rule 6, would have reduced the time available in which clear-headed decisions leading to the avoidance of collisions could be made. FLEC 310's intentional closing in at high speed to within 600 yards of BRP *Pampanga* and subsequent pass from starboard quarter to the portside of BRP *EDSA II* at 200 yards, which violated the requirement of Rule 8 to take action to avoid collision that results in passing at a safe distance, would not have taken into account human error on the bridge and engine or steering gear failure at the critical phase of maneuver and the interaction between passing vessels. FLEC 310's approaching of BRP *Pampanga* at a distance of 600 yards with a speed of 20.3 knots and passing it on its starboard side failed to comply with the requirement of Rule 16 that every vessel that is directed to keep out of the way of another vessel should take early and substantial action to keep well clear.[322]

These differences of emphasis should not overshadow the high degree of consensus between the two experts. The Tribunal did not, however,

[320] Award of 12 July 2016, 428, para. 1092.

[321] Allen Opinion, 377.

[322] Singhota Report, 3–6, paras. 5–16.

delegate decision-making to the experts and proceeded to analyze the evidence submitted by the two experts.

2. The Tribunal's Critical Assessment of the Technical Evidence Submitted by the Experts

The Tribunal found the evidence for its finding that China repeatedly violated the COLREGS in the descriptions by the crew of the Philippine vessels and the credible assessments in the two expert reports.[323] In its evaluation of the conduct of the Chinese vessels, the Tribunal followed the format adopted by the Allen Opinion, which was organized on the basis of the applicable Rules. Under each Rule the Tribunal discussed the risk of collision associated with the violation of each Rule, as described by the Singhota Report.[324] One can say without fear of exaggeration that the Tribunal considered the two expert opinions to be complementary and that the Tribunal's analysis represented a synthesis of the two reports.[325] The Tribunal's own analysis of the expert evidence submitted by the Philippines and by the independent expert highlighted the international responsibility of China and identified Rule 7 of COLREGS as a logical prerequisite to the analysis of the violations of Rules 8, 15, and 16.

The idea of China's international responsibility for the conduct of its vessels was alluded to in the Allen Opinion, which expressed the view that any breach of the duty to comply with the COLREGS by a government-owned vessel in a manner that harms another State gives rise to international responsibility.[326] When undertaking its analysis of China's conduct, the Tribunal explained in greater detail the basic principle of international responsibility involved. The Tribunal recalled that all the Chinese-flagged vessels in the incidents belonged to the CMS or the FLEC. Because the dangerous conduct was committed by vessels directly under the command and control of the Chinese government, the vessels' conduct constituted official acts of China. The conduct of each Chinese

[323] Award of 12 July 2016, 434, para. 1105.

[324] Ibid., 431–35, paras. 1091–107.

[325] One is somewhat puzzled to read a commentator express the view that the Tribunal considered the Singhota Report to be "persuasive but not necessarily conclusive." Espenilla, "Judicial Fact-Finding Initiatives," 28. A close reading of the two expert reports or of the Award of 12 July 2016, for that matter, would have avoided such a hasty and inaccurate conclusion.

[326] Allen Opinion, 376.

vessel—CMS 71, CMS 84, FLEC 303, FLEC 306, and FLEC 310—was automatically attributable to China as such.[327] In the diplomatic correspondence, China had not denied that the acts of the vessels were attributable to it, nor had it asserted that the vessels were not following official orders. Yet the Tribunal could not have missed the opportunity to reaffirm the basic principle of international responsibility applicable to this situation.

The second step in the Tribunal's critical assessment of the technical evidence submitted by the two experts highlighted the importance of Rule 7, which has been described by two commentators who are also professional mariners as an information collection and analysis rule.[328] Determination of the risk of collision triggers the operation of other rules, notably Rules 15 and 16. Rule 7 warns that if there is any doubt whether a risk of collision exists, the risk should be deemed to exist. Proper use should be made of radar equipment (Rule 7(b)), but

[327] Award of as July 2016, 431, para. 1090; Hearing on the Merits, Transcript, Day 3, 70–72.

[328] Llana and Wisneskey, *Handbook*, 92. The text of Rule 7 (Risk of collision) is as follows:

> (a) Every vessel shall use all available means appropriate to the prevailing circumstances and conditions to determine if risk of collision exists. If there is any doubt such risk shall be deemed to exist.
>
> (b) Proper use shall be made of radar equipment if fitted and operational, including long-range scanning to obtain early warning of risk of collision and radar plotting or equivalent systematic observations of detected objects.
>
> (c) Assumptions shall not be made on the basis of scanty information, especially scanty radar information.
>
> (d) In determining if risk of collision exists the following considerations shall be among those taken into account:
>
> (i) such risk shall be deemed to exist if the compass bearing of an approaching vessel does not appreciably change;
> (ii) such risk may sometimes exist even when an appreciable bearing change is evident, particularly when approaching a very large vessel or a tow or when approaching a vessel at close range.

assumptions should not be made on the basis of scanty information, especially scanty radar information (Rule 7 (c)). Once it has been determined that risk of collision exists, succeeding Rules prescribe the action to be taken by vessels. In particular, Rule 8 provides instructions on the manner in which the collision avoidance maneuvers specified in other Rules are to be executed.[329]

Rule 7, which set out the principles governing the risk of collision, had been invoked by the Philippines in its *Memorial*. The Philippines recalled that in case of doubt, it must be presumed that a risk of collision exists. Therefore, the Chinese vessels were under an obligation to act as if the risk of collision—that was created by the vessels' own maneuvers—existed.[330] During the Hearing on the Merits, the Philippines no longer invoked Rule 7.[331] The two experts did not analyze the conduct of the Chinese vessels in terms of Rule 7, perhaps because what mattered was the actual conduct of the vessels. It could be plausibly argued that such conduct indirectly demonstrated that the Chinese vessels had not used all available means to determine if the risk of collision existed, or that they had proceeded to act in such a way as to risk collision, after having determined that risk of collision existed.

Whatever may have been the reason for the two experts' silence on Rule 7, the Tribunal derived its finding that risk of collision existed on 28 April and 26 May 2012 from Rule 7. The Tribunal went further than did the Philippines in the *Memorial* and during the Hearing on the Merits and identified three instances in which a risk of collision existed: (a) on 28 April, FLEC 303 closed in at high speed within 600 yards of BRP *Pampanga* and passed BRP *EDSA II* within 200 yards; (b) on 26 May, CMS 71, FLEC 303, and CMS 84 passed Philippine vessels at distances of 100 yards or less; and (c) on 26 May, FLEC 306 nearly rammed MCS 3008. Consequently, the Tribunal considered the risk of collision identified under Rule 7 to have been clearly established, imposing on the Chinese vessels further obligations under Rules 7, 15, and 16.

After having surveyed the Tribunal's assessment of the evidence submitted by all the experts appointed by the Philippines in support of its

[329] Llana and Wisneskey, *Handbook*, 37, 38.

[330] *MP*, vol. I, 208, 212, paras. 6.137, 6.143.

[331] Hearing on the Merits, Transcript, Day 3, 66–67.

submissions on the status of features, the environmental consequences of China's island-building, and the dangerous maneuvers of Chinese vessels and the Tribunal's assessment of the opinions rendered by all the independent experts, one can safely dismiss the CSIL's baseless charge that the Tribunal adopted expert reports without further evaluation. Just as unfounded are the attacks on the independence and impartiality of the appointing authority, the members of the Arbitral Tribunal, and the Tribunal as a whole, to which we shall now turn.

References

Agreement Between the International Tribunal for the Law of the Sea and the Government of the Federal Republic of Germany Regarding the Headquarters of the Tribunal and Exchange of Notes, 14 December 2004, https://www.itlos.org/fileadmin/itlos/documents/basic_texts/headquarters_agreement_eofn_eng.pdf, accessed 21 May 2020.

Appazov, Artur. *Expert Evidence and International Criminal Justice*. Cham, Switzerland: Springer International Publishing AG Switzerland, 2016.

Application for Revision and Interpretation of the Judgment of 24 February 1982 in the Case Concerning the Continental Shelf (Tunisia/Libyan Arab Jamahiriya) (Tunisia v. Libyan Arab Jamahiriya). Judgment. I.C.J. Reports 1985, 192–321, https://www.icj-cij.org/files/case-related/71/071-19851210-JUD-01-00-BI.pdf, accessed 21 May 2020.

Armed Activities on the Territory of the Congo (Democratic Republic of the Congo v. Uganda). Judgment. I.C.J. Reports 2005, 168–283, https://www.icj-cij.org/files/case-related/116/116-20051219-JUD-01-00-BI.pdf, accessed 27 May 2020.

Beckman, Robert C., and Clive H. Schofield. "Defining EEZ Claims from Islands: A Potential South China Sea Change." *The International Journal of Marine and Coastal Law* 29 (2014): 193–243.

Bell, Evan. "Judicial Assessment of Expert Evidence." *Judicial Studies Institute Journal* 2 (2010): 55–96, https://www.ijsj.ie/assets/uploads/documents/pdfs/2010-Edition-02/article/judicial-assessment-of-expert-evidence.pdf, accessed 7 November 2019.

Bennouna, Mohamed. "Experts Before the International Court of Justice: What for?" *Journal of International Dispute Settlement* 9 (2018): 345–51.

Benzing, Markus. *Das Beweisrecht vor internationalen Gerichten und Schiedsgerichten in zwischenstaatlichen Streitigkeiten* [The Law of Evidence before International Courts and Arbitral Tribunals in Inter-State Disputes]. Heidelberg: Springer, 2010.

Blair John M. et al. "Ecosystems as Functional Units in Nature." *Natural Resources & Environment* 14 (Winter 2000): 150–55.

Boisson de Chazournes, Laurence, and Guillaume Yvan Jean Gros. "L'expert et le Tribunal international du droit de la mer [The Expert and the International Tribunal for the Law of the Sea]." *Les 20 ans du Tribunal international du droit de la mer* [Twenty Years of the International Tribunal for the Law of the Sea], 181–201. Ed. Guillaume Le Floch. Paris: Editions A. Pedone, 2018.

——— et al. "One Size Does Not Fit All—Uses of Experts Before International Courts and Tribunals: An Insight into the Practice." *Journal of International Dispute Settlement* 9 (2018): 477–505.

Boyes, Grant. "Australia's Approach to Using Remotely Sensed Data to Determine Territorial Sea Baselines." Paper presented at the 6th IHO-IAG-ABLOS [International Hydrographic Organization-International Association of Geodesy-Advisory Board on the Law of the Sea] Conference, International Hydrographic Bureau, Monaco, 25–27 October 2010, https://legacy.iho.int/mtg_docs/com_wg/ABLOS/ABLOS_Conf6/S4P1-B.pdf, accessed 8 July 2017.

——— et al. "Establishing an Australian Marine Spatial Data Infrastructure." Paper presented at the 6th IHO-IAG-ABLOS [International Hydrographic Organization-International Association of Geodesy-Advisory Board on the Law of the Sea] Conference, Monaco, 25–28 October 2010, https://www.iho.int/mtg_docs/com_wg/ABLOS/ABLOS_Conf6.htm, accessed 8 July 2017.

——— et al. "The Universal Digital Marine Cadaster." Paper presented at the 7th ABLOS [Advisory Board on the Law of the Sea] Conference, Monaco, 3–5 October 2012, https://www.iho.int/mtg_docs/com_wg/ABLOS/ABLOS_Conf8/ABLOS8_Abstracts_Programme_v9.2.pdf, accessed 8 July 2017.

Boyle, Alan, and James Harrison. "Judicial Settlement of International Environmental Disputes: Current Problems." *Journal of International Dispute Settlement* 4 (2013): 245–76.

Caddell, Richard. "Annex VIII. Special Arbitration." *United Nations Convention on the Law of the Sea 1982: A Commentary*, 2491–2511. Eds. Alexander Proelss et al. München: C.H. Beck, 2017.

Campbell, James B., and Randolph H. Wynne. *Introduction to Remote Sensing*, 5th ed. New York: The Guilford Press, 2011.

CARIS. *CARIS LOTS Article 76, Product Overview.* Fredericton, New Brunswick: CARIS, 2017, http://www.caris.com/products/lots/overview.cfm, accessed 4 September 2017.

———. *LOTS Brochure.* Fredericton, New Brunswick: CARIS, 2017, http://www.caris.cm/downloads/brochures/lots-en.pdf, accessed 4 September 2017.

Chinese Society of International Law. "The South China Sea Arbitration Awards: A Critical Study." *Chinese Journal of International Law* 17 (2018): 207–748.

Cockcroft, A.N. and J.N.F. Lameijer. *Guide to the Collision Avoidance Rules—International Regulations for Preventing Collisions at Sea, 7th edition Incorporating the 1981, 1987, 1989, 1993, 2001 and 2007 Amendments*. Langford Lane, Kidlington, Oxford: Butterworth and Heinemann, 2012.

COLREGS - International Regulations for Preventing Collisions at Sea. Done at London on 20 October 1972. Entered into force on 15 July 1977, www.mar.ist.utl.pt/mventura/Projecto-Navios-I/IMO-Conventions (copies)/COLREG-1972.pdf, accessed 11 June 2020.

Convention on Biological Diversity. Done at Rio de Janeiro on 5 June 1992. Entered into force on 29 December 1993, https://www.cbd.int/doc/legal/cbd-en.pdf, accessed 9 June 2020.

———. Conference of the Parties. Ninth Meeting. Decision IX/20. Marine and Coastal Biodiversity. Doc. UNEP/CBD/COP/DEC/IX/20 (9 October 2008), https://www.cbd.int/doc/decisions/cop-09/cop-09-dec-20-en.pdf, accessed 9 June 2020.

Convention on Fishing and Conservation of the Living Resources of the High Seas. Done at Geneva on 29 April 1958. Entered into force on 20 March 1966, https://www.gc.noaa.gov/documents/8_1_1958_fishing.pdf, accessed 10 April 2020.

Convention on the International Regulations for Preventing Collisions at Sea, 1972. Consolidated text as amended in 1981, 1987, 1989, 1993, 2001 and 2007, https://www.ecolregs.com/index.php?option=com_k2&view=itemlist&layout=category&Itemid=505&lang=en, accessed 11 June 2020.

Damme, Isabelle Van. "The Assessment of Expert Evidence in International Adjudication." *Journal of International Dispute Settlement* 9 (2018): 401–10.

D'Aspremont, Jean, and Makane Moïse Mbengue. "Strategies of Engagement with Scientific Fact-Finding in International Adjudication." *Journal of International Dispute Settlement* 5 (2014): 240–72.

Davenport, Tara. "Procedural Issues Arising from China's Non-Participation in the *South China Sea Arbitration*." *The South China Sea Arbitration: The Legal Dimension*, 65–98. Eds. S. Jayakumar et al. Cheltenham: Edward Elgar Publishing, 2018.

Delimitation of the Maritime Boundary in the Gulf of Maine Area (Canada/United States). Treaty Between the Government of Canada and the Government of the United States of America to Submit to Binding Dispute Settlement the Delimitation of the Maritime Boundary in the Gulf of Maine Area (25 November 1981). *I.C.J. Pleadings, Delimitation of the Maritime Boundary in the Gulf of Maine Area (Canada/United States)*. Vol. I, 3–26, https://www.icj-cij.org/files/case-related/67/9595.pdf, accessed 24 May 2020.

Différend Héritiers de S.A.R. Mgr le Duc de Guise - Décision no 162 du 20 novembre 1953 [Dispute concerning the Heirs of H.R.H. The Duke of Guise – Decision No. 162 of 20 November 1953]." *Reports of International Arbitral Awards*. Vol. XIII, 150–70. New York: United Nations, 1964, https://legal.un.org/riaa/cases/vol_XIII/150-170_Heritiers.pdf, accessed 1 June 2020.

Différend Industrie Vicentine Elettro-Meccaniche (I.V.E.M.) —Décisions n°s 125 et 183 [Industrie Vicentine Elettro-Meccaniche (I.V.E.M.) Dispute. Decisions Nos. 125 and 183] (1 March 1952 and 7 March 1955). *Reports of International Arbitral Awards*. Vol. XIII, 325–81. New York: United Nations, 2006, http://legal.un.org/docs/?path=../riaa/cases/vol_XIII/325-381.pdf&lang=O, accessed 23 July 2020.

DigitalGlobe. *Accuracy of WorldView Products*. White Paper Accuracy 5/16. Westminster, CO: DigitalGlobe, 16 May 2016, https://dg-cms-uploads-production.s3.amazonaws.com/uploads/document/file/38/DG_ACCURACY_WP_V3.pdf, accessed 3 June 2020.

———. *Base Product Series FAQ*. Westminster, CO: DigitalGlobe, 2017, https://www.c-agg.org/wp-content/uploads/DigitalGlobe-Base-Product-FAQ.pdf, accessed 3 June 2020.

———. *Data Sheet Information Products. Standard Imagery*. Westminster, CO: DigitalGlobe (7 October 2016), https://dg-cms-uploads-production.s3.amazonaws.com/uploads/document/file/21/Standard_Imagery_DS_10-7-16.pdf, accessed 3 June 2020.

Donoghue, Joan E. "Expert Scientific Evidence in a Broader Context." *Journal of International Dispute Settlement* 9 (2018): 379–87.

Dwyer, Déirdre. *The Judicial Assessment of Expert Evidence*. Cambridge: Cambridge University Press, 2009.

The Editors of Encyclopaedia Britannica. "Cay." *Encyclopaedia Britannica* (2020), https://www.britannica.com/science/atoll, accessed 9 October 2020.

———. "Nitrogen Fixation: Chemical Reaction." *Encyclopædia Britannica* (2020), https://www.britannica.com/science/nitrogen-fixation, accessed 10 June 2020.

EOMAP. *EOMAP Provides Bathymetry for South China Sea*. Seefeld, Germany: EOMAP, 16 June 2015, http://www.eomap.com/eomap-provides-bathymetry-for-south-china-sea/, accessed 3 June 2020.

———. *EOMAP Satellite Derived Bathymetry White Paper*. Seefeld, Germany: EOMAP, 10 April 2014, http://www.eomap.com/exchange/pdf/EOMAP_Bathy_20140410.pdf, accessed 3 June 2020.

Espenilla, Jacqueline Joyce F. "Judicial Fact-Finding Initiatives in the *South China Sea Arbitration*." *Asian Journal of International Law* 9 (2019): 20–30.

ESRI. *Fundamentals of Orthorectifying a Raster Dataset*. Redlands, CA: ESRI, 2016, https://desktop.arcgis.com/en/arcmap/10.3/manage-data/raster-and-images/fundamentals-of-orthorectifying-a-raster-dataset.htm, accessed 3 June 2020.

Foster, Caroline E. "New Clothes for the Emperor? Consultation of Experts by the International Court of Justice." *Journal of International Dispute Settlement* 5 (2014): 139–73.

———. *Science and the Precautionary Principle in International Courts and Tribunals: Expert Evidence, Burden of Proof and Finality*. Cambridge: Cambridge University Press, 2011.

Gaja, Giorgio. "Assessing Expert Evidence in the ICJ." *Law and Practice of International Courts and Tribunals* 15 (2016): 409–18.

Gogarty, Brendan. "Conceptions and (Mis)conceptions of Science in International Treaties: The ICJ Whaling Case in Context." *Yearbook of Polar Law* 7 (2015): 607–22.

———, and Peter Lawrence. "The ICJ *Whaling* Case: Missed Opportunity to Advance the Rule of Law in Resolving Science-Related Disputes in Global Commons?" *Heidelberg Journal of International Law* 77 (2017): 261–98.

Gros, Guillaume. "The ICJ's Handling of Science in the *Whaling in the Antarctic* Case: A Whale of a Case?" *Journal of International Dispute Settlement* 6 (2015): 578–620.

Gray, David H. "Technical Standards for Judicial Decisions and Experts Appointed by Courts." Paper presented at the 7th IHO-IAG-ABLOS [International Hydrographic Organization-International Association of Geodesy-Advisory Board on the Law of the Sea] Conference, Monaco, 3–5 October 2012, https://www.iho.int/mtg_docs/com_wg/ABLOS/ABLOS_Conf8/ABLOS8_Abstracts_Programme_v9.2.pdf, accessed 8 July 2017.

Guyana v. Suriname. Award of the Arbitral Tribunal (17 September 2007), https://pcacases.com/web/sendAttach/902, accessed 24 May 2020.

———. Corrected Report on Site Visit (30 July 2007), https://pcacases.com/web/sendAttach/901, accessed 24 May 2020.

———. Hearing Transcripts. Vol. 1 (7 December 2006), https://pcacases.com/web/sendAttach/891, accessed 24 May 2020.

———. Hearing Transcripts. Vol. 2 (8 December 2006), https://pcacases.com/web/sendAttach/892, accessed 24 May 2020.

———. Hearing Transcripts. Vol. 7 (15 December 2006), https://pcacases.com/web/sendAttach/897, accessed 24 May 2020.

He Tiantian. "Commentary on Award on Jurisdiction and Admissibility of the Philippines-Instituted Arbitration Under Annex VII to the UNCLOS: A Discussion on Fact-Finding and Evidence." *Chinese Journal of Global Governance* 2 (2016): 96–128.

International Convention for the Safety of Life at Sea (SOLAS 1974). Done at London on 1 November 1974. Entered into force on 25 May 1980, https://www.refworld.org/docid/46920bf32.html, accessed 12 June 2020.

International Court of Justice. *Rules of Court, adopted on 14 April 1978 and entered into force on 1 July 1978*, https://www.icj-cij.org/en/rules, accessed 22 March 2020.

International Hydrographic Organization. *Hydrographic Dictionary*. Part I. Vol. I. *English*, 5th ed. Monaco: International Hydrographic Organization, 1994, https://www.iho.int/iho_pubs/standard/S-32/S-32-eng.pdf, accessed 19 May 2020.

International Maritime Organization. *Status of Conventions—Comprehensive Information Including Signatories, Contracting States, Declarations, Reservations, Objections and Amendments*. London: IMO, 2020, http://www.imo.org/en/About/Conventions/StatusOfConventions/Documents/Status%20-%202020%20May.pdf, accessed 12 June 2020.

———. Assembly. 24th session. A24/Res. 982, Resolution 982 adopted on 1 December 2005. *Revised Guidelines for the Identification and Designation of Particularly Sensitive Sea Areas*, http://www.imo.org/en/KnowledgeCentre/IndexofIMOResolutions/Assembly/Documents/A.982(24).pdf, accessed 9 June 2020.

International Oceanographic Commission; International Hydrographic Organization; and International Association of Geodesy. *A Manual of Technical Aspects of the United Nations Convention on the Law of the Sea – 1982*. Monaco: International Hydrographic Bureau, 2006, https://www.gc.noaa.gov/documents/gcil_iho_tech_aspects_los.pdf, accessed 24 May 2020.

International Tribunal for the Law of the Sea. *Rules of the Tribunal* (ITLOS/8), *as adopted on 28 October 1997 and amended on 15 March 2001, 21 September 2001, 17 March 2009 and 25 September 2018*, https://www.itlos.org/fileadmin/itlos/documents/basic_texts/Itlos_8_E_25.09.18.pdf, accessed 29 April 2020.

Jennings, Sir Robert. "International Lawyers and the Progressive Development of International Law." *Theory of International Law at the Threshold of the 21st Century. Essays in Honor of Krzysztof Skubiszewski*, 413–24. Ed. Jerzy Makarczyk. The Hague: Kluwer Law International, 1996.

Kojima, Chie. "South China Sea Arbitration and Protection of the Marine Environment: Evolution of UNCLOS Part XII through Interpretation and the Duty to Cooperate." *Asian Yearbook of International Law* 21 (2015): 166–80.

Kpalma, Kidiyo et al. "Recent Trends in Satellite Image Pan-sharpening Techniques." Paper presented at the 1st International Conference on Electrical, Electronic and Computing Engineering, June 2014, Vrniacka Banja, Serbia, https://hal.archives-ouvertes.fr/hal-01116094/document, accessed 3 June 2020.

Kuhn, Thomas. *The Structure of Scientific Revolutions*, 2nd ed., enlarged. Chicago: The University of Chicago Press, 1970.

Land and Maritime Boundary Between Cameroon and Nigeria (Cameroon v. Nigeria: Equatorial Guinea intervening). Judgment. I.C.J. Reports 2002, 303–458, http://www.icj-cij.org/files/case-related/94/094-20021010-JUD-01-00-BI.pdf, accessed 22 July 2020.

Larousse Dictionary of Science and Technology. Edinburgh: Larousse plc, 1995.

Layton, C.W.T. et al. *Dictionary of Nautical Words and Terms*, 2nd ed. Glasgow: Brown Ferguson & Son Ltd., Naval Publishers, 1982.

Lima, Lucas Carlos. "The Evidential Weight of Experts Before the ICJ: Reflections on the *Whaling in the Antarctic* Case." *Journal of International Dispute Settlement* 6 (2015): 621–35.

Lippitt, C.D. "Georeferencing and Georectification." *The Geographic Information Science & Technology Body of Knowledge (3rd Quarter 2020 Edition)*. Ed. John P. Wilson. Ithaca, N.Y.: University Consortium for Geographic Information Science, 2020. https://doi.org/10.22224/gistbok/2020.3.3, https://gistbok.ucgis.org/bok-topics/georeferencing-and-georectification, accessed 9 October 2020.

Llana, Christopher B., and George P. Wisneskey. *Handbook of the Nautical Rules of the Road: A Convenient Take-Along Guide for Sail and Power Boaters*, 3rd. ed. [online], 2009, http://navruleshandbook.com/Rule1.html, accessed 29 June 2018.

London Institute of Space Policy and Law. *Evidence from Space. Study for the European Space Agency on Use of Space-Derived Earth Observation Information as Evidence in Judicial and Administrative Proceedings as Part of its Series of Studies in Support of Actions to Integrate New Developments in the Current EO Services*. Doc. ESA-ISPAL.76/Final. London: London Institute of Space Policy and Law, 2012, https://www.space-institute.org/app/uploads/1342722048_Evidence_from_Space_25_June_2012_-_No_Cover_zip.pdf, accessed 4 June 2020.

Lyons, Youna. "Prospects for Satellite Imagery of Insular Features and Surrounding Marine Habitats in the South China Sea." *Marine Policy* 45 (2014): 146–55.

McManus, John W. et al. "Coral Reef Fishing and Coral-algal Phase Shifts: Implications for Global Reef Status." *ICES Journal of Marine Science* 57 (2000): 572–78.

Magron, Franck. "Shallow Water Bathymetry." *SPC* [Secretariat of the Pacific Community] *Newsletter*, 120 (January/March 2007): 44–48.

Mangel, Marc. "Whales, Science, and Scientific Whaling in the International Court of Justice." *PNAS* [Proceedings of the National Academy of Sciences] 113 (20 December 2016): 14523–27, https://www.pnas.org/content/pnas/113/51/14523.full.pdf, accessed 25 May 2020.

Maritime Delimitation in the Caribbean Sea and the Pacific Ocean (Costa Rica v. Nicaragua). Order of 31 May 2016. I.C.J. Reports 2016, 235–38, https://www.icj-cij.org/files/case-related/157/157-20160531-ORD-01-00-BI.pdf, accessed 27 May 2020.

Marsden, Reginald Godfrey. *A Treatise on the Law of Collisions at Sea*. London: Stevens and Sons, 1880, https://ia800205.us.archive.org/26/items/cu31924022403897/cu31924022403897.pdf, accessed 11 June 2020.

Mbengue, Makane Moïse. "The South China Sea Arbitration Innovation in Marine Environmental Fact-Finding and Due Diligence Obligations." *ASIL* [American Society of International Law] *Unbound* (12 December 2016): 285–89.

Mégret, Frédéric. "International Judges and Experts' Impartiality and the Problem of Past Declarations." *Law and Practice of International Courts and Tribunals* 10 (2011): 31–66.

Mora, Camilo et al. "Dredging in the Spratly Islands: Gaining Land But Losing Reefs." *PLoS Biology* 14 (31 March 2016): 31002422.

Moses, Margaret L. *The Principles and Practice of International Commercial Arbitration*. Cambridge: Cambridge University Press, 2008.

Natural Resources Canada. *Fundamentals of Remote Sensing*. Ottawa: Canada Centre for Remote Sensing, 2016, http://www.nrcan.gc.ca/sites/www.nrcan.gc.ca/files/earthsciences/pdf/resource/tutor/fundam/pdf/fundamentals_e.pdf, accessed 2 June 2020.

Nordquist, Myron H. et al. (eds.). *United Nations Convention on the Law of the Sea 1982: A Commentary*. Vol. V. *Settlement of Disputes, General and Final Provisions and Related Annexes and Resolutions*. Leiden: Brill, 1989.

Odom, Jonathan G. "The True 'Lies' of the Impeccable Incident: What Really Happened, Who Disregarded International Law, and Why Every Nation (Outside of China) Should Be Concerned." *Michigan State University College of Law Journal of International Law*, 18 (2010): 411–52, https://digitalcommons.law.msu.edu/cgi/viewcontent.cgi?article=1025&context=ilr, accessed 11 June 2020.

Oral, Nilufer. "The South China Sea Arbitral Award, Part XII of UNCLOS and the Protection and Preservation of the Marine Environment." *The South China Sea Arbitration: The Legal Dimension*, 223–46. Eds. S. Jayakumar et al. Cheltenham: Edward Elgar, 2018.

Organisation for Economic Co-operation and Development. *Glossary of Statistical Terms*. Paris: OECD, July 2005, https://stats.oecd.org/glossary/detail.asp?ID=6660, accessed 3 June 2020.

Ormsby, Harry. "Judicial Fact-finding and the South China Sea Arbitration." *Kluwer Arbitration Blog*, 6 September 2016, http://kluwerarbitrationblog.com/2016/09/06/judicial-fact-finding-and-the-south-china-sea-arbitration/, accessed 11 September 2020.

Paris-Limouzy, Claire. "Reef Interconnectivity/Larval Dispersal." *Encyclopedia of Modern Coral Reefs: Structure, Form and Process*, 881–89. Ed. David Hopley. Dordrecht: Springer Netherlands, 2011.

Parlett, Kate. "Parties' Engagement with Experts in International Litigation." *Journal of International Dispute Settlement* 9 (2018): 440–52.

Pattanaik, Amitansu et al. "Estimation of Shallow Water Bathymetry Using IRS-Multispectral Imagery of Odisha Coast, India." *Aquatic Procedia* 4 (2015): 173–81, https://www.sciencedirect.com/science/article/pii/S2214241X15000255, accessed 3 June 2020.

Perez, Oren. "Judicial Strategies for Reviewing Conflicting Expert Evidence: Biases, Heuristics, and Higher-order Evidence." *American Journal of Comparative Law* 64 (2016): 75–120.

Plakokefalos, Ilias. "Environmental Law Aspects of the South China Sea Arbitration Award." Paper presented at the Symposium on the South China Sea Award, Netherlands Institute for the Law of the Sea. Utrecht Centre for Oceans Water and Sustainability Law, School of Law, Utrecht University, 7 December 2016, https://papers.ssrn.com/sol3/papers.cfm?abstract_id=2880624, accessed 5 June 2020.

Pulp Mills on the River Uruguay (Argentina v. Uruguay). Judgment. I.C.J. Reports 2010, 14–107, http://www.icj-cij.org/files/case-related/135/135-20100420-JUD-01-00-BI.pdf, accessed 26 May 2020.

———. Declaration of Judge Yusuf. *I.C.J. Reports 2010*, 216–20, https://www.icj-cij.org/files/case-related/135/135-20100420-JUD-01-05-BI.pdf, accessed 21 May 2020.

———. Joint Dissenting Opinion of Judge Al-Khasawneh and Judge Simma. *I.C.J. Reports 2010*, 108–20, https://www.icj-cij.org/files/case-related/135/135-20100420-JUD-01-01-BI.pdf, accessed 22 July 2020.

———. Separate Opinion of Judge Greenwood, 221–32, https://www.icj-cij.org/files/case-related/135/135-20100420-JUD-01-06-BI.pdf, accessed 26 May 2020.

———. Verbatim Record, CR 2009/14 (16 September 2009), http://www.icj-cij.org/files/case-related/135/135-20090916-ORA-01-00-BI.pdf, accessed 2 June 2020.

———. Verbatim Record, CR 2009/16 (21 September 2009), http://www.icj-cij.org/files/case-related/135/135-20090921-ORA-01-00-BI.pdf, accessed 2 June 2020.

———. Verbatim Record, CR 2009/19 (24 September 2009), http://www.icj-cij.org/files/case-related/135/135-20090924-ORA-01-00-BI.pdf, accessed 26 May 2020.

———. Verbatim Record, CR 2009/20 (28 September 2009), http://www.icj-cij.org/files/case-related/135/135-20090928-ORA-01-00-BI.pdf, accessed 2 June 2020.

———. Verbatim record, CR 2009/21 (29 September 2009), https://www.icj-cij.org/files/case-related/135/135-20090929-ORA-01-01-BI.pdf, accessed 21 May 2020.

Ranjeva, Raymond. "Le règlement des différends [Dispute Settlement]." *Traité du nouveau droit de la mer* [Treatise on the New Law of the Sea], 1105–67. Eds. René-Jean Dupuy and Daniel Vignes. Paris: Éditions Economica, 1985.

Riddell, Anna, and Brendan Plant. *Evidence Before the International Court of Justice.* London: British Institute of International and Comparative Law, 2009.

Robles, Alfredo C. Jr. *Endangered Species and Fragile Ecosystems in the South China Sea: The Philippines v. China Arbitration.* Singapore: Palgrave-Macmillan, 2020.

———. *Vessel Collisions in the Law of the Sea: The South China Sea Arbitration.* Singapore: Palgrave Macmillan, 2022.

Rosenne, Shabtai, with the assistance of Yaël Ronen. *The Law and Practice of the International Court 1990–2005.* Leiden: Martinus Nijhoff Publishers, 2006.

Sands, Philippe. "Science and International Litigation." *Unité et diversité du droit international. Écrits en l'honneur du professeur Pierre-Marie Dupuy* [Unity and Diversity of International Law. Essays in Honour of Professor Pierre-Marie Dupuy], 891–908. Eds. Denis Alland et al. Leiden: Martinus Nijhoff Publishers, 2014.

Savadogo, Louis. "Le recours des juridictions internationales à des experts [The Recourse of International Jurisdictions to Experts]." *Annuaire français de droit international* [French Yearbook of International Law] 50 (2004): 231–58, https://www.persee.fr/docAsPDF/afdi_0066-3085_2004_num_50_1_3795.pdf, accessed 21 May 2020.

Shalowitz, Aaron L., and Michael W. Reed. *Shore and Sea Boundaries.* Vol. I. Washington, D.C.: U.S. Department of Commerce, Coast and Geodetic Survey, 1962.

Simma, Bruno. "The International Court of Justice and Scientific Expertise." *Proceedings of the Annual Meeting (American Society of International Law)* 106 (28 March 2012): 230–33.

South China Sea Arbitration. Assessment of the Potential Environmental Consequences of Construction Activities on Seven Reefs in the Spratly Islands in the South China Sea. Expert Report of Dr. rer. nat. Sebastian C.A. Ferse, Professor Peter Mumby, PhD and Dr. Selina Ward, PhD (26 April 2016), https://pcacases.com/web/sendAttach/1809, accessed 29 May 2020.

———. Award of 12 July 2016, https://pcacases.com/web/sendAttach/2086, accessed 10 March 2020.

———. Award on Jurisdiction and Admissibility (29 October 2015), https://pcacases.com/web/sendAttach/2579, accessed 10 March 2020.

———. Declaration of Prof. Kent E. Carpenter, Ph.D., 24 April 2016, https://pcacases.com/web/sendAttach/1917, accessed 9 June 2020.
———. Hearing on the Merits and Remaining Issues of Jurisdiction and Admissibility. Transcript, Day 2 (25 November 2015), https://pcacases.com/web/sendAttach/1548, accessed 27 April 2020.
———. Transcript, Day 3 (26 November 2015), https://pcacases.com/web/sendAttach/1549, accessed 13 October 2019.
———. Transcript, Day 4 (30 November 2015), https://pcacases.com/web/sendAttach/1550, accessed 16 April 2020.
———. Letter dated 22 April 2016 from John McManus, https://pcacases.com/web/sendAttach/1917, accessed 9 June 2020.
———. *Memorial of the Philippines*. Vol. I (30 March 2014), https://files.pca-cpa.org/pcadocs/Memorial%20of%20the%20Philippines%20Volume%20I.pdf, accessed 27 March 2019.
———. Annexes. Vol. IV, http://www.pcacases.com/pcadocs/The%20Philippines%27%20Memorial%20-%20Volume%20IV%20%28Annexes%2061-102%29.pdf, accessed 11 June 2020.
———. Annex 78. Report from Commanding Officer, SARV-003, Philippine Coast Guard, to Commander, Coast Guard District Northwestern Luzon, Philippine Coast Guard (28 April 2012), 147–58.
———. Annex 82. Report from Angelito A. Arunco et al., FRPLEU-QRT [Fisheries Resource Protection and Law Enforcement/Quick Response Team] Officers, Bureau of Fisheries and Aquatic Resources, Republic of the Philippines, to Director, Bureau of Fisheries and Aquatic Resources, Republic of the Philippines (28 May 2012), 163–95.
———. Annexes. Vol. VI, https://files.pca-cpa.org/pcadocs/The%20Philippines%27%20Memorial%20-%20Volume%20VI%20%28Annexes%20158-221%29.pdf, accessed 11 June 2020.
———. Annex 209. *Note Verbale* from the Department of Foreign Affairs of the Philippines to the Embassy of the People's Republic of China in Manila, No. 12-1222 (30 April 2012), 393–96.
———. Annex 211. *Note Verbale* from the Embassy of the People's Republic of China in Manila to the Department of Foreign Affairs of the Republic of the Philippines, No. (12) PG-239 (25 May 2012), 401–04.
———. Annexes. Vol. VII, https://files.pca-cpa.org/pcadocs/The%20Philippines%27%20Memorial%20-%20Volume%20VII%20%28Annexes%20222-255%29.pdf, accessed 19 May 2020.
———. Annex 239. Opinion of Craig H. Allen, Judson Falknor Professor of Law, University of Washington (19 March 2014), 371–88.
———. Annex 240. Kent E. Carpenter, Ph.D., Eastern South China Sea Environmental Disturbances and Irresponsible Fishing Practices and their Effects on Coral Reefs and Fisheries (22 March 2014), 389–437.

———. Annexes. Vol. VIII, http://www.pcacases.com/pcadocs/The%20Philippines%27%20Memorial%20-%20Volume%20VIII%20%28Annexes%20256-275%29.pdf, accessed 9 June 2020.
———. Annex 262. F. Moberg and C. Folke, "Ecological Goods and Services of Coral Reef Ecosystems", *Ecological Economics*, Vol. 29, No. 2 (1999), 229–34.
———. *The Philippines' Annexes cited during Merits Hearing* (30 November 2015), https://files.pca-cpa.org/pcadocs/Annexes%20cited%20during%20Hearing%20on%20Jurisdiction%20%28Annexes%20574-583%29.pdf, accessed 24 April 2020.
———. Annex 821. China State Oceanic Administration, "Construction Work at Nansha Reefs Will Not Harm Oceanic Ecosystems" (18 June 2015), 11–14.
———. Annex 850. John McManus, "Offshore Coral Reef Damage, Overfishing and Paths to Peace in the South China Sea," 578–608.
———. *Responses of the Philippines to the Tribunal's 5 February 2016 Request for Comments* (11 March 2016), https://pcacases.com/web/sendAttach/1849, accessed 7 July 2020.
———. *(Annexes 864–892)* (11 March 2016), https://files.pca-cpa.org/pcadocs/The%20Philippines%27%20Written%20Responses%20%2811%20March%202016%29%20%28Annexes%20864-892%29.pdf, accessed 3 May 2020.
———. Annex 864. China State Oceanic Administration, The Guidance for the Assessment of Coastal Marine Ecosystem Health, Marine Industry Standards of the People's Republic of China, No. HY/T 087-2005 (2005), 5–7.
———. Annex 865. China State Oceanic Administration, "2012 Communique [sic] on Marine Environment of China, Part 2: Marine Biodiversity and Ecological Conditions" (1 April 2013), 8–21.
———. Annex 866. China State Oceanic Administration, Code of Practice for Marine Monitoring Technology, Part 5: Marine Ecology, Marine Industry Standards of the People's Republic of China, No. HY/T 147.5-2013 (25 April 2013), 22–24.
———. Annex 867. China State Oceanic Administration, "2013 Communique [sic] on Marine Environment of China, Part 2: Conditions of Marine Ecology" (25 March 2014), 25–36.
———. Annex 868. China State Oceanic Administration, Technical Guidelines for Environmental Impact Assessment of Marine Engineering, National Standards of the People's Republic of China, No. GB/T 19485 -2014 (1 April 2014), 37–128.
———. Annex 869. China State Oceanic Administration, South China Sea Branch, "Communique [sic] on the Oceanic Conditions of the South China Seas Region in 2013" (14 August 2014), 129–59.

———. Annex 870. China State Oceanic Administration, "2014 Communique [sic] on Marine Environment of China, Part 2: Conditions of Marine Ecology" (16 March 2015), 160–70.
———. Annex 871. China State Oceanic Administration, South China Sea Branch, "Communique [sic] on the Oceanic Conditions of the South China Sea Region in 2014" (28 May 2015), 171–200.
———. Annex 872. China State Oceanic Administration, "Construction Activities at Nansha Reefs Did Not Affect the Coral Reef Ecosystem" (10 June 2015), 201–08.
———. Captain Gurpreet S. Singhota, *Report of the International Navigational Safety Expert Appointed by the Permanent Court of Arbitration* [sic], *The Hague, The Netherlands*, 15 April 2016, https://pcacases.com/web/sendAttach/1810, accessed 29 May 2020.
———. Rules of Procedure (27 August 2013), https://pcacases.com/web/sendAttach/233, accessed 11 May 2020.
———. *Supplemental Documents of the Philippines* (19 November 2015). Vol. I, https://files.pca-cpa.org/pcadocs/The%20Philippines%27%20Supplemental%20Documents%20-%20Volume%20I%20%28Annexes%20607-667%29.pdf, accessed 27 April 2020.
———. Vol. II, https://files.pca-cpa.org/pcadocs/The%20Philippines%27%20Supplemental%20Documents%20-%20Volume%20II%20%28Annexes%20608-709%29.pdf, accessed 19 May 2020
———. Annex 699. K.E. Carpenter & L.M. Chou, Environmental Consequences of Land Reclamation Activities on Various Reefs in the South China Sea (14 November 2015), 235–93.
———. Vol. V, http://www.pcacases.com/pcadocs/The%20Philippines%27%20Supplemental%20Documents%20-%20Volume%20III%20%28Annexes%20710-756%29.pdf, accessed 2 June 2020.
———. Annex 807. EOMAP GmbH & Co, Satellite Derived Bathymetry for Selected Features in the South China Sea (18 November 2015), 8–27.
———. *Supplemental Written Submission of the Philippines* (16 March 2015). Vol. I, https://files.pca-cpa.org/pcadocs/Supplemental%20Written%20Submission%20Volume%20I.pdf, accessed 23 April 2020.
———. Annexes. Vol. IX, https://files.pca-cpa.org/pcadocs/The%20Philippines%27%20Supplemental%20Written%20Submission%20-%20Volume%20IX%20%28Annexes%20500-521%29.pdf, accessed 19 May 2020.
———. Annex 513. C. Schofield et al., An Appraisal of the Geographical Characteristics and Status of Certain Insular Features in the South China Sea (March 2015), 143–245.
Stephens, Tim. "The Collateral Damage from China's 'Great Wall of Sand': The Environmental Dimensions of the South China Sea Case." *Australian Yearbook of International Law* 24 (2017): 41–56.

Talmon, Stefan. *The South China Sea Arbitration: Is There a Case to Answer?* Bonn: Universität Bonn, Institute for Public International Law, 2014, https://papers.ssrn.com/sol3/papers.cfm?abstract_id=2393025, accessed 13 March 2020.

Tams, Christian J. "Article 50." *The Statute of the International Court of Justice: A Commentary*, 3rd ed., 1287–99. Eds. Andreas Zimmermann et al. Oxford: Oxford University Press, 2019.

———. "Article 51." *The Statute of the International Court of Justice: A Commentary*, 3rd ed., 1441–52. Eds. Andreas Zimmermann et al. Oxford: Oxford University Press, 2019.

Tanaka, Yoshifumi. "The South China Sea Arbitration: Environmental Obligations Under the Law of the Sea Convention." *Review of European, Comparative and International Environmental Law* 27 (2018): 90-96.

Tempfli, Klaus et al. (eds.). *Principles of Remote Sensing. An Introductory Textbook.* Enschide, The Netherlands: The International Institute for Geo-Information Science and Earth Observation, 2009.

Torge, Wolfgang. *Geodesy*, 2nd ed. Berlin: Walter de Gruyter, 1991.

Trail Smelter Case (United States, Canada). Awards of 16 April 1938 and 11 March 1941. *Reports of International Arbitral Awards.* Vol. III, 1905–82. New York: United Nations, 2006, https://legal.un.org/riaa/cases/vol_III/1905-1982.pdf, accessed 11 October 2020.

Treves, Tullio. "Article 289. Experts." *United Nations Convention on the Law of the Sea 1982: A Commentary*, 1863–66. Eds. Alexander Proelss et al. München: C.H. Beck, 2017.

———. "La navigation [Navigation]." *Traité du nouveau droit de la mer* [Treatise on the New Law of the Sea], 687–808. Eds. René-Jean Dupuy and Daniel Vignes. Paris: Éditions Economica, 1985.

Turner, Woody et al. "Remote Sensing for Biodiversity Science and Conservation," *Trends in Ecology and Evolution* 18 (June 2003): 306–14.

United Nations Convention on the Law of the Sea. Concluded at Montego Bay on 10 December 1982. Entered into force on 16 November 1994, http://www.un.org/Depts/los/convention_agreements/texts/unclos/closindx.htm, accessed 21 March 2020.

United Nations. Division for Ocean Affairs and the Law of the Sea. *Annex VIII. Special Arbitration*, https://www.un.org/depts/los/convention_agreements/texts/unclos/annex8.htm, accessed 22 May 2020.

———. *List of Experts in the Field of Fisheries Maintained by the Food and Agriculture Organization of the United Nations (Communicated on 12 January 2017)*, https://www.un.org/Depts/los/settlement_of_disputes/expertsunclosVIIIjan2017fao.pdf, accessed 5 February 2020.

———. *List of Experts in the Field of Marine Scientific Research Maintained by the Intergovernmental Oceanographic Commission of UNESCO (as at 28 January*

2016), https://www.un.org/Depts/los/settlement_of_disputes/expertsunclosVIII_iocunesco.pdf, accessed 5 February 2020.

———. *List of Experts in the Field of Navigation, Including Pollution from Vessels and by Dumping, Maintained by the International Maritime Organization (as at 8 April 2019)*, https://www.un.org/Depts/los/settlement_of_disputes/expertsunclosVIIIimo2019.pdf, accessed 5 February 2020.

———. *List of Experts in the Field of Protection and Preservation of the Marine Environment Maintained by the United Nations Environment Programme (Communicated on 8 November 2002)*, https://www.un.org/Depts/los/settlement_of_disputes/expertsunclosVIIInov2002unep.pdf, accessed 5 February 2020.

———. General Assembly. Resolution 41/65. Principles Relating to Remote Sensing of the Earth from Space. UN Doc. A/RES/41/65 (3 December 1986), https://digitallibrary.un.org/record/126423?ln=en, accessed 2 June 2020.

United States. Department of Commerce. National Oceanic and Atmospheric Administration. National Ocean Service. *What Is Bathymetry?* Silver Spring, MD: National Ocean Service, 6 July 2017, https://oceanservice.noaa.gov/facts/bathymetry.html, accessed 3 June 2020.

———. Geological Survey. *Landsat - Earth Observation Satellites*. Fact Sheet 3015–3081 (November 2015), http://pubs.usgs.gov/fs/2015/3081/fs20153081.pdf, accessed 3 June 2020.

University of Minnesota. Polar Geospatial Center. *Introduction to Stereoscopic Imagery. Collection Mode*. St. Paul, MN: Polar Geospatial Center, University of Minnesota College of Science and Engineering, 23 February 2017, https://www.pgc.umn.edu/guides/stereo-derived-elevation-models/introduction-to-stereoscopic-imagery/?print=pdf, accessed 4 June 2020.

Watts, Arthur. "Enhancing the Effectiveness of Procedures of International Dispute Settlement." *Max Planck Yearbook of United Nations Law* 5 (2001): 21–40.

Whaling in the Antarctic (Australia v. Japan: New Zealand Intervening). Judgment. I.C.J. Reports 2014, 226–300, http://www.icj-cij.org/files/case-related/148/148-20140331-JUD-01-00-BI.pdf, accessed 26 May 2020.

———. *Memorial of Australia* (9 May 2011), https://www.icj-cij.org/files/case-related/148/17382.pdf, accessed 28 May 2020.

———. Lars Walløe, *Scientific Review of Issues Raised by the Memorial of Australia, including Its Two Appendices* (9 April 2013), http://www.icj-cij.org/files/case-related/148/17418.pdf, accessed 26 May 2020.

———. Verbatim Record. CR 2013/14 (3 July 2013), https://www.icj-cij.org/files/case-related/148/148-20130703-ORA-02-00-BI.pdf, accessed 26 May 2020.

Zhang Duo, and Zhang Renping. "Chinese Law Enforcement Activities in Its Own Territorial Waters Legitimate and Justifiable." *China Daily*, 31 May 2016, http://www.chinadaily.com.cn/opinion/2016-05/30/content_25522234.htm, accessed 4 December 2018.

CHAPTER 5

The Defaulting State, the Appointing Authority, and the Judges in the *South China Sea Arbitration*

It is not unexpected that a State defaulting in international judicial proceedings protests when the court hearing the case continues the proceedings. Furthermore, one might understand that a defaulting State that denies jurisdiction will criticize a judgment affirming jurisdiction and a judgment on the merits that dismisses its claims. In the *South China Sea Arbitration* China's conduct went beyond the limits of that of defaulting States in cases before the International Court of Justice ("ICJ"). In the early phase of the proceedings, China attempted to undermine the independence of the Arbitral Tribunal through secret approaches. After the issuance of the Award on Jurisdiction, it mobilized pressure from non-parties to the disputes, seemingly ignoring that such pressure could have no impact on the Award. In a campaign launched nearly three and a half years into the proceedings and continued after their conclusion, China accused the Tribunal of bias, on several grounds. China alleged that the Tribunal, in the absence of a Chinese or Asian member, lacked representative character. It also accused the appointing authority, who had appointed four of the Tribunal's five members, of manipulating the Tribunal's composition. Finally, China attributed to financial considerations the Tribunal's decisions on procedure and on the merits that were favorable to the Philippines. These charges were dutifully echoed by individual Chinese scholars and by the Chinese Society for International Law ("CSIL").

A. C. Robles Jr., *The Defaulting State and the South China Sea Arbitration*, https://doi.org/10.1007/978-981-19-6394-0_5

The *Institut de droit international* ("IDI," Institute of International Law), which had recommended a procedure for fact-finding in cases of default in its resolution on non-appearance before the ICJ, surely had not anticipated conduct of the kind that China exhibited and for that reason had not made (and could not have made) any recommendation, procedural or otherwise, that could have addressed it.[1] Clearly, the Philippines had no means of redress against China's attempts to undermine the Tribunal's independence, but the Rules of Procedure of the *South China Sea Arbitration* had offered China a procedure for challenging the independence and impartiality of the arbitrators prior to and during the proceedings.[2] It may be recalled that each one of the arbitrators signed a declaration of independence and impartiality that was transmitted to the parties for their responses. At this stage, China could already have raised objections to the independence and impartiality of one or more arbitrators. Under Article 7 of the Rules of Procedure, China could have challenged one or more arbitrators if there were circumstances that gave rise to justifiable doubts as to his or their impartiality or independence, within 30 days after it had become aware of such circumstances. Under Article 8, China should have sent notice of the challenge to the Philippines, to the arbitrator(s) being challenged, the other arbitrators, and the Permanent Court of Arbitration ("PCA"), the Registry in the case. Several outcomes were possible. The two parties could have agreed to the challenge, the challenged arbitrator could have withdrawn from the Tribunal, or if neither of these outcomes occurred, China could have, within 30 days of its notice of challenge, sought a decision on the challenge by the President of the International Tribunal for the Law of the Sea ("ITLOS").

A challenge procedure was implemented in the *Chagos Marine Protected Area Arbitration*, when Mauritius expressed concern, two weeks after receiving the arbitrators' declaration of independence and impartiality. at the long-standing and close working relationship of the arbitrator appointed by the UK with the latter. Mauritius requested additional disclosure from the arbitrator, after which it challenged the arbitrator's

[1] *Institut de Droit International* [Institute of International Law], Session de Bâle [Basel Session], *Non-Appearance Before the International Court of Justice* (1991), https://www.idi-iil.org/app/uploads/2017/06/1991_bal_01_en.pdf, accessed 16 March 2020.

[2] *South China Sea Arbitration*, Rules of Procedure (27 August 2013), https://pcacases.com/web/sendAttach/233, accessed 5 April 2020.

appointment. There ensued two rounds of written submissions and a hearing on the challenge by Mauritius. In the end the challenge was dismissed by the Tribunal's other members.[3] A State that proclaimed its aim "to safeguard the solemnity and integrity of international law" would have and should have emulated the example of Mauritius.[4]

China could argue that it "discovered" the arbitrators' lack of independence and impartiality only when the proceedings had been concluded. Obviously, charges of lack of independence and impartiality made in such circumstances are motivated by dissatisfaction with the decisions and can hardly be taken seriously. Furthermore, any grounds for challenge could no longer have been entertained, as China had failed to raise a challenge following the procedures established in the Rules of Procedure and could be deemed to have waived its right to do so. In short, there would be no need to pay any attention to any charges of lack of independence and impartiality raised after the conclusion of the proceedings. Like Chapter 4, this Chapter could end here. Any attempt to respond to China's charges might appear to be "trying too hard."

Other considerations must weigh in the balance. One can hardly exaggerate the extraordinary nature of China's charges of lack of independence and impartiality of the Tribunal and its members, which as unexpectedly and as inexplicably extended to the appointing authority. It was observed over sixty years ago that in the ICJ context, States whose claims had been rejected by the Court "generally refrained from impugning the integrity of its motives."[5] The only major instance remotely resembling an exception to this observation seems to have occurred when the US withdrew from the merits phase of the *Nicaragua Case*. One rationale for the US withdrawal was the alleged national security risk that it would run by presenting highly sensitive intelligence material on Nicaragua's actions

[3] *Chagos Marine Protected Area Arbitration (Mauritius v. United Kingdom)*, Reasoned Decision on Challenge (1 December 2011), 1–4, paras. 9–25, https://pcacases.com/web/sendAttach/1792, accessed 16 June 2020.

[4] Ministry of Foreign Affairs of the People's Republic of China ("Foreign Ministry"), *Briefing by Xu Hong, Director-General of the Department of Treaty and Law on the South China Sea Arbitration Initiated by the Philippines 2016/05/12*, https://www.fmprc.gov.cn/nanhai/eng/wjbxw_1/t1364804.htm, accessed 16 January 2020.

[5] Oliver James Lissitzyn, *The International Court of Justice. Its Role in the Maintenance of International Peace and Security* (New York: Carnegie Endowment for International Peace, 1951), 55.

"in public or before a Court that includes two judges from Warsaw Pact nations."[6]

China's conduct during and after the proceedings compares unfavorably with that of the defaulting State in another arbitration under Annex VII of the Convention. Following an award affirming jurisdiction in the *"Arctic Sunrise" Arbitration*, Russia simply declared that it maintained its decision not to participate in the proceedings.[7] Upon the issuance of the Award on the Merits in August 2015, Russia merely reiterated its position that the Tribunal had no jurisdiction in the case and asserted that the Award was "not impeccable by a whole range of parameters and contain[ed] obvious inaccuracies, for instance, in its interpretation of Russia's legal status as a State successor to the Soviet Union."[8] At no point during and after the proceedings did Russia criticize the *"Arctic Sunrise"* Tribunal for its non-representative character or impugn the motivations of the Tribunal or the integrity of its members and of the appointing authority.[9]

Most importantly, an assessment of China's accusations will be valuable when seen in the context of the heightened scholarly interest in the last two decades in the status, independence, and impartiality of international judges. This interest, stimulated by the proliferation of international courts and tribunals, has manifested itself in the launching of research projects,[10] the publication of numerous scholarly books and articles, the teaching of a course on the independence of international judges at the

[6] "Text of U.S. Statement on Withdrawal from Case before the World Court," *New York Times*, 19 January 1985, http://www.nytimes.com/1985/01/19/world/text-of-us-statement-on-withdrawal-from-case-before-the-world-court.html?pagewanted=all&pagewanted=print, accessed 16 June 2020. The judges concerned were Judge Morozov, a USSR national, and Judge Lach, a Polish national.

[7] *The Arctic Sunrise Arbitration (Netherlands v. Russia)*, Award on the Merits (14 August 2015), 4, para. 18, https://pcacases.com/web/sendAttach/1438, accessed 17 March 2020.

[8] Interfax, "Russian Foreign Ministry: Arctic Sunrise Arbitration Court Lacks Proper Jurisdiction," *Russia Beyond the Headlines*, 25 August 2015, https://www.rbth.com/news/2015/08/25/russian_foreign_ministry_arctic_sunrise_arbitration_court_lacks_proper_j_48720.html, accessed 16 June 2020.

[9] The Tribunal consisted of nationals of Ghana, the Netherlands, Mexico, Poland, and Australia. The appointing authority was the ITLOS President, Judge Yanai.

[10] Project on International Courts and Tribunals ("PICT"), launched in 1997 by a consortium of British and American universities. http://www.pict-pcti.org, accessed 4 January 2018.

Hague Academy of International Law,[11] the establishment of an Institute of International Judges at Brandeis University,[12] and the adoption by the International Law Association ("ILA") of principles on the independence of the international judiciary.[13] An analysis of Chinese critiques of the independence and impartiality of the appointing authority and the members of the Arbitral Tribunal in the *South China Sea Arbitration* provides the opportunity to bring to bear the insights derived from this scholarly literature on some of the gravest accusations that have yet been formulated against international judges.

This Chapter will be divided into three parts. The first examines China's charge that the Arbitral Tribunal lacked representative character. It argues that representation of major civilizations, legal systems, and nationals of the parties is not an inherent requirement of international arbitration in general or of arbitration under Annex VII of the United Nations Convention on the Law of the Sea ("Convention") in particular.[14] The second and third parts examine separately the issues of independence and impartiality of the appointing authority and of the judges in the *South China Sea Arbitration.* Admittedly judicial independence and judicial impartiality are often conflated. Ironically, it is China's litigation strategy that makes it possible to distinguish clearly between judicial independence and judicial impartiality. The second part draws on insights from international caselaw and the scholarly literature in order to assess the degree of independence of the appointing authority and of the judges in the *South China Sea Arbitration* and draws parallels

[11] Jiři Malenovský, "L'indépendance des juges internationaux [The Independence of International Judges]," *Recueil des Cours de l'Académie de droit international de La Haye* [Collected Courses of the Hague Academy of International Law], vol. 349 (2010-IV), 9–276 ("*RCADI*").

[12] Brandeis University, International Center for Ethics, Justice and Public Life, *A Forum for International Judges* (Waltham, MA.: International Center for Ethics, Justice and Public Life, 2018), https://www.brandeis.edu/ethics/internationaljustice/biij/index.html, accessed 16 June 2020. The Institute holds sessions approximately every eighteen months. Its reports for 2002, 2003, 2004, 2006, 2007, 2009, 2010, 2012, 2013, 2015, 2015 and 2018 may be found on its website.

[13] Philippe Sands et al., "The Burgh House Principles on the Independence of the International Judiciary," *Law and Practice of International Courts and Tribunals* 4 (2005): 247–60 ("*LPICT*").

[14] *United Nations Convention on the Law of the Sea*, concluded at Montego Bay on 10 December 1982, entered into force on 16 November 1994, http://www.un.org/Depts/los/convention_agreements/texts/unclos/closindx.htm, accessed 21 March 2020.

between China's conduct toward the Tribunal and the conduct of the Chinese government and the Chinese Communist Party ("CCP") toward Chinese judges. The third part examines the charges of lack of impartiality against the appointing authority and individual members of the Arbitral Tribunal, on the one hand, and against the Tribunal as a whole, on the other. It assesses China's mendacious allegations on the basis of standards or conceptions of impartiality derived from the caselaw of inter-State courts and from the scholarly literature and explains China's allegations by referring to judicial corruption in China.

I. The Defaulting State and the Representative Character of the Arbitral Tribunal

One year into the proceedings, China started to argue that the selection of four members of the Tribunal was biased and resulted from manipulation by the appointing authority designated by Annex VII of the Convention, the ITLOS President, who at the time was Judge Shunji Yanai.[15] In its Notification and Statement of Claim, the Philippines had appointed Judge Wolfrum, then an ITLOS member, as its arbitrator.[16] Following China's failure to appoint its arbitrator, the Philippines requested, under the terms of Article 3(c) of Annex VII of the Convention, that the appointing authority designate the four other arbitrators. The ITLOS President duly

[15] It seems that the first scholar to call attention to the nationality of the ITLOS President was an American scholar. Julian Ku, "What Happens if China Tries to Boycott UNCLOS Arbitration? A Japanese Guy Gets to Appoint the Tribunal," *opiniojuris.org*, 25 January 2013, http://opiniojuris.org/2013/01/25/what-happens-if-china-tries-to-boycott-unclos-arbitration-a-japanese-guy-gets-to-appoint-the-tribunal/, accessed 17 June 2020. The use of the word "guy" in the title of the article suggests that Ku was speaking tongue-in-cheek. The charge of manipulation of the Tribunal's composition was apparently first raised by a Chinese newspaper in 2014, although it did not give any explanation of the charge. "Manila's Scheme Abuses Law," *China Forum (China Daily)*, 1 April 2014, http://europe.chinadaily.com.cn/opinion/2014-04/01/content_17394014_2.htm, accessed 17 June 2020. See also Julian Ku, "So How is China Reacting to the Philippines Arbitration Submission? Not Very Well," *opiniojuris.org*, 3 April 2014, http://opiniojuris.org/2014/04/03/china-reacting-philippines-arbitration/, accessed 17 June 2020.

[16] *South China Sea Arbitration*, *Memorial of the Philippines* (30 March 2014), Annex 1, Notification and Statement of Claim of the Republic of the Philippines (22 January 2013), vol. III, 13–34, https://files.pca-cpa.org/pcadocs/The%20Philippines%27%20Memorial%20-%20Volume%20III%20%28Annexes%201-60%29.pdf, accessed 15 March 2020.

appointed the four others and designated the fourth, M.C.W. Pinto, a Sri Lankan national, president of the Tribunal. Judge Pinto subsequently resigned because his wife was a Filipino national.[17] One wonders how the Philippines and the ITLOS President could have overlooked the nationality of Pinto's wife, and one is even more astonished that it took Pinto two weeks to acknowledge the fact. Be that is it may, the ITLOS President proceeded to nominate Judge Mensah, a Ghanaian national, in Pinto's place.[18]

The appointing authority was described as follows by no less than a Chinese Vice-Minister of Foreign Affairs:

> Who is Shunji Yanai? He is a judge of the ITLOS now and before [sic] as well as the Chairman of [the] Advisory Panel on Reconstruction of the Legal Basis for Security set by the Shinzo Abe administration. He plays [sic] an important role in helping Shinzo Abe with the lifting of the ban on collective self-defense and challenging international order after World War II. He was also former Japanese Ambassador to the US.[19]

The Chinese press, not to be outdone, described Judge Yanai as a "manipulator."[20]

The result of the alleged manipulation was an arbitral tribunal that did not have a Chinese or Asian member:

[17] Michaela del Callar, "For Having Pinay Wife, Sri Lankan Judge in PHL Arbitral Proceedings vs China Resigns," *GMA News*, 7 June 2013, http://www.gmanetwork.com/news/story/311870/news/nation/for-having-pinay-wife-sri-lankan-judge-in-phl-arbitral-proceedings-vs-china-resigns, accessed 17 June 2020.

[18] International Tribunal for the Law of the Sea ("ITLOS"), *New Arbitrator and President Appointed in the Arbitral Proceedings Instituted by the Republic of the Philippines against the People's Republic of* China, ITLOS/Press 197 (24 June 2013), https://www.itlos.org/fileadmin/itlos/documents/press_releases_english/PR_197_E.pdf, accessed 17 June 2020.

[19] Foreign Ministry, *Veil of the Arbitral Tribunal Must Be Tore* [sic] *Down* [sic], 13 July 2013, http://www.fmprc.gov.cn/mfa_eng/wjbxw/t1381879.shtml, accessed 18 July 2016. As this extraordinary interview is no longer available on the Foreign Ministry website, the complete text is reproduced in Annex 5.1. Could the Foreign Ministry be regretting the message or the errors in translation?

[20] Xinhua. "Shunji Yanai, Manipulator Behind Illegal South China Sea Arbitration," *Xinhua.net*, 17 July 2016, http://en.people.cn/n3/2016/0717/c90000-9087223.html, accessed 17 June 2020.

> Four of them (the arbitrators) come from Europe....The fifth judge is from Ghana...but he lived [sic] in Europe permanently. So does a court like this have any representativeness?....[N]one of the five judges...is from Asia, let alone China. Do they know Asia? Do they understand Asian cultures? Do they know the South China Sea issue? Do they understand the complicated geographical politics in Asia? Do they know the history of the South China Sea? On what basis can they make a fair award?[21]

Two years later, this charge was faithfully reprised by the CSIL. The latter further muddied the discussion by alleging that the composition of the Tribunal should have represented the main forms of civilization and the principal legal systems or geographic regions of the world, which it claimed to be a generally accepted idea. The CSIL was forced to admit that Annex VII of the Convention did not expressly provide for the representative character of the composition of the Tribunal, but the CSIL, not one to let itself be deterred by the explicit text of an international treaty, alleged that if there was no agreement between the parties, the general rules and practices of international courts should have been followed. The CSIL referred to the ICJ and the ITLOS, which established such requirements for their composition.[22]

Taking a tack different from that of the Vice Foreign Minister, Xinhua alleged that the arbitrators' selection was careless. The ICJ, with 15 members, and the ITLOS, with 21 members, supposedly had strict procedures for election, involving in the former case election by the UN General Assembly and the UN Security Council, and in the latter case by the States parties to the Convention. Xinhua set great store by the fact that unlike the ICJ and the ITLOS, the Arbitral Tribunal's members were appointed and that it consisted of only five members. This meant that only three out of the five were needed to make an award.[23]

For some unfathomable reason, Sienho Yee found it significant that two of the five arbitrators were nationals of former colonial powers in

[21] Foreign Ministry, *Veil*.

[22] Chinese Society of International Law ("CSIL"), "The South China Sea Arbitration Awards: A Critical Study," *Chinese Journal of International Law* 17 (2018): 624–26, paras. 903–906 ("*CJIL*").

[23] Xinhua, "Ad hocism [sic] Guided S China Sea Arbitral Tribunal," *China Daily*, 18 July 2016, https://www.chinadailyasia.com/special/southchinasea/2016-07/18/content_15464647_2.html, accessed 17 June 2020.

Southeast Asia.[24] Like China's Vice Foreign Minister and the CSIL, he criticized the Tribunal's composition for not representing the main forms of civilization or the principal legal systems of the world and for not reflecting the need for a national arbitrator. He argued that if States parties to an arbitration could not agree on the appointment of the tribunal's members, the Tribunal should still have been representative and should have had a national arbitrator. He feigned ignorance about the reason for not constituting a representative tribunal and not appointing a Chinese arbitrator. The ITLOS Special Chamber, created to settle the dispute concerning the delimitation of the maritime boundary between Ghana and the Côte d'Ivoire and consisting of members from Algeria, Germany, South Korea, Ghana, and France, appeared to him as the model of a representative tribunal.[25]

Whether expressed crudely or dressed up in scholarly garb, China's objections to the composition of the Tribunal for not representing the major civilizations and legal systems of the world and for not having a Chinese arbitrator fail to distinguish between arbitration and judicial settlement by a permanent international court and erroneously assume that the presence of a "national" arbitrator is an inherent requirement of arbitration. Close reading of Annex VII of the Convention and a survey of the practice of Annex VII tribunals reveal that representation of major civilizations, principal legal systems, and nationals of parties to the arbitration is not an indispensable condition for the constitution of Annex VII arbitral tribunals.

[24] Sienho Yee, "The South China Sea Arbitration Decisions on Jurisdiction and Rule of Law Concerns," *CJIL* 15 (2016): 224. The former colonial powers in question are France, of which Judge Cot is a national, and the Netherlands, of which Judge Soons is a national. Yee also alleged that the ITLOS President appointed "just anyone (222)."

[25] Ibid. *Dispute Concerning Delimitation of the Maritime Boundary between Ghana and Côte d'Ivoire in the Atlantic Ocean (Ghana/Côte d'Ivoire)*, Special Agreement and Notification of 3 December 2014 and the Minutes of Consultation, annexed thereto, https://www.itlos.org/fileadmin/itlos/documents/cases/case_no.23_merits/special_agreement_and_notification.pdf, accessed 17 June 2020. One is hard put to explain why Sienho Yee was not bothered that France was the former colonial power in Côte d'Ivoire. Notwithstanding Yee's approval, it is possible to question the representativeness of the Special Chamber's composition. Africa and Western Europe are over-represented; Eastern Europe, North America and other States, and Latin America and the Caribbean are not represented at all.

A. Representation and the Composition of Permanent International Courts and International Arbitral Tribunals

Representation of civilizations and legal systems was never a consideration in the constitution of tribunals when arbitration was the only mode for judicial settlement of inter-State disputes. It emerged as a requirement only when the first permanent international court with universal jurisdiction, the Permanent Court of International Justice ("PCIJ") was established in 1922; it was also incorporated in the ICJ Statute in 1945. It will be discussed first, as it is more implausible and for this reason easier to dismiss. What Sienho Yee qualifies as the "need for a national arbitrator" will then be analyzed in the context of the evolution of the notion of representation of the parties in the composition of an arbitral tribunal.

1. The Representation of Civilizations and Legal Systems in the PCIJ and the ICJ

Under Article 9 of the ICJ Statute, the representation of "the main forms of civilization and of the principal legal systems of the world should be assured" in the Court's composition.[26] We may understand the rationale for this twin requirement by reviewing the drafting history of the PCIJ Statute, from which it was drawn. This review will make it obvious that the considerations that led to the incorporation of the requirement in the PCIJ Statute do not and cannot play any weight in the establishment of arbitral tribunals.

The PCIJ differed from ad hoc arbitral tribunals in that it was a permanent court that had general jurisdiction—it had jurisdiction over disputes with an international character. To be sure, members of the League of Nations were not under a duty to submit their disputes to the PCIJ. For States that accepted the PCIJ's compulsory jurisdiction, their acceptance meant that States that had also accepted the PCIJ's compulsory jurisdiction could unilaterally file cases against them. The Great Powers who would accept the PCIJ's jurisdiction could not avoid this risk. In the Advisory Committee of Jurists that drafted the PCIJ Statute, they declared

[26] International Court of Justice ("ICJ"), *Statute*, http://www.icj-cij.org/en/statute, accessed 10 March 2020.

that their citizens would not consent to have their States submit to judgments of a court on which they were not represented.[27] They admitted candidly that they feared having to submit to the judgment of a court in which most members were representatives of small States.[28] They stressed that they possessed the material force necessary to ensure the execution of the PCIJ's decisions.[29] Japan, which saw itself as the principal representative of Asian civilizations, insisted that all different forms of civilization had to be represented in the PCIJ, otherwise its citizens would never consent to submit to the PCIJ's jurisdiction.[30] For these reasons the Great Powers demanded permanent representation in the PCIJ. As was to be expected, the Great Powers met with the determined opposition of the "small" powers, who emphasized the principle of equality of sovereign States.[31]

The compromise between the two positions was found in the need to assure the representation of the great legal systems and the main forms of civilization on the PCIJ.[32] The main legal systems were identified in the minds of Committee members with distinct systems of legal education. In the first system, judges attached more importance to precedent; in the second system, to logical deduction and to the logical sequence of inference from authorities and principles. It was said that by requiring representation of the principal legal systems, any and all points of national law involved in international disputes would be comprehended.[33] The reference to "main forms of civilization" was intended not just to accommodate the Japanese perspective but also to ensure that there could be French and Italian judges, and not just one judge representing civil law

[27] League of Nations, Advisory Committee of Jurists, *Procès-verbaux of the Proceedings of the Committee, June 16th–July 24th, 1920, with Annexes* (The Hague: Vanangenhuysen, 1920), 105, https://ia600900.us.archive.org/6/items/procsverbauxof00leaguoft/procsverbauxof00leaguoft.pdf, accessed 19 June 2020 ("*Procès-verbaux*").

[28] Ibid., 108.

[29] Ibid., 105.

[30] Ibid., 136.

[31] Ibid., 103, 363, 366, 369, 639.

[32] Ibid., 111, 370.

[33] Ibid., 710.

systems.[34] The two requirements resulted in an increase in the proposed number of PCIJ members from seven to 15.[35]

Neither "the main forms of civilization" nor "the principal legal systems of the world" were defined in the PCIJ Statute and they remain undefined in the ICJ Statute. The expression "main forms of civilization," which smacks of a Eurocentric world view and implies an idea of hierarchy incompatible with the legal equality of States, is now understood as a metaphor for cultural diversity.[36] Some ICJ judges have attempted to shed some light on the meaning of this twin requirement, without reference to the drafting history. The principal legal systems of the world were identified by Judge Ammoun as the law of Western Europe and of Latin America, common law, Muslim law, Chinese law, Soviet law, Hindu law, the law of other Asian States. and the law of African States, but the ICJ itself has not had the occasion to pronounce on this matter.[37] In Judge Weeramantry's view, the twin requirements impose on the Court "the particular obligation to search in all these legal traditions and legal systems for principles and approaches that enrich the law it administers."[38] Judge Ammoun believed that the fact that the Court represents the main forms of civilization and the principal legal systems of the world lends greater authority to the opinions of the judges.[39] Academic commentary has explained that as the Court has jurisdiction over disputes

[34] Bardo Fassbender, "The Representation of the 'Main Forms of Civilization' and of 'the Principal Legal Systems of the World' in the International Court of Justice," in Denis Alland et al. (eds.), *Unité et diversité du droit international. Ecrits en l'honneur du professeur Pierre-Marie Dupuy* [Unity and Diversity of International Law. Essays in Honour of Professor Pierre-Marie Dupuy] (Leiden: Martinus Nijhoff Publishers, 2014), 583.

[35] Advisory Committee of Jurists, *Procès-verbaux*, 173, 175.

[36] Fassbender, "The Representation," 586, 588.

[37] *North Sea Continental Shelf*, *Judgment*, Separate Opinion of Judge Fouad Ammoun, *I.C.J. Reports 1969*, 140, para. 38, http://www.icj-cij.org/files/case-related/51/051-19690220-JUD-01-06-BI.pdf, accessed 18 June 2020.

[38] *Maritime Delimitation in the Area between Greenland and Jan Mayen*, *Judgment*, Separate Opinion of Judge Weeramantry, *I.C.J. Reports 1993*, 273, para. 234, www.icj-cij.org/files/case-related/50/050-19700205-JUD-01-10-BI.pdf, accessed 19 June 2020.

[39] *Barcelona Traction, Light and Power Company, Limited*, *Judgment*, Separate Opinion of Judge Ammoun, *I.C.J. Reports 1970*, 3, http://www.icj-cij.org/files/case-related/50/050-19700205-JUD-01-10-BI.pdf, accessed 19 June 2020.

of many different States, it has to consist of judges from diverse States and not just the States parties to the dispute.[40]

Whatever our understanding of "main forms of civilization" and "principal legal systems," it is obvious that the rationales for these requirements are not relevant to international arbitration. The latter is an ad hoc form of legally binding dispute settlement to which two States parties to a dispute have recourse to resolve a particular dispute. An individual arbitral tribunal does not have jurisdiction over disputes of many different States or general jurisdiction over disputes of an international character. A Great Power that has not given its consent to arbitration does not run the risk that a small State will unilaterally initiate arbitral proceedings against it. The material force of the Great Powers is not necessary to ensure the execution of each and every arbitral award. A dispute before an individual arbitral tribunal does not necessarily require understanding of the main forms of civilization or of the principal legal systems of the world. For all these reasons, there is no need for the representation of the main forms of civilization or the principal legal systems of the world in every arbitral tribunal, and there is no need for an arbitral tribunal of 15 or 21 members, as Xinhua seemed to imply.[41] It is no accident that no requirements of the representation in arbitral tribunals of the main forms of civilization and the main legal systems of the world kind may be found in the Conventions for the Pacific Settlement of International Disputes of 1899 and 1907, the General Act of Arbitration (Pacific Settlement of International Disputes) of 1928, the Revised General Act for the Pacific Settlement of International Disputes of 1949, the UN Draft Convention

[40] Eric A. Posner and John C. Yoo, "Judicial Independence in International Tribunals," *California Law Review* 93 (2005): 25, https://chicagounbound.uchicago.edu/cgi/viewcontent.cgi?article=2758&context=journal_articles, accessed 19 June 2020.

[41] Xinhua, "Ad hocism." One can say without fear of contradiction that there has never existed an arbitral tribunal with 15 or 21 members. If the parties to a dispute wished to have their dispute settled by such a large tribunal, they might as well submit it to the ICJ or to the ITLOS, as the case may be, and save themselves the expense.

on Arbitral Procedure of 1955, Annex VII of the Convention on arbitration, and Annex VIII of the Convention on special arbitration.[42] Nor do any of these instruments contain the least allusion to an alleged need for parties to a dispute to be represented by nationals in arbitral tribunals.

2. The Representation of "National" Arbitrators in International Arbitration

Sienho Yee's conception of "the need for a national arbitrator" seems to be a manifestation of what Adam M. Smith calls "judicial nationalism," States' assumption that national judges will vote with them and that other States' judges will follow their masters.[43] Whether or not national judges always vote with the State of nationality, the assertion of "the need for a national arbitrator" ignores arbitral practice, which has not always recognized such a need and which has progressively diminished the element of national representation in the composition of arbitral tribunals.

The familiar model of the arbitral tribunal traces its origin to the mixed commissions established by the Treaty of Amity, Commerce, and Navigation between the US and Great Britain of 1794 (known in the US as "the Jay Treaty"). In these commissions, each party appointed two members; to avoid ties, an additional member, the umpire, was appointed, but the umpire was also a national of one of the parties and he was chosen by

[42] *1899 Convention for the Pacific Settlement of International Disputes* ("*1899 Hague Convention*"), https://pca-cpa.org/wp-content/uploads/sites/6/2016/01/1899-Convention-for-the-Pacific-Settlement-of-International-Disputes.pdf, accessed 3 April 2020; *1907 Convention for the Pacific Settlement of International Disputes* ("*1907 Hague Convention*"), https://pca-cpa.org/wp-content/uploads/sites/6/2016/01/1907-Convention-for-the-Pacific-Settlement-of-International-Disputes.pdf, accessed 3 April 2020; *General Act of Arbitration (Pacific Settlement of International Disputes)*, done at Geneva, 26 September 1928, https://cil.nus.edu.sg/wp-content/uploads/2017/08/1928-General-Act-of-Arbitration.pdf, accessed 19 June 2020; *Revised General Act for the Pacific Settlement of International Disputes*, done at New York, 28 April 1949, https://www.un.org/ruleoflaw/blog/document/revised-general-act-for-the-pacific-settlement-of-international-disputes/, accessed 19 June 2020; United Nations, *Commentary on the Draft Convention on Arbitral Procedure Adopted by the International Law Commission at its Fifth Session, Prepared by the Secretariat*, UN Doc. A/CN.4/92 (New York: United Nations, 1955) ("*Draft Convention on Arbitral Procedure*"), https://legal.un.org/ilc/documentation/english/a_cn4_92.pdf, accessed 18 June 2020.

[43] Adam M. Smith, "'Judicial Nationalism' in International Law: National Identity and Judicial Autonomy at the ICJ," *Texas International Law Journal* 40 (2005): 199.

the other members.[44] In this model, the commissioners for the most part saw themselves as representatives of the State that appointed them. Less well-known is the model of the single arbitrator, who until the beginning of the twentieth century was almost always a monarch. The latter seemed the only authority satisfactory to States that did not recognize any authority higher than themselves.[45] In reality, the head of State entrusted the responsibility of judging the legal issues to a committee, whose judgment he/she then endorsed. Obviously in this model there is no question of national representation in the tribunal.[46] Arbitration by a single arbitrator was progressively replaced by that of the mixed commission, but it survived until the first decades of the twentieth century, with a jurist replacing the sovereign.[47]

The model of the mixed commission itself evolved from the second half of the nineteenth century onward. In the *Alabama Arbitration* between the US and Great Britain, only two of the five Tribunal members were nominated by the parties; the Tribunal's three other members were appointed by the heads of State of third States—the emperor of Brazil, the King of Italy, and the President of the Swiss Confederation.[48] As a result, the two "national" arbitrators constituted a minority in the Tribunal. The advantage of a tribunal constituted in this way was that the influence of the nationals of the parties was minimized, making it possible

[44] *Treaty of Amity, Commerce, and Navigation* (Jay Treaty), 19 November 1894, Articles V, VI, and VII, https://www.loc.gov/law/help/us-treaties/bevans/b-gb-ust000012-0013.pdf, accessed 3 April 2020.

[45] Albert Geouffre de Lapradelle and Nicolas Socrate Politis (eds.), *Recueil des arbitrages internationaux* [Collection of International Arbitrations], vol. I, *1798–1855* (Paris: A. Pedone, Éditeur, 1905), xxxvii-xxxviii, https://archive.org/details/recueildesarbit00laprgoog/page/n8/mode/2up, accessed 19 June 2020; Jackson H. Ralston, *International Arbitration from Athens to Locarno* (Stanford: Stanford University Press, 1929), 54, https://archive.org/details/in.ernet.dli.2015.166200, accessed 18 June 2020; Malenovský, "L'indépendance," 50.

[46] Edgar Rouard de Card, *L'arbitrage international dans le passé, le présent et l'avenir* [International Arbitration in the Past, Present, and Future] (Paris: A. Durand et Pedone-Lauriel, 1877), 52, https://ia902706.us.archive.org/14/items/droitinternatio01cardgoog/droitinternatio01cardgoog.pdf, accessed 21 June 2020.

[47] Ralston, *International Arbitration*, 54; Manley O. Hudson, *The Permanent Court of International Justice. A Treatise* (New York: The Macmillan Company, 1934), 25–26.

[48] *Treaty between Her Majesty and the United States of America, signed at Washington, May 8, 1871 (ratified and ratifications exchanged June 17, 1871)*, Article 1, https://archive.org/details/cihm_45724/page/n1/mode/2up, accessed 19 June 2020.

to render a decision without the "national" arbitrators' agreement.[49] A further innovation was introduced by some of the first arbitral tribunals that were constituted under the auspices of the newly-created PCA. In the very first case, *The Pious Fund of the Californias*, concerning Mexico's obligation to pay interest on the sale of Pious Fund properties in Mexico to bishops in California (1902), the two parties agreed that none of the members of the tribunal would be a national of either party. As arbitrators, the US-appointed nationals of Russia and the UK, Mexico designated two Dutch nationals, and the four selected as the umpire a Danish national.[50] The parties to two subsequent cases, the *Preferential Claims* (Germany, Great Britain, and Italy/Venezuela, 1903), concerning the three European States' demands for preferential treatment of their claims to Venezuelan customs revenues over those of other creditor States, and the *Orinoco Steamship* (US/Venezuela, 1910), concerning payment by Venezuela of the financial claim of the steamship company Orinoco, established tribunals consisting of three members, none of whom was to be a national of either party.[51]

Since 1945, multilateral treaties with provisions on arbitration provide for tribunals consisting of one member, three members (one each selected by the parties and one neutral member appointed by the two arbitrators or by both States), or five members (one or two each appointed by the parties, with three neutrals or one neutral, respectively, appointed by the other two or four arbitrators or by both States).[52] Sienho Yee's alleged "need for national arbitrators" is not—or is no longer—universally recognized by States. In practice it often occurs that arbitrator(s) appointed by a party is(are) not national(s) of the appointing party. This is usually the case of small States who lack competent jurists whom they could appoint as arbitrators.[53] If the States to the dispute agree, it is

[49] Louis B. Sohn, "The Role of Arbitration in Recent International Multilateral Treaties," *Virginia Journal of International Law* 23 (1982–83): 180.

[50] Ralston, *International Arbitration*, 32.

[51] Hudson, *The Permanent Court of International Justice* 13, 18.

[52] Sohn, "The Role," 179.

[53] This is also the rationale for appointing non-nationals as judges ad hoc at the ICJ. Nicolas Valticos, "Rôle et éthique d'un judge ad hoc à la Cour internationale de justice [The Role and Ethics of a Judge Ad Hoc at the International Court of Justice]," in Nisuke Ando et al. (eds.), *Liber Amicorum Judge Shigeru Oda*, vol. I (The Hague: Kluwer Law International, 2002), 109.

possible that a three- or five-member tribunal will be composed entirely of nationals of third States.[54] In such a situation, the nationality of the arbitrators ceases to be a factor in a tribunal's deliberations. In a scenario in which the arbitrators appointed by the two parties in a three-member tribunal see themselves as representatives of the States appointing them, the party-appointed arbitrators will cancel out each other's votes, and it is the neutral member—the member appointed by the other arbitrators or by the two States—who decides the outcome of the case.[55] The neutral member may decide wholly in favor of a party in order to obtain a majority, or may attempt to reconcile the theses of the opposing parties. Similar scenarios may be envisaged in a five-member tribunal in which there is only one neutral member. They are less likely if the majority of the tribunal's members consists of neutrals (three out of the five members) or if all of the members are neutrals.[56]

All this might seem irrelevant to Sienho Yee, whose concern was with the appointment of a "national" arbitrator in instances of disagreement of the parties. Upon closer examination, it appears that his formulation of the problem is misleading. In the *South China Sea Arbitration*, it was China's default that was the obstacle to the appointment of a Chinese arbitrator. Until the mid-twentieth century, arbitral practice offered no precedent of the appointment of an arbitrator, whether a national of a party or not, in lieu of a party. Default in inter-State arbitral proceedings

[54] The tribunal in the Guinea-Bissau/Senegal arbitration consisted of nationals of Argentina (president), France, and Algeria. *Case concerning the delimitation of maritime boundary between Guinea-Bissau and Senegal, 31 July 1989, Reports of International Arbitral* Awards, vol. XX (New York: United Nations, 2006), 119–213 ("*RIAA*"), https://legal.un.org/riaa/cases/vol_XX/119-213.pdf, accessed 11 December 2019. The five-member tribunal in the *Beagle Channel Arbitration (Argentina/Chile)* consisted of nationals of the UK (president), France, Sweden, Nigeria, and the US, all of whom were ICJ judges at the time of the proceedings. *Dispute between Argentina and Chile concerning the Beagle Channel, 18 February 1977, RIAA*, vol. XXI (New York: United Nations, 2006), 53–264, http://legal.un.org/riaa/cases/vol_XXI/53-264.pdf, accessed 19 June 2020.

[55] Ralston, *International Arbitration*, 29; Malenovský, "L'indépendance," 54.

[56] Lucius Caflisch, "L'avenir de l'arbitrage interétatique [The Future of Inter-State Arbitration]," *Annuaire français de droit international* [French Yearbook of International Law] 25 (1979): 18 ("*AFDI*"), http://www.persee.fr/web/revues/home/prescript/article/afdi_0066-3085_1979_num_25_1_2149, accessed 19 June 2020.

did not occur when arbitration was organized through a special agreement between the parties.[57] A State that refused to appear before an arbitral tribunal manifested its attitude by not concluding an agreement in the first place. This option was not open to China as a State party to the Convention, under which China was deemed to have accepted arbitration as the compulsory dispute settlement procedure for disputes over the interpretation and application of the Convention. To answer the question of why in the circumstances of China's default a Chinese or Asian arbitrator was not appointed, one must examine Annex VII of the Convention and State practice.

B. Representation and the Composition of Annex VII Arbitral Tribunals

Annex VII of the Convention contains no provision comparable to Article 2 of the ITLOS Statute (Annex VI of the Convention), which mandates "the representation of the principal legal systems of the world" and "equitable geographical distribution."[58] Annex VII does allow a State party to appoint a national as an arbitrator, but whether or not both States participate in the proceedings, non-nationals of the parties will normally be the majority in a tribunal. State practice confirms this conclusion, although it also demonstrates that some attention is paid to the diversity of geographical origins of the arbitrators.

1. Annex VII and the Appointment of Nationals of the Parties

Annex VII arbitral tribunals consist in general of five members (Article 3(a)). Under Articles 3(b) and 3(c) of Annex VII, the State initiating the arbitration and the respondent State each have the right to appoint

[57] Albert Geouffre de Lapradelle and Nicolas Socrate Politis (eds.), *Recueil des arbitrages internationaux* [Collection of International Arbitrations], vol. II, *1856–1872* (Paris: A. Pedone, Éditeur, 1923), xxiv, https://ia802607.us.archive.org/3/items/recueildesarbitr02lapruoft/recueildesarbitr02lapruoft.pdf, accessed 21 June 2020; Christine Gray and Benedict Kingsbury, "Developments in Dispute Settlement: Inter-State Arbitration Since 1945," *British Yearbook of International Law* 63 (1992): 97–134.

[58] The latter expression replaces the Eurocentric, borderline racist concept of "main forms of civilization." United Nations Division for Ocean Affairs and the Law of the Sea, *Annex VI*, *Statute of the International Tribunal for the Law of the Sea*, http://www.un.org/depts/los/convention_agreements/texts/unclos/annex6.htm, accessed 18 September 2020.

nationals as arbitrator. The arbitrators should preferably be chosen from a list of arbitrators that is drawn up on the basis of nominations by States parties to the Convention and maintained by the UN Secretary-General. The persons on the list should be "experienced in maritime affairs" and enjoy "the highest reputation for fairness, competence and integrity."[59] As the Tribunal in the *Chagos Marine Protected Area Arbitration* explained, the arbitrators appointed by the parties are not required to be drawn from the list, although the requirements of fairness, competence, and integrity still apply to them.[60] These qualifications are equivalent to those required for election to the ITLOS.[61] In a scenario in which both States participate in the proceedings, and *a fortiori* in a scenario in which the respondent State defaults, the majority of the members of the Tribunal will consist of non-nationals of the parties.

Within the scenario in which both States participate in the proceedings, one may distinguish two further situations. In the first, the two parties cooperate in the appointment of the three remaining arbitrators. The latter should preferably be chosen from the list maintained by the UN Secretary-General. However, they must be nationals of third States, unless the parties agree otherwise (Article 3(d)). The assumption is that the experience and the reputation for fairness, competence, and integrity will enable the arbitrators to bring to bear the principles and rules of the law of the sea on specific problems of particular States, obviating the need for judges who are nationals of the parties. In this situation, assuming that each party appoints a national, three of the five arbitrators will still be nationals of third States. If one of the parties does not nominate a national, or if both do not nominate nationals, then four or five of the tribunal's members will not be nationals of the parties.

[59] United Nations Division for Ocean Affairs and the Law of the Sea, *Annex VII*, Article 2(1), http://www.un.org/depts/los/convention_agreements/texts/unclos/annex7.htm, accessed 7 April 2020. The list may be found in United Nations Treaty Collection, Law of the Sea, *United Nations Convention on the Law of the Sea, Montego Bay, 10 December 1982 Notifications made under article 2 of annexes V and VII (List of conciliators and arbitrators)* (2020), https://treaties.un.org/pages/ViewDetailsIII.aspx?src=TREATY&mtdsg_no=XXI-6&chapter=21&Temp=mtdsg3&clang=_en, accessed 21 June 2020.

[60] *Chagos Marine Protected Area Arbitration*, Reasoned Decision, 24, para. 135.

[61] *Statute of the ITLOS*, Article 2, para. 1.

In the second situation, the two parties, despite their efforts, fail to agree on the nomination of one or more of the three remaining arbitrators. In that situation, the power to appoint one or more arbitrators falls to an appointing authority designated by Annex VII of the Convention, the ITLOS President, or to any third person or third State to whom the parties have granted that power.[62] In this situation, the requirements concerning the qualifications and nationality of the three neutral arbitrators are more complex. As regards qualifications, the three neutral arbitrators must be drawn from the list maintained by the UN Secretary-General. The appointing authority has no choice in the matter. As for the nationality of the neutral members, Annex VII mandates not only that they should be of "different nationalities," but also that they may not be nationals, "not be in the service of" nor be "ordinarily resident in the territory" of any of the parties to the dispute."[63] Under these conditions and depending on whether one or both parties have appointed nationals, the tribunal may end up with a majority of three, four, or five members who are not nationals of either party.

In a scenario in which the respondent State defaults and fails to appoint an arbitrator, the appearing State has the right to request that the appointing authority appoint the arbitrator in lieu of the defaulting State.[64] In this situation, Article 3(e) of Annex VII also applies. The arbitrator appointed in this manner must be drawn from the list maintained by the UN Secretary-General. The appointing authority has no choice in the matter. As in the case of arbitrators appointed in the event of disagreement between the parties, the arbitrator may not be a national of either the appearing State or the defaulting State, ordinarily resident in the territory of either the appearing State or the defaulting State, or in the service of either the appearing State or the defaulting State (Article 3(e)). In a situation of default, it is to be assumed that the defaulting State will not only refuse to appoint its arbitrator but will also refuse to participate in the appointment of the three other arbitrators. The appointing authority is also authorized to appoint, upon the request of the appearing party, the three remaining arbitrators. Assuming the appearing party appoints a

[62] *Annex VII*, Article 3(e).

[63] Ibid., Article 3(c).

[64] A situation in which the State initiating the arbitration fails to appoint the arbitrator is inconceivable.

national, there will be at least four arbitrators who are not nationals of either party. If the appearing party does not appoint a national, then all the members of the tribunal will be nationals of third States.

Herein lies the explanation of the absence of a Chinese arbitrator in the Tribunal. In view of China's failure to appoint an arbitrator, the ITLOS President exercised the power to appoint the arbitrator in lieu of China, but Annex VII prohibited him from appointing one who was in China's service, who was ordinarily resident in China, or who was a national of China. In addition, because of China's default, the appointing authority was called upon to appoint the three neutral arbitrators, none of whom could be a national of China or the Philippines, or ordinarily resident on the territory of China or the Philippines, or in the service of China or the Philippines.

These conditions might appear to upset the equality of the parties and create an advantage in favor of the appearing party, who after all, has the right to appoint a national. The rationale for these conditions is not explained in commentaries on the Convention. One commentary merely remarks that the ease with which Annex VII was agreed upon was partly due to the existence of international instruments on dispute settlement and to the Model Rules on Arbitral Procedure of 1958, drafted by the International Law Commission.[65] It cannot be excluded that the purpose of these conditions is to protect the arbitrator appointed by the appointing authority in lieu of the defaulting State from pressures that may be exerted or sanctions that may be imposed by the defaulting State on his/her person or on his/her family, pressures to which a person who is a national of or ordinarily resident in or in the service of the defaulting State would be vulnerable. One can very well imagine China's reaction if a Chinese national had agreed to be a member of the Arbitral Tribunal, in defiance of China's official policy of default. From this perspective, the rules are not "strange," as a Chinese scholar contends.[66]

The absence of an Asian arbitrator in the *South China Sea* Tribunal is an unexpected consequence of the requirement that in the event of

[65] Myron H. Nordquist et al. (eds.), *United Nations Convention on the Law of the Sea 1982: A Commentary*, vol. V, *Settlement of Disputes, General and Final Provisions and Related Annexes and Resolutions* (Leiden: Martinus Nijhoff Publishers, 1989), 421–22.

[66] Jianjun Gao, "Appointment of Arbitrators by the President of the ITLOS pursuant to Article 3 of Annex VII to the LOS Convention: Some Tentative Observations," *CJIL* 16 (2017): 741.

default, the appointing authority must appoint the remaining arbitrators from the list maintained by the UN Secretary-General. Initially, the ITLOS President had appointed M.C.W. Pinto, a Sri Lankan national, but he had to resign from the Tribunal. Assuming that the ITLOS President had sought to replace him with members from Asia, it is not sure that the composition of the tribunal would have escaped the strictures of China. The potential arbitrators—those who were on the list established in accordance with Annex VII, Article 2(1)—would have been nationals of Indonesia, Japan, Lebanon, the Republic of Korea, and Singapore. Three of these States (Indonesia, Japan, and the Republic of Korea) have territorial and/or maritime disputes with China. Indonesia and Singapore are member States of the Association of Southeast Asian Nations ("ASEAN"), of which the Philippines is also a member. That would have left only a national of Lebanon, who at the time was an ITLOS member. Even had the latter been appointed to the tribunal, the ITLOS president would still have been compelled to appoint three members who were not from Asia.

This rapid review of the provisions of Annex VII demonstrates that Sienho Yee's assertions that the ITLOS President appointed "just any one" and that no information was available as to why a more representative tribunal could not have been constituted or why no Chinese national could have been appointed are baseless. Since China had failed to appoint a Chinese national and refused consultations with the Philippines on the appointment of the three neutral arbitrators, the ITLOS President made the appointment in its place and appointed the three neutral arbitrators. Annex VII of the Convention specifically excludes the possibility that the arbitrator appointed in China's place and the three arbitrators appointed in a situation of default could be a national or resident or person in the service of China. Contrary to Sienho Yee's assertion, there is no need for additional information that would explain why no Chinese national was appointed. This overview of the provisions of Annex VII also allows us to dismiss Xinhua's frivolous and absurd assertion that the appointment of the arbitrators was careless.[67]

We should note in passing that China's international campaign to criticize the Award of 12 July 2016 drew heavily on opinions of academics

[67] Xinhua, "Ad Hocism.".

from Argentina,[68] Egypt,[69] Ghana,[70] Italy,[71] Malagasy [sic],[72] the US,[73] and Venezuela.[74] None is a Chinese national or even an Asian. Following China's own logic, none of them would know Asia, understand Asian cultures, know the South China Sea issue, understand the complicated geographical politics in Asia, and know the history of the South China Sea.[75] They would meet the criteria of not being nationals or ordinarily resident in or persons in the service of China. However, none would satisfy the criteria of experience in maritime affairs and a reputation for fairness, competence, and integrity. They would therefore have had no basis "to make a fair award."

A survey of State practice on the constitution of Annex VII arbitral tribunals belies assertions made by the CSIL and Chinese scholars

[68] Ibid., "Argentine Expert Says South China Sea Award Riddled with Inconsistencies," *xinhuanet.com*, 15 July 2016, https://www.linkedin.com/pulse/south-china-sea-argentine-expert-ferrara-says-award-riddled-ferrara, accessed 19 June 2020. The article is no longer available on the Xinhua website. Could the reason for this be the disappearance of the inconsistencies in the Award?

[69] Ibid., "World Should Heed U.S. Interests in South China Sea Arbitration—Egyptian Experts," *China.org.cn*, 16 July 2016, http://www.china.org.cn/world/Off_the_Wire/2016-07/16/content_38896347.htm, accessed 19 June 2020. The use of the word "heed" in the title is obviously a mistranslation.

[70] Ibid., "South China Sea Arbitration Award 'Unfair': Ghanaian Analysts," *Global Times*, 16 July 2016, http://www.globaltimes.cn/content/994650.shtml, accessed 19 June 2020.

[71] Ibid., "Tribunal Award on S. China Sea Complicates Things But Further Talks Can Take Place: Italian Expert," *Global Times*, 14 July 2016, http://www.globaltimes.cn/content/994356.shtml, accessed 19 June 2020.

[72] Ibid., "China Is Right to Reject International Court's South China Sea Decision: Malagasy (sic) Experts," *xinhuanet.com*, 13 July 2016, http://news.xinhuanet.com/english/2016-07/13/c_135510262.htm, accessed 18 July 2016. The article is no longer available on the Xinhua website. Either the "Malagasy" experts no longer think China is right to reject the decisions, or Xinhua realized that there is no State named "Malagasy.".

[73] Ibid., "Arbitral Tribunal's Award on South China Sea Creates Bad Precedent, Says U.S. Expert," *ecns.com*, 15 July 2016, http://www.ecns.cn/2016/07-15/218514.shtml, accessed 19 June 2020.

[74] Ibid., "World Leaders, Experts Voice Support for China's Stance on South China Sea," *xinhuanet.com*, 15 July 2016, http://news.xinhuanet.com/english/2016-07/15/c_135516383.htm, accessed 18 July 2016. The article is no longer available on the Xinhua website. Do world leaders and experts no longer voice support for China's stance on the South China Sea?

[75] Foreign Ministry, *Veil*.

regarding the composition of Annex VII arbitral tribunals. Representation of major civilizations, principal legal systems, and nationals of the parties is not perceived by States to be a requirement in the constitution of Annex VII tribunals.

2. *State Practice and the Composition of Annex VII Arbitral Tribunals*

Table 5.1 provides an overview of the composition of Annex VII arbitral tribunals that were effectively constituted by 2020.[76] The identification of regions in the table follows informal ICJ practice, which identifies six regions: African, Asian, Eastern European, Western European, Latin American-Caribbean, and other States (this last comprising the US, Canada, Australia, and New Zealand). Two conclusions may be derived from Table 5.1. First, the appointment of nationals of both parties is the exception rather than the rule. Second, while efforts are made to ensure diversity of regions of origin of the arbitrators, rare indeed is the tribunal whose composition satisfies the criterion of equitable regional distribution.

The analysis of the representation of nationals of parties in the composition of Annex VII tribunals would hardly lend support to Sienho Yee's assertion of a putative "need for a national arbitrator." Of eight tribunals constituted prior to 2013, four (3, 4, 5, and 9) had no members who were nationals of either party; four (1, 2, 6, and 7) had members who were nationals of one party; none had members that were nationals of the two parties. If we now take 12 tribunals, excepting the two (10 and 12) in which the arbitrator of a party was appointed by the ITLOS President in lieu of that party, the number of tribunals with no "national" members remains unchanged (3, 4, 5, and 9), while that of tribunals in which at least one national is a member nearly doubles to seven (1, 2, 6, 7, 11, 14, and 15). It was only in 2015 that a tribunal comprising nationals of both parties (13) was constituted. What is one to make of these figures? Should one say that both parties were mistaken in four cases for not appointing nationals, that one party in seven cases failed to perceive its self-interest by not appointing a national, and that only in one case did both parties

[76] Table 5.1 excludes the *"M/V Saiga" (Saint Vincent and the Grenadines v. Guinea)* arbitration, the dispute on conservation and sustainable exploitation of swordfish stocks in the South-Eastern Pacific Ocean (Chile/European Union) and Ghana/Côte d'Ivoire maritime delimitation dispute, all of which were transferred to the ITLOS.

Table 5.1 Composition of Annex VII Tribunals

Case and PCA Case No	*Party 1*	*Party 2*	*Africa*	*Asia*	*Eastern Europe*	*Latin America-Caribbean*	*Western Europe*	*Other States*
(1) Southern Bluefin Tuna	New Zealand Australia (Others)	Japan (Asia) Japan (Asia)		Feliciano (Philippines) Yamada (Japan)			Tresselt (Norway)	Schwebel * (US) Keith (Australia)
(2) MOX Plant [2002–01]	Ireland (Western Europe)	UK (Western Europe)	Mensah *(Ghana)				Hafner (Austria) Lord Mustill (UK)	Crawford (Australia) Fortier (Canada)
(3) Land Reclamation by Singapore in and around the Straits of Johor [2004–05]	Malaysia (Asia)	Singapore (Asia)		Pinto * (Sri Lanka) Hossain (Bangladesh)			Watts (UK)	Oxman (US) Shearer (Australia)
(4) Delimitation of EEZ and continental shelf [2004–02]	Barbados (Latin America and the Caribbean)	Trinidad & Tobago (Latin America and the Caribbean)				Orrego Vicuña (Chile)	Brownlie (UK) Vaughan Lowe (UK) Watts (UK)	Schwebel * (US)
(5) Delimitation of maritime boundary [2004–04]	Guyana (Latin America and the Caribbean)	Suriname (Latin America and the Caribbean)		Hossain (Bangladesh)		Nelson * (Grenada)		Franck (US) Shearer (Australia) Smit (US)

(continued)

Table 5.1 (continued)

Case and PCA Case No	*Party 1*	*Party 2*	*Africa*	*Asia*	*Eastern Europe*	*Latin America-Caribbean*	*Western Europe*	*Other States*
(6) Bay of Bengal Maritime Boundary [2010–16]	Bangladesh (Asia)	India (Asia)	Mensah (Ghana)	Rao (India)			Wolfrum * (Germany) Cot (France)	Shearer (Ausralia)
(7) Chagos Marine Protected Area [2011–03]	Mauritius (Africa)	UK (Western Europe)	Hoffmann (South Africa) Kateka (Tanzania)				Wolfrum (Germany) Greenwood (UK)	Shearer *(Australia)
(8) South China Sea [2013–19]	Philippines (Asia)	China (Asia)	Mensah * (Ghana)		Pawlak (Poland)		Wolfrum (Germany) Soons (Nether-lands) Cot (France)	
(9) Atlanto-Scandian Herring [2013–30]	Denmark in respect of Faroe Islands (Western Europe)	EU (Western Europe)	Mensah *(Ghana)	Pinto (Sri Lanka)		Orrego Vicuña (Chile)	Hafner (Austria) Wolfrum (Germany)	
(10) "Arctic Sunrise" [2014–02]	Netherlands (Western Europe)	Russian Federation (Eastern Europe)	Mensah *(Ghana)		Symonides (Poland)	Szekely (Mexico)	Soons (Nether-lands)	Burmester (Australia)

Case and PCA Case No	*Party 1*	*Party 2*	*Africa*	*Asia*	*Eastern Europe*	*Latin America-Caribbean*	*Western Europe*	*Other States*
(11) ARA Libertad [2013–11]	Argentina (Latin America - Caribbean)	Ghana (Africa)	Mensah (Ghana)	Al-Khasawneh (Jordan)		Kelly (Argentina)	Simma * (Austria)	Oxman (US)
(12) The Duzgit Integrity[2014–07]	Malta (Western Europe)	São Tomé and Príncipe (Africa)	Kateka (Tanzania)				Soons * (Nether-lands) Treves (Italy)	
(13) 'Enrica Lexie' Incident [2015–28]	Italy (Western Europe)	India (Asia)		Paik (South Korea) Rao (India)	Golitsyn* (Russian Federa-tion)	Robinson (Jamaica)	Francioni (Italy)	
(14) Coastal State Rights in the Black Sea, Sea of Azov, and Kerch Strait [2017–06]	Ukraine (Eastern Europe)	Russian Federation (Eastern Europe)	Bouguetaia (Algeria)	Paik * (South Korea)	Golitsyn (Russian Federa-tion)	Gómez-Robledo (Mexico)	Vaughan Lowe (UK)	
(15) Detention of Ukrainian Naval Vessels and Servicemen [2019–28]	Ukraine (Eastern Europe)	Russian Federation (Eastern Europe)			Golitsyn (Russian Federa-tion)		Eiriksson (Iceland) Wolfrum (Germany) Greenwood (UK)	McRae *(Canada)

*Presiding arbitrator. *Source* Compiled by the author

behave rationally by appointing nationals? Obviously, statements of this kind would make no sense, yet this is the conclusion to which arguments alleging the need for a "national arbitrator" ineluctably lead.

As regards the representation of regions in the tribunals, the ITLOS President made appointments in lieu of the respondent State in three cases (8, 10, and 12); in nine cases (3, 6, 7, 8, 10, 11, 12, 13, and 15), he appointed the neutral arbitrators; and in two cases (6 and 8), he appointed an arbitrator to replace another arbitrator.[77] Of the eight arbitral tribunals that were constituted prior to 2013, six (1, 2, 3, 4, 5, and 7) had members originating from three of the six regions; in only two tribunals (6 and 9) were four regions represented. If the Western European group and the group of other States are considered as one group, constituting the Western States, then only two of the six regions were represented in eight tribunals, while arbitrators from three regions were members of two tribunals. Were one to consider all fourteen tribunals (still excluding the *South China Sea Arbitration*), one finds only three tribunals with members originating from five regions (10, 11, and 14). The total number of tribunals with members from four regions increases slightly to three (6, 9, and 13) and the number of tribunals with members from three regions rises to eight (1, 2, 3, 4, 5, 7, 12, and 15). Again, if the "Western European" and "other" groups are considered one group, one should adjust the figures accordingly. Clearly, an effort is made either by the parties or the ITLOS President to ensure that in a tribunal members from at least three (two if "Western Europe" and "other" are counted as one) regions are included. In spite of such efforts, no tribunal has been able to ensure the equitable representation of all six regions. "Equitable geographical distribution" enters the realm of the possible only if "Western Europe" and "other" are considered to be one group. Even then, only one tribunal (14) would achieve that outcome. Otherwise "equitable geographical distribution" is mathematically impossible. Insisting on such a criterion to assess the composition of these tribunals would lead to the conclusion that none of the fourteen arbitral tribunals constituted under Annex VII of the Convention had a satisfactory composition.

Sienho Yee's assessment of the composition of the ITLOS Special Chamber in the maritime delimitation dispute between Ghana and the

[77] Jianjun Gao, "Appointment," 728–31.

Côte d'Ivoire as being "in better shape" [sic] is inapposite.[78] The Special Chamber comprised members from Africa (Algeria and Ghana), Western Europe (Germany and France), and Asia (South Korea). The assessment of the case is rendered inapposite not so much because it comprised members from only three regions but because the two parties to the dispute explicitly agreed on the composition of the Special Chamber by means of a Special Agreement.[79] The agreement between the parties clearly differentiates this case from the *South China Sea Arbitration*, in which the respondent State defaulted. It was the defaulting State's failure to appoint an arbitrator and to engage in consultations with the appearing State on the appointment of the three remaining arbitrators that permitted the ITLOS President to appoint arbitrators drawn from the list established in accordance with Article 2(1) of Annex VII, with all the constraints that have already been noted.

The assumptions of China and Chinese scholars that nationals of the parties or representatives of regions must be members of arbitral tribunals is based on a "judicial nationalism" that runs counter to the ideals of the independence and impartiality of international judges.

II. The Defaulting State and the Independence of the Appointing Authority and of the Judges in the *South China Sea Arbitration*

At first glance it might not make sense to distinguish between independence and impartiality. Statutes or regulations of international courts, international caselaw, declarations signed by arbitrators, codes of conduct formulated by international and nongovernmental organizations, and the few challenges raised by a party or by a defendant in an international criminal case speak of independence and impartiality in the same breath. Undoubtedly, judicial independence and judicial impartiality are interrelated. For our purposes, judicial independence is to be understood in relation primarily to States and to the parties, while impartiality denotes

[78] Sienho Yee, "The South China Sea Arbitration Decisions," 222.

[79] *Delimitation of the Maritime Boundary between Ghana and Côte d'Ivoire in the Atlantic Ocean*, 9, para. 4.

the judges' relation to the subject matter. Independence is a necessary but not sufficient condition of impartiality.[80]

Historically, the independence of the judiciary as a separate branch of government was understood to entail impartiality. In the eighteenth century, Montesquieu sought to ensure the independence of the judiciary by elevating it to the third branch of government and separating its powers from those of the other two other branches.[81] In the US Declaration of Independence of 1776, the attempt by George III to make judges dependent on his will alone was one of the reasons for denouncing him.[82] The French Declaration of the Rights of Man and of the Citizen of 1789 had affirmed the separation of powers among the branches of government.[83] In the twentieth century, the Universal Declaration of Human Rights proclaimed that everyone has a right "in full equality to a fair and public hearing by an independent and impartial tribunal, in the determination of his [sic] rights and obligations and of any criminal charge against him [sic]."[84] The United Nations, the Council of Europe, and

[80] Mr. Fromageot, Seventh Meeting, 14 March 1929, League of Nations, *Committee of Jurists on the Statute of the Permanent Court of International Justice, Minutes of the Session held at Geneva, March 11th-19th, 1929*, League Doc. C. 166. M. 66. 1929.V. (1 May 1929), 43, https://www.icj-cij.org/files/permanent-court-of-international-justice/serie_D/D_minutes_statut_PCIJ_11au19march_1929.pdf, accessed 3 July 2020; Malenovský, "L'indépendance," 29; Helen Keller and Severin Meier, "Independence and Impartiality in the Judicial Trilemma," *American Journal of International Law* 111 (217): 345 ("*AJIL*").

[81] Giacomo Oberto, "Die richterliche Unabhängigkeit in Europa und ihre Sicherung durch einen obersten Richterrat [The Independence of Judges in Europe and Its Protection through Supreme Judicial Councils]," Vortrag zur Jahrestagung des Hessischen Richterbundes, Arnoldshain [Paper presented at the Annual Meeting of the Association of Judges of Hesse, Arnoldshain, Germany], 1–3 July 2004, 1–2, http://hefam.de/koll/oberto-200407.pdf, accessed 22 June 2020.

[82] United States Citizenship and Immigration Services, *The Declaration of Independence & the Constitution of the United States*, Doc. M-654 (rev. 07/08), 2, https://www.uscis.gov/sites/default/files/USCIS/Office%20of%20Citizenship/Citizenship%20Resource%20Center%20Site/Publications/PDFs/M-654.pdf, accessed 22 June 2020.

[83] *Déclaration des Droits de l'Homme et du Citoyen de 1789*, Article 16, https://www.legifrance.gouv.fr/contenu/menu/droit-national-en-vigueur/constitution/declaration-des-droits-de-l-homme-et-du-citoyen-de-1789, accessed 22 June 2020.

[84] Oberto, "Die richterliche Unabhängigkeit," 1–2.

nongovernmental organizations such as the International Bar Association have all adopted principles and standards of judicial independence applicable at the domestic level.

At the international level, the ideal of the independence of international judges did not emerge until the establishment of the first permanent international court with general jurisdiction in the twentieth century. In the late eighteenth and nineteenth centuries, moral authority and scholarly reputation, rather than independence, were the qualities explicitly demanded of arbitrators, who tended to see themselves as "national" arbitrators, representing the States of which they were nationals and which appointed them. It is significant that the word "independence" did not appear in major writings on arbitration.[85] The Hague Convention of 1907 and the Convention establishing the Central American Court of Justice did not innovate in this respect.[86] It was only in the PCIJ Statute that the ideal of independence was formally enshrined. The PCIJ was to be composed of "a body of independent judges" who fulfilled certain other conditions specified in the Statute.[87] The ideal of independence was preserved in Article 2 of the ICJ Statute. Neither Statute provided criteria for ascertaining the independence of judges. The proliferation of international courts since the late twentieth century has compelled States

[85] See, for example, Alexandre Mérignhac, *Traité théorique et pratique de l'arbitrage international: le rôle du droit dans le fonctionnement actuel de l'institution et dans ses destinées futures* [A Theoretical and Practical Treatise on International Arbitration: The Role of Law in the Present Operation of the Institution and in Its Future Destiny](Paris: Librairie du Recueil général des Lois et des arrêts et du Journal du Palais, 1895), 219, https://ia601407.us.archive.org/14/items/traitthoriqueet00mrgoog/traitthoriqueet00mrgoog.pdf, accessed 3 April 2020; Ferdinand Dreyfus and Frédéric Passy, *L'arbitrage international* [International Arbitration](Paris: Calmann Lévy, 1892), https://ia902703.us.archive.org/29/items/larbitrageinter00passgoog/larbitrageinter00passgoog.pdf, accessed 24 June 2020; Card, *L'arbitrage international*; Thomas de Saint -Georges d'Armstrong, *Principes généraux du droit international public: De l'utilité de l'arbitrage* [General Principles of Public International Law: On the Usefulness of Arbitration] (Paris: L. Larose et Forcel, 1890), https://archive.org/details/principesgnraux00dargoog, accessed 24 June 2020.

[86] 1907 Hague Convention, Article 44; *Convention for the Establishment of a Central American Court of Justice*, *AJIL*, *Supplement: Official Documents* 2 (1908): 231–43.

[87] PCIJ, *Statute and Rules of Court*, Article 2, 1st Edition, Series D. No.1 (1926), https://www.icj-cij.org/files/permanent-court-of-international-justice/serie_D/D_01_1e_edition.pdf, accessed 3 April 2020.

and scholars to explore the scope of the concept of independence and the appropriate mechanisms for guaranteeing it.[88]

Despite the interrelationship between independence and impartiality, it is possible to assess the independence of the appointing authority and of the judges in the *South China Sea Arbitration* by referring to judicial and scholarly conceptions. Paradoxically it is China's efforts to exert pressure on the Arbitral Tribunal through secret approaches and mobilization of non-parties to the dispute that make it possible to comprehend the essence of the concept of independence.

A. The Independence of the Appointing Authority and of the Judges in the South China Sea Arbitration

Once we have properly grasped the scope of the ideal of independence, it is relatively easy to apply it to the appointing authority and the judges in the *South China Sea Arbitration.*

1. The Scope of the Independence of Judges and Arbitrators

At the core of the ideal of the independence of international judges is the freedom of the judge to decide free from external pressure emanating from States, the parties to the dispute, public opinion, and other external bodies. While the measures designed to guarantee independence have been designed primarily having in mind the members of permanent international courts, the practice of ad hoc arbitral tribunals demonstrates that the ideal is also deemed relevant for arbitrators.

From the drafting history of the PCIJ Statute one may conclude that independence was conceptualized mainly in relation to the States of nationality of the judges. Judges were to make judgments independent of their States and were not to consider themselves State representatives.[89] At the Conference of San Francisco, which drafted the UN Charter and the ICJ Statute in 1945, this understanding was confirmed, with the clarification that judges should also be independent of UN control.[90] During

[88] Malenovský, "L'indépendance," 19–20.

[89] Mr. Hagerup (Norway), Mr. Loder (the Netherlands), and Mr. Altamira (Spain), in Advisory Committee of Jurists, *Procès-verbaux*, 121, 363, 369.

[90] Shabtai Rosenne, with the assistance of Yaël Ronen, *The Law and Practice of the International Court 1990–2005*, vol. I, *The Court and the United Nations* (4th ed.; Leiden: Martinus Nijhoff Publishers, 2006), 359.

the Cold War it was the relationship of judges with States that appeared to be the essence of independence. Independence was taken by scholars to mean that a judge did not act on instructions from superior authority, which in this context could only be a State.[91] The charge of lack of independence of ICJ judges often heard from Soviet scholars, who described them as pliable instruments in the hands of imperialist powers, was rooted in this understanding of independence.[92]

Over time a broader conception of independence started to evolve. In 1970, Judge Tanaka expressed in a separate opinion the view that.

> [t]he judicial independence of courts and judges must be safeguarded not only from other branches of the government, that is to say, the political and administrative power, but also from any other external power, for instance, political parties, trade unions, mass media and public opinion. Furthermore, independence must be defended as against various courts and as between judges.[93]

Judge Tanaka subsequently explained in a scholarly article that independence is inherent in the concept of judge, whether domestic or international. It refers to a mental attitude to carry out his/her duty without being subjected to any external or internal influence; the judge is dependent solely on his/her conscience and on the law.[94] In 1971, his understanding of independence, expressed in his individual opinion of 1970, was endorsed by the ICJ in its Advisory Opinion on Namibia, which explicitly declared that the Court "acts only on the basis of the law, independently of all outside influence or interventions whatsoever, in the exercise of the judicial function entrusted to it alone by the Charter and its Statute."[95] The Code of Judicial Conduct of one of the latest

[91] Ibid., 382.

[92] Zigurds L. Zile, "A Soviet Contribution to International Adjudication: Professor Krylov's Jurisprudential Legacy," *AJIL* 58 (1964): 356.

[93] *Barcelona Traction, Light and Power Company, Limited, Judgment*, Separate Opinion of Judge Tanaka, *I.C.J. Reports 1970*, 154, https://www.icj-cij.org/files/case-related/50/050-19700205-JUD-01-05-BI.pdf, accessed 23 June 2020.

[94] Kotaro Tanaka, "Independence of International Judges," *Comunicazioni e studi* [Communications and Studies] 14 (1975): 858–60.

[95] *Legal Consequences for States of the Continued Presence of South Africa in Namibia (South West Africa) notwithstanding Security Council Resolution 276 (1970), Advisory*

international courts to be established, the Caribbean Court of Justice, incorporated this conception of independence into positive law:

> A judge shall exercise the judicial function independently on the basis of the judge's assessment of the facts and in accordance with a conscientious understanding of the law, free of any extraneous influences, pressures, threats or interference, direct or indirect, from any quarter or for any reason.[96]

Formulated in this way, the scope of the independence of the international judge is identical to that of domestic judges, as enunciated in the Basic Principles on the Independence of the Judiciary endorsed by General Assembly resolutions 40/32 of 29 November 1985 and 40/146 of 13 December 1985.[97] This is not to say that a judge will not be subject

Opinion, *I.C.J. Reports 1971*, 23, para. 29, https://www.icj-cij.org/files/case-related/53/053-19710621-ADV-01-00-BI.pdf, accessed 23 June 2020.

[96] Caribbean Court of Justice, *Judicial Code of Conduct*, *adopted on the 25th of July* 2013, Code 2.1, 7, https://ccj.org/wp-content/uploads/2011/11/CCJ-Judicial-Code-of-Conduct-reduced.pdf, accessed 23 June 2020.

[97] *Basic Principles on the Independence of the Judiciary, Adopted by the Seventh United Nations Congress on the Prevention of Crime and the Treatment of Offenders held at Milan from 26 August to 6 September 1985 and endorsed by General Assembly resolutions 40/32 of 29 November 1985 and 40/146 of 13 December 1985*, https://www.ohchr.org/EN/ProfessionalInterest/Pages/IndependenceJudiciary.aspx, accessed 3 February 2020. This definition of independence is now routinely referred to in the scholarly literature. Tom Dannenbaum, "Nationality and the International Judge: The Nationalist Presumption Governing the International Judiciary and Why it Must be Reversed," *Cornell International Law Journal* 45 (2012): 168, http://scholarship.law.cornell.edu/cgi/viewcontent.cgi?article=1786 &, accessed 23 June 2020; Jeffrey L. Dunoff and Mark A. Pollack, "The Judicial Trilemma," *AJIL* 111 (2017): 226; Giorgios Dimitropoulos, "Measuring Judicial Independence," *Maastricht Journal of European and Comparative Law* 24 (2017): 540; Keller and Meier, "Independence and Impartiality," 345; Paul Mahoney, "The International Judiciary—Independence and Accountability," *LPICT* 7 (2008): 319; Malenovský, "L'indépendance," 26; Theodor Meron, "Judicial Independence and Impartiality in International Criminal Tribunals," *AJIL* 99 (2005): 359; Sandra Szurek, "La composition des juridictions internationales permanentes: de nouvelles exigences de qualité et de représentativité [The Composition of International Tribunals: New Demands for Quality and Representativeness]," *AFDI* 56 (2010): 46, https://www.persee.fr/docAsPDF/afdi_0066-3085_2010_num_56_1_4602.pdf, accessed 23 June 2020; and Anna Torres Pérez, "From Judicial Independence to Interdependence in the International Sphere," *Maastricht Journal of European and Comparative Law* 24 (2017): 463. The Burgh House Principle is more succinct: "The court and the judges shall exercise their functions free from direct and indirect interference or influence by any person or entity." *LPICT* 4 (2005): 252.

to any influence whatsoever. What is to be avoided is the specific influence over a particular decision, rather than the diffuse or historical influence over the judge's general approach to legal or moral reasoning, achieved by parents, professors, colleagues, and peers. Equally to be proscribed is influence other than that achieved through persuasive legal argument, whether by counsel presenting before the court, by the judges alongside whom the judge is hearing the case, by *amicus curiae*, or by appropriate legal authority.[98]

Permanent international courts establish conditions for ensuring the independence of their members. These relate to the manner of their appointment, the security of tenure, salaries and remuneration, privileges and immunities, institutional and operational independence, financing and resources, and the integrity and control of the proceedings.[99] These mechanisms for ensuring the independence of international judges can hardly apply to arbitrators. The latter are appointed for a specific case, sometimes (not always) by the State of which they are nationals, not by the assembly of an international organization that also provides for the financing and resources of the court. Unlike ICJ and ITLOS members, arbitrators continue to exercise their profession while arbitral proceedings are ongoing. They resume their professional activities after a case has been decided. In such circumstances, one might legitimately ask in what sense arbitrators may be considered independent.[100]

In the traditional/diplomatic conception of arbitration, the arbitrators appointed by either party were regarded (and regarded themselves) as representatives of the party appointing them. They were "national"

[98] Dannenbaum, "Nationality," 108.

[99] Mahoney, "The International Judiciary," 324; Margaret Allars, "Disqualification for Bias and International Tribunals: Room for a Common Test," *Missouri Law Review* 78 (2013): 392, https://scholarship.law.missouri.edu/cgi/viewcontent.cgi?article=4033&context=mlr, accessed 20 November 2019; Dannenbaum, "Nationality," 109; Posner and Yoo, "Judicial Independence," 7; and Torres Pérez, "From Judicial Independence," 471.

[100] Yuval Shany argues that many of the rules and principles that sustain judicial independence and impartiality are unrealistic or irrelevant to party-appointed arbitrators. He does not distinguish between inter-State arbitration and State-investor arbitration. It seems that his skepticism is justified in the latter context but not (always) in the former. Yuval Shany, "Squaring the Circle? Independence and Impartiality of Party-Appointed Adjudicators in International Legal Proceedings," *Loyola of Los Angeles International and Comparative Law Review* 30 (2008): 186, http://digitalcommons.lmu.edu/ilr/vol30/iss3/8, accessed 24 June 2020.

judges, who maintained close and uninterrupted contact with the agents and counsel of the State that appointed them; in reality, they were not so much judges as counsel.[101] Occasionally, individual arbitrators in the nineteenth century contradicted this conception, urging their colleagues not to see themselves as counsel for one or the other State but as judges.[102] Nearly a century later, when the UN International Law Commission was codifying arbitral procedure, the Special Rapporteur, French scholar Georges Scelle, still felt compelled to emphasize the need to counter "the all too common practice of appointing arbitrators who do not aspire to be genuine judges but remain representatives or advocates of their respective governments."[103] To this conception the Special Rapporteur opposed the "jurisprudential conception," under which "national" judges cease to be so from the time when the tribunal is finally constituted. From his perspective, the mere fact that arbitrators are accepted by both parties or that they are designated by an appointing authority already makes them appointed judges—members of an international "judicial organ," albeit temporary.[104] Their awards have the same binding force as judgments of permanent international courts. The implication is that since their authority is identical to that of members of permanent international courts, arbitrators will also be held to the same standards of conduct as the latter.[105]

[101] United Nations International Law Commission ("ILC"), *Draft on Arbitral Procedure Adopted by the Commission at its Fifth Session. Report by Georges Scelle, Special Rapporteur (with a Model Draft on Arbitral Procedure Annexed)*, UN Doc. A/CN.4/113 (6 March 1958), in *Yearbook of the International Law Commission 1958*, vol. II, *Documents of the Tenth Session, including the Report of the Commission to the General Assembly*, UN Doc. A/CH.4/SER.A/1958/Add. 1 (New York: United Nations, 1958), 13, para. 41, http://legal.un.org/docs/index.asp?path=../ilc/documentation/english/a_cn4_113.pdf&lang=EFS&referer=http://legal.un.org/ilc/guide/10_1.shtml, accessed 24 June 2020.

[102] US-Ecuadorian Claims Commission [1862], Opinion of Mr. Hassaurek, in John Bassett Moore, *History and Digest of the International Arbitrations to which the United States Has Been a Party*, vol. III (Washington, D.C.: Government Printing Office, 1898), 2733–34, https://ia800204.us.archive.org/18/items/historyanddiges01moorgoog/historyanddiges01moorgoog.pdf, accessed 2 April 2020.

[103] ILC, *Draft on Arbitral Procedure*, 6, para. 41.

[104] Ibid., 7, para. 42.

[105] Ibid., *Arbitral Procedure. Rapport par Georges Scelle, rapporteur spécial* [Report by Georges Scelle, Special Rapporteur], UN Doc. A/CN.4/18 (21 March 1950), in *Yearbook of the International Law Commission 1950*, vol. II, *Documents of the*

This second conception has gained wider currency among arbitrators themselves. Mohamed Bedjaoui, a former ICJ judge who has on several occasions also served as an arbitrator, put forward a vision of the arbitrator's role that is practically identical to that of a member of a permanent international court. He argues that since an arbitrator fulfills the same task as a judge, he/she should follow the same code of behavior. An arbitrator should not be influenced by external pressure, public opinion and rumor, fear of criticism, or the desire to indulge personal interests.[106] One indicator that arbitrators are held to the same standards of independence and impartiality as members of permanent international courts is that they file declarations of independence and impartiality upon their appointments. Declarations of this kind are comparable to the solemn declaration that Article 20 of the ICJ Statute requires every member of the ICJ to make in open court, before taking up his/her duties, under the terms of which he/she will exercise his/her powers impartially and conscientiously.

Procedures for challenges to arbitrators are provided for in the Rules of Procedure of several arbitrations under Annex VII of the Convention.[107] As mentioned in the Chapter introduction, the only formal challenge, which became the object of incidental proceedings and resulted in a reasoned decision by an arbitral tribunal, concerned the arbitrator appointed by the UK, Judge Christopher Greenwood, in the *Chagos Marine Protected Area Arbitration*. The challenge of Mauritius argued

Second Session including the Report of the Commission to the General Assembly, UN Doc. A/CN. 4/SER.A/1950/Add. 1 (New York: United Nations, 1957), 121, para. 21, http://legal.un.org/docs/?path=../ilc/documentation/french/a_cn4_18.pdf&lang=F, accessed 25 June 2020. This document is available only in French.

[106] Mohammed Bedjaoui, "Arbitrator: One Man-Three Roles—Some Independent Comments on the Ethical and Legal Obligations of an Arbitrator," *International Arbitration* 5 (1988): 13.

[107] *MOX Plant Case (Ireland v. United Kingdom)*, Rules of Procedure (25 October 2001), Article 6, 3, https://pcacases.com/web/sendAttach/848, accessed 12 May 2020; *Chagos Marine Protected Area Arbitration (Mauritius v. United Kingdom)*, Rules of Procedure (29 March 2012), Article 6, 4, https://pcacases.com/web/sendAttach/1567, accessed 14 January 2020; *The ARA Libertad Arbitration (Argentina v. Ghana)*, Rules of Procedure (31 July 2013), Article 6, 4, https://pcacases.com/web/sendAttach/427, accessed 12 May 2020; *South China Sea Arbitration* (Rules of Procedure (27 August 2013), Articles 7, 8, and 9, 4–5; *The Atlanto-Scandian Herring Arbitration (The Kingdom of Denmark in respect of the Faroe Islands v. The European Union)*, Rules of Procedure (15 March 2014), Article 4, 4–5, https://pcacases.com/web/sendAttach/305, accessed 12 May 2020; *"Arctic Sunrise" Arbitration*, Rules of Procedure (17 March 2014), Article 7, 4–5, https://pcacases.com/web/sendAttach/1317, accessed 29 April 2020.

that his representation of the UK in a great number of cases before national and international courts and his participation in an Appointment Board that selected the Legal Adviser of the UK's Foreign and Commonwealth Office ("FCO") were evidence of his long-standing and close professional relationship with the UK and were incompatible with the objective appearance of independence.[108] Judge Greenwood and the UK explained that he had been nominated to the Board prior to the initiation of the *Arbitration* and his appointment by the UK, he had been appointed to the Board precisely because he was independent of government, he had performed his role independently from the UK government, he had received no remuneration for his service on the Board, he no longer played a role in it, and he had not been party to or aware of any discussion relating to the arbitral proceedings, the Chagos Archipelago, or the law of the sea.[109] The UK believed that he had fulfilled the standard laid down in Article 3 of Annex VII of the Convention, in that he was not in the service of the UK. Strictly speaking, the conditions set out in Article 3(e) of Annex VII apply only to arbitrators who are appointed by the appointing authority. This implies that the arbitrator appointed by a party may not only be a national of that party but that he/she may also be in the service of that party. However, the UK believed that the standard set for the neutral arbitrators could also be applied to the arbitrator appointed by a party. The Tribunal agreed with the UK, finding that Judge Greenwood's participation in the Appointment Board was advisory, did not entail any advice on legal issues, was confined to advising on one aspect of the suitability of the candidates for the post of Legal Adviser, and was of considerably limited duration, lasting only two days. His participation in the process, which did not involve giving advice on legal issues, was restricted to that particular purpose and was limited to brief participation in a panel, neither constituted nor continued an already existing relationship.[110] For these and other reasons, which will be discussed in the next part of this Chapter, the challenge to Judge Greenwood was dismissed by the Tribunal.

If we now turn to the *South China Sea Arbitration*, we realize that China did not criticize the lack of independence of the appointing

[108] *Chagos Marine Protected Area Arbitration*, Reasoned Decision, 1, para. 10.

[109] Ibid., 2, 16, paras. 12, 88–89.

[110] Ibid., 34, paras. 181–82.

authority and of the members of the Tribunal and that the reason for this was that there were no possible grounds for doing so.

2. The Assessment of the Independence of the Appointing Authority and of the Judges in the South China Sea Arbitration

The starting point of the assessment of the independence of the appointing authority is the fact that he did not play a judicial role at all in the *South China Sea Arbitration*. The members of the Arbitral Tribunal, for their part, were not in the service of either party.

The role in the constitution of arbitral tribunals conferred by Annex VII of the Convention on the appointing authority, the ITLOS President, is non-judicial or extra-judicial. The fact that the appointing authority is a judge is irrelevant in the fulfillment of this role.[111] A similar role is conferred by other multilateral treaties to the ICJ President and the UN Secretary-General. The purpose of the provisions of Annex VII that govern the appointing authority's role is to avoid the proceedings being paralyzed by a party's failure to name its arbitrator or the two parties' failure to agree on the appointment of the neutral arbitrators. Analogous provisions are found in two other annexes of the Convention. Annex V, on Conciliation, and Annex VIII, on special arbitration relating to fisheries, protection and preservation of the marine environment, marine scientific research, and navigation, assign a similar role to the UN Secretary-General.[112]

The ITLOS President's role is one of selection, and not of the decision itself. Following former ICJ President Muhammad Zafrullah Khan, one may describe the appointing authority's role as "ministerial," in the sense of "relating to or possessing delegated executive authority," "(of an office, duty, etc.) requiring the following of instructions, without power

[111] The following paragraphs rely heavily on Mohammed Zafrullah Khan, "The Appointment of Arbitrators by the President of the International Court of Justice," *Comunicazioni e studi* [Communications and Studies] 14 (1975): 1021–42. The author was a former ICJ President (1970–1973); as such he had to act as appointing authority for a number of arbitrations.

[112] United Nations Division for Ocean Affairs and the Law of the Sea, *Annex V, Conciliation*, Articles 3(c), (d) and (e), https://www.un.org/Depts/los/convention_agreements/texts/unclos/annex5.htm, accessed 24 June 2020; United Nations Division for Ocean Affairs and the Law of the Sea *Annex VIII*, *Special Arbitration*, Article 3(e), https://www.un.org/Depts/los/convention_agreements/texts/unclos/annex8.htm,, accessed 24 June 2020.

to exercise any personal discretion in doing so," or "acting as an agent or cause; instrumental."[113] He/she is not asked to settle the dispute, but simply to choose the suitable person(s) to act as arbitrators. The fact that the appointing authority is a judge is irrelevant, as no more is expected of him/her than of the UN Secretary-General under Annexes V and VIII of the Convention. In the event a State refuses to appoint an arbitrator alleging that the dispute settlement clause is not applicable, the appointing authority is not in a position to judge whether it is indeed applicable.

What then are the duties of an appointing authority? First, he/she must satisfy himself/herself that the two parties have agreed to give him/her a part in the constitution of the tribunal. The party or parties requesting the appointment must prove the existence of the treaty conferring the power to act to him/her. As former ICJ President Zafrullah Khan put it, "the possibility of it [the treaty] being a mere fiction is hardly conceivable."[114] Next, if the treaty sets any time limits within which a party must request the appointing authority to act, then he/she must ensure that these provisions have been complied with. Third, the appointing authority must be satisfied that the entity making the application is the party entitled to do so. This problem is not likely to arise in the case of inter-State disputes, but it may be an issue if a contract between a State and private corporation confers a power of appointment on an appointing authority.[115] It is understood that the clause providing for the appointment of arbitrators by the ITLOS President or the ICJ President or the UN Secretary-General means appointment by the persons holding those positions at the time of the appointment and not those who occupied them at the time of the conclusion of the agreement.

There can be no doubt that Judge Yanai, the ITLOS President at the time the Philippines initiated proceedings against China, complied with

[113] *Collins English Dictionary* (Glasgow: HarperCollins Publishers, 2020), https://www.collinsdictionary.com/dictionary/english/ministerial, accessed 4 June 2020.

[114] Zafrullah Khan, "The Appointment," 1031–32.

[115] It was the ICJ President who, upon the request of two private companies, appointed the single arbitrator in the *Texaco Overseas Petroleum Company/California Asiatic Oil Company v. The Government of the Libyan Arab Republic Arbitration* when Libya failed to appoint its arbitrator and defaulted in the proceedings. Ad hoc Award of January 19, 1977, https://www.trans-lex.org/261700/_/texaco-overseas-petroleum-company-v-the-government-of-the-libyan-arab-republic-yca-1979-at-177-et-seq-/, accessed 24 June 2020.

these duties. Determining the existence of the treaty that conferred the power of appointment to him would have posed no difficulty—the treaty in question was the Convention, which had also established the ITLOS. The Philippines complied with the time limits set by the Convention. The ITLOS President would have had to verify that neither the Philippines nor China had made a declaration under Article 287 of the Convention opting for a particular mode of compulsory dispute settlement entailing binding decisions and that consequently, arbitration was deemed to be the mode of dispute settlement for disputes between them concerning the interpretation and application of the Convention. Any attempt to impugn the independence of the ITLOS President must provide evidence that the Philippines, one or more States parties to the Convention, or a Convention body had given him instructions to appoint the four arbitrators that he appointed. Any attempt of this kind must fail, as there is no such evidence.

As for the four arbitrators appointed by the ITLOS President and the arbitrator appointed by the Philippines, it is quite obvious that by definition, all of them are independent. Following the precedent of the *Chagos Marine Protected Area Arbitration*, a decisive consideration in this assessment is that Judge Pawłak, who was appointed as a result of China's default, was not in the service of China. Unlike Judge Greenwood, who was a national of the appointing State and was habitually resident in that State's territory, Judge Pawłak was neither a national of nor ordinarily resident in China, as required by Article 3(e) of Annex VII of the Convention. As for the arbitrator appointed by the Philippines and the three arbitrators appointed by the ITLOS President, none was a national of either the Philippines or China, none was in the service of either State, and none was ordinarily resident in the territory of either State.

Chinese scholars argued that the five arbitrators were influenced by Yanai's political views: "it is only natural to believe that the five arbitrators shared similar views with those who appointed them or were inclined to be influenced by those who had appointed them."[116] In the first place, it is worth recalling that Judge Wolfrum was not appointed by the appointing authority, but by the Philippines. In the second place, if we base ourselves on the definitions of independence provided by Judge

[116] Fei Liena and Han Mo, "Commentary: Puppet Tribunal in S. China Sea Case Does Not Represent int'l [sic] Law," *ecns.cn*, 14 July 2016, http://www.ecns.cn/voices/2016/07-15/218364.shtml, accessed 7 July 2020.

Tanaka, the ICJ, and the Caribbean Court of Justice, one could point out that the four arbitrators appointed by the ITLOS President, and for that matter, the Tribunal as a whole, were not answerable for their decisions to the ITLOS President. Nor were they accountable to the States that had nominated them for the list of conciliators and arbitrators maintained by the UN Secretary-General in accordance with Article 2 of Annex VII of the Convention. Judges Mensah, Pawłak, and Soons had been nominated by the States of which they were nationals; Judges Cot and Wolfrum had both been nominated by Mongolia. None of them was accountable for their decisions in the *South China Sea Arbitration* to the States that nominated them for inclusion in the list. One would have to enter the realm of the absurd to think that Ghana, Poland, the Netherlands, and Mongolia, respectively, had given them instructions as to the decisions concerning the claims of the Philippines.

China, which did not and could not question the independence of the ITLOS President and the five members of the Arbitral Tribunal, instead attempted to undermine the Tribunal's independence.

B. China's Threats to the Independence of the Tribunal in the South China Sea Arbitration

Neither specialists of China writing on the *South China Sea Arbitration*[117] nor specialists of Chinese smear campaigns[118] have paid any attention to China's threats to the independence of the Tribunal in the *South China Sea Arbitration. A fortiori* no attempt has been made to relate them to the conduct of the Chinese government and the CCP toward Chinese judges.

[117] Julian Ku, "The Significance of China's Rejection of the *South China Sea Arbitration* for Its Approach to International Dispute Settlement and International Law," *Chinese (Taiwan) Yearbook of International Law and Affairs* 34 (2016): 74, 88; Isaac B. Kardon, "China Can Say 'No': Analyzing China's Rejection of the South China Sea Arbitration. Toward a New Era of International Law with Chinese Characteristics," *University of Pennsylvania Asian Law Review* 13 (2019): 3, https://scholarship.law.upenn.edu/cgi/viewcontent.cgi?article=1037&context=alr, accessed 23 March 2020.

[118] Heather Timmons and Ilaria Maria Sala, "How to Smear Your Enemies and Silence Your Critics, Chinese Communist Party Style," *Quartz*, 23 June 2016, https://qz.com/712187/how-to-smear-your-enemies-and-silence-your-critics-chinese-communist-party-style/, accessed 28 June 2020.

The starting points of an understanding of China's conduct toward Chinese and international judges should be two sets of declarations by the Chinese government and CCP officials. First, The Supreme People's Court ("SPC") and its President have unequivocally declared that judicial independence is a Western trap to be avoided.[119] Second, the CCP has decreed that in deciding a case, judges must take into account three "supremes": the supremacy of the party, the supremacy of the interest of the people, and the supremacy of the constitution and the law.[120] The lack of judicial independence in China will not be news to most outsiders, who assume this to be the case in one-party systems or authoritarian systems. Less well-known are the mechanisms of dependence and the way in which China's conduct in the *South China Sea Arbitration* replicates that of the State and the CCP toward Chinese judges. The following discussion does not claim to be an exhaustive study of the independence (or lack of it) of Chinese judges or of the Chinese judiciary. It will focus on two manifestations of dependence that are relevant for understanding the conduct of China in the *South China Sea Arbitration.* In the early stages of the proceedings, China attempted to manipulate the judges through secret lobbying. Following the issuance of the Award on Jurisdiction, China organized an international campaign that may be considered an international manifestation of "judicial populism."

1. The Defaulting State's Attempt to Manipulate the Tribunal in the South China Sea Arbitration

The little we know of the circumstances of China's clandestine efforts to lobby the judges in the *South China Sea Arbitration* cannot fail to convince us that China was hoping to manipulate them in the way that the Chinese government and the Chinese Communist Party ("CCP") manipulates judges at the domestic level.

[119] Reuters, "China's Top Court Rejects Judicial Independence as 'Erroneous Thought'," *The Guardian*, 26 February 2015, https://www.theguardian.com/world/2015/feb/26/chinas-top-court-rejects-judicial-independence-as-erroneous-thought, accessed 28 June 2020; Zheping Huang, "Xi Jinping Promised Legal Reform in China, But Forget About Judicial Independence," *Quartz*, 18 January 2017, https://qz.com/886665/xi-jinping-promised-legal-reform-in-china-but-forget-about-judicial-independence/, accessed 28 June 2020.

[120] Randall Peerenboom, "Fly High the Banner of Socialist Rule of Law with Chinese Characteristics!" *Hague Journal on the Rule of Law* 7 (2015): 55.

The only source of factual information on China's actions is the Award on Jurisdiction and Admissibility, which reveals that "on 14 November 2013, after the Chinese Ambassador to the UK requested a meeting with the President of the Tribunal," the Tribunal wrote to China and the Philippines to remind them of their obligation to refrain from *ex parte* communications.[121] It turns out that on two previous occasions, China had also attempted to contact the PCA, the Registry in the case: "The Tribunal recalled that the Registry had on two prior occasions discussed informal questions of a procedural nature with a representative of the Chinese Embassy [in the Netherlands]."[122] The Tribunal's restraint in the matter is remarkable. It did not publicize China's request at the time that it was made. The public was to learn of China's maneuver only two years later, upon the issuance of the Award on Jurisdiction. The Chinese Ambassador's letter and the Chinese Embassy's informal queries were not posted on the PCA website, nor is it likely that they will ever be. The Chinese maneuvers were no longer mentioned in the Procedural History section of the Award of 12 July 2016. In all probability, the Tribunal wished to avoid humiliating China, inflaming public opinion in China and the Philippines, and heightening the tension between the two States. There can be no doubt, though, that the Philippines was informed of China's maneuvers.

China's conduct contradicts its oft-repeated claim that its conduct in not accepting or participating in the arbitral proceedings has a "solid basis" in international law. The Rules of Procedure of the *Arbitration* unambiguously state:

> The Parties shall not engage in any *ex parte* oral or written communications with any member of the Arbitral Tribunal in connection with the subject matter of the arbitration or any procedural issues which are related

[121] *South China Sea Arbitration*, Award on Jurisdiction and Admissibility, 29 October 2015, 18, para. 40 ("Award on Jurisdiction"), https://pcacases.com/web/sendAttach/2579, accessed 10 March 2020. An *ex parte* communication is defined by Canon 2, Rule 2.9 of the *Model Code of Judicial Conduct* of the American Bar Association ("ABA") as communication "made to the judge outside the presence of the parties or their lawyers, concerning a pending or impending matter" (Chicago: American Bar Association, 2020), https://www.americanbar.org/groups/professional_responsibility/publications/model_code_of_judicial_conduct/model_code_of_judicial_conduct_canon_2/rule2_9expartecommunications/, accessed 28 June 2020.

[122] Award on Jurisdiction, 18, para. 40.

> to the proceedings. A written communication shall not be considered *ex parte* if the Party also sends a copy of the written communication to the other Party. An oral communication shall not be considered *ex parte* if it is made in a meeting, teleconference, videoconference or hearing of which the other Party has been notified, but in which it has decided not to participate.[123]

By November 2013, China must have been aware of the prohibition of *ex parte* communications, simply because it had been receiving copies of all communications sent by the Philippines to the Tribunal and all decisions of the Tribunal, including the Rules of the Procedure and other procedural orders. In the Award on Jurisdiction, the Tribunal reminded China and the Philippines that

> [i]f a Party wishes to express its position on matters in dispute, it should be aware that such statements will be made available to all members of the Tribunal, the Registry and the other party, in accordance with the Rules of Procedure and the need to ensure that the Parties are treated with equality.[124]

The unmistakable conclusion to be derived from the reminder is that China attempted to conceal its actions from the Philippines. Finally, the Tribunal "encouraged the Parties to direct any questions of a procedural nature to the Registry."[125] Obviously, it was only China that was being "reminded" and "encouraged" but the Tribunal did not single out China, in order to avoid humiliating it further.

The Tribunal did not explain in the Award on the Jurisdiction the reason(s) for China's request. The reader is thus left to wonder whether the aim that China hoped to achieve through such contacts was the termination of the proceedings; and whether China believed it could more easily sway the President of the Tribunal rather than the Tribunal as a whole—or the Philippines, for that matter. The Tribunal is also silent on the nature of China's procedural inquiries and the PCA's and/or the Tribunal's responses to them. China's contacts with the Registry prompt one to ask why China had procedural questions if it defaulted; whether

123 *South China Sea Arbitration*, Rules of Procedure, Article 12(1), 6.

124 Award on Jurisdiction, 18, para. 40.

125 Ibid.

it would have been simpler to participate in the proceedings rather than informally asking questions; and whether the subsequent intervention of China's Ambassador to the UK can be explained by the failure of the maneuvers of China's Embassy in the Netherlands. No light is shed on these matters in the five-hundred-page critique of the Awards published by the CSIL.[126] The circumstance that puts China's conduct in the worst possible light is the attempt to conceal these maneuvers from the Philippines. Had China's aims had a "solid basis" in international law," surely there would have been no need to resort to underhanded maneuvers.

One may draw a parallel between China's clumsy attempt to manipulate the Tribunal President, on the one hand, and the conduct of the Chinese State and the CCP toward judges in the domestic sphere, on the other. As a result of the dependence of Chinese courts on government agencies, notably for their financing and other resources, government agencies in China can intervene directly in individual cases.[127] For instance, local governments do not hesitate to give instructions to courts at the same level on the decisions to be adopted in certain cases, notably those in which a non-local entity is involved.[128] A judge who refuses to follow instructions may be the object of sanctions ranging from remonstrance to dismissal.[129]

When Chinese government agencies are defendants in a case, they send messages to the courts to pressure them into demanding that plaintiffs withdraw the case.[130] Once a court accepts a case, government agencies pressure the court to find in their favor. They also refuse to cooperate with the courts: they refuse to accept summons, to appear in court, to respond to the complaint, to provide evidence, and to comply with court

[126] CSIL, "The South China Sea Arbitration Awards," 207–748.

[127] Katrin Blasek, *Rule of Law in China: A Comparative Approach* (Berlin: Springer-Verlag, 2015), 63.

[128] Ting Gong, "Dependent Judiciary and Unaccountable Judges: Judicial Corruption in Contemporary China," *China Review* 4 (2004): 43.

[129] Yuwen Li, *The Judicial System and Reform in Post-Mao China: Stumbling Towards Justice* (Farnham, Surrey: Ashgate Publishing Co., 2014), 71; Qianfan Zhang, "Judicial Reform in China: An Overview," in John Garrick and Yan Chang Bennett (eds.), *China's Socialist Rule of Law Reforms Under Xi Jinping* (Milton Park, Abingdon, Oxon: Routledge, 2016), 19.

[130] Yuwen Li, *The Judicial System*, 58.

decisions. Some government agencies go so far as to destroy or fabricate evidence.[131]

Like government agencies, the CCP is in a position to give instructions on policy to the judiciary as a whole and on individual cases to individual judges or courts. The CCP instructs courts on judicial policies, whether on its own initiative or upon the request of the courts or other agencies. It is the CCP that warns judicial officials against being misled by the Western concept of the independence of the judiciary.[132] The CCP also solves disputes between the courts and State agencies and among different judicial organs.[133] At both central and local levels, the Party Political-Legal Committees ("PPLC") oversee the courts and indeed the entire government branch of law enforcement.[134] The PPLCs' control over judicial affairs gives it direct access to decision-making in individual cases so that the CCP can control the outcome of a case. The PPLCs control decision-making through case coordination, whereby they summon the institutions handling a case to report to them in coordination meetings, and through case inspection, whereby they investigate and solve complaints about non-compliance with CCP policies and State laws.[135] The PPLCs do not intervene in the over 10 million cases that Chinese courts hear every year that are not politically sensitive. They focus on a small number of cases that are "sensitive"—those that threaten national security and challenge CCP authority to rule.[136] In these cases the PPLCs can issue specific

[131] Randall Peerenboom, "A Government of Laws: Democracy, Rule of Law, and Administrative Law Reform in China," in Suisheng Zhao (ed.), *Debating Political Reform in China: Rule of Law vs. Democratization* (Armonk, N.Y.: M.E. Sharpe, 2006), 67.

[132] Willy Lam, "The Politicisation of China's Law Enforcement and Judicial Apparatus," in Jean-Philippe Béja (ed.) *The Impact of China's 1989 Tiananmen Massacre* (Milton Park, Abingdon, Oxon: Routledge, 2011), 130.

[133] Ling Li, "The Chinese Communist Party and People's Courts: Judicial Dependence in China," *American Journal of Comparative Law* 64 (2016): 59; Ting Gong, "Dependent Judiciary," 42.

[134] Chongyi Feng, "China's Socialist Rule of Law: A Critical Appraisal of the Relationship between the Communist Party and Comprehensive Law Reform," in John Garrick and Yan Chang Bennett (eds.), *China's Socialist Rule of Law Reforms Under Xi Jinping* (Milton Park, Abingdon, Oxon: Routledge, 2016), 48.

[135] Yuwen Li, *The Judicial System*, 66.

[136] Peerenboom, "Fly High," 71; Ling Li, "The Chinese Communist Party," 71; Yuwen Li, *The Judicial System*, 55.

instructions to courts on the outcomes of cases. These instructions are not subject to judicial scrutiny.[137]

The Chinese judiciary's lack of independence from government organizations is inherent in the structure of government in China. Local People's Congresses elect and dismiss the presidents of local courts at the same level. The Standing Committee of the Local People's Congresses elects court vice presidents, heads of divisions, and judges. People's Congresses at all levels approve the annual reports of courts on their work; review judicial interpretations to ensure that they are in compliance with the law; and handle petitions and complaints against unlawful conduct of judicial officials.[138] Local people's courts are responsible to the local people's congresses. At the highest level, the SPC is accountable to the National People's Congress ("NPC") and its Standing Committee. The dependence of courts on government organizations arises in part from the fact that the latter provide most of the salaries and funds of the courts at the same level.[139]

The judiciary's dependence on the CCP is embedded in the structure of China's political system. The overwhelming majority of judges, including court presidents and vice presidents, are CCP members, who have to adhere unconditionally to the party line on all issues.[140] In each court, there is a party group, whose head is the president of the court. The court party group is the highest decision-making body in courts, which carries out CCP commands and gives instructions to court leaders. The latter in turn take these instructions to the courts. Since court leaders are CCP members, CCP leaders can dictate rulings in selected cases, without the need for legal justification. Judges must implement instructions unconditionally.[141]

This rapid survey gives rise to two impressions. First, the conduct of State agencies who are defendants in legal cases in China seems to have set a pattern for China's litigation strategy in the *South China Sea Arbitration*. Second, and more importantly, China is accustomed to giving

[137] Yuwen Li, *The Judicial System*, 70.

[138] Ibid., 37.

[139] Zhang, "Judicial Reform," 19.

[140] Yuwen Li, *The Judicial System*, 51.

[141] Ling Li, "The 'Production' of Corruption in China's Courts: Judicial Politics and Decision-Making in a One-Party State," *Law and Social Inquiry* 37 (2012): 854–56.

instructions to judges on politically sensitive cases through government agencies and the CCP and to receiving unconditional obedience. This mindset explains China's attempts to manipulate the Tribunal, and particularly its President, in the *South China Sea Arbitration.* Unfortunately for China—and fortunately for international justice—the relationship between China and the Tribunal, and particularly its President, is in no way comparable to that between the Chinese government and the CCP, on the one hand, and Chinese judges, on the other. It seems that China did not fully comprehend this, for it resorted to another strategy that had gained some currency among Chinese victims and/or defendants in the first decade or so of this century—judicial populism.

2. The Defaulting State's Strategy of Judicial Populism in the South China Sea Arbitration

One tactic deployed by China in the wake of the issuance of the Award on Jurisdiction to gain international support for its position on the *Arbitration* was to portray itself as a victim. This tactic justifies a description of this element of China's litigation strategy as one of judicial populism, in which victims, as well as defendants, mobilize public opinion for the purpose of exerting pressure on judges and courts.

Prior to the Tribunal's decisions on jurisdiction and admissibility in October 2015, China's informal communications to the Tribunal, which restated the arguments of the Position Paper against the Tribunal's jurisdiction, made sense.[142] More puzzling is the fact that well after the Tribunal had affirmed jurisdiction and indeed, after the oral proceedings on the merits had concluded, at a time when strictly speaking it was futile to do so, China continued to write to the Tribunal to insist that the latter

[142] *South China Sea Arbitration, Supplemental Written Submission of the Philippines*, Annex 470, Letter from H.E. Ambassador Chen Xu, Embassy of the People's Republic of China in The Hague, to H.E. Judge Thomas A. Mensah (6 Feb. 2015), vol. VIII, 73–84 ("*SWSP*"), https://files.pca-cpa.org/pcadocs/The%20Philippines%27%20Supplemental%20Written%20Submission%20-%20Volume%20VIII%20%28Annexes%20466-499%29.pdf, accessed 10 March 2020; *South China Sea Arbitration, The Philippines' Annexes cited during Hearing on Jurisdiction (Annexes 574–583)*(13 July 2015), Annex 574, Letter from H.E. Chen Xu, Ambassador of the People's Republic of China to the Kingdom of the Netherlands, to H.E. Judge Thomas A. Mensah (1 July 2015), 1–3, https://files.pca-cpa.org/pcadocs/Annexes%20cited%20during%20Hearing%20on%20Jurisdiction%20%28Annexes%20574-583%29.pdf, accessed 24 April 2020; cited in the Award of 12 July 2016, 15, 17, paras. 42, 51.

lacked jurisdiction.[143] The Tribunal could do no more than acknowledge receipt of these letters and transmit them to the Philippines. It seems to us that the series of Letters provided China with grounds for portraying the Tribunal as unresponsive to China's arguments. In other words, China could portray itself as a victim of a Tribunal that allegedly lacked impartiality. It is not very likely that the ordinary observer, whether inside or outside China, could understand the legal niceties that prevented the Tribunal from reconsidering its jurisdiction upon the request of one of the parties to the dispute when the Tribunal had already settled the question of its jurisdiction. From the very beginning of the proceedings, China had portrayed itself as a victim of the Philippines, which it accused of an abuse of the compulsory dispute settlement procedures of the Convention and a "grave challenge to the solemnity [sic]" of these procedures.[144] China had also consistently portrayed itself, directly or indirectly, as a victim of the US, which allegedly instigated the Philippines to go back on its alleged agreement with China to resolve their disputes exclusively through bilateral negotiations and which manipulated public opinion to smear China.[145] A few weeks prior to the issuance of the Award of 12 July 2016, a former Foreign Minister asserted that China was suffering "injustice at the hands of the US and rival claimants" and that China was "perhaps the biggest victim of the South China Sea issue."[146] To the Philippines and the US one could now add the Tribunal. As the *People's Daily* succinctly put it, the *Arbitration* was a "ruse against China which

[143] Letters of 20 May, 3 June, 8 June, and 10 June 2016 from the Chinese Ambassador to the Netherlands. Award of 12 July 2016, 34–7, paras. 97, 100, 102, 103.

[144] *SWSP*, Annex 467, People's Republic of China Position Paper of the Government of the People's Republic of China on the Matter of Jurisdiction in the South China Sea Arbitration Initiated by the Republic of the Philippines (7 December 2014), vol. VIII (16 March 2015), 30, para. 74.

[145] Foreign Ministry, *Foreign Ministry Spokesperson Lu Kang's Regular Press Conference on June 14, 2016*, https://www.fmprc.gov.cn/nanhai/eng/fyrbt_1/t1372136.htm, accessed 29 June 2020.

[146] Former Chinese Foreign Minister Li Zhaoxing, quoted in "China Is Perhaps the 'Biggest Victim' in South China Sea, Says Former Foreign Minister," *asiasociety.org*, 23 June 2016, https://asiasociety.org/blog/asia/china-perhaps-biggest-victim-south-china-sea-says-former-foreign-minister, accessed 9 April 2020.

was instigated and manipulated by the US, initiated by the Philippines, with cooperation from the Arbitral Tribunal."[147]

China adapted its portrayal of itself as a victim to its audience. At a meeting of think tanks during the 5th China-Africa Conference in China in April 2016, when China sought African support for its position on the *South China Sea Arbitration*, China described Africa and China as good friends. As such they had to support each other on issues concerning their vital interests, because they had all been victims of colonization.[148] The last statement was, of course, not literally true. China had undoubtedly been a victim of Western imperialism from the mid-nineteenth century onwards, but it had never been a formal colony, as had been the case with almost all African States. Should one wish to overlook this inconvenient historical detail, one is compelled to point out that there is no reason for China and Africa to adopt a common stand against the Philippines, which was in no way responsible for imperialist actions against China and the colonization of Africa. Indeed, the Philippines had also been a colony, and if one wished to score points for being a victim, it could claim two, for having been a colony of two Western powers, and maybe half a point each for occupation by Great Britain during the Seven Years' War (1762–1764) and by Japan during the Second World War (1941–1945).

[147] Xinhua, "Major Chinese Newspapers Slam South China Sea Arbitration," *Global Times*, 11 July 2016, http://www.globaltimes.cn/content/993590.shtml, accessed 1 July 2020.

[148] Laouali Soleymane, "Conférence de Presse du Directeur général en charge du département Afrique du Ministère des Affaires Etrangères de la République Populaire de Chine: Des clarifications sur la question de la mer de Chine méridionale [Press Conference of the Director General of the Africa Department of the Ministry of Foreign Affairs of the People's Republic of China. Clarifications on the South China Sea Issue]," *Nigerdiaspora. La communauté virtuelle du Niger* [Nigerdiaspora. The Virtual Community of Niger], 20 April 2016, https://nigerdiaspora.net/index.php/politique-archives/item/73676-conference-de-presse-du-directeur-general-en-charge-du-departement-afrique-du-ministere-des-affaires-etrangeres-de-la-republique-populaire-de-chine-des-clarifications-sur-la-question-de-la-mer-de-chine-meridionale?tmpl=component&print=1, accessed 29 June 2020.

One cannot help but be struck by the peculiar strategy of this fictitious victim of Western colonization. Instead of seeking legal redress from the proper authorities—which is what one would have expected from a victim, at least within the domestic sphere—China sought solace in the opinion of other States. By June 2016, China's media was claiming that over 40 States supported China's position that the Tribunal lacked jurisdiction. There was some debate over the exact figure. The Asian Maritime Transparency Initiative ("AMTI"), a US-based thinktank, identified 31 States that had publicly voiced support for Beijing's position prior to the issuance of the Award of 12 July 2016, along with four that had denied any such support and 26 that had remained publicly silent despite China's claim of support or had issued statements that were considerably more ambiguous than indicated by China. In contrast, 40 States had said that the Arbitral Award would be legally binding and had called on both China and the Philippines to respect it.[149] The AMTI identified States countries that had publicly called for the Arbitral Award to be respected after the conclusion of the proceedings, 33 that had issued generally positive statements noting the Award but had refrained from calling on the parties to abide by it, nine that had made extremely vague or neutral statements without addressing the Award, and six that had publicly rejected it.[150] In contrast, Chinese media claimed that after the issuance of the Award of 12 July 2016, the number of States supporting its position rose from 40 to 66. Chinese researchers attempting to verify the figure after the issuance of the Award claimed that the real number was even higher, at 70.[151] They contended that it was not always possible to find the statements of

[149] Asian Maritime Transparency Initiative ("AMTI"), *Who Is Taking Sides After the South China Sea Ruling?* 15 August 2016, https://amti.csis.org/sides-in-south-china-sea/, accessed 1 July 2020.

[150] Ibid.

[151] Wang Wen and Chen Xiaochen, "Who Supports China in the South China Sea and Why," *The Diplomat*, 27 July 2016, https://thediplomat.com/2016/07/who-supports-china-in-the-south-china-sea-and-why/, accessed 16 March 2020.

support, because they were in languages other than English.[152] Sometimes enthusiasm got the better of the Chinese media, which announced that Fiji and Slovenia were among China's supporters, only for the two to issue denials immediately.[153] At other times, the support is more apparent than real. For example, a communiqué issued by Russia, India, and China called for the full respect of the Declaration on the Conduct of the Parties in the South China Sea of 2002 ("DOC"), which for China excluded the recourse to arbitration, as well as all provisions of the Convention, and which in the Philippine view would have permitted recourse to arbitration.[154] China's Foreign Ministry did not give an exact figure, declaring

[152] The statements of some African countries are available online. For Burundi, see "Ambassade de Chine > Présentation de la position de la Chine sur la Mer de Chine méridionale [Embassy of China > Presentation of the Position of China on the South China Sea]," *Publications de Presse Burundaise* [Publications of Burundi's Press], 11 May 2016, http://www.ppbdi.com/index.php/extras/politique-cooperation-actualite-internationales/4137-ambassade-de-chine-presentation-de-la-position-de-la-chine-sur-la-mer-de-chine-meridionale, accessed 29 June 2020; for Mozambique, see Ministério dos Negócios Estrangeiros e Cooperação [Ministry of Foreign Affairs and Trade], *Moçambique e China estabelecem parceria estratégica para cooperação global* [Mozambique and China Establish a Strategic Strategy for Overall Cooperation], 20 May 2016, http://www.minec.gov.mz/index.php/imprensa/destaques/91-mocambique-e-china-estabelecem-parceria-estrategica-para-cooperacao-global, accessed 1 June 2016; for Niger, see *Communiqué de presse du Ministère en charge des Affaires Etrangères, relatif au différend entre la République Populaire de Chine et les Philippines en Mer de Chine Méridionale* [Press Communiqué of the Ministry of Foreign Affairs, on the Dispute between the People's Republic of China and the Philippines in the South China Sea], 19 May, 2016, http://news.aniamey.com/h/72663.html, accessed 29 June 2020; for Togo, see "Pékin apprécie la position togolaise [Beijing Appreciates the Togolese Position]," *Republic of Togo*, 19 May 2016, https://www.republicoftogo.com/Toutes-les-rubriques/Diplomatie/Pekin-apprecie-la-position-togolaise, accessed 29 June 2020.

[153] Agence France Presse, *Mer de Chine* [sic]*: Pékin en quête d'alliés diplomatiques, de Kaboul à Niamey* [China Sea (sic): Beijing in Search of Diplomatic Allies, from Kabul to Niamey], 25 May 2016, http://fr.annahar.com/article/390379-mer-de-chine-pekin-en-quete-dallies-diplomatiques-de-kaboul-a-niamey, accessed 29 June 2020; Caroline Lafargue, "Mer de Chine [sic]: le Vanuatu apporte un soutien de poids-plume à Pékin [China Sea (sic): Vanuatu Gives Featherweight support to Beijing]," *francetvinfo.fr*, 31 May 2016, https://la1ere.francetvinfo.fr/nouvellecaledonie/mer-de-chine-le-vanuatu-apporte-un-soutien-de-poids-plume-pekin-365317.html, accessed 29 June 2020. In spite of its denial, Slovenia still appears in the map provided by Wang Wen and Chen Xiaochen, "Who Supports China.".

[154] "South China Sea Dispute: China Claims Support of 40 Countries," *The India Times*, 12 July 2016, https://economictimes.indiatimes.com/news/defence/south-china-sea-dispute-china-claims-support-of-40-countries/articleshow/52363836.cms?from=mdr, accessed 29 June 2020.

that the States that supported China far outnumbered the seven or eight States that opposed China's position.[155] The Foreign Ministry claimed that the States that supported it "cared about China," and that after having worked out rights and wrongs, they were "willing to speak out from a sense of justice." The moral of the story, according to the Foreign Ministry, was that "a just cause enjoys abundant support and people have a sense of natural justice."[156] For the Chinese newspaper *People's Daily*, "public opinion is the best judge."[157]

The notions that "abundant support" from people or States and "public opinion" are the judges of a legal case would immediately make sense to a Chinese domestic audience. In China, public opinion sometimes plays an influential and sometimes decisive role in judicial decisions, particularly those involving the death penalty, a phenomenon that scholars have called "judicial populism"[158] or "penal populism." The two terms refer to victim-generated public opinion, which is proactive, aggressive, and effective in its mobilization.[159] A survey of the main features of the phenomenon is worthwhile, for China's campaign to mobilize in its favor international public opinion, represented by States that were not parties to the dispute, arguably reflects a strategy of judicial populism.

The trigger for judicial or penal populism is a tragic event, which may range from a death in a road rage incident to a death in police custody. Judicial populism is hardly spontaneous. Public opinion is mobilized through the Internet, petitions, and protests by families and supporters

[155] Foreign Ministry, *Foreign Ministry Spokesperson Lu Kang's Regular Press Conference on June 16, 2016*, 16 June 2016, https://www.fmprc.gov.cn/nanhai/eng/fyrbt_1/t1372802.htm, accessed 29 June 2020.

[156] Ibid., *Foreign Ministry Spokesperson Lu Kang's Regular Press Conference on June 14, 2016*, 14 June 2016, https://www.fmprc.gov.cn/nanhai/eng/fyrbt_1/t1372136.htm, accessed 29 June 2020.

[157] "South China Sea Arbitration Case Today the Results of People's Daily Nearly [sic]," 12 July 2016, http://www.hubgold.com/2016/07/12/south-china-sea-arbitration-case-today-the-results-of-people-s-daily-nearly, accessed 25 April 2017.

[158] Ira Belkin, "Justice in the PRC. How the Chinese Communist Party Has Struggled with Managing Public Opinion and the Administration of Criminal Justice in the Internet Age," in Flora Sapio et al., *Justice (The China Experience)* (Cambridge: Cambridge University Press, 2017), 198–99.

[159] Fu Hualing, "Between Deference and Defiance: Courts and Penal Populism in Chinese Capital Cases," in Bin Liang and Hong Lu (eds.), *China's Death Penalty in Transition: Theory, Policy, Practice and Reform* (New York: Columbia University Press, 2015), 276.

of both victims and defendants, often with the help of professional protesters.[160] Great pressure is brought to bear on courts, sometimes in favor of the death penalty and at others for a more lenient sentence.[161] If public opinion is mobilized after a sentence has been delivered, then the court may be pressured to change its decision.[162] Judicial populism does not necessarily result in compliance with the law. On the contrary, it may lead to a kind of mob justice, where the emotion of the online crowd of the moment can literally make the difference between life and death.[163]

Chinese judges and courts feel vulnerable to public opinion and threats of protest because they lack independence.[164] It is extremely difficult for courts to defy public opinion.[165] The influence of public opinion on judicial decisions is graphically illustrated by a murder case stemming from a road rage incident in 2006. The judge conducted a public opinion poll among the classmates of the defendant, a student at a music conservatory, to determine if the court should sentence him to death. The classmates' vote in favor of a life sentence enraged netizens, who conducted their own poll and voted overwhelmingly in favor of the death penalty. The court then imposed the death sentence on the defendant, who was executed immediately.[166]

The influence of public opinion on Chinese courts is channeled through the CCP when the latter realizes that a case may have a "large social impact," leading to public protests and challenges to the CCP's authority. The CCP may then give instructions to the courts to decide the case in a certain way, it has happened that the instructions were

[160] Belkin, "Justice," 219.

[161] Fu Hualing, "Between Deference and Defiance," 278.

[162] Benjamin Liebman, "A Populist Threat to China's Courts?" in Margaret Y.K. Woo and Mary E. Gallagher (eds.), *Chinese Justice: Civil Dispute Resolution in Contemporary China* (New York: Cambridge University Press, 2011), 294; Lin Feng, *The Future of Judicial Independence in China*, Center for Judicial Education and Research, City University of Hong Kong, Working Paper Series, No. 2 (2016), 19, http://www.cityu.edu.hk/cjer/lib/doc/paper/WK2_The_Future_of_Judicial_Independence_in_China.pdf, accessed 1 July 2020.

[163] Belkin, "Justice," 196.

[164] Fu Hualing, "Between Deference and Defiance," 275.

[165] Ibid., 284, 289.

[166] Belkin, "Justice," 195.

given even before the trial began.[167] In compliance with CCP policy, the SPC President instructed courts in April 2008 to consider, among other factors, people's feelings in deciding whether the death sentence should be imposed.[168] In February 2010, an SPC notice on sentencing in criminal cases instructed courts to consider, among other factors, if the handling of the case would win the broad support of the masses, preserve social stability, and diminish social protest. In considering severity or leniency, courts had to take into account whether the reaction of the masses was particularly strong.[169] The policy of listening to people's feelings was part of the CCP's broader effort to prioritize social stability above all.[170] In conformity with this policy, the SPC has instructed middle-level courts to change sentences.[171] In one instance, the SPC took the unprecedented step of reviewing a case on its own and ordered the immediate execution of the defendant, in line with public demand.[172]

Belkin believes that under Xi Jinping the policy of "judicial populism" has been in practice rejected.[173] Whether or not this is the case, the parallels between the conduct of victims and their supporters at the domestic level and China's litigation strategy in the *South China Sea Arbitration* are uncanny. China considered itself to be the victim—of the Philippines, the US, and the Tribunal. As such, it considered itself authorized to mobilize on its behalf international public opinion, represented by States not parties to the dispute. The unanimous Award on Jurisdiction was dismissed as null and void by the putative victim, who saw itself as the judge in its own case. The letters that China continued to send to the Tribunal long after the Tribunal had ruled that it had jurisdiction, reiterating its position that the Tribunal lacked jurisdiction, may be compared to the petitions that families of victims send to courts to protest against their decisions. Like the families of victims and their supporters, China actively sought to mobilize support for its position. The "professional protesters" were Chinese diplomats and journalists. What was important

[167] Ibid., 188, 202; Fu Hualing, "Between Deference and Defiance," 188.

[168] Qianfan Zhang, "Judicial Reform," 24.

[169] Belkin, "Justice," 211.

[170] Ibid., 197.

[171] Qianfan Zhang, "Judicial Reform," 23.

[172] Belkin, "Justice," 195.

[173] Ibid., 224.

for the victim was the number of States that supported it. One could almost say that China was conducting an opinion poll in order to bolster its position. The difference, of course, was that at the international level, there was no CCP or SPC to instruct the Arbitral Tribunal to listen to China's feelings and the Tribunal did not feel vulnerable to the opinion of China or that of its supporters. As a solitary Chinese scholar admitted, the members of the Tribunal were legal experts who highly valued their independence. Hence, China was not in a position to influence their judgment on jurisdiction or to persuade them to change it.[174]

Not content with its strategy of undermining the Tribunal's independence, and perhaps considering its failure, China at the same time sought to impugn the impartiality of the appointing authority, the judges, and the Tribunal.

III. The Defaulting State and the Impartiality of the Appointing Authority, the Judges, and the Tribunal in the *South China Sea Arbitration*

The ideal of impartiality is indissociably linked with that of independence in the Universal Declaration of Human Rights of 1948, which proclaimed the right of everyone "in full equality to a fair and public hearing by an independent and impartial tribunal, in the determination of his [sic] rights and obligations and of any criminal charges against him [sic]." International judges emphasize that impartiality is defined in relation to issues.[175]

According to Sir Hersch Lauterpacht, impartiality is a function of human will and of the individual sense of moral duty and enlightened interest.[176] Judge Malenovský, a former member of the European Court

[174] Xue Li, "How China Views the South China Sea Arbitration Case," *The Diplomat*, 14 July 2015, http://thediplomat.com/2015/07/how-china-views-the-south-china-sea-arbitration-case/, accessed 30 June 2020.

[175] Malenovský, "L'indépendance," 29.

[176] Hersch Lauterpacht, *The Function of Law in The International Community* (Oxford: Oxford University Press, 2011), 211.

of Human Rights ("ECtHR") defined impartiality as the absence of prejudice or conceived bias when rendering judgments.[177] States profess adherence to the ideal of impartial international judges. At the same time, they justify their reluctance to submit their disputes to international judicial settlement by claiming that impartiality is difficult, if not impossible, to achieve. At a meeting in April 1907 of the US National Arbitration and Peace Congress, US Secretary of State Elihu Root declared that"[t]he great obstacle to universal adoption of arbitration is not the unwillingness of civilized nations to submit their disputes to the decision of an impartial tribunal, it is rather the apprehension that the tribunal selected will not be impartial."[178] Writing in the 1930s, the future ICJ judge Hersch Lauterpacht agreed that "the problem of the impartiality of the international judge is the Cape Horn of international judicial settlement."[179]

Impartiality is not specifically mentioned in the Statutes of the PCIJ, the ICJ, and the ITLOS. The first two mandate that their members are to be of "high moral character;"[180] the last requires that its members enjoy "the highest reputation for fairness and integrity."[181] Similarly, members of arbitral tribunals constituted under Annex VII of the Convention, whether or not they are drawn from the list maintained by the UN Secretary-General under Article 2(1) of Annex VII, must enjoy "the

[177] Malenovský, "L'indépendance," 29.

[178] Quoted by James Brown Scott, at the Ninth Meeting of the First Subcommission of the First Commission, 1 August 1907, in Scott (ed.), *The Proceedings*, vol. II, 315. It was not Root himself who made the statement at the Hague Peace Conference, contrary to the assertion of Edward Gordon, "The Independence and Impartiality of International Judges," *Proceedings of the Annual Meeting (American Society of International Law)* 83 (1989): 509.

[179] Hersch Lauterpacht, *The Function of Law in The International Community* (Oxford: Oxford University Press, 1933), 202, https://ia601603.us.archive.org/31/items/in.ernet.dli.2015.459090/2015.459090.The-Function-Of-Law-In-The-International-Community.pdf, accessed 3 July 2020. The quotation is on 211 of the 2011 reprint. Cape Horn is "a rocky headland on an island at the extreme S [southern] tip of South America, belonging to Chile. It is notorious for gales and heavy seas; until the building of the Panama Canal, it lay on the only sea route between the Atlantic and the Pacific." *Collins English Dictionary*, https://www.collinsdictionary.com/dictionary/english/cape-horn, accessed 4 June 2020.

[180] PCIJ, *Statute*, Article 2, in *Statute and Rules of Court*, 2; ICJ, *Statute*, Article 2.

[181] *ITLOS Statute*, Article 2(1).

highest reputation for fairness, competence and integrity."[182] The ideal of impartiality is enshrined in the solemn declarations that international judges must make upon assuming office, under the terms of which they will exercise their powers and duties "honorably and faithfully, impartially and conscientiously,"[183] or "honourably, faithfully, impartially and conscientiously."[184] It has also become the practice for members of Annex VII arbitral tribunals for which the PCA serves as a Registry to make declarations of independence and impartiality, notwithstanding the fact that this is not a requirement of Annex VII.[185] The arbitrator declares that he/she is impartial with respect to each of the parties and intends to remain so. In one variant of the declaration, he/she declares that there are no facts, past or present, that need to be disclosed because they are likely to give rise to justifiable doubts as to his/her impartiality and independence. In the second variant, the arbitrator declares "past and present professional, business and other relationships with the parties and...any other relevant circumstances," and affirms that those circumstances do not affect his/her independence and impartiality. He/she undertakes to "promptly notify the parties and the other arbitrators of any such further relationships or circumstances that may subsequently come to his/her attention during the arbitration."[186]

The conduct of States and their representatives sometimes creates the impression that it is the impartiality of international judges, rather than

[182] *Annex VII*, Article 2(1); *Chagos Marine Protected Area* Arbitration, Reasoned Decision, 24–25, para. 135.

[183] PCIJ, *Rules of Court*, Article 5, in *Statute and Rules of Court*, 35, https://www.icj-cij.org/files/permanent-court-of-international-justice/serie_D/D_01.pdf, accessed 3 July 2020.

[184] ICJ, *Rules of Court, adopted on 14 April 1978 and entered into force on 1 July 1978*, Article 4(1), https://www.icj-cij.org/en/rules, accessed 22 March 2020; ITLOS, *Rules of the Tribunal (ITLOS/8), as adopted on 28 October 1997 and amended on 15 March 2001, 21 September 2001, 17 March 2009 and 25 September 2018*, Article 5(1), 4, https://www.itlos.org/fileadmin/itlos/documents/basic_texts/Itlos_8_E_25.09.18.pdf, accessed 7 November 2019.

[185] *Chagos Marine Protected Area Arbitration*, Reasoned Decision, 25, para. 136.

[186] PCA, *Arbitration Rules 2012*, 23, https://pca-cpa.org/wp-content/uploads/sites/6/2015/11/PCA-Arbitration-Rules-2012.pdf, accessed 5 July 2020.

partiality, that they fear.[187] The fear of impartiality degenerated into violence at the Iran–US Claims Tribunal ("IUSCT"), which had been established in 1980 to settle US claims against Iran as part of the settlement for the liberation of US hostages in Teheran. In 1982, Iran filed a complaint against a judge of Swedish nationality, Nils Mangard, with the IUSCT appointing authority, Judge Charles M.J.A. Moons, a former Chief Justice of the Netherlands Supreme Court, alleging that Judge Mangard had made statements against executions in Iran. Western reports suggest that the real reason for Iran's complaint was Iran's belief that as a neutral judge of the IUSCT, Mangard was responsible for awarding substantial compensation to US companies.[188] The Iranian challenge was dismissed for failing to provide a sufficiently clear description of the circumstances on which the accusation was based or even the date on which the event that was the basis of the accusation took place.[189] In September 1984, two months following the award of $50 million plus interest to a US company, two Iranian judges of the IUSCT grabbed Judge Mangard's necktie, twisted and shook him, prodded him on the back, and shoved him toward the door of the IUSCT premises; one issued a death threat in the event Judge Mangard returned to the Tribunal.[190] The two Iranian judges refused to apologize for their behavior. The US subsequently filed a challenge to the continued service of the two judges, a challenge that Iran accepted.[191]

Fortunately, in the *South China Sea Arbitration*, China confined itself to verbal assaults against the appointing authority, individual judges, and the Tribunal. But verbal assaults they were, for one is bound to conclude that China's charges of partiality are mendacious, whether one

[187] Richard Falk, "The Independence and Impartiality of International Judges," *Proceedings of the Annual Meeting (American Society of International Law)* 83 (1989): 516.

[188] William Drozdiak, "Hostilities Threaten Future of Tribunal on U.S.-Iran Claims," *Washington Post*, 3 October 1984, https://www.washingtonpost.com/archive/politics/1984/10/03/hostilities-threaten-future-of-tribunal-on-us-iran-claims/ef19e86d-8548-4bb7-9692-41454253cb71/, accessed 3 July 2020.

[189] Rahmatullah Khan, *The Iran-United States Claims Tribunal—Controversies, Cases and Contribution* (Dordrecht: Martinus Nijhoff Publishers, 1990), 69–70.

[190] Drozdiak, "Hostilities.".

[191] Charles N. Brower, "The Iran-United States Claims Tribunal," *RCADI*, vol. 224 (1990-V), 165.

considers the charges of partiality directed at the appointing authority and individual judges, or those aimed at the Tribunal as a whole.

A. The Impartiality of the Appointing Authority and of Individual Judges in the **South China Sea Arbitration**

One common academic approach to assessing the impartiality of an international judge examines his/her voting record in cases in which his/her State of nationality is a party. In this approach, great significance is attached to a judge's vote against the interest of the State of which he/she is a national.[192] Judge Manfred Lachs, who was a member of the ICJ from 1967 to 1993 and its President from 1973 to 1976, contends that it is a gross simplification to identify a judge's views on a legal issue with his nationality.[193] However, a series of statistical studies carried out over the years suggests otherwise.[194] A 2005 study covering 76 cases from 1946 to 2004 found that ICJ judges vote with their State of nationality approximately 85–90 percent of the time when their State is a party to a case.[195] Another study published in 2005, covering the years 1949–2000, found that 70 percent of the time, judges elected for a fixed term (as opposed to judges ad hoc) voted with their State of nationality when the latter was a party to the case. In what might be seen as a favorable development, by the end of the period, approximately 24 percent of the votes were cast against the State of nationality.[196] The limitations of this approach are obvious if the State of the nationality of the judge has never been party to a dispute submitted before the ICJ.

[192] Zile, "A Soviet Contribution," 387; Manfred Lachs, "A Few Thoughts on the Independence of Judges of the International Court of Justice," *Columbia Journal of Transnational Law* 25 (1987): 596.

[193] Lachs, "A Few Thoughts," 595.

[194] William Samore, "National Origins v. Impartial Decisions: A Study of World Court Holdings," *Chicago-Kent Law Review* 34 (1956):193–221, http://scholarship.kentlaw.iit.edu/cgi/viewcontent.cgi?article=1859&context=cklawreview, accessed 13 December 2019; Thomas R. Hensley, "National Bias and the International Court of Justice," *Midwest Journal of Political Science* 12 (1968): 568–86; Il Ro Suh, "Voting Behavior of National Judges in International Courts," *AJIL* 63 (1969): 224–36.

[195] Eric A. Posner and Miguel F. P. de Figueiredo, "Is the International Court of Justice Biased?" *Journal of Legal Studies* 34: (2005): 615.

[196] Smith, "'Judicial Nationalism'," 218.

Interesting as these studies might be, international courts have eschewed an approach to determining the impartiality of their members that focuses exclusively on nationality. It is the approaches that courts themselves have adopted that will be the focus of the following discussion. Once we have a clear understanding of the way in which international courts ascertain the impartiality of international judges, it becomes an easy matter to assess the impartiality of the appointing authority and of individual judges in the *South China Sea Arbitration*.

1. The Scope of the Impartiality of International Judges and Arbitrators

Impartiality is normally understood to mean the absence of prejudice or bias.[197] There are two distinct approaches to the assessment of a judge's impartiality derived from the statutes and case law of international courts: the subjective approach, which aims to determine the personal convictions of a judge in a given case, and the objective approach, which seeks to determine whether a judge offers guarantees sufficient to exclude any legitimate doubt in this respect.[198] The first approach seeks proof of actual bias; the second focuses on the appearance of bias.[199]

The subjective approach is that adopted by the ICJ and other international courts, such as the ITLOS, whose provisions on this matter have been strongly influenced by those of the ICJ Statute. The latter stipulates that

> [n]o member may participate in the decision of any case in which he [sic] has previously taken part as agent, counsel, or advocate for one of the parties, or as a member of a national or international court, or of a commission of enquiry, or in any other capacity.[200]

[197] *The Prosecutor v. Anto Furundžija, Judgment, International Criminal Tribunal for the Former Yugoslavia, Appeals Chamber*, Case No. IT–95–17/1-A (21 July 2000), 55, para. 181, http://www.icty.org/x/cases/furundzija/acjug/en/fur-aj000721e.pdf, accessed 6 July 2020.

[198] Ibid.

[199] Ibid., 55, para. 179.

[200] ICJ, *Statute*, Article 17(2); ITLOS, *Statute*, Article 8(1): No member of the Tribunal may participate in the decision of any case in which he [sic] has previously taken part as agent, counsel or advocate for one of the parties, or as a member of a national or international court or tribunal, or in any other capacity.

Should a judge consider that "for some special reason," he/she should not take part in the decision of a case, he/she recuses himself.[201] It should be noted that the nationality of a judge does not constitute a reason for prohibiting a judge from participating in the decision of any case. Self-recusals have become quite common among judges who have served as legal advisers to a party in a case or members of international commissions of inquiry that have dealt with matters related to a case.[202] If a judge who is a national of a party does not recuse himself/herself, the solution adopted by the ICJ Statute is to authorize the party without a judge having its nationality to appoint a judge ad hoc. Alternatively, under the Rules of Court, a party to a case may write confidentially to the ICJ President to bring to the attention of the Court facts unknown to it that may affect a judge's impartiality.[203]

In conformity with the Rules of Court, Israel wrote to the Court in 2003 in the proceedings relating to the UN General Assembly request for an advisory opinion on the legal consequences of the construction of a wall in the Occupied Palestinian Territory. Israel challenged the judge of Egyptian nationality, Judge El-Araby, on the basis of his active, official, and public role as an advocate for the Palestinian cause (e.g., as Egyptian delegate to the UN General Assembly Emergency Session that formulated the request for an advisory opinion) and of an interview that he gave to an Egyptian newspaper in August 2001. The Court dismissed the challenge, on the grounds that Judge El-Araby could not be regarded as having previously taken part in the case in any capacity. He had performed his activities in his capacity as an official representative of Egypt, he had ceased to participate in the UN General Assembly Special Session when

[201] ICJ, *Statute*, Article 24(1).

[202] Chiara Giorgetti, "The Challenge and Recusal of Judges at the International Court of Justice," in Chiara Giorgetti (ed.), *Challenges and Recusals of Judges and Arbitrators in International Courts and Tribunals* (Leiden: Brill, 2015), 17–25.

[203] ICJ, *Rules of Court*, Article 34(2). Karl Doehring believes that it does not make sense that a party may only bring to the ICJ's attention facts that are unknown to the latter and that a party may only do so confidentially. Karl Doehring, "Zur Befangenheit internationaler Richter [On the Partiality of International Judges]," in Nisuke Ando et al., *Liber Amicorum Judge Shigeru Oda*, vol. I (The Hague: Kluwer Law International, 2002), 27.

the request for an advisory opinion was formulated, and he had not expressed any opinion on the question put in the case in the interview.[204]

The subjective approach was also adopted by the Arbitral Tribunal in its Reasoned Decision to the challenge raised by Mauritius to the arbitrator appointed by the UK in the *Chagos Marine Protected Area Arbitration*. Mauritius had justified its challenge by referring to the arbitrator's long-standing and close professional relationship with the UK, as counsel of the UK in a great number of cases before national and international courts and as a member of a board that selected the legal adviser of the UK's FCO.[205] The Tribunal agreed with the UK that the standard to be applied in determining the independence and impartiality of the challenged arbitrator was Annex VII of the Convention, specifically the requirements that arbitrators enjoy the highest reputations for fairness, independence, and integrity and that they should not be in the service of any of the parties.[206] Annex VII was to be supplemented by the law and practice of international courts and tribunals in inter-State cases, particularly the ICJ, the ITLOS, and Annex VII arbitral tribunals.[207] The *Chagos* Tribunal stressed the fact that Judge Greenwood had not been involved in the dispute before his appointment as arbitrator.[208] The ICJ's conditions concerning the activities of judges led the *Chagos* Tribunal to conclude that Judge Greenwood's record of frequent service as counsel to the UK did not give rise to justifiable doubts as to his independence and impartiality.[209] His participation in the selection of the FCO Legal Adviser was restricted to that purpose, was limited to brief participation in the selection panel, did not involve advice on legal issues, and thus neither constituted or continued an already existing relationship.[210] In passing the *Chagos* Tribunal noted that no judge had ever been successfully challenged on the grounds that he/she had held senior government positions

[204] *Legal Consequences of the Construction of a Wall in the Occupied Palestinian Territory, Order of 30 January 2004, I.CJ. Reports 2004*, 4–5, paras. 2, 4, 8, http://www.icj-cij.org/files/case-related/131/131-20040130-ORD-01-00-BI.pdf, accessed 6 July 2020.

[205] *Chagos Marine Protected Area Arbitration*, Reasoned Decision, 13, para. 71.

[206] Ibid., 6, 8, 10, 11, paras. 39, 47–48, 58, 63.

[207] Ibid., 30, paras. 165, 167, 169.

[208] Ibid., 32, para. 172.

[209] Ibid., 32, para. 173.

[210] Ibid., 34, para, 183.

or had acted as counsel before being elected as a judge or nominated as arbitrator.[211]

The subjective approach, which searches for actual bias, runs up against the difficulty of ascertaining the mental state of an individual.[212] It cannot be excluded that a judge who has not participated previously in a case will still lack impartiality, evidence of which may be found in views that he/she has expressed or positions that he/she has taken. These may create the impression that he/she has prejudged one or more of the issues in the dispute before a court.[213] The objective approach to determining the impartiality of a judge requires that the judge is not only genuinely impartial but also appears to be impartial.[214] The objective approach is embodied in Rule 28(2) of the ECtHR, which adds to previous participation in a case a comprehensive list of circumstances that may create the appearance of bias on the part of a judge:

a. he or she has a personal interest in the case, including a spousal, parental or other close family, personal or professional relationship, or a subordinate relationship, with any of the parties;
b. he or she has previously acted in the case, whether as the Agent, advocate or adviser of a party or of a person having an interest in the case, or as a member of another national or international tribunal or commission of inquiry, or in any other capacity;
c. he or she, being an ad hoc judge or a former elected judge continuing to sit by virtue of Rule 26 § 3, engages in any political or administrative activity or any professional activity which is incompatible with his or her independence or impartiality;
d. he or she has expressed opinions publicly, through the communications media, in writing, through his or her public actions or otherwise, that are objectively capable of adversely affecting his or her impartiality;

[211] Ibid., 32, para. 174.

[212] Dannenbaum, "Nationality," 117.

[213] *Legal Consequences*, *Order*, Dissenting Opinion of Judge Buergenthal, 9, para. 11, https://www.icj-cij.org/files/case-related/131/131-20040130-ORD-01-01-BI.pdf, accessed 6 July 2020; Yuval Shany and Sigall Horovitz, "Judicial Independence in The Hague and Freetown: A Tale of Two Cities," *Leiden Journal of International Law* 21 (2008): 115, 126.

[214] *The Prosecutor v. Anto Furundžija*, 56, para. 182.

e. for any other reason, his or her independence or impartiality may legitimately be called into doubt.[215]

Similar provisions govern the disqualification of judges at the International Criminal Court ("ICC"). Like the ICJ Statute, the Rome Statute of the ICC expressly provides that "[a] judge shall not participate in any case in which his or her impartiality might reasonably be doubted on any ground."[216] It provides that a judge is prohibited from participating in the hearing of a case if he/she "has previously been involved in any capacity in that case before the Court or in a related criminal case at the national level involving the person being investigated or prosecuted."[217] Like the ECtHR, the Rome Statute also makes provision for additional grounds for disqualification, which are laid down in the ICC Rules of Procedure and Evidence:

(a) Personal interest in the case, including a spousal, parental or other close family, personal or professional relationship, or a subordinate relationship, with any of the parties;
(b) Involvement, in his or her private capacity, in any legal proceedings initiated prior to his or her involvement in the case, or initiated by him or her subsequently, in which the person being investigated or prosecuted was or is an opposing party;
(c) Performance of functions, prior to taking office, during which he or she could be expected to have formed an opinion on the case in question, on the parties or on their legal representatives that, objectively, could adversely affect the required impartiality of the person concerned;

[215] European Court of Human Rights, Registry of the Court, *Rules of Court* (Strasburg: European Court of Human Rights, Registry of the Court 2019), 15, https://www.echr.coe.int/Documents/Rules_Court_ENG.pdf, accessed 1 May 2020.

[216] International Criminal Court ("ICC"), *Rome Statute of the International Criminal Court*, Article 42(2) (a), (The Hague: ICC, 2011), 27, https://www.icc-cpi.int/nr/rdonlyres/add16852-aee9-4757-abe7-9cdc7cf02886/283503/romestatuteng1.pdf, accessed 5 July 2020.

[217] Ibid.

(d) Expression of opinions, through the communications media, in writing or in public actions, that, objectively, could adversely affect the required impartiality of the person concerned.[218]

The objective approach was the basis for assessing the impartiality of a judge undertaken by the International Criminal Tribunal for the Former Yugoslavia ("ICTY") and the Special Court for Sierra Leone ("SCSL"). At the ICTY, the Appeals Chamber had to decide whether to disqualify Judge Florence Mumba, who had presided over a trial chamber that had found Anto Furundžija guilty of aiding and abetting in outrages upon personal dignity, including rape, on the grounds of her former involvement as a representative of Zambia in the UN Commission on the Status of Women ("UNCSW").[219] When Judge Mumba was a member of the UNCSW, it had condemned mass and systematic rape in the former Yugoslavia and urged the ICTY to give them priority by prosecuting those allegedly responsible.[220] Without alleging actual bias, Furundžija argued that the appearance had been created that Judge Mumba had sat in judgment in a case that "could advance and did in fact advance the legal and political agenda that she helped to create" while she was an UNSCW member.[221]

The Appeals Chamber found that there was a general rule that a judge should not only be subjectively free from bias but also that there should be nothing in the surrounding circumstances that objectively gives rise to the appearance of bias. It adopted a two-pronged approach. First, a judge is not impartial if it is shown that actual bias exists. Second, there is an unacceptable appearance of bias if:

i. a Judge is a party to the case, or has a financial or proprietary interest in the outcome of a case, or if the Judge's decision will

[218] ICC, *Rules of Procedure and Evidence*, Rule 34(1), 13, ICC Doc. 10ICC-ASP/1/3 (2002), https://www.icc-cpi.int/iccdocs/pids/legal-texts/rulesprocedureevidenceeng.pdf, accessed 5 July 2020.

[219] International Criminal Tribunal for the Former Yugoslavia ("ICTY"), *Furundžija Case: The Judgement of the Trial Chamber. Anto Furundzija Found Guilty on Both Charges and Sentenced to 10 Years in Prison*, ICTY Doc. JL/PIU/372-E (10 December 1998), http://www.icty.org/en/sid/7609, accessed 6 July 2020.

[220] *The Prosecutor v. Anto Furundžija*, 50, para. 160.

[221] Ibid., 51–52, para. 169.

lead to the promotion of a cause in which he or she is involved, together with one of the parties. Under these circumstances, a Judge's disqualification from the case is automatic; or

ii. the circumstances would lead a reasonable observer, properly informed, to reasonably apprehend bias.[222]

As actual bias was not alleged, the Appeals Chamber examined whether Judge Mumba's membership in the UNCSW would lead a reasonable and informed observer to apprehend bias.[223] The Appeals Chamber pointed out that a presumption of impartiality, recognized in the ICTY caselaw and in municipal law, attaches to judges.[224] In the absence of evidence to the contrary, it must be assumed that judges can "disabuse their minds of any irrelevant personal beliefs or disposition." The threshold to reach in order to rebut the presumption of impartiality is high.[225] The Appeals Chamber ruled that Judge Mumba, as a UNCSW member, acted as a representative of her State and therefore served in an official capacity. She was subject to the instruction and control of her government. When she spoke at the UNCSW, she spoke on behalf of her State.[226] Even if she had expressly shared UNCSW goals and objectives, the inclination was of a general nature and was to be distinguished from the inclination to implement them in a particular case.[227]

At the SCSL, a motion for disqualification of Justice Robertson was filed in February 2004 by Issa Hassan Sesay on the basis of Robertson's previous writings, rather than his previous activities. The SCSL was established in 2002 following a request to the UN in 2000 by Sierra Leone for a "special court" to try serious crimes against civilians and UN peacekeepers committed during the country's civil war (1991–2002). The Special Court's Prosecutor was empowered to bring charges for war crimes, crimes against humanity, other serious violations of international humanitarian law, and certain serious violations

[222] Ibid., 58, para. 189.

[223] Ibid., 60, para. 195.

[224] Ibid., 60, para. 196.

[225] Ibid., 60, para. 197.

[226] Ibid., 61, para. 199.

[227] Ibid., 61, para. 200.

of Sierra Leonean law.[228] Issa Hassan Sesay was a senior officer and Commander in the Revolutionary United Front ("RUF"), the Armed Forces Revolutionary Council ("AFRC") and their joint forces called the Junta, operating within Sierra Leone from 1993 to 2003. During this period, the RUF and the AFRC, acting in concert with Sesay or under his orders, allegedly carried out armed attacks against civilian population as well as humanitarian assistance personnel and UN peacekeepers throughout Sierra Leone. These raids, designed to terrorize the civilian population, consisted of unlawful killings, physical and sexual violence, looting of property, abductions of girls and women for sexual slavery, and enforced recruitment of child soldiers.[229] Sesay's motion for disqualification alleged that Justice Robertson had expressed the clearest and most grave bias against both the RUF and the AFRC and thereby displayed a lack of impartiality against him and other members of these groups. Alternatively, Sesay alleged that the comments and opinions expressed in Robertson's book *Crimes against Humanity: the Struggle for Global Justice* (2002) objectively gave rise to an appearance of bias.[230] The Prosecutor conceded that there were valid arguments for an appearance of bias on the part of Justice Robertson; his opinions and comments could lead a reasonable observer, properly informed, to apprehend bias.[231] The Appeals Chamber agreed that "a reasonable man" [sic] would apprehend bias and disqualified Justice Robertson from adjudicating on cases involving RUF members before the Appeals Chamber.[232]

The objective approach to determining the potential bias of a judge, particularly that resulting from past declarations, has been examined in some depth by Mégret and Brubaker. As mentioned in the previous Chapter, in Mégret's conception, a judge, like an expert, is impartial when he/she lacks prior emotional attachment to a case and has no personal

[228] *Special Court for Sierra Leone and Residual Special Court for Sierra Leone* (2020), http://www.rscsl.org/, accessed 6 July 2020.

[229] Hague Justice Portal, "Sesay, Issa Hassan," *haguejusticeportal.net* (2016), http://www.haguejusticeportal.net/index.php?id=8320, accessed 6 July 2020.

[230] *Prosecutor v. Isa Hassan Sesay. Decision on Defence Motion Seeking the Disqualification of Justice Robertson from the Appeals Chamber* [2004] SCSL 1 (13 March 2004), 2, paras. 1–2, https://sierralii.org/sl/judgment/special-court/2004/1-0, accessed 6 July 2020.

[231] Ibid., 6, para. 7.

[232] Ibid., 8, para. 18.

interest in the case. A judge is also impartial when he/she approaches a case free of obvious ethnic, racial, and religious biases. Finally, a judge is impartial when he/she has the ability to approach issues with a fresh mind.[233] The question that interested Mégret was the extent to which the past declarations of a judge demonstrate bias. He identified four factors or conditions that have to be taken into account to determine a lack of impartiality. First, the judge must have actually expressed a view on the matter. One cannot attribute views to him/her merely on the basis of religion, ethnic or national origins, gender, age, class, means, or sexual orientation. This is exactly what the US did in the *Nicaragua Case*, when it implied that two ICJ members could not be trusted with sensitive intelligence information on conflicts in Central America simply because they were nationals of Warsaw Pact member States. In response to the US allegation, Judge Lachs, a Polish national who was an ICJ member from 1967 to 1993 and was one of the two judges alluded to, had objected that it was unseemly to doubt a judge on account of the place where he was born or his passport.[234] Second, the form taken by the opinion and the forum in which it is expressed should be considered. An opinion expressed in an academic symposium is likely to be more strongly held than one expressed in a chat show and could become a source of bias. Third, the substance of the previous opinion is crucial. There must be a clear connection between that opinion and the issue in the case. The opinion may create a psychological incentive not to contradict oneself or it may lead others to find it difficult to believe that he/she is impartial. Fourth, the context should also be taken into consideration, as words can be taken out of context. The context may be further analyzed in terms of a series of dichotomies: unrelated/related, general/specific, old/recent, relative/absolute, consensual/polemical, legal/factual, official/personal capacity, expert/activist, and private/public. The second element of each dichotomy affords some presumption that the opinion expressed in the past declaration is strongly held and may be a source of bias.[235]

[233] Frédéric Mégret, "International Judges and Experts' Impartiality and the Problem of Past Declarations," *LPICT* 10 (2011): 33.

[234] *Military and Paramilitary Activities in and against Nicaragua (Nicaragua v. United States of America), Merits, Judgment*, Separate Opinion of Judge Lachs, *I.C.J. Reports 1986*, 160, http://www.icj-cij.org/files/case-related/70/070-19860627-JUD-01-02-BI.pdf, accessed 5 July 2020.

[235] Mégret, "International Judges," 48–66.

Brubaker examines the factors that have to be analyzed if we are to determine whether issue conflicts—between the prior opinions or commitments of a judge and issue(s) raised in a dispute—can create the appearance of bias on the part of a judge. Opinions expressed as a State representative, expert, academic, or member of an advocacy group may create such issue conflicts.[236] In his view, the three crucial factors in the analysis are the proximity, depth, and timing of the opinion. The appearance of bias is greater when a prior legal or factual opinion is closely related to an issue in dispute, when the personal involvement in the issue is greater in terms of duration and responsibility, and when the opinion has been formed in recent years.[237]

Whether we apply the academic, subjective, or objective approaches to the appointing authority and the judges in the *South China Sea Arbitration*, the conclusion is inescapable that they were impartial.

2. The Assessment of the Impartiality of the Appointing Authority and of the Judges in the South China Sea Arbitration

It should be reiterated here that the appointing authority is brought into the picture only because his impartiality was questioned by China. As has already been indicated several times, his role in the proceedings was not judicial, but purely ministerial; the fact that he happened to be a judge is immaterial. That having been said, the following paragraphs will first employ the three approaches to assess the impartiality of the appointing authority and then proceed with a comparable examination of the members of the *South China Sea* Tribunal. Despite the fact that it is eschewed by international courts, the academic approach will be applied, because it yields interesting information. This will be followed by an assessment of impartiality based on the subjective and objective approaches. All three approaches confirm the impartiality of the appointing authority and of the five members of the Arbitral Tribunal.

It is possible to apply the academic approach to assess the impartiality of the appointing authority, for he was a judge in a case in which his State of nationality was a party. As an ITLOS member, he participated in the hearing of a case filed by Japan on 6 July 2007 for the prompt

[236] Joseph R. Brubaker, "The Judge Who Knew Too Much: Issue Conflicts in International Adjudication," *Berkeley Journal of International Law* 26 (2008): 112.

[237] Ibid., 135–40.

release of a Japanese vessel, the *Tomimaru*, detained by Russia for alleged infringement of national fisheries legislation in its Exclusive Economic Zone ("EEZ"). Japan alleged that Russia had not complied with Article 73(2) of the Convention concerning the prompt release of a vessel upon the posting of a reasonable bond or other financial security. The vessel had been confiscated by a decision of the Petropavlovsk-Kamchatskii City Court on 28 December 2006; the decision was upheld by the Kamchatka District Court on 6 January 2007. Russia informed the ITLOS that the Russian Supreme Court had dismissed the complaint concerning the confiscation of the vessel and argued that the confiscation rendered Japan's application without object. The reason was that Article 292(3) of the Convention authorized the ITLOS to deal only with the question of release, without prejudice to the merits of the case before a domestic court against the vessel, its owner, or its crew. Russia pointed out that the case had been considered by domestic courts on the merits, a decision had entered into force, and the decision had been executed. The ITLOS decided unanimously, i.e., with the concurring vote of Judge Yanai, that the Russian courts' decision to confiscate the vessel eliminated the provisional character of the detention of the vessel, rendering the procedure for prompt release without object.[238] Judge Yanai not only agreed with the other ITLOS judges that Japan's application for prompt release no longer had any object. He also issued a separate declaration in which he criticized Japan for waiting too long before filing its application with the ITLOS. The vessel had been boarded and inspected by Russian authorities on 31 October 2006 in the Russian EEZ and detained thereafter, but it was not until 6 July 2007 that Japan had filed its application with the ITLOS.[239] In short, Judge Yanai voted against the State of which he was a national.

The application of the subjective approach adopted by the ICJ and the *Chagos* Tribunal also leads to the conclusion that Judge Yanai is impartial. He had never been involved in any capacity in the dispute prior to

[238] ITLOS, *Tribunal Delivers Judgment in Case No 15. Tribunal Finds that the Application in the Tomimaru Case Is without Object*, ITLOS Doc. ITLOS/Press 113 (6 August 2007), https://www.itlos.org/fileadmin/itlos/documents/press_releases_english/PR_113_E.pdf, accessed 7 July 2020.

[239] *"Tomimaru" (Japan v. Russian Federation), Prompt Release, Judgment*, Declaration of Judge Yanai, *ITLOS Reports 2005–2007*, 102, para. 2, https://www.itlos.org/fileadmin/itlos/documents/cases/case_no_15/15_judgment_060807_dec_Yanai_en.pdf, accessed 7 July 2020.

his election to the ITLOS, whether as agent, counsel, or member of a national or international commission of inquiry. He had never given the Philippines (or China) legal advice, nor had he ever been in any other way in the service of the Philippines (or China).

The application of the objective approach, which stresses the need to avoid the appearance of bias, does not yield a different conclusion. The appointing authority had no personal interest in the outcome of the case or expressed any opinions publicly that could adversely affect his impartiality. China and Chinese scholars derive unjustified conclusions from the fact that the appointing authority was a national of Japan who had played an "important role in helping [Japanese Prime Minister] Shinzo Abe with the lifting of the ban on collective self-defense and challenging the international order after World War II" and was a former ambassador to the US.[240] Some Chinese writers contended that in view of Japan's dispute with China over the Diaoyu Islands/Senkaku Islands, Yanai was not able to maintain an "objective and just attitude."[241]

Regardless of the nationality or of the position formerly occupied by the appointing authority in the State of which he is a national, the fact remains that he had not expressed any opinions in previous writings on the South China Sea dispute. Judge Yanai's role in the formulation of Japan's foreign policy and the existence of a territorial dispute between Japan and China are not relevant considerations, as they are unrelated to the South China Sea disputes. Even were we to grant that there existed some such relation—of which China gave no proof—he should be assumed to have acted in an official capacity and his acts should be attributed to his government rather than to himself. Any acts that he carried out in an official capacity cannot constitute evidence to rebut the presumption of impartiality that attaches to an international judge, which was emphasized by the ICTY Appeals Chamber in the *Furundžija Case*. As Mégret pointed out, it is simply not permissible to attribute an opinion to a judge solely on the basis of national origins. To impugn the impartiality of a judge because of past declarations, one must prove that such declarations had actually been made. China, the CSIL, and Chinese

[240] Foreign Ministry, *Veil*.

[241] Xinhua, "Ad hocism;" Xinhua, "Spotlight: Unmasking the Ragtag South China Sea Arbitral Tribunal," *Global Times*, 18 July 2016, http://www.globaltimes.cn/content/994907.shtml, accessed 7 July 2020.

scholars have simply failed to provide evidence that Judge Yanai had made any declarations pertinent to the *South China Sea Arbitration*.

In passing, it is worth noting that China's reaction to the appointment of arbitrators by the appointing authority compares unfavorably with that of Russia to the same acts by the same appointing authority in the *"Arctic Sunrise" Arbitration*. Following Russia's refusal to appoint its arbitrator and a request from the Netherlands, the then ITLOS President, Judge Yanai, nominated the second arbitrator, and subsequently, the three remaining arbitrators. There appears to be no record of any criticism on the part of Russia regarding the constitution of the Tribunal or the role of the ITLOS President as appointing authority. Russia did not at any time invoke Russia's territorial dispute with Japan going back to 1945 over the islands occupied by Russia as the successor State of the former USSR, in order to call into question the ITLOS President's appointment of arbitrators. Despite Russia's default, Russia probably understood that Judge Yanai as ITLOS President was merely performing an institutional function.[242]

Turning now to the members of the Tribunal, the academic approach may be of some value in assessing the impartiality of three of them. Judge Mensah, the President of the Tribunal, has been a judge in two cases in which his State of nationality, Ghana, was a party. He was judge ad hoc, appointed by Ghana, in the *"ARA Libertad"* case filed by Argentina with the ITLOS. In October 2012, Ghana had prevented the departure of the Argentine warship frigate *ARA Libertad* from the port of Tema, pursuant to a decision of the High Court of Accra.[243] Argentina requested that the ITLOS prescribe a provisional measure ordering Ghana to authorize the departure of the vessel from Tema.[244] Ghana submitted that the ITLOS should reject Argentina's request and that Argentina should be ordered to pay all the costs incurred by Ghana in connection

242 Chinese scholars have failed to note this difference in conduct. See Jun Zhao and Jiang Li, "The *Arctic Sunrise* Case and Its Implications for China," in Shicun Wu and Keyuan Zou (eds.), *Arbitration concerning the South China Sea. Philippines versus China* (London: Routledge 2016), 105–25.

243 ITLOS, *Tribunal Orders Release of Argentine Frigate ARA Libertad*, ITLOS Doc. ITLOS/Press 188 (15 December 2012), https://www.itlos.org/fileadmin/itlos/documents/press_releases_english/PR_188_E.pdf, accessed 8 July 2020.

244 *"ARA Libertad" (Argentina v. Ghana)*, *Final Submissions of Argentina* (30 November 2012), https://www.itlos.org/fileadmin/itlos/documents/cases/case_no.20/C20_final_subs_Ghana.pdf, accessed 8 July 2020.

with the request.[245] Judge Mensah joined all the other members of the ITLOS in ordering that Ghana authorize the departure of the Argentine warship and that each party should bear its costs.[246] Subsequently, Judge Mensah was appointed in 2014 by Ghana to be an ad hoc member of a Special Chamber of ITLOS created to delimit its maritime boundary with the Côte d'Ivoire in the Atlantic Ocean.[247] One of Ghana's submissions was that a tacit agreement existed between the two States to delimit their territorial sea, EEZ, and continental shelf both within and beyond 200 nautical miles.[248] Judge Mensah voted with the Special Chamber's four other members to dismiss this submission of Ghana. In his separate opinion, he explained that Ghana had not met the high standard of proof required to prove that a tacit agreement existed between the two States. Ghana had been unable to show that there was anything in the oil practice of the parties, in bilateral exchanges or negotiations, or in their submissions to the Commission on the Limits of the Continental Shelf ("CLCS") that would constitute compelling proof that there was in fact a tacit agreement between the two States on their maritime boundary.[249]

Judge Soons has also been a judge in arbitral proceedings involving the State of which he is a national, the Netherlands. In the *"Arctic Sunrise" Arbitration*, one of the Dutch requests was that Russia be ordered to pay compensation for, among others, expenses incurred by the Netherlands relating to a vessel survey report, an accountants' report fee, and the costs of procuring the Audited Claims Statement by the accountants.[250] Judge Soons agreed with the Tribunal's four other members that these claims

[245] Ibid., *Final Submissions of the Republic of Ghana* (30 November 2012), https://www.itlos.org/fileadmin/itlos/documents/cases/case_no.20/C20_final_subs_Ghana.pdf, accessed 8 July 2020.

[246] *"ARA Libertad" (Argentina v. Ghana), Provisional Measures, Order of 15 December 2012, ITLOS Reports 2012*, 350, para. 8, https://www.itlos.org/fileadmin/itlos/documents/cases/case_no.20/published/C20_Order_151212.pdf, accessed 8 July 2020.

[247] *Delimitation of the Maritime Boundary in the Atlantic Ocean (Ghana/Côte d'Ivoire), Judgment, ITLOS Reports 2017*, 9, para. 4, https://www.itlos.org/fileadmin/itlos/documents/cases/case_no.23_merits/C23_Judgment_20170923.pdf, accessed 8 July 2020.

[248] Ibid., 34, para. 102.

[249] Ibid., Separate Opinion of Judge ad hoc Mensah, 1, para. 4.

[250] *"Arctic Sunrise" Arbitration (Netherlands v. Russia)*, Notification and Statement of Claim dated 4 October 2013, 5, para. 14, https://pcacases.com/web/sendAttach/1314, accessed 10 March 2020.

arose from the *Arbitration* itself and that the Netherlands should bear them.[251]

Like Judges Mensah and Soons, Judge Cot has participated in the decision of a case involving the State of which he is a national. He was appointed by France as a judge ad hoc in the proceedings filed against it by Belize with the ITLOS in 2001 for the prompt release of the fishing vessel *Grand Prince*, flying the flag of Belize. The vessel, accused of illegal fishing in the EEZ of the Kerguelen Islands in the French Southern and Antarctic Territories, had been arrested by the French authorities on 26 December 2000. Belize maintained that the bond set by France for the release of the vessel was not reasonable and that the vessel should be released upon the posting of a bond or other security in a much smaller amount.[252] France denied that the ITLOS had jurisdiction to hear the case, because a French court had already issued a judgment on the merits ordering the confiscation of the vessel. Therefore, it was no longer possible to initiate a prompt release proceeding before the ITLOS.[253] The majority of the ITLOS, which included Judge Cot, decided that it lacked jurisdiction to hear the case, but not for the reason that France had advanced. While France had not questioned that Belize was the flag State of the vessel, the ITLOS had decided to examine the issue *proprio motu*, and it came to the conclusion that Belize was not the flag State of the vessel when the proceedings were initiated. It was for this reason that the ITLOS lacked jurisdiction. Judge Cot voted with the majority on this point.[254]

If one goes back in time, one finds that Judge Cot has not hesitated to go on record as opposing French legal positions. In the *Nuclear Tests Cases*, France had asserted that the dispute with Australia and New

[251] *"Arctic Sunrise" Arbitration*, Award on the Merits, 99, para. 401 K.

[252] ITLOS, *Application Filed on Behalf of Belize against France for Release of Arrested Fishing Vessel*, ITLOS Doc. ITLOS/Press 46 (21 March 2001), https://www.itlos.org/fileadmin/itlos/documents/press_releases_english/press_release_46_en.pdf, accessed 8 July 2020.

[253] *"Grand Prince" (Belize v. France), Prompt Release, Judgment*, *ITLOS Reports 2001*, 35, para. 57, https://www.itlos.org/fileadmin/itlos/documents/cases/case_no_8/published/C8-J-20_apr_01.pdf, accessed 8 July 2020.

[254] Ibid., 38–44, paras. 66–92. For a commentary, see Caroline Laly-Chevalier, "Activité du Tribunal international du droit de la mer (2001–2002) [The Activities of the International Tribunal for the Law of the Sea]," *AFDI* 48 (2002): 362–67, https://www.persee.fr/docAsPDF/afdi_0066-3085_2002_num_48_1_3706.pdf, accessed 8 July 2020.

Zealand concerning French atmospheric nuclear tests in the Pacific was a political, not a legal, dispute; that the French decision not to appear in the proceedings was the most clear-cut and honorable choice; that the circumstances compelled France to conclude that it could no longer trust the ICJ to declare that it had no jurisdiction in the cases excluded by France in its declaration of acceptance of the ICJ's compulsory jurisdiction; and that by withdrawing that declaration, France had resigned itself to modifying its relations with the ICJ, but that the reason was that the ICJ itself had changed.[255] Professor Cot (as he was then) took issue with each and every one of these claims, He argued that the distinction between legal and political disputes was highly questionable; that French non-participation in the proceedings seriously weakened the principle of international justice, which France had traditionally supported; that French non-participation amounted to taunting the international judge; and that France had demonstrated contempt for the ICJ throughout the entire proceedings, leaving a bitter taste in the mouth.[256]

Judge Wolfrum has not been a member of any international court to which a case involving his State of nationality, Germany, has been submitted. However, he was appointed by Mauritius as a member of the Arbitral Tribunal in the *Chagos Marine Protected Area Arbitration*. Yet he voted with the three other arbitrators to dismiss the challenge raised by Mauritius to the independence and impartiality of the arbitrator appointed by the UK.[257] The academic approach is of no assistance in assessing the impartiality of Judge Pawłak, who has not (yet) had the occasion to participate in the decision of a case involving his State of nationality.

Application of the subjective approach, which seeks evidence of actual bias, fails to yield evidence of partiality on the part of all of the members of

[255] Guy de Lacharrière, "Commentaires sur la position juridique de la France à l'égard de la licéité de ses expériences nucléaires [Commentaries on the Legal Position of France with respect to the Legality of Its Nuclear Tests]," *AFDI* 19 (1973): 235–51, http://www.persee.fr/doc/afdi_0066-3085_1973_num_19_1_2212, accessed 23 July 2019.

[256] Jean-Pierre Cot, "Affaire des Essais nucléaires (Australie c. France et Nouvelle-Zélande c. France). Demandes en indication de mesures conservatoires. Ordonnances du 22 juin 1973 [The Nuclear Tests Case (Australia v. France and New-Zealand v. France. Requests for the Indication of Provisional Measures. Orders of 22 June 1973]," *AFDI* 19 (1973): 252–71, https://www.persee.fr/docAsPDF/afdi_0066-3085_1973_num_19_1_2213.pdf, accessed 1 April 2020.

[257] *Chagos Marine Protected Area* Arbitration, Reasoned Decision, 35.

the Tribunal. None had ever been involved in any capacity in the dispute prior to their appointment to the Tribunal, whether as agent, counsel, or member of a national or international commission of inquiry. None had ever given the Philippines (or China) legal advice or had ever been in any other way in the service of the Philippines (or China). Without such evidence, Chinese writers' assertion that the judges were "tilted toward the Philippines"[258] would never be accepted by an international court.

It is possible to apply the objective approach to verify the CSIL's allegation of bias on the part of two arbitrators, Judge Jean-Pierre Cot and Professor Alfred A.H. Soons, who were accused of agreeing in the Award on Jurisdiction to positions that were allegedly inconsistent with their past views that the status and entitlement of maritime features, on the one hand, and maritime delimitation, on the other, are integral and inseparable. The opinion in question of Judge Cot, published in 2011, stated that the definition of legal entitlement and maritime delimitation, distinct as they are, are interrelated. The opinions of Professor Soons, published in 1990 and 2011, stated that the definition of rocks within the meaning of Article 121(3) of the Convention and their entitlement form an inherent part of maritime delimitation between opposite or adjacent States and that the issue of the application of Article 121(3) does not arise in practice unless in the context of maritime delimitation, often intertwined with disputes over sovereignty.[259] China had argued in its Position Paper that the Tribunal had no jurisdiction to determine the status of maritime features as low-tide elevations, rocks, or islands. From China's perspective, determination of the status of maritime features was inseparable from maritime delimitation, which China had excluded from the jurisdiction of any court or tribunal constituted under Part XV of the Convention. In the Award on Jurisdiction, the Tribunal ruled, contrary to China's position, that it indeed had jurisdiction over the Philippine submission. The CSIL accused the two arbitrators of "stealthily" switching their positions to endorse the view that the status and entitlement of maritime

[258] Xinhua, "Arbitral Tribunal on South China Sea Illegal, Ridiculous," *Global Times*, 8 July 2016, http://www.globaltimes.cn/content/993110.shtml, accessed 16 March 2020. One Chinese scholar has been brave enough to admit that he did not question the impartiality of the appointing authority. Xinjun Zhang, "Bifurcation in Inter-State Cases," *University of Pennsylvania Journal of International Law* 40 (2019): 980, https://scholarship.law.upenn.edu/cgi/viewcontent.cgi?article=1991&context=jil, accessed 7 July 2020.

[259] CSIL, "The South China Sea Arbitration Awards," 629, para. 423.

features can be addressed separately from maritime delimitation and for not providing an explanation for their reversal of position.[260]

The charge that the two arbitrators had not explained their alleged change of position is misleading. Since the Award on Jurisdiction was adopted unanimously. the explanation for any alleged change of position is found in the Award itself. On page 61, paragraph 155, the Tribunal agreed with China "that maritime delimitation is an integral and systemic process." The Tribunal then went on to point out that disputes over issues that arise in the process of maritime delimitation, such as "equitable solution," "special circumstances" in respect of the territorial sea, and relevant circumstances in relation to the EEZ and/or the continental shelf, may exist in a context that is different from that of maritime delimitation. The fact that a dispute exists over any one of these issues does not automatically transform the issue into a dispute over maritime delimitation itself: "It does not follow that a dispute over an issue that may be considered in the course of maritime delimitation constitutes a dispute over maritime delimitation itself." This explanation is entirely compatible with the two judges' expressed positions.

Turning now to the alleged change in position, assuming for the sake of argument that the positions expressed in past writings were interpreted properly, a correct understanding of the way in which past declarations may create bias or the appearance of bias will lead to the conclusion that any change of position was a sign of impartiality. As Mégret persuasively argues, past declarations may adversely affect impartiality and create the appearance of bias if they prevent a judge from approaching an issue with an open mind and being receptive to new perspectives and arguments. In this context, the positions imputed to the two judges would have given the Philippines—not China—grounds to perceive the appearance of bias, to the extent that the past declarations of the two judges might have predisposed them to ignore Philippine arguments and evidence. Even assuming that there had been a change in position—an assumption that the explanation in the Award disproves — the acceptance of the idea that the status of maritime features could be determined without undertaking maritime delimitation is a sign that the two judges had indeed approached the issue with an open mind, instead of adhering rigidly

260 Ibid.

to past declarations in the face of fresh arguments and evidence to the contrary.

It cannot be excluded that China sensed that the ground on which its accusations of bias against the appointing authority and the judges stood was weak, or it may have been simply motivated by a desire to implement a comprehensive litigation strategy, Whatever the reason, China also attacked the impartiality of the Tribunal as a whole.

B. The Impartiality of the Tribunal in the South China Sea Arbitration

China's unprecedented attacks on the impartiality of the Tribunal as a whole were made publicly by no less than a Vice-Minister of Foreign Affairs, who at the time was also a member of the PCA.[261] He alleged that the Tribunal rendered an award largely favorable to the Philippine claims in exchange for monetary consideration:

> Who supported the Arbitral Tribunal? The arbitrators are paid by certain parties, but who? Maybe by the Philippines or other countries. This system is completely different from the ICJ or the ITLOS. Judges of the ICJ or the ITLOS receive salaries from the UN for the sake of independence and impartiality. But these five judges of the Arbitral Tribunal are doing it for a profit, and their payments come from the Philippines and probably others, too. We are unsure about the details but they do provide paid services.[262]

The Chinese press put it more crudely, saying that the arbitrators made "much money out of the arbitration." It was recognized that in

[261] A member of the PCA, who is appointed by a party to the Hague Convention of 1899 or the Hague Convention of 1907 and not elected by all parties, forms part of a list of arbitrators from which parties to the two Hague Conventions may select arbitrators in the event they wish to settle a dispute by arbitration. In theory, States parties to either of the two Hague Conventions who are encountering difficulties in identifying arbitrators could decide to choose the Vice Foreign Minister in question, Liu Zhenmin, who was appointed by China, as a member of an arbitral tribunal. PCA, *Members of the Court* (2021), https://pca-cpa.org/en/about/structure/members-of-the-court/, accessed 23 July 2021.

[262] Foreign Ministry, *Veil*. The text of the interview has been removed from the website of China's Foreign Ministry. For the benefit of those who may not have had the opportunity to read it before the website was scrubbed, it is attached to this Chapter as Annex 5.1.

arbitration, the parties normally pay equal shares of the expenses of the proceedings. But since China refused to pay its share, the Philippines, in order to enable the proceedings to continue, was said to have been "generous" enough to offer to pay for China, and the Arbitral Tribunal was said to have "gladly" accepted the money. It was alleged that the Tribunal reciprocated the Philippine "nice gesture" by giving it a favorable ruling.[263]

China's claim that financial interest was the motivation for the Tribunal's adverse rulings against it, implying that the judges were bribed, is so grave that one American writer deemed it tantamount to "defamation"[264] and another equated it with slander.[265] This claim was not a momentary lapse, for it was repeated by Chinese scholars in scholarly publications.[266] We would be remiss if we ignored it. The allegation of corruption against the members of the Arbitral Tribunal is a deliberate and willful misunderstanding of arbitration and a manifestation of the reality of judicial corruption in China.

1. A Deliberate and Willful Misunderstanding of Arbitration

China's "character assassination"[267] of the entire Tribunal in the *South China Sea Arbitration* deliberately ignores the fundamental difference between the workings of a permanent international tribunal, such as the ICJ or the ITLOS, and those of an ad hoc arbitral tribunal. The kind of evidence that would be necessary to prove corruption may be gleaned from the only known case of corruption of arbitrators in the two-hundred year-history of modern arbitration. This evidence China is unable to provide, for the simple reason that it is non-existent.

[263] Fei Liena and Han Mo, "Commentary: Puppet Tribunal;" Xinhua, "Ad hocism.".

[264] Jerome Cohen, "South China Sea Ruling and Defamation," *jeromecohen.net*, 20 July 2016, http://www.jeromecohen.net/jerrys-blog/2016/7/20/south-china-sea-ruling-and-defamation, accessed 9 July 2020.

[265] Julian Ku, "China's Vice-Minister for Foreign Affairs Casually Slanders the South China Sea Arbitral Tribunal," *opiniojuris.org*, 26 July 2016, http://opiniojuris.org/2016/07/26/chinas-vice-minister-for-foreign-affairs-casually-slanders-the-south-china-sea-arbitral-tribunal/, accessed 9 July 2020.

[266] Sienho Yee, "The South China Sea Arbitration Decisions," 224.

[267] Ku, "China's Vice-Minister.".

In proceedings before a permanent international court and an ad hoc arbitral tribunal, each party naturally pays its own expenses. A great advantage of the recourse to a permanent international tribunal such as the ICJ, as a former ICJ President reminds us, is that the costs of operation of the Court, including the services of the Registry and the salaries of the staff, are all free, being paid for out of the UN budget.[268] In the case of an arbitral tribunal, which is established by the two parties to the dispute for the sole purpose of resolving a particular dispute, it is an established principle that each party pays an equal share of the expenses of the tribunal.

The major arbitration treaties of the modern period contain without exception a provision to this effect. Article VIII of the 1794 Treaty of Amity, Commerce, and Navigation (The Jay Treaty) between the US and Great Britain provided that

> [t]he Commissioners...shall be respectively paid in such manner, as shall be agreed between the two parties, such agreement being to be settled [sic] at the Time of the exchange of the Ratifications of this Treaty. And all other Expences [sic] attending the said Commissions shall be defrayed jointly by the two Parties...[269]

Similarly, the 1871 Treaty of Washington that organized the *Alabama Arbitration* provided in its Article VIII that

> [e]ach Government shall pay its own Agent and provide for the proper remuneration of the counsel employed by it, and of the Arbitrator appointed by it, and for the expense of preparing and submitting its case to the Tribunal. All other expenses connected with the arbitration shall be defrayed by the two Governments in equal moieties.[270]

The principle was incorporated in Article 57 of the Hague Convention of 1899 and in Article 85 of the Hague Convention of 1907, to both of

[268] Sir Robert Jennings, "The Difference between Conducting a Case in the ICJ and in an Ad Hoc Arbitration Tribunal: An Inside View," in Nisuke Ando et al., *Liber Amicorum Judge Shigeru Oda*, vol. II (The Hague: Kluwer Law International, 2002), 908.

[269] *Treaty of Amity, Commerce, and Navigation (Jay Treaty).*

[270] *Treaty between Her Majesty and the United States of America.* "Moiety" is an archaic term meaning "half," from Old French "moitié," half. *Collins English Dictionary* (Glasgow: HarperCollins Publishers, 2020), https://www.collinsdictionary.com/dictionary/english/moiety, accessed 12 October 2020.

which China is a party. Article 7 of Annex VII of the Convention merely reaffirms this principle:

> Unless the arbitral tribunal decides otherwise because of the particular circumstances of the case, the expenses of the tribunal, including the remuneration of its members, shall be borne by the parties to the dispute in equal shares.

This provision applies to all arbitrations under Annex VII of the Convention. It is carried over into Article 13(1) of the Rules of Procedure of the *South China Sea Arbitration*.

The earlier treaties, which were concluded at a time when it was assumed that the parties had agreed to the arbitration and would participate in the proceedings, did not contain provisions for one of the two parties shouldering the responsibility for part of all of the other party's share of the expenses. The introduction of arbitration and conciliation as compulsory modes of dispute settlement for the interpretation and application of an increasing number of multilateral treaties from the late 1970s onwards now created the possibility that one of the parties to a dispute would deny that it had given its consent to arbitration or conciliation and would default. Beginning with the second arbitration under Annex VII of the Convention, the Rules of Procedure of arbitral tribunals provided for such an eventuality:

> If the requested deposits are not paid in full within sixty days after the receipt of the request, the Arbitral Tribunal shall so inform the Parties in order that one or another of them may make the required payment. If such payment is not made, the Arbitral Tribunal may order the suspension or termination of the proceedings.[271]

The Rules of Procedure of subsequent Annex VII arbitrations all contained similar language, the main difference being the length of the

[271] *MOX Plant Case*, Rules of Procedure, Article 18(3), 7.

period specified (30 days or 60 days).[272] The period provided for in the *South China Sea Arbitration* was 45 days.

It is obvious from the preceding discussion that the reason the Philippines paid for the two parties' expenses is the same as the reason for the appointment by the ITLOS President of four arbitrators: China's default. The Netherlands found itself in the same situation when Russia defaulted in the *"Arctic Sunrise" Arbitration*. It is remarkable that Russia, in its critique of the Award on the Merits, refrained from attributing the Tribunal's decision, which found Russia in breach of the Convention, to motives of cupidity on the part of the arbitrators.[273] Russia's silence is all the more noteworthy in that the Award on the Merits, upon the request of the Netherlands, ordered Russia "immediately to reimburse the Netherlands the amounts of Russia's share of the deposits paid by the Netherlands" and reiterated that despite Russia's default, "the fees and expenses of the Tribunal incurred to date shall be borne by the Parties in equal shares."[274]

The Philippines and China could have avoided the obligation to shoulder the expenses of the Arbitral Tribunal if they had recognized under Article 287(1) of the Convention the jurisdiction of either the ICJ or the ITLOS, both permanent tribunals, for the settlement of their disputes concerning the interpretation and application of the Convention. The Philippines has recognized the ICJ's compulsory jurisdiction under Article 36(2) of the ICJ Statute, but China has not.[275] Had the Philippines filed an application with the ICJ, the latter would have dismissed it, for lack of jurisdiction. Another way of submitting the dispute to the

[272] *Guyana v. Suriname*, Rules of Procedure (24 February 2004), Article 18(2), 8, http://www.pcacases.com/web/sendAttach/882, accessed 11 May 2020; *Barbados v. Trinidad and Tobago*, Rules of Procedure (16 February 2004), Article 19(3), 8, https://pcacases.com/web/sendAttach/1062, accessed 11 May 2020; *Bay of Bengal Maritime Boundary Arbitration between Bangladesh and India*, Rules of Procedure (8 October 2009), Article 21(3), 12, http://www.pcacases.com/web/sendAttach/375, accessed 11 May 2020; *Chagos Marine Protected Area Arbitration*, Rules of Procedure, Article 20(3), 9; *The ARA Libertad Arbitration*, Rules of Procedure (31 July 2013), Article 28(3), 12; *The Atlanto-Scandian Herring Arbitration*, Rules of Procedure (15 March 2014), Article 28(3), 13; *"Arctic Sunrise" Arbitration*, Rules of Procedure, Article 33(3), 14.

[273] Interfax, "Russian Foreign Ministry.".

[274] *"Arctic Sunrise" Arbitration*, Award on the Merits, 99, paras. 401(I) and 401(J).

[275] ICJ, *Declarations Recognizing the Jurisdiction of the Court as Compulsory: Philippines (18 January 1972)*, https://www.icj-cij.org/en/declarations/ph, accessed 12 July 2020.

ICJ or to the ITLOS would have been through a special agreement for this purpose. China would surely have refused to conclude such a special agreement. Without a declaration under Article 287(1) of the Convention or a special agreement, arbitration under Annex VII of the Convention is deemed to be the mode of dispute settlement that both have accepted under Article 283(3) of the Convention.

Arbitration under Annex VII carries with it the obligation to assume responsibility for the Tribunal's expenses and a risk for one of the parties that the other would refuse to pay its share. Following China's default, the proceedings could have continued only if the appearing party—the Philippines—had agreed to pay both parties' share of the Tribunal's expenses. Sienho Yee believes that a way should have been found to avoid allowing one party to pay the whole cost of the proceedings. He implied that for the demarcation of the border between Iraq and Kuwait, the UN Security Council paid for Iraq's share of the cost when the latter withdrew from the proceedings.[276] Unfortunately, Sienho Yee provides no evidence for his assertion, nor is there any record of the UN Security Council taking responsibility for Iraq's share of the costs in the demarcation.[277] Assuming for the sake of argument that Sienho Yee is right, this act of the Security Council's could be explained by the peculiar circumstances in which the demarcation took place. Demarcation was an integral part of the settlement of the crisis triggered by the Iraqi invasion of Kuwait in August 1990 and was imposed on Iraq by the UN Security Council. No comparable circumstance existed in Sino-Philippine relations. One might add that there seems to be no instance in the history of inter-State arbitration in which a third party intervened, following the default of one of the parties, to pay the share of the defaulting State's share of the Tribunal's expenses.

Had China intended its accusation against the entire Tribunal to be taken seriously, it would have made efforts to uncover evidence of the type found by the US Congress in the only proven instance of corruption of

[276] Sienho Yee, "The South China Sea Arbitration Decisions," 224.

[277] Hussein Hassouna, "The Kuwait-Iraq Border Problem," in Joseph A. Kechichian (ed.), *Iran, Iraq, and the Arab Gulf States* (New York: Palgrave-Macmillan, 2001), 237–61; Maurice Mendelson and Susan Hulton, "Les décisions de la Commission de démarcation de la frontière entre l'Iraq et le Koweït [The Decisions of the Commission to Demarcate the Border between Iraq and Kuwait]," *AFDI* 39 (1993): 178–231, http://www.persee.fr/doc/afdi_0066-3085_1993_num_39_1_3127, accessed 12 July 2020.

an arbitrator in the modern history of arbitration. This instance occurred in the context of the US-Venezuela Mixed Commission, established by a treaty of 25 April 1866 to settle US claims against Venezuela.[278] The Commission, which sat between August 1867 and August 1868, decided 49 claims, for a nominal amount of $4,823,273.31, and made awards on 24 claims, worth $1,253,31,030. In February 1869, Venezuela protested against the awards, alleging irregularity in the appointment of the umpire and fraud in the proceedings and findings. Initially the US government refused to give credence to the protests of Venezuela and forced it to pay.

Subsequently, a US Congressional investigation between 1875 and 1877 did uncover evidence to support Venezuela's allegations. The name of the umpire, who under the terms of the Treaty was nominated by the Russian minister in Washington, D.C., following the parties' failure to reach an agreement, was in fact the result of a conspiracy that aimed to defraud the claimants by exacting from them a large proportion of their awards in the form of attorney's fees. The conspirators were the umpire, the US Minister in Caracas, the member of the Commission appointed by the US, and the latter's brother-in-law. The last obtained contracts with claimants to represent them before the Commission in exchange for 40 to 60 percent of the award. Certificates of award were made in small amounts and payable to the bearer, so as to pass without endorsement. The US member of the Commission, as joint attorney of his brother-in-law and of the claimants, withdrew the certificates from the Commission. After the claimants had received the certificates representing their share of the award, the rest was divided between the four conspirators. The US finally recognized in 1883 that the alleged commission was a conspiracy, that the proceedings were tainted with fraud, and that there had been no valid Commission as called for by the 1866 Treaty. The solution adopted by the US and Venezuela was to appoint a new Commission to hear US citizens' claims.[279]

China has failed to provide anything remotely resembling evidence to support its denunciations of the Tribunal's impartiality, and indeed China could not provide it, for the simple reason that there is no such evidence. China's allegation rests solely on the fact that the Philippines shouldered

[278] Lauterpacht, *The Function*, 211.

[279] Moore, *History and Digest*, vol. II, 1659–64, https://archive.org/details/historyanddiges08moorgoog/page/n5/mode/2up, accessed 12 July 2020.

all of the costs of the arbitral proceedings. China's denunciations rest on a deliberate and willful misunderstanding of the operation of arbitration; more than anything else, they are a manifestation of the reality of judicial corruption in China.

2. A Manifestation of Judicial Corruption in China

China's totally unfounded allegation of judicial corruption in the *South China Sea Arbitration* reflects the reality of judicial corruption in China. It is a clumsy attempt to graft onto international arbitration a phenomenon that has never been a problem in its modern history.

China's charge that the Tribunal made decisions in favor of the Philippines in exchange for financial consideration makes sense coming from a State where judicial corruption is proteiform, pervasive, institutionalized, and collective. Certainly, an allegation of this kind would make sense to Chinese citizens and lawyers. Ordinary citizens' perceptions of judicial corruption range from the belief that a significant proportion of judges is highly corrupt to the total loss of faith in judges.[280] Chinese lawyers also expect judges to be corrupt.[281] The expectation is born of several main features of judicial corruption in China, which may be described as follows, without any claim to being exhaustive.

First, judicial corruption takes many forms, of which participation in bribery and fraud is only one. It also includes accepting gifts or hospitality from the parties and having improper associations with lawyers, according to SPC rules adopted in 2009.[282] Transparency International identified the following forms of judicial corruption: fabricating rulings in exchange for money; blackmailing litigants into paying for, or excluding, evidence; extorting kickbacks from intermediaries for passing cases to certain judges; trading law enforcement services for personal gain; taking bribes from the plaintiff and defendant (or their lawyers), or both;

[280] Yuwen Li, *The Judicial System*, 86.

[281] At a meeting with Chinese lawyers at Fudan University in Shanghai, an American lawyer was asked how judges were bribed in the US. Jim Zirin, "Question from China: How Do American Lawyers Bribe U.S. Judges?" *forbes.com*, 10 November 2014, https://www.forbes.com/sites/jameszirin/2014/11/10/question-from-china-how-do-american-lawyers-bribe-u-s-judges/#eb31fe8160c7, accessed 12 July 2020. Judges suspected of partiality are the object of public wrath, which has on occasion culminated in the murder of judges. Ling Li, "The 'Production'," 849.

[282] Yuwen Li, *The Judicial System*, 84.

manufacturing court cases; embezzling court funding; bowing to the demands of local officials, criminal networks, local clans, social networks, or economic interests; and abusing the power of judges to order suspension of business operations, the confiscation of property, the eviction of tenants, or fair compensation and labor rights.[283]

Second, judicial corruption takes place at all levels, not excluding the highest levels of the judiciary. Over the years there has been a steady stream of cases involving high court officials in the midst of repeated anti-corruption campaigns. For example, in 2007–2008, the presidents of Higher People's Courts in four provinces were jailed for graft and economic crime.[284] In 2010 a former SPC Vice President, Huang Songyou, was sentenced to life imprisonment for taking RMB 3.9 million in bribes from a law firm in return for favorable rulings on cases between 2005 and 2009 and for embezzling RMB 1.2 million in State funds when he was the president of a city-level court in Southern Guangdong Province in 1997.[285] In the same year, the former Procurator General of Shanghai, Chen Xu, was also sentenced to life imprisonment for accepting money and property worth more than $10.68 million in personal gifts or through family members, orchestrating favorable contracts, and helping beneficiaries to evade prosecution.[286] More recently, a former SPC Vice President, Xi Xiaoming, was jailed for life for accepting RMB 115 million ($16.78 million) in bribes, for breaching confidentiality rules, and for leaking secrets related to judicial work. It may or may not be ironic that Xi Xiaoming, a CCP member for 40 years and fourth ranking member in

[283] Keith Henderson, "The Rule of Law and Judicial Corruption in China: Halfway over the Great Wall," in Transparency International, *Global Corruption Report 2007. Corruption in Judicial Systems* (New York: Cambridge University Press, 2007), 155, https://images.transparencycdn.org/images/2007_GCR_EN.pdf, accessed 13 July 2020.

[284] Willy Lam, "The Politicisation," 137.

[285] Associated Press, "China Jails Former Top Judge for Corruption in Beijing," *The Guardian*, 19 January 2010, https://www.theguardian.com/world/2010/jan/19/china-supreme-court-judge-jailed, accessed 13 July 2020.

[286] Lucy Papachristou, "Jailed Shanghai Prosecutor Implicates 100 Officials in Corruption," *Organized Crime and Corruption Reporting Project*, 12 November 2018, https://www.occrp.org/en/27-ccwatch/cc-watch-briefs/8891-jailed-shanghai-prosecutor-implicates-100-officials-in-corruption, accessed 4 February 2020.

the SPC hierarchy, had been specialized within the SPC in economic law cases.[287]

Third, judicial corruption is institutionalized. It is not attributable to a few bad apples who can be removed by periodic anti-corruption campaigns. It is a phenomenon inherent in the structure of the Chinese judiciary.[288] As explained in Part II of this Chapter, in each court, the court party group, consisting of CCP members, is the highest decision-making body.[289] They are not judges, yet they give instructions to court leaders, who in turn relay them to the frontline judges. The instructions specify the outcome, are devoid of legal reasoning and justification, and must be complied with unconditionally. This mechanism allows party leaders to dictate judgments in cases in which they have a personal or financial interest. The leader judges—presidents, vice presidents, and divisional directors and vice-directors—assign tasks, and monitor, approve and evaluate the work of subordinates. Drafts of judgments prepared by the judges responsible for hearing cases must be approved by the court leaders, who do not necessarily hear the cases. The division of labor allows corrupt leader judges to control the outcome of a much greater number of cases of personal interest to them than they could manage if they were required to participate fully in the entire course of the process. The leader judges give instructions to judges, which often disregard facts or the law but must nevertheless be complied with unconditionally. The frontline judges carry out the judicial functions at the lowest level. As they provide the information that is the basis of decisions by leader judges, the frontline judges acquire some de facto power in cases that are not sufficiently significant to attract the leaders' full attention or that involve groups with low or no political power. The frontline judges, who engage in decision-making on a daily basis, have many opportunities for corruption. Corruption at the lower levels is generally tolerated unless it is exposed by the media and generates public unrest. Some frontline judges engage their superiors in corrupt deals to ensure protection.

[287] Ben Blanchard, "China Jails Former Senior Judge for Life in Graft Case," *reuters.com*, 16 February 2017, https://www.reuters.com/article/us-china-corruption-court/china-jails-former-senior-judge-for-life-in-graft-case-idUSKBN15V10W, accessed 12 July 2020.

[288] Ling Li, "The 'Production'," 850; Ting Gong, "Dependent Judiciary," 51.

[289] The following discussion is based on Ling Li, "The 'Production'," 855–64.

This brings us to the fourth characteristic of judicial corruption in China—it is increasingly becoming a collective enterprise. In response to anti-corruption campaigns, judges forge alliances with each other, with the result that groups of judges collaborate in corrupt activities.[290] It is significant that the former Shanghai Procurator sentenced to life implicated some 100 officials linked to his corruption case.[291] The collective character of the enterprise makes it that much more difficult to detect and expose corruption. Paradoxically, it is competition for enormous profits between groups of corrupt judges that may lead to the exposure of weaker groups.[292]

China's slander of the Arbitral Tribunal assumes that international arbitration is plagued by the same problem of judicial corruption as the Chinese judicial system. Nothing could be further from the truth. In his book published nearly a century ago, Sir Hersch Lauterpacht observed that the question of the integrity and probity of arbitrators and judges had long ceased to occupy writers' minds.[293] The question had attracted some attention in the second half of the nineteenth century, in the context of the validity of arbitral awards and appeals from awards. At the time, corruption was discussed only because authors had nothing better to discuss ("*faute de mieux*," lit. "for want of anything better"), obligatory and permanent arbitration being unknown. The possibility of corruption was only discussed by the IDI as a ground for invalidity of awards. In 1874, draft regulations for international arbitral procedure submitted to the IDI had contained a provision stipulating that "the award is void in case of void compromise or exceeding of powers, or of corruption proved against one of the arbitrators."[294] This provision was incorporated without modification in a draft Russian code of arbitral procedure

[290] Ibid., 865–66.

[291] Papachristou, "Jailed Shanghai Prosecutor."

[292] Ling Li, "The 'Production'," 865–66.

[293] Lauterpacht, *The Function*, 211.

[294] *Annuaire de l'Institut de droit international. Première année* [Yearbook of the Institute of International Law. First Year] (Gand: Bureau de la Revue de droit international, 1877), 133, https://ia802606.us.archive.org/15/items/annuairedelinst20lawgoog/annuairedelinst20lawgoog.pdf, accessed 12 July 2020.

submitted to the 1899 Hague Peace Conference.[295] Neither at IDI meetings nor at the Hague Peace Conference was any actual case of corruption ever cited. As Borel pointed out nearly a century ago, the "extreme care" with which the responsibilities of an arbitrator are entrusted to persons presenting all guarantees of moral authority and qualifications made the eventuality of corruption "infinitely improbable."[296]

One cannot say as much of Chinese judges and the Chinese judicial system. China's accusation of bias resulting from corruption on the part of the entire tribunal in the *South China Sea Arbitration* is a more accurate reflection of the condition of the accuser than that of the accused.

Annex 5.1

Veil of the Arbitral Tribunal Must Be Tore [Sic] Down [Sic]

–Vice Foreign Minister Liu Zhenmin Answers Journalists' Questions on the So-Called Binding Force of the Award Rendered by the Arbitral Tribunal of the South China Sea Arbitration Case 2016/07/13.

China Central Television (CCTV): After the arbitration results were issued, some countries stated that "the arbitration award is valid and has binding force on both parties." If China does not execute the award, they will regard it as a "violation of the international law and damage to the international reputation." What is China's view on that?

Vice Foreign Minister Liu Zhenmin: As for whether the arbitration award has the binding force, the Chinese government and the Ministry

[295] *Draft of Arbitral Code Produced by the Russian Delegation*, Article 26, in James Brown Scott (ed.). *The Proceedings of The Hague Peace Conferences. Translation of the Official Texts. The Conference of 1899* (New York: Oxford University Press, 1920), 183, https://ia802604.us.archive.org/18/items/proceedingshagu02scotgoog/proceedingshagu02scotgoog.pdf, accessed 3 April 2020. The original is in Ministère des Affaires Étrangères [Ministry of Foreign Affairs, Kingdom of the Netherlands], *La Conférence internationale de la paix. La Haye, 18 mai-29 juillet 1899* [The International Peace Conference. The Hague, 18 May-29 July 1899] (The Hague: Martinus Nijhoff, 1907), 106, https://ia902705.us.archive.org/0/items/laconfrenceint00inteuoft/laconfrenceint00inteuoft.pdf, accessed 12 July 2020.

[296] Eugène Borel, "Les voies de recours contre les sentences arbitrales [Remedies for Arbitral Awards]," *RCADI*, vol. 52 (1935-II), 36.

of Foreign Affairs have already stated our position, that is, the arbitration award has no binding force and it is invalid and illegal. China will neither recognize nor execute the arbitration award. Why do we say that? Reasons have been elaborated systematically in statements of the Ministry of Foreign Affairs and the white paper issued today. Now I mainly want to explain to you whether the tribunal is a legitimate "international court" in order to tear down the veil of the Arbitral Tribunal.

First, this Arbitral Tribunal is not an "international court." It has nothing to do with the International Court of Justice (ICJ) under the United Nations (UN) system in The Hague. It has a certain relationship with the International Tribunal for the Law of the Sea (ITLOS) in Hamburg, but it is not a part of the ITLOS. It is not in the system of the Permanent Court of Arbitration (PCA) in The Hague either, but they can be related just because the PCA provided secretarial service for the Arbitral Tribunal. The Arbitral Tribunal also used the hall of the PCA to carry out the court trail [sic] and that is all. The Arbitral Tribunal is by no means an "international court," which I believe is worth noting.

Second, the establishment of the Arbitral Tribunal is in fact the result of political manipulation. The Arbitral Tribunal consists of five arbitrators. Apart from Professor Rüdiger Wolfrum from Germany, the arbitrator designated by the Philippines, the other four arbitrators were appointed by the Japanese judge Shunji Yanai, who was the then ITLOS President. Who is Shunji Yanai? He is a judge of the ITLOS now and before as well as the Chairman of Advisory Panel on Reconstruction of the Legal Basis for Security set by the Shinzo Abe administration. He plays an important role in helping Shinzo Abe with the lifting of the ban on collective self-defense and challenging the international order after World War II. He was also a former Japanese Ambassador to the US. Various sources prove that the composition of the Arbitral Tribunal was completely manipulated by him. Moreover, he also exerted his influence on the proceedings of the Arbitral Tribunal afterward.

Third, there are big problems in the composition of the Arbitral Tribunal. As the media have seen, among the five arbitrators of the Arbitral Tribunal, four of them come from Europe: one from Germany, one from France, one from the Netherlands, and one from Poland. All these four countries are members of the European Union (EU). The fifth judge is from Ghana, who was the president of the ITLOS when the court was first established, but he lived in Europe permanently. So does a court like this have any representativeness? Do the judges know well about Asian cultures? Do they know the South China Sea issue well? These factors matter to representativeness and fairness of an arbitral tribunal or court, which has been a problem attracting high attention from the international community in the past few decades. When the UN Charter was signed in 1945 and the Statute of The International Court of Justice was enacted, one of the articles explicitly provided that the composition of international courts must represent all major cultures and all main legal systems in the whole world. When the ITLOS was set up afterward, there was also such a requirement. Why? Because it can ensure that international courts established in the future would have representativeness and authority. The ICJ, the ITLOS, and the PCA all have Chinese judges. I myself am one of the four Chinese arbitrators of the PCA. However, none of the five judges of the Arbitral Tribunal is from Asia, let alone China. Do they know Asia? Do they understand Asian cultures? Do they know the South China Sea issue? Do they understand the complicated geographical politics in Asia? Do they know the history of the South China Sea? On what basis can they make a fair award?

Fourth, there is something interesting in the proceedings of the Arbitral Tribunal, which shocked the international legal community. Original viewpoints of some judges convinced people that they would safeguard relevant interests, but during the proceedings of the Arbitral Tribunal, these judges turned their backs on the academic opinions they once held on to. What are the true viewpoints and stances of these judges? They proposed one point of view in their academic articles and showed another one in the Arbitral Tribunal. It makes people question their academic consciousness and set positions. Moreover, as for witnesses approved by the Arbitral Tribunal, one witness once mentioned in his writings that "at least 12 ocean terrains can be classified as islands in Nansha Qundao, so 200 nautical miles of exclusive economic zone can be claimed." However, when stood as the witness in the Arbitral Tribunal, he withdrew his previous view and said that "none of them are islands." What an expert! Unfortunately, the Arbitral Tribunal admitted such evidence without carrying out any investigations or authentication.

Besides, who supported the Arbitral Tribunal? The arbitrators are paid by certain parties, but who? Maybe by the Philippines or other countries. This system is completely different from the ICJ or the ITLOS.

Judges of the ICJ or the ITLOS receive salaries from the UN for the sake of independence and impartiality. But these five judges of the Arbitral Tribunal are doing it for a profit, and their payments come from the

Philippines and probably others, too. We are unsure about the details but they do provide paid services. That is to say, this case was the first of its kind that led to the establishment of the temporary arbitration tribunal in self-alleged accordance of [sic] the Annex VII of the United Nations Convention on the Law of the Sea (UNCLOS) since the UNCLOS took effect. Nevertheless, this Arbitral Tribunal operates in a way against all expectations and anticipations of the drafters of UNCLOS, setting an unhealthy precedent. I once said last year that this arbitration might become a notorious case in the history of the international law. All the performances of the Arbitral Tribunal show that mandatory arbitral procedures can hardly succeed and this Arbitral Tribunal turns out to be a failure. I cannot see the effectiveness, credibility, and impartiality of the award rendered by such an Arbitral Tribunal. Some countries said that it is a binding award that requires implementation of concerned parties. This is a sheer lie. Who would enforce a verdict that has no credibility? The position of the Chinese government is clear: the award is null and void and has no binding force. China neither accepts nor recognizes it.

Source: Ministry of Foreign Affairs of the People's Republic of China, Veil of the Arbitral Tribunal Must Be Tore [sic] Down [sic], 13 July 2013, http://www.fmprc.gov.cn/mfa_eng/wjbxw/t1381879.shtml, accessed 18 July 2016.

References

1899 Convention for the Pacific Settlement of International Disputes, https://pca-cpa.org/wp-content/uploads/sites/6/2016/01/1899-Convention-for-the-Pacific-Settlement-of-International-Disputes.pdf, accessed 3 April 2020.

1907 Convention for the Pacific Settlement of International Disputes, https://pca-cpa.org/wp-content/uploads/sites/6/2016/01/1907-Convention-for-the-Pacific-Settlement-of-International-Disputes.pdf, accessed 3 April 2020.

Agence France Presse. *Mer de Chine* [sic]: *Pékin en quête d'alliés diplomatiques, de Kaboul à Niamey* [China Sea (sic): Beijing in Search of Diplomatic Allies, from Kabul to Niamey], 25 May 2016, http://fr.annahar.com/article/390379-mer-de-chine-pekin-en-quete-dallies-diplomatiques-de-kaboul-a-niamey, accessed 29 June 2020.

Allars, Margaret. "Disqualification for Bias and International Tribunals: Room for a Common Test." *Missouri Law Review* 78 (2013): 379–411, https://scholarship.law.missouri.edu/cgi/viewcontent.cgi?article=4033&context=mlr, accessed 20 November 2019.

"Ambassade de Chine > Présentation de la position de la Chine sur la Mer de Chine méridionale [Embassy of China > Presentation of the Position of China on the South China Sea]." *Publications de Presse Burundaise* [Publications of Burundi's Press], 11 May 2016, http://www.ppbdi.com/index.php/extras/politique-cooperation-actualite-internationales/4137-ambassade-de-chine-presentation-de-la-position-de-la-chine-sur-la-mer-de-chine-meridionale, accessed 29 June 2020.

American Bar Association. *Model Code of Judicial* Conduct. Chicago: American Bar Association, 2020, https://www.americanbar.org/groups/professional_responsibility/publications/model_code_of_judicial_conduct/model_code_of_judicial_conduct_canon_2/rule2_9expartecommunications/, accessed 28 June 2020.

Annuaire de l'Institut de droit international. Première année [Yearbook of the Institute of International Law. First Year]. Gand: Bureau de la Revue de droit international, 1877, https://ia802606.us.archive.org/15/items/annuairedelinst20lawgoog/annuairedelinst20lawgoog.pdf, accessed 12 July 2020.

"ARA Libertad" Arbitration (Argentina v. Ghana). Final Submissions of Argentina (30 November 2012), https://www.itlos.org/fileadmin/itlos/documents/cases/case_no.20/C20_final_subs_Ghana.pdf, accessed 8 July 2020.

_________. *Final Submissions of the Republic of Ghana* (30 November 2012), https://www.itlos.org/fileadmin/itlos/documents/cases/case_no.20/C20_final_subs_Ghana.pdf, accessed 8 July 2020.

_________. *"ARA Libertad" (Argentina v. Ghana). Provisional Measures. Order of 15 December 2012. ITLOS Reports 2012*, 332–51, https://www.itlos.org/fileadmin/itlos/documents/cases/case_no.20/published/C20_Order_151212.pdf, accessed 8 July 2020.

_________. Rules of Procedure (31 July 2013), https://pcacases.com/web/sendAttach/427, accessed 12 May 2020.

"Arctic Sunrise" Arbitration (Netherlands v. Russia). Award on the Merits (14 August 2015), https://pcacases.com/web/sendAttach/1438, accessed 17 March 2020.

_________. Notification and Statement of Claim dated 4 October 2013, https://pcacases.com/web/sendAttach/1314, accessed 10 March 2020.

_________. Rules of Procedure (17 March 2014), https://pcacases.com/web/sendAttach/1317, accessed 29 April 2020.

Asian Maritime Transparency Initiative. *Who Is Taking Sides After the South China Sea Ruling?* 15 August 2016, https://amti.csis.org/sides-in-south-china-sea/, accessed 1 July 2020.

Associated Press. "China Jails Former Top Judge for Corruption in Beijing." *The Guardian*, 19 January 2010, https://www.theguardian.com/world/2010/jan/19/china-supreme-court-judge-jailed, accessed 13 July 2020.

The Atlanto-Scandian Herring Arbitration (The Kingdom of Denmark in respect of the Faroe Islands v. The European Union). Rules of Procedure (15 March 2014), https://pcacases.com/web/sendAttach/305, accessed 12 May 2020.

Barbados v. Trinidad and Tobago. Rules of Procedure (16 February 2004), https://pcacases.com/web/sendAttach/1062, accessed 11 May 2020.

Barcelona Traction, Light and Power Company, Limited. Judgment. Separate Opinion of Judge Ammoun. *I.C.J. Reports 1970*, 286–333, http://www.icj-cij.org/files/case-related/50/050-19700205-JUD-01-10-BI.pdf, accessed 19 June 2020.

__________. Separate Opinion of Judge Tanaka, *I.C.J. Reports 1970*, 114–60, https://www.icj-cij.org/files/case-related/50/050-19700205-JUD-01-05-BI.pdf, accessed 23 June 2020.

Basic Principles on the Independence of the Judiciary, Adopted by the Seventh United Nations Congress on the Prevention of Crime and the Treatment of Offenders held at Milan from 26 August to 6 September 1985 and endorsed by General Assembly resolutions 40/32 of 29 November 1985 and 40/146 of 13 December 1985, https://www.ohchr.org/EN/ProfessionalInterest/Pages/IndependenceJudiciary.aspx, 3 February 2020.

Bay of Bengal Maritime Boundary Arbitration between Bangladesh and India. Rules of Procedure (8 October 2009), http://www.pcacases.com/web/sendAttach/375, accessed 11 May 2020.

Bedjaoui, Mohammed. "Arbitrator: One Man-Three Roles - Some Independent Comments on the Ethical and Legal Obligations of an Arbitrator." *International Arbitration* 5 (1988): 7–20.

Belkin, Ira. "Justice in the PRC. How the Chinese Communist Party Has Struggled with Managing Public Opinion and the Administration of Criminal Justice in the Internet Age." *Justice (The China Experience)*, 195–228. Eds. Flora Sapio *et al.* Cambridge: Cambridge University Press, 2017.

Blanchard, Ben. "China Jails Former Senior Judge for Life in Graft Case." *reuters.com*, 16 February 2017, https://www.reuters.com/article/us-china-corruption-court/china-jails-former-senior-judge-for-life-in-graft-case-idUSKBN15V10W, accessed 12 July 2020.

Blasek, Katrin. *Rule of Law in China: A Comparative Approach.* Berlin: Springer-Verlag, 2015.

Borel, Eugène. "Les voies de recours contre les sentences arbitrales [Remedies for Arbitral Awards]." *Recueil des cours de l'Académie de droit international de La Haye* [Collected Courses of the Hague Academy of International Law]. Vol. 52 (1935-II), 1–104.

Brandeis University. International Center for Ethics, Justice and Public Life. *A Forum for International Judges.* Waltham, MA: International Center for Ethics, Justice and Public Life, 2018, https://www.brandeis.edu/ethics/internationaljustice/biij/index.html, accessed 16 June 2020.

Brower, Charles N. "The Iran-United States Claims Tribunal." *Recueil des Cours de l'Académie de Droit International de La Haye* [Collected Courses of the Hague Academy of International Law]. Vol. 224 (1990-V), 123–396.

Brubaker, Joseph R. "The Judge Who Knew Too Much: Issue Conflicts in International Adjudication." *Berkeley Journal of International Law* 26 (2008): 111–52.

Caflisch, Lucius. "L'avenir de l'arbitrage interétatique [The Future of Inter-State Arbitration]." *Annuaire français de droit international* [French Yearbook of International Law] 25 (1979): 9–46, http://www.persee.fr/web/revues/home/prescript/article/afdi_0066-3085_1979_num_25_1_2149, accessed 19 June 2020.

Card, Edgar Rouard de. *L'arbitrage international dans le passé, le présent et l'avenir* [International Arbitration in the Past, Present, and Future]. Paris: A. Durand et Pedone-Lauriel, 1877, https://ia902706.us.archive.org/14/items/droitinternatio01cardgoog/droitinternatio01cardgoog.pdf, accessed 21 June 2020.

Caribbean Court of Justice. *Judicial Code of Conduct, adopted on the 25th of July 2013*, https://ccj.org/wp-content/uploads/2011/11/CCJ-Judicial-Code-of-Conduct-reduced.pdf, accessed 23 June 2020.

Case concerning the Delimitation of Maritime Boundary between Guinea-Bissau and Senegal, 31 July 1989. Reports of International Arbitral Awards. Vol. XX, 119–213. New York: United Nations, 2006, https://legal.un.org/riaa/cases/vol_XX/119-213.pdf, accessed 11 December 2019.

Chagos Marine Protected Area Arbitration (Mauritius v. United Kingdom). Reasoned Decision on Challenge (1 December 2011), https://pcacases.com/web/sendAttach/1792, accessed 16 June 2020.

_________. Rules of Procedure (29 March 2012), https://pcacases.com/web/sendAttach/1567, accessed 14 January 2020.

"China Is Perhaps the 'Biggest Victim' in South China Sea, Says Former Foreign Minister." *asiasociety.org*, 23 June 2016, https://asiasociety.org/blog/asia/china-perhaps-biggest-victim-south-china-sea-says-former-foreign-minister, accessed 9 April 2020.

China, People's Republic of. Ministry of Foreign Affairs. *Foreign Ministry Spokesperson Lu Kang's Regular Press Conference on June 14, 2016*, 14 June 2016, https://www.fmprc.gov.cn/nanhai/eng/fyrbt_1/t1372136.htm, accessed 29 June 2020.

_________. *Foreign Ministry Spokesperson Lu Kang's Regular Press Conference on June 16, 2016*, 16 June 2016, https://www.fmprc.gov.cn/nanhai/eng/fyrbt_1/t1372802.htm, accessed 29 June 2020.

_________. *Veil of the Arbitral Tribunal Must Be Tore* [sic] *Down* [sic]. 13 July 2013, http://www.fmprc.gov.cn/mfa_eng/wjbxw/t1381879.shtml, accessed 18 July 2016.

Chinese Society of International Law. "The South China Sea Arbitration Awards: A Critical Study." *Chinese Journal of International Law* 17 (2018): 207–748.

Cohen, Jerome A. "South China Sea Ruling and Defamation." *jeromecohen.net*, 20 July 2016, http://www.jeromecohen.net/jerrys-blog/2016/7/20/south-china-sea-ruling-and-defamation, accessed 16 March 2020.

Collins English Dictionary. Glasgow: HarperCollins Publishers, 2020, https://www.collinsdictionary.com/dictionary/english, accessed 24 June 2020.

Convention for the Establishment of a Central American Court of Justice. American Journal of International Law Supplement: Official Documents 2 (1908): 231–43.

Cot, Jean-Pierre. "Affaire des Essais nucléaires (Australie c. France et Nouvelle-Zélande c. France). Demandes en indication de mesures conservatoires. Ordonnances du 22 juin 1973 [The Nuclear Tests Case (Australia v. France and New-Zealand v. France. Requests for the Indication of Provisional Measures. Orders of 22 June 1973]." *Annuaire français de droit international* [French Yearbook of International Law] 19 (1973): 252–71, https://www.persee.fr/docAsPDF/afdi_0066-3085_1973_num_19_1_2213.pdf, accessed 1 April 2020.

Dannenbaum, Tom. "Nationality and the International Judge: The Nationalist Presumption Governing the International Judiciary and Why it Must be Reversed." *Cornell International Law Journal* 45 (2012): 77–184, http://scholarship.law.cornell.edu/cgi/viewcontent.cgi?article=1786&, accessed 23 June 2020.

Déclaration des Droits de l'Homme et du Citoyen de 1789 [Declaration of the Rights of Man and of the Citizen], https://www.legifrance.gouv.fr/contenu/menu/droit-national-en-vigueur/constitution/declaration-des-droits-de-l-homme-et-du-citoyen-de-1789, accessed 22 June 2020, accessed 22 June 2020.

Del Callar, Michaela. "For Having Pinay Wife, Sri Lankan Judge in PHL Arbitral Proceedings vs China Resigns." *GMA News*, 7 June 2013, http://www.gmanetwork.com/news/story/311870/news/nation/for-having-pinay-wife-sri-lankan-judge-in-phl-arbitral-proceedings-vs-china-resigns, accessed 17 June 2020.

Delimitation of the Maritime Boundary in the Atlantic Ocean (Ghana/Côte d'Ivoire). Judgment. ITLOS Reports 2017, 4–177, https://www.itlos.org/fileadmin/itlos/documents/cases/case_no.23_merits/C23_Judgment_20170923.pdf, accessed 8 July 2020.

Dimitropoulos, Giorgios. "Measuring Judicial Independence." *Maastricht Journal of European and Comparative Law* 24 (2015): 531–51.

Dispute between Argentina and Chile concerning the Beagle Channel, 18 February 1977. Reports of International Arbitral Awards. Vol. XXI, 53–264. New York:

United Nations, 2006, http://legal.un.org/riaa/cases/vol_XXI/53-264.pdf, accessed 19 June 2020.

Dispute Concerning Delimitation of the Maritime Boundary between Ghana and Côte d'Ivoire in the Atlantic Ocean (Ghana/Côte d'Ivoire). Special Agreement and Notification of 3 December 2014 and the Minutes of Consultation, annexed thereto, https://www.itlos.org/fileadmin/itlos/documents/cases/case_no.23_merits/special_agreement_and_notification.pdf, accessed 17 June 2020.

Doehring, Karl. "Zur Befangenheit internationaler Richter [On the Partiality of International Judges]." *Liber Amicorum Judge Shigeru Oda*. Vol. I, 23–39. Eds. Nisuke Ando *et al.* The Hague: Kluwer Law International, 2002.

Dreyfus, Ferdinand, and Frédéric Passy. *L'arbitrage international* [International Arbitration]. Paris: Calmann Lévy, 1892, https://ia902703.us.archive.org/29/items/larbitrageinter00passgoog/larbitrageinter00passgoog.pdf, accessed 24 June 2020.

Drozdiak, William. "Hostilities Threaten Future of Tribunal on U.S.-Iran Claims." *Washington Post*, 3 October 1984, https://www.washingtonpost.com/archive/politics/1984/10/03/hostilities-threaten-future-of-tribunal-on-us-iran-claims/ef19e86d-8548-4bb7-9692-41454253cb71/, accessed 3 July 2020.

Dunoff, Jeffrey L., and Mark A. Pollack. "The Judicial Trilemma." *American Journal of International Law* 111 (2017): 255–76.

European Court of Human Rights. Registry of the Court. *Rules of Court*. Strasburg: European Court of Human Rights, Registry of the Court 2019, https://www.echr.coe.int/Documents/Rules_Court_ENG.pdf, accessed 1 May 2020.

Falk, Richard. "The Independence and Impartiality of International Judges." *Proceedings of the Annual Meeting (American Society of International Law)* 83 (1989): 516–19.

Fassbender, Bardo. "The Representation of the 'Main Forms of Civilization' and of 'the Principal Legal Systems of the World' in the International Court of Justice." *Unité et diversité du droit international. Écrits en l'honneur du professeur Pierre-Marie Dupuy* [Unity and Diversity of International Law. Essays in Honour of Professor Pierre-Marie Dupuy], 581–98. Eds. Denis Alland *et al.* Leiden: Martinus Nijhoff Publishers, 2014.

Fei Liena and Han Mo. "Commentary: Puppet Tribunal in S. China Sea Case Does Not Represent int'l [sic] Law." *ecns.cn*, 14 July 2016, http://www.ecns.cn/voices/2016/07-15/218364.shtml, accessed 7 July 2020.

Feng, Chongyi. "China's Socialist Rule of Law: A Critical Appraisal of the Relationship between the Communist Party and Comprehensive Law Reform." *China's Socialist Rule of Law Reforms Under Xi Jinping*, 45–58. Eds. John

Garrick and Yan Chang Bennett. Milton Park, Abingdon, Oxon: Routledge, 2016.

Fu Hualing. "Between Deference and Defiance: Courts and Penal Populism in Chinese Capital Cases." *China's Death Penalty in Transition: Theory, Policy, Practice and Reform*, 274–99. Eds. Bin Liang and Hong Lu. New York: Columbia University Press, 2015.

Gao Jianjun. "Appointment of Arbitrators by the President of the ITLOS pursuant to Article 3 of Annex VII to the LOS Convention: Some Tentative Observations." *Chinese Journal of International Law* 16 (2017): 723–49.

General Act of Arbitration (Pacific Settlement of International Disputes). Done at Geneva, 26 September 1928, https://cil.nus.edu.sg/wp-content/uploads/2017/08/1928-General-Act-of-Arbitration.pdf, accessed 19 June 2020.

Giorgetti, Chiara. "The Challenge and Recusal of Judges at the International Court of Justice." *Challenges and Recusals of Judges and Arbitrators in International Courts and Tribunals*, 3–31. Ed. Chiara Giorgetti. Leiden: Brill, 2015.

Gong, Ting. "Dependent Judiciary and Unaccountable Judges: Judicial Corruption in Contemporary China." *China Review* 4 (2004): 33–54.

Gordon, Edward. The Independence and Impartiality of International Judges. *Proceedings of the Annual Meeting (American Society of International Law)* 83 (1989): 508–12.

"Grand Prince" (Belize v. France). Prompt Release. Judgment. ITLOS Reports 2001, 17–46, https://www.itlos.org/fileadmin/itlos/documents/cases/case_no_8/published/C8-J-20_apr_01.pdf, accessed 8 July 2020.

Gray, Christine, and Benedict Kingsbury. "Developments in Dispute Settlement: Inter-State Arbitration Since 1945." *British Yearbook of International Law* 63 (1992): 97–134.

Guyana v. Suriname. Rules of Procedure (24 February 2004), http://www.pcacases.com/web/sendAttach/882, accessed 11 May 2020.

Hague Justice Portal. "Sesay, Issa Hassan." *haguejusticeportal.net* (2016), http://www.haguejusticeportal.net/index.php?id=8320, accessed 6 July 2020.

Hassouna, Hussein. "The Kuwait-Iraq Border Problem." *Iran, Iraq, and the Arab Gulf States*, 237–61. Ed. Joseph A. Kechichian. New York: Palgrave-Macmillan, 2001.

Henderson, Keith. "The Rule of Law and Judicial Corruption in China: Halfway over the Great Wall." *Global Corruption Report 2007. Corruption in Judicial Systems*, 151–58. Transparency International. New York: Cambridge University Press, 2007, https://images.transparencycdn.org/images/2007_GCR_EN.pdf, accessed 13 July 2020.

Hensley, Thomas R. "National Bias and the International Court of Justice." *Midwest Journal of Political Science* 12 (1968): 568–86.

Huang Zheping. "Xi Jinping Promised Legal Reform in China, But Forget About Judicial Independence." *Quartz*, 18 January 2017, https://qz.com/886665/xi-jinping-promised-legal-reform-in-china-but-forget-about-judicial-independence/, accessed 28 June 2020.

Hudson, Manley O. *The Permanent Court of International Justice. A Treatise.* New York: The Macmillan Company, 1934.

Institut de droit international [Institute of International Law]. Session de Bâle [Basel Session]. *Non-Appearance Before the International Court of Justice* (1991), https://www.idi-iil.org/app/uploads/2017/06/1991_bal_01_en.pdf, accessed 16 March 2020.

Interfax. "Russian Foreign Ministry: Arctic Sunrise Arbitration Court Lacks Proper Jurisdiction." *Russia Beyond the Headlines* (25 August 2015), https://www.rbth.com/news/2015/08/25/russian_foreign_ministry_arctic_sunrise_arbitration_court_lacks_proper_j_48720.html, accessed 16 June 2020.

International Court of Justice. *Declarations Recognizing the Jurisdiction of the Court as Compulsory: Philippines (18 January 1972)*, https://www.icj-cij.org/en/declarations/ph, accessed 12 July 2020.

________. *Statute*, http://www.icj-cij.org/en/statute, accessed 10 March 2020.

International Criminal Court. *Rome Statute of the International Criminal Court*. The Hague: International Criminal Court, 2011, https://www.icc-cpi.int/nr/rdonlyres/add16852-aee9-4757-abe7-9cdc7cf02886/283503/romestatuteng1.pdf, accessed 5 July 2020.

________. *Rules of Procedure and Evidence*. ICC Doc. 10ICC-ASP/1/3 (2002), https://www.icc-cpi.int/iccdocs/pids/legal-texts/rulesprocedureevidenceeng.pdf, accessed 5 July 2020.

International Criminal Tribunal for the Former Yugoslavia. *Furundžija Case: The Judgement of the Trial Chamber. Anto Furundžija Found Guilty on Both Charges and Sentenced to 10 Years in Prison*. ICTY Doc. JL/PIU/372-E (10 December 1998), http://www.icty.org/en/sid/7609, accessed 6 July 2020.

International Tribunal for the Law of the Sea. *Application Filed on Behalf of Belize against France for Release of Arrested Fishing Vessel*. ITLOS Doc. ITLOS/Press 46 (21 March 2001), https://www.itlos.org/fileadmin/itlos/documents/press_releases_english/press_release_46_en.pdf, accessed 8 July 2020.

________. *New Arbitrator and President Appointed in the Arbitral Proceedings Instituted by the Republic of the Philippines against the People's Republic of* China. ITLOS/Press 197 (24 June 2013), https://www.itlos.org/fileadmin/itlos/documents/press_releases_english/PR_197_E.pdf, accessed 17 June 2020.

________. *Rules of the Tribunal* (ITLOS/8), *as adopted on 28 October 1997 and amended on 15 March 2001, 21 September 2001, 17 March 2009 and 25 September 2018*, https://www.itlos.org/fileadmin/itlos/documents/basic_texts/Itlos_8_E_25.09.18.pdf, accessed 29 April 2020.

_________. *Tribunal Delivers Judgment in Case No 15. Tribunal Finds that the Application in the Tomimaru Case Is without Object*. ITLOS Doc. ITLOS/Press 113 (6 August 2007), https://www.itlos.org/fileadmin/itlos/documents/press_releases_english/PR_113_E.pdf, accessed 7 July 2020.

_________. *Tribunal Orders Release of Argentine Frigate ARA Libertad.*, ITLOS Doc. ITLOS/Press 188 (15 December 2012), https://www.itlos.org/fileadmin/itlos/documents/press_releases_english/PR_188_E.pdf, accessed 8 July 2020.

Jennings, Sir Robert. "The Difference between Conducting a Case in the ICJ and in an *Ad Hoc* Arbitration Tribunal: An Inside View." *Liber Amicorum Judge Shigeru Oda*. Vol. II, 893–909. Eds. Nisuke Ando *et al.* The Hague: Kluwer Law International, 2002.

Kardon, Isaac B. "China Can Say 'No': Analyzing China's Rejection of the South China Sea Arbitration. toward a New Era of International Law with Chinese Characteristics." *University of Pennsylvania Asian Law Review* 13 (2019): 1–46, https://scholarship.law.upenn.edu/cgi/viewcontent.cgi?article=1037&context=alr, accessed 23 March 2020.

Keller, Helen, and Severin Meier. "Independence and Impartiality in the Judicial Trilemma." *American Journal of International Law* 111 (217): 344–47.

Khan, Rahmatullah. *The Iran-United States Claims Tribunal—Controversies, Cases and Contribution*. Dordrecht: Martinus Nijhoff Publishers, 1990.

Ku, Julian. "China's Vice-Minister for Foreign Affairs Casually Slanders the South China Sea Arbitral Tribunal." *opiniojuris.org*, 26 July 2016, http://opiniojuris.org/2016/07/26/chinas-vice-minister-for-foreign-affairs-casually-slanders-the-south-china-sea-arbitral-tribunal/, accessed 16 March 2020.

________. "The Significance of China's Rejection of the South China Sea Arbitration for Its Approach to International Dispute Settlement and International Law." *Chinese (Taiwan) Yearbook of International Law and Affairs* 34 (2016): 73–103.

_________. "So How is China Reacting to the Philippines Arbitration Submission? Not Very Well." *opiniojuris.org*, 3 April 2014, http://opiniojuris.org/2014/04/03/china-reacting-philippines-arbitration/, accessed 17 June 2020.

_________. "What Happens if China Tries to Boycott UNCLOS Arbitration? A Japanese Guy Gets to Appoint the Tribunal." *opiniojuris.org*, 25 January 2013, http://opiniojuris.org/2013/01/25/what-happens-if-china-tries-to-boycott-unclos-arbitration-a-japanese-guy-gets-to-appoint-the-tribunal/, accessed 17 June 2020.

Lacharrière, Guy de. "Commentaires sur la position juridique de la France à l'égard de la licéité de ses expériences nucléaires [Commentaries on the Legal Position of France with respect to the Legality of Its Nuclear

Tests].” *Annuaire français de droit international* [French Yearbook of International Law] 19 (1973): 235–51, http://www.persee.fr/doc/afdi_0066-3085_1973_num_19_1_2212, accessed 2 April 2020.

Lachs, Manfred. “A Few Thoughts on the Independence of Judges of the International Court of Justice.” *Columbia Journal of Transnational Law* 25 (1987): 593–600.

Lafargue, Caroline. “Mer de Chine [sic]: le Vanuatu apporte un soutien de poids-plume à Pékin [China Sea (sic): Vanuatu Gives Featherweight Support to Beijing].” *francetvinfo.fr*, 31 May 2016, https://la1ere.francetvinfo.fr/nouvellecaledonie/mer-de-chine-le-vanuatu-apporte-un-soutien-de-poids-plume-pekin-365317.html, accessed 29 June 2020.

Lam, Willy. “The Politicisation of China’s Law Enforcement and Judicial Apparatus.” *The Impact of China’s 1989 Tiananmen Massacre*, 125–41. Ed. Jean-Philippe Béja. Milton Park, Abingdon, Oxon: Routledge, 2011.

Laly-Chevalier, Caroline. “Activité du Tribunal international du droit de la mer (2001–2002) [The Activities of the International Tribunal for the Law of the Sea].” *Annuaire français de droit international* [French Yearbook of International Law] 48 (2002): 362–80, https://www.persee.fr/docAsPDF/afdi_0066-3085_2002_num_48_1_3706.pdf, accessed 8 July 2020.

Lapradelle, Albert Geouffre de, and Nicolas Socrate Politis (eds.). *Recueil des arbitrages internationaux* [Collection of International Arbitrations]. Vol. I. *1798–1855*. Paris: A. Pedone, Éditeur, 1905, https://archive.org/details/recueildesarbit00laprgoog/page/n8/mode/2up, accessed 19 June 2020.

_________. *Recueil des arbitrages internationaux* [Collection of International Arbitrations]. Vol. II. *1856–1872*. Paris: A. Pedone, Éditeur, 1923, https://ia802607.us.archive.org/3/items/recueildesarbitr02lapruoft/recueildesarbitr02lapruoft.pdf, accessed 21 June 2020.

Lauterpacht, Hersch. *The Function of Law in The International Community*. Oxford: Oxford University Press, 1933, https://ia601603.us.archive.org/31/items/in.ernet.dli.2015.459090/2015.459090.The-Function-Of-Law-In-The-International-Community.pdf, accessed 3 July 2020.

_________. *The Function of Law in The International Community*. Oxford: Oxford University Press, 2011.

League of Nations. Advisory Committee of Jurists. *Procès-verbaux of the Proceedings of the Committee, June 16th-July 24th, 1920, with Annexes*. The Hague: Van Langenhuysen, 1920, https://ia600900.us.archive.org/6/items/procsverbauxof00leaguoft/procsverbauxof00leaguoft.pdf, accessed 19 June 2020.

_________. *Committee of Jurists on the Statute of the Permanent Court of International Justice. Minutes of the Session held at Geneva, March 11th–19th, 1929*. League Doc. C. 166. M. 66. 1929.V (1

May 1929), https://www.icj-cij.org/files/permanent-court-of-international-justice/serie_D/D_minutes_statut_PCIJ_11au19march_1929.pdf, accessed 3 July 2020.

Legal Consequences for States of the Continued Presence of South Africa in Namibia (South West Africa) notwithstanding Security Council Resolution 276 (1970). Advisory Opinion. I.C.J. Reports 1971, 16–66, https://www.icj-cij.org/files/case-related/53/053-19710621-ADV-01-00-BI.pdf, accessed 23 June 2020.

Legal Consequences of the Construction of a Wall in the Occupied Palestinian Territory. Order of 30 January 2004. I.CJ. Reports 2004, 3–6, http://www.icj-cij.org/files/case-related/131/131-20040130-ORD-01-00-BI.pdf, accessed 6 July 2020.

_________. Dissenting Opinion of Judge Buergenthal. *I.CJ. Reports 2004*, 7–10, https://www.icj-cij.org/files/case-related/131/131-20040130-ORD-01-01-BI.pdf, accessed 6 July 2020.

Li Ling. "The Chinese Communist Party and People's Courts: Judicial Dependence in China." *American Journal of Comparative Law* 64 (2016): 37–74.

_________. "The 'Production' of Corruption in China's Courts: Judicial Politics and Decision-Making in a One-Party State." *Law and Social Inquiry* 37 (2012): 848–77.

Li Yuwen. *The Judicial System and Reform in Post-Mao China: Stumbling Towards Justice*. Farnham, Surrey: Ashgate Publishing Co, 2014.

Liebman, Benjamin. "A Populist Threat to China's Courts?" *Chinese Justice: Civil Dispute Resolution in Contemporary China*, 269–313. Eds. Margaret Y.K. Woo and Mary E. Gallagher. New York: Cambridge University Press, 2011.

Lin Feng. *The Future of Judicial Independence in China*. Center for Judicial Education and Research, City University of Hong Kong, Working Paper Series, No. 2 (2016), http://www.cityu.edu.hk/cjer/lib/doc/paper/WK2_The_Future_of_Judicial_Independence_in_China.pdf, accessed 1 July 2020.

Ling, Bing. *China's Attitude to the International Legal Order in the Xi Era: The Case of South China Sea Arbitration*. Sydney Law School Research Paper No. 19/04 (6 February 2019), https://papers.ssrn.com/sol3/papers.cfm?abstract_id=3329614, accessed 28 June 2020.

Lissitzyn, Oliver James. *The International Court of Justice. Its Role in the Maintenance of International Peace and Security*. New York: Carnegie Endowment for International Peace, 1951.

Mahoney, Paul. "The International Judiciary—Independence and Accountability." *Law and Practice of International Courts and Tribunals* 7 (2008): 713–49.

Malenovský, Jiři. "L'indépendance des juges internationaux [The Independence of International Judges]." *Recueil des cours de l'Académie de droit international de La Haye* [Collected Courses of the Hague Academy of International Law]. Vol. 349 (2010-IV), 9–276.

"Manila's Scheme Abuses Law." *China Forum (China Daily)*, 1 April 2014, http://europe.chinadaily.com.cn/opinion/2014-04/01/content_17394014_2.htm, accessed 17 June 2020.

Maritime Delimitation in the Area between Greenland and Jan Mayen. Judgment. Separate Opinion of Judge Weearamantry. *I.C.J. Reports 1993*, 211–79, www.icj-cij.org/files/case-related/50/050-19700205-JUD-01-10-BI.pdf, accessed 19 June 2020.

Mégret, Frédéric. "International Judges and Experts' Impartiality and the Problem of Past Declarations." *Law and Practice of International Courts and Tribunals* 10 (2011): 31–66.

Mendelson, Maurice, and Susan Hulton. "Les décisions de la Commission de démarcation de la frontière entre l'Iraq et le Koweït [The Decisions of the Commission to Demarcate the Border between Iraq and Kuwait]." *Annuaire français de droit international* [French Yearbook of International Law] 39 (1993): 178–231, http://www.persee.fr/doc/afdi_0066-3085_1993_num_39_1_3127, accessed 12 July 2020.

Mérignhac, Alexandre. *Traité théorique et pratique de l'arbitrage international: le rôle du droit dans le fonctionnement actuel de l'institution et dans ses destinées futures* [A Theoretical and Practical Treatise on International Arbitration: The Role of Law in the Present Operation of the Institution and in Its Future Destiny]. Paris: Librairie du Recueil général des Lois et des arrêts et du Journal du Palais, 1895, https://ia601407.us.archive.org/14/items/traitthoriqueet00mrgoog/traitthoriqueet00mrgoog.pdf, accessed 3 April 2020.

Meron, Theodor. "Judicial Independence and Impartiality in International Criminal Tribunals." *American Journal of International Law* 99 (2005): 359–69.

Military and Paramilitary Activities in and against Nicaragua (Nicaragua v. United States of America). Merits. Judgment. Separate Opinion of Judge Lachs. *I.C.J. Reports 1986*, 158–73, http://www.icj-cij.org/files/case-related/70/070-19860627-JUD-01-02-BI.pdf, accessed 5 July 2020.

Ministère des Affaires Étrangères [Ministry of Foreign Affairs, Kingdom of the Netherlands]. *La Conférence internationale de la paix. La Haye, 18 mai-29 juillet 1899* [The International Peace Conference. The Hague, 18 May–29 July 1899]. The Hague: Martinus Nijhoff, 1907, https://ia902705.us.archive.org/0/items/laconfrenceint00inteuoft/laconfrenceint00inteuoft.pdf, accessed 12 July 2020.

Moore, John Bassett. *History and Digest of The International Arbitrations to which The United States Has Been A Party*. Vol. III. Washington,

D.C.: Government Printing Office, 1898, https://ia800204.us.archive.org/18/items/historyanddiges01moorgoog/historyanddiges01moorgoog.pdf, accessed 2 April 2020.

MOX Plant Case (Ireland v. United Kingdom). Rules of Procedure (25 October 2001), https://pcacases.com/web/sendAttach/848, accessed 12 May 2020.

Mozambique. Ministério dos Negócios Estrangeiros e Cooperação [Ministry of Foreign Affairs and Trade]. *Moçambique e China estabelecem parceria estratégica para cooperação global* [Mozambique and China Establish a Strategic Strategy for Overall Cooperation], 20 May 2016, http://www.minec.gov.mz/index.php/imprensa/destaques/91-mocambique-e-china-estabelecem-parceria-estrategica-para-cooperacao-global, accessed 1 June 2016.

Niger. *Communiqué de presse du Ministère en charge des Affaires Etrangères, relatif au différend entre la République Populaire de Chine et les Philippines en Mer de Chine Méridionale* [Press Communiqué of the Ministry of Foreign Affairs, on the Dispute between the People's Republic of China and the Philippines in the South China Sea], 19 May, 2016, http://news.aniamey.com/h/72663.html, accessed 29 June 2020.

Nordquist, Myron H. *et al* (eds.). *United Nations Convention on the Law of the Sea 1982: A Commentary*. Vol. V. *Settlement of Disputes, General and Final Provisions and Related Annexes and Resolutions*. Leiden: Brill, 1989.

North Sea Continental Shelf. *Judgment*. Separate Opinion of Judge Fouad Ammoun. *I.C.J. Reports 1969*, 100–53, http://www.icj-cij.org/files/case-related/51/051-19690220-JUD-01-06-BI.pdf, accessed 18 June 2020.

Oberto, Giacomo. "Die richterliche Unabhängigkeit in Europa und ihre Sicherung durch einen obersten Richterrat [The Independence of Judges in Europe and Its Protection through Supreme Judicial Councils]." Vortrag zur Jahrestagung des Hessischen Richterbundes, Arnoldshain [Paper presented at the Annual Meeting of the Association of Judges of Hesse, Arnoldshain, Germany], 1–3 July 2004, http://hefam.de/koll/oberto-200407.pdf, accessed 22 June 2020.

Papachristou, Lucy. "Jailed Shanghai Prosecutor Implicates 100 Officials in Corruption." *Organized Crime and Corruption Reporting Project*, 12 November 2018, https://www.occrp.org/en/27-ccwatch/cc-watch-briefs/8891-jailed-shanghai-prosecutor-implicates-100-officials-in-corruption, accessed 4 February 2020.

Peerenboom, Randall. "Fly High the Banner of Socialist Rule of Law with Chinese Characteristics!" *Hague Journal on the Rule of Law* 7 (2015): 49–74.

__________. "A Government of Laws: Democracy, Rule of Law, and Administrative Law Reform in China." *Debating Political Reform in China: Rule of Law vs. Democratization*, 58–78. Ed. Suisheng Zhao. Armonk, N.Y.: M.E. Sharpe, 2006.

Permanent Court of Arbitration. *Members of the Court* (2021), https://pca-cpa.org/en/about/structure/members-of-the-court/, accessed 23 July 2021.

_________. *Members of the Permanent Court of Arbitration. Current List* (2021), https://docs.pca-cpa.org/2017/07/2017/07/09fe252a-pca-184006-v91-current_list_annex_1_members_of_the_court.pdf, accessed 12 July 2021.

Permanent Court of International Justice. *Statute and Rules of Court*, 1st Edition. Series D. No. 1 (1926), https://www.icj-cij.org/files/permanent-court-of-international-justice/serie_D/D_01_1e_edition.pdf, accessed 3 April 2020.

Posner, Eric A., and Miguel F. P. de Figueiredo. "Is the International Court of Justice Biased?" *Journal of Legal Studies* 34: (2005): 599–630.

_________, and John C. Yoo. "Judicial Independence in International Tribunals." *California Law Review* 93 (2005): 1–74, https://chicagounbound.uchicago.edu/cgi/viewcontent.cgi?article=2758&context=journal_articles, accessed 19 June 2020.

The Prosecutor v. Anto Furundžija. Judgment. International Criminal Tribunal for the Former Yugoslavia. Appeals Chamber. Case No. IT-95-17/1-A (21 July 2000), http://www.icty.org/x/cases/furundzija/acjug/en/fur-aj000721e.pdf, accessed 6 July 2020.

Prosecutor v. Isa Hassan Sesay. Decision on Defence Motion Seeking the Disqualification of Justice Robertson from the Appeals Chamber [2004] SCSL 1 (13 March 2004), https://sierralii.org/sl/judgment/special-court/2004/1-0, accessed 6 July 2020.

Ralston, Jackson H. *International Arbitration from Athens to Locarno.* Stanford: Stanford University Press, 1929, https://archive.org/details/in.ernet.dli.2015.166200, accessed 18 June 2020.

Reuters. "China's Top Court Rejects Judicial Independence as 'Erroneous Thought'." *The Guardian*, 26 February 2015, https://www.theguardian.com/world/2015/feb/26/chinas-top-court-rejects-judicial-independence-as-erroneous-thought. accessed 28 June 2020.

Revised General Act for the Pacific Settlement of International Disputes. Done at New York, 28 April 1949, https://www.un.org/ruleoflaw/blog/document/revised-general-act-for-the-pacific-settlement-of-international-disputes/, accessed 19 June 2020.

Rosenne, Shabtai, with the assistance of Yaël Ronen. *The Law and Practice of the International Court 1990–2005*. Leiden: Martinus Nijhoff Publishers, 2006.

Samore, William. "National Origins v. Impartial Decisions: A Study of World Court Holdings." *Chicago-Kent Law Review* 34 (1956):193–221, http://scholarship.kentlaw.iit.edu/cgi/viewcontent.cgi?article=1859&context=cklawreview, accessed 13 December 2019.

Sands Philippe et al. "The Burgh House Principles on the Independence of the International Judiciary." *Law and Practice of International Courts and Tribunals* 4 (2005): 247–60.

Scott, James Brown (ed.). *The Proceedings of the Hague Peace Conferences. Translation of the Official Texts. The Conference of 1907*. Vol. II. *Meetings of the First Commission*. New York: Oxford University Press, 1920, https://ia802704.us.archive.org/1/items/proceedingsofhag02inteuoft/proceedingsofhag02inteuoft.pdf, accessed 3 July 2020.

Shany, Yuval. "Squaring the Circle? Independence and Impartiality of Party-Appointed Adjudicators in International Legal Proceedings." *Loyola of Los Angeles International and Comparative Law Review* 30 (2008): 176–90, http://digitalcommons.lmu.edu/ilr/vol30/iss3/8, accessed 24 June 2020.

_________, and Sigall Horovitz. "Judicial Independence in The Hague and Freetown: A Tale of Two Cities." *Leiden Journal of International Law* 21 (2008): 113–29.

Smith, Adam M. "'Judicial Nationalism' in International Law: National Identity and Judicial Autonomy at the ICJ." *Texas International Law Journal* 40 (2005): 197–232.

Sohn, Louis B. "The Role of Arbitration in Recent International Multilateral Treaties." *Virginia Journal of International Law* 23 (1982–83): 171–89.

Soleymane, Laouali "Conférence de Presse du Directeur général en charge du département Afrique du Ministère des Affaires Etrangères de la République Populaire de Chine: Des clarifications sur la question de la mer de Chine méridionale [Press Conference of the Director General of the Africa Department of the Ministry of Foreign Affairs of the People's Republic of China. Clarifications on the South China Sea Issue]." *Nigerdiaspora. La communauté virtuelle du Niger* [Nigerdiaspora. The Virtual Community of Niger], 20 April 2016, https://nigerdiaspora.net/index.php/politique-archives/item/73676-conference-de-presse-du-directeur-general-en-charge-du-departement-afrique-du-ministere-des-affaires-etrangeres-de-la-republique-populaire-de-chine-des-clarifications-sur-la-question-de-la-mer-de-chine-meridionale?tmpl=component&print=1, accessed 29 June 2020.

South China Sea Arbitration. Award on Jurisdiction and Admissibility (29 October 2015), https://pcacases.com/web/sendAttach/2579, accessed 10 March 2020.

_________. *Memorial of the Philippines* (30 March 2014). Vol. III. Annexes, https://files.pca-cpa.org/pcadocs/The%20Philippines%27%20Memorial%20-%20Volume%20III%20%28Annexes%201-60%29.pdf, accessed 15 March 2020.

_________. Annex 1. Notification and Statement of Claim of the Republic of the Philippines (22 January 2013), 13–34.

_________. *The Philippines' Annexes cited during Hearing on Jurisdiction (Annexes 574–583)*(13 July 2015), https://files.pca-cpa.org/pcadocs/Annexes%20cited%20during%20Hearing%20on%20Jurisdiction%20%28Annexes%20574-583%29.pdf, accessed 24 April 2020.

_________. Annex 574. Letter from H.E. Chen Xu, Ambassador of the People's Republic of China to the Kingdom of the Netherlands, to H.E. Judge Thomas A. Mensah (1 July 2015), 1–3.

_________. Rules of Procedure (27 August 2013), https://pcacases.com/web/sendAttach/233, accessed 11 May 2020.

_________. *Supplemental Written Submission of the Philippines* (16 March 2015). Vol. VIII. Annexes, https://files.pca-cpa.org/pcadocs/The%20Philippines%27%20Supplemental%20Written%20Submission%20-%20Volume%20VIII%20%28Annexes%20466-499%29.pdf, accessed 10 March 2020.

_________. Annex 470. Letter from H.E. Ambassador Chen Xu, Embassy of the People's Republic of China in The Hague, to H.E. Judge Thomas A. Mensah (6 February 2015), 73–84.

"South China Sea Arbitration Case Today the Results of People's Daily Nearly [sic]." 12 July 2016, http://www.hubgold.com/2016/07/12/south-china-sea-arbitration-case-today-the-results-of-people-s-daily-nearly, accessed 25 April 2017.

"South China Sea Dispute: China Claims Support of 40 Countries." *The India Times*, 12 July 2016, https://economictimes.indiatimes.com/news/defence/south-china-sea-dispute-china-claims-support-of-40-countries/articleshow/52363836.cms?from=mdr, accessed 29 June 2020.

Special Court for Sierra Leone and Residual Special Court for Sierra Leone (2020), http://www.rscsl.org/, accessed 6 July 2020.

Suh, Il Ro. "Voting Behavior of National Judges in International Courts." *American Journal of International Law* 63 (1969): 224–36.

Szurek, Sandra. "La composition des juridictions internationales permanentes: de nouvelles exigences de qualité et de représentativité [The Composition of International Tribunals: New Demands for Quality and Representativeness]." *Annuaire français de droit international* [French Yearbook of International Law] 56 (2010): 41–78, https://www.persee.fr/docAsPDF/afdi_0066-3085_2010_num_56_1_4602.pdf, accessed 23 June 2020.

Tanaka, Kotaro. "Independence of International Judges." *Comunicazioni e studi* [Communications and Studies] 14 (1975): 855–72.

Texaco Overseas Petroleum Company/California Asiatic Oil Company v. The Government of the Libyan Arab Republic Arbitration. Ad hoc Award of January 19, 1977, https://www.trans-lex.org/261700/_/texaco-overseas-petroleum-company-v-the-government-of-the-libyan-arab-republic-yca-1979-at-177-et-seq-/, accessed 24 June 2020.

"Text of U.S. Statement on Withdrawal from Case before the World Court." *New York Times*, 19 January 1985, http://www.nytimes.com/1985/01/19/world/text-of-us-statement-on-withdrawal-from-case-before-the-world-court.html?pagewanted=all&pagewanted=print, accessed 16 June 2020.

Thirlway, H.W.A. *Non-appearance before the International Court of Justice*. Cambridge: Cambridge University Press, 1985.

Timmons, Heather, and Ilaria Maria Sala. "How to Smear Your Enemies and Silence Your Critics, Chinese Communist Party Style." *Quartz*, 23 June 2016, https://qz.com/712187/how-to-smear-your-enemies-and-silence-your-critics-chinese-communist-party-style/, accessed 28 June 2020.

Togo. "Pékin apprécie la position togolaise [Beijing Appreciates the Togolese Position]." *Republic of Togo*, 19 May 2016, https://www.republicoftogo.com/Toutes-les-rubriques/Diplomatie/Pekin-apprecie-la-position-togolaise, accessed 29 June 2020.

"Tomimaru" (Japan v. Russian Federation). Prompt Release. Judgment. Declaration of Judge Yanai. *ITLOS Reports 2005–2007*, 102–04, https://www.itlos.org/fileadmin/itlos/documents/cases/case_no_15/15_judgment_060807_dec_Yanai_en.pdf, accessed 26 July 2020.

Torres Pérez, Anna. "From Judicial Independence to Interdependence in the International Sphere." *Maastricht Journal of European and Comparative Law* 24 (2017): 462–83.

Treaty between Her Majesty and the United States of America, signed at Washington, May 8, 1871 (ratified and ratifications exchanged June 17, 1871), https://archive.org/details/cihm_45724/page/n1/mode/2up, accessed 19 June 2020.

Treaty of Amity, Commerce, and Navigation, 19 November 1894, https://www.loc.gov/law/help/us-treaties/bevans/b-gb-ust000012-0013.pdf, accessed 3 April 2020.

United Nations. *Commentary on the Draft Convention on Arbitral Procedure Adopted by the International Law Commission at its Fifth Session, prepared by the Secretariat*. UN Doc. A/CN.4/92. New York: United Nations, 1955, https://legal.un.org/ilc/documentation/english/a_cn4_92.pdf, accessed 18 June 2020.

United Nations. Division for Ocean Affairs and the Law of the Sea. *Annex V. Conciliation*, https://www.un.org/Depts/los/convention_agreements/texts/unclos/annex5.htm, accessed 24 June 2020.

_________. *Annex VI. Statute of the International Tribunal for the Law of the Sea*, http://www.un.org/depts/los/convention_agreements/texts/unclos/annex6.htm, accessed 11 March 2020.

_________. *Annex VII. Arbitration,* http://www.un.org/depts/los/convention_agreements/texts/unclos/annex7.htm, accessed 10 March 2020.

_________. *Annex VIII. Special Arbitration*, https://www.un.org/Depts/los/convention_agreements/texts/unclos/annex8.htm, accessed 24 June 2020.

_________. International Law Commission. *Arbitral Procedure. Rapport par Georges Scelle, rapporteur special* [Report by Georges Scelle, Special Rapporteur]. UN Doc. A/CN.4/18 (21 March 1950). *Yearbook of the International Law Commission 1950*. Vol. II. *Documents of the Second Session including the Report of the Commission to the General Assembly*, 114–51. UN Doc. A/CN. 4/SER.A/1950/Add. 1, New York: United Nations, 1957, http://legal.un.org/docs/?path=../ilc/documentation/french/a_cn4_18.pdf&lang=F, accessed 25 June 2020.

_________. *Draft on Arbitral Procedure Adopted by the Commission at its Fifth Session. Report by Georges Scelle, Special Rapporteur (with a Model Draft on Arbitral Procedure Annexed)*. UN Doc. A/CN.4/113 (6 March 1958). *Yearbook of the International Law Commission 1958*. Vol. II. *Documents of the Tenth Session, including the Report of the Commission to the General Assembly*, 1–15. UN Doc. A/CH.4/SER.A/1958/Add. 1. New York: United Nations, 1958, http://legal.un.org/docs/index.asp?path=../ilc/documentation/english/a_cn4_113.pdf&lang=EFS&referer=http://legal.un.org/ilc/guide/10_1.shtml, accessed 24 June 2020.

United States Citizenship and Immigration Services. *The Declaration of Independence & the Constitution of the United States*. Doc. M-654 (rev. 07/08), https://www.uscis.gov/sites/default/files/USCIS/Office%20of%20Citizenship/Citizenship%20Resource%20Center%20Site/Publications/PDFs/M-654.pdf, accessed 22 June 2020.

United States Diplomatic and Consular Staff in Tehran. Order of 24 December 1979. I. C.J. Reports 1979, 23–24, http://www.icj-cij.org/files/case-related/64/064-19791224-ORD-01-00-BI.pdf, accessed 10 July 2020.

Valticos, Nicolas. "Rôle et éthique d'un judge ad hoc à la Cour internationale de justice [The Role and Ethics of a Judge Ad Hoc at the International Court of Justice]." *Liber Amicorum Judge Shigeru Oda*. Vol. I, 107–16. Eds. Nisuke Ando *et al.* The Hague: Kluwer Law International, 2002.

Wang Wen, and Chen Xiaochen. "Who Supports China in the South China Sea and Why." *The Diplomat*, 27 July 2016, https://thediplomat.com/2016/07/who-supports-china-in-the-south-china-sea-and-why/, accessed 16 March 2020.

Xue Li. "How China Views the South China Sea Arbitration Case." *The Diplomat*, 14 July 2015, http://thediplomat.com/2015/07/how-china-views-the-south-china-sea-arbitration-case/, accessed 30 June 2020.

Xinhua. "Ad hocism Guided S China Sea Arbitral Tribunal." *China Daily*, 18 July 2016, https://www.chinadailyasia.com/special/southchinasea/2016-07/18/content_15464647_2.html, accessed 17 June 2020.

_________. "Arbitral Tribunal's Award on South China Sea Creates Bad Precedent, Says U.S. Expert." *ecns.com*, 15 July 2016, http://www.ecns.cn/2016/07-15/218514.shtml, accessed 19 June 2020.

_________. "Arbitral Tribunal on South China Sea Illegal, Ridiculous." *Global Times*, 8 July 2016, http://www.globaltimes.cn/content/993110.shtml, accessed 16 March 2020.

_________. "Argentine Expert Says South China Sea Award Riddled with Inconsistencies." *xinhuanet.com*, 15 July 2016, https://www.linkedin.com/pulse/south-china-sea-argentine-expert-ferrara-says-award-riddled-ferrara, accessed 19 June 2020.

_________. "China Is Right to Reject International Court's South China Sea Decision: Malagasy [sic] Experts." *xinhuanet.com*, 13 July 2016, http://news.xinhuanet.com/english/2016-07/13/c_135510262.htm, accessed 18 July 2016.

_________. "Major Chinese Newspapers Slam South China Sea Arbitration." *Global Times*, 11 July 2016, http://www.globaltimes.cn/content/993590.shtml, accessed 1 July 2020.

_________. "Shunji Yanai, Manipulator Behind Illegal South China Sea Arbitration." *Xinhua.net*, 17 July 2016, http://en.people.cn/n3/2016/0717/c90000-9087223.html, accessed 17 June 2020.

_________. "South China Sea Arbitration Award 'Unfair': Ghanaian Analysts." *Global Times*, 16 July 2016, http://www.globaltimes.cn/content/994650.shtml, accessed 19 June 2020.

_________. "Spotlight: Unmasking the Ragtag South China Sea Arbitral Tribunal." *Global Times*, 18 July 2016, http://www.globaltimes.cn/content/994907.shtml, accessed 7 July 2020.

_________. "Tribunal Award on S. China Sea Complicates Things But Further Talks Can Take Place: Italian Expert." *Global Times*, 14 July 2016, http://www.globaltimes.cn/content/994356.shtml, accessed 19 June 2020.

_________. "World Leaders, Experts Voice Support for China's Stance on South China Sea." *Xinhuanet.com*, 15 July 2016, http://news.xinhuanet.com/english/2016-07/15/c_135516383.htm, accessed 18 July 2016.

_________. "World Should Heed U.S. Interests in South China Sea Arbitration—Egyptian Experts." *China.org.cn*, 16 July 2016, http://www.china.org.cn/world/Off_the_Wire/2016-07/16/content_38896347.htm, accessed 19 June, 2020.

Yee, Sienho. "The South China Sea Arbitration Decisions on Jurisdiction and Rule of Law Concerns." *Chinese Journal of International Law* 15 (2016): 219–37.

Zafrullah Khan, Mohammed. "The Appointment of Arbitrators by the President of the International Court of Justice." *Comunicazioni e studi* [Communications and Studies] 14 (1975): 1021–42.

Zhang Qianfan. "Judicial Reform in China: An Overview." *China's Socialist Rule of Law Reforms Under Xi Jinping*, 17–29. Eds. John Garrick and Yan Chang Bennett. Milton Park, Abingdon, Oxon: Routledge, 2016.

Zhang Xinjun. "Bifurcation in Inter-State Cases." *University of Pennsylvania Journal of International Law* 40 (2019): 937–88, https://scholarship.law.upenn.edu/cgi/viewcontent.cgi?article=1991&context=jil, accessed 7 July 2020.

Zhao Jun, and Jiang Li. "The *Arctic Sunrise* Case and Its Implications for China." *Arbitration concerning the South China Sea. Philippines versus China*, 105–25. Eds. Shicun Wu and Keyuan Zou. London: Routledge 2016.

Zile, Zigurds L. "A Soviet Contribution to International Adjudication: Professor Krylov's Jurisprudential Legacy." *American Journal of International Law* 58 (1964): 359–88.

Zirin, Jim. "Question from China: How Do American Lawyers Bribe U.S. Judges?" *forbes.com*, 10 November 2014, https://www.forbes.com/sites/jameszirin/2014/11/10/question-from-china-how-do-american-lawyers-bribe-u-s-judges/#eb31fe8160c7, accessed 12 July 2020.

CHAPTER 6

Summary and Conclusions

The *South China Sea Arbitration* was the first occasion on which a respondent State defaulted in arbitral proceedings under Annex VII of the United Nations Convention on the Law of the Sea ("the Convention"), and indeed within the framework of compulsory dispute settlement established by the Convention. This book has focused on the legal issues raised by China's default and its practical consequences. Based on an examination of the history of default in cases before the International Court of Justice ("ICJ") between 1948 and the 1980s, it accepts that in certain respects, China behaved as did other defaulting States, but argues that in other respects, China's litigation strategy departed significantly from that of these States. Faced with the conduct of the defaulting State, the Arbitral Tribunal made full use of its procedural powers with a view to fulfilling its obligation under Article 9 of Annex VII of the Convention to satisfy itself that it had jurisdiction and that the Philippine claims were well founded in fact and in law.

Chapter 1 presented the legal framework of default of appearance, the practical consequences of default for the appearing State, the defaulting State, and the Tribunal, and a historical survey of China's default. Under Article 9 of Annex VII, default is no bar to the continuation of the proceedings if the appearing party requests that they continue. The defaulting party remains a party to the case and will be bound by any decisions of the Arbitral Tribunal. These provisions protect the appearing

A. C. Robles Jr., *The Defaulting State and the South China Sea Arbitration*, https://doi.org/10.1007/978-981-19-6394-0_6

State's right to have its claim adjudicated notwithstanding the respondent State's default. Annex VII protects the rights of the defaulting State by imposing on the Tribunal the obligation to satisfy itself that it has jurisdiction and that the appearing State's claims are well founded in fact and in law.

Default obliges the appearing State to "guess," as the Philippines put it, the defaulting State's arguments, the better to refute them. For the defaulting State, default may be advantageous if an arbitral tribunal feels bound to act as its de facto counsel. For an arbitral tribunal, the main practical consequences of default are those identified by the *Institut de droit international* (Institute of International Law, "IDI") in 1991, an acquisition of knowledge of the facts and the upholding of the equality of the parties. Following ICJ caselaw, default should not create advantages or disadvantages for either State. Nevertheless, Philippine counsel informally admitted that the Tribunal did act as China's counsel but did not protest against the Tribunal's conduct.

Chapter 1 divided the history of China's default into three periods: the initiation of the *Arbitration*; the period from the constitution of the Arbitral Tribunal to the issuance of the Award on Jurisdiction and Admissibility in October 2015; and the period from October 2015 to the issuance of the Award on the merits in July 2016. The Chapter highlighted anecdotal evidence that some officials within China's Foreign Ministry and some academics argued for participation in the jurisdictional phase and withdrawal from the proceedings if the Tribunal declared that it had jurisdiction, as the US had done in the *Nicaragua Case* before the ICJ in 1984. A creative and imaginary explanation for China's default attributed partial responsibility for it to the Philippine timing of the Notification and Statement of Claim shortly before the Lunar New Year Holiday, allegedly leaving China little time in which to negotiate with the Philippines. The second period is marked by China's refusal to respond to communications from the Tribunal soliciting its views on all procedural matters and China's informal participation in the proceedings, through the publication of a Position Paper on jurisdiction and admissibility (December 2014), informal communications to the Tribunal, Foreign Ministry statements, an attempt to manipulate the Tribunal in November 2013 without informing the Philippines, and possibly the hacking of the website of the Permanent Court of Arbitration ("PCA"), the Registry in the case. The third period is marked by China's continued refusal to respond to the Tribunal's requests for its views on all procedural matters and China's informal participation in the proceedings through further communications to the Tribunal and public statements denying the jurisdiction of the Tribunal, at a time when it was futile to make such statements, China's failure to object to submissions by surrogates (Taiwan in 2015 and 2016 and a shadowy Asia Pacific Institute of International Law ["APIIL"] in June 2016), China's efforts to exert pressure on the Tribunal through mobilization of third States; and the launching of a campaign of defamation against the appointing authority and the members of the Arbitral Tribunal.

Chapter 2 detailed the defaulting State's attitude to the jurisdiction of Annex VII arbitral tribunals and, in particular, China's efforts to deny the jurisdiction of the Arbitral Tribunal in the *South China Sea Arbitration*, in spite of the unambiguous text of Annex VII of the Convention. International legal scholarship largely agrees on the absence of a duty to appear before an international court but the reason for this consensus lies in the very nature of the obligation undertaken by States. Once a State has given its consent to the compulsory jurisdiction of an international court, the latter is empowered to render a judgment even in the event of the default of the respondent State (the State against which proceedings are initiated). The idea of a"right not to appear" so stridently proclaimed by China had already been rejected over three decades ago by the IDI, precisely for the very conclusion that China attempted to derive from it—the denial of the *compétence de la compétence*, the inherent power of an international court to determine its own jurisdiction. China's denial of this principle, which has been established for over one hundred fifty years, belies its assertion that its position has a "solid basis" in international law.

The Tribunal, following ICJ caselaw, decided to treat China's Position Paper as a preliminary objection and bifurcated the proceedings, despite the opposition of the Philippines. The complaint of some Chinese scholars that the Tribunal treated it as a defaulting State rather than dismissing the case immediately recalls the demand made by some defaulting States at the ICJ that the case be immediately removed from the ICJ's General List for the alleged lack of jurisdiction of the ICJ. This complaint ignores the fact that the ICJ removes cases from the General List only when there is manifestly no basis for jurisdiction. In the *South China Sea Arbitration*, there was a basis for jurisdiction that the Philippines was able to invoke.

China would have been well within its rights to exempt itself permanently from the risk of being subject to the jurisdiction of an Annex VII arbitral tribunal by withdrawing from the Convention if it had wished to do so, the possibility of withdrawal being provided for in Article 317 of the Convention. Withdrawal was informally discussed among scholars; in the end, China remained within the Convention. The withdrawal would not have released China from the obligation to comply with the Tribunal's decisions and could have prompted a rush to institute proceedings against China during the one-year period prior to the withdrawal taking effect. Withdrawal would have been tantamount to rejecting a Convention that China had welcomed in the 1980s as a first step in the Third World's efforts to achieve a new international economic order. It would have deprived China of the opportunity to participate in the further development of the law of the sea and hampered its efforts to obtain international recognition of its claim to an extended continental shelf.

Chapter 3 discussed at length the procedural steps taken by the Tribunal to enable it to acquire knowledge of the facts in the *South China Sea Arbitration*. The first part discussed the Tribunal's handling of China's informal communications and public statements as well as the supplemental written submissions of the Philippines. A defaulting State's informal communications and public statements upset equality between the parties, since they are exempt from the procedural rules that are applicable to the appearing State's submissions. Yet they may serve to inform both the appearing State and the Tribunal of the defaulting State's arguments and the supporting evidence. China's most important informal communication to the Tribunal was its Position Paper, which the Philippines welcomed. Treating the Position Paper as a plea on jurisdiction, the Tribunal decided to bifurcate the proceedings, contrary to the wishes of the Philippines, and not to limit the scope of the Hearing on Jurisdiction to the arguments raised in the Position Paper, contrary to a proposal by the Philippines. The Tribunal seemed to attach significance to the absence of informal communications from China when the latter failed to communicate to it in one way or another any Environmental Impact Assessment ("EIA") conducted prior to undertaking the island-building that in the Philippine view had caused harm to the marine environment in the South China Sea.

As a result of China's default, the task of collecting China's public statements fell to the Philippines and to the Tribunal. Contrary to a widespread impression, China did not publish public statements on the merits of the Philippine submissions—or at least public statements comparable to the French *Livre Blanc* (White Paper) in the *Nuclear Tests Cases* or the US *Revolution Beyond Borders* in the *Nicaragua Case*. The handful of public statements that touched on issues related to the merits of the Philippine submissions did not serve China's cause. For example, the statement that China respected two traditional freedoms of the high seas, the freedom of navigation and overflight, in the South China Sea was interpreted by the Tribunal as evidence that China's infamous "nine-dash line" did not amount to a claim to sovereignty over much of the South China Sea.

In response to the difficulty identified by the Philippines of having to "guess" the defaulting State's arguments, the Tribunal set in place in Article 25(2) of the Rules of Procedure an innovative mechanism, whereby the Tribunal would authorize the Philippines to make a supplemental written submission ("*SWSP*") or would pose questions to it on issues that in the Tribunal's view had not been sufficiently canvassed or had not been canvassed at all by the Philippines. This procedure had been requested by appearing States in the *Nuclear Tests Cases* and the *Aegean Sea Continental Shelf Case*, to no avail. It was proposed by scholars in the 1980s and endorsed by the IDI in 1991 as a means of reestablishing the equality of the parties and obviating the difficulties in fact-finding created by default. This procedure has sometimes been misunderstood as penalizing the Philippines for China's default, to the detriment of the equality of the parties. Perusal of the *SWSP* shows that in formulating many of its questions, the Tribunal was largely inspired by China's Position Paper and was in fact acting as China's counsel.

Chapter 3 also discussed the Tribunal's response to attempts by three non-State entities, Taiwan, the Chinese (Taiwan) Society of International Law ("C(T)SIL") and the APIIL to present submissions as self-proclaimed or de facto *amici curiae* ("friends of the court"). Some supporters of China had advocated the acceptance of such submissions as a way of alleviating the consequences of China's default. What is remarkable is that the Tribunal did not reject them outright. In the case of the submissions by Taiwan and the C(T)SIL, it examined them as part of the evidence for the status of Itu Aba in the Spratly Islands as a fully entitled island or a rock within the meaning of Article 121(3) of the Convention. The Tribunal did not go so far as to make formal decisions explicitly granting them the status of *amici curiae*, for which there is no precedent in Annex VII arbitrations. The chapter relied on criteria identified in investor-State arbitration under the rules and in the caselaw of the North America Free Trade Agreement ("NAFTA") and the International Centre for the Settlement of Investment Disputes ("ICSID") for the purpose of assessing their contribution to the Tribunal's fact-finding. These criteria are interest in the proceedings and independence from the parties; the ability to help the Tribunal; and the avoidance of burden to a party and disruption of the proceedings. Only Taiwan and the C(T)SIL seemed to fulfill all three criteria: their interest was the determination of the status of Itu Abu; they were undoubtedly independent from China and the Philippines; they could provide information on the status of Itu Aba, which was occupied by Taiwan; and the Philippines, conscious of the difficulties created for the Tribunal by China's default, did not object to the Tribunal's consideration of their submissions. In contrast, the APIIL's interest in the proceedings, described as the preservation of the dispute settlement system of the Convention, was vague. Its identity was doubtful, having been founded only a few weeks before the preparation of its submission and not having undertaken any activities prior to and after the submission. The usefulness of its submission, which merely repeated China's arguments against the Tribunal's Award on Jurisdiction and proposed a vast research program on the history of imperialism and colonialism in East Asia, was questionable. Consideration of its submission, submitted over six months after the oral proceedings, would undoubtedly have disrupted the proceedings and caused prejudice to the Philippines. These considerations probably account for the Tribunal's conclusion that the APIIL did not provide any assistance to it.

The last part of Chapter 3 discussed the Tribunal's exercise of other fact-finding powers. The Tribunal made liberal use of the power to put questions to the parties during the oral proceedings. Prior to the Hearings on Jurisdiction and on the Merits, the Tribunal had also forwarded to the Philippines, upon the latter's request, questions that the Philippines answered during the oral proceedings. The Tribunal's questions took the place of arguments that the respondent State could have put forward in a *Counter-Memorial*. Following the first round in the two oral hearings, the Tribunal, also in response to a Philippine request, put questions to the latter that replaced the rebuttals that a respondent State would have put forward in a first round and that the Philippines had to answer in the second round. The rationale for this procedure was undoubtedly identical to the rationale for Article 25(2) of the Rules of the Procedure: to obviate the practical difficulties caused for the appearing State by default.

The Tribunal also exercised its power to appoint independent experts. The first, a hydrographer, was engaged at an early stage of the proceedings. Three coral reef experts and a navigational safety expert were appointed following the closure of the oral proceedings. Prior to their appointment, the Tribunal communicated their terms of reference, qualifications, and declarations of independence and impartiality to China and the Philippines. An innovative procedure established by the Rules of Procedure would have provided either of the two parties the opportunity to raise objections to the qualifications and declarations of independence and impartiality of the expert(s). A further innovative procedure was set in place for the evaluation of the independent experts' reports following the transmission of the reports to the parties and of the parties' comments on the experts' reports. If a disagreement had arisen between the parties and the experts concerning the experts' reports, the Tribunal would have been empowered to call a hearing at the request of one of the parties or if the Tribunal considered it necessary. During a hearing, the parties could have questioned the independent experts and presented their own experts. The existence of these twin sets of procedures belies the charges made by the Chinese Society of International Law ("CSIL") that the procedures for the appointment of the experts were opaque and that the Tribunal adopted the coral reef experts' reports without evaluation.

Following the closure of the oral proceedings, the Tribunal undertook several fact-finding initiatives that can only be justified on the basis of its exercise of the power to take all appropriate measures in order to establish the facts. Commentators agree that international courts possess wide-ranging powers to establish the facts, but most would doubt that the scope of such powers includes independent fact-finding. That said, some ICJ statements do admit the possibility of independent fact-finding in cases of default. The Tribunal's first initiative was to search for Chinese official publications relating to the environmental impact of China's island-building activities in the South China Sea. It is possible that this initiative has been ignored by the CSIL because it was carried out on China's behalf. The Philippines stressed that whether taken singly or as a whole, the documents did not amount to an EIA. The thoroughness of the Tribunal's fact-finding was confirmed when the CSIL admitted in 2018 that China had not carried out an EIA.

In succeeding initiatives the Tribunal obtained pre-World War II British and Japanese surveys of the Spratly Islands from the UK Hydrographic Office and reports on the Spratly Islands from the *Bibliothèque Nationale de France* (French National Library) and the *Archives Nationales d'Outremer* (National Overseas Archives), all of which formed the basis for its assessment of the status of maritime features in the Spratly

Islands as low-tide elevations or rocks within the meaning of Article 121(3) of the Convention. The CSIL and other authors have misunderstood this initiative as tantamount to the Tribunal's taking over of the burden of proof on behalf of the Philippines. In reality, the Tribunal's independent fact-finding was motivated by a different approach to determining the status of maritime features. The Philippine approach relied heavily on satellite imagery and satellite-derived bathymetry. The analysis of Taiwan and the C(T)SIL took as their starting point the present state of Itu Aba. Both approaches were unsatisfactory in the eyes of the Tribunal, which followed a different line of inquiry, one emphasizing the importance of original survey data. The Tribunal, therefore, sought out such data and submitted them to both China and the Philippines for their responses. If the Tribunal had rejected the Philippine submissions without informing it of the basis of the rejection or giving it the opportunity to comment on the Tribunal's approach, the procedural rights of the Philippines would have been violated and it would have been surprised by the decision. This would explain why the Philippines was allowed to make written submissions well after the conclusion of the written proceedings and why China was given exactly the same opportunity to comment on the archival materials, a fact that the CSIL conveniently forgets.

Chapters 4 and 5 address attacks by the CSIL and individual Chinese scholars on the independence and impartiality of the experts appointed by the Philippines, of the independent experts, of the appointing authority, of the judges, and of the Tribunal in the *South China Sea Arbitration*. Where both parties appear before an arbitral tribunal, challenges to the independence and impartiality of the independent experts and/or the judges would not be admissible once the proceedings had concluded. There is no reason why, in case of a default, they should be entertained either. From this perspective, the two chapters would be unnecessary. Nevertheless, Chapters 4 and 5 do tackle the Chinese accusations for at least two reasons. The growth of scholarly interest in the independence and impartiality of experts and of judges in the last two decades would justify a detailed examination of charges of lack of independence and impartiality that are rarely formulated explicitly during or after inter-State judicial proceedings. Moreover, tackling China's accusations head-on will preempt further charges of a desire to avoid substantive issues by hiding behind legal technicalities.

Chapter 4 began by providing a sampling of the complex scientific and technical evidence that the Philippines submitted concerning the status of maritime features, the harm to the marine environment caused by China's island-building, and the risk of collision caused by Chinese vessels. The CSIL's objection to the engagement of five experts by the Tribunal assumes that the practice of the ICJ, which had engaged experts only twice in 70 years, is a binding norm, whereas it is no more than that—a practice. Chapter 4 pointed out that the Convention accords particular roles to experts as members of a court or tribunal under Article 289 or as members of special arbitral tribunals under Annex VIII of the Convention. A survey of the practice of Annex VII tribunals reveals that the appointment of an expert hydrographer is a common practice in maritime delimitation cases; in one instance, a tribunal did not hesitate to engage a legal expert to resolve a side dispute between the parties concerning access to archival materials.

Chapter 4 then proceeded to assess the independence and impartiality of two categories of experts: the experts appointed by the Philippines and the experts appointed by the Tribunal, which designated them as "independent experts." An expert may be deemed independent if he/she does not depend on any authority other than his/her own. Independence is a precondition of impartiality, but there may be other sources of partiality (bias) than lack of independence. These other sources may be personal, intellectual, and financial. Impartiality requires that an expert approach a case with an open mind, free of bias, and if necessary, the expert should be willing to change his/her opinion. Cross-examination of experts constitutes the main procedure through which international courts determine the independence and impartiality of experts appointed by the parties. The independence and impartiality of experts appointed by international courts are examined by the parties upon the experts' appointment and through an evaluation of their reports.

In the *South China Sea Arbitration*, the experts appointed by the Philippines on the status of maritime features, coral reefs, and navigational safety may be deemed independent and impartial. None was in the service of the Philippines. All were senior academics with international experience and reputations to lose if they tailored their expert opinions to the needs of the case. For instance, the expert on navigational safety is the author of one of the two standard texts in the US on the Convention on the International Regulations for Preventing Collisions at Sea, 1972 ("COLREGS"). The fact that he and the other experts were engaged by the Philippines did not mean that they necessarily endorsed all Philippine arguments. For example, the experts on the status of features did not agree with all of the Philippine characterizations of the maritime features in the Spratly Islands. During the oral hearings, the Tribunal, which put a very large number of questions to one coral reef expert and one expert on the status of maritime features, had the opportunity to probe their expert opinion and ascertain their independence and impartiality. As for the independent experts, their qualifications and their international experience provide the guarantees of their independence and impartiality.

The three remaining parts of Chapter 4 examined in some detail scientific and technical expert evidence submitted by the Philippines, the independent experts' expert evidence, and the Tribunal's evaluation of the evidence submitted by the two categories of experts. This exercise has rarely been undertaken in a satisfactory fashion by previous commentators, undoubtedly because of the complexity and technical nature of the issues that they involved. On the status of maritime features, the Tribunal accepted the expert hydrographer's assessment of the limitations of satellite imagery and satellite-derived bathymetry as means for determining whether a feature is a low-tide elevation or a high-tide elevation. As regards the impact of China's island-building on coral reefs, the Tribunal noted that the findings of the experts appointed by the Philippines and the independent experts largely agreed with each other. One reason that the Tribunal seemed to place greater reliance on the opinion of the independent experts might be that the materials placed at their disposal were not available to the experts appointed by the Philippines. Be that as it may, the Tribunal did not simply adopt the independent experts' report. Rather it categorized its findings and used the resulting framework as the basis for its decisions. On navigational safety, the Tribunal considered the reports of the expert appointed by the Philippines and the independent expert to be complementary. The Tribunal's evaluation of the two expert reports stressed the international responsibility of China. The Tribunal also highlighted the importance of Rule 7 of the COLREGSs, which had not been invoked by either the expert appointed by the Philippines or the independent expert, as the basis for the finding of risk of collision during the two incidents of 2012 reported by the Philippines.

Chapter 5 discusses issues that have so far escaped the attention of scholars outside China, who might be inclined to think that China's attacks on the composition of the Arbitral Tribunal and on the independence and impartiality of the appointing authority, the judges, and the Tribunal as a whole, which began late in the proceedings, are merely the result of momentary pique at the Tribunal's decisions and for this reason are not to be taken seriously. Yet these attacks are so extraordinary that they cannot be swept under the rug.

Chapter 5 first discussed Chinese objections that the Tribunal did not have a Chinese or Asian member and did not represent the main forms of civilization and principal legal systems of the world. The objection neglects deliberately the differences between a permanent international court and an ad hoc arbitral tribunal. The requirements of representation of the main forms of civilization and of the principal legal systems of the world, first imposed on the Permanent Court of International Justice ("PCIJ"), represented a compromise between great powers who wished to have permanent representation in the PCIJ and small powers who defended the principle of equality of States; obviously, this consideration is irrelevant for international arbitration. It is also a mistake to argue that Annex VII arbitral tribunals must have "national" arbitrators or that their composition must be based on equitable geographical distribution. Each State party to the dispute has the right to appoint a national as an arbitrator, but in the event of default, Annex VII prohibits the appointing authority, the President of the International Tribunal for the Law of the Sea ("ITLOS"), from appointing arbitrators who are nationals of, or ordinarily resident in, or in the service of either of the two parties. The rationale for this restriction might be the protection of the national, resident, or person in the service of the defaulting State against sanctions for accepting an appointment to an arbitral tribunal. Once China had refused to appoint its arbitrator, it was impossible for a Chinese arbitrator to be appointed to the Tribunal. It was also practically impossible to appoint an Asian to the tribunal, for Annex VII requires that in the event of default, the arbitrators must be chosen from a list maintained by the UN Secretary-General, and at the time of the appointments, all but one of the Asians on the list were from States that had territorial and/or maritime disputes with China or had close ties with the Philippines. If one now turns to the practice of Annex VII arbitral tribunals, one realizes that very few had nationals of both parties as members and that very few had members from more than three different regions.

Chapter 5 then went on to examine the independence of judges, which is conceptualized in relation to external powers, such as other branches of government, political parties, trade unions, mass media, and public opinion. If one keeps this conception in mind, one quickly comes to the conclusion that there are no possible grounds for questioning the independence of the appointing authority and the five members of the Arbitral

Tribunal. The appointing authority was not even a judge in the case and is in any event in no relation of subordination to the States parties to the Convention, nor are the arbitrators accountable to the appointing authority or the States that put forward their names for inclusion in the list of arbitrators and conciliators maintained by the UN Secretary-General under Annex VII of the Convention. Furthermore, none of the five arbitrators is a national, a resident, or a person in the service of either China or the Philippines. Instead of criticizing the judges for their lack of independence, China threatened their independence by secretly lobbying them and by exerting pressure on them through the mobilization of the support of third States for its position that the Tribunal lacked jurisdiction. The secret lobbying reminds us that in China the government and the Chinese Communist Party ("CCP) give instructions to judges that must be followed unconditionally. China's international campaign is comparable to "judicial populism," which pressures judges to decide cases, or to modify decisions, particularly cases involving the death penalty, in accordance with the wishes of public opinion.

Finally, Chapter 5 addressed the issue of the impartiality of international judges, which is understood to refer to the absence of bias and the willingness to approach issues with an open mind. Academics ascertain the impartiality of an international judge by examining his/her voting record in cases in which his/her State of nationality is a party. This approach is of limited value if the State of nationality of the judge has not been a party to a case before the court of which the judge is a member. To this academic approach, international courts themselves prefer either a subjective approach or an objective approach. The subjective approach seeks to determine whether the judge is actually biased. Previous participation in the case in any capacity would constitute evidence of bias. The objective approach examines whether circumstances exist that could create the impression that the judge is biased. Among these circumstances are personal, professional, or financial interest in the outcome of the case as well as previous declarations. Whichever of the three approaches one adopts, one cannot but conclude that China's accusations of bias directed against the appointing authority and the individual judges are totally groundless. The appointing authority was not even a judge in the case; he was merely the appointing authority. At any rate, he had voted as an ITLOS member against the State of which he is a national, Japan, in a prompt release case brought by the latter against Russia. He had never been previously involved in any capacity in the South China Sea disputes, and he had never made any previous declarations, whether as a representative of his State or as an academic, concerning the South China Sea disputes. Similar observations apply to each of the five members of the arbitral tribunal. Three of them had voted against the States of which they were nationals in cases in which these States were parties. None of the five had been previously involved in any capacity in the dispute. The alleged change in opinion of two of the arbitrators on the subject of the relationship between maritime delimitation and the identification of the status of features, assuming there was indeed a change, may be properly considered as a sign of open-mindedness and impartiality, rather than being a sign of bias.

The gravest charge against the Tribunal as a whole is that its bias toward the Philippines was motivated by financial interest. China's accusation of corruption rests on a deliberate and willful misunderstanding of the difference between adjudication by a permanent international court, on the one hand, and arbitration, on the other. In the former, the expenses of the court are borne by the international organization of which the court is a part or by the parties to its statute. In the latter, the expenses of the tribunal are shouldered by the parties. When one party defaults, the other party is obliged to cover the defaulting party's share if the proceedings are to continue. This difference is well known to specialists; the only reason for restating the obvious is that China is counting on the ignorance or gullibility of its audience to make its accusation appear plausible. China is unable to prove its charge of corruption for it would have had to find evidence of the type uncovered after a thorough investigation in the only known case of corruption in the modern history of arbitration. China's accusation of corruption against the five arbitrators can only be understood against the background of proteiform, pervasive, institutionalized, and collective corruption of judges in China, which would make the accusation immediately comprehensible to a Chinese audience. It would not make sense in the context of the history of modern arbitration, in which corruption of arbitrators is a mythical problem.

One may conclude from this study that as anticipated by the scholarly literature, the defaulting State reaped many of the advantages of its default. The transmittal of its Position Paper was cause for the bifurcation of the proceedings, contrary to the wishes of the appearing State. Its public statements were collected and scrutinized by the appearing State and the Tribunal. Its informal communications and public views were the basis of questions that the Tribunal posed to the Philippines, to which the Tribunal added questions that China itself had never formulated. Its views on the merits of Philippine claims became the object of diligent research on the part of both the Philippines and the Tribunal. Evidence that could have supported its position was gathered by the Philippines and the Tribunal. Entities who claimed to be "friends of the court" but who in reality were "friends of China" were courteously entertained instead of being immediately dismissed; at least two of them were taken seriously. These measures undoubtedly contradict the principle that default should not upset the equality of the parties and place either the defaulting State or the appearing State at an advantage or at a disadvantage. Nevertheless, it cannot be denied that these and other procedural steps enabled the Tribunal to successfully address one of the practical difficulties that are caused by default for an international court and that were identified by the IDI, the difficulty in acquiring knowledge of the facts.

The Tribunal managed to some extent to reestablish the relative equality of the parties, upholding of which was the other major practical difficulty identified by the IDI in a situation of default. Unlike the ICJ, the Tribunal explicitly recognized the difficulties that default created for the appearing State and implemented an innovative procedure that had first been put forward in the scholarly literature in the 1980s and endorsed by the IDI in the 1990s. Still, one is not surprised that counsel for the Philippines informally admitted that in practice the Tribunal had acted as China's de facto counsel, while generally refraining from raising any objections against the Tribunal's conduct on behalf of China. The fact is that it was thanks to these procedural measures that the Tribunal's decisions, which were largely favorable to the Philippine claims, had a sound factual basis.

China's contribution to international arbitral practice must be judged negatively. It asserted the existence of a "right not to participate" that had been rejected over thirty years ago by the IDI. It denied the existence of the principle of *compétence de la compétence*, which has been established for over 150 years. It sought to undermine the independence and question the impartiality of the arbitrators and Tribunal by lobbying it secretly, mobilizing States not parties to the dispute, and when all this failed, orchestrating a campaign of defamation against the appointing authority, individual arbitrators, and the Tribunal as a whole. Through these elements in its litigation strategy, China transposed to the international level conceptions and practices associated with the dependent and corrupt judiciary of China.

China experts may seek to reassure their readers that China's conduct during the *South China Arbitration* does not necessarily signal a fundamental change in China's attitude toward international law. But China's conduct cannot be excused, much less justified, by pointing out that in other international forums, such as the World Trade Organization ("WTO"), China participates in binding dispute settlement. Such reassurances are hardly convincing. At the WTO, China has no choice. Its default in proceedings would expose it to sanctions. On the contrary, within the framework of the Convention, which provides no sanctions for default, China had a choice. Its decision to default, and even more importantly, its recourse to the litigation strategy and tactics that have worked so well for the authoritarian State and the CCP in the domestic sphere, provide the observer with more accurate indicators of its commitment to international law. The course of action that a State adopts when it has a choice between legitimate and illegitimate means should be more accurate and eloquent evidence of its attitude toward international law and international legal order than its conduct in circumstances where compliance is unavoidable.

Faced with such a formidable party, the Tribunal had only its procedural powers at its disposal. It drew on the full range of these powers, with the aim of fulfilling the obligation imposed on it by Annex VII of the Convention to satisfy itself that it had jurisdiction and that the claims of the Philippines were well founded in fact and in law. Like the ICJ in cases of default, the Tribunal took cognizance of the defaulting State's informal communications and public statements. Unlike the ICJ, the Tribunal posed a large number of written questions to the Philippines prior to the two Hearings; it posed a large number of questions to the experts presented by the Philippines during the second round of both Hearings; it took into account the views of two self-proclaimed *amici curiae*, both of whom supported China's positions; it appointed independent experts; it conducted its own fact-finding on behalf of China and in pursuit of its own line of inquiry; and it took steps to ensure that through its fact-finding it would not spring a surprise on either party. Unlike the ICJ, the Tribunal explicitly recognized the unfavorable consequences of default for the appearing State and took steps to address them by implementing an innovative mechanism that permitted the appearing State to make a supplemental submission and posing a large number of questions to the Philippines during the second round of both Hearings. Unlike dependent and corrupt Chinese judges, the Tribunal, confronted with the legal challenges and practical difficulties caused by China's default as well as the pressures exerted by the defaulting State, was able to perform successfully the judicial function.

Index

A. C. Robles Jr., *The Defaulting State and the South China Sea Arbitration*, https://doi.org/10.1007/978-981-19-6394-0

E

SPRINGER NATURE

GPSR Compliance

The European Union's (EU) General Product Safety Regulation (GPSR) is a set of rules that requires consumer products to be safe and our obligations to ensure this.

If you have any concerns about our products, you can contact us on ProductSafety@springernature.com

In case Publisher is established outside the EU, the EU authorized representative is:

Springer Nature Customer Service Center GmbH
Europaplatz 3
69115 Heidelberg, Germany

The manufacturer's authorised representative in the EU is Springer Nature Customer Service Centre GmbH, Europaplatz 3, 69115 Heidelberg, Germany. If you have any concerns regarding our products, please contact ProductSafety@springernature.com

Printed and bound by CPI Group (UK) Ltd, Croydon, CR0 4YY

01/10/2026

02225861-0008